Reading for Results

Tenth Edition

Laraine E. Flemming

Ann Marie Radaskiewicz
Contributing Writer

HOUGHTON MIFFLIN COMPANY
Boston   New York

Executive Publisher: Patricia A. Coryell
Sponsoring Editor: Joann Kozyrev
Executive Marketing Manager: Annamarie Rice
Senior Development Editor: Judith Fifer
Senior Project Editor: Margaret Park Bridges
Art and Design Manager: Gary Crespo
Cover Design Manager: Anne S. Katzeff
Senior Photo Editor: Jennifer Meyer Dare
Composition Buyer: Chuck Dutton
New Title Project Manager: Susan Brooks-Peltier
Editorial Assistant: Daisuke Yasutake
Marketing Assistant: Bettina Chiu

Cover image: © Erik Dreyer / Getty Images

Acknowledgments and credits appear on pages 725–726, which
constitutes an extension of the copyright page.

Printed in the U.S.A.

Library of Congress Control Number: 2006934186

Instructor's Annotated Edition
  ISBN-10: 0-618-83079-0
  ISBN-13: 978-0-618-83079-4
For orders, use student text ISBNs
  ISBN-10: 0-618-76677-4
  ISBN-13: 978-0-618-76677-2

123456789-DOC-11 10 09 08 07

 C O N T E N T S

Preface   x

 **Chapter 1   Strategies for Mastering Your Textbooks**   *1*

Introducing *SQ3R*: Survey, Question, Read, Recite, Review   *2*

S: Survey to Get a General Overview   *2*

   Surveying Goals   *4*

   Breaking an Assignment into Manageable Parts   *4*

   Skimming versus Reading   *4*

   Focusing Your Survey   *4*

Q: Use Questions to Guide Your Attention   *7*

   Major and Minor Headings   *8*

   Making Graphs, Tables, Timelines, and Charts Part of Your Survey   *8*

   Expand Prior Knowledge by Using the Web   *9*

R: Read   *9*

   Read to Answer Specific Questions   *9*

   Write While You Read   *9*

   Be Selective with Underlining   *12*

   Vary Your Reading Rate According to the Material   *13*

R: Recite   *15*

   Test Your Understanding   *15*

   Write Out the Answers   *15*

R: Review   *16*

   Immediate Review   *16*

   Review Several Times Over the Course of the Semester   *18*

   The Role of Informal Outlining in Review   *19*

Mining the Web for Background Knowledge   *21*

   The Role of Background Knowledge in Comprehension   *21*

   The World Wide Web Makes a Difference   *22*

   Why Bother?   *22*

   Pick a Search Engine Right for the Job   *22*

   Indexes and Directories   *23*

   The Right Search Term Is Critical, or Never Use a Single Word to Search the Web   *23*

   Some Websites Are More Trustworthy Than Others   *29*

Introducing Bonus Questions   *33*

Sample Chapter: The Cold War Abroad and at Home,
1945–1952   *34*

Test 1: Strategies for Reading Textbooks   *53*

Test 2: Vocabulary Review   *54*

Chapter 2   Word Power   *56*

Using Context   *57*

   Example Clues   *57*

   Contrast Clues   *58*

   Restatement Clues   *58*

   General Knowledge Clues   *60*

Context and Meaning   *67*

Defining Words from Their Parts   *68*

   Learning Roots, Prefixes, and Suffixes   *68*

Combine Forces: Use Context Clues *and* Word Parts   *71*

More Pointers About Specialized Vocabulary   *74*

   Recognizing Key Terms   *74*

   Paragraphs Devoted to Definitions   *74*

   Checking the Glossary   *75*

Connotations and Denotations of Words   *76*

   Connotation, Denotation, and Context   *77*

The Difference Between Reading and Writing Vocabularies   *78*

Digging Deeper: Words Are Like Bullets   *80*

Test 1: Using Context Clues   *83*

Test 2: Using Context Clues   *85*

Test 3: Using Context Clues   *87*

Test 4: Word Analysis and Context Clues   *89*

Test 5: Word Analysis and Context Clues   *91*

Test 6: Word Analysis and Context Clues   *93*

Chapter 3   Relating the General to the Specific in Reading and Writing   *96*

General and Specific Words   *97*

   Putting the Terms *General* and *Specific* into Context   *99*

Understanding the Difference Between General and Specific
Sentences   *103*

   Defining Terms   *103*

   Recognizing Levels of Generality and Specificity in
Sentences   *106*

The Writer's Responsibility   *110*

The Reader's Response   *110*

Connecting General and Specific Sentences in Paragraphs   *118*

   General Sentences in First Position   *118*

   General Sentences in Last Position   *119*

Digging Deeper: Going Global   *124*

*Test 1: Distinguishing Between General and Specific
Sentences*   **127**

*Test 2: Distinguishing Between General and Specific
Sentences*   **128**

Test 3: Recognizing the Most General Sentence   **129**

Test 4: Recognizing the Most General Sentence   **131**

Test 5: Identifying General Sentences in Paragraphs   **133**

Test 6: Vocabulary Review   **136**

Chapter 4   Discovering Topics, Main Ideas, and Topic Sentences   *138*

Identify the Topic   *139*

Use the Topic to Discover the Main Idea   *149*

Topic Sentences and Main Ideas   *151*

   Locating Topic Sentences   *152*

   The Role of Reversal Transitions   *153*

   Expanding the Introduction   *155*

   Transitional Sentences   *156*

More Topic Sentence Locations   *161*

   Opening Question and Topic Sentence Answer   *161*

   Topic Sentence at Mid-Point   *162*

   Topic Sentence in Last Position   *162*

   Doubling Up on Topic Sentences   *164*

Paraphrasing Topic Sentences   *178*

   Accurate and Inaccurate Paraphrasing   *178*

   Paraphrasing Pitfalls   *180*

   Adapt Your Paraphrasing to the Material   *180*

A Two-Step Method for Paraphrasing Complex Ideas   *180*

   Step 1: Identify Agents and Actions   *181*

   Step 2: Add Key Details   *181*

   Reading versus Writing Paraphrases   *181*

Digging Deeper: Jury Dodgers Beware!   *194*

Test 1: Identifying Topics and Topic Sentences   *197*

Test 2: Recognizing Topics and Topic Sentences   *200*

Test 3: Recognizing Topics, Topic Sentences, and Transitions *203*

Test 4: Recognizing Accurate Paraphrases *206*

Test 5: Recognizing Accurate Paraphrases *209*

Test 6: Identifying and Paraphrasing Topic Sentences *213*

Test 7: Vocabulary Review *216*

Chapter 5   Inferences and Main Ideas   *219*

Inferences in Everyday Life   *220*

   Cartoons   *220*

   Quips and Quotes   *221*

Filling in the Gaps in Topic Sentences   *221*

Inferring Main Ideas   *226*

Five Types of Paragraphs Likely to Imply the Main Idea   *238*

   Just the Facts   *239*

   Question and Answer   *240*

   Competing Points of View   *241*

   Comparison and Contrast   *242*

   Results of Research   *243*

More on Evaluating Your Inferences   *252*

Digging Deeper: Black Baseball *261*

Test 1: Recognizing the Implied Main Idea *265*

Test 2: Recognizing the Implied Main Idea *268*

Test 3: Recognizing the Implied Main Idea *271*

Test 4: Recognizing the Implied Main Idea *274*

Test 5: Recognizing the Implied Main Idea *276*

Test 6: Vocabulary Review *279*

Chapter 6   More on the Function of Supporting Details   *283*

Supporting Details Develop Topic Sentences   *284*

Understanding the Difference Between Major and Minor Details   *290*

   The Role of Minor Details   *291*

   Evaluating Minor Details   *292*

Topic Sentences Help Identify Major Details   *299*

Transitions and Major Details   *301*

Reader-Supplied Inferences and Supporting Details   *314*

Visual Aids as Supporting Details   *321*

   Identify the Function of the Visual Aid   *324*

   Bar Graphs   *325*

Concluding Sentences and Supporting Details   *330*

Digging Deeper: Challenging the Digital Divide   *334*

Test 1: Recognizing Supporting Details   *337*

Test 2: Distinguishing Between Major and Minor Details   *339*

Test 3: Recognizing Topic Sentence Clues to Major Details   *344*

Test 4: Recognizing Supporting Details and Concluding Sentences   *346*

Test 5: Topics, Topic Sentences, and Inferring Supporting Details   *348*

Test 6: Visual Aids as Supporting Details   *352*

Test 7: Vocabulary Review   *355*

Chapter 7   Beyond the Paragraph: Reading Longer Selections   *357*

Moving Beyond the Paragraph   *358*

   Titles and Headings Are Tip-offs   *358*

   One Main Idea Controls and Unifies the Others   *358*

   Topic Sentences versus "Thesis Statements"   *359*

   Double Vision Is Essential   *359*

   Implied Main Ideas Are Slow to Emerge   *359*

   Major Supporting Details Expand Their Territory   *360*

   Concluding Paragraphs Fulfill More Functions   *360*

   The Writer's Purpose Becomes Clearer   *361*

Diagramming Major and Minor Details   *361*

Implied Main Ideas in Longer Readings   *372*

Monitoring Comprehension with Informal Outlines   *389*

   Making a Sentence Outline   *389*

Taking Notes with Informal Outlines   *391*

   Making an Informal Outline   *391*

Introducing Graphic Organizers   *399*

Digging Deeper: Legal Rights for Animals   *407*

Test 1: Recognizing Controlling Main Ideas and Supporting Details   *411*

Test 2: Recognizing Controlling Main Ideas and Supporting Details   *417*

Test 3: Recognizing the Main Idea, Supporting Details, and Author's Purpose   *423*

Test 4: Vocabulary Review   *428*

Chapter 8 Recognizing Patterns of Organization in Paragraphs 431

Pattern 1: Definition 432

Pattern 2: Time Order 437

Sequence of Dates and Events 438

Process 446

Pattern 3: Comparison and Contrast 453

Pattern 4: Cause and Effect 461

Pattern 5: Classification 468

Identifying the "Primary" Pattern 475

Digging Deeper: Types of Love 483

Test 1: Predicting Patterns 487

Test 2: Patterns and Transitions 490

Test 3: Recognizing Primary Patterns 492

Test 4: Recognizing Primary Patterns 495

Test 5: Recognizing Primary Patterns 498

Test 6: Recognizing Primary Patterns 501

Test 7: Vocabulary Review 504

Chapter 9 Combining Patterns in Paragraphs and Longer Readings 507

Combining Patterns in Paragraphs 508

Not All Patterns Are Equal 509

Seeing Patterns in Longer Readings 515

Taking Notes on Mixed Patterns 517

Digging Deeper: The Development of Self in Childhood 537

Test 1: Identifying Main Ideas and Patterns of Organization 540

Test 2: Identifying Main Ideas and Patterns of Organization 548

Test 3: Identifying Main Ideas and Patterns of Organization 555

Test 4: Identifying Main Ideas and Primary Patterns 561

Test 5: Vocabulary Review 569

Chapter 10 More on Purpose, Tone, and Bias 572

Why Think About Purpose? 573

Informative Writing 573

Persuasive Writing 576

On the Meaning of "Primary Purpose" 578

Separating Fact and Opinion   586

  Facts   586

  Opinions   587

Combining Opinions with Facts   590

Evaluating Bias in Persuasive Writing   596

  When Bias Goes Overboard   596

  An Example of Acceptable Bias   598

Backing Opinions with Arguments   606

  Opinions and Sound Arguments   607

  Shaky Arguments   608

Digging Deeper: Critical Thinking and Pseudo-Psychologies—Palms, Planets, and Personality   621

Test 1: Fact or Opinion   627

Test 2: Fact, Opinion, or Both   628

Test 3: Identifying Tone   630

Test 4: Recognizing Tone and Purpose   636

Test 5: Recognizing Tone and Excessive Bias   641

Test 6: Locating Errors in Logic   645

Test 7: Vocabulary Review   648

Putting It All Together   651

Reading 1: *The Altruistic Personality*, Sharon S. Brehm, Saul M. Kassin, and Steven Fein   652

Reading 2: *A Hero Scorned*, USA Today Editorial   659

Reading 3: *Does America Need a Third Party?* Ann O'M. Bowman and Richard C. Kearney   664

Reading 4: *The Stereotype Trap*, Sharon Begley   669

Reading 5: *Where Does Free Speech End?* Ann Marie Radaskiewicz and Laraine Flemming   676

Reading 6: *Memory, Perception, and Eyewitness Testimony*, Douglas A. Bernstein, Louis A. Penner, Alison Clarke-Stewart, and Edward J. Roy   681

Reading 7: *Kohlberg's Six Stages of Moral Judgment*, Kelvin L. Seifert, Robert J. Hoffnung, and Michele Hoffnung   689

Reading 8: *Marla Ruzicka: An Activist Angel*, Ann Marie Radaskiewicz   696

Reading 9: *The Wolf Children*, David Wallechinsky   702

Reading 10: *Nuclear Power and Waste Disposal*, James T. Shipman, Jerry D. Wilson, and Aaron W. Todd   707

Appendix: Reading Pie Charts and Graphs   713

Index   727

PREFACE

It's always a pleasure to write the preface for a new edition of *Reading for Results*. A new preface means that the book continues to meet the needs of both instructors and students.

In response to comments and questions from instructors across the country, I have retained all of the successful elements of previous editions. The explanations, for instance, still model every reading skill: They tell students not just what to do but how to do it. Also very much the same is the step-by-step approach to comprehension and critical reading, with each chapter building on previous explanations and skills. As soon as students can identify topics, they advance to main ideas and from there to identifying supporting details and organizational patterns. The complexity of the exercises steadily increases until students are ready for critical reading skills such as recognizing purpose, noticing tone, identifying bias, and evaluating arguments.

The exercises and tests remain numerous, enough for both practice and review. As always, all the reading selections were carefully chosen to illustrate what a stimulating experience reading can be.

Having briefly reviewed what's the same in this edition, let me now say what it's not.

New to the Tenth Edition

End-of-Chapter Vocabulary Quizzes

One of the most important challenges of a reading course is helping students broaden their vocabulary. To meet this challenge, nine chapters now end with vocabulary quizzes that review words defined in chapter exercises and footnotes. The fill-in-the-blank, paragraph-length passages have a three-fold purpose. On the most obvious level, the quizzes have been added to make vocabulary-building an ongoing feature of the book. However, they also illustrate an important point about using context clues: Some of the most useful clues to a new word can come long after the word has been introduced. Thus students need to practice using context clues in longer passages rather than in isolated sentences. Last, the quizzes were created to broaden students' general knowledge about people and events that might be discussed or alluded to in their textbooks. Among the many people and events covered are Galileo's struggle with the church, Darwin's journey to the Galapagos, Elizabeth Cady Stanton's fight for the right to vote; and the early muckrakers' use of exposés to win social justice.

Emphasis on Academic Vocabulary

To help students learn words appropriate to an academic setting, many of the words introduced in Chapter 2 were drawn from the *Academic Word List*, the list created by the Victoria University of Wellington, New Zealand. The list was compiled based on how frequently words appeared in textbooks from different disciplines. (To see the full list, go to **www.vuw.ac.nz/lals/research/awl/index.html.**)

Additional Material on Inferring Supporting Details and Sentence Connections

Because so many students need practice in inferring main ideas, *Reading for Results* has always devoted a good deal of attention to inferring main ideas. It still does; however, a number of exercises now ask students to draw inferences about the supporting details and sentence relationships that writers rely on readers to contribute. As always, the emphasis is on drawing *logical inferences* that are consistent with the author's explicit statements and context.

Graphic Organizers

The addition of graphic organizers reinforces the book's emphasis on the importance of adapting note-taking formats to the characteristics of the textbook material. There are times when a drawing or diagram is more appropriate than an outline.

Drawing Conclusions

In this edition, critical reading assignments focus on two kinds of conclusions. Some questions call for personal conclusions such as how students might apply what the author says to their own life. Others ask readers to infer how an author might react to situations related to but not specifically addressed in the reading, for example, "Given what the authors say about eyewitness testimony, what advice might they offer to jurors in a murder trial?"

Brief Reading and Learning Tips

College students need exposure to a wide range of learning techniques so that they'll have a variety at their disposal. Thus it seemed useful to cull learning tips from a number of books on comprehension and critical reading—among my sources are Robert J. Gula's *Nonsense*, Larry Wright's *Critical Reading*, and Frank Smith's *Understanding Reading*—and thread them through the chapters.

Predictions About Topic Sentence Locations

Building on the skills introduced in Chapter 3, "Relating the General to the Specific in Reading and Writing," Chapter 4, "Discovering Topics, Main Ideas, and Topic Sentences," shows how the knowledge of general and specific relationships can help in predicting topic sentence locations. New diagrams in the text reinforce the different shapes paragraphs can take, depending on the topic sentence location and the distribution of general and specific information.

Internet Literacy and Background Knowledge

Today's students need to be prepared to access online resources and process information in electronic formats. To help develop these abilities, a new section in Chapter 1 describes exactly how the Internet can supply the background knowledge that speeds up textbook comprehension. Titled "Mining the Web for Background Knowledge," this section explains how to find and evaluate websites without wading through a lot of useless information.

Internet Bonus Questions and Resources

Internet Bonus Questions, which appear throughout the chapters, encourage students to practice what they have learned about evaluating websites. Boxed references to Internet resources also show students some terrific websites they can access to improve their learning skills.

Reading Rate and Flexibility

Because students don't always know when it's appropriate to speed up or slow down their reading, a new section on reading rate underscores the importance of being a flexible reader, who adjusts his or her approach to the material at hand. Students also learn how adjusting rate is a key element of overall reading flexibility.

More Attention to Visual Literacy

This edition of *Reading for Results* pays more attention than ever before to the way pictures and diagrams, both the writer's and reader's, contribute to comprehension.

Recognizing Hasty Generalizations

Chapter 10 offers a foundation in critical thinking with new material on a common error in logic—the hasty generalization. Drawing on what they have already learned about generalizations, students now concentrate on distinguishing between generalizations that are solidly grounded in enough specifics and those that teeter precariously on one or two examples.

Revised Explanations Focusing on Readers Thinking Like Writers

It's important for students to make the connection between the writer's intent and the reader's response. Inspired by Doug Brent's *Reading as Rhetorical Invention* and Martha Kolln's *Rhetorical Grammar*, several of this book's key explanations have been rewritten—particularly in Chapters 3 and 4—to emphasize how crucial it is for readers to think like writers. The more readers can infer the reasons why a writer chose to follow one sentence with another, the better they are at recreating an intended meaning.

New Sample Chapter on Truman and the Cold War

Because students need practice with textbook format and content, this edition includes a new sample chapter drawn from a popular history text, *The Enduring Vision*. This sample chapter should prove useful in a number of ways. The chapter's authors use several common textbook conventions to highlight the main points introduced, making it an ideal illustration of how the textbook format can guide the reader's search for meaning. The sample chapter also defines important terms that have become part of the culture's store of shared allusions, for example, "Cold War," "Iron Curtain," "McCarthyism," and "GI Bill."

Many New Readings

As in the past, the high-interest readings in this edition will supply students with the motivation they need to complete their assignments. This edition covers topics such as the first face transplant, the international success of Spanish telenovelas, imaginative excuses used by jury dodgers, the origins of Hurricane Katrina's devastation, and the pitfalls inherent in eyewitness testimony.

Eight of the ten extended readings appearing at the end of the book are also new, and five of them are from textbooks. Among the topics covered are the roots of altruism, the need for a third political party, and the pros and cons of nuclear power.

Pointers on Reading Flexibility and Monitoring Comprehension

To reinforce the idea that the reader should be flexible and adapt his or her reading rate to a particular type of reading, all ten extended readings in the book's final section now open with a suggestion for matching reading strategy to both the subject matter and writing style. The readings also end with a specific suggestion for monitoring comprehension.

Student Websites for Independent Practice and Review

Students often enjoy using websites for additional information and practice, particularly when the practice is interactive, with immediate results and feedback. *Reading for Results* has two websites where students can find many additional exercises to follow up on those introduced in the text. Introduced by a computer icon, references to the two websites (**college.hmco.com/pic/flemmingRFR10e** and **laflemm.com**) appear in every chapter. All exercises and tests are self-correcting, with the rejoinders explaining exactly why an answer is right or wrong, allowing students to work independently. While the Houghton Online Study Center for this book offers three levels of tests—"Getting Down the Basics," "Checking Your Progress," and "Taking the Challenge," the author's personal website provides additional exercises, some with click-on vocabulary reviews. Instructors can pick and choose from both sites to individualize both lab and homework.

Instructor's Website with Password-Protected and Downloadable Quizzes

For security and to provide as much instructor assistance as possible, Houghton Mifflin provides an Online Teaching Center for *Reading for Results,* a password-protected instructor's website at **college.hmco.com/pic/flemmingRFR10e** that provides an

Instructor's Resource Manual and Test Bank with suggestions for teaching, additional exercises, and vocabulary handouts, as well as a complete Answer Key for all exercises in the text. The Instructor's Resource Manual is also available in hard copy upon request.

Many Thanks to Reviewers

This edition, like all the previous ones, would have been all but impossible to complete without the help of the reviewers, whose suggestions I relied on to steer my way through this latest revision: Daryl Ann Bettcher of Illinois Valley Community College, Marylin Burke of Austin Community College, Helen R. Carr of San Antonio College, Barbara Fagg of The Community College of Baltimore County–Catonsville, Lesley S. Fredericks of Camden County College, Margot Haynes of Delta College, Joan Hellman of The Community College of Baltimore County–Catonsville, Joycelyn Jacobs of Lee College, Joyce Kevetos of Palm Beach Community College, Susie Khirallah-Johnston of Tyler Junior College, Dina Levitre of Community College of Rhode Island, Barbara M. Migden of Middlesex County College, Calisa A. Pierce of Southern West Virginia Community and Technical College, Carrie H. Pyhrr of Austin Community College, Candace Ready of Piedmont Technical College, Theodore Ridout of Bunker Hill Community College, Dawn Sedik of Valencia Community College, Deborah Spradlin of Tyler Junior College, and Barbara Jean Van Meter of Montgomery College.

Also Available in Laraine Flemming's Series: *Reading Keys* and *Reading for Thinking*

Written as an introduction to *Reading for Results*, *Reading Keys* offers a clear, step-by-step approach to the fundamentals of reading comprehension. Students start by reading single paragraphs and then move on to longer, multiparagraph readings. In contrast to *Reading for Results*, *Reading Keys* provides briefer explanations and more repetition of key concepts.

For those teaching a more advanced reading course, *Reading for Thinking* begins with a review of the comprehension skills covered in *Reading for Results* but quickly expands the scope and complexity of those skills by placing them in the context of learning strategies like annotating, summarizing, and synthesizing.

Part Two of *Reading for Thinking* explains, in more depth, many of the critical thinking skills introduced in *Reading for Results*, such as distinguishing between fact and opinion, recognizing the author's purpose, identifying tone, and responding to bias. Also included are a complete chapter on analyzing arguments and a final selection of readings that encourage students to make evaluating an author's ideas as important as understanding them. *Reading for Thinking* can be used independently. However, in format, terminology, and coverage, it is an excellent follow-up to *Reading for Results*.

Vocabulary Supplements

Instructors who would like additional vocabulary work for their students might be interested in *Words Count* (basic) and *Words Matter* (advanced). Both books use a contextual approach to teaching vocabulary. The ten words in each chapter revolve around a common theme, such as government, friendship, food, or marriage. The common thread of each chapter helps students make connections among the words and store them in long-term memory. Like the three-book reading series, the vocabulary books feature numerous exercises and lively readings that focus on topics of current and historical importance.

Additional Online and Electronic Supplements

Eduspace® With Houghton Mifflin's online learning tool powered by Blackboard, students get exercises with immediate feedback, chat rooms and discussion boards that encourage interaction, and 24-hour access to all assignments. Instructors receive a classroom management system that allows them to assign, distribute, track, and grade student assignments all online as well as post additional class assignments, announcements, and syllabi. Go to **www.edu space.com** for additional information.

Getting Focused A program for reading improvement available as a CD-ROM, "Getting Focused" was created by Ulrich and Laraine Flemming. The step-by-step program features a carefully sequenced series of exercises, tests, and tutorials that take students from basic comprehension to more advanced critical reading. Like Flemming's texts, "Getting Focused" features clear, comprehensive explanations and lively, informative readings.

Reading Space This web-based program fosters improved reading comprehension through a progressive sequence of Pre-, Practice, and Mastery Tests.

HM Reading CD-ROM Three diagnostic tests cover a total of 180 questions, as well as additional practice exercises. Each question focuses on one of twelve reading skills areas.

HM Vocabulary CD-ROM The CD features 800 questions comprising eighty drills. Four types of drills (matching, multiple-choice, fill-in-the-sentence, and fill-in-the-paragraph formats) ensure students have ample opportunities to practice new terms.

Vocabulary Enrichment Exercises for Reading (VEER) CD-ROM Eighty tests include matching, multiple-choice, fill-in-the-sentence, and fill-in-the-paragraph. The program features two modes, Practice and Test, so students can choose to either build their skills or gauge their progress.

Expressways 5.0 CD-ROM Expressways is a self-paced paragraph- and essay-level writing tutorial that provides students with extra practice on the writing process. Fourteen modules each include sections on prewriting and drafting, revising, and analyzing a reading, as well as a writing lab with three additional topics drawn from the earlier reading.

Additional Print Supplements

***Houghton Mifflin Guide to Reading Textbooks*, Second Edition** This guide helps students develop their reading skills, specifically for textbook reading in an academic environment.

***The American Heritage College Dictionary*, Fourth Edition** With 7,500 new words and meanings, along with 2,500 new illustrations, the fourth edition is the most up-to-date college dictionary available.

The American Heritage ESL Dictionary The first English as a second language (ESL) dictionary of its kind to be based on one of the most respected and authoritative American language dictionaries available, this resource is specially designed to meet the needs of ESL students.

Words Count This basic vocabulary book by Laraine Flemming uses a contextual approach to vocabulary building.

Words Matter This is a more advanced vocabulary book than *Words Count* and is also by Laraine Flemming.

Strategies for Mastering Your Textbooks

In this chapter, you'll learn

- how to use *SQ3R*, a reading method created specifically for learning from textbooks.

- how to adapt your reading rate when necessary, speeding up or slowing down to suit the text and your purpose in reading.

- how to prepare for difficult assignments by developing background knowledge with the help of the World Wide Web.

Chapter 1 introduces a system for study reading called *SQ3R*. Invented by psychology instructor Francis Robinson around half a century ago, the system has stood the test of time. One reason for its success is that it can

1

easily be adapted to both individual learning styles and different textbook assignments.

Chapter 1 also emphasizes reading rate and tells you when to skim at a high rate of speed or slow down to do a close, almost phrase-by-phrase reading. In addition, it illustrates how the World Wide Web can provide you with background knowledge, one of the keys to efficient reading. In short, Chapter 1 will get you started on the path to academic success.

Introducing *SQ3R*: Survey, Question, Read, Recite, Review

If you are reading a bestseller by a writer like Dan Brown or Anne Rice, you probably aren't inclined to look ahead to see how the story ends. Nor, for that matter, will you begin by asking yourself questions about plot, character, or atmosphere. When you read solely for pleasure, you more than likely let your mind drift along with the story, almost as if you were dreaming it.

Yet this dreamy, unfocused approach, so perfect for leisure reading, is not appropriate for textbooks. With textbooks, you need a systematic but flexible system for study reading, one that can take into account your assignment, the difficulty of the material, and the author's style of writing. *SQ3R* is flexible enough to take all three elements into account.

S: Survey to Get a General Overview

When you begin to work on a textbook assignment, don't just open up your textbook and start reading. Instead, **survey** or preview the material using the general sequence of steps described in the box below. Although your survey steps might increase or decrease according to how difficult the text is and how much you know about the subject, these seven steps are almost always essential. Take ten or twenty minutes to complete them before officially starting to read.

Seven Basic Steps

1. Read the title.
2. Read all introductory material. Pay close attention to chapter outlines, lists of questions, goals, or objectives, all of which identify what the author expects readers to learn.
3. Use the title and introduction to form a general question or two about the chapter's content. Check your memory to see if you have any prior knowledge or previous experience with the topic discussed.*
4. Read the heading of each chapter section as well as the opening sentence. If the material is especially difficult or unfamiliar, you can expand this step to read the last sentence of every chapter section or even the first and last sentence of every paragraph. If the chapter introduces a new section with an introductory overview, as the sample chapter does (see page 34), read these as well when the material is unfamiliar and dense with details.
5. Look at all visual aids. Visual aids include pictures, photos, maps, charts, boxes, and graphs. If captions or explanations accompany the visual aids, read them, too. Try to figure out before you begin reading why the visual aids might be important to the chapter.
6. Pay attention to words printed in boldface or in the margin of the page. With particularly important or difficult courses, expand this step to include jotting boldface or italicized terms in the margins. As you read, you can then add definitions to the terms written in the margins.
7. Read end-of-chapter summaries and questions. If there is no end-of-chapter summary, read the last page.

Reading Tip

Collect key vocabulary words—the ones highlighted with italics, boldface, or colored ink—chapter by chapter in order to develop a master list for each course. After finishing an assignment, transfer your vocabulary notes from the margins of your text to a vocabulary notebook. Review one page per day.

*More on developing prior knowledge using the World Wide Web on pages 21–31.

Surveying Goals

Brief as it is, a survey should still give you (1) a general overview of the chapter's contents, (2) a sense of the writer's style and organization, (3) a feeling for what's important in the chapter, and (4) an idea of the chapter's natural breaks or divisions, which can then be used to organize the number and length of your study sessions.

Breaking an Assignment into Manageable Parts

This fourth and last benefit of surveying is particularly important to those of you who feel you have trouble concentrating. Knowing that you are sitting down to read fifty pages over a period of two hours may leave you feeling exhausted before you start. But if you divide a chapter into two manageable portions of, say, twenty to twenty-five pages each and allot each segment to a different night, your chances of staying focused and alert while reading are likely to improve.

Skimming versus Reading

Surveys are meant to be short, ten to twenty minutes depending on the length and difficulty of the material. A survey can be this brief because you are actually skimming the material instead of reading it. When you **skim**, you look only at certain pre-selected sections of text in order to get a *general idea* of the content. Your reading rate while skimming can be as high as 600 or 800* words per minute. At that speed, you can get a chapter overview, which is all you want to accomplish in this pre-reading step.

Focusing Your Survey

As you skim selected portions of the chapter, keep questions like those that follow in mind. Knowing what you are looking for or trying to understand will make your survey productive because you will be attentive to the answers when you spot them.

---

*There are discussions of reading rate that cite figures as high as 1200 wpm, but I'd reserve that rate for scanning, i.e., looking for a particular piece of information.

Ten Questions to Guide Your Survey

1. What does the title suggest about the author's emphasis or focus?
2. According to the headings, what issues or topics will the author address?
3. Are there any visual aids? What do they suggest about chapter content and focus?
4. Do any sections look especially difficult?
5. Does any of the material look familiar?
6. Does the author use **boldface**, marginal annotations, color, or *italics* to emphasize important words and ideas?
7. How many pages should I plan to complete during each study session?
8. What background knowledge do I have about the topics or issues addressed in this chapter?
9. Are there any questions in the headings I can use to focus my attention while reading?
10. Is there a summary I can use to figure out what's central to the chapter?

EXERCISE 1 **Surveying a Chapter**

DIRECTIONS Survey the sample chapter on pages 34–52. Then answer the following questions by circling either the correct response or the letter of the correct response. *Note*: In this case, your survey should include the first and last sentence of every paragraph.

1. Based on the introductory material, you should read to answer which question?
   a. How did the Cold War affect the U.S. at home and overseas?
   b. What brought an end to the Cold War?
   c. How long did the Cold War last?

2. Which is the best question to ask about the heading on page 36 "The Economic Boom Begins"?
   a. What caused the economic boom following World War II?
   b. When did the economic boom begin?
   c. When did the economic boom following World War II

Please explain your answer. _It tells you in the heading that in the reading you will find out when it begins._

3. If you followed the directions for surveying, you would know that Congress enacted the GI Bill in

   (a.) 1944.   b. 1945.   c. 1946.

4. Based on your survey, which of the following is true?

   a. The majority of returning servicemen wanted to use their GI benefits for higher education and purchasing a home.

   b. Many returning servicemen wanted to use their GI benefits to buy luxuries that could convince them they were really home again and living in peacetime.

   c. Most returning servicemen found it difficult to accept money from the federal government, even if they had more than earned it by going to war.

5. Based on your survey, which of the following is true?

   a. The postwar boom benefited only returning soldiers, who received help from the government in order to resume their lives.

   b. The postwar boom benefited business more than ordinary working people.

   c. Following the war, people from all walks of life benefited from the postwar boom.

6. Based on your survey, identify the following statement as *True* or *False*.

   True or *False.* The African-American civil rights movement began just before the Cold War started.

7. Based on your survey, identify the following statement as *True* or *False*.

   True or *False*. A. Philip Randolph was a civil rights activist.

8. Based on your survey, which of the following people was accused of being a communist?

   a. Jackie Robinson

   b. A. Philip Randolph

   c. Alger Hiss

   d. Dan Collins

9. Based on your survey, what was the effect of the Truman Doctrine and the Marshall Plan on the Soviet Union?

   a. The Soviet Union realized it had to compete more with the West when it came to providing goods and services.

   b. The Soviet Union became even more determined to maintain control over Eastern Europe.

   c. The Soviet Union recognized that its control over Eastern Europe could not possibly last in the face of American power.

10. Based on your survey, identify the following statement as *True* or *False*.

    True or *False*. The Cold War also had a profound effect on Asia.

 # *Q*: Use Questions to Guide Your Attention

Once you complete your survey, you'll have plenty of material for **questions** to help guide your reading of the chapter. Here again, reading to answer questions will keep you alert to what's important. Say, for instance, that you were assigned the sample chapter appearing on pages 34–52. Once you finished your survey, you'd know the questions the authors expect you to answer from your reading. Those questions appear in the chapter introduction.

> **1.** How did the postwar policies of the United States and the Soviet Union contribute to the beginnings of the Cold War?
>
> **2.** What was the doctrine of containment, and how was it implemented from 1947 to 1952?
>
> **3.** How did the Cold War affect the rights of African Americans?
>
> **4.** What were the main domestic and international factors leading to the postwar Red Scare, and why did so many Americans react to it as they did?

You could also use the headings you skimmed to frame more questions of your own; the heading **The GI Bill of Rights** on page 36 is a good example. Unless you already know the answer, that heading should prompt questions like "What was the GI Bill of Rights?" "How did it originate?" "What was the public's reaction to the GI Bill?"

Major and Minor Headings

Most textbooks use **MAJOR** and **minor** headings to organize chapter content. Major headings identify the broad general topics or issues covered in the chapter. Minor headings follow major ones and help subdivide the larger, more general topic into smaller, more manageable subtopics. Use both major and minor headings as the basis of your questions.

A Note on *Who*, *When*, and *Where*

By all means use the words *who*, *when*, and *where* to develop questions. Just don't rely on them too heavily. Instead of an in-depth understanding of the author's ideas, they often produce questions that generate brief, factual answers. What you need are questions that help you probe and explore the chapter in depth. Question openers such as *what*, *why*, *how*, and *in what way* can help you get in tune with the author's thinking.

Making Graphs, Tables, Timelines, and Charts Part of Your Survey

Like headings, graphs, tables, timelines, and charts can be the basis for questions. Line graphs (like the one on page 42 in the sample chapter) typically trace changes over time—in this case the amount spent on defense between 1940 and 1961. You can tell the time span from the dates that run along the bottom line, or horizontal axis, of the graph. (See page 718 of the Appendix.)

Although you don't need to study visual aids closely until you actually read the text and can match graphic information to text statements, you can still pose survey-based questions, for example, "Why do the authors include a graph that reflects changes in defense spending?" "What would defense spending have to do with the topic of the chapter, the Cold War?"

Expand Prior Knowledge by Using the Web

During your survey you may discover that you have little or no prior knowledge about the topic being discussed. If that's the case and you want to dramatically improve your mastery of the chapter, you can always turn to the World Wide Web discussed on pages 21–31. But for now let's finish the steps in *SQ3R*.

 *R*: Read

Once you have completed your survey, it's time to read the twenty pages or so that you have decided to cover in your first study session. This is the time to be totally focused on what you are doing. If you are not, it's easy to read the words without grasping the meaning.

Read to Answer Specific Questions

Every time you start a chapter section, consciously consider the questions generated by your survey. Reading with specific questions in mind will help you locate key points. It will also help you **monitor**, or check, your comprehension. If you can't answer any of the survey questions, take a brief break and start from scratch because you may not be concentrating.

When you can answer a question, you'll feel a sense of accomplishment. This sense of accomplishment will motivate you to keep reading even the most difficult assignments.

Write While You Read

If I personally could give one piece of advice to student readers, it would be this one: *Keep a pen in your hand and write while you read*. This doesn't mean you should mindlessly copy the author's words into a notebook. Instead, underline selectively, take marginal notes, record personal associations, and use symbols to highlight essential names, dates, and terms.

Marking Your Textbooks

1. Underline (sparingly) the key words in sentences, "The <u>psychological problems of readjustment</u> faced <u>by veterans</u> were <u>intensified by</u> a drastic <u>housing shortage</u> and <u>soaring divorce</u> rate."

2. Take marginal notes, paraphrasing the author's ideas by putting them into your own words.

3. Draw arrows connecting specific examples to broad general statements: "Truman was in trouble early on (generalization).

    unions furious at him ◄───┐

4. Make small diagrams showing how one event (the cause) created or produced another (the effect).

    | Marshall Plan | ──provokes──► | Russians into using more force to maintain control. |

5. Write comments based on your own prior knowledge or personal experience, e.g., "My grandfather went to school on the GI Bill."

6. Mark passages where you don't agree with the author's ideas (see the chart on page 11 for symbols): "It's crazy to say Truman needed to drop the atomic bomb!!"

7. Identify confusing passages so that you can give them a second reading, e.g., ? ? or RR (for reread).

8. List opposing points of view (yours or someone else's), "Compare Howard Zinn on the role of the Marshall Plan."

9. Circle, star, or box key names and dates, e.g., George Kennan.

10. Jot down verbatim, or word for word, statements that seem perfectly phrased and have a nice ring to them: "If you can't stand the heat, get out of the kitchen [Harry Truman]."

11. Identify potential test questions, e.g., "What role did A. Philip Randolph play in the Pullman strike?"

The following chart offers you some suggestions for marking a text. However, you can certainly create your own symbol system. Just be sure to use it consistently.

Symbols for Marking a Text

Broken underlining for key words in important statements.	— — —
Abbreviations to show the type of support: examples, reasons, statistics	Ex, R, Stat
Numbers to itemize examples, reasons, steps, or studies	1, 2, 3
Stars for particularly important statements or quotations	★ ★
Boxes for transitional words or key terms	☐
Circles for key names, dates, or terms	○
Exclamation points to show surprise	! !
Question marks to indicate an unclear sentence or passage	? ?
The letters *TQ* to identify potential test questions; the letters *RR* to indicate the the need for a second reading	TQ and RR
Connected arrows to highlight related statements	⇄
Vertical marks or brackets to emphasize a key passage	‖ [ ]
Marginal notes to record comments and questions	Argument doesn't make sense
Equal signs to identify definitions following key words	cognition = thinking

---

Three Benefits of Writing While Reading

1. **Maintains your concentration.** The physical act of writing will keep you more mentally alert even if you are reading a chapter assignment that you would never have read on your own.
2. **Improves comprehension.** Taking marginal notes requires you to paraphrase, or translate the author's words into your own. When you paraphrase you have to thoroughly understand the meaning before you can find the language to match. Paraphrase regularly and you won't have a chance to go on automatic pilot and read without thinking, one of the chief causes for failed comprehension.
3. **Ensures remembering.** Your brain needs both effort and time to transfer new information into your long-term memory, where it can stay for months, years, maybe even forever. Whenever you jot down your disagreements, note your confusion, or reword the author's ideas, you are giving long-term memory a chance to process and store information it has never seen before.

Be Selective with Underlining

Be selective about what you consider important enough to underline, highlight, or note in margins. With very difficult or unfamiliar text, you may want to underline and take notes *after* a second reading. At that point, you understand the material and can decide what's important and what's not. If you underline before you are clear on the meaning, you might end up with pages that look like this:

> **The GI Bill of Rights.** In 1944 Congress had enacted the Servicemen's Readjustment Act. Commonly called the GI Bill of Rights or GI Bill, it was designed to forestall the expected . . . [economic downturn] by easing veterans back into the work force, as well as to reward the "soldier boys" and reduce their fears of female competition. The GI Bill gave veterans priority for many jobs, occupational guidance, and, if need be, fifty-two weeks of unemployment benefits. It also established veterans' hospitals and provided low-interest loans to returning GIs who were starting businesses or buying homes or farms. Almost four million veterans bought homes with government loans, fueling a baby boom, suburbanization, and a record demand for new goods and services.

Underlining everything defeats the purpose, because the most important elements don't stand out. Everything seems equally important, and that's rarely the case. Your goal should be to mark pages so that a quick glance tells you what's important.

T.Q. What was the purpose of the GI Bill, and what did it do for veterans?

The GI Bill of Rights. In 1944 Congress had <u>enacted</u> the <u>Ser-vicemen's Readjustment Act</u>. Commonly called the GI Bill of Rights or GI Bill, it was designed ①<u>to forestall the expected . . . economic downturn</u> by <u>easing veterans</u> back <u>into</u> the <u>work force,</u> as well as ②<u>to reward</u> the "soldier boys" and ③<u>reduce</u> their <u>fears</u> of <u>female competition</u>. The GI Bill <u>gave veterans priority for</u> many <u>jobs</u>, <u>occupational guidance</u>, and, if need be, fifty-two weeks of <u>unemployment benefits</u>. It also <u>established veterans' hospitals</u> and provided <u>low-interest loans</u> to returning GIs who were starting businesses or buying homes or farms. Almost four million veterans <u>bought homes</u> with government loans, fueling a baby boom, suburbanization, and a record demand for new goods and services.

GI Bill benefits

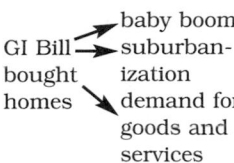

GI Bill bought homes → baby boom → suburbanization → demand for goods and services

---

Reading Tip

Selectively underlining words will help you understand and remember what you read. But a better method is to combine underlining with marginal notes, diagrams, symbols, and personal comments. Using a variety of page-marking techniques will keep you focused and sharp. It will also help you remember what you read.

Vary Your Reading Rate According to the Material

Unless you are reading a science text, where the difficulty level of the material forces you to consistently maintain a low reading rate (see the following chart), you should always adjust your rate to the material. While rereading the introduction you already surveyed, feel free to speed up to 500 or 600 words a minute.

With material that is familiar and not that difficult—introductions in textbooks, for instance, are often lists of single sentences rather than paragraphs—your rate can be on the boundary between skimming and reading. If you are reading, say, a chapter on childhood nutrition and already know the material from another course, then keep your reading rate fairly high, between 350 and 400 words per minute. If the text becomes difficult, don't be afraid to slow down and do an analytical or close reading, probably at 100 or 150 words per minute.

Reading Rates

Good readers are flexible about reading rate.
They vary it to suit the material and their reading purpose.

Scanning	Purpose	Type of Assignment	Rate
Scanning	To locate a specific piece of information	You are searching for a specific fact, statistic, or study.	700 to 1000 words per minute
Skimming	To get a general overview of an article or a chapter	You are preparing to read a chapter and previewing it to determine how much time and how many study sessions you will need to master the material.	400 to 800 words per minute
Study Reading	To understand an author's message or follow the plot of a novel or short story	You are reading a detailed but clearly written chapter in preparation for class.	250 to 400 words per minute
Close or Analytical Reading	To understand a hard-to-read passage or unfamiliar and complex material	You are trying to understand a chapter filled with new ideas and written in a hard-to-read style.	100 to 250 words per minute

INTERNET RESOURCE

For more on the four reading rates, see **laflemm.com**.

 # *R*: Recite

Unfortunately, most students think they can skip this step in *SQ3R*. Yet, *reciting*, or mentally answering questions about each chapter section, is a key step to understanding and remembering what you read.

Test Your Understanding

Reciting immediately after reading is a great way to monitor, or test, your comprehension. If you can't recite answers to such questions as "What was this section about?" or "What did the author say about the Marshall Plan?" then you probably haven't understood the material. Similarly, if you can't answer any of the questions from your survey, you should definitely mark portions of the chapter section for a later rereading.

Reading Tip   Reciting after reading gives your mind a chance to go over the material a second time. Repetition of new information is what helps you remember it.

Write Out the Answers

In describing the second *R* in *SQ3R*, its creator, Francis Robinson, suggested that readers go beyond reciting and actually write out answers to their questions. He believed that writing the answers is a better test of comprehension because you can't fool yourself into accepting vague or only half-formed answers.

Although you might not want to follow Robinson's advice for every reading assignment, do consider it for assignments that are difficult and have special importance. If, for example, you are struggling with biology, and biology is your major, you probably should write out the answers to your questions about each chapter section.

EXERCISE 2 Testing Your Understanding

DIRECTIONS Test your understanding of the material you have just read by writing answers to the following three questions.

1. Why is it a good idea to recite after reading?

_____

_____

2. If you can't recite answers to any of your questions, what should you do?

_____

_____

3. Why did Francis Robinson believe that students should actually write answers to the questions they posed about a chapter section?

_____

_____

R: Review

Like reciting after you finish a chapter section, *reviewing* the entire chapter after you complete it is a critical step. Reviewing tells you which chapter sections you understood and which ones you need to reread. Because reviewing gives you another chance to think about the author's ideas, it also slows down the rate of forgetting— a bonus you can't ignore.

Immediate Review

Reviews you do immediately after finishing a chapter should be brief—no more than fifteen minutes. During this time, you can choose from several different ways to review. The type of review you do depends on how difficult the material is, how thoroughly you need to know it, and your preferred learning style.

Methods of Review

1. Look over the headings to see how much you can recall about each one.
2. Skim only the words you've underlined. See if you can mentally fill in what's missing.
3. Ask a friend to read the chapter headings to you so you can say aloud what you remember about each one.
4. Write out answers to the survey questions you asked before actually reading the material.
5. Look at the visual aids to see if you can explain why they are in the chapter.
6. Diagram the chapter to show its key points. (For more on informal outlines and graphic organizers, or diagrams, see pages 19–20 and pages 399–402.)

Visual aids can be especially useful during reviews. For instance, if a chapter has a timeline like the following, you can review by just looking at the dates and seeing how well you can recall the events that occurred at those times.

Chronology, 1948–1952

1948 Communist coup in Czechoslovakia.
State of Israel founded.
Soviet Union begins blockade of Berlin; United States begins airlift.
Congress approves Marshall Plan.
Truman orders an end to segregation in the armed forces.
Communist leaders put on trial under the Smith Act.
Truman elected president.

1949 North Atlantic Treaty Organization (NATO) established.
East and West Germany founded as separate nations.
Communist victory in China; People's Republic of China established.
Soviet Union detonates an atomic bomb.

1950 Truman authorizes building a hydrogen bomb.
Soviet spy ring at Los Alamos uncovered.

> Alger Hiss convicted of perjury.
> Joseph McCarthy launches anticommunist crusade.
> Korean War begins.
> Julius and Ethel Rosenberg arrested as atomic spies.
> McCarran Internal Security Act.
> Truman accepts NSC-68.
> China enters the Korean War.
> **1951** Douglas MacArthur dismissed from his Korean
>   command.
> Supreme Court upholds Smith Act.
> Rosenbergs convicted of espionage.
> **1952** First hydrogen bomb exploded.
> Dwight D. Eisenhower elected president;
>   Republicans win control of Congress.

Study Tip   Consider creating your own timelines as a way of studying the
dates and events in a chapter.

Review Several Times Over the Course of the Semester

As early as the nineteenth century, researchers on memory knew
that repeated reviews over an extended period of time were the key
to mastering and remembering new information. Thus, if you want
to be prepared for exams and avoid cramming, you should plan on
several chapter reviews carried out over time.

Check Your Understanding
1. Why is reviewing an important step in *SQ3R*?
_____
_____
2. What are some of the techniques you can use to review?
_____
_____

The Role of Informal Outlining in Review

To get a head start on preparing for exams, make an informal outline of the chapter sections as part of your long-term review. When you make an **informal outline**—as opposed to a formal one in which the organization and symbols are rigidly prescribed—don't worry about how you use numbers, letters, phrases, or sentences. At this stage in your reading and test preparation, you don't want, or need, to be too detailed. Each time you review, you will be able to add to your informal outline, making it more detailed each time. Initially, all you want or need is a list of the major and minor headings, along with a brief statement about each chapter section. Here is an illustration of a partial outline based on pages 35–39 of the sample chapter.

1. The postwar political setting, 1945–1946

In the aftermath of World War II, America prospered.

   a. Demobilization

   Americans wanted their soldiers home, but once back, it wasn't clear how the country could readjust to peace.

   b. Truman's Domestic Program

     (1) Truman vetoed bill for extending price controls; within a week, food prices go up 16%.

     (2) Everyone hates Truman at this point, particularly labor.

   c. Anticommunism and Containment, 1946–1952

   Stalin declares there can be no lasting peace with U.S.

See those big spaces separating each item in the outline. They are there for a reason. Over time, those spaces would be filled in based on your rereading of difficult chapter sections, your reviews of underlined text and marginal jottings, and the addition of information from lecture notes. When exam time rolled around, you would no longer have to look at your textbook. You'd have a complete and detailed outline to review in preparation for the exam.

■ EXERCISE 3 Practicing the *R* in *SQ3R*

DIRECTIONS To answer these questions, turn to page 35 and read the chapter section beginning with the heading "The Postwar Political Setting, 1945–1946" and ending with "The Economic Boom Begins" (page 36). You can return to these pages as you answer the questions, but first a thorough reading is necessary. Then answer the questions by circling the letter of the correct response or filling in the blanks.

1. The first minor heading in the chapter is "Demobilization." Based on the paragraph that follows (paragraph 2), circle the letter of the sentence that best defines the word "demobilization."

    a. Demobilization refers to Truman's giving in to public pressure.

    b. Demobilization refers to Truman's removing millions of soldiers from active duty.

    c. Demobilization refers to huge numbers of soldiers asking for and getting transport ships with the threat of "no boats, no votes."

2. At the end of paragraph 4, the authors refer to a question from a popular women's magazine. The question was "Isn't a Woman's Place in the Home?" The question is there to illustrate which point?

    a. Women's magazines were slow to recognize women's new role in the economy that emerged after the end of World War II; the magazines still tended to picture women as homemakers.

    b. Women's magazines remained popular with women even after women began to take more jobs modeled on Rosie the Riveter.

    c. When men returned home, they replaced women in the work force, and women were encouraged to return to the home rather than compete with men.

3. According to the authors, what benefits did the GI Bill of Rights give to returning veterans? (Please paraphrase first without looking back at the text. Then check your answers against what's stated in the chapter (paragraphs 5 and 6).

_____

_____

4. What's the connection between the authors' description of the GI Bill of Rights (paragraphs 5 and 6) and the reference to new state and community colleges (paragraph 7)?

_____

_____

INTERNET RESOURCE

For a clear and complete review of *SQ3R* as well as explanations of every study skill or strategy imaginable, go to **www.study.gs.net**, a great site. Be sure to bookmark it.

 Mining the Web for Background Knowledge

". . . a reader's *schema*, or organized knowledge of the world, provides much of the basis for comprehending, learning, and remembering the ideas in stories and texts."
—Reading Researcher Richard Anderson, University of Illinois at Urbana

Earlier in this chapter, you learned that the Web could be used to enlarge and enhance background knowledge. It's now time to show you why and how to use the Web to improve reading.

The Role of Background Knowledge in Comprehension

Around 1970, reading researchers began focusing on the relationship between background knowledge and comprehension. Almost unanimously they came to one conclusion: The more readers know about a subject *before* they begin reading, the more their comprehension improves. At the time this was hardly cause for celebration among student readers. College students are constantly confronted by textbooks featuring topics they know little or nothing about. That's why they are in college—to learn what they don't know and need to know in order to enhance both their personal and professional lives. In the 1970s student readers couldn't really put theory into practice and broaden their background knowledge as part of their prereading; research was necessary, and that required time and effort. Fortunately, though, the arrival of the Internet and the World Wide Web has changed everything.

The World Wide Web Makes a Difference

Nowadays, if you survey a textbook chapter and think, "Oh no, this reads as if it were written in a foreign language, that's how little I know about the subject," you can turn to the World Wide Web, a huge network of computerized documents linked together in cyberspace. The Web has information on just about any topic you can think of. With the Web, it's possible to get a general framework (that's the schema referred to above) about whatever subject you are studying.

For instance, if you surveyed the sample chapter and thought to yourself, "The only thing I know about Harry Truman is that my grandfather considered him a hero while my grandmother thought he was the devil," you probably need to get some background knowledge about Truman and the role he played in the Cold War before reading in earnest.

Why Bother?

Could you read the chapter without any background knowledge? Absolutely. But will you get more out of it if you already have some information about Truman's role in the long-running tension between the United States and Russia? Without a doubt. Using the Web as part of your prereading preparation for detailed and unfamiliar texts pays huge dividends. And it certainly doesn't hurt to supplement your text with Web research *while* you are reading as well. That means using a **search engine**, or software for navigating the Web.

Pick a Search Engine Right for the Job

Google is a search engine that has a great track record for coming up with sites relevant to the topic being researched, so we will use it to illustrate the explanations provided here.

However, when doing Web searches, it's often a good idea to use at least two search engines so that you can compare the results and decide which one is better suited to your task. Search engines vary in their capabilities, ease of use, and organizational clarity.

Indexes and Directories

There are two kinds of search engines: directories and indexes. Like all **directories**, Google's is created by people—as opposed to software—who organize websites into listings of general topics. These general, or broad, topics are then further broken down into more specific, or restricted, subcategories, for example: Recreation → Tourism → Specialty Travel → Ecotourism.* Directories are terrific for those times when you have a broad category in mind but don't quite know what you are looking for within that general grouping. A directory can help you see how others think about a topic, making it easier for you to develop your own focus. While a directory might prove useful once you have finished a chapter and are thinking about a research paper, an index is a better choice for generating background knowledge about chapter headings, which are already fairly specific, or limited in scope.

Indexes are huge collections of websites and webpages. They are created by something called a *web crawler*, an automated tool that searches out and collects sites related to a specific topic. The crawler then sends that information on to an indexer (software, not a person) to be analyzed and categorized. When you type words into a search box, the search engine browses its own index (or indexes), not the entire Web. This means that a search engine is only as good as its index, and some indexes are either better than others or more appropriate to specific tasks.

INTERNET RESOURCE
To get a detailed explanation of what you can do with the Internet and the World Wide Web, go to **learnthenet.com** and click on "Glossary" and "Animated Internet." You won't be disappointed.

The Right Search Term Is Critical, or Never Use a Single Word to Search the Web

Computers are sometimes compared to dogs. The joke is that they are faithful, friendly, and not too bright. But in addition to being unfair to dogs, that simile, or comparison, is unfair to computers.

Ecotourism: Tourism devoted to nature and how to preserve its resources.

The categories come from an excellent book on Google: Sarah Milstein and Rael Dornfest. *The Missing Manual.* Sebastapol, CA: O'Reilly Media, 2004.

Computers only give back what people put into them. A vague, general search term probably won't get what you want. Or more to the point, you won't get what you want fast. Look, for instance, what comes up on Google when the search term is just "Truman."

[1] **Truman** State University
Truman State University Missouri's Public Liberal Arts & Sciences University.
www.truman.edu/

[2] The H. **Truman** Scholarship Foundation I Home
Scholarships for college juniors who show leadership potential and have an interest in government or public sector service.
www.truman.gov/

[3] President **Truman** - Harry S. **Truman** Presidential Museum and Library
Truman Presidential Museum & Library hosts documents, photographs, virtual exhibits, audio files, oral histories, digital archives, kids page, . . .
www.trumanlibrary.org/

[4] Biography of Harry S. **Truman**
Biography of Harry S. **Truman**, the thirty-third President of the United States (1945–1953).
www.whitehouse.gov/history/presidents/ht33.html

[5] The **Truman** Show (1998)
The **Truman** Show - Cast, Crew, Reviews, Plot Summary, Comments, Discussion, Taglines, Trailers, Posters, Photos, Showtimes, Link to Official Site, Fan Sites.
www.imdb.com/title/tt0120382/

[6] Harry S. **Truman** - Wikipedia, the free encyclopedia
Truman's presidency was eventful, seeing the atomic bombings of . . .
Truman was a folksy, unassuming president, and popularized phrases such as "The buck . . .
en.wikipedia.org/wiki/Harry_S._Truman

[7] The Avalon Project: **Truman** Doctrine
Complete text of the March 12, 1947, address before a joint session of Congress.
www.yale.edu/lawweb/avalon/trudoc.htm

[8] **Truman** College
Apply online, admissions, programs, continuing education, departments, financial aid, class schedule, news.
www.trumancollege.cc/

[9] Project WhistleStop: Harry S **Truman**
Features original source material from the Harry S **Truman** Presidential Library.

With a good deal of trial and error this list of websites might get you the background knowledge you need. However, why bother even thinking about websites devoted to the schools and scholarship named after Truman, (websites 1, 2, 3, and 8). And, for sure, you won't be able to use the website about the movie *The Truman Show* (website 5). When you are trying to develop background knowledge, you want several *relevant*, or related, resources. And you want them as quickly as possible. To save time, you need to use a precise search term, which almost always consists of more than one word. Here, we can skim the sample chapter for terms that consistently appear and use them to create a more focused *search phrase*. Although several possibilities might come to mind when you look at the chapter, the term "Truman's Cold War Policies" should get you relevant material. Look at what that phrase turned up with Google.

[1] **Cold War Policies** 1945-1991
Narrative outline of United States and other **policies** during the **Cold War**. Includes various photographs and related links.
history.sandiego.edu/gen/20th/coldwar0.html

[2] CNN **Cold War** - Historical Document: **Truman** Doctrine
In this famous address to Congress, President **Truman** stressed the duty of the . . . The foreign **policy** and the national security of this country are involved. . . .
www.cnn.com/SPECIALS/cold.war/episodes/03/documents/truman/

[3] Documents Related to the **Cold War**
Documents Relating to American Foreign **Policy**. The **Cold War** . . . **Truman** Library, Interviews in 1971–73. Early **Cold War** History . . .
www.mtholyoke.edu/acad/intrel/coldwar.htm

[4] John Kennedy and the **Cold War**
Throughout his pre-presidential career, JFK was an active **Cold** Warrior. As noted, his first Congressional campaign boasted of taking on the anti-**Cold War** . . .
mcadams.posc.mu.edu/progjfk5.htm

[5] 79.02.01: The Foreign **Policies** of Harry S. **Truman**
First Lesson: **Truman** Takes Over the Presidency. Day 1: Foreign **Policies**: Ending the **War** in . . . How the **Cold War** Was Played in Foreign Affairs, Vol. 51, No. . . .
www.yale.edu/ynhti/curriculum/units/1979/2/79.02.01.x.html

[6] The American President: Harry **Truman**
Truman's policies abroad, and especially toward the Soviet Union in the emerging **Cold War**, would become staples of American foreign **policy** for generations. . . .
www.americanpresident.org/history/harrytruman/

[7] **Cold War**: 14 to 18 years
Harry S. **Truman**: The Presidential Years: At the **Truman** Presidential Museum . . . **Cold War Policies** 1945-1991: A collection of illustrated articles and outline . . .
www.spartacus.schoolnet.co.uk/REVhistoryCOLD3.htm

[8] Harry S. **Truman**
I recommend it for additional web file material on **Cold War policy**. In particular for the **Truman** years, use the Documents subfile to see Documents Related . . .
cstl-cla.semo.edu/Renka/Modern_Presidents/truman.htm

[9] The **Cold War**
HIS 122 Research Brief The US **Cold War Policy** of Containment. George C. Marshall. The **Truman** Administration proposed to rebuild the continent in the . . .
www.vw.vccs.edu/vwhansd/HIS122/ColdWar.html

Now most of these websites do look relevant to our search for background knowledge. Some, however, will be more relevant than others, and the last thing you want to do is to just start at the beginning and work your way down the list by clicking on every single one.* That could take a good deal of time, and you shouldn't spend more than an hour or so building background knowledge in preparation for reading. At this point, you should skim the list and make some decisions about which websites might be more useful than others. To help you decide which websites to look at first, here are several pointers:

How to Choose a Website

1. **Read the website descriptions carefully. Look for references to words in your search term, or people and events relevant to your chapter topics.** Search engines introduce each link with a title, description, and web address. The most relevant links will generally include at least one or two words from your search term. The least relevant ones will either not contain any words from your search term or describe people and places that have little to do with the topic you're interested in. Based on this pointer, you could already eliminate website number 4 since we know that the sample chapter does not address the presidency of John F. Kennedy.

2. **Eliminate those sites where the description refers to documents, conference proceedings, addresses, interviews, and journal articles.** There is a chance that sites referring to, say, President Truman's Inaugural Address might prove useful. However, there is a greater possibility that they will be too limited in scope to fulfill your pre-reading purpose: to enlarge your general background knowledge about "Truman's Cold War Policies" and their effects. Based on this second pointer, we can eliminate sites 2 and 3 from our search.

---

*Some research suggests that this start-at-the-beginning-and-keep-reading method is the reason why some people don't grasp the Web's value as a research tool. Laura A. Henry, "The Critical Role of New Literacies while Reading on the Internet." *The Reading Teacher*, April 2006, pp. 614–615.

3. **Hold off clicking on websites referred to as outlines.** Websites set up as outlines or timelines are great for reviews. But they are usually too abbreviated to be valuable as prereading preparation. Outlines and timelines pare information down to its most basic elements. While such abbreviated versions of events are fine once you have mastered the material covered in a chapter, they are less useful for building background knowledge in preparation for reading.

4. **Avoid sites that end in *gov*.** If the Uniform Resource Locator (URL), which is a fancy phrase for website address, ends in *gov*, the U.S. government is the source of the webpage. While resources from the government are fine for researching a term paper, they tend to be long, dry, and sometimes hard to read. For the purpose of gaining background knowledge, you want websites that provide information in a lively and easy-to-read manner. To broaden your background knowledge, you would be better off with URLs ending in or including *edu* (the source is an educational institution); *org* (nonprofit organization); and *com* (commercial organization). *Note*: *htm* and *html* do not tell you anything about the source of the information. These letters describe *how* the pages were created.

5. **Don't bother with sponsored sites.** Sponsored sites weren't just found by the web crawler searching the Web. Someone paid a fee to make them come up in response to a particular set of search terms. You will very likely have to pay to use them. They are also likely to be **biased**, or inclined to show favoritism. With Google, sponsored sites generally appear on the right-hand side of the screen, but they can also make their way into the list of sites compiled randomly, or without plan, by the web crawler. If a site seems to be selling products of any kind, cross it off the list of links to look at.

Now that we have narrowed the number of seemingly relevant sites down to the five, let's make a decision about which one to look at first. Probably the best choice to start with is website 6, The American President: Harry Truman (www.americanpresident.org/history/harrytruman). The website's title suggests that the site will have the general focus we are looking for. As a first start, it is certainly preferable to website 5, The Foreign Policies of Harry S. Truman, which might be too limited in scope to help with a chapter that focuses heavily on domestic events.

As it turns out, website 6 is a very good choice. Look at the home page that comes up for that web address.

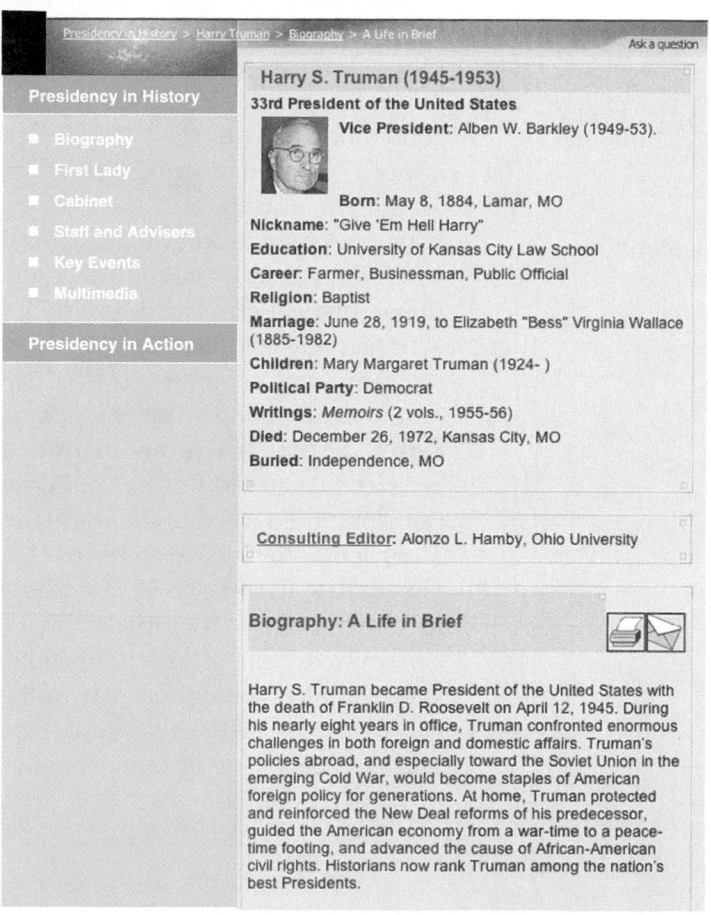

The list on the left of the home page identifies the topics covered on the website. Clearly this site can tell you a lot about Harry Truman's personal and professional life. But to help you get background knowledge for the sample chapter, hitting the link titled "Key Events" would get you the information you need, as the following web excerpt illustrates:

Truman and Post-War America

Truman took office as World War II in Europe drew to a close. The German leader Adolf Hitler committed suicide in Berlin only two weeks into Truman's presidency and the allies declared victory in Europe on May 7, 1945. The war in the Pacific, however, was far from being over; most experts believed it might last another year and require an American invasion of Japan. The U.S. and British governments, though, had secretly begun to develop the world's most deadly weapon -- an atomic bomb. Upon its completion and successful testing in the summer of 1945, Truman approved its use against Japan. On August 6 and 9, 1945, the U.S. Army Air Force dropped atomic bombs on two cities, Hiroshima and Nagasaki, immediately killing upwards of 100,000 people (with perhaps twice that number dying from the aftereffects of radiation poisoning). Japanese emperor Hirohito agreed to surrender days later, bringing World War II to a close.

Truman faced unprecedented and defining challenges in international affairs during the first years of his presidency. American relations with the Soviet Union -- nominal allies in the battle against Germany and Japan -- began to deteriorate even before victory in World War II. Serious ideological differences -- the United States supported democratic institutions and market principles, while Soviet leaders were totalitarian and ran a command economy -- separated the two countries. But it was the diverging interests of the emerging superpowers in Europe and Asia which sharpened their differences.

In response to what it viewed as Soviet threats, the Truman administration constructed foreign policies to contain the Soviet Union's political power and counter its military strength. By 1949, Soviet and American policies had divided Europe into a Soviet-controlled bloc in the east and an American-supported grouping in the west. That same year, a communist government sympathetic to the Soviet Union came to power in China, the world's most populous nation. The Cold War between the United States and the Soviet Union, which would last for over forty years, had begun.

As the above excerpt shows, the website is a gold mine of background knowledge relevant to the sample chapter. However, that doesn't mean that you should read everything on the website. Instead, browse the site selectively, guided by a list of topics drawn from the chapter, for instance, "GI Bill" and "Containment." Using the chapter topics to focus your search, you can scroll the site, stopping and reading about those key terms. When you sit down to read the chapter, you'll be amazed at how readily the author's words seem to sink in and make sense.

Some Websites Are More Trustworthy Than Others

Much of the time, website information your search engine turns up will be current and backed by solid research and evidence. Keep in mind, though, that some websites are maintained by people who don't care about currency, accuracy, or evidence. Their goal is to convince others to share their opinions, even if those opinions are completely irrational. For instance, there are websites claiming that the Holocaust never happened and that NASA never made it to the moon. Because some websites are maintained by people who rewrite history and current events to suit their own beliefs, you need to evaluate websites by asking questions like the following:

Questions for Evaluating a Website

1. **Is the source of information an established expert?** Find out as much as you can about where the website's information originated. Often you will get that information at the bottom of the last webpage, but if you don't, make sure to look at any information labeled *Bio* or *About Us*. If you are pursuing a personal hobby or interest on the Web, feel free to look at websites created by a single individual who has no special credentials, or proof of training and expertise, beyond a passion for the subject matter. But for background knowledge related to your textbooks, stick with individuals and institutions that supply their credentials. If those credentials are completely unknown to you, make sure you check them out. For instance, if the creator of the website says she is the author of a book on global warming, go to Powell's or Amazon.com and look up the book to see what you can learn about it and its author. Similarly, if you have never heard of the institution or group posting the website, type the name into a search engine box to see what comes up.

2. **Does the source reveal a bias?** Talking about bias is always tricky because the word has such negative associations. But, in fact, revealing a bias is not necessarily bad. If the bias expressed is based on accurate information and sound arguments, the website can still be relevant to your research. What you really want to know is if the information on the website is too biased to be trusted. If your search lands you on a site where opinions—personal points of view that cannot be checked for accuracy—overwhelm hard facts that can be verified, or checked, with *outside sources*, you might want to close the window and continue your search. The same holds true for websites where the language is so emotionally charged it suggests the writer has abandoned all willingness to hear an opposing point of view. Here again, clicking on the *About Us* link, if there is one—and there usually is with institutions—can

tell you a lot. This is where the creators of the website might more readily reveal the slant of their thinking.

3. **What are the links to other sites like?** Most websites offer links to other sites. Always check some of these out to see where they lead. If the other links give you information from reliable sources, that's a good indication that the website you are using for background knowledge is a solid and equally reliable source of information.

4. **Does a second reliable source verify the information?** If you find that the links to other sites are good ones, make it a point to check the information from the website you are using with one of the other sites listed. If necessary, search out a similar and equally reliable website in order to compare what each one says about the same topic. If they agree, you can be pretty sure that your information is accurate. If they disagree, you will have to find another site to see which one got it right and which one didn't.

5. **When was the site last updated?** If you are reading a chapter on crime investigation techniques like fingerprint analysis and want to get some background knowledge, you cannot rely on a site that hasn't been updated within the last year, never mind within the last four or five years. The controversy over the accuracy of fingerprint analysis has been raging since 1993, and every year brings new challenges and new rebuttals. To find information about rapidly changing, or evolving, topics, you need a website that is regularly updated. And even for historical information like the material in the sample chapter, you would do well to rely on a site that is revised on a regular basis since history does get rewritten when new information comes to light.

■ **EXERCISE 4**   **Using the Web**

DIRECTIONS Circle either the letter of the correct response or the response itself. Fill in the blanks where necessary.

1. *True* or *False.* Search engine indexes are created by software, but directories are put together by people.

2. Imagine that you are trying to determine the origin of the term "Iron Curtain," the phrase used to refer to the boundary between western, democratic countries and the communist countries in Eastern

Europe. What search term would be the quickest route to getting that information?

a. Iron Curtain

b. Communist

c. First Use Term Iron Curtain

d. Iron Curtain Dividing Europe

3. *True* or *False*. Websites that provide outlines or timelines are perfect when you are in pursuit of background knowledge.

4. *True* or *False*. Many search engines are available to you, but they all do much the same thing.

5. The letters *edu* at the end of a website address tell you that the

website information is posted by _____ .

6. *True* or *False*. Sponsored sites are probably the most reliable because someone is responsible for the information.

7. Imagine that your instructor tells you to use the Internet to find the name of the U.S. president who said, "I don't give 'em hell; I make them think they are in hell." What will you type into your search

engine box? _____

8. Looking at website links labeled "Home" or "About Us" is important

because it can help you _____ .

9. When a list of websites comes up in response to your search question

or term, you should read the _____ carefully to see if either contains any references to _____

_____ .

10. *True* or *False*. Web information is not the same as information in books. You can quote anything from the Web without naming your source.

 **Introducing Bonus Questions**

Throughout this book, you'll see **Internet Bonus Questions** and just plain **Bonus Questions**, which your instructor may (or may not) use to give you extra credit. What follows is an example. Find the answer and you may get some extra credit points added to your grade on an exercise or a test.

 INTERNET BONUS QUESTION

Who first used the term "Cold War"?

Bernard Mannes Baruch

Let us not be deceived—we are today in the midst

of a cold war

George Orwell

CHAPTER 26

The Cold War Abroad and at Home, 1945–1952

Dan Collins grew up in Boston's South End community. Like most other Irish-American Catholic teenagers from families that had a hard time during the Great Depression. Dan could not wait to enlist once the Second World War began. He served with the U.S. First Army in North Africa and the Tenth Army in Okinawa, witnessing, as he put it, "more than I care to talk about." His body intact, although he suffered recurring nightmares, Dan returned to Boston in 1946 and stashed his uniform in the attic, "hoping to relax, get rich, and enjoy a bit of the good life."

Qualifying under the GI Bill of Rights for a small business loan, Collins started a Massachusetts construction company. He married, had a family, and, like many veterans, fretted about his wife's working outside the home, consulted Dr. Benjamin Spock's child-care manual, took his children's pictures with the first Polaroid camera, bought a Ford with automatic transmission, and moved to a split-level house in the suburbs. Dan earned more money in construction during the postwar housing boom than he had ever dreamed possible, and gained reassurance by attending church regularly and unfurling his flag on holidays. But he couldn't shake the nightmares, and peace of mind seemed as elusive as peace in the world. The decisive changes at home and abroad brought about by the Second World War intruded on and disturbed Dan Collins and most other Americans. . . .

CHAPTER OUTLINE

The Postwar Political Setting, 1945–1946

Anticommunism and Containment, 1946–1952

The Truman Administration at Home, 1945–1952

The Politics of Anticommunism

Containing communism abroad profoundly affected American thoughts and actions at home. It directly affected the economy, minority rights, and domestic politics. The anxieties provoked by fears of communist aggression and domestic subversion, moreover, spawned a second "Red Scare" reminiscent of the first one in 1919, with witch hunts undermining civil liberties. The reckless hurling of unfounded charges of disloyalty added "McCarthyism" to the American vocabulary. McCarthyism destroyed careers, silenced criticism, fueled intolerance, and discredited both the American Left and the Truman administration.

Dan Collins and many Americans thought McCarthyism made sense. The presence of communist spies at home and American setbacks abroad convinced him that "McCarthy must be on target in attacking those liberals in Washington." In 1952, believing the Truman administration to be "riddled with Reds and corruption," Collins, whose family had been staunch Democrats, decided that "it was time to give the other guys a chance." He turned to his hero, Dwight D. Eisenhower, the favorite general of most of his GI buddies, as the man needed in dangerous times.

This chapter focuses on [four] major questions:

■ **How did the postwar policies of the United States and the Soviet Union contribute to the beginnings of the Cold War?**

■ **What was the doctrine of containment, and how was it implemented from 1947 to 1952? . . .**

■ **How did the Cold War affect the rights of African-Americans?**

■ **What were the main domestic and international factors leading to the postwar Red Scare, and why did Americans react to it as they did?**

THE POSTWAR POLITICAL SETTING, 1945–1946

1 After going without during the Great Depression and World War II, Americans like Dan Collins looked forward to the postwar era. The emerging Cold War, however, profoundly changed the United States for better and for worse. It spurred a quarter of a century of economic growth and prosperity, the longest such period in American history. It propelled research in medicine and science that, for the most part, made lives longer and better. And it contributed to a vast expansion of higher education that enabled many Americans to become middle class.

Demobilization

2 As soon as the war ended, GIs and civilians alike wanted those who had served in the military "home alive in '45." Troops demanding transport ships barraged Congress with threats of "no boats, no votes." On a single day in December 1945, sixty thousand postcards arrived at the White House with the message "Bring the Boys Home by Christmas." Truman bowed to popular demand. American military strength dropped from 12 million men at war's end to just 1.5 million by 1948.

3 The psychological problems of readjustment faced by veterans were intensified by a drastic housing shortage and soaring divorce rate. By 1950 more than a million couples who had married during the war had gotten divorced. Some veterans could not reestablish prewar ties with family and friends or adjust to the greater independence of once-submissive wives. Some experienced profound loneliness, missing the companionship and community of their wartime buddies. Others worried that automation—machines performing industrial operations faster and more accurately than human workers—would displace them, or that the stalled unionization drive, especially in the South and West, would depress wages. As war plants closed, reviving memories of the hard times immediately after World War I, many feared unemployment and economic depression. Defense spending dropped from $76 billion in 1945 to under $20 billion in 1946, and more than a million defense jobs vanished.

4 "What's Become of Rosie the Riveter?" asked the *New York Times Magazine* in May 1946. She had probably lost her job in war industry, married that year, and had a child and/or had gone back to work. By the end of the decade more women were working outside the home than during World War II. Most women did not enter heavy industry, as they had during the war, or surge into the professions. Rather, they took jobs in traditional women's fields, especially office work and sales, to pay for family needs. Although the postwar economy created new openings for women

in the labor market, many public figures urged women to seek fulfillment at home. With feminist ideology* and organizations at low ebb, popular culture romanticized married bliss and demonized career women as a threat to social stability. Having endured depression and war, many women looked forward to traditional roles in a secure, prosperous America, and few answered negatively when popular magazines asked, "Isn't a Woman's Place in the Home?"

The GI Bill of Rights

5   In 1944 Congress had enacted the Servicemen's Readjustment Act. Commonly called the GI Bill of Rights or GI Bill, it was designed to forestall the expected . . . [economic downturn] by easing veterans back into the work force, as well as to reward the "soldier boys" and reduce their fears of female competition. The GI Bill gave veterans priority for many jobs, occupational guidance, and, if need be, fifty-two weeks of unemployment benefits. It also established veterans' hospitals and provided low-interest loans to returning GIs who were starting businesses or buying homes or farms. Almost four million veterans bought homes with government loans, fueling a baby boom, suburbanization, and a record demand for new goods and services.

6   Most vitally in the long run, the government promised to pay Dan Collins and millions of others who had served in the armed forces for up to four years of further education or job training. Not all Americans approved. Some opposed it as opening the door to socialism* or to demands by minorities to special entitlements. Many university administrators, fearing that riffraff would sully their bastions* of privilege, echoed the complaint of the University of Chicago president that their hallowed* halls of learning would become "educational hobo jungles."

7   In 1946, flush with stipends of sixty-five dollars a month—ninety dollars for those with dependents—and up to five hundred dollars a year for tuition and books, 1.5 million veterans were attending college, spurring a huge increase in higher education and the creation of many new state and community colleges. Almost immediately, California State University established addi-

tional campuses in Fullerton, Hayward, Long Beach, Los Angeles, Northridge, Sacramento, and San Bernardino. Various "normal schools" for the training of teachers were upgraded into full-fledged colleges to create the State University of New York in 1948. Veterans made up over half of all college students in 1947. Often married and the fathers of young children, they were less interested in knowledge (frequently asking "what good will it do me?") than in a degree and a higher-paying job. To accommodate them, colleges converted old military barracks and Quonset huts into so-called Veterans Village housing units and featured accelerated programs and more vocational or career-oriented courses. Campus life, at least for a time, became less social and less fun, as the survivors of Normandy spurned* fraternity high-jinks in favor of "learning and earning," getting on with life.

8   To make room for the millions of GIs pursuing higher education after the war, many colleges limited the percentage of women admitted or barred students from out of state. The percentage of college graduates who were women dropped from 40 percent in 1949 to 25 percent in 1950. By then most women students were the working wives of the eight million veterans who were taking advantage of the GI Bill to go to college.

9   The GI Bill democratized higher education. It allowed many more Americans (most the first in their families to attend) to go to college. Later they expected their children to follow suit, and higher education became an accepted part of the American Dream. Speaking for many other veterans, the president of a Midwest publishing firm would later say that "the GI Bill made all the difference in the world" to him; otherwise he "could never have afforded college." No longer a citadel* of privilege, universities awarded almost half-million degrees in 1950, more than twice as many as in 1940. . . .

The Economic Boom Begins

10   In addition to the assistance given returning servicemen, a 1945 tax cut of $6 billion spurred corporate investment in new factories and equipment and helped produce an economic boom that began in late 1946. Boosting postwar growth and prosperity, Americans spent much of the $135 billion they had saved from wartime work and service pay to satisfy their desire for consumer goods formerly beyond their means or not produced during the war. As

*ideology: the ideas and beliefs that guide a society or an individual, as in capitalist or socialist ideology.
*socialism: a political system that values the group's welfare over the individual's.
*bastions: well-defended positions.
*hallowed: holy, sacred.

*spurned: rejected.
*citadel: well-defended place.

advertisements promising "a Ford in your future" and an "all-electric kitchen of the future" furthered the rage to consume, sales of homes, cars, and appliances skyrocketed. Scores of new products—televisions, high-fidelity phonographs, filter cigarettes automatic transmissions, freezers, and air conditioners—soon defined the middle-class lifestyle.

11   In 1944 representatives of the wartime Allies had met in Bretton Woods, New Hampshire, to hammer out a framework for the global economy in the postwar world. The Bretton Woods Agreement created the International Monetary Fund (IMF) to stabilize rates by valuing ("pegging") other currencies in relation to the U.S. dollar. The agreement established the International Bank for Reconstruction and Development (World Bank) to help rebuild war-battered Asia and Europe. It also laid the groundwork for the 1947 General Agreement on Tariffs and Trade (GATT) to break up closed trading blocs and expand international trade. Since the United States largely controlled and funded these powerful economic institutions, they further aided the speedy reconversion of the American economy and gave the United States an especially favorable position in international trade and finance. . . .

Truman's Domestic Program

12 The hunger to enjoy the fruits of affluence* left Americans with little appetite for more New Deal reforms, and Truman agreed. "I don't want any experiments," he confided to an aide. "The American people have been through a lot of experiments and they want a rest." Accordingly, the only major domestic accomplishment of the Seventy-ninth Congress was the Employment Act of 1946. The act committed the federal government to ensuring economic growth and established the Council of Economic Advisers to confer with the president and formulate policies for maintaining employment, production, and purchasing power. Congress gutted both the goal of full employment and the enhanced executive powers to achieve that objective, blocking Truman's main effort to advance beyond the New Deal.

13   Congressional eagerness to dismantle wartime controls worsened the nation's chief economic problem: inflation.* Consumer demand outran the

President Truman with Union Supporters

Following his veto of the Taft-Hartley bill and 1948 election victory, won, in large part, by the strong backing of organized labor, a smiling Truman dons a hard hat with copper miners in Butte, Montana. © Bettmann/Corbis.

supply of goods, intensifying the pressure on prices. The Office of Price Administration (OPA) sought to hold the line by enforcing price controls, but food producers, manufacturers, and retailers* opposed continuing wartime controls. While some consumers favored the OPA, others deplored it as an irksome relic of the war. In June 1946 Truman vetoed a bill that would have extended the OPA's life, but deprived it of power, effectively ending all price controls. Within a week food costs rose 16 percent and the price of beef doubled. "PRICES SOAR, BUYERS SORE, STEERS JUMP OVER THE MOON," headlined the *New York Daily News.*

14   Congress then passed, and Truman signed, a second bill extending price controls in weakened form. Protesting any price controls, farmers and meat producers threatened to withhold food from the market. Knowing that "meatless voters are opposition voters," "Horsemeat Harry," as some now referred to Truman, lifted controls on food prices just before the 1946 midterm elections. When Democrats fared poorly anyway, Truman ended all price controls. By then the consumer price index had jumped nearly 25 percent since the end of the war.

15   This staggering increase in the cost of living, coming on top of the end of wartime bonuses and overtime, intensified organized labor's demand for the higher wages that had been disallowed during

---

*affluence: wealth.
*inflation: rise in prices and devaluation of the dollar.

---

*retailers: people who supply goods to consumers.

the war. More than 4.5 million workers went on strike in 1946. When a United Mine Workers walkout paralyzed the economy for forty days, Truman ordered the army to seize the mines. A week later, after Truman had pressured owners to grant most of the union's demands, the miners returned to work, only to walk out again six months later. Meanwhile, on the heels of the first mine workers settlement, railway engineers and trainmen announced that they would shut down the nation's railroad system for the first time in history. "If you think I'm going to sit here and let you tie up this whole country," Truman shouted at the heads of the two unions, "you're crazy as hell." In May he asked Congress for authority to draft workers who struck vital industries. Before he could finish his speech, the unions gave in. Still, Truman's threat alienated most labor leaders.

16 By fall 1946, Truman had angered virtually every major interest group. Less than a third of the Americans polled approved of his performance. "To err is Truman," some gibed.* One commentator suggested that the Democrats nominate Hollywood humorist W. C. Fields for president: "If we're going to have a comedian in the White House, let's have a good one." Summing up the public discontent Republicans asked, "Had enough?" In the 1946 elections they captured twenty-five governorships and, for the first time since 1928, won control of both houses of Congress.

17 The public mood reflected more than just economic discontent. Under the surface laughter at stores advertising atomic sales or bartenders mixing atomic cocktails ran a new, deep current of fear, symbolized by the rash of "flying saucer" sightings that had begun after the war. . . . Some schoolchildren wore dog tags in order to be identified after an atomic attack, while also practicing crawling under their desks and putting their hands over their heads—"Duck and Cover"—to protect themselves from the bomb. The end of World War II had brought an uneasy peace.

ANTICOMMUNISM AND CONTAINMENT, 1946–1952

18 By late 1946 the simmering antagonisms between Moscow and Washington had come to a boil. With the Nazis defeated, the "shotgun wedding" between the United States and the U.S.S.R. dissolved into a struggle to fill the power vacuums left

by the defeat of Germany and Japan, the exhaustion of Western Europe, and the crumbling of colonial empires in Asia and Africa. Misperception and misunderstanding mounted as the two powers sought greater security, each feeding the other's fears. The Cold War was the result.

Polarization and Cold War

19 The destiny* of Eastern Europe, especially Poland, stood at the heart of the strife* between the United States and the U.S.S.R. Wanting to end the Soviet Union's vulnerability to invasions from the West, Stalin insisted on a buffer zone of nations friendly to Russia along its western flank, and sought a demilitarized and deindustrialized Germany. He considered a Soviet sphere* of influence in Eastern Europe essential to Russian security, a just reward for bearing the brunt of the war against Germany, and no different than the American spheres of influence in Western Europe, Japan, and Latin America. Stalin also believed that Roosevelt and Churchill had implicitly accepted a Soviet zone in Eastern Europe at the Yalta Conference.

20 With the 10-million-strong Red Army occupying most of Eastern Europe at war's end, Stalin had installed pro-Soviet puppet governments in Bulgaria and Romania by the time of the Potsdam Conference in July 1945, and supported the establishment of communist regimes in nominally independent Albania and Yugoslavia. Ignoring the Yalta Declaration of Liberated Europe, Stalin barred free elections in Poland and brutally suppressed Polish democratic parties. Poland, he said, was "not only a question of honor for Russia, but one of life and death." . . .

21 Truman also thought that accepting the "enforced sovietization" of Eastern Europe would betray American war aims and condemn nations rescued from Hitler's tyranny to another totalitarian* dictatorship. He worried, too, that a Soviet stranglehold on Eastern Europe would hurt American businesses dependent on exports and on access to raw materials. Truman understood that the Democratic party would invite political disaster if he reneged on the Yalta agreements. The Democrats counted on winning most of the votes of the 6 million Polish-Americans and millions of other Americans of Eastern European origin, who remained keenly interested

---

*gibed: insulted, made rude comments about, taunted.

---

*destiny: fate.
*strife: battle.
*sphere: area.
*totalitarian: characteristic of a political system that concentrates power in the hands of one person or group, demands total obedience, and is not reluctant to use force.

in the fates of their homelands. Not appearing "soft on communism" was a political necessity.

22   Combativeness fit the temperament of the feisty* Truman. Eager to prove he was in command, the president matched Stalin's intransigence* on Polish elections with his own demands for Polish democracy. Encouraged by America's monopoly of atomic weapons and its position as the world's economic superpower, the new president hoped that the United States could, in the words of a November 1945 State Department document, "establish the kind of world we want to live in."

The Iron Curtain Descends

23   As Stalin's and Truman's mistrust of one another grew, Stalin tightened his grip on Eastern Europe, stepping up his confiscation* of materials and factories from occupied territories and forcing his satellite nations (countries under Soviet control) to close their doors to American trade and influence. In a February 1946 speech that the White House considered a "declaration of World War III," Stalin asserted that there could be no lasting peace with capitalism and vowed to overcome the American lead in weaponry no matter what the cost.

24   Two weeks later, George F. Kennan, an American diplomat in Moscow, wired a long telegram to his superiors at the State Department. A leading student of Russian affairs, Kennan described Soviet expansionism as moving "inexorably* along a prescribed path, like a toy automobile wound up and headed in a given direction, stopping only when it meets some unanswerable force." Therefore, he concluded, U.S. policy must be the "long-term, patient but firm and vigilant containment of Russian expansive tendencies." The idea that only strong, sustained U.S. resistance could "contain" Soviet expansionism suited the mood of Truman, who a month earlier had insisted that the time had come "to stop babying the Soviets" and "to get tough with Russia." If they did not like it, the president added, they could "go to hell." "Containment"—a doctrine* uniting military, economic, and diplomatic strategies to prevent communism from spreading and to enhance America's security and influence abroad—became Washington gospel.

25   In early March 1946 Truman accompanied former British Prime Minister Winston Churchill to Fulton, Missouri. In an address at Westminister College, Churchill warned of a new threat to Western democracies, this time from Moscow. Stalin, he said, had drawn an iron curtain across the eastern half of Europe. The threat of further Soviet aggression required an alliance* of the English-speaking peoples and an Anglo-American monopoly of atomic weapons: "There is nothing the Communists admire so much as strength and nothing for which they have less respect than for military weakness."

26   Truman agreed. In spring 1946 he threatened to send in American combat troops unless the Soviets withdrew from oil-rich Iran. In June he submitted an atomic-energy control plan to the United Nations requiring the Soviet Union to stop all work on nuclear weapons and to submit to U.N. inspections before the United States would destroy its own atomic arsenal. As expected, the Soviets rejected the proposal and offered an alternative plan equally unacceptable to the United States. With mutual hostility escalating, the Soviets and Americans rushed to develop their own doomsday weapons. In 1946 Congress established the Atomic Energy Commission (AEC) to develop nuclear energy and nuclear weaponry. The AEC devoted more than 90 percent of its effort to atomic weapon development. By 1950, one AEC adviser reckoned, the United States "had a stockpile capable of somewhat more than reproducing World War II in a single day."

27   Thus, less than a year after American and Soviet soldiers had jubilantly* met at the Elbe River to celebrate Hitler's defeat, the Cold War had begun. It would be waged by economic pressure, nuclear intimidation, propaganda, proxy wars, and subversion rather than by direct U.S.-Soviet military confrontation. It would be viewed by many Americans as an ideological conflict pitting democracy against dictatorship, freedom against totalitarianism, religion against atheism, and capitalism against socialism. It would affect American life as decisively as any military engagement that the nation had fought.

Containing Communism

28   On February 21, 1947, the British informed the United States that they could no longer afford to assist Greece and Turkey in their struggles against communist-supported insurgents and Soviet pressure for access to the Mediterranean. A stricken

---

*feisty: hot tempered.
*intransigence: stubbornness.
*confiscation: the act of seizing or taking by force.
*inexorably: in an unstoppable, or relentless, manner.
*doctrine: policy.

---

*alliance: union, combined effort.
*jubilantly: happily.

Britain asked the United States to bear the costs of thwarting communism in the eastern Mediterranean. The harsh European winter, the most severe in memory, intensified the sense of urgency in Washington. The economies of Western Europe had come to a near-halt. Famine and tuberculosis plagued the Continent. European colonies in Africa and Asia had risen in revolt. Cigarettes and candy bars circulated as currency in Germany, and the communist parties in France and Italy appeared ready to topple democratic coalition governments. Truman resolved to meet the challenge.

29   Truman first had to mobilize support for a radical departure from the American tradition of avoiding entangling alliances. In a tense White House on February 27, the new secretary of state, former army chief of staff George C. Marshall, presented the case for aid to Greece and Turkey to key congressional leaders. They balked, more concerned about inflation at home than civil war in Greece. But Dean Acheson, the newly appointed undersecretary of state, seized the moment. The issue, he said, was not one of assisting the Greek oligarchy* and Turkey's military dictatorship, but rather a universal struggle of freedom against tyranny. "Like apples in a barrel infected by the corruption of one rotten one," he warned, the fall of Greece or Turkey would open Asia, Western Europe, and the oil fields of the Middle East to the Red menace. "The Soviet Union [is] playing one of the greatest gambles in history," Acheson concluded. "We and we alone are in a position to break up this play." Shaken, the congressional leaders agreed to support the administration's request if Truman could "scare hell out of the country."

30   Truman did. On March 12, 1947, addressing a joint session of Congress, he asked for $400 million in military assistance to Greece and Turkey. In a world endangered by communism, Truman said, the United States must support free peoples everywhere "resisting attempted subjugation by armed minorities or by outside pressures." If we fail to act now, the president concluded, "we may endanger the peace of the world—and we shall surely endanger the welfare of our own nation." His rhetoric* worked. Congress appropriated funds that helped the Greek monarchy defeat the rebel movement and helped Turkey stay out of the Soviet orbit.

31   Truman's statement of a new policy of active U.S. engagement to contain communism, soon known as the Truman Doctrine, persisted long after the crisis in the Mediterranean. It became as comprehensive as the Monroe Doctrine's "Keep Out" sign posted on the Western Hemisphere. It laid the foundation for American Cold War policy for much of the next four decades.

32   To back up the new international initiative, Congress passed the National Security Act of 1947. It created the National Security Council (NSC) to advise the president on strategic matters. It established the Central Intelligence Agency (CIA) to gather information abroad and to engage in covert activities in support of the nation's security. And it began the processes of transforming the old War and Navy Departments into a new Department of Defense and combining the leadership of the army, navy, and air force (now a separate and equal military service) under the Joint Chiefs of Staff.

33   Congress also approved the administration's proposal for massive U.S. assistance for European recovery in 1947. Advocated by the secretary of state, and thus called the Marshall Plan, it was to be another weapon in the arsenal against the spread of communism. With Europe, in Churchill's words, "a rubble heap . . . a breeding ground of pestilence and hate," Truman wanted to end the economic devastation believed to spawn communism. Truman correctly guessed that the Soviet Union and its satellites would refuse to take part in the plan, because of the controls linked to it, and accurately foresaw that Western European economic recovery would expand sales of American goods abroad and promote prosperity in the United States.

34   Although denounced by the Left as a "Martial Plan" and by isolationist voices on the Right as a "Share-the-American-Wealth Plan," the Marshall Plan more than fulfilled its sponsors' hopes. . . .

Confrontation in Germany

35   Reacting to the Truman Doctrine and the Marshall Plan, the Soviet Union tightened its grip on Eastern Europe. Communist takeovers added Hungary and Czechoslovakia to the Soviet sphere in 1947 and 1948. Stalin then turned his sights on Germany. The 1945 Potsdam Agreement had divided Germany into four separate zones (administered by France, Great Britain, the Soviet Union, and the United States) and created a joint four-power administration for Germany's capital, Berlin, lying 110 miles within the Soviet-occupied eastern zone. As the Cold War intensified, the Western powers moved toward uniting their zones into an anti-Soviet West German state to help contain communism. Stalin viewed that with alarm. Demanding a powerless Germany that could never attack the Soviet Union

---

*oligarchy: rule of the few.
*rhetoric: mode of speech designed to persuade.

The Berlin Airlift, 1948
German children watching an American plane in "Operation Vittles" bring food and supplies to their beleaguered city. The airlift kept a city of 2 million people alive for nearly a year and made West Berlin a symbol of the West's resolve to contain the spread of Soviet communism. © Bettmann/ Corbis.

again, he responded in June 1948 by blocking all rail and highway routes through the Soviet zone into Berlin. He calculated that the Western powers would be unable to provision the 2 million Berliners under their control and would either have to abandon plans to create a West German nation or accept a communist Berlin.

36   Truman resolved neither to abandon Berlin nor to shoot his way into the city and possibly trigger World War III. Instead he ordered a massive airlift to provide Berliners with the food and fuel necessary for survival. American cargo planes landed at West Berlin's Tempelhof Airport every three minutes around the clock, bringing a mountain of supplies. To prevent the Soviets from shooting down the U.S. planes, Truman ordered a fleet of B-29s, the only planes capable of delivering atomic bombs, to bases in England in July 1948. Truman hinted that he would use "the bomb" if necessary. Tensions rose. The president confided to his diary that "we are very close to war." Meanwhile, for nearly a year, "Operation Vittles" provided the blockaded city with a precarious lifeline.

37   In May 1949 the Soviets ended the blockade.* Stalin's gambit had failed. The airlift highlighted American determination and technological prowess,* revealed Stalin's readiness to starve innocent people to achieve his ends, and dramatically heightened anti-Soviet feeling in the West. U.S.

---

*blockade: closing off a city, an area, or a nation by force to prevent commerce.
*prowess: skill.

public opinion polls in late 1948 revealed an overwhelming demand for "firmness and increased 'toughness' in relations with Russia." . . .

The Cold War in Asia

Moscow-Washington hostility also carved Asia into   38
contending camps. The Russians created a sphere of influence in Manchuria; the Americans occupied and imposed a U.S.-written democratic constitution on Japan; and both partitioned a helpless Korea.

As head of the U.S. occupation forces in Japan,   39
General Douglas MacArthur oversaw that nation's transformation from an empire in ruins into a prosperous democracy. By 1948 the Cold War had caused American policy to shift from keeping Japan's economy and government weak, thereby preventing it from threatening peace again, to making it as strong as possible an ally in a vital part of the world. The Japanese economy flourished, and, although the official occupation ended in 1952, a military security treaty allowed the U.S. to retain its Japanese bases and brought Japan under the American "nuclear umbrella." In further pursuit of containment, the United States helped crush procommunist insurgency in the Philippines and aided the efforts of France to reestablish its colonial rule in Indochina (Vietnam, Laos, and Cambodia), despite American declarations in favor of national self-determination and against imperialism.

In China, however, U.S. efforts to block com-   40
munism failed. The Truman administration first tried to mediate the civil war between the Nationalist government of Jiang Jieshi (Chiang Kai-shek)

and the communist forces of Mao Zedong (Mao Tse-tung). It also sent nearly $3 billion in aid to the Nationalists between 1945 and 1949. American dollars, however, could not force Jiang's corrupt government to reform itself and win the support of the Chinese people, whom it had widely alienated. As Mao's well-disciplined and motivated troops marched south, Jiang's soldiers mutinied or surrendered without fighting. Unable to stem revolutionary sentiment or to hold the countryside—where the communists, in Mao's words, "swam like fishes in the peasant sea"—Jiang's regime collapsed, and he fled to exile on the island of Taiwan (Formosa), off the coast of southeast China.

41   Mao's establishment of the communist People's Republic of China (PRC) shocked Americans. The most populous nation in the world, imagined by Washington as a counterforce to Asian communism and a market for American exports, had become "Red China." Although the Truman administration explained that it could have done nothing to alter the outcome and placed the blame for Jiang's defeat on his failure to reform China, most Americans were unconvinced. China's "fall" especially embittered conservatives who believed that America's power in the world rested on Asia, not Europe. . . .

42   In September 1949, as the "Who lost China" debate raged, the president announced that the Soviet Union had exploded an atomic bomb, ending the American monopoly* on nuclear weapons. Suddenly the world had changed, shattering illusions of American invincibility. While military leaders and politicians pressed Truman to develop an even more powerful weapon, ordinary Americans sought safety in civil defense. Public schools held air-raid drills. "We took the drills seriously," recalled novelist Annie Dillard; "surely Pittsburgh, which had the nation's steel, coke, and aluminum, would be the enemy's first target." Four million Americans volunteered to be Sky Watchers, looking for Soviet planes. More than a million purchased or constructed their own family bomb shelters. Those who could not afford a bomb shelter were advised by the Federal Civil Defense Administration to "jump in any handy ditch or gutter . . . bury your face in your arms . . . never lose your head."

43   On January 31, 1950, stung by charges that he was "soft on communism," Truman ordered the development of a fusion-based hydrogen bomb (H-bomb).

In November 1952 the United States exploded its first thermonuclear bomb, nicknamed Mike, containing ten times more power than the Hiroshima atomic bomb. The blast, equal to more than 10 million tons of TNT, completely vaporized one of the Marshall Islands in the Pacific, carved a mile-long crater in the ocean floor, and spilled radioactive dust over thousands of square miles. Nine months later the Soviets detonated their own H-bomb. The danger of thermonuclear terror escalated.

44   Truman also called for a top-secret review of defense policy by the National Security Council in early 1950. Completed in April, its secret report, NSC-68, emphasized the Soviet Union's military strength and aggressive intentions. To counter what the NSC saw as the U.S.S.R.'s "design for world domination"—the mortal challenge posed by the Soviet Union "not only to this Republic but to civilization itself"—NSC-68 urged a militarized anticommunist offensive, not merely containment. It endorsed massive increases in America's nuclear arsenal, a large standing army, vigorous covert* actions by the CIA, and a quadrupling of the defense budget. Truman hesitated. An aide to Secretary of State Acheson recalled, "We were sweating over it, and then, with regard to NSC-68, thank God Korea came along." By the end of 1950 NSC-68 had become official U.S. policy (see Figure 1).

FIGURE 1

National Defense Spending, 1940–1961

In 1950 the defense budget was $13 billion, less than a third of the total federal outlay. In 1961 defense spending reached $47 billion, fully half of the federal budget and almost 10 percent of the gross national product.

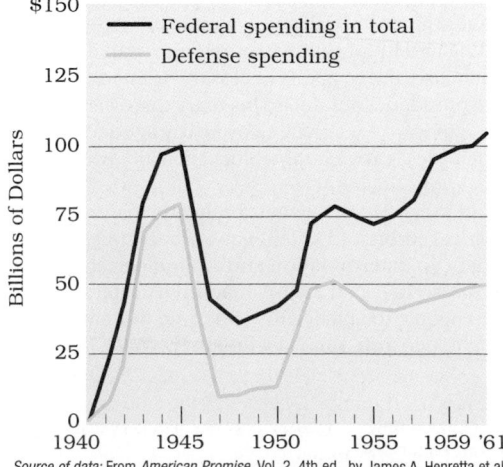

Source of data: From *American Promise*, Vol. 2, 4th ed., by James A. Henretta et al.

---

*monopoly: total control or ownership.
*covert: secret.

The Korean War, 1950–1953

45 After World War II the United States and Soviet Union temporarily divided Korea, which had been controlled by Japan since the Russo-Japanese War of 1904, at the thirty-eighth parallel for purposes of military occupation. This line then solidified into a political frontier between the American-supported Republic of Korea, or South Korea, and the Soviet-backed Democratic People's Republic of Korea in the north, each claiming the sole right to rule all of Korea.

46 On June 24, 1950, North Korean troops swept across the thirty-eighth parallel to attack South Korea. Truman decided to fight back, viewing the assault as a Soviet test of U.S. will and containment. "Korea is the Greece of the Far East," Truman maintained. "If we are tough enough now, if we stand up to them like we did in Greece . . . they won't take any next steps." Mindful of the failure of appeasement at Munich in 1938, he believed that the communists were doing in Korea exactly what Hitler and the Japanese had done in the 1930s: "Nobody had stood up to them. And that is what led to the Second World War." Having been accused of "selling out" eastern Europe and "losing" China, Truman needed to prove he could stand up to "the Reds."

47 Without consulting Congress, Truman ordered air and naval forces to Korea from their bases in Japan on June 27. That same day he asked the United Nations to authorize action to repel the North Korean attack. Fortunately for Truman, the Soviet delegate was boycotting the Security Council to protest the U.N.'s unwillingness to seat a representative from Mao's China, and Truman gained approval for a U.N. "police action" to restore South Korea's border. He appointed General Douglas MacArthur to command the U.N. effort and ordered American ground troops into the battle. The Cold War had turned hot.

48 North Korean forces initially routed the disorganized American and South Korean troops. "All day and night we ran like antelopes," recalled Sergeant Raymond Remp. "We didn't know our officers. They didn't know us. We lost everything we had." Then, in mid-September, with U.N. forces cornered on the tip of the peninsula around Pusan, struggling to avoid being pushed into the sea, MacArthur's troops landed at Inchon in a brilliant amphibious maneuver. Within two weeks, U.S. and South Korean forces drove the North Koreans back across the thirty-eighth parallel. Seeking an all-out victory, MacArthur persuaded Truman to let him cross the border to liberate all of Korea from communism.

49 As U.N. troops swept across the thirty-eighth parallel and neared the Yalu River—the boundary between Korea and China—the Chinese warned that they would not "sit back with folded hands and let the Americans come to the border." Dismissing the threat as "hot air," an overconfident MacArthur deployed his forces in a thin line south of the river. On November 25 thirty-three Chinese divisions (about three hundred thousand men) counterattacked. Within two weeks they had driven the U.N. forces south of the thirty-eighth parallel. By winter's end the contending forces were deadlocked at roughly the original dividing line between the two Koreas. "We were eyeball to eyeball," recalled Bev Scott, one of the first black lieutenants to head a racially integrated infantry squad.

> Just 20 meters of no man's land between us. We couldn't move at all in the daytime without getting shot at . . . It was like World War I. We lived in a maze of bunkers and deep trenches. . . . There were bodies strewn all over the place. Hundreds of bodies frozen in the snow. We could see the arms and legs sticking up. Nobody could get their dead out of there.

50 Stalemated* Truman reversed course. In spring 1951 he sought a negotiated peace based on the original objective of restoring the integrity of South Korea. MacArthur rocked the boat, however, pressing for authority to blockade and bomb Mao's China and to "unleash" Jiang Jieshi's forces to invade the mainland. "In war" MacArthur insisted "there is no substitute for victory." But Truman, fearing such actions would bring the Soviet Union into the conflict, shot back, "We are trying to prevent a world war—not start one."

51 When MacArthur continued to criticize Truman's limited war—publicly blasting his decision to keep the fight confined to one area and not use nuclear weapons—the president fired the general on April 10, 1951. The Joint Chiefs endorsed Truman's decision, but public opinion backed the general. The very idea of limited war, of containing rather than defeating the enemy, baffled many Americans; and the mounting toll of American casualties in pursuit of a stalemate angered them. It seemed senseless. Despite the warning by General Omar Bradley, Chairman of the Joint Chiefs of Staff, that MacArthur's proposals "would involve us in the

---

*stalemated: stuck in a situation in which no further action can be taken.

wrong war at the wrong place in the wrong time and with the wrong enemy," a growing number of Americans listened sympathetically to Republican charges that communist agents were in control of American policy.

52 After two more years of fighting, the two sides reached an armistice in July 1953 that left Korea as divided as it had been at the start of the war. . . .

53 The so-called forgotten war also had significant consequences. It accelerated implementation of NSC-68 and the expansion of containment into a global policy. From 1950 to 1953 defense spending zoomed from $13 billion to $60 billion—from one-third to two-thirds of the entire federal budget—and the American atomic stockpile mushroomed from 150 to 750 nuclear warheads. The United States acquired new bases around the world, committed itself to rearm West Germany, and joined a mutual-defense pact with Australia and New Zealand. Increased military aid flowed to Jiang Jieshi on Taiwan, and American dollars supported the French army fighting the communist Ho Chi Minh in Indochina (Vietnam, Laos, and Cambodia). By 1954 the United States would be paying three-quarters of the cost of France's war in Indochina.

54 Truman's intervention in Korea preserved a precarious balance of power. It stepped up the administration's commitment to the anticommunist struggle as well as the shift of that struggle's focus from Europe to Asia. Containment, originally advanced to justify U.S. aid to Greece and Turkey, had become the ideological foundation for a major war in Korea and, ominously, for a deepening U.S. involvement in Vietnam. Truman's actions enhanced the powers of an already powerful presidency and set the precedent for later undeclared wars. It helped spark an economic boom and added fuel to a second Red Scare.

THE TRUMAN ADMINISTRATION AT HOME, 1945–1952

55 Since 1929 most Americans had known little but the sufferings and shortages of depression and war. They wanted to enjoy life. The Cold War both hindered that and helped create a postwar affluence that changed dreams into reality. Americans flocked to the suburbs, launched a huge baby boom, and rushed to buy refrigerators and new cars. Sales of TV sets soared from fewer than seven thousand in 1946 to more than 7 million by 1949, and by 1953 half of all U.S. homes had at least one television. Not all Americans shared these good times. Poverty remained a stark fact of life for millions. Minorities experienced the grim reality of racism. Yet a major movement by African-Americans for equality emerged from these Cold War years.

56 Family and career, not public issues, interested most Americans. The New Deal's reform energies subsided into complacency. Although Truman occasionally sought liberal measures, the mood of the times was against him. An increasingly conservative political order wanted to reduce taxes, not raise them, and to contract, not expand, the power of government and organized labor. Anticommunism bred repression, stifled dissent, and rewarded conformity, further undercutting efforts for progressive change.

The Eightieth Congress, 1947–1948

57 The Republicans of the Eightieth Congress interpreted the 1946 elections as a mandate to reverse the New Deal. As "Mr. Republican," Senator Robert A. Taft of Ohio, declared, "We have got to break with the corrupting idea that we can legislate prosperity, legislate equality, legislate opportunity." Congress defeated Democratic bills to raise the minimum wage and to provide federal funds for education and housing.

58 Truman and the GOP waged their major battle over the pro-union Wagner Act of 1935. The massive postwar strikes by miners and railway workers had created a consensus for curbing union power. In 1947 more than twenty states passed laws to restrict union activities. Most important, Congress passed the Taft-Hartley Act (officially the Labor-Management Relations Act), which barred the closed shop, outlawed secondary boycotts, required union officials to sign loyalty oaths, and permitted the president to call a cooling-off period to delay any strike that might endanger national safety or health. Although hardly the "slave labor bill" that unions characterized it, the Taft-Hartley Act weakened organizing drives in the nonunion South and West, hastening the relocation of labor-intensive industries, such as textiles, from the Northeast and Midwest to the Sunbelt. It also helped drive communists and other leftists out of CIO leadership positions, making organized labor less of a social justice movement and more of a special-interest group.

59 Eager for labor's support in the upcoming presidential election. Truman vetoed the bill. Congress overrode the veto. But Truman had taken a major step toward reforging FDR's majority coalition. He played the role of a staunch New Dealer to the hilt, urging Congress to repeal Taft-Hartley; raise the minimum wage, social-security benefits, and price

supports for farmers; enact federal aid to education and housing; and adopt a federal health insurance program. . . .

The Politics of Civil Rights and the Election of 1948

60 In 1947 Jackie Robinson, the grandson of a slave, joined the Brooklyn Dodgers, breaking major-league baseball's color barrier. It would not be an easy trip around the bases to interracial harmony. Unhappy fans insulted Robinson and mailed death threats. Opposition pitchers tried to bean him and runners to spike him. The humiliations and stress injured him physically and psychologically. But Robinson endured and triumphed, winning Rookie of the Year and then going on to win Most Valuable Player in the National League, inducted into the Baseball Hall of Fame, and see every major-league team integrated by the late 1950s. Robinson's example also led to the start of integration by the Cleveland and Los Angeles franchises of the All-American Football Conference and the Boston Celtics of the National Basketball Association. African-Americans took heart and pressed assertively for an end to racial discrimination.

61 In 1945 Walter White, the head of the NAACP had noted, "World War II has immeasurably magnified the Negro's awareness of the disparity between the American profession and practice of democracy." The war had heightened African-American expectations for racial equality, and numerous blacks, especially veterans, were actively demanding a permanent Fair Employment Practices Commission (FEPC), the outlawing of lynching, and the end of the poll tax. Voter-registration drives raised the percentage of southern blacks registered to vote from 2 percent in 1940 to 12 percent in 1947.

62 Fearful of further gains as well as of a bold new spirit among African-Americans, some southern whites turned to violence. In 1946 whites killed several black war veterans who had voted that year in rural Georgia, flogged to death an "uppity" black tenant farmer in Mississippi, blowtorched a young black in Louisiana for daring to enter a white woman's house, and blinded a black soldier for failing to sit in the rear of a bus in South Carolina. In Columbia, Tennessee, in 1946 whites rioted against blacks who insisted on their rights. The police then arrested seventy blacks and did nothing as a white mob broke into the jail to murder two black prisoners.

63 In September 1946 Truman met with a delegation of civil-rights leaders. Believing that every American should enjoy the full rights of citizenship

and knowing the political importance of the growing black vote, particularly in northern cities, he promised action. Truman realized, too, that white racism damaged U.S. relations with much of the world. The U.S.S.R. highlighted the mistreatment of African-Americans, both to undercut U.S. appeals to the nonwhites of Africa, Asia, and Latin America, and to counter criticism of its own repression behind the Iron Curtain. Accordingly, Truman established the first President's Committee on Civil Rights. Its 1947 report, *To Secure These Rights,* dramatized the inequities of life in Jim Crow America and emphasized all the compelling moral, economic, and international reasons for the government to enact federal legislation outlawing lynching and the poll tax, establish a permanent FEPC, desegregate the armed forces, and support a legal assault on segregation in education, housing, and interstate transportation.

64 Southern segregationists reacted immediately, accusing Truman of "stabbing the South in the back" and warning of a Dixie boycott of the national Democratic ticket. Truman backtracked. Cowed by the prospect of losing the Solid South, he dropped plans to submit civil-rights bills to Congress and endorsed a weak civil-rights plank for the Democratic platform. But liberals and urban politicians who needed the votes of African-Americans rejected the president's feeble civil-rights plank at the Democratic convention in July 1948 and committed the party to act on Truman's original proposals. Thirty-five delegates from Alabama and Mississippi stalked out, joining other southern segregationists to form the States' Rights Democratic party which nominated Governor Strom Thurmond of South Carolina for the presidency. The "Dixiecrats" hoped to win enough electoral votes to deny Truman reelection, restore their dominance in the Democratic party, and preserve the segregationist "southern way of life." They placed their electors on the ballot as the regular Democratic ticket in several states, posing a major roadblock to Truman's chances of victory.

65 Truman's electoral hopes faded further when left-wing Democrats joined with communists to launch a new Progressive party, which nominated former Vice President Henry A. Wallace for president and called for friendly relations with the Soviet Union. The Wallace candidacy threatened Truman's chances in key northern states, where many urban Democrats saw Wallace as the true heir of New Deal liberalism. The divisions in the Democratic party heartened Republicans. To play it safe they bypassed conservative, controversial

senator Robert A. Taft and nominated moderate, bland governor Thomas E. Dewey of New York. Confident of victory, Dewey ran a complacent campaign designed to offend the fewest people. Truman, in contrast, campaigned tirelessly, blasting the "no-good, do-nothing" Republican-controlled Eightieth Congress. To shouts of "Give 'em hell, Harry," the president crisscrossed the country hammering away at the GOP as the party of "privilege, pride, and plunder," Political pundits applauded Truman's spunk, but all fifty of the experts polled by *Newsweek* predicted a sure Dewey victory.

66 A surprised nation awoke the day after the election to learn that the president had won the biggest upset in electoral history and that his party had regained control of both houses of Congress. Ironically, the Progressives and Dixiecrats had helped Truman. Their radicalism had kept moderate Democrats safely in the fold. The Berlin crisis, a coup in Czechoslovakia, and Wallace's failure to repudiate communist support forced most liberals away from the Progressives. Although the support for Thurmond signaled the first cracks in the solid South, few southern Democrats felt sufficiently threatened by Truman's civil-rights stand to desert the party in 1948. "The only sane and constructive course to follow is to remain in the house of our fathers—even though the roof leaks, and there be bats in the belfry, rats in the pantry, a cockroach in the kitchen and skunks in the parlor," explained a southern officeholder. Moreover, Dixiecrat defections had freed Truman to campaign as a champion of civil rights. In July 1948 he had issued executive orders barring discrimination in federal employment and requiring "equality of treatment and opportunity for all persons in the armed services without regard to race, color, religion or national origin." Truman had also benefited from Supreme Court decisions declaring segregation in interstate bus transportation unconstitutional (*Morgan* v. *Virginia*) and outlawing restrictive housing covenants that forbade the sale or rental of property to minorities (*Shelley* v. *Kraemer*). . .

The Fair Deal

67 Proclaiming in his inaugural address of 1949 that "every segment of our population . . . has a right to expect from our government a fair deal," Truman proposed a domestic agenda that included civil rights, national health care legislation, and federal aid to education, among many other measures. Unlike the New Deal, the Fair Deal was based on the belief in continual economic growth: the constantly expanding economic pie would mean a

A. Philip Randolph

Leading a group of protesters at the 1948 Democratic national convention, Randolph vowed: "I am prepared to oppose a Jim Crow army till I rot in jail." Soon after, however, President Truman issued Executive Order 9981, asserting equality of treatment and opportunity for all members of the armed services, and a pleased Randolph called off his protest. © Bettmann/Corbis.

progressively bigger piece for most Americans (so they would not resent helping those left behind) and for the government (so it would have the revenue to pay for social welfare programs.

68 The Eighty-first Congress complied with Truman's requests to extend existing programs but rejected new Fair Deal measures. It raised the minimum wage; increased social-security benefits and coverage; expanded appropriations for public power, conservation, and slum clearance; and authorized the construction of nearly a million low-income housing units. It also enacted the Displaced Persons Act, which allowed entry to 205,000 survivors of the Nazi forced-labor and death camps. But Congress rejected federal aid to education, national health insurance, civil-rights legislation, larger farm subsidies, and repeal of the Taft-Hartley Act. . . .

THE POLITICS OF ANTICOMMUNISM

69 As the Cold War worsened, many Americans came to believe that communist spies and traitors at home were the cause of setbacks for the United States abroad. How else could the communists have defeated Jiang in China and built an atomic bomb? Millions of fearful Americans enlisted in a crusade that equated dissent with disloyalty and

sought scapegoats to blame for the nation's problems. . . .

Loyalty and Security

70 American fear of a war with the Soviet Union and of other countries' going communist raised legitimate concerns about security in the United States. The Communist party had claimed eighty thousand members in the United States during the Second World War, and far more sympathizers. No one knew how many party members occupied sensitive government and military positions. In mid-1945 a raid on the offices of a procommunist magazine, *Amerasia*, revealed that classified documents had been given to the periodical by two State Department employees and a naval intelligence officer. Then the Canadian government exposed a major spy network that had passed American atomic secrets to the Soviets during the war. Republicans accused the Democratic administration of being "soft on communism."

71 A week after his Truman Doctrine speech of March 1947, the president issued Executive Order 9835, establishing the Federal Employee Loyalty Program to root out subversives in the government. The first such peacetime program, it barred members of the Communist party and anyone guilty of "sympathetic association" with it from federal employment. "Reasonable grounds for belief that the person is disloyal," such as being homosexual, led to dismissal. Those suspected were allowed neither to face their accusers nor to require investigators to reveal sources. Instead of focusing on potential subversives in high-risk areas, review boards extended the probe to the associations and beliefs of every government worker.

72 Mere criticism of American foreign policy could result in an accusation of disloyalty. Clouds of suspicion hovered over those who liked foreign films and favored the unionization of federal workers or civil rights for blacks. "Of course the fact that a person believes in racial equality doesn't prove he's a communist," mused an Interior Department Loyalty Board chairman, "but it certainly makes you look twice, doesn't it?" Some people lost jobs because they had friends who were radicals or had once belonged to organizations now declared disloyal. People's reading became fair game. An employee was asked if he read the *New Republic*. Another was asked, "What do you think of female chastity?" Tastes in music might trigger concern.

73 Of the 4.7 million jobholders and applicants who underwent loyalty checks by 1952, 560 were fired or denied jobs on security grounds, several thousand resigned or withdrew their applications, and countless were intimidated. Although Loyalty Board probes uncovered no proof of espionage or subversion, they heightened people's fears of what Truman called "the enemy within," adding credibility to the Red Scare. "Why lead with your chin?" became a dominant reflex. "If communists like apple pie and I do," claimed one federal worker, "I see no reason why I should stop eating it. But I would."

The Anticommunist Crusade

74 The fear of disloyalty generated by Truman's inquest fed mounting anticommunist hysteria. It promoted fears of communist infiltrators and legitimated a witch hunt for subversives. FBI chief J. Edgar Hoover claimed that colleges were centers of "red propaganda," and a senator, decrying "communist-line textbooks" and professors, accused colleges of admitting "good Americans" and returning them "four years later as wild-eyed radicals." At Yale the FBI, with the consent of the college administration, spied on students and faculty, screening candidates for jobs and fellowships. Many universities banned controversial speakers, and Truman's Office of Education introduced a "Zeal for Democracy" campaign, providing local school boards with curriculum materials to combat "communist subversion." New York State's Department of Education added a new unit on "How Can We Fight Communism?" to its *Teaching American History* curriculum. Popular magazines featured articles like "Reds Are After Your Child." Comics joined the fray: "Beware, commies, spies, traitors, and foreign agents! Captain America, with all loyal, free men behind him, is looking for you, ready to fight until the last one of you is exposed for the yellow scum you are." The Ford Motor Company put FBI agents on its payroll to look for communists on the assembly line.

75 By the end of Truman's term, thirty-nine states had created loyalty programs, most with virtually no procedural safeguards. Schoolteachers, college professors, and state and city employees throughout the nation had to sign loyalty oaths or lose their jobs. No one knows for sure how many were dismissed, denied tenure, or quietly drifted away, leaving behind colleagues too frightened to speak out.

76 In 1947 the House Un-American Activities Committee began hearings to expose communist influence in American life. HUAC's probes blurred distinctions between dissent and disloyalty,

between radicalism and subversion. Those called to testify were in a bind. When asked whether they had ever been members of the Communist party, witnesses could say yes and be forced to reveal the names of others; say no and be vulnerable to charges of perjury; or refuse to answer, pleading the First or Fifth Amendments, and risk being viewed by the public as a communist. In Washington, D.C., a man who invoked the Fifth Amendment lost his license to sell secondhand furniture, and his livelihood. A woman who did the same suffered a boycott that destroyed her once-thriving drugstore. A Stanford University biochemist poisoned himself rather than respond to HUAC's questions. In a suicide note he blasted the committee for wrecking careers and lives: "The scientific mind cannot flourish in an atmosphere of fear, timidity and imposed conformity."

77   To gain publicity for itself and to influence the content of movies, HUAC also probed Hollywood. In its hearings on "Communist infiltration of the motion picture industry," HUAC listened to testimony by "friendly witnesses," such as conservative novelist Ayn Rand, film producer Walt Disney, and Screen Actors Guild president Ronald Reagan. They saw as proof of communist activity wartime films about the Soviet Union showing Russians smiling, or movies featuring the line "share and share alike, that's democracy." In 1947, HUAC cited for contempt of Congress a group of prominent film directors and screenwriters who, claiming the freedom of speech and assembly guaranteed by the First Amendment, refused to say whether they had been members of the Communist party. The so-called Hollywood Ten—some of them Communists, all of them leftists—were convicted of contempt and sent to prison. The threat of further investigations prompted the movie colony, financially dependent on favorable press and public opinion, to deny work to them as well as to other "unfriendly witnesses," such as directors Orson Welles and Charlie Chaplin. Soon the studios established a blacklist barring the employment of anyone suspected of communism.

78   Between 1947 and 1952 Hollywood brought out almost fifty anticommunist movies. One studio canceled a film on Longfellow, explaining that Hiawatha had tried to stop wars between Indian tribes and that some might see the effort as communist propaganda for peace. Another withdrew plans to film the story of Robin Hood because he took from the rich and gave to the poor.

HUAC also frightened the labor movement into   79
expelling communists and avoiding progressive causes. Fearful of appearing "red," or even "pink," most unions focused on securing better pay and benefits for their members.

The 1948 presidential election campaign also   80
fed national anxieties. Truman lambasted Henry Wallace as a Stalinist dupe and accused the Republicans of being "unwittingly the ally of the communists." In turn, the GOP dubbed the Democrats "the party of treason." Republican Congressman Richard Nixon of California charged that Democrats bore responsibility for "the unimpeded growth of the communist conspiracy in the United States."

To blunt such accusations, Truman's Justice   81
department prosecuted eleven top leaders of the American Communist party under the Smith Act of 1940, which outlawed any conspiracy advocating the overthrow of the government. In 1951, in *Dennis* v. *United States,* the Supreme Court affirmed the conviction and jailing of the communists, despite the absence of any acts of violence or espionage, declaring that Congress could curtail freedom of speech if national security required such restriction.

Ironically, the Communist party was fading into   82
obscurity at the very time when politicians magnified its threat. By 1950 its membership had shrunk to fewer than thirty thousand. Yet Truman's attorney general warned that American Reds "are everywhere—in factories, offices, butcher stores, on street corners, in private businesses—and each carries in himself the germ of death for society."

Alger Hiss and the Rosenbergs

Nothing set off more alarms of a Red conspiracy   83
in Washington than the case of Alger Hiss. Amid the 1948 political campaign, HUAC conducted a hearing in which Whittaker Chambers, a *Time* editor and former Soviet agent who had broken with the communists in 1938, identified Hiss as belonging to a secret communist cell in the 1930s.

A rumpled, repentant, former communist and   84
college dropout, Chambers appeared to be a tortured soul crusading to save the West from the Red peril. The elegant Hiss, in contrast, seemed the very symbol of the liberal establishment. He was a Harvard-trained lawyer who had clerked for Supreme Court Justice Oliver Wendell Holmes, served FDR in the New Deal and later as a State Department official, and presided over the inaugural meeting of the United Nations. For

Left and Right in Cold War America

Arrested in 1950 and charged with being members of a Soviet atomic spy ring during World War II, American communists Julius and Ethel Rosenberg were found guilty of conspiring to commit espionage and were executed in 1953. Although they and their defenders protested their innocence, Soviet documents made public in the 1990s identified Julius Rosenberg as a secret communist agent. © Elliot Erwitt/Magnum Photos

conservative Republicans, a better villain could not have been invented. Hiss denied any communist affiliation or even knowing Chambers, and most liberals believed him. They saw him as a victim of conservatives bent on tarnishing New Deal liberalism. Truman denounced Chambers's allegation* as a "red herring" being used to deflect attention from the failures of the Eightieth Congress.

85 To those suspicious of the Roosevelt liberal tradition, Chambers's persistence and Hiss's bizarre notions—"Until the day I die, I shall wonder how Whitakker Chambers got into my house to use my typewriter"—intensified fears that the Democratic administration teemed with communists. Under relentless questioning by Congressman Richard

Nixon, Hiss finally admitted that he had known Chambers and had even let Chambers have his car and live in his apartment. But he still denied ever having been a communist. Chambers then broadened his accusation, claiming that Hiss had committed espionage in the 1930s by giving him secret State Department documents to be sent to the Soviet Union. To prove his charge, Chambers led federal agents to his farm in Maryland where, in a hollowed-out pumpkin, he had microfilm copies of confidential government papers that had been copied on a typewriter traced to Hiss. A grand jury then indicted Hiss for perjury. (The statute of limitations for espionage prevented a charge of treason.) After one trial ended in a hung jury, a second resulted in a conviction and a five-year prison sentence for Hiss. While prominent Democrats continued to defend Hiss, Republican conservatives were emboldened. Who knew how many other bright young New Dealers had betrayed the country?

Hard on the heels of the Hiss conviction, 86 another spy case shocked Americans. In February 1950 the British arrested Klaus Fuchs, a German-born scientist involved in the Manhattan Project, for passing atomic secrets to the Soviets during the Second World War. Fuchs's confession led to the arrest of his American accomplice, Harry Gold, who then implicated* David Greenglass, a machinist who had worked at Los Alamos. Greenglass named his sister and brother-in-law, Ethel and Julius Rosenberg, as co-conspirators in the wartime spy network. The children of Jewish immigrants, the Rosenbergs insisted that they were victims of anti-Semitism and were being persecuted for their leftist beliefs. In March 1951 a jury found both of them guilty of conspiring to commit espionage. The trial judge, declaring their crime "worse than murder," sentenced them to die in the electric chair. Offered clemency if they named other spies, neither Rosenberg would confess. On June 19, 1953, they were executed—the first American civilians to lose their lives for espionage.

Both the Rosenbergs and Alger Hiss protested 87 their innocence to their end, and their defenders continued to do so for decades. Soviet secret documents released by the National Security Agency in the 1990s—called the Venona Intercepts—lent weight to Chambers's charges against Hiss and confirmed Julius Rosenberg's guilt. (Ethel's role in her husband's spying remained uncertain.)

---

*allegation: accusation.

*implicated: involved in or raised suspicions about.

McCarthyism

88 At the time, when few Americans could separate fact from fantasy, the Hiss and Rosenberg cases tarnished liberalism and fueled other loyalty investigations. Only a conspiracy, it seemed, could explain U.S. weakness and Soviet might. Frustrated by their unexpected failure to win the White House in 1948, Republicans eagerly exploited the fearful mood and abandoned restraint in accusing the "Commiecrats" of selling out America.

89 No individual would inflict as many wounds on the Democrats as Republican Senator Joseph R. McCarthy of Wisconsin. Falsely claiming to be a wounded war hero, "Tail-Gunner Joe" won a Senate seat in the 1946 Republican landslide, and promptly gained a reputation for lying and heavy drinking. His political future in jeopardy, McCarthy decided to imitate Republicans like Richard Nixon who had gained popularity by accusing Democrats of being "soft on communism." In February 1950 McCarthy told an audience in Wheeling, West Virginia, that the United States found itself in a "position of impotency" because of "the traitorous actions" of high officials in the Truman administration. "I have here in my hands a list of 205," McCarthy claimed as he waved a laundry ticket, "a list of names known to the Secretary of State as being members of the Communist party and who nevertheless are still working and shaping policy." Although McCarthy offered no evidence, the newspapers printed his charges, giving him a national forum. McCarthy soon repeated his accusations, reducing his numbers to 81, to 57, and to "a lot," and toning down his rhetoric from "card-carrying communists" to "subversives" to "bad risks." A Senate committee found McCarthy's charges "a fraud and a hoax," but he persisted.

90 Buoyed by the partisan* usefulness of Senator McCarthy's onslaught, Republicans encouraged even more accusations. "Joe, you're a dirty s.o.b.," declared Ohio Senator John Bricker, "but there are times when you've got to have an s.o.b. around, and this is one of them." Even the normally fair-minded Robert Taft, who privately dismissed McCarthy's charges as "nonsense," urged him "to keep talking, and if one case doesn't work, try another." He did just that, and "McCarthyism" became a synonym for personal attacks on individuals by means of indiscriminate* allegations, especially unsubstantiated charges.

---

*partisan: the biased support of a party, a cause, a person, or an idea.
*indiscriminate: lacking in thought or judgment.

91 As the Korean War dragged on, McCarthy's efforts to "root out the skunks" escalated. He ridiculed Secretary of State Dean Acheson as the "Red Dean," termed Truman's dismissal of MacArthur "the greatest victory the communists have ever won," and charged George Marshall with having "aided and abetted a communist conspiracy so immense as to dwarf any previous such venture in the history of man."

92 Such attacks appealed most to Republicans indignant about the Europe-first emphasis of Truman's foreign policy and eager to turn the public's fears into votes for the GOP. For many in the American Legion and the Chambers of Commerce, anticommunism was a weapon of revenge against liberals and internationalists, as well as a means to regain the controlling position that conservative forces had once held. McCarthy also won a devoted following among blue-collar workers who identified with his charge that a person was either a true American who detested "communists and queers" or an "egg sucking phony liberal." Laborers praised his demand that the war against communism be fought with brass knuckles, not kid gloves, while both small and big businessmen sniffed an opportunity to destroy the power of organized labor. McCarthy's flag-waving appeals held a special attraction for traditionally Democratic Catholic ethnics, who sought to gain acceptance as "100 percent Americans" by their anticommunist zeal, especially after such tactics had won the blessings of New York's Cardinal Francis Spellman and television personality Bishop Fulton J. Sheen. Countless Americans also shared McCarthy's scorn for privilege and gentility, for the "bright young men who are born with silver spoons in their mouths," for the "striped-pants boys in the State Department."

93 While McCarthy's conspiratorial explanation offered the public an appealingly simple answer to the perplexing questions of the Cold War, his political power rested on the support of the Republican establishment and on Democrats' fears of antagonizing him. McCarthy appeared invincible after he helped GOP candidates in the 1950 congressional elections unseat Democrats who had denounced him. "Look out for McCarthy" became the Senate watchword. "Joe will go that extra mile to destroy you," warned the new majority leader, Democrat Lyndon B. Johnson of Texas. Few dared incur McCarthy's wrath.

94 In 1950, over Truman's veto, federal lawmakers adopted the McCarran Internal Security Act, which required organizations deemed communist by the

attorney general to register with the Department of Justice. It also authorized the arrest and detention during a national emergency of "any person as to whom there is reason to believe might engage in acts of espionage or sabotage." As part of this effort, a Senate committee sought to root out homosexuals holding government jobs. The linking of disloyalty with homosexuality in turn legitimated the armed forces' effort to dismiss "queers" and the raiding of gay bars by city police. The McCarran-Walter Immigration and Nationality Act of 1952, also enacted over Truman's veto, maintained the quota system that severely restricted immigration from southern and eastern Europe, increased the attorney general's authority to prevent homosexuals from entering the country, and gave the Justice Department the power to exclude or deport aliens suspected of sympathy for communism.

The Election of 1952

95 In 1952 public apprehension about the loyalty of government employees combined with frustration over the Korean stalemate to sink Democratic electoral prospects to their lowest level since the 1920s. Both business and labor also resented Truman's decision to freeze wages and prices during the Korean conflict. Revelations of bribery and influence peddling by some of Truman's old political associates gave Republicans ammunition for charging the Democrats with "plunder at home, and blunder abroad."

96 With Truman too unpopular to run for reelection, dispirited Democrats drafted Governor Adlai Stevenson of Illinois. But Stevenson could not separate himself politically from Truman, and his lofty speeches failed to stir most voters. An intellectual out of touch with the common people, he was jokingly referred to as an "egghead," someone with more brains than hair. Above all, Stevenson could not overcome the widespread sentiment that twenty years of Democratic rule was enough.

97 Compounding Democratic woes, the GOP nominated popular war hero Dwight D. Eisenhower. In 1948 Eisenhower had rejected Democratic pleas that he head their ticket, insisting that "lifelong professional soldiers should abstain from seeking higher political office." But in 1952 he answered the call of the moderate wing of the Republican party and accepted the nomination. As a concession to the hard-line anticommunists in the party, "Ike"

chose as his running mate Richard Nixon, who had won a seat in the Senate in 1950 by red-baiting his opponent, Helen Gahagan Douglas, as "pink right down to her underwear."

98 Eisenhower and Nixon proved unbeatable. With his captivating grin and unimpeachable record of public service, Eisenhower projected both personal warmth and the vigorous authority associated with military command. His smile, wrote one commentator, was one "of infinite reassurance." At the same time, Nixon kept public apprehensions at the boiling point. Accusing the Democrats of treason, he charged that the election of "Adlai the appeaser. . . who got a Ph.D. from Dean Acheson's College of Cowardly Communist Containment" would bring "more Alger Hisses, more atomic spies." . . .

Conclusion

99 The 1952 election ended two decades of Democratic control of the White House. It also closed the first phase of the Cold War, in which an assertive United States, eager to protect and expand its influence and power in the world, sought to contain a Soviet Union obsessed with its own security and self-interest. In the name of containment—the policy to prevent further Soviet, and eventually Chinese, communist advances in the world—the United States aided Greece and Turkey, established the Marshall Plan, airlifted supplies into Berlin for a year, approved the creation of the Federal Republic of Germany (West Germany), established NATO, and went to war in Korea.

100 American fear of global communism spawned anxieties at home as well. Truman's Cold War rhetoric and loyalty probe encouraged others to seek scapegoats and legitimated conservative accusations that equated dissent with disloyalty. The postwar Red Scare, combined with economic prosperity and pent-up demand for consumer goods, weakened the appeal of liberal reform. New Deal measures stood, but Truman's Fair Deal initiatives in education, health insurance, and civil rights failed. Although bold proposals to end racial discrimination and segregation had little chance in the midst of the Great Fear, the need of the United States to appeal to the nonwhites of the world during the Cold War brought racial issues to the fore in American politics. They would remain there as a Republican assumed the presidency.

CHRONOLOGY, 1945-1952

1944 Servicemen's Readjustment Act (GI Bill).

1945 Postwar strike wave begins.

1946 Employment Act.
George Kennan's "long telegram."
Winston Churchill's "iron curtain" speech.
Coal miners' strike.
More than a million GIs attend college.
Inflation soars to more than 18 percent.
Republicans win control of Congress.

1947 Truman Doctrine.
Federal Employee Loyalty Program.
Jackie Robinson breaks major league baseball's color line.
Taft-Hartley Act.
National Security Act
Marshall Plan to aid Europe proposed.
President's Committee on Civil Rights issues
To Secure These Rights.
HUAC holds hearings on Hollywood.

1948 Communist coup in Czechoslovakia.
State of Israel founded.
Soviet Union begins blockade of Berlin; United States begins airlift.
Congress approves Marshall Plan.
Truman orders an end to segregation in the armed forces.

Communist leaders put on trial under the Smith Act.
Truman elected president.

1949 North Atlantic Treaty Organization (NATO) established,
East and West Germany founded as separate nations.
Communist victory in China; People's Republic of China established.
Soviet Union detonates an atomic bomb.

1950 Truman authorizes building a hydrogen bomb.
Soviet spy ring at Los Alamos uncovered.
Alger Hiss convicted of perjury.
Joseph McCarthy launches anticommunist crusade.
Korean War begins.
Julius and Ethel Rosenberg arrested as atomic spies.
McCarran Internal Security Act.
Truman accepts NSC-68.
China enters the Korean War.

1951 Douglas MacArthur dismissed from his Korean command.
Supreme Court upholds Smith Act.
Rosenbergs convicted of espionage.

1952 First hydrogen bomb exploded.
Dwight D. Eisenhower elected president;
Republicans win control of Congress.

Websites

Cold War International History Project of the Woodrow Wilson International Center for Scholars
http://cwihp.si.edu/default.htm

National Archives and Records Administration (NARA)
http://www.nara.gov/publications/rip/rip107/rip107.html

Two sites rich in documents of the Cold War.

Jackie Robinson
http://www.nara.gov/education/teaching/robinson/robmain.html

A website on Jackie Robinson's quest for racial justice.

McCarthyism
http://expert.cc.purdue.edu/~phealy/mccarthy.html

A good site on the rise and fall of McCarthyism, with many links.

Adapted from Paul S. Boyer et al., *Enduring Vision:
A History of the American People.* Boston:
Houghton Mifflin, 2004, pp. 815–841.

INTERNET RESOURCE

For a test to evaluate your understanding of this chapter, go to
college.hmco.com/pic/flemmingRFR10e.

Test 1: Strategies for Reading Textbooks

DIRECTIONS Fill in the blanks or circle the correct response.

1. How can you use the World Wide Web to improve your comprehension?

_____

_____

2. In the 1970s, researchers discovered that what factor played a big role in ease of comprehension?

_____

3. The three goals of a survey are

a general overview of the chapter - a sense of
the style + organization - a feeling of whats important in chpt.

4. Explain the relationship between major and minor headings.

major - identify the broad general topics or issues covered
in chapter minor - follow major ones + help subdivide
the larger more general topics into smaller more manageable

5. What are three reasons for writing while reading? *Subtopics.*

Maintains you concentration - Improves Comprehension
+ Ensures remembering

6. Explain what it means to paraphrase.

To put thing in your own words

7. When using questions to guide and focus our reading, what are the best *kinds* of questions to use?

Questions that help you Probe + explore the chapter
what - why - how - + in what way.

8. *True* or *False*. Really good readers can read everything at reading rates as high as 500 words per minute.

9. *True* or *False*. People who are very efficient readers do not ever have to read a passage more than once.

10. *True* or *False*. SQ3R should always be used exactly as it is described in this chapter or it will not be effective.

 **Test 2: Vocabulary Review**

DIRECTIONS Here are twenty of the words introduced in the sample chapter. Use them to fill in the blanks. *Note*: The form of the word used here may differ from the form used in the chapter, e.g. *affluent* instead of *affluence*. To fill in the blanks, it may help to check the chapter for definitions and jot those definitions next to the words listed below.

Militant supporter
Happy-joyful
Not able to be persuaded
Superior skill or ability

partisans	spurned	affluent	allegations
jubilantly	stalemate	citadel - *blocked*	feisty
inexorably	ideology	intransigent	bastions
prowess	totalitarian	doctrine	blockade
alliance	rhetoric	gibes	oligarchy

1. Built in 1370 as a ___Citadel___ to defend the city of Paris, the towers of the Bastille (French for "castle" or "stronghold") were converted into a prison in the fifteenth century. By the late eighteenth century, the Bastille had become, according to the ___Partisans___ of the French Revolution, a symbol of everything that was wrong with France, a country where an ___affluent___ few ___spurned___ the notion of democracy and imprisoned those who dared complain. But as the eighteenth century wound down, France's ___Oligarchy___ was coming to what would be a bloody end. On July 14, 1789, French rebels stormed the Bastille and freed those inside. They then went in search of anyone who looked wealthy enough to be a supporter of the king. Those they found were subject to, at the very least, ___gibes___ and insults. Anyone who could not disprove ___allegations___ of favoring royalty was executed on the spot.

2. The U.S. presidential election of 2000 was one of the closest elections in U.S. history, decided by only 527 votes. On election night,

the _feisty_ Republican candidate George W. Bush _jubilantly_ claimed victory; however, Democratic candidate Al Gore challenged the results, and for a month, both men were _intransigent_, refusing to admit defeat. Although _rhetoric_ of both parties insisted their man had won, the U.S. Supreme Court finally settled the _stalemate_, voting 5–4 to declare George W. Bush the winner.

3. According to communist _doctrine_, the best economic system is one in which the means of production are owned by all citizens rather than private individuals. Although many countries—such as Poland, East Germany, Czechoslovakia, and Romania—have abandoned communist _ideology_ for capitalism, a few have not. Today, the last _bastions_ of the communist system include Cuba, China, and North Korea.

4. After communist dictator Fidel Castro seized control of Cuba in 1959, he formed a close political and economic _alliance_ with the _totalitarian_ Soviet Union, another communist country. He even went so far as to allow the Soviets to begin building missile bases in his country. But these bases put nuclear weapons within range of American cities, so President John F. Kennedy ordered a naval _blockade_ to cut off supplies to Cuba. For thirty-eight terrifying days in 1962, the "Cuban Missile Crisis" escalated tensions between the United States and Soviet Union, and nuclear war seemed _inexorably_ near. But Kennedy, despite his inexperience, was not without political _prowess_. Aided by behind-the-scenes diplomacy from his brother Robert, Kennedy skillfully pulled the country away from the brink of war.

 C H A P T E R 2

Word Power

In this chapter, you'll learn

- how the *context*, or setting, of a word can help you determine a definition.

- how a knowledge of word parts can help you define a word.

- how to recognize specialized vocabulary words in textbooks.

- how context can change word meaning.

- how reading and writing vocabularies differ.

Words are the building blocks of comprehension. Enlarge your vocabulary while sharpening your comprehension skills, and you'll be amazed at your increased ability to understand and remember what you read. As Wilfred Funk, one of the great dictionary makers of all time, aptly expressed it, "The more words you know, the more clearly and powerfully you will think . . . the more ideas you will invite into your mind."

◢◣●│ Using Context

What do you do when you come across an unfamiliar word? Do you just skip over it? Or do you pick up your dictionary and look for the definition? You probably already know that the first method is not recommended. Yet actually, the second one—turning to the dictionary every time—also has drawbacks. Looking up too many words can hurt your concentration. If you look up too many words, you can lose track of where you were on the page.

Fortunately, there are other alternatives to ignoring new words or looking them up. One alternative is to search the *context*, or setting, of the word to see if it contains a clue or clues to word meaning. Frequently, the sentence or passage in which the word appears can help you determine an **approximate definition** that allows you to keep reading without interruption. An approximate definition may not perfectly match a dictionary's definition. Still, it is close enough so that you can continue reading without interruption.

> When Russia was under the control of Josef Stalin, *dissidents* were routinely shot or imprisoned in hospitals for the mentally ill. Stalin did not allow anyone to express disagreement or discontent with his policies.

If you didn't know what the word *dissidents* in the first sentence meant, you could probably **infer**, or figure out, a definition from the sentence that follows. That sentence offers an example of what dissidents do: They disagree with their government.

Although there are several different kinds of context clues, most fall into one of four categories: example, contrast, restatement, and general knowledge.

Example Clues

As you already know from the previous illustration, the context of an unfamiliar word sometimes provides you with an example of the behavior or thinking associated with the word. Here's another sentence in which an example can lead you to a definition, this time of the word *ambivalent.*

> His feelings for his cousin were *ambivalent:* Sometimes he delighted in her company; at other times, he couldn't stand the sight of her.

What's an example of ambivalent feelings? They are in conflict with one another. Because this is an example of what it feels like to be ambivalent, we can infer the following approximate definition: To be ambivalent is to experience conflicting emotions.

Contrast Clues

Context clues can also tell you what a word does not mean. Fortunately, knowing what a word doesn't mean can often lead you to a good approximate definition. Here's an example of a passage that provides a contrast clue:

> As a child, she liked to be alone and was fearful of people; but as an adult, she was remarkably *gregarious*.

This sentence suggests that someone who is *gregarious* does not exactly flee the company of others. In fact, the sentence implies just the opposite: People who are gregarious like to be in the company of others. Thus, "liking the company of others" would be a good approximate definition.

Words That Signal Contrast Clues

In addition to knowing what a contrast clue is, you should also know that words such as *but, yet, nevertheless,* and *however* frequently introduce contrast clues. These words are all **transitions**—verbal bridges that help readers connect ideas. The transitions mentioned here tell readers to be on the lookout for a shift or change in thought. Note how the word *however* in the following sentence changes the author's train of thought and paves the way for a contrast clue that helps define the word *frivolous*.

> After having had a really bad day, she wanted to read something *frivolous*. Normally, however, she preferred serious novels.

So what does the word *frivolous* mean? "Silly," "light," or "not serious" are all good approximate definitions.

Restatement Clues

To avoid tedious word repetition, authors often use a word and then follow it with a **synonym**, a word or phrase similar in meaning:

The journalist had the *audacity* to criticize the president to his face. Oddly enough, her boldness seemed to amuse rather than irritate him.

In this case, the author doesn't want to overuse the word *audacity*, so she follows it with a synonym, *boldness*. For readers not sure what *audacity* means, the synonym *boldness* restates the word in language they can understand and provides them with a definition.

Restatement Clues in Textbooks

Intent on supplying readers with the **specialized vocabulary** essential to mastering an academic subject, textbook authors often introduce a word and then carefully define it. For example, the authors of the following passage want to be sure that their readers have exact definitions for the terms *brand recognition* and *ad recognition*. To make sure their readers have no doubt what these two terms mean, the authors define them in parentheses:

> Two important types of recognition in marketing are *brand recognition* (we remember having seen the brand before) and *ad recognition* (we remember having seen the ad before). (Hoyer and MacInnis, *Consumer Behavior*, p. 17.)

In addition to parentheses, authors use other devices to tell readers, "Here is the definition for the word I just introduced." Dashes, for instance, are also common.

> Reconversion—the transition from wartime production to the manufacture of consumer goods—ushered in a quarter century of ever-expanding prosperity. (Boyer et al., *The Enduring Vision*, p. 790.)

In this case, the authors realize their readers might not know what *reconversion*, particularly in this context, means. To avoid confusion, they enclose the definition in dashes right after the word first appears.

In addition to dashes or parentheses, textbook authors like to signal a restatement clue by first introducing the word being defined, in either boldface or italics. Then they follow the word with a comma and a definition. Here's an example:

> A major buzzword in leadership and management is *vision*, the ability to imagine different and better conditions and the ways to achieve them. (Dubrin, *Leadership*, p. 62.)

Here, the author is well aware that readers might think they know the meaning of the word *vision*—the ability to see. Yet within this particular context, the author has a specialized definition in mind, and he is careful to provide it right after he introduces the word.

Textbook authors go to great lengths to make sure you have the right definitions for the words essential to their academic field. In turn, your job as a reader is twofold: (1) Pay attention to the devices that signal the presence of restatement or definition clues; and (2) When those definitions appear, read them carefully. Consider as well jotting both words and definitions in a notebook for later review. The chances are good that the definitions will not reappear in later chapters, though the words themselves will.

General Knowledge Clues

Example, contrast, and restatement context clues are important. However, some context clues are not so obvious. Often your knowledge of the situation or events described will be your only real clue to word meaning. The following passage illustrates this point:

> For months he had dreamed of being able to *redeem* his medals. He had been unable to think of anything else. Now, with the vision of the medals shimmering before him, he hurried to the pawnshop.

None of the context clues previously discussed appears in the passage. However, your general knowledge should tell you that the word *redeem,* in this context at least, means "reclaim" or "recover." Most people go to a pawnshop to buy or to sell, and the man described as hurrying to the pawnshop probably wouldn't be in such a rush to sell something he had dreamed of for months. He is going to buy back what he has already sold.

Four Common Context Clues	
Type	**Definition and Examples**
Example	The author includes the behavior, attitude, or event associated with the word, as in "The discussion was becoming increasingly *belligerent*; no matter what was said, someone in the group would challenge it in an angry voice."

Contrast	The author tells you what the word does not mean, as in "At first the smell was almost flowerlike, but in a matter of minutes it became harsh and *acrid.*"
Restatement	(a) The author gives you a synonym or word close in meaning, as in "His behavior was *eccentric*; but in New York, it wasn't all that unusual for people to be odd." (b) In textbooks, the authors are more likely to give you an exact definition introduced by a comma or enclosed in parentheses or dashes: "*Cognition*—thinking or knowing—has been the subject of numerous studies."
General Knowledge	The passage describes an experience or event with which you are familiar, as in "Football and basketball coaches are frequently known for their *volatile* tempers."

◄■ EXERCISE 1　Using Context Clues

DIRECTIONS Use context clues to develop an approximate meaning for each italicized word.

EXAMPLE To the old dog lying under the table, the smell of frying bacon was almost unbearably *tantalizing*, and he stared at the pan with obvious longing.

Tantalizing means _appealing, exciting; desirable but out of reach_

_____.

EXPLANATION In this case, the sentence offers a general knowledge clue. Even readers who don't have pets would undoubtedly know that to a dog, the smell of frying bacon is extremely appealing or exciting. While the *American Heritage College Dictionary* offers a more detailed definition for *tantalize*—"to excite (another) by exposing something desirable while keeping it out of reach"—the definitions above would certainly do in a pinch.

1. According to the myth, the hero Achilles was *vulnerable* in just one area of his body. He could be killed only if he was wounded in the heel.

   Vulnerable means _easily hurt_.

2. The candidate had expected to win but instead she was *trounced* by her opponent, who won by a landslide.

   Trounced means _beat by large margin_.

3. Forced to sell their lands and homes at whatever prices they could obtain, Japanese Americans were herded into barbed wire-encircled detention camps in the most desolate areas of the West. Sadly, few Americans protested the *incarceration* of their Japanese-American countrymen. (Boyer et al., *The Enduring Vision*, p. 778.)

   Incarceration means _imprisonment_.

4. Before allowing someone to deliver a personal opinion on the air, most television news programs issue a *disclaimer* denying all responsibility for the views expressed.

   Disclaimer means _warning_.

5. Killed by an obsessed fan in 1995, the Latina entertainer Selena was deeply mourned because she was so much more than an entertainer: Selena was the *embodiment* of Mexican-American culture—representing devotion to the family, hard work, and a sense of community. (Adapted from Hoyer and MacInnis, *Consumer Behavior*, p. 295.)

   Embodiment means _physical representation_.

6. Unfairly accused of spying, Captain Alfred Dreyfus* (1859–1935) was convicted and sentenced to life in prison on the ill-famed Devil's Island; pardoned in 1899, Dreyfus was fully *exonerated* of all charges in 1906.

   Exonerated means _forgiven / found innocent_.

*The famous Dreyfus affair, fueled by anti-Semitism, tore France apart.

7. The Chinese novelist Ha Jin is an amazingly *perceptive* writer: he understands human behavior in a way that few novelists do.

   Perceptive means <u>smart easily notice</u>.

8. Confusion and *delusions* (false and distorted beliefs) are typical signs of sleep deprivation. (Coon, *Essentials of Psychology*, p. 34.)

   Delusions means <u>false belief</u>.

9. Queen Marie Antoinette's *hedonistic* ways was one of the things that made her hated by the people of France; close to starvation themselves, they could not love a queen who seemed to care about nothing but pleasure.

   Hedonistic means <u>evil ways</u>.

10. In his 1939 novel *The Grapes of Wrath*, novelist John Steinbeck movingly describes the *plight* of migrant farm workers in California forced to work under brutal and dehumanizing conditions.

    Plight means <u>the troubles</u>.

■─ EXERCISE 2 **Using Context Clues**

DIRECTIONS Use context clues to develop an approximate mean ing for each italicized word.

1. The reporters were sent out to cover the fighting that had broken out in the streets, but under no condition were they to get involved in the *upheaval*.

   Upheaval means <u>Sudden violence</u>.

2. The millionaire did not expect the judge to hand down such a *punitive* sentence.

   Punitive means <u>Punishment harsh</u>.

3. All over the country, people were starving and desperately *scavenging* for food.

   Scavenging means <u>Search or collect material</u>.

4. Looking filthy and *disreputable* after being lost for a month in the woods, the children were finally discovered by a team of hunting dogs.

   Disreputable means <u>poor condition</u>.

5. Her boss didn't need to make an effort to be nasty; he was *inherently* so and thought nothing of publicly humiliating his employees.

   Inherently means _____.

6. Since I can't spell very well, I was happy to learn there is no apparent *correlation* between the ability to spell and a high IQ.

   Correlation means _not related_____.

7. The jockey hoped that *submersing* himself in the hot tub would soothe his aching body.

   Submersing means _Cover with water liquid_____.

8. Inventors don't necessarily care if their inventions are *lucrative*; often they just have an idea they are desperate to make a reality, and money doesn't matter.

   Lucrative means _Profitable_____.

9. Research on people who have lived to be more than eighty years old has consistently revealed a connection between low body weight and *longevity*.

   Longevity means _long life_____.

10. How is it that so many doctors who *advocate* diet and exercise are overweight couch potatoes?

    Advocate means _Support_____.

EXERCISE 3   Using Context Clues

DIRECTIONS Use context clues to develop an approximate definition for each italicized word.*

EXAMPLE People driven by *intrinsic* motivation don't need external rewards such as praise from others; instead, they find satisfaction in simply completing a task.

Intrinsic means _internal; inside or within oneself_

EXPLANATION In this case, the sentence offers a contrast clue. If people do not need external rewards, they must be motivated by

---

*The italicized words in exercises 3 and 4 are all from the Academic Word List developed by the School of Linguistics and Applied Language Studies at Victoria University of Wellington in New Zealand.

rewards that are internal, or inside or within themselves. These are all good approximate definitions of the word *intrinsic*.

1. African-American novelist Richard Baldwin was an outspoken advocate of civil rights, who did not believe that racism would disappear on its own. Friends enjoyed relaying *anecdotes* about Baldwin's fiery and often funny responses to anyone claiming it would.

   Anecdotes means ___Stories___.

2. Emperor Justinian gathered together all of Rome's disorganized laws and made them into a *coherent* legal system.

   Coherent means ___Organized___.

3. Corporate raiders spend their days figuring out how to acquire new companies while offering the previous owners as little *compensation* as possible.

   Compensation means ___the giving of something for a loss___

4. By embracing drug use, rock music, "free love," and non-Western religions, the rebellious hippies of the 1960s and 1970s rejected *conventional* rules.

   Conventional means ___Customary___.

5. If *preliminary* testing of a new drug indicates potential benefits, the drug is then tested again for a longer period of time and on a larger sample population.

   Preliminary means ___first test trial period___.

6. Electricity is *generated* from a variety of different energy sources, including coal, oil, wood, nuclear reactors, wind, sunlight, and water.

   Generated means ___produced___.

7. *Proponents* of the bill were disheartened when the vote was put off until spring; the bill's critics, however, were jubilant.

   Proponents means ___Supporters of Something___.

8. Milton Hershey certainly didn't invent chocolate, but his *innovations* to the recipe and manufacture turned a luxury for the affluent into an affordable treat for all.

   Innovations means ___trying Something New___.

9. The lawyer's *cogent* argument convinced the court, and she was allowed to submit the fibers as evidence.

   Cogent means ___persuasive___.

10. Franklin D. Roosevelt was elected president four times; however, after the Twenty-second Amendment to the U.S. Constitution took effect in 1951, all *ensuing* presidents were limited to two terms each.

    Ensuing means ___following___.

EXERCISE 4 Using Context Clues

DIRECTIONS Use context clues to develop an approximate definition for each italicized word.

1. Although global warming has been *attributed* to the burning of fossil fuels, a few scientists argue that it's actually caused by natural climate cycles.

   Attributed means ___Blamed___.

2. U.S. military officials believed that dropping atomic bombs on Japan was the only way to save millions of American lives and end World War II; however, others have argued that there was no *justification* for killing more than 140,000 Japanese citizens and injuring another 100,000.

   Justification means ___reason___.

3. Based on research and observation, scientists propose theories, or explanations, of events, then they conduct experiments that either prove a theory's *validity* or else reveal its inaccuracy.

   Validity means ___value   worth___.

4. In the U.S. Army, a general is the highest rank of officer, whereas the most *subordinate* officer rank is second lieutenant.

   Subordinate means ___higher   ranking___.

5. The final event of the American Civil War occurred on April 9, 1865; Confederate General Robert E. Lee officially *terminated* the conflict by surrendering to Union commander Ulysses S. Grant at the Appomattox, Virginia, courthouse.

   Terminated means ___ended___.

6. Medical research rules require that human subjects know they are participating in an experiment; therefore, scientists must obtain each subject's *consent*, or permission, before giving him or her any treatment.

   Consent means ___permission aggre___.

7. When scientists attempt to create a clone, they *extract* the DNA from the cell of one organism and then insert it into the egg cell of another organism of the same species.

   Extract means ___take out___.

8. The kilometer is the unit of length used in Europe, Canada, and other countries; it is *equivalent*, or equal, to 0.62 miles.

   Equivalent means ___same as___.

9. Because they can explode when mixed together, *incompatible* chemicals spelled with the same first letter, like cadmium chlorate and cupric sulfide, must be kept apart; they should never be stored alphabetically in a laboratory.

   Incompatible means ___not able to get (along) mix___.

10. A paperback dictionary includes only some of our language's most commonly used words; the *Oxford English Dictionary*, however, aims to present all words from the earliest records to the present day. Its over 400,000 entries make it our language's most *comprehensive* dictionary.

    Comprehensive means ___complete___.

Context and Meaning

There are few situations in life where context isn't important. Certainly, words are no exception. Change a word's context and you are likely to change its meaning. For instance, if you are buying a new air conditioner, you might ask the salesperson how big a room the unit can *cool*. Here the word means "lower the temperature." But if someone asks your opinion of the The Black Eyed Peas' new CD, you might say, "It's cool," and you wouldn't be talking about the group's temperature.

BONUS QUESTION

Can you come up with five more words that can have dramatically different meanings when the context changes? If you can, put all five into sentences that show how the meaning changes with the context.

_____

_____

_____

Defining Words from Their Parts

In addition to using context clues to determine approximate meanings for unfamiliar words, check to see if you know any of the word's parts. For example, imagine you read this sentence and were initially puzzled by the word *dermatitis*: "The deadly disease began with a seemingly minor symptom—a light *dermatitis* on the arms and legs." Even if you had never heard or used the word *dermatitis*, you could come up with a definition simply by knowing that *derma* means skin and *itis* means inflammation, or outbreak. Given the context and your knowledge of the word's parts, you would be correct to say that *dermatitis* means "inflammation of the skin," or "rash."

Learning Roots, Prefixes, and Suffixes

To determine meaning from word parts, you need to know some of the most commonly used roots and prefixes, along with a few suffixes. The exercises in this chapter will introduce you to a good many, but you can find many more on this website: **www.southhampton .liu.edu/academic/pau/course/webesl.htm**.

It's worth your while to learn a few new word parts every day, averaging about twenty a week. Then review them regularly. You will be amazed at how quickly your vocabulary expands.

1. **Roots** give words their fixed meaning. Prefixes and suffixes can then be attached to the roots to form new words. For example, the following words are all based on the root *spec*, which means "look" or "see": re*spec*t, in*spec*tion, *spec*tacles, *spec*ulation.
2. **Prefixes** are word parts that appear at the *beginning* of words and modify the root meaning, as in *in*clude and *ex*clude or *in*voke and *re*voke.
3. **Suffixes** are word parts that appear at the *end* of many words. Although suffixes do occasionally affect word meaning, they are more likely to reveal what part of speech a word is, as in quick*ness* and quick*ly*. Words ending in *ness* are usually nouns. Those ending in *ly* are usually adverbs.

Study Tip

When you make a list of word parts, put the definitions on the far right. Each time you review, cover one side of the list and *recall from memory* either the word part or the definition.

EXERCISE 5   Learning Word Parts

DIRECTIONS Read each sentence and note what meaning the missing or partial word should convey. Then fill in the blanks with one—or in some cases, two—of the word parts listed below.

Prefixes	Roots
bi = two	*chron* = time
im = not	*gam* = marriage
per = through	*lat* = side
poly = many	*mob* = move
	pel = force
	popul = people
	rect = straight, straighten

EXAMPLE When we talk about events being ordered according to time, we are talking about events that are described in *chron*ological order.

EXPLANATION The partially completed word needs to say something about "time." Thus, we need a word part that brings that meaning to the blank. The obvious choice would be the root *chron*, meaning "time."

1. When a situation can't be fixed or straightened out, we say that it cannot be _just_ified. rect

2. If a city is filled with people, it can be described as _poly_ous.

3. When a disease goes away and repeatedly comes back over time, it is called _____ic.

4. Human skin is called _per_meable because substances, both good and bad, can pass through it.

5. An interesting book that almost forces you to keep reading is often described as com_pel_ling.

6. An agreement that has to be signed by two sides is called _bi_ _lat_eral.

7. Being married to two people at the same time is called _bi_ _gam_y.

8. Being married to several people at the same time is called _poly_ _gam_y.

9. If someone or something can move, we say that he or it is _mob_ile.

10. In contrast, someone or something that cannot move would be described as _im_ _mob_ile.

Study Tip	Because the word parts introduced in the previous exercise appear in many different words, you should start learning them right now. Repeated reviews done over an extended period of time are the key to mastery.

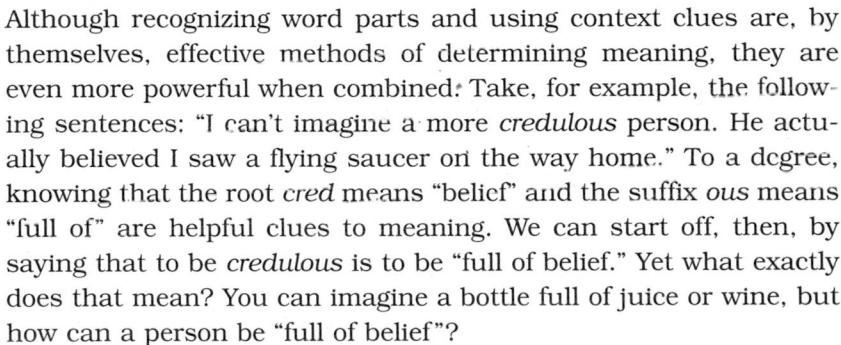

Combine Forces: Use Context Clues *and* Word Parts

Although recognizing word parts and using context clues are, by themselves, effective methods of determining meaning, they are even more powerful when combined. Take, for example, the following sentences: "I can't imagine a more *credulous* person. He actually believed I saw a flying saucer on the way home." To a degree, knowing that the root *cred* means "belief" and the suffix *ous* means "full of" are helpful clues to meaning. We can start off, then, by saying that to be *credulous* is to be "full of belief." Yet what exactly does that mean? You can imagine a bottle full of juice or wine, but how can a person be "full of belief"?

This is where context comes in. Look at the example clue the author offers: "He actually believed I saw a flying saucer on the way home." Apparently, a credulous person is likely to believe a story that most people might laugh at or question. After a closer look at the context, we can come up with a more precise definition of *credulous*: "gullible" or "easily fooled."

A knowledge of word parts can also help you sharpen or improve an approximate definition derived from context. Suppose you are not sure how to define the word *ambiguous* in a sentence like this one: "The finest poems are usually the most *ambiguous*, suggesting that life's big questions defy easy answers." Relying solely on context, you might decide that *ambiguous* means *puzzling* or *difficult*. Those definitions are certainly acceptable. But once you know that the prefix "ambi" means "both," you could make your definition more precise by defining *ambiguous* as "open to more than one interpretation," which would, in fact, be a better definition.

━ EXERCISE 6   Using Word Parts and Context Clues

DIRECTIONS Use context clues and word parts to develop an approximate definition for each italicized word. *Note:* Some of the words in the following sentences employ prefixes or roots from the previous exercise.

Prefixes	Roots	Suffixes
mono = one	*for* = to bore into	*ism* = state, condition, or quality
pseudo = false	*the* = god	
mal = bad	*vit* = life	*ize* = to cause to be, to treat or affect
re = again, back		
syn, sym = together		*onym* = name, word

1. The Egyptian pharaoh Akhenaton rejected *polytheism,* advocating *monotheism* instead, but his decision to worship one god over many led to his downfall.

   Monotheism means ⟨one god state⟩ .

   Polytheism means ⟨many god state⟩ .

2. The International Olympic Committee took a long time to acknowledge how difficult it is for *synchronized* swimmers to execute the same movement at the same time while submersed in water.

   Synchronized means ⟨together time affect⟩ .

3. The kidnapper's actions were so *repellent,* it was hard to have any sympathy for her. Most agreed with the prosecution and hoped to see her incarcerated for a very long time.

   Repellent means ⟨again force⟩ .

4. During the operation, the surgeon's knife almost *perforated* the patient's lung.

   Perforated means   ⟨through to bore into⟩ .

5. The injection had completely *immobilized* the bear, allowing the ranger to approach it without fear.

   Immobilized means _Not move_.

6. Amazingly, the drug had *revitalized* him after everyone thought he would not last the night.

   Revitalized means _back life_.

7. In the nineteenth century, many women writers used *pseudonyms* because they were afraid of being labeled "unladylike" and didn't want their real names to be known.

   Pseudonyms means _false name_.

8. The long illness had *vitiated* his once lively spirit, and the sad plight he endured on a daily basis was obvious even to strangers.

   Vitiated means _life out_.

9. In an effort to win elections, politicians spend too much time *maligning* one another.

   Maligning means _bad talk_.

10. *Acronyms* are words formed from the first or sometimes first two letters of several words; the words *SEAL* (SEa, Air, Land) and *NATO* (North Atlantic Treaty Organization) are two examples.

    Acronyms means _Name_.

INTERNET RESOURCE
See **www.acronymfinder.com** for more common acronyms.

Study Tip

Create acronyms to learn disconnected pieces of information that are hard to store in memory because they don't have an obvious connection to one another. For instance, an acronym for the mathematical order of operations is PEMDAS.*

---

*PEMDAS: parentheses, exponents, multiplication, division, addition, subtraction. The source of the acronym is Rick Wormelli's *Summarizing in Any Subject: 50 Techniques to Improve Student Learning*, great for students and instructors alike.

More Pointers About Specialized Vocabulary

Pages 59–60 introduced some common methods textbook authors use to highlight and define specialized vocabulary. But, in fact, there are several other important devices textbook authors employ to highlight the words and terms essential to their discipline, or subject.

Recognizing Key Terms

Each time you open a textbook, you should immediately determine how an author signals to readers that a particular word or term is significant. Some authors consistently boldface key words or terms and then follow with a definition. Others introduce specialized vocabulary in boldface or italics, follow it with a definition, and then repeat both word and definition in the margin. Look, for example, at the following passage:

Goal-Setting Theory: A theory of motivation suggesting that employees are motivated to achieve goals they and their managers establish together.

Goal-setting theory suggests that employees are motivated to achieve goals they and their managers establish together. The goal should be very specific, moderately difficult, and one the employee will be committed to achieve. Rewards should be directly tied to goal achievement. (Pride, Hughes, and Kapoor, *Business*, p. 232.)

Here the authors use three different devices to highlight the term *goal-setting theory*: They introduce it in boldface, provide a definition, and repeat that definition in a marginal annotation, or note. Whenever a word or phrase gets so much attention, it's important, and you should add both the word and the definition to your notes.

Paragraphs Devoted to Definitions

Although many textbook authors use multiple devices to make specialized vocabulary stand out, not all of them do. Sometimes, the only real clue to key terms is how much space the author has devoted to defining them. Any word or phrase that gets a whole paragraph to itself is bound to be essential to the subject you are studying. Look, for example, at the following paragraph, in which the author not only defines *stereotyping* but also gives you a brief history of its meaning.

Stereotyping occurs when members of one group attribute characteristics to members of another group. Typically, these characteristics carry a positive or negative evaluation. In the United States, race and gender groups are often stereotyped. The meaning of the word *stereotype*, however, has changed considerably since its introduction in 1824 by James Morier, when it was used to describe a printing process. A century later Walter Lippmann defined stereotypes as "pictures in our heads" and argued that stereotypes are not merely descriptions of others, but include an emotional component* that is driven by one's self-respect and value orientations. In more recent times, the word *stereotype* has taken on negative connotations, or associations. (Adapted from Neulip, *Intercultural Communication*, p. 150.)

Typically for the definition paragraph, this one opens with the word that is being defined; the definition follows right on its heels. The opening focus on word and definition is the key characteristic of a definition paragraph. What follows after that can vary, ranging from examples of the word in action to a brief history of its meanings. The main thing to remember is any word that earns a paragraph deserves your close attention. (For more on definition paragraphs, see pages 432–434.)

Checking the Glossary

If you feel unsure about any definitions of specialized vocabulary, check to see if your textbook has a glossary in the back. Most do. **Glossaries** list all the specialized terms in a textbook. If a definition is vague or unclear in the text, referring to the glossary will usually help clear up any confusion.

Study Tip	Make separate lists of specialized vocabulary for each of your courses. Review one list per day by covering up the definitions and looking only at the words. Try to recall the definitions from memory. Look at them only to check that your definition is correct or to double check a definition you can't seem to recall.

*component: element.

Connotations and Denotations of Words

The more words you add to your reading vocabulary, the more inclined you will be to try them out in your own writing. That's wonderful. However, to use words effectively, you need to know more than their **denotation**, or dictionary definitions. You also need to know whether a word carries with it any connotations. **Connotations** are the associations or implications some words develop over time.

For example, the words *pruning* and *slashing* both refer to the act of cutting. Their connotations, however, are very different, as you can see from the following brief passage. "My wife asked me why I was *slashing* her rose bushes. I told her I was just *pruning* them." By using the word *pruning,* the husband suggests he is shaping the bushes, whereas the wife's use of the word *slashing* implies he is destroying them.* Yet if you look up the two words in the dictionary and find their definitions—also known as their *denotations*—you will see that the definitions are not all that different. What gives *pruning* and *slashing* different meanings in the above sentences are the connotations the words carry with them. Pruning is associated with gardening, whereas slashing has a long history of being linked to violent acts (there's a genre of movies, after all, known as "slasher" films).

In the following pairs of sentences, you have two words to choose from in parentheses. In the first pair, underline the word that would encourage readers to have a positive response to the person or group under discussion.

a. Over the years, the lawyer Gloria Allred has taken on some truly (off-the-wall *or* unconventional) cases.

b. The students managed to (spend *or* waste) a few hours at the library.

Now underline the words that would encourage readers to react negatively.

c. (Gobbling *or* Eating) lunch at her desk, the receptionist was clearly not pleased to see so many new arrivals.

---

*This example comes from Joseph Trimmer, *Writing with a Purpose.*

d. Henry Wallace, Franklin Delano Roosevelt's third-term vice president, was famous in Washington for his (weird *or* unusual) interests and hobbies.

Connotation, Denotation, and Context

Not all words have positive or negative connotations. Words like *table, chair,* and *molecule,* for instance, usually carry with them only their denotation. Then, too, some words have strong connotations in one context and no connotations in another. Take, for example, the word *pill* in the following sentence: "Can you give me some water so I can take a *pill*?" Here, the word *pill* has no positive or negative associations. Yet in the next sentence, the word has a distinctly negative connotation: "My boss is a real *pill*; every time I sit down, she finds something else for me to do."

When learning new words, pay attention to and record examples of how they are used so that you begin to develop a sense for the appropriate context. Yes, a *domicile* is a house, but it is a rather formal word for house, more likely to be used in insurance or tax forms than in everyday conversation. So you might see a sentence like the following: "The company's *domicile* should not affect its tax advantage." But it would be rare for you to see a sentence like this one: "The dog hated to sleep in his *domicile*; he preferred his owner's bed." The word *domicile* is at home in the first sentence, out of place in the second.*

■ EXERCISE 7   Understanding Connotation

DIRECTIONS Underline the word with more positive connotations.

1. (Crude, Direct) in the way he expressed himself, he often offended people even when he meant no harm.

2. She (giggled, guffawed) her amusement at her husband's quick-witted response.

3. Today's fashion models are almost always tall and (slender, emaciated).

---

*Thanks to one of the finest teachers I have ever met, Joan Hellman of Catonsville Community College, for this example.

4. He didn't expect to pay such a high price for a (preowned, used) vehicle.

5. Clothes for (overweight, husky) boys are located on the second floor.

 **EXERCISE 8 Understanding Connotation**

DIRECTIONS Underline the word with more negative connotations.

1. The student (called, blurted) out the answer before the teacher had finished reading the question.

2. The couple spent days (deliberating, disputing) how to spend their tax refund.

3. She was (stubborn, determined) and refused to change her mind.

4. His (carelessness, recklessness) caused the accident.

5. He (tossed, hurled) her suitcase out the window.

The Difference Between Reading and Writing Vocabularies

Mastering new vocabulary, whether for reading or writing, involves the regular collecting and reviewing of new words. However, with your reading vocabulary, the goal is to develop *automatic* word recognition: You see the word; you know its meaning, without having to consciously think about it. Learning researchers call this *automaticity.* That's a fancy way of saying your grasp of word and meaning are so firmly embedded in your memory that you don't have to mentally search for a definition. Understanding words at this automatic level is like driving a car for a long time. After a certain point, you have practiced your driving skills to such a degree, they feel like a natural instinct rather than a learned activity.

Mastering new vocabulary for writing is a little different. Your writing vocabulary should *not* involve automatic word choices. When you are looking for words to express your thoughts, you may need to think a bit about the most appropriate ones. The ones that come automatically to mind may be those you have heard so often, they are considered *clichés*—overused expressions which suggest the writer has given up on original thought and shifted into automatic pilot. This is never the impression you want to create as a writer. Whatever *tone,* or attitude, you convey with words, you want those words to seem fresh and carefully chosen. Thus, adding words to you writing vocabulary requires more than collection and review.

Study Tip

Use *mnemonic devices,* or memory tricks, to learn new words. Associate new words with images or examples; connect them to sample sentences or to people, e.g., "The word *anecdote* reminds me of how my dad gives advice. He always starts with an anecdote."

■ DIGGING DEEPER

WORDS ARE LIKE BULLETS

LOOKING AHEAD Author Thomas Whissen uses an interesting simile—a comparison using *like* or *as*—to describe words. He says, they are similar to bullets. See if you agree.

> "The question is," said Alice, "whether you *can* make words mean so many different things."
>
> "The question is," said Humpty Dumpty, "which is to be master—that's all."
>
> —Lewis Carroll, *Through the Looking Glass*

1   Since the first dictionary was compiled by Samuel Johnson over two hundred years ago, it has been all too easy to fall back on the dictionary as the ultimate authority and pretend to let the matter rest there. But nobody today would dream of relying on Johnson's original dictionary for anything but enjoyment and curiosity. In his day he had the last word. Lexicographers don't make up meanings (although Johnson did); at best they can only record what a word means to literate people at the time the dictionary is being compiled. Even as the book is coming off the press, parts of it are becoming obsolete.

2   Words are like bullets. Fire one into a mattress and you get a predictable reaction. That's denotation. Fire one into a crowded auditorium and you can't be sure what reaction you will get beyond the noise. Will people freeze or panic? Will the sound echo or go dead? Will there be backfiring, ringing, reverberation?* Whatever the result, that's connotation. It's the echo and backfire, the ringing and reverberation that give words their vitality. It's the added meaning that ignites a word and makes it explode in several directions at once.

Sharpening Your Skills

DIRECTIONS Answer the following questions by circling the letters of the correct response or filling in the blanks.

---

*reverberation: echo.

1. Explain how bullets resemble words.

_____

_____

_____

2. The author's explanation of why words are like bullets illustrates a point made in the chapter. The point is that
   a. words have more than a dictionary meaning.
   b. words have more denotations than connotations.
   c. word meaning can change with the context.

3. Based on the context, what is a lexicographer?

_____

4. In addition to the opening simile, the author also uses *metaphors* in the last few sentences. Like similes, metaphors compare unlike things to reveal a resemblance. They just don't use the words *like* or *as*. In this case, the author compares the connotation of a word

   to a(n) _____.

   In the last sentence, he uses a metaphor that compares

_____.

5. The excerpt opens with an *allusion*, or reference, to author Lewis Carroll's book *Through the Looking Glass*, where language no longer plays by normal rules and nonsense is king. What does Humpty Dumpty mean when he says, "The question is, which is to be master—that's all"?
   a. Questions are more important than answers.
   b. Do we control words, or do they control us?
   c. What is the meaning of life during times of confusion?
   d. Words have far too many meanings and cause confusion.

INTERNET BONUS QUESTION

Create a search term that will help you answer the question that follows: In one of his most famous similes, Samuel Johnson*

compared a woman preaching to a _____

_____. What was the point of Johnson's simile? _____

_____.

INTERNET RESOURCE

For more practice with context clues and vocabulary, go to **college.hmco.com/pic/flemmingRFR10e**.

---

*Samuel Johnson: Some scholars have challenged the notion that the eighteenth-century writer was sexist. Johnson's interest in the rights of women is, in fact, the subject of a book by Kathleen Nulton Kermerer.

 **Test 1: Using Context Clues**

DIRECTIONS Use context clues to select an approximate definition for each italicized word.

1. In the face of real danger, he didn't even try to display his usual *bravado:* When the bull charged, he ran like a scared rabbit.

   a. extreme shyness

   b. love of animals

   c. false bravery

   d. quick wit

2. With age, the financial wizard and penny pincher Hazel Green grew increasingly eccentric: she wore *bizarrely* unfashionable clothes, trusted no one, went on strange diets, and generally seemed to be out of step with the world.

   a. stingily

   b. weirdly

   c. colorful

   d. cleverly

3. In *The Country of the Pointed Firs*, the nineteenth-century writer Sarah Orne Jewett created the remarkable and compelling Mrs. Todd, a country woman who uses her vast store of herbal *lore* to cure the ailing and aging.

   a. knowledge

   b. mystery

   c. myths

   d. poisons

4. After her face was *disfigured* by an automobile accident, the super-model realized that there really were people in the world who could love her for who she was rather than what she looked like.

   a. enriched

   b. abandoned

   c. rebuilt

   d. ruined

5. In order to justify his claim to visitation rights, Adam was willing to undergo a *paternity* test that would prove David was indeed his son.

   a. relative

   b. brotherhood

c. fatherhood

d. chemical

6. In the nineteenth century, girls and boys were rigidly *socialized:* Girls were encouraged to be subordinate to boys and boys were told they could conquer the world.

a. restricted by class

b. punished for misbehavior

c. taught to obey

d. taught appropriate social roles

7. Although the curse of Tutankhamen's tomb has never been scientifically proven, the *irrational* belief persists that those who discovered the tomb met an early death.

a. dishonest

b. sensational

c. fast-spreading

d. unreasonable

8. In the fairy tale, the wolf tried to disguise his *predatory* nature by dressing up as Little Red Riding Hood's elderly grandmother.

a. insensitive

b. youthful

c. dangerous

d. wild

9. He wanted to work on their relationship by regularly seeing a therapist; she opted for a more *radical* solution and filed for divorce.

a. insignificant

b. drastic

c. quiet

d. expensive

10. The lawyer *systematically* worked his way through the document and eliminated all references to the coauthor.

a. casually

b. slowly

c. quickly

d. carefully

 **Test 2: Using Context Clues**

> **DIRECTIONS** Use context clues to develop an approximate definition for each italicized word.

1. The artist, who is clearly a Democrat, uses his *satirical* cartoons to expose the follies of Republican politicians.

Satirical means <u>Sarcasm</u>   <u>make fun</u>.

2. They decided against buying the house because of its *proximity* to the airport.

Proximity means <u>location</u>   <u>near</u>.

3. Having a child outside of marriage no longer carries the punitive *stigma* it did twenty-five years ago.

Stigma means <u>reputation</u>.

4. On the highway running through the city, a vehicle accident can cause *gridlock* that stretches for miles.

Gridlock means <u>Standstill</u>   <u>traffic jam</u>.

5. To provide her children with intellectual *stimulation*, the young mother often took them to museums, bookstores, and concerts.

Stimulation means <u>activate</u>.

6. When Martha asked her husband if she was getting fat, he said "yes" without thinking and quickly regretted his *candor*.

Candor means <u>openness</u>.

7. George Washington was the first and last U.S. president to govern from Philadelphia; all *subsequent* presidents have resided in the White House in Washington, D.C.

Subsequent means <u>succeeding</u>.

8. When the *Apollo 11* astronauts landed on the moon, they found a rocky, *barren* landscape.

Barren means <u>empty</u>.

9. The count had a *supercilious* expression on his face and seemed to be looking down his nose at the other guests.

Supercilious means _proud_____.

10. Rev. Martin Luther King Jr.'s *charismatic* leadership inspired millions of people to demand civil rights for black Americans.

Charismatic means _powerful energect_____.

 **Test 3: Using Context Clues**

> **DIRECTIONS** Use context clues to develop an approximate definition for each italicized word.*

1. The 1938 Fair Labor Standards Act signed by Franklin D. Roosevelt prevents the *exploitation* of children; it prohibits anyone under the age of thirteen from working in most jobs.

   Exploitation means ___miss use of___.

2. The Louisiana Purchase, President Thomas Jefferson's *acquisition* of 5.3 million acres of French territory in 1803, doubled the size of the United States.

   Acquisition means ___purchases___.

3. Wilbur and Orville Wright succeeded in building the first "flying machine" because they systematically *modified* their design, making changes and improvements following each test flight.

   Modified means ___Changed___.

4. By the end of the twentieth century, America's economy had begun to shift from one based *predominantly* on manufacturing to one based mostly on employees' knowledge and skills.

   Predominantly means ___mostly mainly___.

5. The Common Era, also known as the Christian Era, began with the year Jesus was believed to be born; the years *preceding* this date are followed by *B.C.*, an abbreviation for "Before Christ."

   Preceding means ___before___.

6. The American Civil War *commenced* on April 12, 1861, when the South fired the first shots at Union troops in Charleston, South Carolina, and ended on April 9, 1865.

   Commenced means ___began___.

---

*The italicized words are all from the Academic Word List developed by the School of Linguistics and Applied Language Studies at Victoria University of Wellington in New Zealand.

7. According to one *hypothesis,* the impact of an asteroid 65 million years ago led to the extinction of the dinosaurs, but this explanation is not a proven fact.

   Hypothesis means _____theroy_____.

8. The legal document known as a "living will" provides *explicit* instructions about what caregivers should and should not do in the event that a person becomes comatose or requires long-term life support.

   Explicit means __detailed_____.

9. According to many scientists, global warming could have dangerous *implications* for the future, including a destructive rise in sea levels, damage to ecosystems and agriculture, and an increase in extreme weather events like hurricanes.

   Implications means ___results_____.

10. In economics, *fluctuations* in the prices of goods are caused by similar increases and decreases in the availability of and demand for those goods.

    Fluctuations means ___changes_____.

 **Test 4: Word Analysis and Context Clues**

DIRECTIONS Use context clues and word parts to develop an approximate definition for each italicized word.

Prefixes		Roots	
anti = against		*cred* = belief	
extra = over, outside, beyond		*dict* = say or speak	
dis = apart from, not, without		*sect* = cut, divide	
ad = to, toward		*here* = stick	

1. The doctors were fearful the boy would die because they had no *antidote* for the snakebite.

   Antidote means <u>against (cure)</u>.

2. The girl refused to *dissect* the frog because she couldn't bear the thought of wasting a frog's life just so some student could cut up the body.

   Dissect means <u>apart from cut divide</u>.

3. Because the Shaker religion forbade sex even in marriage, it had a hard time keeping *adherents*.

   Adherents means <u>to, toward stick (supporters)</u>.

4. The report included too much *extraneous* information: The committee wanted only the essential facts of the situation, not silly gossip about dress and personal behavior.

   Extraneous means <u>over</u>.

5. If she wants to run in the next campaign, she needs to *disassociate* herself from well-known gamblers and gangsters.

   Disassociate means <u>apart from</u>.

6. Dr. Sorenson thinks of himself as an expert on ocean environment, but he lacks the proper *credentials:* He's a dentist, not a marine biologist.

   Credentials means <u>belief</u>.

7. My mother always told me to follow the *dictum* "neither a borrower nor a lender be," but I am always borrowing money from my friends.

   Dictum means Say or speak .

8. The bank official desperately tried to *extricate* himself from the financial crisis he had helped to create, but all his influence couldn't get him out of trouble this time.

   Extricate means over, outside .

9. Once the suspect gave a *credible* account of his actions the night before, the police decided to let him go.

   Credible means belief .

10. Even with the glue in place, the pictures simply would not *adhere* to the shiny wallpaper.

    Adhere means to, toward .

Test 5: Word Analysis and Context Clues

DIRECTIONS Use context clues and word parts to develop an approximate definition for each italicized word.

Prefixes	Roots
in, im = in, into, not	*clin* = lean
multi = many	*plac* = calm, please
omni = all	*ven* = come
circum = around	*sci* = know
	vor = eat

1. As my uncle got older, he became less *implacable;* more mellow with age, he was much easier to please.

   Implacable means ⎯not⎯calm⎯⎯⎯⎯⎯⎯⎯⎯⎯.

2. The entertainer Lena Horne was determined to *circumvent* the racist rules that once ruled Las Vegas. When hotel owners told her they didn't allow African Americans to rent rooms, Horne told them no room, no performance. As usual, Lena got her way.

   Circumvent means ⎯around⎯come⎯⎯⎯⎯⎯⎯⎯.

3. President Lyndon B. Johnson's first *inclination* in a difficult situation was to sweet-talk whomever he needed on his side; if that didn't work, he could quickly turn into a bully.

   Inclination means ⎯into⎯⎯⎯⎯⎯⎯⎯⎯⎯⎯.

4. In George Orwell's famous novel *1984*, "Big Brother" is an *omniscient* political leader, so all-knowing that privacy simply doesn't exist in the world he controls.

   Omniscient means ⎯all⎯⎯⎯⎯⎯⎯⎯⎯⎯⎯⎯.

5. The United States had a *multiplicity* of reasons for not entering World War II, but after Japan bombed Pearl Harbor, every one of those reasons disappeared like smoke.

   Multiplicity means ⎯many⎯⎯⎯⎯⎯⎯⎯⎯⎯⎯.

6. When millions died during the civil war in Rwanda, both Europe and the United States were harshly criticized for not *intervening* early on, when lives might have been saved.

Intervening means _no come_.

7. Roaches have survived for centuries because they are *omnivorous;* they eat anything and everything—from paste to nail filings.

Omnivorous means _all eat full of_.

8. While the angry *multitudes* shouted outside the gates of the palace, the frightened king and queen tried to leave in secret, knowing full well that there was no way to calm their starving subjects.

Multitudes means _many_.

9. The mother *placated* the child with a chocolate chip cookie; in a matter of seconds, he went from tears to giggles.

Placated means _calm_.

10. Not anxious to return to work, the boy took the most *circuitous* route he could think of, and a fifteen-minute trip took him three-quarters of an hour.

Circuitous means _around_.

 **Test 6: Word Analysis and Context Clues**

DIRECTIONS Use context clues and word parts to develop an approximate definition for each italicized word.

Prefixes	Roots
pre = before or preceding, prior to	*locut, loqu* = speech
super = over, beyond, above	*voc* = voice, call
sub = under, from below, put under	*fic, fact, fect* = to make, to do
	gen = to give birth to, to produce, to cause

1. She has an amazing mind; in a single class session, she can *generate* one original idea after another, and most of them are quite good.

   Generate means produce .

2. After having their reports censored by military officials, the reporters were *vocal* in their complaints; they told anyone who would listen that their right to free speech had been ignored by the high command.

   Vocal means voice .

3. As a *prelude* to his speech, the scientist told a silly joke; as he had hoped, the comic introduction warmed up the audience and made them more attentive.

   Prelude means before .

4. Patricia Henley's novel *Hummingbird House* wonderfully *evokes* the lush and beautiful landscape of Guatemala; she is particularly good at describing the country's colorful birds and gorgeous flowers.

   Evokes means calls .

5. What exactly is the *genesis* of the word *bedlam*? I've heard two different stories about its origin, and I am not sure which one is accurate.

   Genesis means give birth .

6. Although the two men work together very well, they couldn't be more different: Bob is relaxed and *loquacious*, whereas Will is tense and silent most of the time.

Loquacious means ___full of___ .

7. To avoid being followed by reporters, the famous couple used *fictitious* names when they checked into the hotel, but they used their real names after they had crossed over the border into Mexico.

Fictitious means ___to make full of___ .

8. In an effort to trim her speech down to no more than fifteen minutes, the union organizer carefully crossed out any *superfluous* details that weren't directly related to her message.

Superfluous means ___over full of___ .

9. The previous group leader encouraged independent thought; unfortunately, the current leader tries to *subdue* all signs of it.

Subdue means ___put under___ .

10. Sometimes truth is stranger than *fiction*, and the real world can be odder than the one you find in books.

Fiction means ___make___ .

INTERNET RESOURCE
For more work on vocabulary and context clues, go to
laflemm.com and click on *Words Count* and *Words Matter*.

Prefixes, Roots, and Suffixes Introduced in Chapter 2

Prefixes	Roots	Suffixes
ad = to, toward	*bellum* = war	*ism* = state, condition, or quality
anti = against	*chron* = time	
bene = well, good	*clin* = lean	*itis* = inflammation
bi = two	*cred* = belief	*ize* = to cause to be, to treat or affect
circum = around	*derma* = skin	
dis = apart from, not, without	*dict* = say or speak	
	fic, fact, fect = to make or to do	*onym* = name, word
extra = over, outside, beyond		*ous* = full of
im = not	*for* = to bore into	
in, im = in, into, not	*gam* = marriage	
	gen = to give birth to, to produce, to cause	
mal = bad		
mono = one		
multi = many	*here* = stick	
omni = all	*lat* = side	
per = through	*locut, loqu* = speech	
poly = many	*mob* = move	
pre = before, preceding, prior to	*pel* = force	
	plac = calm, please	
pseudo = false	*popul* = people	
re = again, back	*rec, rect* = straight, straighten	
syn, sym = together	*sci* = know	
sub = under, from below, put under	*sect* = cut, divide	
	the = god	
super = over, beyond, above	*ven* = come	
	vi, vit, viv = life	
	voc = voice, call	
	vor = eat	

CHAPTER 3

Relating the General to the Specific in Reading and Writing

In this chapter, you'll learn

- how to tell the difference between general and specific words.

- how to tell the difference between general and specific sentences.

- how writers and readers cooperate to create meaning.

- how general and specific sentences team up in paragraphs.

Many of the explanations in *Reading for Results* assume you have an immediate understanding of the terms *general* and *specific*. Because these two terms are so crucial, Chapter 3 defines them in some detail. Equally important, it also explains how they apply to reading and writing.

 General and Specific Words

You'll soon be working with general and specific sentences, but let's begin with general and specific words. Once you learn to distinguish, or see the difference, between general and specific words, it's easy to identify general and specific sentences.

Here are two lists of words, one labeled *general,* the other *specific.* As you read each list, think about these two questions: How do the words in each list differ? What makes one word general and another one specific?

General	Specific
creatures	dogs
silver	nickels
expression	smile
object	statue
liquid	ink
flower	daisy
machine	computer

Did you notice that the words on the left can be interpreted, or understood, in a variety of ways? The word *creatures,* for example, is broad enough to include everything from cows to children. The word *dogs,* however, quickly eliminates both the cows *and* the children. We are now talking about a specific type of creature—one that barks, has four legs, and wags its tail.

Similarly, the word *silver* can refer to table settings or to money. The word *nickels,* however, quickly eliminates all other possibilities. It refers to coins rather than forks.

With these illustrations in mind, we can sum up the differences between general and specific words.

> **General words** are broad in scope. They refer to or include a wide variety of different things and thus can be understood in several ways. **Specific words**, in contrast, are much narrower in focus. They cover less territory and can't be understood in so many different ways. General words expand meaning; specific words narrow or focus it. To make ourselves understood, we need both kinds of words. We need general words to sum up our experiences and specific words to explain or clarify them.

Let's look at two more pairs of words. This time, it's up to you to label them. Write a *G* next to the general word. Write an *S* next to the more specific one.

sound _____   scream _____

dance _____   movement _____

Did you put a *G* next to *sound* and an *S* next to *scream*? If you did, you're on the right track. The word *sound* covers everything from a meow to a giggle. Thus it's the more general of the two.

If you put an *S* next to the word *dance* and a *G* next to the word *movement,* you again labeled the words correctly. The word *movement* refers to many activities, from playing baseball to doing a tango. The word *dance,* however, eliminates playing baseball along with a host of other possibilities, such as kicking a football or waving good-bye.

EXERCISE 1   Coming Up with Specifics

DIRECTIONS After each general word, list at least three more specific words that could be included under that heading.

EXAMPLE

communication

speech _____

signs _____

television _____

EXPLANATION Because all three words refer to a specific type of communication, we can include all three under the more general heading.

1. feelings

<u>Sad</u>

<u>happy</u>

<u>mad</u>

2. music

<u>R+B /hip hop</u>

<u>Country</u>

<u>Jazz</u>

Putting the Terms *General* and *Specific* into Context

To be meaningful, the terms *general* and *specific* need a context. Sure, *dog* seems like a general word, but if you place it next to the word *animals*, it's the more specific of the two. Similarly, if you put the word *dog* next to the name of a specific dog, say, a labrador retriever named *Tonka* the word *dog* becomes the more general of the two.

For an illustration of how a word can become more general or specific with context, see the following diagram:

animals	The word *animals* refers to all kinds of living beings. Members of the group called *animals* are very different from one another; they are more dissimilar than similar.
quadrupeds	The term *quadrupeds* refers only to those animals having four legs; all other animals are excluded. Members of the group are more dissimilar than similar.
dogs	The word *dogs* refers to one particular group of animals. Members of the group called *dogs* are more similar to one another than are members of the group called four-legged animals.
pedigrees	The word *pedigrees* now includes only dogs whose parentage is clear; all mixed breeds have been excluded.
labs	The word *labs* refers to one particular pedigree, the labrador retriever. The members of this group look alike. At this level, all other breeds are excluded.
Tonka	The word *Tonka* refers only to labs bearing the name "Tonka." All other labrador retrievers are excluded from this level.

Check Your Understanding

Explain the difference between general and specific words.

_____

_____

_____

_____

_____

■ EXERCISE 2 **Seeing the Difference Between General and Specific Words**

DIRECTIONS Underline the more specific word in each pair.

EXAMPLE

a. entertainment, <u>movies</u>

b. *Newsweek*, magazines

EXPLANATION The word *movies* is more specific than the word *entertainment*. It refers to a fewer number of things, and the things to which it refers are more alike than unlike. The word *Newsweek* is more specific than the word *magazines*. It refers to one particular magazine rather than to a variety of publications.

1. architecture, churches

2. crimes, robbery

3. Usher, rapper

4. Congress, government

5. documents, Constitution

━ ▇ EXERCISE 3 **Seeing the Difference Between General
and Specific Words**

DIRECTIONS Underline the more general word in each pair.

1. creature, person

2. earth, planet

3. pollution, smog

4. phobia, claustrophobia

5. flag, symbol

━ ▇ EXERCISE 4 **Finding a General Category**

DIRECTIONS Find one word or term *general enough* to include all
the other words listed.

EXAMPLE *academic subjects*

American history
English composition
sociology
algebra

EXPLANATION In this case, all four items can be included under
the heading "academic subjects." Now it's your turn.

1. _____ movies

The Da Vinci Code
Harry Potter and the Half-Blood Prince
Memoirs of a Geisha
The Kite Runner

2. Artiest /musicans

Shakira
Jessica Simpson
Kelly Clarkson
Alicia Keys

3. fictional charters

Superwoman
Buffy the Vampire Slayer
Xena
Cat Woman

4. _Cartoons_

Snoopy
Calvin and Hobbes
Dilbert
Batman

5. _Movies_

The Ring
Night of the Living Dead
The Texas Chainsaw Massacre
The Silence of the Lambs

EXERCISE 5 General and Specific in Context

DIRECTIONS Fill in the accompanying diagrams with the appropriate letters. The letter of the most general word goes on top. The letter of the most specific word goes on the bottom.

EXAMPLE

a. musician

b. artist

c. violinist

b	(most general)
a	(more specific)
c	(most specific)

EXPLANATION The word *artist* can refer to many different kinds of people, for example, painters, sculptors, or writers. As the most general word, it goes on the top level. *Musician* is somewhat more specific than *artist*. It excludes all people who are not concerned with music. Therefore, it goes on the middle rung. *Violinist* is the most specific word; it refers only to people who play the violin.

1. a. flu
   b. disease
   c. swine flu

2. a. water
   b. Indian Ocean
   c. ocean

3. a. detergent
   b. product
   c. Tide

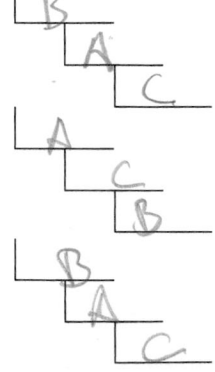

4. a. continent
   b. land mass
   c. South America

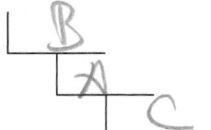

 # Understanding the Difference Between General and Specific Sentences

To test your understanding of the terms *general* and *specific* when they are applied to sentences, read the two examples below. See if you can explain what makes the first sentence more general than the second.

General Sentence   **1.** Anger can take many different forms.

Specific Sentence   **2.** Some people grow quiet when they get angry, while others scream and shout.

Did you notice that the more general sentence, like more general words, could be interpreted, or understood, in several ways? Based on sentence 1, we could assume that anger might be expressed in tears, shouts, silence, or laughter. It all depends on how readers choose to interpret the key phrase "many different forms." The more specific sentence brings the general one into focus. It narrows, or limits, expressions of anger to just two responses: being quiet or noisy.

Defining Terms

Now that we have looked at an example, here are two more detailed definitions that should nail down the meanings of *general* and *specific* when used in reference to sentences.

> **General sentences** combine and comment on a number of different, but in some way related, events, ideas, or experiences. In the previous sentence, for instance, experiences as different as silence and shouting are brought together in the general phrase "many different forms" of anger. Precisely because general sentences are broad in meaning, they can be misinterpreted or misunderstood. They need, therefore, to be accompanied by more specific sentences.

> **Specific sentences** cover less ground than general ones. They focus on a smaller number of events, ideas, and experiences. Specific sentences help explain or clarify general ones, answering questions readers might raise, such as "What are some of the forms anger can take?"

Here's another pair of sentences. Put a *G* next to the general sentence and an *S* next to the more specific one.

> **1.** When they are in a classroom, many people are afraid to ask questions or disagree. _____
> **2.** Our behavior is often affected by the presence of others. _____

If you labeled sentence 1 specific and sentence 2 general, you are correct. Sentence 2 says that our behavior is affected by the presence of others, but it doesn't zero in on any one situation. Instead, it sums up and includes any and all situations where people are present.

Sentence 1, in contrast, focuses on one particular setting—the classroom. It also identifies two particular kinds of behavior—asking questions or disagreeing. Sentence 1 clarifies and helps us understand sentence 2, making sentence 1 the more specific sentence.

Reading Tip

As soon as you spot a general sentence check to see which of the sentences that follow clarify or explain it.*

---

*This advice will become crucial in Chapter 4, when you look for the main idea or message of a paragraph.

EXERCISE 6   Recognizing General and Specific Sentences

DIRECTIONS Read each pair of sentences. Then label the general sentence *G* and the specific one *S*.

EXAMPLE

a. The focus in elementary schools has switched from girls to boys, and researchers now have a whole new set of educational concerns. _*G*_

b. In the 1990s, educational research focused on how to help girls excel in science and math, but now the emphasis is on helping boys become better readers and writers. _*S*_

EXPLANATION Sentence *a* is more general because we don't have specific meanings for the words *focus* and *concerns*. Note how sentence *b*, the more specific sentence, defines both terms and puts limits on how they can be understood.

1. a. Early in U.S. history, newspapers didn't pretend to be without political bias. _S_

   b. In the eighteenth century, American politicians funded and openly controlled newspapers. _G_

2. a. In the past twenty years, health care around the world has markedly improved, especially for infants. _G_

   b. Thanks to improved health care, the number of babies who die in the first year of life has decreased markedly over the last twenty years. _S_

3. a. In Japan, readily revealing one's emotions to others is not encouraged, but in America the opposite is true. _S_

   b. Culture affects behavior in a number of ways, particularly within the context of personal relations. _G_

4. a. Like many of his victims, Jesse James was shot in the back.

_S_

b. The outlaw Jesse James met what some have called a fitting end.

_6_

5. a. The Fourth Amendment to the Constitution guarantees Americans the right to privacy. ___S___

b. Americans value the right to privacy so much that they made it a law. _6_

Recognizing Levels of Generality and Specificity in Sentences

The previous examples compared only two sentences. However, most paragraphs consist of more than two sentences. As you might expect, those sentences can range from the very general to the very specific. Look, for example, at the four sentences that follow. Each one is on a different level of specificity.

1. Famous performers are inclined to be demanding.

2. Famous pop divas often have very special requirements for their dressing rooms.

3. When pop diva Christina Aguilera performs, her contract requires that her dressing room be well-stocked with her favorite food and drinks.

4. According to a clause in her contract, Aguilera has to have, among other things, ten bottles of water (not Evian), a six-pack of Coke (not diet), assorted raw almonds, full-fat soymilk, a bottle of Echinacea capsules, one small tray of processed meats, and one small tray of fresh fruit.*

Sentence 1 makes a general statement about famous performers. At this point, the sentence could be referring to all kinds of performers, from pianists to ballerinas. Sentence 2, though, is narrower in

*For the full list of requirements, see www.thesmokinggun.com/backstage/aguilera4.html.

Check Your Understanding

Why do general sentences need to be accompanied by specific sentences?

_____

_____

_____

_____

---

scope. It tells us the writer is discussing only one particular type of performer—the female pop singer. We also now know more about the meaning of "demanding." In sentence 1, the writer could have meant that famous performers fuss over their equipment, the place where they perform, their costumes, and so on. But by sentence 2, we know we are talking solely about dressing room demands.

Sentence 3 is even more specific because the writer refers to one particular performer, Christina Aguilera, and what she requires for her dressing room. By sentence 4, we know, in part at least, exactly what Aguilera expects to have if she is to go on stage. We also have a much clearer idea of what the writer means with her opening claim about famous performers.

EXERCISE 7 Recognizing Levels of Generality and Specificity

DIRECTIONS Fill in the accompanying diagrams with the appropriate letters. The letter of the most general sentence goes on the top level. The letter of the most specific sentence goes on the bottom level.

EXAMPLE

a. We use our teeth to prepare food for digestion.

b. To prepare food for digestion, molars crush and grind food; incisors cut large pieces of food into smaller ones.

c. In the process of preparing food for digestion, different teeth have different functions.

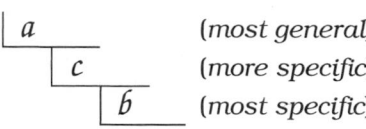

a (*most general*)
c (*more specific*)
b (*most specific*)

> **EXPLANATION** Sentence *a* is the most general. It tells us that our teeth prepare food for digestion. Sentence *c* tells us more about the way the teeth prepare the food for digestion. Sentence *b* is the most specific sentence. It identifies specific kinds of teeth and their functions.

1. a. The biggest change in the American work force involves gender.

   b. The American work force is changing.

   c. Since 1960, the number of women in the American work force has nearly doubled.

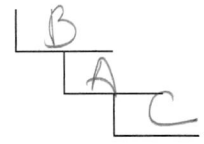

2. a. In mathematics, for example, some words have meanings that are different from their usual ones.

   b. In mathematics, a *curve* is the path between two points and a curve can be straight rather than rounded.

   c. Changing the context of a word can change its meaning.

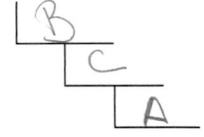

3. a. There are many ways to fight insomnia and fall asleep more easily.

   b. The more carbohydrates—sugars, starches, and grains—you eat at night, the more easily you will fall asleep.

   c. Diet can help you fight insomnia.

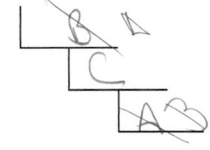

4. a. Both President Franklin D. Roosevelt and President Harry S Truman made the decision to wage war during their terms in office.

   b. American presidents have enormous power.

   c. American presidents have declared war without congressional approval.

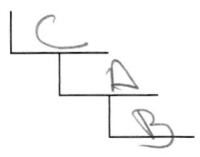

5. a. Forests play an important part in controlling flooding and erosion.*

   b. Forests are a valuable resource.

   c. The network of roots in a forest floor soaks up heavy rains; this prevents flooding and halts erosion.

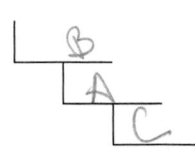

---

*erosion: the process of wearing away.

6. a. The early American colonists borrowed words from the Native Americans.

b. The early American colonists borrowed the names of plants and animals from the Native Americans they met.

c. Americans have always borrowed from other languages.

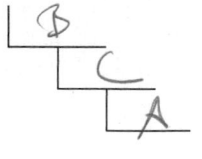

7. a. In the nineteenth century, anti-vivisectionists* demonstrated against the use of animals in research.

b. The animal-rights movement has a long history.

c. As early as the nineteenth century, people demonstrated in support of animal rights.

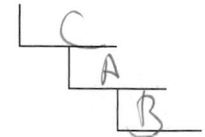

8. a. The great opera singer Maria Callas was known not just for her gorgeous voice but also for being an explosive prima donna.*

b. On several occasions, Callas halted a performance because she didn't think her audience was appreciative enough.

c. Opera singers are famous for being temperamental.*

9. a. Our attitudes toward childhood have changed over time.

b. In Puritan America, children were expected to behave like small adults and do their share of the household work.

c. In Puritan America, childhood was not considered a time to be lighthearted and carefree as it is today.

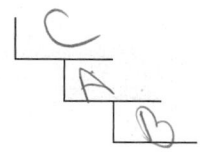

10. a. In ancient times, France was ruled by the Romans, who had a strong influence on the French language.

b. Most cultures are the product of many different influences.

---

*anti-vivisectionists: people opposed to the cutting up of live animals for scientific research.
*prima donna: a talented but demanding performer, usually used in reference to women.
*temperamental: emotional, moody.

c. Like most European cultures, France was
invaded by many different groups that
influenced the country's language and culture.

The Writer's Responsibility

To explain or argue an idea, writers need to **generalize**. They need
to make broad statements that cover a number of specific people,
ideas, or events, for example, "The current popularity of poker among
teenagers is a disturbing trend that could have long-term consequences"; "Animal-rights activists have used some controversial tactics to discourage children from eating meat"; "Head Start programs
for children have a history of both success and controversy."

Writers, however, also need to be specific. So that readers don't get
confused, writers need to include sentences that will clarify and limit
possible interpretations. Specific sentences are a writer's way of
saying to readers, "I mean this, not that." For an illustration, look at
how the following more specific sentences help restrict the meanings
of the three general statements already introduced: "True, some
teenagers have won huge sums of money playing poker, but many
more have lost large sums yet continue to play, inspired by stories of
their peers' financial success"; "In some cases, animal-rights activists
have scared children with pictures of animals suffering from the tor-
tures of factory farming"; "Children who work their way through Head
Start programs usually end up reading at the appropriate grade level
or above, but that doesn't stop critics from insisting that education
should be a local rather than a federal concern."

Without general sentences, writers would have a hard time making
a larger point that went beyond individual experience. Without specific sentences, they couldn't explain an idea or argue a point of view.

The Reader's Response

For their part, readers need to follow the writer's train of thought
through all of its twists and turns. On the most basic level, this
means being on the lookout for general statements that sum up a
variety of people, events, or ideas. Having spotted those statements,
readers need to connect them to the more specific sentences used
as clarification or proof. It's only by connecting the two kinds of
sentences that the reader can determine the author's meaning.

Fulfilling the reader's role and making the right connections come naturally to readers who keep the following three questions in mind while reading:

---

1. Where are the most general statements in the reading?
2. What questions do they raise?
3. Where are the specific sentences that answer those questions?

If they cannot answer one of these three questions, *experienced readers are quick to retool their approach* and ask different questions. For instance, if they can't find any general statements, they start asking what general idea or point is suggested, or implied, by the specific sentences in the passage (more about implied main ideas in Chapter 5). Should the specific sentences in the reading seem unrelated to the general sentence that initially appeared to be the focal point of the passage, experienced readers start looking for another general sentence (more on this in Chapter 4).

Reading Tip

Take a flexible approach to reading. If one question doesn't work, try another. If a first reading doesn't give you the author's meaning, read the passage a second time.

EXERCISE 8   Clarifying General Sentences

DIRECTIONS Read the three specific sentences. Then look at the general sentences that follow. Put a check next to the one general statement that the specific sentences could best support.

EXAMPLE

Specific Sentences a. Before 1980, most doctors worked alone, but today more than half are salaried employees who work for medical companies.

b. Twenty-five years ago, doctors could count on the respect of their patients, but recent polls show a decline in patients' respect for physicians.

c. Increasingly, doctors must seek permission from government agencies or insurance companies to give special treatments to patients.

General   _____ **1.** The number of women and minorities applying to medical
Sentences   school has increased greatly.

       _✓_ **2.** The professional life of physicians has changed dramatically in
                    the past twenty-five years.

       _____ **3.** Most people who enter medical school do so because they have
                    been influenced by family doctors.

EXPLANATION General sentences 1 and 3 are not good choices
because the specific sentences do not mention medical schools or
why people apply to them.

Specific   **1.** a. The tradition of using candles at funerals began with the
Sentences   Romans, who used them to frighten away evil spirits.

            b. Tombstones originated as a way of keeping the dead in the
               underworld.

            c. The original purpose of coffins was to keep the dead safely
               underground.

General   _____ **1.** Anthropologists have found evidence that funeral traditions
Sentences   existed during the Neanderthal age (100,000–40,000 BC).

       _____ **2.** Different cultures have different ways of mourning their dead.

       _✓_ **3.** Many of the modern customs associated with mourning came
                    from a fear of the dead and what they might do to the living.

Specific   **2.** a. The citizens of Sparta, a city-state of ancient Greece, were not
Sentences   allowed to become farmers; they were made to train as warriors
                       instead.

            b. Family life in Sparta was severely limited because both boys and
               girls spent long hours in physical training.

            c. From age seven to age thirty, the boys received instruction in the
               art of waging war.

General   _✓_ **1.** The Spartans were obedient to the laws of their land.
Sentences
       _____ **2.** The Spartan life was hard and devoted to war.

       _✗_ **3.** Spartan men and women were known for their heroism in war.

Specific   **3.** a. During World War II, German invaders destroyed Russia's rich-
Sentences   est agricultural regions.

General Statement = Topic

b. According to official reports, more than seven million Russians were killed while defending their country against German attacks.

c. Many Russians lost their lives in concentration camps.

General *Sentences*	___✓___	**1.** The Russians suffered heavy losses in World War II.
	_____	**2.** Russia suffered more losses than any of the other great powers.
	_____	**3.** Russia has never recovered from the tragedy of World War II.

Specific *Sentences* **4.** a. During World War II, the War Department finally approved the training of African-American pilots.

b. In 1941 Benjamin O. Davis Jr. became the first African American to lead a squadron of pilots.

c. President Franklin D. Roosevelt's Executive Order 8802 required employers in defense industries to make jobs available "without discrimination* because of race, creed* or color."

General *Sentences*	___✓___	**1.** For many African Americans, World War II offered a chance to break down racial barriers.
	_____	**2.** During World War II, racial violence broke out on several military bases.
	_____	**3.** World War II brought out the best in Americans.

Specific *Sentences* **5.** a. Between 1933 and 1939, about 150,000 square miles of U.S. farmland lost its topsoil.

b. Huge dust storms turned day into night all over the Great Plains.

c. During the same period, more than 500 million tons of rich earth dried out and turned to powder.

General *Sentences*	_____	**1.** American land has been overplowed and overplanted for decades.
	___✓___	**2.** In the 1930s, a large part of the United States turned into what came to be called the "Great Dust Bowl."
	_____	**3.** Poor farming techniques cause hardships for many countries.

---

*discrimination: the act of showing prejudice in favor of or against a particular group.
*creed: belief, religion.

Specific Sentences **6.** a. If you're curious about the future, one site on the World Wide Web offers visitors a free tarot card* reading.

b. The Ragu spaghetti sauce company sponsors a website overflowing with free recipes, plus a basic course in the Italian language.

c. An Oakland University website lets Internet users transfer hundreds of useful programs to their home computers without spending a penny.

General Sentences ___✓___ **1.** Computer users can find a wealth of free information and services on the World Wide Web.

_____ **2.** Surveys indicate that a growing number of American families own a home computer.

_____ **3.** Thousands of companies have been trying to find new ways to make money on the Internet.

Specific Sentences **7.** a. When actor Robert Coates liked the lines in one of Shakespeare's death scenes, he would repeat the scene over and over until angry theatergoers pelted him with oranges.

b. Coates forgot his lines every night, so he made up his own for well-known plays such as *Hamlet* and *King Lear*.

c. England's theater critics laughingly called the actor "Romeo" Coates because he would stop the show to wave to friends and chat with people in the audience.

General Sentences ___✓___ **1.** Robert Coates, a nineteenth-century stage performer, may have been the most incompetent Shakespearean actor who ever lived.

_____ **2.** Actor Robert Coates played many of Shakespeare's most famous characters during the early 1800s.

_____ **3.** Handsome costumes mattered very much to British actor Robert Coates.

Specific Sentences **8.** a. A blue fireball exploded above central Siberia when an asteroid hit near the Tunguska River on June 30, 1908.

b. A mushroom cloud bloomed in the air, and trees were uprooted and scorched for dozens of miles.

c. An entire herd of reindeer died because of the heat the asteroid produced, while its impact shattered windows as far away as 600 miles.

———————————
*tarot card: a card used in fortune telling.

General Sentences _____ 1. Scientists believe that asteroids are ancient chunks of matter that never clumped together to become planets.

_____ 2. Most asteroids are grouped into belts that hang in space.

___✓___ 3. When an asteroid crashed to earth in 1908, it caused great damage.

Specific Sentences 9. a. In sign language, we use hands and other body parts to make gestures that stand for letters, words, and concepts.

b. Morse code requires a wire telegraph machine to produce sounds—dots and dashes—that are translated into letters, numbers, and punctuation.

c. Often seen at airports, the semaphore, or flag signaling system, works this way: A person stands holding a flag in each hand, then moves his or her arms to positions that indicate letters and numbers.

General Sentences _____ 1. Mass communication means that messages are sent to large audiences.

___✓___ 2. Some communication methods do not rely on written language.

_____ 3. Simple writing systems date back to the Sumerians of 3000 BC.

Specific Sentences 10. a. Using the milk from 6,000 cows, a 13,440-pound cheese was produced for an exhibit at the 1937 New York State Fair.

b. In 1801, a Massachusetts preacher, John Leland, presented President Andrew Jackson with a 1,200-pound Cheshire cheese made in Leland's hometown.

c. The Wisconsin Cheese Foundation collected 183 tons of milk for its display in the 1964 World's Fair: a cheese wedge that weighed more than 34,500 pounds and stood six feet high.

General Sentences _____ 1. Ancient Romans who created huge cheeses were considered quite eccentric.

_____ 2. Canadians proudly show their skill at cheese making during the annual Toronto Fair.

___✓___ 3. Over the years, cheese-loving Americans have produced some pretty big cheeses.

EXERCISE 9   Clarifying General Sentences

DIRECTIONS Read each general sentence. Then circle the letters of the specific sentences that help explain the general one.

EXAMPLE

General Sentence   After interviewing eighty-five couples who had been married at least fifteen years, author Francine Klagsbrun identified several characteristics that make a happy marriage.

Specific Sentences

(a.) The ability to change and to tolerate change was high on the list of characteristics that make a happy marriage.

b. Married men tend to live longer than single ones do.

c. Women usually marry men who are a few years older than themselves.

(d.) According to Klagsbrun, a belief that marriage is a long-term commitment* appears to be essential to a happy marriage.

(e.) Many married couples insisted that "trust" is a key characteristic of a happy marriage.

f. Compared with Europeans, Americans are more likely to get married.

EXPLANATION The general sentence leaves readers wondering what characteristics make a happy marriage. Specific sentences *a*, *d*, and *e* answer that question, whereas sentences *b*, *c*, and *f* do not.

General Sentence   1. The German psychologist Hermann Ebbinghaus was the first person to systematically study the process of forgetting.

Specific Sentences

a. One theory of forgetting suggests that we forget when new information interferes with old.

b. Ebbinghaus spent thousands of hours memorizing nonsense syllables.

c. After learning the nonsense syllables, Ebbinghaus measured the time it took to forget them.

d. Another theory of forgetting stresses that we forget whenever we don't intend to remember.

*commitment: the state of being bound emotionally or intellectually to another person.

e. As a result of his research, Ebbinghaus discovered that the greatest memory loss occurs right after learning.

f. Another memory researcher, A. P. Bumstead, discovered that several learning sessions stretched out over time actually decreased forgetting.

General Sentence

Specific Sentences

2. It's easy to understand why the threat of rabies inspires great fear.

a. In its final stages, rabies produces hallucinations.

b. Few people recover from rabies once symptoms appear.

c. Rabies has been around a long time; there are references to it as early as 700 BC.

d. Once the disease takes hold, the victim can neither stand nor lie down comfortably.

e. Recently, scientists have improved the treatment for rabies; the new treatment is much less painful than the old.

f. In the early stages of rabies, a dog is likely to appear tired and nervous; it will try to hide, even from its master.

General Sentence

Specific Sentences

3. Many people believe that mystery stories are a product of modern times, but the mystery story actually has a long history.

a. Historians of the detective story claim to have found elements of the mystery story in the pages of the Bible.

b. Dorothy Sayers was for some years an enormously popular mystery writer.

c. Poe's "The Murders in the Rue Morgue," published in 1841, presented the classic mystery problem of a dead body found in a sealed room.

d. Mystery historians are continually arguing about which books may or may not be classified as true mystery stories.

e. In the nineteenth century, Charles Dickens created a highly amusing character, Inspector Bucket, who in many ways resembles modern-day detectives.

f. Some mystery writers do not use their real names.

General Sentence

Specific Sentences

4. Muhammad, the spiritual leader of the Muslims,* had an enormous influence on world history.

a. Muhammad was born somewhere around the year AD 570.

---

*Muslims: believers in Islam, a religion based on the teachings of Muhammad. Muslims believe in one God (Allah). They also believe in paradise and hell.

b. Muhammad founded a religion, Islam, which was to become a major world religion.

c. Until his fortieth year, Muhammad lived the ordinary life of a well-to-do merchant.

d. Muhammad's teachings were the source of the Koran, the sacred text of the Muslims, which is still accepted by Muslims as the final authority on all spiritual matters.

e. Muhammad founded an empire that included lands in Syria, northern Africa, and Spain.

f. Muhammad was born in Mecca.

 ## Connecting General and Specific Sentences in Paragraphs

The exercises you have completed so far were to prepare you for what we'll be doing in this section of the chapter as well as in the chapters that follow—understanding how general and specific sentences connect to create meaning.

General Sentences in First Position

Writers always have to make choices about how to approach their readers. Scholarly writers, for instance, often begin by reviewing what other authors have said about the topic or subject. Reviewing past research is the writer's way of giving readers a context so that they can better judge his or her contribution to the discussion. Writers of newspaper editorials, in contrast, might well open with a colorful anecdote to attract readers and make them keep reading until they get to the point of the article. Textbook writers, however, know they have to pass on many new ideas to their readers. Thus they are inclined to open paragraphs with the general thought they want to communicate. Here's an example:

General Sentence

[1]Anthropologists who study line-forming behavior have concluded that the way people wait in line reveals a good deal about cultural

Specific Sentences

values. [2]In some Arab countries, where women do not have equal rights, men routinely cut in front of women waiting in line. [3]They see no reason why a man should wait in back of a woman. [4]In Britain and the U.S., where men and women are at least officially considered equal, few men would dare cut ahead of a woman who was standing ahead of them in line. [5]In countries like Italy and

Spain, where individuality is highly prized above social conformity,* lines are little more than an annoyance to be ignored at will. [6]Men and women routinely jostle for the best position in line, and the poor soul who stands and waits his or her turn is considered to be lacking in spirit.

In this example, the first sentence is a general sentence that announces the paragraph's **main idea** or central point. The remaining more specific sentences then define phrases like "line-forming behavior" and "cultural values." The writer uses the general opening sentence to announce the point of the paragraph and the remaining more specific sentences for clarification and support.

General Sentences in Last Position

Writers of essays sometimes reverse the previous approach. They open with a series of specific sentences leading up to a general one. It's the writer's way of stimulating audience interest. Here's an illustration:

Specific Sentences

[1]Speed dating is currently popular among single men and women in pursuit of a mate. [2]On a "speed date," the women sit at tables while the men circulate, spending anywhere from two to five minutes with any number of females. [3]When the prescribed time is up, the men move on with the temporary couple having decided either to meet again or forget the brief encounter. [4]In another widely reported-on trend, high school students don't talk about "dating," "going steady," or "courting," all of which are considered old-fashioned and uncool. [5]Instead, more and more teenagers agree to be "friends with benefits." [6]This means there will be a certain amount of physical contact, maybe even intercourse, but the two friends are not, or claim not to be, emotionally involved. [7]The physical part of the relationship is the "benefit," and that benefit can end as soon as one friend or the other decides they are no longer interested. [8]There are also anecdotal* reports among women that men no longer bring flowers on a first date while the men complain that young women are more interested in a male's financial success than they are in romantic behavior or courting techniques.

General Sentence

[9]To those of us who remember an earlier time, it's sad but seemingly true that romance is disappearing from the lives of the young and single.

*conformity: obedience, willingness to follow rules.
*anecdotal: not scientific, based on personal stories.

Here the sentences start out specific and build to a general statement of what those specific details mean.

Reading Tip

If the second sentence in a paragraph explains the first, the chances are good that the opening general sentence expresses the main idea.

EXERCISE 10 Locating General Sentences

DIRECTIONS Read each paragraph. Then underline the general sentence, deciding if it's the first sentence in the paragraph or the last.

EXAMPLE [1]<u>Senator Joseph McCarthy, the man who did untold harm to the country in the 1950s, pretended to be a dedicated patriot, but all he truly cared about was his own personal ambition.</u> [2]In the early 1940s and 1950s, Americans were anxious about the spread of Communism within their country. [3]At the same time, McCarthy was looking for an attention-getting campaign platform. [4]Taking advantage of the country's fearful mood, the senator decided to launch a modern-day witch-hunt. [5]Claiming to possess a list of Communists who were secretly working inside the U.S. government, McCarthy falsely accused not only civil servants* but people in the military, academia, and even Hollywood's film industry. [6]Ultimately, the senator's relentless investigation failed to produce even one Communist. [7]But McCarthy had gotten the publicity he so desperately wanted and, more importantly for his ambitious ego, he had become a powerful man in Washington. (Sources of information: Norton et al., *A People and a Nation*, 5th ed., pp. 821–822; "Echoes of a Shameful Era," *USA Today*, May 6, 2003, p. 14A.)

EXPLANATION In this passage, the first sentence is general enough to sum up and include all the others. The more specific supporting sentences explain how McCarthy "pretended to be a dedicated patriot" when he was really dedicated to "his own personal ambition."

1. [1]<u>Several types of pollutants are turning the earth's oceans into a toxic dumpsite.</u> [2]Rain that washes over the world's cities and farmland carries contaminants such as grease, pesticides, fertilizers,

---

*civil servants: people working for state and local government.

and many other kinds of toxic chemicals into storm drains and then out to sea. [3]Spills from oil tankers also pollute the ocean as does sewage from cities and boats. [4]Although most developed countries treat sewage at waste-water facilities, many cities in the world's poorer areas have little or no sewage treatment, so human waste goes directly into the ocean. [5]Even in countries that treat sewage, flooded pipes often back up into storm drains allowing untreated waste to flow directly out to sea. [6]Solid garbage also fouls our oceans. [7]People all over the world dump their household, boating, or commercial trash directly into the sea itself or into streams and rivers that carry the garbage to the ocean. [8]As a result, plastic bags and bottles routinely float in mid-ocean. [9]On one day in 2000, more than 800,000 people took part in an ocean cleanup and removed some 13.5 million pounds of trash from coastal waters. (Sources of information: "Oceanic Pollution," www.learning-network.org/global/issues/o/oceans/; "Ocean Pollution," www.ocean .com/Conservation/OceanPollution.asp.)

2. [1]Many of the world's most famous artists were either undervalued or ignored during their lifetime. [2]Nineteenth-century impressionist* painter Vincent van Gogh, whose paintings now sell for millions of dollars, sold only one painting in his lifetime and died penniless. [3]One of van Gogh's contemporaries, the now-famous painter Paul Gauguin, also died in poverty. [4]The seventeenth-century Dutch painter Rembrandt van Rijn had to file for bankruptcy at age fifty because the art critics of his time dismissed his work as unfashionable. [5]While he was alive, another celebrated Dutch painter, Jan Vermeer, found few buyers for his paintings. [6]Vermeer fell into complete obscurity* after his death in 1675. His work was not rediscovered until the nineteenth century. [7]Of the more than 1,000 works of musical genius Johann Sebastian Bach (1685–1750), only eight were published during his lifetime. [8]Considered a good organ player, Bach was viewed as a mediocre composer. [9]The nineteenth-century poet Emily Dickinson wrote 1,775 poems, but only ten of these were published during her lifetime. [10]Dickinson's slightly older contemporary, *Moby-Dick* author Herman Melville was forced to abandon the idea of earning a living from writing when the public showed little enthusiasm for his writing. [11]The sage* of Concord, Henry David Thoreau, sold only 1,700 copies of *Walden* in 1855,

---

*Impressionist: an artist who creates a personal impression or sense of the world rather than a realistic picture.
*obscurity: the state of being unknown.
*sage: wise person; also, wise.

the year after it was published. [12]Fewer than 300 copies sold over the next five years, so the publisher did not reprint it. (Source of information: Lucius Furius, "Genius Ignored," www.serve.com/Lucius/GI.index.html.)

3. [1]In addition to the $1, $2, $5, $10, $20, $50, and $100 bills that circulate today, the U.S. Federal Reserve Board once issued and circulated bills in the amount of $500, $1,000, $5,000, and $10,000. [2]On July 14, 1969, however, the Treasury Department announced that these four bills would no longer be printed because they were rarely used. [3]As a result, the $100 bill is the highest denomination* in circulation today. [4]Over the years, the Federal Reserve Board has also stopped producing several coin denominations. [5]The denominations include the half-cent, two-cent, three-cent, and twenty-cent copper coins, as well as a small silver coin that was called a half-dime (replaced by the nickel). [6]Although half-dollar and dollar coins are still in circulation, they are no longer either gold or silver as they were in the past. [7]As these examples illustrate, the Federal Reserve Board can and does discontinue or alter both coin and paper currency.

4. [1]In 1968, Billie Jean King joined with several other female tennis players to negotiate professional contracts that would increase their income. [2]Angered that male players received more prize money than females, King was the guiding force in making the women's Virginia Slims Tour a reality in 1970. [3]The next year, she became the first female athlete to win more than $100,000. [4]And no one will forget her 1973 victory over Bobby Riggs in the match that came to be known as the "Battle of the Sexes." [5]King beat Riggs in three sets and forever laid to rest the notion that women choked under pressure. [6]Not surprisingly, Billie Jean King is considered one of the most influential women in the history of tennis.

5. [1]In Poland, soup lovers can now choose from eight different varieties of Campbell's *zupa*, including *flaki*—tripe soup spiced with lots of pepper. [2]In Australia, Campbell's best seller is pumpkin. [3]To please Mexican palates, Campbell came up with hot and spicy *crema de chile poblano* and *flor de calabaza* (squash soup). [4]Working in its Hong Kong test kitchen, Campbell concocted some recipes it hoped would appeal to the more than two billion consumers in

---

*denomination: a group of units having specific values.

Malaysia, Indonesia, Thailand, the Philippines, Vietnam, and Japan. [5]What did Campbell chefs come up with? [6]Successes include watercress and duck gizzard soup, radish-carrot soup, fig soup, and date soup. [7]The soup maker also developed several flavors of corn soup specifically for markets in Taiwan, Hong Kong, and Singapore. [8]What Campbell discovered is that Asian consumers are willing to buy lots of canned soup if the right soup is in the can. [9]Encouraged by the successful efforts of its chefs in Hong Kong, Campbell decided to launch seventeen varieties of soup in the Chinese province of Guangdong. [10]Clearly, the Campbell Soup Company is trying hard to please an international market. (Adapted from Pride, Hughes, and Kapoor, *Business*, p. 319.)

■ **DIGGING DEEPER**

GOING GLOBAL

LOOKING AHEAD Here's another selection describing how American businesses are wooing an international market. As you read it, look carefully at the sentences to see which ones are more general and which ones are more specific.

1 Ken Krusensterna, owner of a Dallas trucking company, had driven across the border into Mexico for business reasons every week for five years without mishap. The trip was simply part of his routine—until the day he was kidnapped, beaten, and held for ransom. Although he was rescued after two weeks, Krusensterna sold his company rather than return to Mexico on business again.

2   Kidnapping and robbery are relatively remote but real dangers for multinational firms' employees and managers who work in or travel to other countries. Kidnappers in parts of Mexico, Brazil, Argentina, Colombia, and other developing nations sometimes target foreign business people whose employers seem able to pay ransoms totaling thousands or millions of dollars. Thieves also may assault and rob foreign business people. Now companies doing business in other countries are taking a number of precautions to keep their personnel safe.

3   Many firms educate their employees about the risks of working and traveling abroad through seminars and frequent updates. Nova Chemicals, based in Canada, sends out regular e-mail warnings about problem areas so that employees know what to expect when they travel. Employees of Nortel Networks know to check the company's intranet for comprehensive safety information before and during an international business trip. Nortel also gives its employees a toll-free phone number to call from any country, at any hour, if they run into trouble and need emergency assistance.

4   Other multinationals go even further. For example, Japanese companies with operations near Tijuana often require transferred executives to live in southern California and travel to their factories on buses protected by armed guards. Some companies hire security specialists to teach their business travelers how to survive if they are attacked or kidnapped, even conducting mock kidnappings to reinforce the skills. At a minimum, experts say that employees who work or travel in other nations should not call attention to themselves. They also should avoid flashing cash in public and keep corporate symbols hidden. Finally, varying the daily routine will make it more difficult for criminals to plan a

kidnapping or robbery. (Adapted from Pride, Hughes, and Kapoor, *Business*, p. 317.)

Sharpening Your Skills

DIRECTIONS Answer the questions by circling the letters of the correct response.

1. In paragraph 1, would you say that
   a. the first sentence is the most general?
   b. the last sentence is the most general?
   c. the first and last sentences are equally specific?

2. Which description fits paragraph 2?
   a. The first sentence is the most general sentence in the paragraph; it sums up the more specific details that follow.
   b. The last sentence is the most general sentence with the more specific sentences illustrating it.

3. In paragraph 3, the more specific sentences answer which question?
   a. What are the risks of traveling abroad?
   b. How often do companies provide frequent updates?
   c. How do firms educate employees about risks?

4. Which of the following is the general statement that sums up the entire reading?
   a. Although he was rescued after two weeks, Krusensterna sold his company rather than return to Mexico on business again.
   b. Thieves may assault and rob foreign businesspeople.
   c. Companies doing business in other countries are now taking a number of precautions to keep their personnel safe.
   d. Many firms educate their employees about the risks of working and traveling abroad through seminars and frequent updates.

INTERNET RESOURCE

For more practice with general and specific sentences, go to **college.hmco.com/pic/flemmingRFR10e**, where you will find three levels of interactive quizzes: *Getting Down the Basics*, *Checking Your Progress*, and *Taking the Challenge*. You can also find additional interactive practice at **laflemm.com**, *Reading for Results*: Online Practice for Chapter 3.

Test 1: Distinguishing Between General and Specific Sentences

DIRECTIONS Read each pair of sentences. Then mark the general sentence with a *G* and the more specific one with an *S*.

1. a. In wintertime, the body temperature of a woodchuck undergoes a steep drop of many degrees. _G_

   b. In wintertime, the body temperature of a woodchuck drops from 90°F to around 40°F. _S_

2. a. The fats found in fish, nuts, and vegetables may actually help protect you from heart disease. _S_

   b. Not all fats are bad; in fact, some may be good for you. _G_

3. a. The temperature of Antarctica is changing; it is not as cold as it used to be. _G_

   b. Current Antarctic temperatures are nine degrees higher than they were fifty years ago. _S_

4. a. Heart disease is the leading cause of death in the United States. _S_

   b. Heart disease is a killer. _G_

5. a. Many records claim that baseball was first played in 1846, but there is evidence suggesting that the game is older than that. _G_

   b. In her 1818 novel *Northanger Abbey*, author Jane Austen refers to a game called baseball, suggesting that the game was played before 1846. _S_

 **Test 2: Distinguishing Between General and Specific Sentences**

DIRECTIONS Read each pair of sentences. Then mark the general sentence with a *G* and the more specific one with an *S*.

1. a. We tend to take birds for granted, but birds, like most living creatures, can surprise us with their unusual abilities. ___ *G*

   b. The ruby-throated hummingbird has the rare ability to fly back-ward and upside-down. ___ *S*

2. a. The California sculptor Ned Kahn specializes in large artworks that imitate violent happenings in nature so realistically they can be terrifying. ___ *G*

   b. Ned Kahn, a San Francisco sculptor, uses swirling water, fog, and sand to create room size tornadoes and earthquakes that leave visitors shaking in their shoes. ___ *S*

3. a. Around the Caribbean island of Bequia, ten-man teams hunt forty-ton humpback whales in wooden sailboats, armed only with harpoons the fishermen throw by hand. ___ *S*

   b. In the Caribbean, a small group of fishermen pursue their prey much like their ancestors once did, using old-fashioned methods and tools. ___ *G*

4. a. In the 1970s, the first U.S. space shuttle got its name from a popular science fiction television series. ___ *G*

   b. In 1977, urged by fans of the TV series *Star Trek*, President Gerald Ford asked NASA to name the first U.S. space shuttle *Enterprise*. ___ *S*

 ## Test 3: Recognizing the Most General Sentence

DIRECTIONS In each group of sentences, one is more general than the others. Circle the letter of the most general statement.

1. a. When a Hmong* person dies, a string must be knotted around his or her finger and tied to a slaughtered cow or pig.

b. Hmong mourners burn small boats folded from gold or silver paper, and do so very close to the dead person's body.

c. One Hmong death ritual is to play a mouth organ with long reed pipes, pound on a drum, and strike a metal gong.

d. When the Hmong, a mountain people from Southeast Asia, settled in the United States, they brought with them their funeral customs.

e. At a Hmong funeral two relatives dress in the dead person's clothes and pretend to be him or her, greeting guests who come to view the body.

f. Hmong mourning starts with a twenty-four-hour vigil attended by hundreds of people who chant, wail, and cry as loudly as possible.

2. a. In ancient Britain, gathering and hanging mistletoe were winter traditions.

b. During feasts, the ancient Romans draped their homes with mistletoe.

c. The custom of kissing or embracing under a branch of mistletoe has been around for centuries and is part of many cultures.

d. The early Scandinavians considered mistletoe a symbol of love.

e. In ancient Britain, if enemies met under the mistletoe, they would have to lay down their weapons and embrace.

f. In the fourth century, the Christian Church outlawed the hanging of mistletoe because it was associated with pagan traditions, but many people ignored the church's law.

3. a. In Mexican-American families, young children are rarely separated from their mothers.

b. Unless forced to by financial need, Mexican-American mothers generally stay home with their children.

---

*Hmong: a group of people who made their home in Laos and who supported the United States during the Vietnam war (1954–1975).

c. In Mexican-American families, the children usually come first.

d. Although the children are mainly the mother's responsibility, fathers are deeply involved in decisions about the children's upbringing and future.

e. Fathers often work two or more jobs so that mothers can stay home with the children.

f. When a baby is born to a Mexican-American couple, both parents frequently rearrange their lives to care for the child.

4. a. In AD 1466, Pope Gelasius ordered a celebration in honor of the martyred Saint Valentine.

b. The earliest known valentine was written in 1415.

c. Saint Valentine's Day has been celebrated for centuries.

d. By the sixteenth century, it had become a tradition for lovers to exchange gifts on Saint Valentine's Day.

e. It was in the sixteenth century that the image of Cupid became associated with Saint Valentine's Day.

f. In 1797, a British publisher put together *The Young Man's Valentine Writer*, a collection of verses for young men who needed help writing their own valentines.

5. a. People who use amphetamines tend to perceive situations unrealistically and as a result don't handle them well.

b. People who use large doses of amphetamines have trouble sleeping.

c. People who use amphetamines often find that they are unable to stop talking.

d. Under the influence of amphetamines, people usually feel they are working more efficiently; unfortunately, this impression is seldom accurate.

e. Amphetamines, also known as *speed*, are dangerous drugs with serious side effects.

f. Loss of appetite is a common side effect of amphetamines.

Test 4: Recognizing the Most General Sentence

DIRECTIONS In each group of sentences, one is more general than the others. Circle the letter of the most general statement.

1. a. In the African country of Dahomey, music historians were carefully trained to preserve important records.

    b. There was a time when the music of Africa was also the history of the African people.

    c. In the African country of Burundi, singers followed soldiers to war and recorded great actions in song.

    d. Many African countries trained men and women to be living books who could record important events in song.

    e. If the songs contained important information, some African musicians had to learn them in secret.

    f. In the Sudan, singers recited the history of the nation at public gatherings and sang the deeds of great heroes.

2. a. Tornadoes are clouds shaped like funnels: they reach all the way to the ground, doing enormous damage.

    b. Although all storms have fearful aspects, tornadoes are the most frightening.

    c. Winds within the funnel of the tornado can reach speeds of more than several hundred miles per hour.

    d. Tornadoes strike without warning: they seem to come out of nowhere.

    e. Sometimes buildings actually blow up as the tornado passes over them.

    f. The heavy rain and hail that accompany a tornado also do much damage.

3. a. Because of the way he looked, John Merrick could not go into the street without being mobbed by curious strangers who stared at and ridiculed him.

    b. Before he came under a doctor's care, John Merrick was exhibited in the circus, like an animal.

c. The victim of a terrible and disfiguring* disease, John Merrick could not sleep like other people; he had to sit up with his heavy head resting on his knees.

d. The head of the Elephant Man was enormous and misshapen.

e. John Merrick, also known as the Elephant Man, had a brief and all too painful life.

f. John Merrick never forgot the brutal beatings and terrible humiliation of his life in the circus.

4. a. It took a while for L. Frank Baum, author of *The Wonderful Wizard of Oz*, to find just the right title for his masterpiece.

b. While the book was in production, Baum changed the title to *From Kansas to Fairyland*.

c. An author sometimes has great difficulty choosing the title of a book.

d. When Baum first submitted his manuscript in 1899, it was called *The Emerald City*.

e. Just before the book appeared in print, Baum changed the title again, this time to *The City of the Great Oz*.

f. In the end, the book was published in 1900 as *The Wonderful Wizard of Oz*.

5. a. Supervisors at the Levi Strauss company patrol hallways, making sure no one wears tank tops or flip-flops.

b. When major corporations relax their dress codes, they still use a variety of methods to let employees know what's acceptable.

c. The S. C. Johnson Wax firm prints a pamphlet with "What's Hot and What's Not" clothes guidelines, then distributes it with paychecks.

d. Two Sears mannequins are dressed in casual clothing, then placed in the cafeteria of the company's headquarters.

e. Salomon Smith Barney, an investment firm, issues formal memos that outline changes in policy—for example, allowing women executives to shed their pantyhose in warm weather.

f. The Society of Human Resources Management holds an "outfits" fair for employees, offering information booths, trivia games, and prizes.

---

*disfiguring: ruining, spoiling, or deforming.

Test 5: Identifying General Sentences in Paragraphs

DIRECTIONS Read each paragraph and underline the general sentence that opens or closes the paragraph.

1. [1]One of the ancient world's seven wonders, the Great Pyramid of Giza, was the tallest structure in the world for forty-three centuries. [2]Consisting of about two million blocks of stone, each weighing two tons, the Great Pyramid was pushed or pulled into place with human muscle alone. [3]The other tomb on the list of seven wonders, the 140-foot-tall Mausoleum at Halicarnassus, was not only gigantic but also adorned with beautiful statues and carvings. [4]Another wonder, the Hanging Gardens of Babylon, consisted of tiers of terraces that were supported with stone columns. [5]Each terrace was watered with a complex irrigation system so that lush plant life would thrive above ground level and over visitors' heads. [6]The Lighthouse at Alexandria, which was as tall as a 40-story building, was covered with white marble and contained a mirror that could reflect light for miles. [7]Among the seven wonders were two statues considered wondrous for both size and artistry. [8]Made of ivory and gold, the statue of Zeus stood as tall as a 4-story building. [9]The statue of the sun god Apollo, called the Colossus of Rhodes, was a 110-foot-high bronze structure that took twelve years to build. [10]The seventh wonder, the Temple of Artemis at Ephesus, was widely considered to be the most beautiful structure in the world. [11]Built to honor the Greek goddess of hunting, nature, and fertility,* this marble building included 127 columns, each 60 feet high, and housed paintings and statues created by the greatest artists of the time. [12]The Seven Wonders of the Ancient World were all massive marvels of engineering genius. (Source of information: Alaa Ashmawy, "The Seven Wonders of the Ancient World," http://ce.eng.usf.edu/pharos/wonders/.)

2. [1]Federalist* architecture was designed to reflect democratic ideals. [2]The government buildings erected in the Federalist style from 1790 to 1820 were inspired by the temples of Greece and Rome because America's founders admired these two ancient civilizations. [3]Like the structures they were modeled after, Federalist

---

*fertility: the ability to reproduce or grow.
*Federalist: related to the belief that individual states should recognize the authority of a central government.

buildings were constructed of materials such as stone, brick, and marble to symbolize the enduring nature of democracy. [4]The huge buildings' columns and domes suggested the grand and dignified proceedings that were to take place within them. [5]Their Roman porticos, or porches, were designed to draw citizens to the great meeting places where they could participate in government. [6]And the buildings' shapes and symmetry reflected the equality, order, and stability of republican values. [7]The rectangular floor plans and the balanced, parallel features of the structures' exteriors signified the democratic nature of the government functions they housed. [8]The round shapes of the rotundas and circular windows stood for the eternal nature of democratic principles.

3. [1]Odd as it may seem, in the past decade, several journalists who plagiarized* or in some cases simply invented their stories ultimately profited from their wrongdoing. [2]In 2003, reporter Jayson Blair was fired by the *New York Times* when it was found that he had plagiarized news stories and made up dozens of others. [3]Just months after the scandal broke, however, Blair was in discussion with television producers about selling his story. [4]He had also begun writing a book expected to bring him handsome profits. [5]Another fraud, writer-editor Stephen Glass, made up stories and printed them as fact. As a result, he was fired in 1998 by his employer, *New Republic* magazine. [6]Five years later Glass had six-figure movie and book deals based on his life story. [7]Then there was *Boston Globe* columnist Mike Barnicle, who was forced to resign in 1998 when his plagiarism became public knowledge. [8]Today, Barnicle is a columnist for the *Boston Herald* and he regularly appears on television as a critic and commentator. [9]Barnicle's fellow *Boston Globe* columnist Patricia Smith was fired for inventing quotes in her stories, yet she now writes for various publications. [10]Elizabeth Wurtzel was fired by the *Dallas Morning News* for plagiarism, too, but she went on to write for *New York* magazine as well as *The New Yorker*, and she has authored a number of best-selling books. (Source of information: Maria Puente, "Disgrace, Dishonor, Infamy: They're Not So Bad Anymore," *USA Today*, May 22, 2003, p. 1D, www.usatoday.com/usatonline/20030522/5180112x.htm.)

4. [1]Textbooks have long taught that the seventeenth-century English settlement at Jamestown, Virginia, struggled and almost perished because the colonists didn't like hard work. [2]Historians believed

---

*plagiarized: took the ideas of others and presented them as if they were the writer's.

that the colonists were more interested in finding gold than getting their hands dirty. [3]However, when scientists analyzed the rings of Jamestown cypress trees during a 1998 climate study, they found that the trees' growth was significantly stunted between 1606 and 1612. [4]Based on this information, the study's authors argued that when Jamestown was founded in 1607, a lack of rain caused fresh water supplies to dry up and parched corn to turn brown on the stalk. [5]The subsequent food shortage would have aggravated relations between the colonists and the Powhatan Indians, who were also forced to compete for scarce resources. [6]In 1608, Captain John Smith noted in his journal that the Indians would not trade corn for colonists' goods because that year's crop had been poor, and the Indians did not have enough for themselves. [7]Based on current research, it now seems very possible that a drought, rather than laziness or greed, was to blame for Jamestown's troubles. (Source of information: Jeffery L. Sheler, "Rethinking Jamestown," *Smithsonian*, January 2005, pp. 48–56.)

Test 6: Vocabulary Review

DIRECTIONS Here are ten of the words introduced in Chapter 3. Use them to fill in the blanks. Words introduced in previous chapters are marked with an asterisk. *Note*: The form of the word used here may differ from the form used in the chapter.

anecdotal   discrimination
conformity   fertility
sage wisdom   creed
commitment   obscurity
temperamental   prima donna

1. Based on _anecdotal_ evidence, Mariah Carey, the pop singer who rose from _obscority_ to fame and fortune in the 1990s, is said to be extremely _temperamental_ and has a tendency toward being a _prima donna_. In fact, stories of her tantrums, breakdowns, and demands abound. However, even her critics admit that her _commitment_ to music is central to her personal _creed_, and Carey is known for giving her all at every single performance. Because of her talent, determination, and hard work, she now has one of the most successful and most lucrative careers in show business. Carey currently holds the record as the female artist with the highest number of number one hits.

2. Rural African culture is dependent on manual labor. Therefore, it emphasizes the importance of female _fertility_. Failing to become a mother, particularly the mother of a boy, is a source of _discrimination_. In fact, any woman who cannot conceive a child or does not consent* to become a wife and mother is systematically* shunned by the men of the community. While African cities share the values of the other urban areas around the

world and permit women more freedom of choice, in rural areas, _conformity_ is the rule. Any woman, regardless of how lovely or _Sage_ she might be, is considered inherently* flawed if she has no interest in motherhood. In fact, few women would run the risk of voicing such an opinion, for fear of the punitive* measures that might be taken against her.

BONUS QUESTION

McCarthyism became a word following the brief and ugly career of Senator Joseph McCarthy (described on page 120). Given what you know about the senator, what do you think McCarthyism is?

_____

_____

Which of the following sentences do you think uses the word correctly?

a. Although everyone believes that the battle against terrorists has to be waged, few want to see a new wave of McCarthyism wash over the country.

b. Thanks to an enthusiastic rise in McCarthyism among students, almost everyone now believes that schools are safer places for children.

Discovering Topics, Main Ideas, and Topic Sentences

In this chapter, you'll learn

- how to identify the *topic* of a paragraph.

- how to ask questions that lead you to the *main idea.*

- how to recognize *topic sentences.*

- how *transitions* can signal a topic sentence.

- how to *paraphrase* an author's language by changing the words without altering the meaning.

Chapter 4 offers you a step-by-step strategy for understanding paragraphs. It also gives you a chance to apply everything you have learned about general and specific sentences.

 ## Identify the Topic

Somewhere along the way, I began to realize that reading skills are simply thinking skills applied to a reading situation.
—Dr. Kylene Beers, Reading Researcher, Yale University

Identifying the **topic** is the first step you need to take toward understanding a paragraph. The topic is the subject under discussion. It's the person, place, event, or experience most frequently mentioned or referred to by the author. Usually you can discover the topic by asking a simple question: "Who or what is most frequently mentioned or referred to in this paragraph?" The following paragraph illustrates how that one question can lead you to the topic:

> The doctrine of the Jehovah's Witnesses, a religious group founded by Charles Taze Russell, is based on the belief that there will be a second coming of Christ. According to this doctrine, the coming of Christ is not far off, and his arrival is eagerly awaited because only he can conquer the devil. Once the devil is conquered, peace and harmony will come to the world. Anxious to explain their doctrine to the public, Jehovah's Witnesses publish and sell two magazines, *Watchtower* and *Awake.*

Every sentence in this paragraph mentions or refers to the doctrine of the Jehovah's Witnesses. This is the topic of the paragraph. The topic is not "Charles Taze Russell" or "*Watchtower.*" The man and the magazine are each mentioned only once. They are not repeated or constantly referred to and don't dominate the paragraph.

Notice, too, that we needed five words—"doctrine of the Jehovah's Witnesses"—to express the topic. Occasionally, the topic of a paragraph can be expressed in a single word. Most of the time, however, you will need two or more words to fully express the topic, as in the following paragraph:

> Charles Lindbergh's strong and independent character shaped every event in his altogether spectacular life. In 1927, when he decided to fly nonstop over the Atlantic, everyone said it was

impossible. But Lindbergh would not listen and flew anyway, becoming an international hero. In 1933, when the public demanded that he return a medal given to him by the Nazis, Lindbergh refused. No matter how unpopular his decision, he would not bend to the opinion of others. True to character, Lindbergh also planned his own funeral. Typically, he was not about to leave such an important event in anyone else's hands. Charles Lindbergh wanted to die just as he had lived—on his own terms.

At first glance, you might say that the topic of this paragraph is "Lindbergh." Yet actually, that topic is too general. The paragraph does not mention the many different subjects that might fall under such a broad heading—subjects like Lindbergh's family, hobbies, or illnesses. The focus of the paragraph is more specific than "Lindbergh." The paragraph concentrates on Lindbergh's independent character, making "Lindbergh's independent character" the precise topic. That phrase is general enough to include everything discussed at length in the paragraph. It is also specific enough to exclude anything not discussed in detail.

---

1. The **topic** is the subject under discussion in the paragraph. It's the person, place, event, or experience most frequently mentioned or referred to in the paragraph.
2. You can usually discover the topic by asking yourself "Who or what is most frequently mentioned or referred to throughout the paragraph?"
3. The topic you decide on should be general enough to include everything discussed in the paragraph. It should also be specific enough to exclude anything not discussed in detail.

EXERCISE 1   Choosing the Best Topic

DIRECTIONS Read each paragraph. Put a *T* next to the word or phrase that best expresses the topic. Then label the other topics either *G* for too general or *S* for too specific.

EXAMPLE In the nineteenth century, American and British fishermen nearly wiped out the Antarctic seal. However, the seals have made an astonishing comeback, and the current seal population is rapidly increasing. Although scientists admit there may be other factors responsible for the return of the Antarctic seal, they are convinced that the severe decrease in the baleen whale population is a major cause. The baleen whale and the Antarctic seal once competed for the same food source—a tiny shellfish called krill. With the baleen whale practically extinct, the seals now have an almost unlimited food supply. That increase in the food supply is clearly one reason for the seals' comeback.

a. seals around the world   _G_

b. the disappearance of the baleen whale   _S_

c. the comeback of the Antarctic seal   _T_

EXPLANATION The phrase mentioned or referred to most often in this paragraph is "the comeback of the Antarctic seal." Just about every sentence in the paragraph describes the seals' return. Answer *a* is too general because the author clearly focuses on one type of seal rather than seals all over the world. Answer *b* is too specific. The paragraph deals with more than the disappearance of the baleen whale.

1. Socrates was a philosopher, a person who searches for the truth and the meaning of life. A well-known teacher in ancient Athens,* his method of teaching was to pose questions that made his students examine and question their beliefs. Socrates' method, however, upset many Athenian leaders. They thought that by teaching the young to question, Socrates was challenging the authority of the government. Consequently, Socrates was sentenced to death.

a. philosophy   _G_

b. the Athenian leaders   _S_

c. Socrates' method of teaching   _T_

2. Gender roles are taught throughout the life cycle, but parents probably have the greatest influence, especially when children are very young. Early on, parents reinforce the roles considered appropriate to their child's gender with such remarks as "What a good, sweet girl!" or "What a big, strong boy!" Such statements are usually accompanied by smiles and nods of approval or pleasure. Actually, most, if not all, of the forces of socialization* in our culture—parents, teachers, peers, movies, television, and books for children and adults—reinforce the notion that boys and girls play different roles

_____
*Athens: a city in Greece.
*socialization: teaching behavior appropriate to a particular society.

based on their gender. The resulting set of traits is what we call masculinity and femininity. (Adapted from Greenberg et al., *Sexuality,* p. 375.)

a. masculinity   _____

b. gender roles   _____

c. social roles   _____

3. Some societies have a custom called the *couvade.* The couvade is a ceremony in which the husband acts as if he is suffering from labor pains at the same time that his wife actually gives birth. Although no one seems able to explain fully the meaning of the couvade, there are several theories. According to one, the couvade is a way of warding off evil spirits. In effect, the husband directs attention away from his wife and toward himself. Another theory speculates that the couvade is a way of publicly identifying the father so that his paternity will not be in doubt.

a. ceremony and ritual   _____

b. theories about the couvade   _____

c. the belief in evil spirits   _____

4. In sudden infant death syndrome (SIDS), a sleeping baby stops breathing and dies. In the United States, SIDS strikes about two of every thousand infants, usually when they are two to four months old. SIDS is less common in cultures where infants and parents sleep in the same bed, suggesting that sleeping position may be important. Indeed, about half of apparent SIDS cases may be accidental suffocations caused when infants lie face down on soft surfaces. Other SIDS cases may stem from problems with brain systems regulating breathing or from exposure to cigarette smoke. (Bernstein et al., *Psychology,* p. 173.)

a. infant deaths   _____

b. SIDS   _____

c. the incidence of SIDS in other cultures   _____

5. If two people with sharply different spending styles commit to a relationship, problems usually arise. This is particularly true in a marriage. For example, the conflict of "his" and "her" money may come into play, and whoever earns the larger salary may want to tell the other how to spend. In disagreements over money, the larger earner may think or say, "I earned it and I'll spend it." (Adapted from Garman and Forgue, *Personal Finance,* p. 119.)

a. conflicting spending styles _____

b. money _____

c. fights about "his" money _____

▪ EXERCISE 2 Choosing the Best Topic

DIRECTIONS Read each paragraph. Then circle the appropriate letter to identify the best topic.

EXAMPLE In ancient times, Roman warriors used loud noise to frighten their enemies. Beating their swords against their shields, they'd yell taunts and insults, blow horns, and pound drums. During the Civil War, Union soldiers reportedly got chills when they heard their Confederate opponents' blood-curdling "rebel yell." Throughout history, then, loud noise has been employed as a weapon. Today, for instance, the U.S. Army uses noise to unsettle enemies and drive them out of hiding. Soldiers also play heavy metal or hard rock music to intimidate the enemy. In 1989, U.S. troops blasted high-volume rock music at the Vatican Embassy in Panama, where General Noriega, the Panamanian military leader wanted on drug charges, had taken refuge. During the Gulf and Iraq wars, right before an attack, American soldiers played grunge rock from mounted loudspeakers. Soldiers also sometimes use a "noise gun," the Long Range Acoustical Device (LRAD), which blasts a focused stream of harsh sound so loud it can trigger nausea and fainting. (Source of information: Anjula Razdan, "The Father of Acoustic Ecology," *Utne*, July–August 2005, p. 57.)

Who or what is frequently mentioned or referred to in the paragraph?

Topic a. Roman warriors' scare tactics

(b.) loud noise used as a weapon

c. high-volume rock music

d. ancient weapons

EXPLANATION Every sentence in the paragraph mentions or refers to how loud noise, from verbal taunts to rock music, has been used by warriors to intimidate enemies. Thus answer *b* is the correct choice. "High-volume rock music" is mentioned only in sentences 6 through 8. The rest of the time, other kinds of noise are described. Answer *a*, "Roman warriors' scare tactics," could not be the correct answer because that topic is referred to only twice, in sentences 1 and 2. Similarly answer *d* won't work because ancient weapons are only discussed in the first two sentences.

1. From around 1690 until 1730, history's most notorious pirates—men like Blackbeard and Captain William Kidd—terrorized sailors and voyagers on the high seas. However, not all of those who made names for themselves during the Golden Age of Piracy were men. Anne Bonny, for example, was one of the seventeenth century's best known female pirates. Headstrong and hot-tempered, young Anne emigrated from Ireland to America with her parents but quickly grew bored by life on her father's Charleston plantation. At age sixteen she eloped with a penniless sailor, James Bonny. After their marriage, the couple sailed to the Bahamas, where Anne found that she enjoyed the company of the island's pirate society. She was particularly enthralled* by the dashing John Rackham, known as Calico Jack for his love of striped pants. Before long, Anne abandoned her husband and joined Rackham's crew aboard the pirate ship *Revenge*. For almost a year, Anne and another woman on board, Mary Read, daringly wielded sword and pistol in combat as they sailed the Caribbean, boarding and looting ships. Taking only a short break to give birth to Rackham's baby, Anne then abandoned the child to return to her life on the *Revenge*. In 1720, when the ship was captured by the Jamaican governor's troops, Rackham was hanged. But Anne, pregnant again, was imprisoned and eventually pardoned. At this point, her name disappeared from official records. (Source of information: "Anne Bonny," Wikipedia, http://en .wikipedia.org/wiki/Anne_Bonny.)

Who or what is frequently mentioned or referred to in the paragraph?

Topic a. notorious pirates

b. the pirate Anne Bonny

c. female pirates

d. notorious women

2. With a huge white horn planted firmly in the middle of its head, the rhinoceros is a comical-looking animal. Unfortunately, there is nothing funny about what presently appears to be the rhino's

---

*enthralled, fascinated, delighted.

unhappy fate: Pursued by poachers who sell the rhino's horns for profit, the animals are rapidly being destroyed. Laws to stop poaching have been enacted in parts of Africa where the animals are found. But so far those laws have not been very successful; poachers continue to hunt rhinos with impunity.* In fact, only a few individual poachers have been arrested. Large-scale poaching rings, responsible for much of the slaughter, remain intact. Free of significant interference, they continue to kill the animals in order to make their horns into fancy daggers or useless aphrodisiacs.*

Who or what is frequently mentioned or referred to in the paragraph?

Topic a. the preservation of endangered animals

   b. rhino poaching

   c. poaching in Africa

   d. slaughtering animals

3. Like most people, you probably know what a yuppie is. However, have you ever heard of a "NIMBY"? Like yuppie, the word *NIMBY* is an acronym; it comes from the words *Not In My Back Yard*. NIMBYs are quick to respond if anyone invades their territory with a project or plan they consider dangerous or displeasing. When that happens, NIMBYs use any number of means to respond. Among other things, they might stage a demonstration, take their opponent to court, or call a press conference. In 2002, for instance, many Nevada NIMBYs began battling federal officials who had chosen their state's Yucca mountain as a site for nuclear waste disposal. Other NIMBYs throughout the country have opposed WalMart stores, landfills, low-income housing, prisons, homeless shelters, power lines, and chemical waste companies. Although some NIMBYs have come in for criticism and even ridicule—it's hard to sympathize with wealthy suburbanites who reject low-cost housing because it spoils their view—NIMBYism is not always a movement for the well-heeled. In some cases, NIMBYs have been poor people who banded together to protest the presence of waste dumps in their neighborhood. In instances like these, it seems perfectly legitimate to say "Not In My Back Yard."

---

*impunity: without fear of punishment.
*aphrodisiacs: substances that supposedly increase sexual desire.

Who or what is frequently mentioned or referred to in the paragraph?

Topic a. NIMBYs

       b. Yuppies versus NIMBYs

       c. criticism of NIMBYs

       d. NIMBYs and WalMart

4. Research in learning suggests that good grades depend more on effective study skills than on a high IQ. For instance, students with high grades are likely to prepare for exams in advance and do several complete reviews before the exam. Students with low grades tend to review once before an exam, and they review at the last minute, often cutting back on sleep in order to complete the review. Unfortunately, this method (or, should we say, lack of method) seldom produces high grades. Overall, students who get high grades have good time-management skills. They know exactly what they hope to have accomplished in a month or more, and they plan their days and weeks accordingly. Students who get poor grades seldom have long-term goals and think daily to-do lists are a waste of time. Sad to say, their grades are a clear indicator that time-management skills are essential to college success.

Who or what is frequently mentioned or referred to in the paragraph?

Topic a. daily to-do lists

       b. cramming

       c. regular reviews

       d. effective study skills

Reading Tip

Look for a topic general enough to include everything discussed in a paragraph but still specific enough to exclude anything not mentioned or discussed in detail.

INTERNET RESOURCE

For tips on managing, rather than wasting, your time, see **laflemm.com**, *Reading for Results*: Online Practice for Chapter 4.

◼ EXERCISE 3 Defining the Topic

DIRECTIONS Read each paragraph. Then in the blank that follows write a word or phrase that sums up the topic.

EXAMPLE Joseph Boulogne, the eighteenth-century black composer, led a life so active and so exciting, it is surprising that he still found the time to write music. Son of an African slave and a French official, Boulogne was born in Guadeloupe* but was educated in Paris, where he acquired all the graces of an accomplished gentleman. By the age of eighteen, he could skate, dance, fence, and ride with any man in Paris. When the French Revolution bloodied the streets of Paris, Boulogne commanded an all-black regiment, proving himself a brilliant military strategist. However, none of these activities interfered with the composer's love of music. Boulogne wrote and performed music throughout his lifetime, stopping only when he was imprisoned for a brief period after the Revolution.

Topic   *The exciting life of Joseph Boulogne* _____

EXPLANATION The paragraph describes in detail the varied and active life of Joseph Boulogne. This is the subject to which the author repeatedly returns.

1. When Americans think of the Wild West, they don't usually imagine it inhabited by African Americans. Yet this image of the West— without the presence of black people—is completely inaccurate. In truth, thousands of African Americans helped settle the West, even though few Hollywood films have acknowledged their existence. In the 1940s, for example, Hollywood released a movie called *Tomahawk*. The white actor Jack Oakie played a character named James Beckworth. Beckworth was actually a black cowboy who became famous during the California gold rush. Similarly, Oklahoma, the location for many Westerns, was the site of several African-American communities, none of which has ever appeared on film. It's time for Hollywood to acknowledge its historical error and make films showing African Americans taking part in the westward movement.

Topic _____

2. If you could choose whether your baby would be male or female, would you do it? What about selecting your baby's eye and hair color, or deciding whether the child would be a talented athlete or an

_____
*Guadeloupe: French islands in the West Indies.

accomplished musician? If the polls are to be believed, many people would like the chance to make these decisions. Unfortunately, in a relatively short time, reproductive technology may well be available so that parents can, in fact, create the designer babies of their dreams. However, having the ability to create designer babies does not mean that we should allow parents to treat children as if they were cars. While it's perfectly acceptable to go to the car dealer and select the options we want our cars to have, this same principle should never be applied to human beings. It is morally wrong to create the child of our choice. In effect, this attitude toward human life amounts to playing God since God is the only one who should decide such matters.

Topic _____

3. Technology companies like Turnitin.com would have you believe that online plagiarism is rampant, with students taking papers off the Internet from what are commonly known as "cheatsites." For a price, these sites provide students with quick-fix homework and term-paper solutions. And while Turnitin.com, which calls itself the "standard in online plagiarism prevention," may have its own slightly cynical reasons for raising the alarm about online plagiarism, the company doesn't seem to be that off the mark. A report published in the May/June 2002 issue of the *Journal of College Student Development* found that 24.5 percent of the 698 students interviewed had "sometimes," "very frequently," or "often" cut passages found on the Internet and pasted them into their own papers. They had not, however, included sources for the quotes. Similarly, Andrea L. Foster in the *Chronicles of Higher Education* (November 20, 2002) reports that out of 1,925 papers run through Turnitin.com, 14 percent were found to have been plagiarized. Statistics like these are cause for serious concern.

Topic _____

4. The Japanese word *kimono* actually means "clothing," but the word is used primarily to refer to robelike garments with wide-angle sleeves. According to tradition, kimonos for men were made of black silk and decorated with the family crest.* Women had more choices. The color of their kimonos could vary with the occasion. Both sexes bound or tied their kimono with a large sash called the "obi," and the sash itself, along with the way it was tied, was a good indicator of social class. Prior to the nineteenth century, the upper classes in

_____
*crest: symbol or sign.

Japan dressed almost exclusively in kimonos, but in modern Japan, kimonos are worn only for special occasions.

Topic ───────────────────────────────────

INTERNET RESOURCE

If you think you need a little more work with identifying topics, see **laflemm.com**, *Reading for Results*: Online Practice for Chapter 4 and "Definitions of Key Concepts."

Use the Topic to Discover the Main Idea

Imagine that you overheard two of your friends chatting, and during the conversation, your name came up repeatedly. When you asked them what they were talking about, they replied in unison, "you." It's doubtful you would be satisfied with that answer. After all, you wouldn't know what they were saying *about* you. Your friends' response gives you the topic of the conversation but leaves out the point, that is, Were they saying what a generous, good-hearted person you are or complaining that you are mean-spirited and rude? More than likely, you would ask, maybe even demand, to know the point of the conversation in addition to the topic.

Much the same principle holds true for paragraphs. You won't be satisfied with knowing just the topic. All that gives you is the subject under discussion, for example, Internet plagiarism, rhino poaching, designer babies, or the Socratic method. As soon as you get a sense of the topic, you need to start thinking about the author's comment *about* the topic. You need, that is, to discover the **main idea**. As you know from Chapter 3, the main idea is the central message or point of the paragraph. It's the underlying thought that connects the individual sentences. Sentences in a paragraph not united around a main idea usually don't make sense. They read like a list, rather than a unified paragraph.

For an illustration of how to use the topic to arrive at the main idea, let's look at a sample paragraph and start with the question that will lead us to the topic: What subject does the author repeatedly mention or refer to throughout the paragraph?

[1]For a period of about seventy-five years (1765–1840), the Gothic novel, an early relative of the modern horror story, was popular

throughout Europe. [2]Many of the most popular Gothic novels—those written by Horace Walpole, Ann Radcliffe, and Monk Lewis—sold in the thousands. [3]They were quickly translated, and frequently plagiarized. [4]Gothic novels were the object of fascination because they described a world where mysterious happenings were a matter of course, and ghostly, hooded figures flitted through ruined buildings in the dead of night. [5]Because Gothic novels were read and discussed by men and women of all classes, publishers, ever alert to a ready market, made sure that the books were available at bargain prices. [6]Even the poorest members of the working class could afford to pay a penny to enter the Gothic world of terror, and they paid their pennies in astonishing numbers.

The topic of this paragraph is the Gothic novel. This is the subject to which the author repeatedly returns in every sentence. Knowing the topic, we now have to take the next step and ask two more questions: (1) What idea is developed in both general and specific sentences, and (2) What does the author want to say *about* the topic?

The paragraph opens with a general sentence telling us that the Gothic novel was very popular in Europe between 1765 and 1840. Notice now how sentences 2 through 6 all describe, in more specific detail, the popularity of Gothic novels. We learn whose books were the most popular and who read Gothic novels. Based on the relationship between general and specific sentences, we can now answer our second question: What does the author want to say about the topic? The author wants readers to know that Gothic novels were extremely popular in Europe in the eighteenth and nineteenth centuries. That's the main idea of the paragraph.

Look now at a second sample paragraph. After you finish reading it, fill in the blanks labeled *topic* and *main idea*.

[1]Possessed by the desire to modernize his country and his subjects, Peter the Great, Tzar* of Russia, tried to whip his subjects into living in the style of the modern world. [2]The nobles of his court were told to clip their beards and shorten their robes while their wives were summoned to court. [3]The ladies, who had previously been told to stay at home, were terrified and tended to huddle in a corner. [4]Still, they were forbidden to leave. [5]To import new ideas from the West, Peter demanded that young Russians go abroad to study, and he invited Europeans to come and visit Russia. [6]The Europeans could refuse; his subjects could not. [7]If they rebelled against modern ideas, they were beaten. [8]Continued stubbornness about modernization could lead to execution by a firing squad.

---

*Tzar (or czar): ruler, leader.

Topic _____

Main Idea _____

Did you fill in the topic blank with a phrase like "Peter the Great" or "Peter the Great's desire to modernize Russia"? If you did, you are absolutely right. If for the main idea you wrote something like "Peter the Great used brutally punitive measures to modernize Russia," right again. You already know, then, how to use the topic to get to the main idea.

Reading Tip

Think of the main idea as the author's comment on the topic, e.g., if the author's topic is "designer babies," the main idea or comment on the topic might be "Parents using reproductive technology to create the baby of their dreams are making a mistake."

INTERNET RESOURCE

For additional pointers on using the topic to discover the main idea, go to **laflemm.com** and click on "main idea" under "Definitions of Key Concepts."

Topic Sentences and Main Ideas

Notice how the first sentence in both of the sample paragraphs (pages 149–150) sum up the main idea? That sentence is worth noticing because many paragraphs are likely to include one like it. These sentences are called **topic sentences**, and, yes, the opening and closing sentences in Chapter 3 (pages 118–123) are also topic sentences. Broader in meaning than most of the sentences in the paragraph, topic sentences put main ideas into words. And, no, the topic sentence and the main idea are not one and the same. The main idea is the thought that unites or links all the sentences in the paragraph. The topic sentence is the author's way of "languaging" that idea. Think of it this way: You can and should paraphrase, or translate the main idea of the paragraph into your own words, but your paraphrase still won't be a topic sentence. The only one who can write the topic sentence of a paragraph is the author.

Because topic sentences frequently appear in writing, particularly in textbooks, you should know how to identify them when you see them. The following pointers will help you do precisely that.

---

1. The topic sentence is more general than most of the other sentences in the paragraph.
2. The topic sentence answers the question "What's the point of this paragraph?"
3. The topic sentence is developed by both general and specific sentences throughout the paragraph.
4. The topic sentence can be used to sum up the entire paragraph.
5. Anyone can paraphrase the main idea, but only the author can write a topic sentence.

Locating Topic Sentences

| Topic Sentence |
| Specific Details |

| Specific Details |
| Topic Sentence |

As you know from Chapter 3, topic sentences can move around. In Chapter 3, the topic sentences summing up the paragraphs were in first and last position. Let's look now at some other locations for topic sentences.

Topic Sentences in Second Position

Read the following paragraph. Then ask yourself which sentence, first or second, fulfills the criteria of a topic sentence.

Topic Sentence

[1]Observing learning behavior in humans is not all that easy. [2]For precisely that reason, scientists often use animals to determine when and where learning takes place. [3]In perhaps the most famous such study, the Russian psychologist Ivan Pavlov used a dog to discover the learning principle called *operant conditioning.* [4]Immediately after ringing a bell, Pavlov placed some meat powder on a dog's tongue. [5]After several repetitions of the sound of the bell followed by food, the dog began to salivate*

---

*salivate: digestive juices enter the mouth.

whenever he heard the bell ring. [6]The dog had *learned* that the bell meant food. [7]In another famous series of experiments, this time with space flight, chimpanzees and dogs were sent into orbit* so scientists could find out if living beings were able to carry out regular activities while whirling through space. [8]Research with animals showed that they learned to adjust to life in space. [9]From that point on, it was only a matter of time before humans orbited the earth.

Try to use the first sentence to summarize the point of the paragraph, and you'll find it won't work. Yes, the first sentence is the most general sentence. However, that's only one of the criteria for topic sentences listed on page 152 that the first sentence fits. It fails on all the others. It doesn't answer the question, "What's the point of the paragraph?" It's also not developed by the other more specific sentences in the paragraph. Nor could it be used as a one-sentence summary of the passage. The first sentence fails all those criteria because it's not the topic sentence. That title goes to the second sentence.

Sentence 2 is the general sentence developed by the more specific sentences that follow. It does answer the question, "What's the point of the paragraph?" And it could function as a one-sentence summary of the passage. Sentence 2 is the topic sentence, which means that sentence 1 is an introductory sentence. Introductory sentences fulfill two functions: (1) encourage readers' interest and (2) set the stage for the topic sentence, often by providing background knowledge. What the **introductory sentences** don't do is sum up the paragraph, and they are never developed by the more specific sentences in the paragraph.

| Introductory Sentence |
| Topic Sentence |
| Specific Details |

The Role of Reversal Transitions

Here's another illustration of a paragraph in which a topic sentence follows an introductory one. This time, though, pay particular attention to the word *yet* opening the second sentence. This was one of the transitional words that signaled the presence of a contrast clue in Chapter 2 (page 58). It does much the same thing here. *Yet* is a contrast or reversal transition telling readers that the author is moving away from the idea in the first sentence and about to introduce the real main idea of the paragraph, an idea that is likely to reverse or modify the point made in the introductory sentence.

———————
*orbit: the path of one thing around another in space.

Introductory Sentence

Reversal transition followed by topic sentence.

[1]In the past twenty years, it's repeatedly been claimed that low self-esteem causes numerous social and psychological ills. [2]**Yet, as it turns out, low self-esteem does not seem to be all that prevalent; on the contrary, exaggerated self-esteem seems to be more common and the source of more problems.** [3]In a wide range of studies, participants consistently gave themselves higher ratings than they gave others; overestimated their personal contribution to team efforts; exaggerated their ability to control life's events; and predicted unrealistically rosy futures for themselves (Taylor, 1989). [4]Similar research also shows that many people overestimate their intellectual and social skills. [5]What's particularly interesting about this tendency is that those who had the poorest intellectual and social skills were the most likely to overrate their performance in both areas. [6]For instance, researchers Justin Kruger and David Dunning (1999) found that college students with the lowest scores on tests of logic and grammar generally assumed that their scores would be high. [7]Interestingly enough, when these same students were schooled to become more competent in both grammar and logic, their self-assessments became less confident and more realistic. (Source of information: Brehm et al., *Social Psychology*, p. 138.)

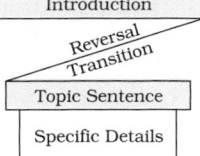

As you can see, the transition *yet* starts the movement away from the author's opening point: Low self-esteem has been cited as the source of numerous problems. That idea is pure introduction. What the author really wants to communicate comes in the second sentence: Exaggerated self-esteem is the real problem. This is the idea developed throughout the paragraph.

Transitions such as *however, nevertheless*, and *still* frequently turn up in paragraphs where the first sentence is not the topic sentence. Thus you need to be on the lookout for these transitions. If the second sentence of a paragraph doesn't explain the first, you can rightly predict that the second sentence might be a topic sentence. When the second sentence opens with a reversal transition, you can be pretty sure that the second sentence is the topic sentence. And if the third sentence continues the thread of the second, you can be dead sure that the topic sentence is in second rather than first position.

Expanding the Introduction

Introduction
Topic Sentence
Specific Details

Writers sometimes need several introductory sentences to pave the way for the topic sentence. Look, for example, at the following paragraph:

> [1]*In the third century BC, the Chinese were the first to sight Halley's comet.* [2]*In the fourteenth, the Florentine painter Giotto put the whirling ball of light into one of his paintings; in the sixteenth, William Shakespeare mentioned it in two of his plays.*
>
> *Topic Sentence* [3]**But it took the eighteenth-century astronomer Edmund Halley (1656–1742) to recognize that the comet seen by the Chinese, the Italians, and the British was the same comet returning on a fixed schedule.** [4]While studying what seemed to be the appearance of many different comets, Halley realized that there might be only one comet that regularly appeared every seventy-six years. [5]As a result of his studies, he predicted that the comet would return in 1758. [6]His prediction was proven correct when the comet showed up on schedule. [7]From that moment on, the comet bore his name. [8]Unfortunately, Halley died without knowing that his prediction had come true.

In this case, the first two sentences provide background knowledge, and it isn't until the third sentence that the writer introduces a topic sentence to summarize the main idea.

Reversal Transitions

Be that as it may	On the contrary
But	On the other hand
Conversely	Regardless
Even so	Still
However	That fact notwithstanding
In contrast	Tragically
In spite of	Unfortunately
Nevertheless	Yet
Nonetheless	

Check Your Understanding

What's the difference between topic sentences and introductory sentences?

_____

_____

Transitional Sentences

In addition to transitional words and phrases, be prepared as well for **transitional sentences**. These are complete sentences that help readers connect one thought to another. Like all transitions, they function as verbal bridges connecting sentences and paragraphs. For an example, see the following:

Introductory Sentence
Transitional Sentence
Topic Sentence

¹Jury duty is an essential part of living in a democratic society. ²But you'd never know it from the way some American citizens behave. ³**For many, jury duty is a burdensome inconvenience they try to avoid.** ⁴At the least complicated level, there are those who simply throw away the summons to jury duty. ⁵They know that if the state authorities come after them, it's easy enough to claim the notice never arrived. ⁶Should the authorities pursue the issue—and they often don't—it's up to the state to prove that the notice actually got into the potential juror's hands, and that's not easy to do. ⁷For those who lack the nerve to just chuck the notice into the wastebasket, there's a second choice. ⁸During the interview stage of jury selection, jury dodgers can display their acting skills. ⁹An agitated tone, much eyeball rolling, and excessive hand-wringing will signal that the potential juror is overly biased or else mentally unbalanced. ¹⁰Both states of mind are reason for dismissal.

Here again, note that the paragraph opens with a general sentence. But that sentence is not developed in the remaining sentences. Instead, the transition—in this case a complete sentence—signals a shift in point of view, and paves the way for the topic sentence.

Reading Tip

✔ A reversal transition opening the second sentence of a paragraph is a strong clue that the topic sentence is *not* in first position.

> **Reading Tip**
>
>
>
> Think of the main idea as the headline you would write if the paragraph were a newspaper article, e.g., "Citizens Blow Off Jury Duty" or "Gothic Novels Were Early Best Sellers."

EXERCISE 4 **Identifying Topics, Main Ideas, and Topic Sentences**

DIRECTIONS Read each paragraph. Circle the appropriate letter to identify the topic and main idea. Then write the number of the topic sentence in the blank. *Note:* All of the paragraphs use one of the three topic sentence locations just introduced.

EXAMPLE [1]When we read or hear about the suffering of wild animals illegally caught, shipped, and sold, we are likely to sigh deeply for about fifteen seconds, then forget both the animals and their suffering. [2]However, we shouldn't be so casual about the wild animal trade, particularly right now. With the threat of bird flu hanging in the air, worldwide illegal trafficking in wild animals can have immediate and disastrous effects. [3]Imported animals don't come into the country alone. [4]They carry with them parasites, germs, and diseases. [5]In 2005, for instance, British inspectors identified a parrot carrying the bird flu virus. [6]Because the parrot was being imported legally, it was under quarantine.* [7]But many of the parrots sold in Britain come into the country illegally and are never checked for disease. [8]One of those birds could also be infected with bird flu and spread the virus to a human owner.

Topic a. exotic animals

b. illegal wild animal trade

c. the suffering of animals

d. the dangers of importing parrots

Main Idea a. If bird flu continues to spread, there may be a worldwide epidemic.

b. The possibility of catching bird flu means we can't ignore illegal trafficking in wild animals.

c. Imported animals can bring with them a range of parasites and diseases.

d. Concerned only with themselves, human beings don't care enough about the suffering of their fellow creatures.

*quarantine: period of isolation to prevent the spread of disease.

Topic Sentence __2__

> **EXPLANATION** In this paragraph, the first sentence, or introductory sentence, encourages the readers to think, "Yes, I have done that." Once potential readers feel personally drawn into the situation, they might just keep reading. Or so the writer hopes. The real point or main idea of the paragraph comes in the second sentence. This is where the topic sentence introduced by the reversal transition, *however,* announces the real issue addressed in the paragraph: It's dangerous to ignore the illegal trafficking in wild animals.

1. [1]Communal movements* are almost as old as America itself. [2]In the mid-1800s Ralph Waldo Emerson remarked that every other person seemed to carry in his pocket a plan for the "perfect society." [3]Indeed, Emerson's friends at Brook Farm had "gone back to the land," and New York newspapers were running ads for people interested in forming communal associations. [4]Communal movements have been most prominent during times of social unrest like the 1840s and 1850s. [5]In the seventies they tended to occur along with other radical movements such as feminism and civil rights activism. [6]During the nineteenth century, more than one hundred communities with nearly 10,000 men, women, and children experimented with alternative social arrangements for living. (McNeil, *The Psychology of Being Human*, p. 604.)

Topic a. Ralph Waldo Emerson

b. American responses to social unrest

(c.) the history of American communal movements

d. alternative social arrangements

Main Idea a. Ralph Waldo Emerson liked to make fun of communal movements.

(b.) Communal movements have a long history in the United States.

c. Most communal experiments have been failures.

d. Communal movements are linked to social unrest.

Topic Sentence __1__

---

*communal movements: social experiments that try other living arrangements outside the traditional family.

2. [1]Men and women show that they're listening in different ways. [2]A woman is more apt to give lots of listening cues such as murmuring "Yeah" or "Uh-uh," nodding in agreement, and smiling. [3]When listening, women also make more eye contact than do men, whose eyes are likely to wonder away from the speaker (Brownell, 2002). [4]In contrast to a woman, a man is more likely to listen quietly, without giving lots of listening cues as feedback. [5]An analysis of calls to a crisis center in Finland revealed that calls taken by a female counselor were significantly longer for both male and female callers (Salminen & Glad, 1992). [6]It's likely that the greater number of listening cues given by the women encouraged the callers to keep talking. (Adapted from Joseph A. DeVito, *The Interpersonal Communication Book.* Boston and New York: Pearson Education Inc., 2004, pp. 128–130.)

Topic a. differences in how men and women listen

b. listening behaviors in men

c. conversational styles

d. making eye contact while listening

Main Idea a. Women and men differ in the way they listen.

b. Women are better listeners than men.

c. Concentration is critical to all kinds of listening.

d. Both men and women could improve their listening behavior.

Topic Sentence _____

3. [1]Most Americans are accustomed to thinking of lie detectors as foolproof. [2]They assume that lie detectors, because they are machines, can, without error, separate guilty from innocent. [3]But, in fact, nothing could be further from the truth. [4]Lie detectors can and do make mistakes. [5]For one thing, those who administer the tests are not necessarily qualified experts. [6]Many states don't employ licensed examiners trained to read and interpret lie detector printouts. [7]In addition, many subjects react to a lie detector test by becoming anxious. [8]As a result, their bodies behave as if the subjects were lying even when telling the truth. [9]Unfortunately, some people are smart enough to use relaxation techniques or tranquilizers to remain calm when they are telling a string of lies.

Topic a. lie detector examiners

b. errors made by lie detectors

c. lie detector printouts

d. lie detector subjects who lie

Main Idea a. Lie detector experts are often badly trained, which makes it hard to trust lie detector results as evidence.

b. Licensing for lie detector experts varies from state to state.

c. Lie detector printouts are hard to read and therefore are not always reliable.

d. Lie detectors are more prone to error than most people realize.

Topic Sentence _____

4. ¹Researchers use interviews, rating scales, and inventories to identify observable psychological traits. ²However, when seeking to uncover hidden or unconscious wishes, psychologists are likely to turn to *projective tests*. ³In some projective tests, the subject is asked to tell a story about a picture or an image. ⁴With others, subjects are told to respond to a word by calling up their associations. ⁵Perhaps the most famous projective test is the Rorschach technique. ⁶Developed by Swiss psychologist Hermann Rorschach, the test consists of ten inkblots. ⁷Subjects look at the inkblots and then describe what they see. ⁸Yet another example of a projective test is the Thematic Apperception Test (TAT). ⁹During the TAT, subjects are shown pictures and asked to make up stories about the people depicted. ¹⁰Although projective tests like the Rorschach and the TAT have been popular for decades, many psychologists now question their reliability as diagnostic instruments.

Topic a. psychological testing

b. unconscious wishes

c. projective tests

d. the Thematic Apperception Test

Main Idea a. The Rorschach is the most famous projective test in use.

b. The Thematic Apperception Test requires those taking the test to make up stories about pictures.

c. Psychologists often use projective tests to explore hidden or secret thoughts.

d. Projective tests are unreliable.

Topic Sentence _____

5. ¹For centuries earthquakes were considered warnings from the gods. ²Both the suddenness of the quakes and the damage they left behind were enough to convince even the unbelieving that such things must be the work of supernatural beings. ³It is only recently

that a comprehensive theory, called *plate tectonics*, seems to adequately explain the cause of earthquakes. [4]According to this theory, the earth's surface consists of about a dozen giant rock plates, each seventy miles thick. [5]Propelled by unknown forces, the plates are constantly in motion. [6]Sometimes they collide and temporarily lock together. [7]The locking of the plates builds up stress on the plate edges, causing the rock to fracture. [8]The fracture causes the plates to resume their motion, but the sudden release of energy can produce an earthquake.

Topic a. plate tectonics

b. myths surrounding earthquakes

c. multiple causes of earthquakes

d. earthquakes as warning from the gods

Main Idea a. Earthquakes are so terrifying they seem to be supernatural.

b. The amount of damage caused by earthquakes is the main reason they are so feared.

c. Scientists now have a theory that seems to explain why earthquakes occur.

d. No one knows what propels the Earth's plates into motion.

Topic Sentence 3 ____

 ## More Topic Sentence Locations

Here are some more common methods writers rely upon to introduce their topic sentences. When you finish reading the description of each one, look closely at the accompanying diagram.

Opening Question and Topic Sentence Answer

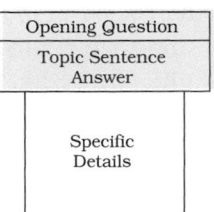

Opening Question
Topic Sentence Answer

Specific Details

Writers, particularly textbook writers, are fond of opening paragraphs with questions. The opening question serves the same function as an introductory sentence: It's there to grab readers' attention and help them focus on the point of the paragraph. The question, however, is not the topic sentence. If a stated answer is present (Chapter 5 will introduce paragraphs with unstated or implied answers), it follows fairly quickly on the heels of the opening question, within the first two or three sentences. Here's a good example:

Question [1]What determines our long-term satisfaction, and why are some
Answer of us happier than others? [2]**Seeking the roots of happiness, Ed**

Diener and his colleagues (1999) reviewed years of research and found that there are three key predictors of happiness. [3]The first is social relationships; people with an active social life, close friends, and a happy marriage are more satisfied than those who lack these intimate connections. [4]The second is employment status. [5]Regardless of income, employed people are happier than those who are out of work. [6]Finally, people who are physically healthy are happier than those who are not. (Adapted from Brehm et al., *Social Psychology*, p. 536.)

As is typical for this kind of paragraph, the sentence that answers the opening question is also the topic sentence of the paragraph.

Topic Sentence at Mid-Point

Specific Details
Topic Sentence
Specific Details

As the paragraph about Halley's Comet on page 155 suggests, the topic sentence can start inching toward the middle of a paragraph. Topic sentences can, in fact, appear smack in the middle of a paragraph, as the following passage illustrates:

[1]Most people know the gruesome story of Baron Frankenstein, the mad doctor who created a living creature from the bodies of corpses. [2]The story has been told and retold. [3]It has also been the subject of numerous films, and most people are familiar with the tale. [4]**What many people don't know, however, is that the chilling story of Dr. Frankenstein and his creature was written by a nineteen-year-old woman named Mary Shelley.** [5]As a young bride, Shelley liked to take part in storytelling competitions with her husband, poet Percy Bysshe Shelley, and his friend and fellow-poet George Gordon Byron. [6]On one particularly long evening, Byron suggested that everyone write and read a ghost story. [7]Mary Shelley responded with the story of Frankenstein, and the rest, as they say, is history.

Topic sentences in the middle of a paragraph are not nearly as common as topic sentences at the beginning. But if a paragraph starts out specific, becomes general in the middle, and then returns to being specific, that general sentence in the middle is very likely the topic sentence.

Topic Sentence in Last Position

If no topic sentence turns up by the time you reach the middle of the paragraph, you have two choices to consider. Either the main idea is implied, or suggested, rather than stated (more about that

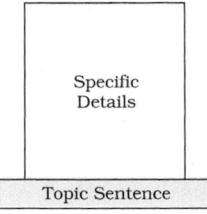

Specific
Details

Topic Sentence

in Chapter 5), or else you are dealing with a paragraph where the topic sentence appears at the very end. Here's an example of a paragraph in which the topic sentence arrives last.

[1]Some people express their personal philosophies by tattooing themselves with phrases like "Live Hard" or "Love Thy Neighbor." [2]Others consider tattoos a way of displaying their taste in art. [3]They might tattoo a William Blake* etching* or a Georgia O'Keeffe* flower on some part of their bodies. [4]But in different cultures and eras, tattoos have also served religious purposes. [5]Mexico's Mayan people expressed their religious beliefs by tattooing themselves with images of jaguars, snakes, turtles, and toads. [6]From the 1700s until the present, many Muslims tattooed themselves to show their devotion to Allah. [7]Some Native American tribes used tattooing for medicinal purposes, believing that tattoos would ward off illness. [8]The Cree, for instance, would tattoo a cross on each cheek to protect against toothaches, and members of the Ojibwa tribe tattooed small circles on their temples to prevent headaches. [9]Throughout history tattooing has been widely used as a means of identification. [10]Before 787 AD, early Christians used tattoos to identify members of their faith. [11]Similarly, members of the military or fraternities may have themselves tattooed to publicly show their commitment. [12]Some cultures have tattooed prisoners, the most sinister example being the Nazis, who tattooed numbers on the arms of concentration camp victims during World War II. [13]**Tattoos, it's clear, have served many different purposes.** (Source of information: "Tattooing," http://salc.wsu.edu/Fair F02/FS18/ Tattooing/tattooing.htm.)

Sentences 1 through 12 are too specific to summarize the paragraph. Only the very last sentence fits all the criteria of a topic sentence.

Reading Tip

If a paragraph maintains a consistent level of specific detail and suddenly branches out into a general statement at the end, that last sentence is probably the topic sentence.

---

*William Blake (1757–1827): British artist whose drawings and paintings have a fantastic otherworldly quality.
*etching: art made by imprinting an image on a metal plate.
*Georgia O'Keeffe (1887–1986): American artist known for her focus on flowers.

Doubling Up on Topic Sentences

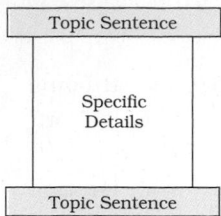

To make sure that they get their point across, writers sometimes double up on topic sentences, stating the main idea at the beginning and the end of a paragraph. Here's an example:

> [1]**The career of George Smith Patton Jr., the much decorated four-star army general, ended because he didn't know how to control his temper.** [2]During World War II, in August 1943, Patton visited ailing and wounded soldiers in two separate army hospitals. [3]On each visit, he publicly slapped a soldier who complained of losing the nerve to fight. [4]Patton considered the men despicable* and insisted that "real" soldiers should not have to look at gutless cowards afraid of battle. [5]Although Patton thought his behavior perfectly appropriate, his commanding officer, Dwight D. Eisenhower, did not. [6]Eisenhower forced Patton to apologize publicly to the hospital staff and to the men themselves. [7]He also saw to it that Patton rose no higher in the chain of military command. [8]**Thanks to his uncontrollable temper, General George Patton never climbed any higher on the military ladder.**

Reading Tip

If a paragraph opens with a general statement, becomes more specific, and then turns more general again at the end, check to see if the opening and closing sentences say much the same thing. If they do, you are reading a paragraph with a double topic sentence.

■ EXERCISE 5 **Identifying Topics, Main Ideas, and Topic Sentences**

> DIRECTIONS Read each paragraph. Circle the appropriate letter to identify the topic and main idea. Then write the number of the topic sentence in the blank.

> EXAMPLE [1]During World War I and again during World War II, the U.S. Congress required Americans to observe daylight saving time (DST) to save energy for the production of war supplies. [2]After U.S. Department of Transportation studies indicated that DST reduced the need for artificial light and decreased Americans' electricity

---

*despicable: beneath contempt.

usage, DST became permanent in most states. [3]In addition to the energy savings, DST extended the daylight hours during warmer months when people were more inclined to be out of doors. [4]DST is also said to prevent traffic accidents by allowing more people to return home from work or school in daylight. [5]There is evidence, too, that DST reduces crime by decreasing the amount of time when people can move about in darkness. [6]Clearly, there are some good reasons for observing daylight saving time. (Source of information: "Daylight Saving Time," Wikipedia, http://en.wikipedia.org/wiki/Daylight_savings_time.)

Topic a. U.S. Department of Transportation studies

b. time changes

c. the history of daylight saving time

(d.) benefits of daylight saving time

Main Idea (a.) Daylight saving time offers a number of bonuses.

b. Observing daylight saving time saves energy.

c. Energy conservation is the best reason to observe daylight saving time.

Topic Sentence   6

EXPLANATION Answer *d* is the correct answer for the topic because almost every sentence in the paragraph mentions a benefit of daylight saving time. None of the other choices for the topic is mentioned as frequently. The only sentence in the paragraph general enough to sum up all of the benefits listed is sentence 6, making that sentence the topic sentence of the paragraph. For the main idea, sentence *a* is the only appropriate choice. Like the author's topic sentence, sentence *a* is general enough to include all the specific details and sum up everything said in the paragraph.

1. [1]The term *instant messaging* (IM) describes a form of communication in which two people use computers to exchange messages in real time. [2]The time element is what distinguishes instant messaging from e-mail. [3]Instant messaging services also generally offer a "presence information" feature, which tells users if the people they want to write to are online and available for conversation. [4]Instant messaging is widely used among college students with kids using instant messaging as naturally as their parents use the telephone. [5]However, that's not to say that they all use instant messaging in the same way. [6]There seems to be a difference in how males and females make use of instant messaging. [7]Researcher Naomi Baron of American University found, for instance, that instant messages from young women are likely to be fairly formal. [8]The women in Baron's study didn't use as many contractions as the men did. [9]Baron also found that the women's punctuation was better. [10]Baron says that female instant messengers use "a more schooled, standard writing style" while men's messages, to put it politely, are likely to be more informal and less restrained by traditional grammar. [11]It may come as no surprise that women also write longer messages than men do. [12]In Baron's study, it took women 41 seconds and nearly ten exchanges to wrap up a conversation. [13]Men took only half that amount of time to finish what they wanted to say. (Source of information: www.livescience.com/technology/050301_internet_language.html.)

Topic
a. females' use of instant messaging

b. grammar usage in instant messaging

c. differences in instant messaging

d. Naomi Baron

Main Idea
a. Unlike their kids, many adults are intimidated by the idea of instant messaging.

b. Nina Baron's study is too small to prove anything significant about instant messaging.

c. Males and females differ in how they use instant messaging.

Topic Sentence _____

2. [1]The life of Supreme Court Justice Oliver Wendell Holmes (1841–1935) was the subject of *The Magnificent Yankee*, a play which later became a Hollywood film (1951). [2]Tall, handsome, self-assured, and athletic, Oliver Wendell Holmes had all the makings of an action movie hero, including courage. [3]Severely wounded on three different occasions during the American Civil War (1861–1865), he repeatedly returned to battle, rising to the rank of captain. [4]In 1864, the twenty-three-year-old Holmes was in the thick of battle at Fort Stevens, near Washington, DC. [5]Spotting a tall, lanky civilian in a top hat who was peering over the fortress wall, Holmes didn't think twice but shouted out in a commanding voice: "GET DOWN, YOU DAMNED FOOL!" [6]Startled, the unknown man dropped to the ground without protest. [7]Holmes later found out that the stranger was President Abraham Lincoln. [8]Holmes, however, was not especially apologetic since the president had, after all, made himself a standing target, an act that Holmes considered foolish. [9]When Holmes disapproved of someone's behavior, he wasn't about to hold

his tongue, even if that someone was the president. [10]In and out of wartime, Holmes always had the courage of his convictions.

Topic a. the life story of Oliver Wendell Holmes

b. Oliver Wendell Holmes and Abraham Lincoln

c. Oliver Wendell Holmes's career on the Supreme Court

d. the courage of Oliver Wendell Holmes

Main Idea a. Oliver Wendell Holmes's heroism on the battlefield made him a legend.

b. Oliver Wendell Holmes was not a man to keep his mouth shut.

c. Oliver Wendell Holmes had all the earmarks of a hero, including bravery.

Topic Sentence ———

3. [1]Why was Hurricane Katrina so disastrous for the city of New Orleans in 2005? [2]The geography of the area around New Orleans, the failure of the levees, and the elimination of wetlands all contributed to the city's devastating destruction at Katrina's hand. [3]Built in a natural bowl that is in some places five feet below sea level, New Orleans is actually lower than the three major bodies of water—the Mississippi River, Lake Pontchartrain, and the Gulf of Mexico—near it. [4]Man-made levees had been built to protect the city from these waters if they overflowed; however, constructing these levees also destroyed natural marshes that had once acted as a buffer, absorbing much of the energy of hurricanes roaring in from the Gulf. [5]Consequently, when Hurricane Katrina hit the coast near New Orleans on August 29, 2005, there was nothing to slow the enormous waves generated by the storm's 125-mile-per-hour winds. [6]A storm surge in Lake Pontchartrain slammed into one levee and broke it, allowing water to pour into the city. [7]For weeks afterward, floodwater soaked New Orleans, ruining what the hurricane's high winds hadn't already demolished. [8]In the end, over 1,300 people were killed, hundreds of thousands lost their homes, and $75 billion in property was destroyed. (Source of information: Katharine Mieszkowski, "Why New Orleans Is Sunk," *Salon*, September 3, 2005, www.salon.com/news/feature/2005/09/03/geology/print.html.)

Topic a. Lake Pontchartrain

b. tragedy in New Orleans

c. man-made levees

d. causes of Hurricane Katrina's destruction

Main Idea a. Hurricane Katrina was one of the century's worst hurricanes.

b. The elimination of wetlands was a major cause of Katrina's destruction.

c. There were three major reasons why Katrina was so destructive to New Orleans.

Topic Sentence —— 2

4. [1]Although various cultures throughout history have adorned themselves with body piercing, Americans never seemed especially interested in piercing their body parts. [2]In fact, even ear piercing fell out of favor in the United States for much of the twentieth century. [3]It only became fashionable again in the 1960s and 1970s, when hippies and punk rockers began piercing their ears. [4]Today, however, many Americans are piercing a number of different body parts. [5]Both men and women now commonly pierce their ears once or even multiple times. [6]Since the 1990s, wearing jewelry on pierced areas of the face, including the nose, the eyebrow, the lip, and the tongue, has been fashionable among the young. [7]More recently, as new clothing styles began to expose the midriff, young women started piercing their navels, too. [8]Some of the bravest of today's trendsetters are even going as far as to pierce their nipples. (Source of information: "Body Piercing," Wikipedia, http://en.wikipedia.org/wiki/Body_piercing.)

Topic a. pierced ears

b. trends in body decoration

c. cultural attitudes toward body piercing

d. body piercing

Main Idea a. Among Americans, body piercing is currently in style.

b. Pierced ears have gone in and out of fashion over the years.

c. Many different cultures from many different eras have used body piercing to signal differences in status.

Topic Sentence ——

5. [1]A blog, short for weblog, is an Internet webpage on which an individual or a group can post anything from personal opinions to photographs or web links. [2]Blog entries appear in reverse chronological order, with the newest additions at the top. [3]Some blogs are personal. [4]They function like an online diary or journal, where the "blogger" writes up thoughts or day-to-day experiences. [5]Other blogs combine news with commentary and focus on particular topics, such as politics, the media, sports, health, travel, or religion. [6]First appearing

in the 1990s, blogs became more popular with the development of new, easy-to-use blog-publishing tools. [7]By 2003, blogs were starting to shape public opinion. [8]By 2004, the growing power and influence of blogs led the *Merriam-Webster's Dictionary* to honor "blog" as word of the year. [9]Currently, millions of blogs are regularly updated, and thousands more created each day. [10]Some of the most widely visited and top rated blogs, with tens of thousands of visitors per day, are www.dailykos.com/, www.instapundit.com/, and http://atrios.blogspot.com.

Topic   a. the Internet

b. personal webpage

c. celebrity blogs

d. blogs

Main Idea   a. Currently, people are relying more on blogs than on newspapers, and the influence of blogs on public opinion has grown dramatically over the last decade.

b. Blogs are regularly posted webpages that can be used for anything from recalling personal experiences to displaying snapshots.

c. The Internet pages known as blogs first appeared in the 1990s.

Topic Sentence _____

EXERCISE 6 **Identifying Topics, Main Ideas, and Topic Sentences**

DIRECTIONS Read each paragraph. Circle the appropriate letters to identify the topic and main idea. Then write the number of the topic sentence in the blank.

1. [1]Outwardly, the arrival of British baby Louise Brown in 1978 seemed like any ordinary birth. [2]But in fact Louise Brown's arrival proved to be an altogether extraordinary event, for Louise's birth was living proof that a scientific procedure known as *in vitro* fertilization could produce normal, healthy babies, even when the actual process of fertilization took place outside the human body. [3]For countless couples who had expected to remain childless because of problems with the initial stages of pregnancy, Louise's birth was a scientific miracle that offered new hope. [4]Since 1978, many more such babies have been born in England, Australia, and the United States, with the result that the term *test-tube babies* has become part of the English language. [5]In the United States there are now entire clinics devoted solely to the process of in vitro fertilization.

Topic a. Louise Brown

b. in vitro fertilization

c. pregnancy

d. reproductive procedures helping infertile couples

Main Idea a. In vitro fertilization is an expensive and complicated procedure that doesn't always work.

b. The birth of Louise Brown proved that in vitro fertilization could produce healthy babies.

c. In both the United States and Europe, there are clinics that help infertile couples have children.

d. For couples who can't have children in vitro fertilization was a godsend.

Topic Sentence _____

2. [1]More than fifty different kinds of sea snakes live in the waters of the Pacific and Indian Oceans. [2]Unlike sea turtles, which must crawl from the water to give birth on land, sea snakes give birth below the surface of the ocean. [3]The only time a sea snake surfaces is when it needs to fill its single lung with air. [4]Once the lung is filled, the sea snake can stay underwater for hours. [5]Although sea snakes are quite beautiful, they are also dangerous. [6]They produce a deadly poison that can kill on contact.

Topic a. the sea

b. sea snakes

c. the poison of sea snakes

d. the lungs of sea snakes

Main Idea a. As many as fifty different kinds of sea snakes make their home in the Pacific and Indian Oceans.

b. Sea snakes can kill on contact by poisoning their victims.

c. Sea snakes have very little in common with sea turtles.

d. Sea snakes are among the loveliest creatures in the ocean.

Topic Sentence _____

3. [1]Nike advertisements featuring superstars like Michael Jordan and snappy slogans like "Just Do It" have made Nike athletic shoes world-famous. [2]But those expensive rubber-soled shoes, now considered a luxury item, had the plainest of beginnings. [3]Nike shoes were the brainchild of two men, Phil Knight and Bill Bowerman of

Oregon. [4]In 1958 Knight was a business major at the University of Oregon. [5]He was also a runner, which is how he got to know coach Bill Bowerman. [6]Bowerman shared Knight's dissatisfaction with American running shoes. [7]Both men believed that the typical running shoe hindered the runner's performance. [8]As a result of their conversations about the perfect running shoe, the two men formed their own company to create and market more comfortable and better fitting shoes for runners. [9]When they formed the company in 1964, marketing for the shoes they sold featured no world-famous superstars. [10]At that time, it meant that Knight went to track meets and personally sold each pair of shoes out of his station wagon. [11]Research and development sometimes took place at home, like the time Bowerman created Nike's famous waffle sole by shaping the rubber with a waffle iron over the stove in his kitchen. [12]Bowerman's and Knight's company was originally called "Blue Ribbon Shoes," and it didn't become Nike until 1968. [13]The name was an allusion to Nike, the Greek goddess of victory, which in hindsight seems an apt, or appropriate, choice for the company name.

Topic   a. Phil Knight

b. Bill Bowerman

c. running shoes

d. Nike's origins

Main Idea   a. Bill Bowerman and Phil Knight are perfect illustrations of the American ability to make something out of nothing.

b. The world-famous Nike company was the inspiration of two men, Phil Knight and Bill Bowerman.

c. The success of Nike shoes is the result of some very smart marketing methods, featuring athlete superstars and catchy slogans.

d. Nike shoes outsell the competition because the shoes were created by two men who knew what runners really wanted.

Topic Sentence _____

4.   [1]Avalanches are among the world's most dangerous natural disasters. [2]Fortunately, avalanches usually occur in remote mountain areas, where they threaten neither human life nor property. [3]Occasionally, however, an avalanche can strike without warning, taking hikers and skiers by surprise. [4]This is precisely what happened more than a century ago when a small group of mountain climbers tried to scale the huge alpine peak Mont Blanc. [5]They were unexpectedly overtaken by an avalanche that left only a few survivors. [6]Three members

of the party were buried in the snow. [7]When, after almost half a century, the bodies were found, they were perfectly preserved. [8]They were so well-preserved, in fact, that a surviving member of the original party, by then an old man, was able to recognize them.

Topic a. natural disasters

b. bodies preserved in ice

c. Mont Blanc

d. sudden avalanches

Main Idea a. For the most part, avalanches occur in remote areas where they don't do much harm to people or property.

b. The bodies of those who died in the Mont Blanc avalanche were so well-preserved they were still recognizable after almost half a century.

c. Avalanches seldom kill huge numbers of people.

d. Deadly avalanches can surprise hikers and skiers.

Topic Sentence ———

5. [1]In 1871, the *New York Herald* sent Henry Morton Stanley to Africa in search of David Livingstone, the English missionary.* [2]Determined to succeed, Stanley courageously faced sickness, hostile natives, and starvation to find the missionary and build a reputation as one of the bravest men in the world. [3]Stanley was indeed brave and generally acted as if he did not know the meaning of fear. [4]For all his bravery, though, Stanley could be both brutal and dishonest. [5]When his real adventures were greeted with disbelief, he made up fantastic stories that were little more than outright lies. [6]Like most men who had suffered great hardship, he considered the world a dangerous battleground, where only the strongest and the most brutal could survive. [7]To exert his authority, he used violence the way other people raise their voice. [8]Those who didn't immediately obey his orders were beaten, even shot. [9]History books may have emphasized the heroic side of Stanley's personality, but he clearly knew how to be a villain as well as a hero.

Topic a. the two sides of Henry Morton Stanley

b. Stanley and Livingstone

c. Stanley's lies

d. the misrepresentation of Stanley in history books

———

*missionary: a person who goes to foreign countries to do religious or charitable work.

Main Idea a. Henry Morton Stanley became famous after discovering the English missionary David Livingstone.

b. Stanley was more villain than hero.

c. Stanley liked pushing people around to show his power and authority.

d. Although Stanley could be heroic, he was also cruel and given to lying.

Topic Sentence ———

6. [1]Between 1857 and 1863, the Franciscan monk Gregor Mendel carefully crossed different varieties of garden peas and studied the results of the crossbreeding. [2]To his delight, he realized that his results explained the rules of heredity,* or biological inheritance. [3]When he completed his experiments, Mendel read an account of his research to a society of naturalists.* [4]To his astonishment, they remained stonily unimpressed. [5]The articles Mendel wrote about his work were greeted with a similar lack of enthusiasm. [6]It was not until sixteen years after Mendel's death that three European scientists who had made similar discoveries decided to investigate the monk's work, and Mendel finally received recognition. [7]The story of Mendel's discoveries is a perfect example of a scientific truth: some of the great scientific discoveries were initially ignored by the experts.

Topic a. the life of Gregor Mendel

b. heredity

c. Gregor Mendel's discoveries

d. scientific discoveries

Main Idea a. Mendel used peas to do experiments that unlocked the laws of heredity.

b. Mendel's account of his experiments left readers and listeners unimpressed, but that did not deter the monk from continuing with his experiments.

c. The response to Mendel's discoveries illustrates a basic truth about scientific research: great scientific breakthroughs are often ignored at first.

d. Gregor Mendel was a dedicated scientist who devoted his life to discovering the laws of heredity.

———

*heredity: the transmission of characteristics from parents to offspring.
*naturalists: people who study plants and animals.

Topic Sentence ──────

7. [1]Because they carry computerized scans of a person's fingerprints, face, and eyes, biometric passports seem crucial to the war on terror. [2]They would guarantee accurate identification of those carrying them, making it hard for a terrorist to slip secretly into any country. [3]No wonder, then, that governments all over the world are spending billions of dollars replacing traditional passports with biometric ones. [4]The question is, Are biometric passports worth the investment? [5]According to a German security consultant named Lukas Grunwald, they are not; Grunwald says that biometric passports are a "waste of money" and the whole design of them is "brain damaged." [6]Appearing at the Black Hat security conference in Las Vegas in August 2006, Grunwald claims to have cloned information stored on biometric passports. [7]Once the data on the passports is cloned, it can be transferred to blank computer chips and implanted in fake passports. [8]If Grunwald is correct, that means the biometric passports could conceivably provide terrorists with precisely the documents they need to enter countries illegally. [9]Grunwald says it took him only two weeks to clone a biometric passport, and the cost of the cloning was a mere $200. [10]He demonstrated the cloning procedure at the conference, using easy-to-buy and readily available computer technology. (Source of information: http://news.com/2061-10789_3-6102333.html.)

Topic
   a. the war on terrorism
   b. Black Hat conference
   c. biometric passports
   d. computerized scans of body parts

Main Idea
   a. Because traditional passports can so easily be forged, security consultant Lukas Grunwald believes we need to find a replacement for them.
   b. Governments around the world are spending billions in the war on terror and repeatedly coming up empty-handed.
   c. Security consultant Lukas Grunwald believes that the huge investment in biometric passports is an enormous waste of money.
   d. When Grunwald showed the conference audience how easily he could clone a biometric passport, everyone at the Black Hat conference was astounded.

Topic Sentence ──────

8. ¹For years, the expression "Sleep Tight, Don't Let the Bed Bugs Bite" was just a cute little rhyme parents said while tucking in their kids. ²But that children's rhyme has taken on new meaning: Over the last four years, bed bugs have made a comeback and invaded cities from New York to Los Angeles. ³The tiny brown insects with the flattened bodies are once again creeping out of mattresses, carpets, and wall and floor cracks to feed on the blood of humans and animals during the dead of night. ⁴Bed bugs had been an all-too-common problem before World War II, but the widespread use of DDT in the 1940s and 1950s wiped them out or so it had seemed. ⁵However, they are back and entomologists, scientists who study the ways of insects, think there are several reasons for the pests' return. ⁶One reason is the change in how bugs in general are controlled. ⁷DDT, once the pesticide of choice, is now prohibited, and less strong substances are used against pests like the bed bug. ⁸Unfortunately bed bugs, like roaches, are hardy creatures, and the less toxic pesticides are not killing them off as the older, more lethal chemicals did. ⁹Then, too, pest control companies, worried about the effect on humans, are spraying more carefully. ¹⁰They don't spray whole rooms unless they absolutely have to, preferring to focus on specific locations. ¹¹People also travel much more than they used to and bed bugs can easily hop a ride in luggage or clothing, spreading from place to place. (Source of information: http://news .yahoo.com/s/ap/20060807/ap_on_re_ us/bedbugs_are_back_4.)

Topic a. DDT

b. pesticides

c. bed bugs

d. the effects of pesticides on humans

Main Idea a. If exterminators would start using DDT again, we wouldn't have a problem with bed bugs.

b. Bed bugs are a sure sign that a hotel or home has not been regularly cleaned.

c. Bed bugs are once again a common problem.

d. Bed bugs have been able to make a comeback because people travel so much more than they used to.

Topic Sentence _____

9. ¹When you hear the word *conflict*, what do you think? ²If you are fairly typical, your list includes such terms as "fight," "dissension," "friction," "strife," and "confrontation." ³These terms all tend to be

negative and many of us have been taught to think of conflict as a totally negative experience—something to be avoided at all costs. [4]Yet in truth, conflict is a natural process that can be negative or positive, depending on how it is used. [5]The Chinese symbol for conflict or crisis is made up of two components. [6]The top half of the symbol means "danger" and the bottom half means "opportunity." [7]Most people recognize the danger in a crisis or conflict, but few recognize the opportunity. [8]Conflict can bring people together, stimulate personal growth, or inspire new solutions to old problems. (Adapted from Berko et al., *Communicating*, p. 179.)

Topic   a. the Chinese view of conflict

       b. negative experience involving conflict

       c. the two meanings of conflict

       d. conflict situations

Main Idea   a. Conflict can be beneficial or damaging; it depends on the situation.

       b. Positive conflict is very different from negative conflict.

       c. The Chinese consider conflict to be a good experience.

       d. Conflict tends to bring people together.

Topic Sentence _____

10. [1]Tejano music originated in the Rio Grande Valley sometime in the late 1800s. [2]Instrumentally it relies on the accordion, while rhythmically it mixes polkas with waltzes. [3]Although initially Tejano music was beloved mainly by working-class Mexican Americans, its appeal has widened over the years. [4]Yearly album sales are now more than 20 million, and sales are not limited to people of Mexican origin. [5]Radio stations in both Europe and Japan regularly feature Tejano music. [6]In part, Tejano music has widened its appeal because Latino culture in general has finally "arrived" in the United States, thanks to the fantastic success of entertainers like Ricky Martin, Marc Anthony, and Christina Aguilera. [7]But another, more tragic reason for the spread of Tejano music was the 1995 death of the entertainer Selena Quintanilla Perez at the age of twenty-three. [8]Killed by an obsessed fan, Selena was known as the queen of Tejano music, and her untimely death drew the public's attention to the songs she made famous. [9]As a result, Tejano music began finding its way into mainstream radio stations and even into mainstream advertisements, like the beer ad that features "Heavy Metal Tejano."

Topic   a. music

b. Selena

c. Tejano music

d. the accordion in Tejano music

Main Idea   a. Thanks to the success of Latino entertainers like Ricky Martin and Christina Aguilera, Tejano music has become widely known.

b. The death of Selena revealed the darkness often hidden behind the bright lights of fame.

c. Over the years, Tejano music has become popular with a wide and varied audience.

d. Selena is solely responsible for the success of Tejano music.

Topic Sentence _____

Check Your Understanding

1. What's the topic?

_____

_____

_____

2. What's the difference between the topic and the main idea of a paragraph?

_____

_____

_____

_____

3. What's the difference between the main idea and the topic sentence?

_____

_____

_____

_____

 # Paraphrasing Topic Sentences

Right after you finish reading a paragraph, it's easy to assume you've understood it because the author's words are still fresh in your memory. However, the real test of your understanding is whether you are able to **paraphrase** the topic sentence. To paraphrase means to express someone else's ideas in your own words.* If you can express the topic sentence in words of your own, you can be sure that you've understood the paragraph.

Accurate and Inaccurate Paraphrasing

For an illustration of accurate and inaccurate paraphrasing, compare the following passages:

Original In a study at the University of Pittsburgh, researchers tried to explain why underachievers, people who don't live up to their ability, are more likely to fail than achievers. According to the study, underachievers fail because they lack persistence in the face of a challenge.

Accurate Paraphrase Researchers at the University of Pittsburgh have been trying to discover why some people don't live up to their ability while others do; the results of their research suggest that underachievers are more likely to give up when faced with obstacles.

The paraphrase is accurate because it uses different language to say the same thing the author says. That is, both the original and the paraphrase contain the same two ideas: (1) that researchers conducted a study of underachievers, and (2) that some people don't achieve because they give up in the face of a challenge.

Let's look now at an example of an inaccurate paraphrase:

Inaccurate Paraphrase A researcher at the University of Pennsylvania has been studying underachievers. His research suggests that underachievers fear failure and therefore give up too easily.

The author of this paraphrase didn't pay close attention to the original passage. The original's "researchers" has become a single person. Even the location of the study has changed. The author of the inaccurate paraphrase has also invented a reason why underachievers give up: they fear failure. Fear of failure may well be why

---

*You should have also learned that paraphrasing someone else's ideas does not free you from the need to cite your sources.

underachievers give up, but that idea is not part of the original passage.

Now read the following group of passages. The first one is the original text. The original is followed by an accurate and an inaccurate paraphrase. Once you have read all three, put an *A* in the blank next to the paraphrase you consider accurate and an *I* next to the one you consider inaccurate.

Original

Executive Order 11246, enacted in 1965, prohibits job discrimination by employers holding federal contracts or subcontracts on the basis of race, color, sex, national origin, or religion.

Paraphrase 1

The 1965 Executive Order 11246 forbids employers with federal contracts to engage in discriminatory practices based on race, color, sex, ethnic background, or religious belief. _____

Paraphrase 2

The government strictly forbids all employers from engaging in discrimination. Employers may not discriminate on the basis of age, race, color, gender, ethnic background, or religious faith. _____

If you put an *A* next to paraphrase 1 and an *I* next to paraphrase 2, you made the right decision. The original text identifies a particular piece of legislation forbidding discrimination. It doesn't refer to the government in general as paraphrase 2 does. Equally important, the second paraphrase fails to be specific about *when* employers begin to face government sanctions for discrimination. The 1965 Executive Order does not take into account *all* employers; it refers only to those who hold government contracts. Paraphrase 2 completely misses that point. It suggests that all employers are affected by Executive Order 11246. The second paraphrase claims that the executive order takes into account discrimination on the basis of age. It doesn't. Overall, the second paraphrase has broken the cardinal rule of paraphrasing: Change the words, but leave the meaning intact.

Paraphrasing Pitfalls

To paraphrase accurately you need to start (1) with a clear understanding of the author's original thought. (2) Then you need to replace the author's words with your own without changing the original meaning. Mistakes in paraphrasing occur when a reader fails one of these requirements.

The author of paraphrase 2, for instance, must have read the original too quickly. She didn't notice that the executive order applies only to a specific group of employers. She was similarly careless in her word choice. For instance, she replaces the word *sex* with the word *gender.* In fact, the original uses the more general word *sex*, in order to take into account discrimination on the basis of sexual preference. The word *gender* is too specific. It refers only to being male or female. Because the word *gender* leaves out the notion of sexual preference, or orientation,* it was a poor choice for a paraphrase.

Adapt Your Paraphrasing to the Material

The amount you paraphrase varies with the material. If your assignment focuses on a familiar subject, and the author's style is easy to read, you might paraphrase the topic sentence and a few specific details for just a few paragraphs. However, when faced with a hard-to-read assignment, you probably need to paraphrase more frequently, perhaps every other paragraph. Like so much else in reading, the amount you paraphrase depends on the particular text. No single rule applies.

 # A Two-Step Method for Paraphrasing Complex Ideas

If you are reading uncomplicated material with which you are fairly familiar, your ability to paraphrase the main idea might seem automatic. You just seem to know, without much thought, exactly how to rephrase the author's language. But as the text becomes more complicated, coming up with a paraphrase might take a little more time and effort. The effort and time, however, aren't wasted because you will also be giving your brain a chance to thoroughly process the information and store it in long-term memory.

_____
*orientation: natural inclination or leaning.

When you encounter paragraphs where you think you know the main idea but are having difficulty coming up with a paraphrase, consider this two-step method. It will sharpen your understanding of the material and supply you with an accurate paraphrase.

Step 1: Identify Agents and Actions

Paraphrasing in chunks, or groups of words, is easier and quicker than trying to paraphrase each word individually. You can start chunking information by breaking a sentence into two parts, the agent(s) and the action(s).* The *agent* is the person, idea, event, or institution essential to the activity or condition mentioned. The *action* is the activity performed or the condition described. Take, for instance, this sentence: "To fully understand the multiple meanings associated with the word *dude,* a linguist from the University of Pittsburgh, Scott Kiesling, taped conversations with members of fraternities; he also had undergraduates write down how the word was used over a three-day period." Reducing that sentence to the agent and actions produces a paraphrase like this one:

agent   **action**

Linguist Scott Kiesling / made tapes of fraternity members' speech and told undergraduates to record use of the word *dude* during a seventy-two-hour period.

Step 2: Add Key Details

If your paraphrase of just the agents and actions doesn't quite sum up the paragraph (and it often won't), you have probably left out a key detail that identifies any one of these sentence elements: (1) location of the action, (2) background or qualifications of the actor, (3) reason or motivation for the action, (4) time or consequences of the action. What's missing in the above paraphrase is the motivation for Kiesling's actions. Add that detail and we have an accurate paraphrase: "In order to determine the various meanings connected to using the word *dude,* linguist Scott Kiesling made tapes of fraternity members' speech and told undergraduates to record use of the word *dude* during a seventy-two hour period."

Reading versus Writing Paraphrases

Paraphrasing for a term paper requires that you be as exact and complete as possible. However, you don't need to be quite so complete

---

*I have adapted the terms to my purposes, but the idea of *agents* and *actions* comes from a fine book by Joseph M. Williams, *Style: Ten Lessons in Clarity and Grace.*

when you are paraphrasing purely to monitor your own comprehension. For instance, if you paraphrased the text on discrimination (page 179) while reading, you might well have come up with something like this: "Executive Order 11246 forbids federally employed contractors from engaging in discrimination on the basis of race, color, sex, and so on." That's fine. To monitor your comprehension, you don't need every detail.

When you take notes or paraphrase for a paper, though, you need to be more precise and account for almost all descriptive details. Thus, a paraphrase written for a paper might look something like this: "Executive Order 11246, enacted in 1965, prohibits employers with government contracts from discriminating against employees because of their religion, race, sex, or ethnic origin."

■ EXERCISE 7 Recognizing an Accurate Paraphrase

DIRECTIONS Read each paragraph, paying special attention to the underlined topic sentence(s). Then circle the letter of the more accurate paraphrase.

EXAMPLE [1]A brief nap is nothing unusual for employees working at Sprint's operation center in Phoenix. [2]Sprint's management encourages napping. [3]This might seem odd given that most U.S. employers take the opposite view: Napping on the job is grounds for dismissal. *Topic Sentence* [4]Sprint, however, might well be on to something, because a good deal of research has confirmed the benefits of power napping. [5]One Harvard University study, for instance, found that after napping on the job for an hour, an employee can perform nearly as well at the end of the workday as at the beginning. [6]An earlier Japanese study reported that a twenty-minute nap improves employee performance. [7]Moreover, the National Sleep Foundation cautions that lack of sleep can take a high toll, leading to errors and accidents on the job as well as absenteeism. [8]This also suggests that naps on the job might be a good thing.

Accurate Paraphrase a. Sleeping on the job is not a bad thing at all; in fact, studies have proven that it is good for business.

b. Because some studies suggest that napping while at work offers some advantages, Sprint may be right to encourage napping at work.

EXPLANATION Sentence *a* won't do because the word *sleeping* is too general as a paraphrase of *napping*. Naps are brief. The word *sleeping* could mean anything from a brief nap to an eight-hour snooze. Studies have shown that quick naps—not sleeping on the job—are good for business.

1. [1]Until the start of the twentieth century, it was assumed the U.S. Supreme Court would never get involved in state criminal trials. [2]However, in 1907 the Supreme Court set a new precedent when it intervened on behalf of Ed Johnson, a black man who had been unfairly convicted of rape and sentenced to death in Chattanooga, Tennessee. [3]Even though several witnesses placed Johnson miles away from the scene of the crime, an all-white jury found him guilty. [4]After hearing about Johnson's unjust conviction, a black lawyer named Noah Parden decided to take the case before the Supreme Court. [5]To everyone's surprise, the court ordered a stay of execution and a new trial. [6]In defiance of the court, the sheriff of Chattanooga, Joseph Shipp, a Ku Klux Klan member, allowed Johnson to be lynched, incorrectly assuming that the Supreme Court would not punish him for flouting* its orders. [7]But when the court learned about Shipp's role in the lynching, the justices tried the sheriff for contempt. [8]Although Joseph Shipp got off with a light sentence, from 1907 on it was clear that the Supreme Court of the United States could and would intervene in state criminal trials.

Accurate
Paraphrase

a. Noah Parden's courageous decision to take Ed Johnson's case before the Supreme Court was a huge civil rights victory.

b. By intervening in the case of Ed Johnson, the Supreme Court set an example: When necessary, it would involve itself in state criminal trials.

2. [1]Despite being hunted every fall, deer are not on the endangered list. [2]Actually, for a number of reasons, the wild deer population in the United States is skyrocketing. [3]Hunting regulations, including hunting bans and strict limits on the number of deer killed, have allowed the animals to thrive. [4]The rate of deer reproduction, too, has contributed to the growing population. [5]One doe usually gives birth to twins every year. [6]Furthermore, reduced numbers of natural predators such as wolves, along with a series of mild winters, have resulted in a lower mortality, or death, rate. [7]Deer have also managed to adapt successfully to human destruction of their habitats.* [8]Even when forests are cut down, deer manage to find enough food and shelter in the remaining vegetation. [9]They also boldly venture into suburbs and snack on tasty garden vegetables and flowers. [10]Because hungry deer can ruin gardens and wipe out plant species, some suburban residents have begun to look more favorably on hunting as a way of keeping the deer population under control.

---

*flouting: showing contempt for or disregarding, commonly confused with *flaunting*, or showing off.

*habitats: living spaces for specific species.

Accurate a. The wild deer population is on the rise mainly due to restrictions
Paraphrase   placed on hunters.

   b. Several factors have contributed to the growing number of wild
       deer.

-▪ EXERCISE 8 Recognizing an Accurate Paraphrase

DIRECTIONS Read each paragraph, paying special attention to the underlined topic sentence. Then circle the letter of the most accurate paraphrase.

1. ^{1}Western visitors to India are often astonished to see stray cows wandering in public places. ^{2}In some areas, cows wander in and out of markets or browse in carefully cultivated gardens, an apparent nuisance to the local populace. ^{3}<u>But for devotees* of Hinduism, cows are never an annoyance; they are held sacred and their presence encouraged.</u> ^{4}In Hindu populated regions of the country, cows are free to gather at the edges of highways even if they occasionally cause traffic snarls. ^{5}Cows are also permitted to wander into the middle of busy intersections, along railroad tracks, and munch on park grass (grass is a staple* of their diet). ^{6}Hindus decorate young cows with garlands of flowers and bring the animals offerings of food. ^{7}Older cows are well taken care of as well. ^{8}They are boarded in homes especially designed for aging bovines.

Accurate a. In India, Hindus treat cows as holy animals and would not dare
Paraphrase   chase the animals away from public places.

   b. Everywhere in India, cows are worshipped like gods.

   c. Westerners are usually dumbfounded by the way cows in India
       casually wander in and out of public places.

2. ^{1}Microbats, the small, insect-eating bats found in North America, have tiny eyes that don't look like they'd be useful to predators navigating in the dark and spotting prey. ^{2}<u>Instead the nocturnal* habits of bats are aided by their powers of *echolocation*, a special ability that makes feeding and flying at night easier than one might think.</u> ^{3}To navigate in the dark, a microbat flies with its mouth open, emitting high-pitched squeaks that humans cannot hear. ^{4}Some of these

---

*devotees: followers.
*staple: essential element.
*nocturnal: nighttime.

sounds echo off flying insects as well as tree branches and other obstacles that lie ahead. [5]The bat listens to the echo and gets an instantaneous mental picture of the object in front of it. [6]From the use of echolocation, or sonar, as it is also called, a microbat can tell a great deal about a mosquito or any other potential meal. [7]With extreme exactness, echolocation allows microbats to perceive motion, distance, speed, movement, and shape. [8]Thanks to echolocation, bats can also detect and avoid obstacles no thicker than a human hair. (Adapted from Pringle, *Batman: Exploring the World of Bats*, pp. 11–12.)

Accurate Paraphrase

a. Thanks to echolocation, bats have superior vision.

b. Echolocation is one of the prime reasons why bats can fly and feed at night.

c. The tiny eyes of microbats are actually very powerful, and they can see better than almost all other nocturnal animals.

■ EXERCISE 9   Recognizing an Accurate Paraphrase

DIRECTIONS Read each paragraph. Circle the correct letter to identify the topic, and write the number of the topic sentence in the blank. Then circle the letter of the most accurate paraphrase.

EXAMPLE [1]Between 1924 and 1933, research on worker productivity* was conducted at Western Electric's plant in Hawthorne, Illinois. [2]The results of the research suggested that productivity would increase anytime workers were the subject of a study, and it didn't much matter which specific workplace conditions were altered. [3]This notion—that workers responded more to attention than to changes in the workplace—came to be known as the "Hawthorne Effect," and in the years since the research was conducted, countless psychology and sociology texts have cited the Hawthorne Effect as if it were a fact. [4]However, as Gina Kolata pointed out in a *New York Times* article, "Scientific Myths That Are Too Good to Die," the Hawthorne Effect is not based on what most scientists would consider good experimental technique; on the contrary, it's an interpretation based on absurdly slim evidence. [5]Only five workers participated in the original study, and two of the five had to be replaced before the study came to an end. [6]This means that the research sample consisted of three people. [7]Even more revealing, though, is the fact that a 1989 examination of eighty-six workplace studies failed to confirm the Hawthorne Effect's existence.

---

*productivity: ability to produce goods.

Topic   a. Gina Kolata

       b. workplace experiments

       (c.) the Hawthorne Effect

Topic Sentence   4

Accurate a. The term "Hawthorne Effect" describes an interesting phenome-
Paraphrase   non: Employee productivity increases any time employees are
          placed under observation.

       (b.) The Hawthorne Effect is based on inadequate scientific evidence
          and probably does not exist.

       c. The Hawthorne Effect was the result of a scientific hoax.

       d. Being the subject of a study has no effect on employees' pro-
          ductivity.

EXPLANATION The first three sentences in the paragraph introduce the Hawthorne Effect, which is the topic of the paragraph. The point of the paragraph comes in sentence 4. Sentence 4 is the topic sentence because it is further explained by the more specific sentences that follow. The most accurate paraphrase of sentence 4 is sentence *b*, which also stresses the lack of evidence for the existence of the Hawthorne Effect.

1. [1]Scientists have long known that some animals use tools. [2]Chimpanzees, for example, use sticks to catch insects, and otters pry open shells with rocks. [3]Recently, though, researchers discovered that some bottlenose dolphins in western Australia use tools to search for food. [4]Before the dolphins root around the ocean floor to find prey hiding in the sand, they stick sea sponges on their snouts. [5]Wearing the sponges allows the dolphins to locate prey they wouldn't otherwise be able to find without the risk of injury. [6]The sponges function as gloves, protecting the dolphins' sensitive skin from hidden dangers, such as poisonous stonefish and stingrays. [7]This behavior, scientists believe, is not instinctive. [8]Rather, the dolphins have learned how to use the sponges, and they pass this knowledge on to their offspring. (Source of information: Liz Szabo, "Dolphins Teach Offspring to Use Tools," *USA Today*, June 7, 2005, p. 9D.)

Topic a. animals that use tools

      (b.) dolphins using tools

      c. sea sponges

Topic Sentence   3

Accurate   a. Dolphins are among the most intelligent of animals. They are
Paraphrase   more intelligent even than chimpanzees.

     b. There's evidence that Australian bottlenose dolphins employ tools when hunting for food.

     c. Unlike chimpanzees, who use sticks to get food, dolphins use sponges.

     d. Dolphins spend a long time teaching their young how to get food.

2. [1]Although the Clean Water Act has been justly credited for improving the condition of the waters in the United States, many lakes, streams, and rivers in the United States still suffer from high levels of toxic pollutants. [2]Among the serious threats posed by water pollutants are respiratory irritation, cancer, kidney and liver damage, anemia, and heart failure. [3]Toxic pollutants also damage fish and other forms of wildlife. [4]In fish they cause tumors or reproductive problems; shellfish and wildlife living in or drinking from toxin-infested waters also develop genetic* defects. (Adapted from Pride et al., *Business*, p. 57.)

Topic   a. Clean Water Act

     b. threatened wildlife

     c. pollutants in water

Topic Sentence _____

Accurate   a. Birth defects among fish is another indication of polluted water.
Paraphrase   b. Thanks to the Clean Water Act, our drinking supply is no longer in danger.

     c. Water sources in the U.S. are still under threat of being polluted.

     d. Polluted water is a main cause of cancerous tumors and birth defects.

3. [1]While making the 1996 hit movie *Evita*, the pop diva Madonna claimed to feel kinship with and admiration for Eva Perón, once one of the most powerful women in Latin America. [2]But Madonna might want to think twice before paying homage* to the wife of Argentinean dictator Juan Perón; glamorous as Maria Eva Duarte (1919–1952) was, she was hardly a role model. [3]Nicknamed "Evita" by the people who loved her, Evita Perón said all the right things about helping

---

*genetic: having to do with biological inheritance.
*homage: show of respect.

the poor and the downtrodden, but her devotion rarely went beyond showing gestures, designed to polish her image as a modern-day saint. [4]As the wife of the president, Evita traveled the country handing out small sums of money to anyone who reached out a hand. [5]Warmed by such seeming generosity, the poor of Argentina did not begrudge Evita the much larger sums of money she spent on clothes, jewelry, and travel abroad. [6]Fond of starting spectacular housing and health projects that were dedicated to helping the poor, Evita usually lost interest in the projects before they reached completion. [7]Nevertheless, her personal charm seemed to protect her from the anger of those she disappointed. [8]For that matter, her beauty and charm still seem to enchant. [9]Even today many people insist, despite all evidence to the contrary, that she was an early feminist and generous philanthropist.

Topic a. Madonna

b. Evita Perón's true character

c. Evita Perón's generosity

Topic Sentence _____

Accurate Paraphrase

a. Like many pop idols, Madonna adopts causes she doesn't really understand.

b. Evita Perón used her beauty and charm to claw her way to the heights of political power.

c. Evita Perón is still beloved by people all over the world.

d. Evita Perón, for all her glamour and power, was not someone to be imitated or admired.

4. [1]Video game players made *Grand Theft Auto* the top-selling game of 2001. [2]Since then, subsequent versions of the game have won awards and critical acclaim. [3]However, because of its violent and sexual content, *Grand Theft Auto* has also generated controversy. [4]Assuming the role of criminal in a big city, a *Grand Theft Auto* player robs banks, sells drugs, commits arson, and assassinates city officials and civilians. [5]Characters commit these crimes with only minor, temporary consequences and are rewarded with cash. [6]In *Grand Theft Auto III*, one mission requires the player to steal a car, have sex with a prostitute, and take her money after murdering her. [7]That same version created additional uproar when it was discovered that players could download online information giving them access to secret, graphic* sex scenes. [8]This kind of content, insisted the

_____

*graphic: vivid and obvious.

game's critics, encourage young people to engage in real-life socio-pathic* behavior; consequently, the United States prohibited anyone under seventeen from buying it, while Australia banned the game altogether. [9]Several car thieves and murderers arrested in America have claimed that the game instigated* their crimes, leading to law-suits against the game's publisher. ("Grand Theft Auto," Wikipedia, http://en.wikipedia.org/wiki/Grand_Theft_Auto_%28 series%29.)

Topic a. *Grand Theft Auto III*

b. controversy over *Grand Theft Auto*

c. violent video games

Topic Sentence ____

Accurate Paraphrase a. Despite its popularity, the video game *Grand Theft Auto* has many critics who detest the game's emphasis on violent crime.

b. Critically successful, *Grand Theft Auto* has also been a financial success, a fact that has aroused envy among its competitors.

c. *Grand Theft Auto* has been shown to encourage crime, and for that reason alone, it should be banned.

d. *Grand Theft Auto* may well be the most popular video game ever created.

5. [1]Although Latin American telenovelas resemble American soap operas in some ways, there are noticeable differences between the two types of melodrama.* [2]Both are highly dramatic, fictional television serials that focus on personal relationships. [3]However, the American soap opera is designed to continue indefinitely; in fact, some of them, such as *As the World Turns* and *The Guiding Light,* have endured for decades. [4]Soap opera writers make up the stories as they go along while individual cast members come and go with time. [5]In contrast, a telenovela usually lasts only six months to a year, and the show's creators know the entire story from the beginning. [6]Telenovela and soap opera story lines differ not only in their duration but also in their focus. [7]While soap operas explore the problems of families and include a number of different and ever-changing plots, telenovelas usually focus on one romantic relationship. [8]The most popular telenovela plot centers on a rich, handsome man who breaks up with his wealthy but evil girlfriend to be with a

---

*sociopathic: lacking all moral or ethical sense.
*instigated: caused, motivated.
*melodrama: highly sensational and emotional dramatic presentation.

poor, beautiful, and kind-hearted heroine. [9]The evil girlfriend and the man's relatives do their best to separate the lovers, but the climactic ending usually sees the villains punished in violent, painful, even gory ways.[10]The hero and the heroine, of course, get married. [11]Soap operas, which are broadcast in the afternoons, are designed to appeal mostly to women; telenovelas, on the other hand, are aired during prime time and attract a much broader and more varied audience. (Source of information: Anthony LaPastina, "Telenovela," The Museum of Broadcast Communications, www.museum.tv/ archives/etv/T/htmlT/telenovela/telenovela.htm.)

Topic a. telenovelas

  b. soap operas

  c. the similarities and differences between telenovelas and soap operas

Topic Sentence _____

Accurate a. Although there are some similarities between soap operas and
Paraphrase   telenovelas, the two also differ a good deal.

  b. Telenovelas have a much wider audience than soap operas do.

  c. Soap operas are a staple of afternoon television, whereas telenovelas are part of prime time.

  d. Telenovelas are the Latin American version of American soap operas.

⊏ EXERCISE 10 Identifying and Paraphrasing Topic Sentences

DIRECTIONS Identify the topic of the paragraph, and write the number of the topic sentence in the blank. Then paraphrase that topic sentence.

EXAMPLE [1]Whether military or civilian, most professional training programs stress the value of self-confidence. [2]Believe in yourself and you will succeed. [3]Yet, in some cases, the opposite is true. [4]There are people whose success stems not from self-confidence but from feelings of failure. [5]Feeling inadequate, these people push themselves hard, forcing themselves to achieve. [6]In this way, failure becomes, paradoxically,* a source of success. [7]At least this was the view of the famed writer and critic Edmund Wilson. [8]As examples of his theory, Wilson cited the philosopher Karl Marx and the

---

*paradoxically: ideas or events seemingly in contradiction, but actually making sense or fitting together.

poet Edna St. Vincent Millay, two people driven to succeed by their feelings of inadequacy and failure.

Topic _Success and fear of failure_

Topic Sentence ___4___

Paraphrase _Fear of failure sometimes drives people to succeed._

EXPLANATION The topic is "success and fear of failure." That's the subject to which the author repeatedly refers. Sentence 4 is the topic sentence because it's the only sentence that sums up the point of the paragraph. As it should, the paraphrase uses different words to make the same point as the topic sentence.

1. ¹Early efforts at developing artificial intelligence (AI) focused on the computer's capabilities for formal reasoning, symbol manipulation, and problem solving. ²Valuable as it is, this logic-based approach to AI has limitations. ³For one thing, expert systems are successful only in narrowly defined fields. ⁴And even then computers show limited ability. ⁵That's because there is no way of putting into computer code all aspects of expert human reasoning. ⁶Sometimes, even the experts can only say, "I know it when I see it, but I can't put it into words." ⁷Second, the vital ability to draw analogies* and make other connections is still beyond the grasp of current computer systems. ⁸Finally, logic-based AI systems depend on "if-then" rules and it is often difficult to tell a computer how to recognize an "if," or under what circumstances, condition in the real world. (Adapted from Bernstein, *Psychology*, p. 299.)

Topic _____

Topic Sentence _2_

Paraphrase _____

_____

2. ¹When it was a republic of the Soviet Union,* Ukraine was sometimes called "Little Russia" or "The Breadbasket of the Soviet Union."

---

*analogies: comparisons between two unlike things that share a similar function, position, or process, suggesting that two things alike in some respect are alike in others.
*Soviet Union: Before the fall of communism in Eastern Europe, this was the common name for Russia and the countries directly under the control of the Russian government.

[2]To the Ukrainians, the nickname must have seemed a cruel joke, given their sufferings under Russian rule. [3]No wonder that the current president of Ukraine, Viktor Yushchenko, is determined to bring attention to the Soviet-created famine that killed millions of Ukrainians between 1931 and 1933, when the Russian dictator Josef Stalin ordered the confiscation of grain. [4]Although the Russians' own agricultural system was in chaos and underproductive, Stalin had another reason for his demand: He wanted to break the rebellious spirit of Ukrainian farmers, who were refusing to participate in his plan for collective farming. [5]Under Stalin's systematic collection of Ukrainian grain and livestock, millions of Ukrainians starved to death. [6]Some even resorted to cannibalism to survive. [7]In a speech given in November of 2005, Yushchenko pressed his case for the United Nations to declare the famine genocide—a conscious plan to destroy the Ukrainian population.

Topic _____

Topic Sentence ~~3~~ ____

Paraphrase _____

_____

3. [1]In his book *Influence*, writer and researcher Robert Cialdini opens with a confession: "I can admit it freely now. [2]All my life I've been timid about asserting myself." [3]Cialdini is not alone. [4]Many people find it difficult to be assertive in interpersonal situations. [5]Faced with an unreasonable request from a friend, spouse, or stranger, they become anxious at the mere thought of putting a foot down and refusing to comply. [6]Indeed, there are times when it is uncomfortable for anyone to say no, and we probably all need a little assertiveness training. (Adapted from Brehm et al., *Social Psychology*, p. 248.)

Topic _Lack being assertive_____

Topic Sentence _4____

Paraphrase _interpersonal situation can make it hard to be assertive_____

4. [1]Few changes accompanying puberty are as explosive for families as the adolescent's increased interest in sex. [2]Still, anthropological* evidence indicates that the majority of cultures tend to permit or at

_____
*anthropological: related to the study of human cultures.

least tolerate some sexual activity during the teenage years. [3]Western societies, however, have generally been more restrictive about sexual expression among teenagers and therefore are slow to recognize its reality. [4]For instance, research suggests that many mothers in the United States underestimate the sexual activity of their children. [5]The children, in turn, tend to underestimate the degree to which their parents disapprove of such activity (Jaccard, Dittus, and Gordon, 1998). [6]Whatever the misunderstandings on either side, it is simply true that large numbers of teenagers are sexually active at an early age. [7]One study reports that 30 percent of the students entering sixth grade in a large urban city had already engaged in sexual intercourse (Kinsman et al., 1998). [8]Levels of sexual activity similar to those found in the United States are also reported in other Western nations. (Adapted from Bukatko and Daehler, *Child Development*, p. 183.)

Topic *adolescents*

Topic Sentence *3*

Paraphrase _____

_____

■ DIGGING DEEPER

JURY DODGERS BEWARE!

LOOKING AHEAD As the paragraph on page 156 explained, some citizens take jury duty very seriously, while others throw away their notices to report. As the following reading suggests, those who shirk jury duty might want to rethink their attitude.

1 Recently, in Passaic County, New Jersey, fourteen citizens were collected by the sheriff's department and brought before a judge at the county courthouse. Their offense? Refusing to respond to multiple notices to report for service as jurors. Their punishment? Fines up to $500 and assignment to jury duty.

2   The keystone of the U.S. justice system is the right to a trial by a jury of one's peers. Recently, however, many courts have experienced serious problems in getting people to perform their civic duty. Only one out of four adults have served as jurors, and jury avoidance is at an all-time high level. It is not uncommon for trials to be delayed because too few jurors are available.

3   Most juries continue to number twelve individuals, although six are sometimes used. Most jury decisions must be unanimous—anything short of that leads to a hung jury and either retrial or dismissal. Potential jurors are summoned by the court for assignment to a jury pool. Jurors usually must be U.S. citizens eighteen years of age or older. Questioning by the judge, prosecuting attorney, and defense attorney—known as *voir dire*—disqualifies individuals with potential conflicts of interest, bias or other factors germane to the case. Once selected the juror may be required to give a day or two to service, or months for the occasional long, complex trial. Remuneration is minimal, ranging from $5 a day in California and New Jersey to $40 in South Dakota and New York.

4   Why has jury-dodging become a problem? First, some individuals suffer a loss of income from not being able to work. Employers may be required to keep employee-jurors on their payroll and are prohibited from firing them for serving jury duty, but abuses occur. For the self-employed, jury duty can be a serious hardship, as it can be for potential jurors with small children and no day care arrangement. Other burdens of jury duty include time spent away from one's job, family, or leisure activities. Jurors in tough criminal cases can suffer psychological disturbances. A relatively minor—but annoying—problem is the uninviting, uncomfortable surroundings of many jury waiting rooms.

5   All states have provisions for excusing or postponing service for people selected for duty, such as old age, disability, undue hardship, extreme inconvenience, military duty, and so on. For those who ignore their summons, judges may respond with a stick, like the Passaic County judge. In Grant County, Washington, two randomly picked jury scofflaws are regularly brought to answer before the judge. In North Dakota, New Jersey, and other states, they are reported in the local newspaper. A judge in Baltimore once placed nonreporting jurors in jail for several hours. A kinder approach is to improve the quality of jury duty by, for instance, installing computer work stations, libraries, and other amenities in the jury lounges.

6   Gradually, courts are incorporating information technology to create a cyberjuror. From basic touch-tone telephone systems to inform members of the jury pool whether they are going to be needed the next day, to on-line, twenty-four-hour interactive systems that qualify potential jurors by administering an electronic *voir dire,* make specific assignments, and process excuse and postponement requests. Postage savings alone can be substantial, and the new cyberjurors appreciate the convenience.

Adapted from Ann O. Bowman and Richard C. Kearney, *State and Local Government,* 5th ed. Boston: Houghton Mifflin, 2002, p. 260.

Sharpening Your Skills

DIRECTIONS Answer the questions by circling the letter of the correct response or filling in the blanks.

1. The topic of this reading is
   a. the right to trial by jury
   b. excuses for jury dodging
   c. the problem of jury dodgers
   d. cyberjuries

2. The overall main idea of the reading is
   a. Jury duty is the responsibility of all good citizens.
   b. Penalties for jury dodgers are becoming harsher because so many people have failed to do their duty.
   c. Brief jail terms are becoming a common punishment for jury dodgers who don't seem to understand the seriousness of their crime.
   d. The punishments and penalties for jury dodgers need to be increased.

3. Using your own words, paraphrase the definition for the term *voir dire*.

_____

4. Paragraph 2 has which shape?

a.

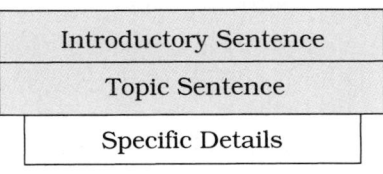

b.

c.

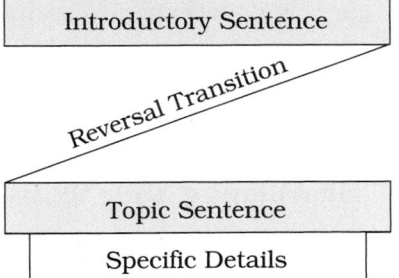

5. Based on the context, how would you define the words *germane* and *remuneration* in paragraph 3?

a. *Germane* means _____.

b. *Remuneration* means _____.

INTERNET RESOURCE

For more practice with main ideas and topic sentences, see **college.hmco.com/pic/flemmingRFR10e**, where you will find three levels of interactive quizzes: *Getting Down the Basics*, *Checking Your Progress*, and *Taking the Challenge*.

 ## Test 1: Identifying Topics and Topic Sentences

DIRECTIONS Read each paragraph. Circle the appropriate letter to identify the correct topic. Then write the number of the topic sentence in the blank.

1. [1]The widespread use of antibiotics began in the 1940s. [2]Since that time, some diseases—for example, tuberculosis—have developed strains of bacteria that are resistant to antibiotics. [3]Once a new strain appears, it can rapidly spread. [4]Scientists also fear that the overuse of antibiotics in both animals and humans has helped destroy other forms of bacteria that would normally control the newer and stronger strains. [5]Thus people are becoming more vulnerable to bacteria that cannot be effectively treated with existing antibiotics.

Topic   a. overuse of antibiotics

b. antibiotics

c. new diseases

Topic Sentence 5

2. [1]Prior to the 1970s, the environmental movement in the United States received relatively little attention or publicity. [2]But, for many people, the environmentalists became a force to be reckoned with* on April 22, 1970—the first Earth Day ever celebrated in the United States. [3]On that day, to the surprise of many, 20 million Americans gathered together to celebrate nature and protest environmental pollution. [4]The first Earth Day also drew attention to the public's desire for environmental legislation, which helped bring about the Federal Water Pollution Control Act (1972), the Endangered Species Act (1973), and several amendments to the Clean Air Act (1977).[5]Perhaps most importantly, Earth Day made lawmakers and politicians realize they had to take preservation of the environment seriously, because failure to do so would anger a large bloc of voters.

Topic   a. the first Earth Day

b. the Clean Water and Clean Air acts

c. the environmental movement

Topic Sentence _____

---

*reckoned with: considered, made aware of.

3. [1]Do you think that buying a new car will make you happy? [2]Are you convinced that marrying your current sweetheart will bring you all the happiness any one person could desire? [3]Well, according to Daniel Gilbert, a psychology professor at Harvard, whatever your prediction, it's probably wrong. [4]Gilbert, along with psychologist Tim Wilson of the University of Virginia and economist George Lowenstein of Carnegie Mellon University, has studied what's called "affective forecasting"—predicting how one will feel or behave if an event does or does not occur—and the results are pretty clear: People aren't very good at predicting how future events will affect them. [5]According to Gilbert, Lowenstein, and Wilson, their studies, conducted over several years, show that most of us consistently under- or overestimate the depth and intensity of our emotional reactions. [6]In other words, the things we think will overwhelm us with joy often don't. [7]By the same token, the things we assume will devastate us often faze us far less than we imagined.

Topic   a. happiness

b. predictions about effects of future events

c. studies by Tom Wilson, George Lowenstein, and Daniel Gilbert

Topic Sentence _____

4. [1]These days, we take spices such as cinnamon, nutmeg, and pepper for granted. [2]To obtain them, we need only head to the nearest supermarket. [3]In the fifteenth century, however, spices were a much sought-after treasure, bringing wealth and power to whoever could obtain them. [4]Thus, in 1497, King Manuel I of Portugal ordered the young navigator Vasco da Gama to find the shortest route between India and Europe. [5]With India a source of every possible spice from ginger to arrowroot, King Manuel knew he could feed the European appetite for spices and make a fortune in the process if da Gama accomplished his task. [6]Da Gama did find the shortest route between India and Europe, and, for a while at least, Portugal cornered the market on spices and became a world power.

Topic   a. Vasco da Gama's accomplishment

b. King Manuel I of Portugal

c. spices in the fifteenth century

Topic Sentence _____

5. [1]Those tricky computer wizards, called hackers,* have pulled off some astounding crimes over the years. [2]Hackers have gotten their kicks by breaking into computer systems, damaging files, and stealing information. [3]They have targeted phone companies and computer systems storing credit card numbers and other valuable information. [4]One of the most notorious hackers, Kevin D. Mitnick,* stole software valued at $1 million from the Digital Equipment Corporation. [5]Another infamous hacker, Robert Tappan Morris,* launched a program on the Internet that copied itself end-lessly, filling the memories of 6,000 computer systems—at the time, about one-tenth of the Internet. [7]Because of Morris's program, sys-tems crashed at major businesses, schools, the U.S. government, the Air Force, and NASA. [8]In one long-running hacker operation that went on between 1998 and 2001, Russian hackers downloaded millions of pages of sensitive data. [9]In 2002 U.S. federal authorities announced that they had cracked the case of an international hacker who broke into roughly 100 unclassified U.S. military net-works.

Topic   a. the Internet

        b. Kevin D. Mitnick

        c. computer hackers

Topic Sentence _____

---

*hackers: The term "hackers" refers to very skillful and devoted computer users. However, the term can have a positive or negative meaning depending on the context.
*Kevin D. Mitnick is now a security consultant. He specializes in helping busi-nesses learn how to keep hackers and other intruders out of their computers.
*Robert Tappan Morris created what is now known as the "Morris worm" while still a student at Cornell. He is now a professor at the Massachusetts Institute of Technology.

 **Test 2: Recognizing Topics and Topic Sentences**

DIRECTIONS Read each paragraph. Circle the appropriate letter to identify the correct topic. Then write the number of the topic sentence in the blank.

1. [1]In the early nineteenth century, many runaway slaves found refuge among Florida's Seminole Indians. [2]Outraged, the U.S. government ordered the Seminoles to leave Florida. [3]But Florida was their home, and they refused. [4]When Osceola, the Seminoles' fierce leader, received the government's order in 1832, he speared it with a dagger, announcing, "This is the only treaty I will make with the whites!" [5]These were not empty words. [6]In 1835, Osceola launched a full-scale rebellion against federal rule that lasted for seven years. [7]Although Osceola outwitted pursuers, he was captured in 1837. [8]Placed in prison, he died the following year. [9]The war, however, raged on. Convinced that Osceola had been murdered, the Seminoles were determined to avenge him. [10]Still, by 1842, even the memory of Osceola was not enough to fuel what had become a bloody and hopeless battle. [11]Defeated, the Seminoles were force-marched to Oklahoma.

Topic a. runaway slaves

b. the U.S. government's treatment of the Seminoles

c. Osceola's leadership of the Seminole rebellion

d. the Seminole Indians' aid to runaway slaves

Topic Sentence ____

2. [1]*Bulimia* is the Greek word for "hunger"; it's also the name of a serious, potentially life-threatening eating disorder that afflicts thousands of people. [2]The disease has numerous triggers, ranging from family conflict to depression, but no one is quite sure of its causes. [3]Victims of the disease are usually young women who engage in binge eating, consuming large quantities of food way past the point when their hunger is satisfied. [4]To avoid gaining weight, they then purge themselves of the food they've consumed. [5]Ninety percent of bulimics purge by vomiting. [6]Others use laxatives or enemas or refuse to eat for long periods of time. [7]Because these behaviors usually occur in secret, bulimic individuals—especially those who maintain an average weight—can be difficult to recognize. [8]Others, though, become alarmingly thin, shrinking to little more than skin

stretched over bones even as they continue to think they are too heavy. [9]Too often, their distorted self-image is fatal. [10]Even bulimics who manage to maintain a normal-looking appearance face severe health problems, including dehydration,* digestive system disorders, ulcers, kidney collapse, heart failure, and even death.

Topic a. eating disorders

b. bulimia

c. causes of bulimia

d. health problems

Topic Sentence _____

3. [1]Today's firefighters battle wildfires with a mixture of science, technology, and old-fashioned physical labor. [2]Some are accompanied by scientists who assist firefighters by tracking climactic changes that will affect the fire's spread. [3]Firefighters are also aided by specialists who study vegetation types and land features to predict the speed and direction of a fire's progress. [4]Technological advancements also help in the fight. [5]Global Positioning Systems can pinpoint the exact location and size of a fire while sophisticated aircraft track the fire, dropping fire-retardant chemicals and water from the sky. [6]Human muscle, though, is a third essential firefighting ingredient. [7]Crews armed with axes, saws, shovels, and hoses still work hard to deter and stop a fire by clearing brush and creating firebreaks by digging bushes and cutting down trees. [8]Modern firefighters use all of the weapons at their disposal—both the new advances and centuries-old techniques—to battle fire's destructive force.

Topic a. modern fire-fighting methods

b. wildfires

c. Global Positioning Systems

d. new technology for battling fires

Topic Sentence _____

4. [1]Daredevil skydivers leap from airplanes at great heights, trusting that training, good equipment, and favorable weather will carry them safely to the ground. [2]Still, skydiving successfully from, say,

_____

*dehydration: loss of fluids.

9,000 feet involves more than courage and luck; it requires real skill. [3]When a skydiver takes the plunge, he or she begins to free fall, traveling through the air with the parachute tightly packed and no way to control the speed. [4]A good skydiver, however, knows how to time the parachute's opening, allowing its dome-shaped canopy* to blossom into the air. [5]The canopy creates surface resistance and slows the diver's descent. [6]Then it's up to the diver to steer the rig to a landing by pulling on lines attached to the parachute. [7]A truly skillful skydiver also knows how to touch down on his or her feet. [8]Still, millions of landings have been made on the knees or other, more delicate, body parts.

Topic a. good and bad landings

b. daredevils

c. daredevil sports

d. skillful skydiving

Topic Sentence _____

5. [1]The white-tailed deer was one of the first animals to be protected by federal legislation. [2]But as it turns out, unlike the passenger pigeon, white-tailed deer were not in much need of protection. [3]They have proven to be highly adaptable creatures, and their population has not diminished despite the loss of wooded areas. [4]Like squirrels and robins, white-tailed deer have adapted quite nicely to life on the edge of suburbia. [5]In fact, they are happy to supplement their regular diets with fruits and vegetables from gardens. [6]In addition, many homeowners are fond of these gentle creatures and put out blocks of deer food that help the animals make it through harsh winters.

Topic a. the diet of white-tailed deer

b. life on the edge of suburbia

c. the survival of white-tailed deer

d. wildlife in the suburbs

Topic Sentence _____

---

*canopy: a cloth cover held or fastened over a person or an object.

 ## Test 3: Recognizing Topics, Topic Sentences, and Transitions

DIRECTIONS Read each paragraph. Circle the appropriate letter to identify the correct topic. Then write the number of the topic sentence in the blank. If the topic sentence is introduced by a reversal transition, circle or underline the transition.

1. [1]Many parents and educators consider the Internet a powerful tool for learning. [2]Others, though, are not so sure; these teachers and parents are concerned about the more than two hundred websites currently selling research papers to students, and they are determined to do something to correct the problem of Internet plagiarism. [3]Websites like CheatHouse, Paper Store, and Cheater sell papers on a variety of subjects, ranging from biology to poetry. [4]Although most of these sites include disclaimers* insisting that the papers are simply "models" along with warnings against plagiarism, it's hard to believe that anyone takes either disclaimer or warning seriously. [5]On the assumption that many students will be tempted to pay for a paper, two instructors at Coastal Carolina University, Margaret Fain and Peggy Bates, have created a list called "Cheating 101: Detecting Plagiarized Papers" (www.coastal.edu/library/presentations/plagiarz.html). [6]Websites like Plagiarism.org have also sprung up to tell teachers how they can spot a stolen term paper.

   Topic a. CheatHouse

   b. plagiarism

   c. the problem of Internet plagiarism

   d. the effects of the Internet on education

   Topic Sentence _____

2. [1]According to the National Center for Education Statistics, today's kids are more likely than kids of thirty years ago to attend college. [2]Now, about 63 percent of high school graduates enroll in some type of post-secondary education program; thirty years ago, only 10 percent of graduating seniors went on to further their education. [3]At the same time, fewer of today's young people are using drugs. [4]In 2002, 25 percent of high school seniors admitted to using an

---

*disclaimers: statements denying an intention, in this case, to encourage plagiarism.

illegal drug in the previous thirty days. [5]In contrast, 37 percent of seniors in 1979 and 1980 had used illegal drugs. [6]Fewer of today's youth are sexually active, too. [7]In 1991, 54 percent of high school students had had sex; by 2001, that number had fallen to 46 percent. [8]According to the Justice Policy Institute, today's young people are also less prone to commit violent crimes. [9]Between the early 1970s and 2000, the juvenile homicide arrest rate dropped 46 percent. [10]Despite all the media's moaning and groaning about the younger generation, the majority of today's kids are making better decisions than their predecessors and avoiding dangerous, risky behavior. (Source of information: Nick Gillespie, "Child Scare," *Washington Post*, May 4, 2003, page BW03, www .washingtonpost.com.)

Topic a. risky sexual behavior among teens

b. youth

c. kids committing violent crimes

d. kids today

Topic Sentence _____

3. [1]In 2005, a team of French surgeons performed a successful face transplant surgery on a thirty-eight-year-old woman, whose face had been savagely ripped apart by a dog. [2]Monstrously disfigured, unable to eat or speak, the woman's only hope was a face transplant to supply her with a new nose, lips, and chin. [3]During a fifteen-hour operation, a team of eight surgeons stitched donated facial tissue on to what was left of their patient's ravaged face. [4]When the operation ended, the doctors pronounced the results to be even better than they'd imagined. [5]With her new face that is a combination of her own and the donor's, the patient does not look as she had before the injury. [6]Nevertheless, the operation is a promising breakthrough for those disfigured by disease or injury. (Source of information: Emma Ross, "First Face Transplant Patient Recovering," Yahoo! News, December 2, 2005, http://news.yahoo .com/s/ap/20051202/ap_on_he_me/face_transplant.)

Topic a. transplants

b. the first successful face transplant

c. transplant surgeons

d. people who have been disfigured in accidents

Topic Sentence _____

4. [1]In the past, young South Koreans of marriageable age relied on their parents or a matchmaker to find them a suitable spouse. [2]But that's no longer the case for the current generation. [3]Nowadays, South Koreans in search of a mate are far more likely to turn to a computerized dating service. [4]Unlike dating services in other parts of the world, those in South Korea don't particularly concern themselves with romance. [5]Their goal is to bring together men and women who share the same social and economic backgrounds. [6]Dating services in South Korea also try to match couples according to the year in which they were born. [7]Tradition claims, for example, that a man born in the year of the monkey would not be happy with a woman born in the year of the tiger. [8]Thus, no respectable dating service would bring together two people born under such incompatible signs.

Topic a. dating services in South Korea

     b. romance in South Korea

     c. the decline of matchmaking in South Korea

     d. dating services

Topic Sentence _____

5. [1]Thirty years ago, scientists and engineers controlled much of the content on the Internet. [2]Today, though, the situation is very different. [3]Almost anyone with a computer can explore the Internet and discover a treasure trove* of bizarre information. [4]Spam lovers, for example, can read poems about their favorite luncheon meat on several websites created for that purpose. [5]If you've ever been furious when an electric can opener won't work, satisfaction is guaranteed on the Home Appliance Shooting site. [6]Here, a Web enthusiast named Daniel C. Benton presents video footage of toasters, blenders, microwaves, and the like as they are reduced to rubble by shotgun blasts and sledgehammer blows. [7]Other sites offer up-to-date information on alien autopsies, slime molds, guillotines, gap-toothed movie stars, and child stars gone astray.

Topic a. weird information found on the Internet

     b. Spam poems

     c. computer technology and the growth of the Internet

     d. the origins of the Internet

Topic Sentence _____

_____

*treasure trove: a collection of great value.

 **Test 4: Recognizing Accurate Paraphrases**

DIRECTIONS Read each paragraph and look carefully at the underlined topic sentence. Then circle the letter of the most accurate paraphrase.

1. [1]Almost as soon as the potato was introduced to Europe, the Irish made it a staple of their daily diet. [2]Historians have estimated, in fact, that at least half of Ireland's population relied on the potato for most of their nutritional needs, and an adult male typically consumed nine to eleven pounds of potatoes per day. [3]Consequently, Ireland was the country most affected when the potato blight* hit Europe in 1845. [4]In less than a year, hundreds of thousands of people died, and before the famine finally ended in 1852, close to a million had lost their lives. [5]Some starved to death. [6]Many more—especially children and the elderly—could not fight off infectious diseases, like typhoid fever and dysentery,* which wasted their already undernourished bodies. [7]Starving and sick, they usually ended up in the country's overflowing poorhouses, where visitors reported seeing skeletons in rags huddled together on filthy straw, moaning as they waited for death to release them from their misery. [8]Those who managed to stay alive faced a different kind of suffering. [9]Plagued by financial ruin, food riots, crime, and despair, many of Ireland's poor abandoned their homes and emigrated to other countries. [10]Some of them collapsed and died by the roadside as they tried to leave. [11]Others, fleeing to crowded, disease-ridden ships bound for places like America, Canada, and Australia, perished during the journey and were tossed into the sea. [12]It's been said that so many bodies were thrown overboard, ships were followed by packs of sharks waiting for their next meal. (Sources of information: Cormac O. Grada, "Ireland's Great Famine," *EH.Net Encyclopedia of Economic History,* edited by Robert Whaples, February 12, 2004, http://eh.net/encyclopedia/article/ograda .famine; "The Hunger Years," *Socialist Review,* Issue 189, September 1995, http://pubs.socialistreviewindex. org.uk/sr189/stack. htm.)

Paraphrase   a. After the potato arrived in Europe, it became the mainstay of the Irish diet.

b. When potatoes grew scarce during the 1845 blight, it was the Irish who suffered most.

c. Thousands died of starvation during Europe's potato blight.

---

*blight: disease.
*dysentery: an infection of the lower intestine.

2. [1]On September 1, 1914, a twenty-nine-year-old bird named Martha died in the Cincinnati Zoo. [2]Martha was the last known passenger pigeon in existence. [3]Yet in the nineteenth century, there were so many passenger pigeons in America that no attempt was made to protect them through legislation. [4]On the contrary, large-scale pigeon shoots were a popular sport. [5]Often the killing went on for days, mainly for the thrill of the kill, because the hunters' need for food had long been satisfied. [6]Throughout the nineteenth century, passenger pigeons also found it harder and harder to locate the wide and uninhabited tracts* of land they needed to raise their young. [7]By the beginning of the twentieth century, Martha the passenger pigeon was all that was left from the huge flocks that had once ranged over the United States, and with her death, the birds became extinct.

Paraphrase a. Martha's lonely, miserable life and death illustrate how horrible it is to confine animals in zoos.

b. At the start of the twentieth century, Martha was all that remained of the large flocks of passenger pigeons that had once darkened the American skies.

c. Martha the passenger pigeon is a good example of how wildlife fared in the early days of this country.

3. [1]By the time Elizabeth I became queen of England in 1558, her half-sister, Mary Tudor, had driven the country into chaos. [2]Mary, a Catholic, opposed the way her six-times-married father, Henry VIII, had broken away from the Catholic faith, so she started a new English church and attempted to force Catholicism on England. [3]She put non-Catholics on trial for heresy* and had some of them burned at the stake. [4]Protestants were forced to flee the country, and the queen became known as "Bloody Mary." [5]It was only after Mary died that peace again returned to England. (Armento et al., *Across the Centuries,* p. 459.)

Paraphrase a. Elizabeth I hated her half-sister Mary Tudor.

b. Mary Tudor resented her father's decision to break away from the Church.

c. When Elizabeth I took over England's throne in 1558, the country was in chaos, thanks to Elizabeth's half-sister, Mary Tudor.

---

*tracts: areas.
*heresy: failure to follow the laws of the Church.

4. [1]Relatives of the nineteenth-century bulldogs used for bull baiting and dog fights, pit bulls can be very scary dogs. [2]Confronted with a threat, most other dogs will stare, growl, bare their teeth, or display other warning signs, fighting only as a last resort. [3]Many pit bulls, however, will just attack without warning. [4]And when they do, they do not behave like German shepherds and other guard dogs that try to restrain their opponent by biting and holding. [5]Instead, pit bulls strike like sharks, clamping down, shaking their heads back and forth, and trying to tear flesh in order to injure and kill. [6]Because of the breed's high pain tolerance, pit bulls are the dog of choice for dog fights. [7]They are greatly prized by those who make money from the so-called "sport" of dog fighting, and their human owners encourage the dogs to be aggressive, punishing and mistreating them if they are not. [8]The timid pit bull—and such dogs do exist—purchased to make an owner money by winning dogfights is unlikely to have a very long life. [9]<u>While pit bulls are inclined to be somewhat aggressive by nature, it's greedy, abusive, and unscrupulous* owners who have made some pit bulls scary and dangerous.</u> (Source of information: Malcolm Gladwell, "Troublemakers," *The New Yorker,* February 6, 2006, www.newyorker.com/fact/content/articles/060206fa_fact.)

Paraphrase a. Pit bulls are aggressive by nature.

b. Inclined to be aggressive by nature, pit bulls can be tamed by gentle treatment.

c. Although pit bulls have been bred to be aggressive, it's abusive owners that make some dogs vicious and threatening.

_____

*unscrupulous: unethical.

 ## Test 5: Recognizing Accurate Paraphrases

DIRECTIONS Read each paragraph and write the number of the topic sentence in the blank. Then circle the letter of the most accurate paraphrase.

1. [1]Cocaine became an outlawed substance in 1914. [2]But, for centuries before that, cocaine was used for a variety of supposedly medicinal purposes. [3]Before the Spanish conquest of Peru, the coca plant was reserved for Inca* royalty, who used it in mystical rituals and celebrations. [4]By the sixteenth century, when Spanish explorers first began arriving in South America, the native inhabitants had a 5,000-year history of chewing coca leaves to fight fatigue and hunger and to increase endurance. [5]The Spanish conquistadors* introduced coca leaves to Europe, where they were smoked or ingested only occasionally until the nineteenth century. [6]In 1860, however, Germany's Albert Niemann isolated the coca plant's active ingredient and processed it into powder and liquid forms. [7]As a result, doctors began dispensing cocaine for a variety of ailments, from toothaches to hay fever. [8]They also used it as an anesthetic during surgery. [9]It wasn't long before cocaine was available over-the-counter and became an ingredient in cigarettes, chocolate, and wine. [10]In 1886, Atlanta surgeon and chemist John Pemberton introduced Coca-Cola, a drink that contained about 60 mg of cocaine and was advertised both as a cure for nervous afflictions and a tonic "offering the virtues of coca without the vices of alcohol." [11]Not until the turn of the century did the medical community begin to understand cocaine's addictive nature, which led to its being banned. (Source of information: "In Search of the Big Bang," www.cocaine.org.)

Topic Sentence _____

Paraphrase a. Because cocaine is a destructive and highly addictive substance, it should remain illegal.

b. Cocaine offers a number of medical benefits, but its dangers far outweigh any of its positive effects.

c. Cocaine should never have been made an illegal drug.

d. For hundreds of years before it was banned, cocaine was used and prescribed without fear of harm.

---

*Inca: Peruvian people who established an empire from Ecuador to central Chile.
*conquistadors: conquerors.

2. [1]We humans spend millions of dollars every year trying to rid ourselves of insects, but some of those annoying bugs are actually
essential to our survival. [2]Some insects, for instance, perform the
vital function of pollinating* flowering plants. [3]Without pollination,
crops could not reproduce. [4]Insects are also essential to maintaining the balance of nature, preventing the uncontrolled spread of vegetation. [5]In addition, diseases spread by insects keep wild animal
populations from growing out of control and destroying entire
ecosystems.* [6]Insects also dispose of animal remains and waste.
[7]Dung beetles, for instance, have prevented Australia's grazing lands
from being ruined by cattle droppings. [8]For some cultures, insects
serve as food with grubs, grasshoppers, and other bugs providing
essential protein. [9]Insects also provide humans with many valuable
products, such as silk, beeswax, and honey. [10]Insects may be pests,
but they also provide us with countless benefits. (Source of information: "Benefits of Insects to Humans," *Encyclopedia Smithsonian*,
www.si.edu/resource/faq/nmnh/buginfo/benefits.htm.)

Topic Sentence _____

Paraphrase a. Insects are essential to a garden; without them, we would have
no flowers.

b. In some cultures, insects are on the menu.

c. Insects may be pesky, but some serve a beneficial purpose.

d. Insects provide us with many of life's luxuries.

3. [1]Many of the young heroes and heroines in children's literature—
including popular characters like J.K. Rowling's Harry Potter, Roald
Dahl's James Henry Trotter of *James and the Giant Peach,* and
Lucy Maud Montgomery's Anne of *Anne of Green Gables*—are
orphans. [2]Although the presence of so many orphans in young
adult fiction may seem to suggest an unnecessarily pessimistic, or
sad, worldview, literature experts say that orphaned characters
actually serve a positive purpose. [3]According to English professor
and children's literature specialist Philip Nel, an orphaned literary
character expresses the powerlessness felt by many young readers.
[4]Still, says Nel, "many literary orphans are resilient characters who,
despite their lack of power, find the emotional resources to beat the
odds and make their way in the world." [5]Thus, orphaned characters make young readers believe it's possible to have some control

---

*pollinating: transferring pollen from flower to flower.
*ecosystems: communities or physical environments in nature that are consid-
ered as a single unit.

over a world dominated by adults. [6]Nel also believes that literary orphans encourage children to think about growing up. [7]He says that a hero or heroine who has been prematurely separated from his or her parents encourages young readers to explore the idea of leaving home and seeking independence. [8]By imagining a world free of their parents, young readers prepare for the transition from child to adult. (Source of information: Deirdre Donahue, "Orphans in Literature Empower Children," *USA Today,* July 3, 2003, p. 7D.)

Topic Sentence _____

Paraphrase a. The large number of orphans in children's fiction has been noted by many experts.

b. Some experts believe that orphaned literary characters help young readers feel more in control of their world.

c. The pessimism in children's literature concerns many.

d. Youthful readers need to express their resentment toward parents; that's why there are so many orphans in children's literature.

4. [1]Men outrank women in all but one (Alzheimer's disease) of the fifteen causes of death, and women live an average of five years longer than men do. [2]Although many people have long believed that the reason for women's longevity was genetic, a new study published in the *American Journal of Public Health* indicates that American males are more likely than women to engage in risky, health-damaging behaviors. [3]For example, 26 percent of men smoke, compared to 22 percent of women; men are also far more likely to abuse drugs, drive without a seat belt, and ride motorcycles without helmets. [4]Thanks to a macho attitude that drives men to tackle danger head-on, they are twice as likely to get hit by lightning or to drown in flood waters. [5]Men also take care of their bodies less than do women, who are twice as likely as men to get an annual physical. [6]Also, men are less likely to seek professional medical help when they experience health problems. [7]Then, too, men work in more dangerous professions than women, so males account for 90 percent of all on-the-job fatalities. [8]Clearly, the study suggests that men's behavior may actually be the reason they don't live as long as women do. (Source of information: Sanjay Gupta, "Why Men Die Young," *Time,* May 12, 2003, www.time.com/time/magazine/printout/0,8816,449501,00.html.)

Topic Sentence _____

Paraphrase a. Men are more likely than women to get Alzheimer's, and scientists are beginning to understand why this is so.

b. Because women live longer than men, research is under way to find out why.

c. Men are risk-takers, whereas women are caretakers, and it is women's social involvement with others that makes them live longer than men.

d. A new study suggests that men's risky behavior results in their having a shorter lifespan than that of women.

5. [1]In the past, snowmobile, motocross, and all-terrain vehicle (ATV) riders were all criticized for damaging the fragile wilderness ecosystems where they practice their sport. [2]Today, another group is being blamed for adversely impacting the landscape. [3]According to environmentalists, the rock-climbing enthusiasts who enjoy scrambling up rock faces and boulders are degrading many wilderness areas. [4]While some climbers are attempting to follow a "leave no trace" policy, many others unthinkingly crush vegetation and interfere with wildlife like nesting birds. [5]In addition to harming wildlife, climbers are also leaving behind trash, climbing gear, and human waste. [6]The chalk they use on their hands to grip rocks, for instance, leaves smudges that do not wash away in the rain. [7]Climbers also damage cliffs by drilling bolts for safety ropes. [8]Some younger climbers paint graffiti on the rocks they scale. [9]In Texas, unruly climbers scrawled graffiti atop ancient rock art, forcing the state's park officials to place restrictions on rock climbing. (Source of information: Terry McCarthy, "Wearing Down the Mountains," *Time*, September 1, 2003, www.time.com/time/magazine/printout/0,8816,477962,00.html.)

Topic Sentence _____

Paraphrase a. Many rock climbers are damaging the wilderness areas.

b. Too many rock climbers are painting graffiti atop ancient landmarks.

c. Rock climbing has become a popular sport, but its popularity shouldn't mask its inherent danger.

d. Rock climbers are worse than snowmobiles when it comes to damaging the environment.

 # Test 6: Identifying and Paraphrasing Topic Sentences

DIRECTIONS Read each paragraph and write the number of the topic sentence in the blank. Then paraphrase that topic sentence.

1. ¹For centuries, people have been fascinated by the story of Atlantis, the advanced civilization that, according to legend at least, mysteriously disappeared into the sea. ²In the fourth century BC, the ancient Greek philosopher Plato claimed that Atlantis was an island located in the Atlantic Ocean, somewhere close to Gibraltar.* ³In Plato's account, the island sinks in a single day, after an earthquake strikes. ⁴In the eighteenth century, Atlantis once again became a popular subject, and attempts were made to prove its existence. ⁵None succeeded, but failure did not kill the legend. ⁶Even today, the story of Atlantis still has its believers. ⁷Convinced by books like Charles Berlitz's *Atlantis* or Shirley Andrew's *Atlantis: Insights from a Lost Civilization*, there are those who believe Atlantis will one day be rediscovered.

Topic Sentence _____

Paraphrase _____

_____

2. ¹Fourteenth-century poet Geoffrey Chaucer, who penned the famous *Canterbury Tales*, is considered one of history's finest writers. ²Yet toward the end of his career, Chaucer apologized for the *Canterbury Tales* and declared them "sinful." ³Worried about the fate of his soul, Chaucer repudiated those works he thought might displease God. ⁴Chaucer is not the only artist who later in life disowned his best work; many other great artists have done the same. ⁵Chaucer's contemporary Giovanni Boccaccio wrote a collection of lively, often sexy tales entitled *Decameron*. ⁶But like Chaucer, Boccaccio expressed embarrassment over the indecent creations of his youth. ⁷He even considered burning his earlier works, but a friend persuaded him not to set them aflame. ⁸Following a long lifetime of amazing artistic output, sixteenth-century painter, sculptor, and architect Michelangelo turned away from art in favor of religious reflection. ⁹Fearing for his soul, he wrote, "I now know how fraught with error was the fond imagination which made Art my idol and my

*Gibraltar: a peninsula on the south central coast of Spain.

king . . . no brush, no chisel will quiet the soul." [10]In the nineteenth century, aging writer Leo Tolstoy underwent a similar spiritual crisis. [11]After turning to religion, Tolstoy labeled as "trash" all of his earlier fiction, including the classics *War and Peace* and *Anna Karenina.* [12]In an essay titled "What Is Art?" written twelve years before he died, he condemned Shakespeare, Beethoven, and Dante for infecting people with immoral desires.

Topic Sentence _____

Paraphrase _____

_____

3. [1]The hypothalamus is the part of the brain that helps us register hunger. [2]The hypothalamus registers hunger by monitoring levels of glucose (sugar) in the blood. [3]When blood sugar is low, the hypothalamus causes us to feel hungry. [4]The hypothalamus also monitors fatty substances in the blood. [5]When the fat content falls below a certain level, called a *set point,* the hypothalamus increases our desire to eat. [6]Conversely,* when the fat content of the blood rises above the set point, the hypothalamus decreases the desire to eat. [7]Much as a thermostat regulates heat, the hypothalamus helps regulate the amount of fat in the body. (Source of information: Rubin et al., *Psychology,* p. 358.)

Topic Sentence _____

Paraphrase _____

_____

4. [1]One early theory likened human memory to a muscle that had to be exercised regularly in order to function properly. [2]This theory was eventually replaced by the idea that remembering was like writing, with experience as the pen and the mind as the blank page. [3]But eventually this idea was also rejected. In its place came another theory—that human memory functioned like a complex and well-stocked library catalog. [4]With a key word, you could look up any piece of stored or cataloged information. [5]Over time, that

_____

*conversely: just the opposite.

theory has also been discarded. [6]Human memory may, in fact, be too sophisticated and too complex to be explained through any one simile or metaphor.

Topic Sentence _____

Paraphrase _____

_____

5. [1]The West's exposure to Muslim women is largely based on Islam's most extreme examples of oppression: Taliban-dominated Afghanistan, Wahhabi*-ruled Saudi Arabia, and post-revolutionary Iran. [2]Under these regimes, women are forced to cover their face and bodies or suffer painful consequences for failing to do so. [3]In addition, many Afghan women are forbidden to attend school, and Saudi women are not allowed to drive. [4]Yet these Islamic societies, with their emphasis on the repression of women, are not typical of the Muslim world. [5]In Egypt, female police patrol the streets. [6]In Jordan, women account for the majority of students in medical school. [7]And in Syria, courtrooms are filled with female lawyers. [8]"Women are out working in every profession, and even expect equal pay," says Leila Ahmed, Harvard Divinity School professor and author of *Women and Gender in Islam.* [9]Though the atmosphere in Muslim countries is becoming more restrictive, no matter how conservative things get, they can't put the genie back into the bottle. (Adapted from Lorraine Ali, "Reform: Not Ignorant, Not Helpless," *Newsweek,* December 12, 2005, p. 33.)

Topic Sentence _____

Paraphrase _____

_____

*Wahhabi: a segment of Islam that allows women few, if any, rights.

 **Test 7: Vocabulary Review**

DIRECTIONS Here are twenty of the words introduced in Chapter 4. Use them to fill in the blanks. Words introduced in previous chapters are marked with an asterisk. *Note*: The form of the word used here may differ from the form used in the chapter.

devotees	naturalists	habitats	pollination
tracts	orbit	graphic	reckoned with
homage	enthralling	paradoxes	analogies
despicable	instigated	heresy	missionary
genetic	staples	sociopathic	flouting

1. In the seventeenth century, Italian scientist Galileo Galilei became a proponent* of the heliocentric model of the universe, the view that all planets, including Earth, ___orbit___ the Sun. Because this idea contradicted the Bible, it was considered ___despicable___ and ___instigated___ the Church's anger. Convinced that he was right, the inherently* stubborn and reckless Galileo persisted in ___missionary___ church teachings by defending his hypothesis.* Although he was willing to pay ___homage___ to church leaders, he refused to deny what he believed until the Inquisition threatened him not just with the confiscation* of everything he owned but also death by being burned at the stake.

2. From 1831 to 1836, Charles Darwin journeyed to South America and the South Seas aboard HMS *Beagle*, a ship conducting scientific research. During this trip, Darwin combed huge ___tracts___ of land in places like Chile and the unspoiled Galapagos Islands, studying plant ___pollination___ and animal ___habitats___. His efforts not only established him as one of Britain's foremost

naturalists but subsequently* led him to develop a theory of development that radically* changed many people's views about their history and origins. Darwin's theory, called "natural selection," implied a _genetic_ link between humans and animals, and it challenged traditional doctrine concerning the origin of human beings. Although Darwin knew his theory would anger many, even he did not _____ the storm of outrage that erupted in response to its publication.

3. Convicted criminal Charles Manson has been called "the most dangerous man in the world." In the 1960s and 1970s, he and "The Family," his group of fiercely loyal _devotees_, brutally murdered as many as thirty-five people. Thanks to _enthralling_ testimony from witnesses who exposed the truth about the group's horrific acts, Manson was convicted and incarcerated.* He is currently serving his life sentence in a California prison. Because of his _sociopathic_ behavior and _floating_ lack of remorse, Manson has been repeatedly denied parole and is likely to die behind bars.

4. The following _analogies_ might be useful when thinking about poetry; it might help to explain why some people say that life without poetry would be so much poorer and duller: Poets are like _Staples_ from the unconscious side of our minds. They write with the intention of converting us to a different way of living, one where the logical, rational* mind is switched off so that we might more readily hear a poem's _graphic_ word music without complaining that it doesn't seem realistic or practical.

Under the spell of a poem, we can let ourselves, for a brief time at least, experience the strangeness and beauty of life. To win us over to their side, poets rely on the _paradoxes_ of their craft— similes* and metaphors,* those imaginative comparisons that make us recognize a connection between two things that, in the real world, would never appear side by side or for that matter in the same sentence. The greatest poets, like the seventeenth-century Christian preacher and poet John Donne, use intriguing _heresy_ that make us think our way into the poem's experience. In perhaps one of his most famous examples, Donne wrote that a Christian cannot be free unless he is captured by God.

BONUS QUESTION

What did John Donne mean when he wrote that freedom could only come through being captured?

_____

_____

_____

_____

INTERNET RESOURCE

To get more illustrations of paradoxes, go to **www.better-english .com/vocabulary/paradoxes.htm**.

 C H A P T E R 5

Inferences and Main Ideas

> **In this chapter, you'll learn**
>
> - about the role of inferences in everyday life.
> - how to infer which words are needed to complete partial topic sentences.
> - how to infer implied main ideas.
> - how to evaluate your inferences.

Chapter 5 shows you how to draw inferences in order to construct complete topic sentences. It also shows you how to infer main ideas that are strongly suggested but never directly stated. Chapter 5 also paves the way for future discussions of inferences in the chapters that follow.

Inferences in Everyday Life

> An inference is a statement about the unknown made on the basis of the known.
>
> S. I. Hayakawa. *Language in Thought and Action,* p. 41

In our practical life, we draw inferences all the time. We draw conclusions, that is, about the unknown based upon the known. If, for instance, neighbors come home with a new baby and shortly afterward start looking tired and worn, we might well infer that the baby was a light sleeper, who kept the parents awake, even if they themselves never complained. If a roommate goes out on a blind date and comes home smiling and whistling, we'd probably assume, before hearing a word, that the date was successful.

Cartoons

Consider, too, how often we draw inferences when reading the comics section of a newspaper. Take, as an example, this Calvin and Hobbes comic strip. What's the boy thinking in the second frame? And what does he mean when he says, "I love loopholes"? In both cases, the cartoon's creator expects you to infer the boy's thoughts.

CALVIN AND HOBBES © 1995 Watterson. Dist. By UNIVERSAL PRESS SYNDICATE. Reprinted with permission. All rights reserved.

In the second frame, readers need to infer that Calvin has suddenly gotten an idea. To make this inference, they have to draw on the message of the first frame, where the boy's expression and the fact that he's reading a test say he's worried because he doesn't know how to answer one of the questions. They also need to know that exclamation points often signal excitement; in this case, the exclamation point suggests Calvin's excitement at finding a solution to his current problem.

To understand the final frame, readers have to infer a connection between Calvin's saying he loves "loopholes" and the gobbledygook he wrote in the previous frame. The inference they need to draw goes something like this: Calvin has interpreted the teacher's instructions to suit his own purposes. The teacher meant that students should paraphrase Newton's Law of Motion. Calvin, however, decides to supply his own meaning and interpret the instructions as "Explain the law in language of your own creation."

If you are thinking at this point that this is a lot of explanation for one simple cartoon, you are absolutely right. But in fact, a lot of explanation is required to describe the number of actual inferences you make when reading a simple cartoon. You just don't know you are doing it. Making inferences to read cartoons is so ingrained, or automatic, we don't realize how often we do it.

Quips* and Quotes

Quotes and quips also rely on you to figure out what was meant but left unsaid. For example, what did American author Mark Twain mean when he said, "Man is the only animal that blushes, or needs to"? And if you know anything at all about a hungry cat, you probably won't have problems understanding this quip: "There is no snooze button on a cat who wants breakfast."* My point is, of course, that you are no stranger to drawing inferences. You do it all the time. All you have to do at this point is think more consciously about how you do it when you read.

 # Filling in the Gaps in Topic Sentences

You may have already noticed that when you look for the topic sentence of a paragraph, you don't always find one that's complete enough to use for later review. In other words, if you read just the underlined topic sentence in preparation for an exam, one or more essential words would be missing from the sentence. Here's an example:

---

*quips: quick one-liners.
*www.re-quest.net/animals/domestic/cats/cat-quotes/index.htm.

Topic Sentence

[1]At one time, the right side of the brain was regarded as the minor hemisphere, or half. [2]<u>We now know, however, that it has its own special set of talents and isn't "minor" at all</u>. [3]The right hemisphere is superior at recognizing patterns, faces, and melodies. [4]It's also involved in detecting and expressing emotions. [5]The right brain is actually better than the left at visualization skills, such as arranging blocks to match a pattern, putting together a puzzle, or drawing pictures.

The first sentence introduces the precise topic of the paragraph—the right side of the brain. However, the first sentence is not the topic sentence. The paragraph does not deal with the earlier notion that the right brain was the minor hemisphere. As the reversal transition "however" suggests, the author is going to revise the opening thought. The real main idea of the paragraph turns up in the second sentence: We now know that the right brain is not inferior to the left; in fact, it has its own unique talents. But if you look at the topic sentence communicating that main idea in the above paragraph, you would notice it has some gaps: "We now know, however, that *it* has *its* own special set of talents and isn't 'minor' at all." Read that sentence a few weeks from now and you might not be so clear about the meanings of those pronouns, *it* and *its*. Then, too, if you want to paraphrase the sentence to take notes, you would first need to draw the correct inference and replace at least one of those pronouns with the right noun. Then you'd have a complete and clear topic sentence: "We now know that the right side of the brain has its own special set of talents and isn't 'minor' at all."

Here's another example of a topic sentence that requires readers to fill in the gaps:

Topic Sentence

[1]In 1911, the English explorer Robert Scott set out to explore the South Pole. [2]<u>Unfortunately, he made a fatal error, and his expedition to the South Pole resulted in tragedy</u>. [3]When Scott left for the Pole, he carried with him not a team of sled dogs but nineteen small ponies. [4]Unlike the more widely used sled dogs, the ponies had a hard time navigating the harsh terrain* and could not withstand the freezing cold. [5]Ultimately, the ponies, along with Scott and his entire team, died in their attempt to reach the South Pole. [6]Roald Amundsen, the explorer who beat Scott to the Pole, later attributed his own success to his team's use of sled dogs rather than ponies.

Because the paragraph focuses on the specific effects of Scott's "fatal error," sentence 2 comes very close to being a complete topic

---

*terrain: an area of ground or land.

sentence. But imagine that you underlined that sentence and reread it to review for an exam, say, six weeks after your first reading. Could it stand on its own as a summary sentence? Well, maybe it could if you were an expert in Antarctic exploration; however, most readers would need to know more. They would need, that is, a completed topic sentence like the following: "Unfortunately, the English explorer Robert Scott made a fatal error, and his 1911 expedition to the South Pole resulted in tragedy."

Reading Tip

✔

Replacing pronouns with the words they refer to is a good way to unravel difficult sentences. Often, just plugging in the nouns will clarify sentence meaning.

 EXERCISE 1 **Completing Topic Sentences**

DIRECTIONS Read each paragraph and locate the partially completed topic sentence that sums up the paragraph. Underline it and write a completed version in the blanks.

EXAMPLE ¹Who was Will Rogers? ²<u>He was the cowboy-philosopher who won America's heart in the 1920s.</u> ³Born in Oklahoma, Rogers began his career on stage playing a rope-twirling cowboy-comedian and in 1915 joined the Ziegfeld Follies.* ⁴Soon his widely quoted wisecracks about the American political scene made him famous nationwide. ⁵The public loved the way he ridiculed politicians: ⁶"I am not a member of any organized party—I am a Democrat." ⁷By the time he died in a plane crash in 1935, Rogers had made more than twenty films, and quotes from his newspaper column had appeared on the front page of the *New York Times.*

Completed Topic Sentence Will Rogers was the cowboy-philosopher who won America's heart in the 1920s.

EXPLANATION Sentence 2 is a partially completed topic sentence. To make it fully convey the author's meaning, readers need to make the connection between the pronoun "he" and the noun "Will Rogers."

---

*Ziegfeld Follies: a famous variety show created by Florenz Ziegfeld.

1. [1]As a relatively young man, Bela Lugosi became rich and famous. [2]Taken by his performance in 1931 as the blood-drinking Count Dracula, audiences willingly paid to see Lugosi's particular brand of elegance and evil. [3]But all that changed as Bela Lugosi grew older. [4]When he died, he had nothing left of the fame and fortune playing Dracula had brought him. [5]Because Lugosi had become so closely identified with the figure of the count, producers were hesitant to cast him in other roles. [6]In addition, his thick Hungarian accent, so effective in *Dracula*, was a handicap for other parts. [7]As a result, Lugosi was reduced to making ridiculous, low-grade thrillers like *Bela Lugosi Meets a Brooklyn Gorilla* and *Mother Riley Meets the Vampire*. [8]By the mid-1950s, Lugosi was all but forgotten by Hollywood and his fans. [9]By 1956, he was dead, a victim of drugs and alcohol.

Completed Topic Sentence _____

_____

2. [1]Throughout the 1800s, explorers had dreamed of reaching the North Pole. [2]But it wasn't until 1909 that anyone claimed to have done it. [3]Who got there first, though, is still the subject of argument. [4]Dr. Frederick Cook claimed that he had reached the Pole on April 21, 1908, spending two days there until drifting ice forced him to move westward. [5]The world press celebrated Cook's achievement until cables began arriving from Robert Peary, who insisted that he had been the first man to reach the Pole. [6]The controversy continued even after the two men had died. [7]In fact, some historians insist that both claims lacked the appropriate proof and therefore cannot be honored. [8]They propose instead that Richard Byrd was the first man to really arrive at the North Pole, flying over it in 1926. [9]Russian historians, for their part, dispute any such claims. [10]They insist that in 1937 the Russian scientist Otto Schmidt was the first person to ever set foot at the North Pole.

Completed Topic Sentence _____

_____

3. [1]Because of research indicating that drinking coffee contributes to diseases ranging from cancer to heart attacks, coffee has long been a guilty pleasure for many. [2]New research, however, suggests that it may actually offer significant health benefits. [3]For instance, researchers at the National Institute of Diabetes and Digestive Diseases found that coffee significantly reduces the risk of chronic liver

disease. [4]Turning old research on its head, two new studies of American nurses have also shown that the biggest coffee drinkers actually have a lower risk for developing high blood pressure. [5]Drinking too much sometimes causes the heart to race, but these palpitations* are apparently harmless. [6]Similarly, coffee's connections to breast cancer, osteoporosis, and dehydration have been exposed as weak and unproven. [7]What coffee does do is improve athletic ability by triggering a release of adrenaline that strengthens muscle contractions while improving speed and endurance. [8]And coffee's benefits aren't just physical. [9]Caffeine, functioning as a mild antidepressant, also helps to chase away the blues. [10]In one Harvard study of 80,000 American women, coffee drinkers were one-third less likely to commit suicide than non-coffee drinkers. (Source of information: Kathleen McAuliffe, "Enjoy!" *U.S. News and World Report*, December 19, 2005, www.usnews.com.)

Completed Topic Sentence

_____

_____

4. [1]Claiming to be the first to clone human stem cells, South Korean biomedical scientist Hwang Woo-Suk rose to worldwide fame. [2]Unfortunately, soon afterward, he stunned the scientific community by admitting that he had faked his pioneering results. [3]Hwang's name first flashed around the world in 2004, when he and his team at Seoul National University announced that they had successfully cloned a human embryo. [4]After publishing a paper about his achievement in the respected magazine *Science*, Hwang became a national hero. [5]In June 2005, Hwang seemed to add to his fame by reporting an even bigger breakthrough: the creation of eleven patient stem cells. [6]What he had really created, though, was a house of cards about to collapse. [7]Shortly after the announcement of his big breakthrough, Hwang's work came under investigation for ethical violations once it was revealed that he had obtained human eggs illegally by paying or coercing women into donating. [8]Adding to Hwang's humiliation, an official probe by Seoul National University revealed that at least nine of Hwang's eleven stem cell lines were fakes and concluded there was no evidence Hwang had ever cloned human stem cells. [9]Now the object of public distrust and ridicule, Hwang resigned from his university position in disgrace. (Source of information: "Hwang's First Human Embryonic Stem Cell Faked," Associated Press, *USA Today*, January 9, 2006,

_____

*palpitations: unusually fast heartbeat.

www.usatoday.com/tech/science/2006-01-09-hwang-human-stem-cells_x.htm.)

Completed Topic
Sentence
_____

_____

_____

 # Inferring Main Ideas

Sometimes writers don't use even partial topic sentences. Instead, they supply a series of specific statements designed to lead their readers to the implied main idea of the paragraph. For an illustration of this method, read the following paragraph:

[1]As a young man, the British soldier and writer T. E. Lawrence took part in an archaeological expedition in the Middle East. [2]The work fascinated him, as did the land, and he became possessed by a dream: The Arabs would overthrow Turkish rule and take control of their own country. [3]Lawrence sought to make his dream become reality during World War I when the British showed an interest in helping the Arabs revolt. [4]Seeing a chance for Arab independence, Lawrence arranged a meeting between British and Arab leaders. [5]Supplied with British arms and aided by Lawrence's military strategy, the Arabs rose up and captured several major Turkish* strongholds. [6]By 1919, the war was over, and the Turks had been defeated. [7]Thrilled by the Arab victory, Lawrence was now sure that his dream of Arab self-rule was about to become reality. [8]But when he was called to the Paris Peace Conference, he was stunned to discover that the British had no intention of giving up their control of the Middle East.

The author hasn't included a topic sentence in the above paragraph. Instead, she leaves a trail of clues and expects readers to infer the implied main idea: "T. E. Lawrence was deeply disappointed at learning that the British were not going to give the Arabs their independence." The basis for that inference are the statements that follow:

---

*In World War I, Britain and Turkey were enemies.

1. Lawrence was, in the writer's words, "possessed" by the dream of Arab independence. The use of this word suggests Lawrence was passionately committed to it.

2. According to the author, Lawrence tried to turn "his dream" into a reality during World War I. The use of "his" suggests Lawrence's attachment to the idea.

3. The author says that Lawrence was "thrilled" to learn about the Arab victory and "sure that his dream of Arab self-rule was to become a reality." The use of the word *thrilled* emphasizes Lawrence's happiness at Arab self-rule.

4. The author uses the contrasting word *stunned* to describe the unpleasant surprise Lawrence felt about learning that the British were not giving up control of the Middle East.

Given the clues shown here it would be hard not to infer that Lawrence was deeply disappointed at the British refusal to give the Arabs self-rule.

Anytime you read a passage and can't find a general sentence that seems to even partially sum up the main idea, look at all the specific statements supplied by the author and ask yourself what these statements combine to suggest about the topic. Look, for instance, at the following paragraph. Study all the specifics given, then at the end write the implied main idea in the blank line that follows.

[1]Ms. B, a twenty-three-year-old woman, complained of a phobia, or fear, of spiders that she had had for as long as she could remember. [2]She had no history of any other psychiatric symptoms. [3]In treatment, when first approached with a closed glass jar containing spiders, she breathed heavily, wept, and rated her distress as extremely high. [4]Suddenly she began scratching the back of her hand, stating she felt as though spiders were crawling under her skin, although she knew this was not really the case. [5]The sensation lasted only a few seconds and did not recur. [6]Her total treatment consisted of four one-hour sessions distributed over the span of a month. [7]At completion, she had lost all fear of spiders and was able to let them crawl freely about her arms, legs, and face, as well as inside her clothing, with no distress. [8]She remained free of fear at a one-year follow-up exam and expressed disbelief that she had allowed such a "silly fear" to dominate her life for so long (Curtis, 1981, p. 1095). (Adapted from Sue et al., *Understanding Abnormal Behavior*, p. 136.)

If your implied main idea goes something like, "Ms. B's treatment helped her overcome her fear of spiders," you drew a logical inference. It's logical because it's solidly based on the following details and how they add up:

1. Ms. B arrives for treatment unable to even look at spiders without having a violent reaction.
2. She then had four one-hour treatments.
3. After the treatments, she did not have a violent reaction and was actually able to let spiders crawl on her body.

Now, of course, you could claim that Ms. B's new response was a miracle. But that wouldn't be a **logical inference.** In other words, it wouldn't be based on the information in the paragraph. To be logical—in the sense of keeping the reader on the same track as the writer—reading inferences have to stem from what's actually said in the paragraph. You must, that is, be able to say: This is the implied main idea because of these words and statements. If you cannot point to anything in the paragraph that supports your version of the implied main idea, you and the author have parted company. Obviously, that's not what readers should be doing. On the contrary, what readers infer and what the author implies should be closely linked.

INTERNET RESOURCE

For a review of implied main ideas, go to
www.cerritos.edu/reading/mainide3.htm.

Reading Tip

Inferring implied main ideas is a two-step process. Your first step is to understand what each sentence contributes to your knowledge of the topic. Next you need to ask yourself what all of the sentences combine to imply as a group. The answer to that question is the implied main idea of the paragraph.

EXERCISE 2 Recognizing the Implied Main Idea

DIRECTIONS Each item in this exercise contains four sentences that combine to imply a main idea. Circle the letter of that implied main idea.

EXAMPLE

a. During the nineteenth century, factory owners hired young orphans, whom they could force to work fifteen hours a day.

b. Many factory owners preferred hiring women, who could move quickly among the machinery and were easily frightened by threats of dismissal.

c. Whenever possible, the employers increased their profits by reducing the workers' wages.

d. Workers who complained about the hours or poor working conditions were promptly fired; whenever possible, employers saw to it that rebellious workers were thrown into jail.

Implied Main Idea

(a.) Nineteenth-century factory owners cruelly exploited the men, women, and children who worked for them.

b. In the nineteenth century, factory owners were quick to hire women, because they were too timid to make any demands.

c. In the nineteenth century, children were expected to work rather than play.

EXPLANATION The first four sentences give examples of the way nineteenth-century employers abused *all* their employees, not just women and children. Thus, *a* is the only implied main idea that follows from all of the specific statements given. It's certainly the only sentence that could summarize the opening four.

1. a. Workplace monitoring of employees is becoming more common thanks to new technology: Employers and supervisors can, if they wish, monitor employees' Web activity; screen their e-mail, and get screen shots of websites that employees visit.

b. All sorts of records—from tax returns to sales receipts—have been digitized for storage in computerized databases, making it easier for people to locate personal information about others.

c. Hackers have hacked into the computerized records of the Veterans Administration and Amazon.com among others.

d. As part of the program for fighting terrorists, the government has asked for and, in many cases, gotten information about the sites computer-users visit with the aid of search engines.

Implied Main Idea

a. Advances in computer technology have made it difficult to keep personal information private.

b. Computers are eliminating the need for paper files, a trend that will undoubtedly continue.

c. Workplace monitoring amounts to a serious, if not illegal, invasion of privacy.

---

2. a. On October 15, 1917, the famed Dutch dancer Mata Hari was taken before a French firing squad and executed as a spy.

b. Although Mata Hari had agreed to spy for the Germans, there is no evidence that she ever gave them any information.

c. Information about a new British tank, said to have been given to the Germans by Mata Hari, was actually provided by a British prisoner of war.

d. The case against Mata Hari was based largely on telegrams supplied by the head of France's espionage agency, who had tampered with them before the trial.

Implied Main Idea

a. Mata Hari was executed not because she was a spy but because she was hated by the head of France's espionage bureau.

b. Mata Hari may not have been guilty of the crimes that earned her a death sentence.

c. There is no evidence Mata Hari agreed to spy for the Germans.

---

3. a. Thanks to Henry Ford's invention of a cheap automobile—called the first "people's car"—farmers from small rural towns were able to sell their products to larger markets located some distance away.

b. Ford's Model T was introduced in 1908 and priced at $850; by 1923 it cost only $290, and people from all walks of life had the chance to own a car.

c. Ford's Model T was so famous, popular songs and jokes alluded to it.

d. In the early part of the twentieth century, almost half the American population lived in the country, but Ford's Model T made access to city life much easier, and the rural population began to diminish.

Implied Main Idea

a. The invention of the Model T had a profound effect on American life.

b. Henry Ford was determined to make a car that even working people could afford.

c. Henry Ford was a genius when it came to making money.

---

4. a. The month of January got its name from Janus, the Roman god of beginnings.

b. Saturday was named after Saturn, the Roman god of agriculture.

c. The sporting goods company Nike took its name from the Greek goddess of victory.

d. The planet Neptune was named after the Roman god of the sea.

Implied Main Idea

a. The gods and goddesses of Greek and Roman mythology had exotic and colorful names.

b. The names of the ancient gods and goddesses live on in our language.

c. Our calendar is a constant reminder of Greek mythology's long-lasting influence.

Reading Tip

The main idea you infer from the specific details should sum up the paragraph in the same way a topic sentence does.

▐ EXERCISE 3 Recognizing the Implied Main Idea

DIRECTIONS Read each paragraph. Then circle the letter of the implied main idea.

EXAMPLE [1]An expectant mother has to avoid alcohol. [2]Alcohol in her blood can deprive the fetus of necessary nutrition, and the baby will be born underweight. [3]Research shows that smoking during pregnancy can permanently damage a baby's health. [4]Children of smokers, for example, tend to have more respiratory* infections throughout their lives. [5]Clearly, mothers-to-be who smoke should try to cut back or quit. [6]They should also be careful about the type of exercise they do. [7]Very vigorous exercise should be avoided. [8]Pregnant mothers also need to monitor their medications. [9]Too often, drugs not harmful to the mother can harm the child. [10]Some drugs can do irreparable,* damage. [11]These are not always the medications one might suspect. [12]In some cases, even aspirin has proved to be dangerous to the unborn child.

Implied Main Idea a. During pregnancy, medication should be carefully monitored because some drugs can do serious harm to the child.

   b. Expectant mothers must take special precautions in order to have a healthy baby.

   c. Women who are pregnant should never smoke.

EXPLANATION Sentence *a* combines information from sentences 8 and 9. However, it does not adequately sum up the paragraph, which addresses more than the need for pregnant women to watch their medications. Smoking is also mentioned as is alcohol. Sentence *c* has the same problem. It's too specific to sum up all that's in the paragraph. Sentence *b* is the correct choice because this inference is general enough to sum up all the specific things pregnant women should avoid.

1. The Russian region of Siberia extends from the Ural Mountains to the Pacific Ocean and embraces more than five million square miles. Winters in Siberia are long with ice and snow covering the region for about six months of the year. Temperatures can be as low as 60°F

---

*respiratory: having to do with breathing.
*irreparable: incapable of being fixed or repaired.

below zero. Several layers of clothing are needed to survive the brutal temperatures. Without them, death by freezing is common. Still there are financial rewards for a Russian who decides to live and work in Siberia. Russians who relocate can increase their salaries by 30 to 40 percent. In addition, foods that are in short supply all over Russia—fruit, fish, and game—are plentiful in Siberia. The shivering population of Siberia, nevertheless, remains small and shows little sign of increasing.

Implied Main Idea a. Despite the rewards of living in Siberia, the country's frigid climate keeps the population from expanding.

b. Although some native Siberians love their country, even they do not deny that the climate is harsh and uninviting.

c. Inhabitants of Siberia are inclined to be depressed for most of the winter.

2. If you are invited to a Southerner's home for New Year's Day, you're likely to find black-eyed peas on your plate. A Southern superstition claims that eating black-eyed peas, which resemble coins, will bring health and wealth in the new year. You are also likely to find bowls of cabbage and collard greens sitting on the table. The color of money, these vegetables are said to bring prosperity to those who eat them. Next to the collard greens and cabbage, there will also probably be a plate of cornbread. The color of gold, cornbread is more insurance that the new year will be a prosperous one.

Implied Main Idea a. In many southern households, New Year's Day is traditionally celebrated with a meal that is colorful, simple, and nutritious.

b. Southerners tend to be more superstitious than people in other parts of the country.

c. On New Year's Day, some Southerners like to serve dishes that are traditionally linked with good fortune.

3. When William Shakespeare's *Macbeth* was first performed in the seventeenth century, the boy actor playing Lady Macbeth fell ill and died. It is often claimed that Shakespeare himself stepped in and played the role. In 1703, a performance of *Macbeth* coincided with one of the worst storms in English history, and the theater was

forced to close down. In the 1920s, when Lionel Barrymore* played Macbeth, he received such terrible notices that he never again had the nerve to perform on Broadway. In 1937, a young actor named Laurence Olivier* was almost killed during a performance of *Macbeth* when a heavy weight crashed to the floor, missing his head by just a few inches.

Implied Main Idea
  a. Over the years, Shakespeare's *Macbeth* has been plagued by bad luck.

  b. When *Macbeth* was first performed in the seventeenth century, Shakespeare himself stepped in and played the title role.

  c. Even the best actors are challenged by playing Shakespeare's *Macbeth*.

4. In 1919, the Eighteenth Amendment made drinking liquor illegal throughout the nation. Still, everyone seemed to know a bar where liquor could be purchased. Some who couldn't afford to buy liquor made it in their bathtubs at home. The liquor, which came to be known as "bathtub gin," tasted terrible, but people drank it anyway, even if it made them sick. The Eighteenth Amendment also gave rise to bootleggers—criminals who supplied the country with liquor by smuggling it in from Canada and the West Indies. Not surprisingly, members of organized crime quickly realized that Prohibition* could be a source of tremendous profit.

Implied Main Idea
  a. The Eighteenth Amendment put money into the hands of hardened criminals.

  b. Many Americans simply ignored the Eighteenth Amendment, and it had little positive effect.

  c. Thanks to the Eighteenth Amendment, alcoholism in the U.S. increased.

---

*American-born Lionel Barrymore went on to become a famous film actor.
*British-born Laurence Olivier became internationally famous.
*Prohibition: the years between 1920 and 1933, when the Eighteenth Amendment was in effect.

Questions for Evaluating Inferences

1. **Is the implied main idea solidly based on statements in the paragraph?**

   If asked to defend your inference, you should be able to point to specific words and sentences that support it.

2. **Are you relying more on the author's words than on your own personal point of view?**

   Even if the author has chosen a topic you think you know quite well, don't infer a main idea based mainly on what you think or feel about the subject. When inferring a main idea, it's the writer's mind you have to read, not your own.

3. **Are you sure that none of the author's statements contradict the main idea you inferred?**

   If any of the sentences in a passage contradict the main idea you inferred, you probably haven't hit upon the main idea the author intended.

4. **Do the sentences in the paragraph connect to your implied main idea?**

   If you jot the implied main idea in the margins, you should immediately see how the supporting details help develop it.

INTERNET RESOURCE

For a comprehensive discussion of inferences, see **www.criticalreading.com** and click on *inference*.

 EXERCISE 4   **Recognizing the Implied Main Idea**

DIRECTIONS Read each paragraph. Then circle the letter of the implied main idea.

1. In the past, many men and women decided to become flight attendants because they were attracted to the glamorous, fun, jet-setting lifestyle that came with the job. Now, however, flight attendants are spending most of their workdays dealing with rude, disgruntled passengers who are frustrated by delays, crowded flights, and the disappearance of perks like free food. These surly travelers often leave their manners in the airport terminal and bombard flight attendants

with complaints. Then, too, flight attendants must worry about the possibility of terrorism. Since the terrorist hijackings of four airliners on September 11, 2001, flight attendants have to scrutinize passengers' behavior, check suspicious baggage, and take many additional security measures. What's more, the crew must endure the stress and anxiety of working in an environment that is a terrorist target. Working in an industry that is struggling financially, flight attendants also now worry constantly about layoffs and wage or benefit cuts. As their employers slash jobs, those flight attendants still working are putting in longer hours as part of understaffed crews. (Source of information: Francine Parnes, "For Flight Attendants, Stress Comes with the Job," *The New York Times*, August 12, 2003, www.nytimes.com/2003/08/12/business/12ATTE.html.)

Implied Main Idea   a. The airline industry is in a shambles.

b. The job of flight attendant has lost much of its glamour.

c. The September 11, 2001, terrorist attacks have significantly affected the airline industry.

d. Flight attendants have the most stressful job in America.

2. Many school officials favor installing Internet-wired video cameras in schools. With video cameras installed throughout the building, administrators would be able to review a videotape to see exactly what happened when a crime—say, a theft—occurred. The cameras could also generate an exact record of all classroom proceedings that could be used to monitor instructor performance as well as interactions between students and teachers. Some teachers want video cameras in their classrooms so that parents can see firsthand how their children behave. Parents think the cameras are a good idea for the opposite reason: They want to see and judge the teachers. Students, for their part, like the idea of being able to view what's going on in their classrooms should they miss a day or two because of illness. (Source of information: Greg Toppo, "Who's Watching the Class?" *USA Today*, August 11, 2003, p. 1D, www.usatoday.com/usatonline/20030811/5396054s.htm.)

Implied Main Idea   a. Video cameras are an excellent tool for improving security in our nation's schools.

b. Technology is improving today's schools in many different ways.

c. Administrators, teachers, and students all have different reasons for wanting to use video cameras in the schools.

d. Internet-wired video cameras in schools make parents more aware of what goes on in the classroom.

3. As far back as 1967, a study done at Harvard Medical School showed that during meditation, people use 17 percent less oxygen, lower their heart rates by three beats per minute, and increase the type of brain waves that occur during the state of relaxation preceding sleep. More recent studies of the brain have confirmed that meditation shifts activity from the right hemisphere of the prefrontal cortex to the left hemisphere. As a result, the brain switches to a calmer, more content state. For this reason, meditation can eliminate the need for medication to treat anxiety, tension, and even pain. As a matter of fact, many individuals are managing the pain of chronic diseases or injuries not with painkillers but with meditation, which helps people learn to accept their discomfort rather than struggle against it. Other patients suffering from diseases like cancer are meditating to actually boost their immune systems. Studies show that people who meditate have higher levels of disease-fighting antibodies in their blood. (Source of information: Joel Stein, "Just Say Om," *Time,* August 4, 2003, p. 48.)

Implied Main Idea   a. Meditation offers some significant health benefits.

b. Meditation is growing in popularity.

c. Meditation can sharpen one's ability to think.

d. Meditation has been shown to boost the immune system.

4. Was the 5,300-year-old, mummified body discovered in 1991 and now known as the "Iceman" killed, or did he freeze to death after being caught in a storm? One of the hikers who discovered the body in the Italian Alps said that before the Iceman was freed from a melting glacier, he had been clutching a knife in one hand. In 2001, an Italian radiologist discovered an arrowhead embedded in the shoulder of the Iceman; its position indicated that he had been hit from behind. Medical examiners have found a deep gash in one of the corpse's hands, in addition to a cut on his other hand and bruises on his body. Furthermore, DNA specialists have analyzed blood found on the arrows the Iceman was carrying. They have also found blood on the back of his cloak and his knife. They say that this blood came from four different people. The blood of two people was found on the same arrow in the Iceman's quiver, suggesting that this arrow had struck two different individuals and then been pulled free. (Source of information: Tim Friend, "'Iceman' Was Murdered, Science Sleuths Say," *USA Today,* August 11, 2003, 6D, www.usatoday.com/usatonline/20030812/5398751s.htm.)

Implied Main Idea   a. Scientists cannot decide if the Iceman froze to death or was murdered.

    b. Evidence suggests that the Iceman was probably killed in a fight.

    c. DNA testing has finally proven that the Iceman died after being shot in the back.

    d. The Iceman discovered in 1991 has proven to be an intriguing and largely unsolvable mystery.

5. Is a diet high in sugar and carbohydrates responsible for American teenagers' acne problems? Although adolescents have long been warned to avoid chocolate and other kinds of junk food, studies in the 1970s and 1980s failed to prove the link between diet and pimples. However, recent research at Colorado State University has revealed that refined foods like bread and cake cause an insulin surge in the body. This insulin stimulates the production of hormones that encourage the skin to secrete large quantities of a greasy substance known as sebum. Sebum promotes bacterial growth that causes the skin to break out. In addition, other studies have shown that for teenagers living in parts of the world where refined foods are uncommon, acne is virtually unknown. Anthropologists have noted that in remote places like Paraguay, Papua New Guinea, and the Amazon, where people eat low-carbohydrate diets, teenagers do not get acne at all, while 95 percent of American eighteen-year-olds do. Scientists also point to Inuit adolescents in Alaska, who began to suffer from acne only when they began eating a Western diet. (Source of information: Helen Pearson, "Chips Means Zits," *Nature,* December 2, 2002, www.nature.com/nsu/021125/021125-10.html.)

Implied Main Idea a. Researchers have failed to prove that eating junk food causes adolescents' acne.

    b. Research suggests that American teenagers' high-carbohydrate diet is causing their acne.

    c. Recent studies have revealed that high levels of insulin are responsible for teenagers' problem with acne.

    d. Research has shown that a sugar-free diet can eliminate acne.

Five Types of Paragraphs Likely to Imply the Main Idea

There's no way to say for sure when a writer will or will not imply the main idea of a paragraph. However, here are five types of paragraphs where it's quite likely that the author will suggest, rather than state, the main idea.

Just the Facts

In the following example, the author uses a series of specific details to describe the public response to a 1938 radio broadcast based on H. G. Wells's book *War of the Worlds*. The passage is limited to specific facts about the broadcast and the audience response. The author does not offer a comment on those specific details. In other words, she does not include a more general topic sentence. That task is left for the reader to do.

> On October 30, 1938, CBS Radio broadcast a dramatized version of H. G. Wells's book *War of the Worlds*. Although announcements before and during the story identified it as a fictional radio play, the broadcast took the form of a newsflash interrupting regular programming. A nationwide audience of about six million listened to a reporter's alarming description of an invasion by Martians, who had landed on Earth and were killing humans with heat-rays and a toxic black gas. Immediately, thousands of hysterical people swamped radio and police stations, requesting advice about how to protect themselves. Frantic listeners began searching for household materials to use as gas masks. In a panic, some people loaded their belongings into their cars. In New York and New Jersey, where the supposed Martian landing had occurred, fleeing residents created massive traffic jams. Thousands of other people hid in their basements and cellars. Hospitals administered sedatives to people suffering from shock and hysteria. All over the country, police stations began to broadcast the message that the radio program was only a dramatization and that there was no cause for alarm. (Sources of information: "Radio Listeners in Panic, Taking War Drama as Fact," *The New York Times*, October 31, 1938, www.war-of-the-worlds.org/ Radio/Newspapers/Oct31/NYT.html; Jennifer Rosenberg, "*War of the Worlds* Radio Broadcast Causes Panic," About.com, http:// history1900s.about.com/od/1930s/a/warofworlds.htm.)

In this case, the specific details lead the reader to infer an implied main idea like the following: "The broadcast of H. G. Wells's *War of the Worlds* caused widespread panic among thousands of radio listeners, who thought they were hearing about a real space invasion."

Reading Tip

If a writer describes an event by piling up specific details without including a more general topic sentence that interprets or evaluates them, it's up to you to infer the main idea implied by the author.

Question and Answer

Writers sometimes open a paragraph with a question that immediately gets answered by the topic sentence (see page 161). Frequently, however, the opening question can't be answered in a single sentence. In this context, the writer leaves it up to readers to infer the answer, and that answer is also the implied main idea. Here's an example:

How did the circle containing a straight line separated into three prongs come to be the symbol or peace sign of the anti-nuclear movement? According to one explanation, an opponent of nuclear power in the 1950s created the peace sign by combining two symbols normally used as railroad signals. One symbol was a horseshoe-shaped curve that stood for the letter *d*. The other was a circle with a slash through it, which represented the letter *n* and the word "no." When these two signs were combined, the modern peace sign emerged to symbolize nuclear disarmament (ND). Yet another explanation says the symbol was designed by the Campaign for Nuclear Disarmament (CND) in the 1950s. The organization's president at the time, British philosopher Bertrand Russell, said that the sign originated with the navy's flag signaling system. In this system, a signaler with two flags holds one flag straight up and one straight down to symbolize the letter *d*. Holding both flags down at a forty-five-degree angle from the body symbolizes the letter *n*. Combining these two signals creates the straight line with three prongs that symbolizes the plea for nuclear disarmament. Still another explanation claims that someone in the campaign for nuclear disarmament mixed two historic Christian symbols, with the outer circle representing Earth and the line with three prongs inside suggesting God reaching down to humans. (Source of information: David J. Danowitz et al., "The History of the Peace Sign," www.abcme.com/peacesigncollection/peacesigncoll.html.)

In this example, the author begins the paragraph with a question that has three different answers, making the implied main idea something like the following: "There are at least three different accounts of how the peace sign originated."

Reading Tip

When the opening question of a paragraph is *not* followed by an immediate answer, it's usually the reader's job to infer an answer that is also the implied main idea.

Competing Points of View

Paragraphs that offer competing points of view about the same event or series of events *without* saying which point of view is more accurate are usually implying, rather than stating, the main idea. Here's an illustration:

> Wilbur and Orville Wright are usually credited with being the first to fly an airplane. On December 17, 1903, in Kitty Hawk, North Carolina, Orville flew the brothers' new invention for twelve seconds. However, some people argue that New Zealand farmer Richard Pearse, who designed his own engine-powered flying machine, was actually the first to fly when his craft rose fifty yards into the air on March 31, 1903, eight months *before* the Wrights' flight. Others argue that Gustave A. Whitehead deserves the credit for making the first powered flight. Although there is no eyewitness evidence for that claim, Whitehead supposedly flew his aircraft for the first time in Bridgeport, Connecticut, on August 14, 1901, more than two years before the Wrights' flight. Then there are those who insist that Brazilian Alberto Santos-Dumont was the first man to achieve powered flight when he flew his invention fifty meters on October 23, 1906. Because the Wrights launched their plane into the air with a catapult* device and Santos-Dumont's plane, which had wheels, took off under its own power alone, his countrymen believe that he is actually the true Father of Aviation. (Sources of information: Debbi Gardiner, "Bamboo Dick, First in Flight," *Salon*, August 22, 2002, www.salon.com/tech/feature/2002/08/22/richard_pearse/; "Were the Wright Brothers Really the First to Fly?" www.didyouknow.cd/wright.htm.)

In this case, the author describes competing points of view but doesn't offer a judgment on any single one. That means it's up to you to infer an implied main idea like the following: "Controversy still exists over who first took flight in an airplane."

Reading Tip

When the author offers several competing points of view but holds back judgment about which one might be better, you need to infer a main idea that expresses the lack of agreement about the issue, person, or event under discussion.

---

*catapult: launch.

Comparison and Contrast

In a comparison and contrast paragraph, the writer points out similarities or differences—or both—between two people, events, objects, or ideas. Sometimes the main idea is stated in a topic sentence. But, frequently the author lets the similarities and differences speak for themselves. Here's an example:

> Most people know about the tragic destruction of the *Titanic*, the luxury ocean liner that sank on April 15, 1912, after hitting an iceberg. They may not know, however, about the *Lusitania*, another "floating palace" that went down a little more than three years later, on May 7, 1915. When the *Titanic* sank, 1,523 people died from injuries, drowning, and exposure to frigid temperatures. That number accounted for 68 percent of those on board. The death toll for the *Lusitania*, which was 1,198 people (or 61 percent of those aboard), was just as devastating. Those victims, too, died from injuries, drowning, and hypothermia.* The *Lusitania*'s destruction also resulted in the loss of treasures as rich as those lost aboard the *Titanic*. And while both disasters had significant consequences, the *Lusitania*'s sinking had an even greater international impact. The *Titanic* accident led to stricter lifeboat rules. The *Lusitania*, torpedoed by a German submarine, generated support for the United States' entrance into World War I.

Here the author compares and contrasts the consequences of the *Titanic* disaster with those arising from the sinking of the *Lusitania*. The writer's point is that the lesser-known *Lusitania* tragedy was as significant as the far more famous sinking of the *Titanic*. The author never specifically says that, however. Instead, the main idea is implied by a series of specific statements comparing and contrasting the two disasters in order to suggest the following main idea: "Although the sinking of the *Titanic* is better known, the sinking of the ship called the *Lusitania* had similar and equally tragic consequences."

Reading Tip	If a paragraph lists similarities and differences between two topics but doesn't tell you what those similarities and differences *mean* or how to evaluate them, you need to infer a main idea that makes a general point about them.

*hypothermia: abnormally low body temperature.

Results of Research

Writers frequently use research to prove a point. However, sometimes they simply cite research and assume readers will figure out what implied main idea the research supports. In the following paragraph, note how the author lets the research results lead readers to her implied main idea:

> Researchers at the Harvard School of Public Health wanted to find out if it's healthier for men to express their anger or to keep their feelings to themselves. So they conducted a study of 23,522 men aged fifty to eighty-five. These participants completed a survey that asked them to identify how they behaved when they got angry, choosing from options such as "I argue with others" and "I do things like slam doors." Then the researchers followed the men over a two-year period. They found that men who expressed their anger in moderate ways were half as likely to suffer from a nonfatal heart attack as men who rarely vented their anger. In addition, the study showed that the risk of stroke decreased as the levels of anger expression increased. (Source of information: Becky Ham, "Expressing Anger May Protect Against Stroke and Heart Disease," Center for the Advancement of Health, January 31, 2003, www.cfah.org/hbns/news/anger01-31-03.cfm.)

In this illustration, the author describes the question being researched: Is it better for men to express their anger or keep it to themselves? The author then explains how the study was conducted and offers up the research results, leading the reader to infer the following main idea: "Research at Harvard suggests it may be healthier for men to express anger instead of keeping it to themselves."

Reading Tip

If the author cites research but doesn't interpret the results, you need to infer what the results suggest about the problem or issue under study.

◀ EXERCISE 5 Recognizing the Implied Main Idea

DIRECTIONS Circle the appropriate letters to identify the implied main idea and the type of paragraph used to suggest it.

EXAMPLE For the last twenty years, the Drug Abuse Resistance Education (D.A.R.E.) program has been encouraging America's schoolchildren to "just say no" to drugs. But until recently no one asked a key question: How effective has this program been in reducing drug use among young people? D.A.R.E. is based on the "gateway," or "stepping stone," theory, which suggests that experimentation with drugs like marijuana leads to the use of more dangerous and addictive drugs like cocaine and heroin. However, the National Academy of Sciences, America's leading scientific organization, says that there is no basis for this theory. And while 80 percent of school districts offer D.A.R.E. to students, close to 50 percent of high school seniors still admit to having tried marijuana, while 80 percent have drunk alcohol. What's more, a 1991 University of Connecticut study of 2,000 students found no difference in the drug use of sixth-grade D.A.R.E. graduates and nongraduates two years after the D.A.R.E. graduates completed the program. Similarly, a 1998 survey of 1,798 students by the University of Illinois again showed no difference in illegal drug use among D.A.R.E. graduates and nongraduates six years later. (Source of information: Brian Braiker, "Just Say Know,' *Newsweek*, April 15, 2003, www .msnbc.com.)

Paragraph Type   a. just the facts

b. question and answer

c. competing points of view

d. comparison and contrast

e. results of research

Implied Main Idea   a. The D.A.R.E. program does not seem to reduce drug use among young people.

b. The D.A.R.E. program is currently being reevaluated.

c. The D.A.R.E. program has been effective despite the lack of statistical evidence.

EXPLANATION In this case, the passage opens with a question about the drug-abuse program called D.A.R.E. However, the answer does not appear in the paragraph. You have to infer the answer, which is also the implied main idea.

1. In 1977, Dr. Alan Scott of the Smith-Kettlewell Eye Research Institute wanted a treatment for lazy eye, a condition in which the eye muscles are hyperactive and cross the eyes. So Dr. Scott became the first to prescribe botulinum toxin, or Botox, which is a poison that destroys nerve function and helps muscles relax. Ten years later, eye doctor Jean Carruthers used the same toxin to treat patients' eye twitches. She began to notice that patients receiving these treatments looked younger, which led to the discovery that Botox smoothes facial wrinkles to produce a more youthful appearance. Then doctors began to notice that patients using Botox stopped having migraine headaches. They also realized that the toxin could help ease the symptoms of cerebral palsy and Tourette's syndrome.* Both disorders are characterized by uncontrollable muscle spasms that can be calmed with Botox injections. Now, researchers have even begun to experiment with Botox as a possible cure for obesity. When injected into patients' stomachs, the toxin makes them feel fuller faster. (Source of information: Elizabeth Weise, "The Little Neurotoxin That Could," *USA Today*, April 21, 2003, p. 1D.)

Paragraph Type   a. just the facts

b. question and answer

c. competing points of view

d. comparison and contrast

e. results of research

Implied Main Idea   a. Botulinum toxin's use as an eye treatment led to discoveries of its effectiveness for a variety of cosmetic and medical uses.

b. Botox has unexpected medical properties, but most of them are related to improving appearance.

c. Medical discoveries often happen by chance, as the history of Botox makes clear.

2. In 1982, the American Cancer Society began evaluating 900,000 people who were cancer free. In this study, researchers examined each participant's body mass index, or BMI, which is calculated using height and weight. Based on BMI, participants were divided into three categories: normal weight, overweight, or obese. During the sixteen years of the study, 57,145 of the participants died of cancer. When researchers compared the mortality rates of the three different groups, they found that the heaviest participants had death rates from all cancers combined that were 52 percent (for men) and 62 percent (for women) higher than the rates in men and women of normal weight. In both men and women, a higher BMI was also linked to higher rates of death due to cancers of the esophagus,

---

*Tourette's syndrome: a disease characterized by involuntary movements and sounds.

colon and rectum, liver, gallbladder, pancreas, and kidney. In addition, men with higher BMIs had higher rates of stomach and prostate cancers, and women had higher rates of cancer of the breast, uterus, cervix, and ovary. (Source of information: Eugenia E. Calle, Ph.D., "Overweight, Obesity, and Mortality from Cancer in a Prospectively Studied Cohort of U.S. Adults," *New England Journal of Medicine,* April 24, 2003, http://content.nejm.org/cgi/content/short/348/17/1625.)

Paragraph Type
a. just the facts

b. question and answer

c. competing points of view

d. comparison and contrast

e. results of research

Implied Main Idea
a. Medical research has repeatedly shown that being overweight leads to an early death.

b. A long-term study by the American Cancer Society suggests that having excess weight increases one's risk of dying of cancer.

c. The American Cancer Society study has not yet been adequately evaluated.

3. Some of today's flightless birds, such as the ostrich, have long legs and feet that are strikingly similar to those of some dinosaurs. Both birds and dinosaurs also have an expanded upper hipbone. As a matter of fact, birds and dinosaurs share more than one hundred different skeletal features. In addition, like many dinosaurs, birds have light, hollow bones and a dense system of blood vessels. Birds' feathers are similar in structure to the scales that covered dinosaurs' bodies, and many scientists believe that some dinosaurs may have had feathers that kept them warm. Furthermore, birds lay eggs, nest in colonies, and care for their young in nests, just as dinosaurs did.

Paragraph Type
a. just the facts

b. question and answer

c. competing points of view

d. comparison and contrast

e. results of research

Implied Main Idea
a. The similarities between birds and dinosaurs suggest that birds may be descendants of dinosaurs.

b. Physical similarities are no proof that dinosaurs and birds are related.

c. Like the dinosaurs they resemble, birds lay eggs and care for their young in nests.

4. Catholics, Jews, and Muslims all regularly practice "intercessory prayer," or praying for someone who is sick or hospitalized. They believe that prayer helps the people being prayed for. To find out if intercessory prayer can heal, scientists have tried to measure the effect of prayer on patients' health. A 1999 study of 1,000 heart patients conducted by University of Missouri professor William Harris found that prayed-for patients fared better than those who were not prayed for. Harris's results seemed to confirm those of a similar 1997–1998 Duke University Medical Center study involving 150 patients who had undergone surgery to open blocked coronary arteries. Unbeknownst to anyone involved, some of these patients were prayed for by seven prayer groups, while other patients weren't prayed for at all. Those who received intercessory prayer turned out to be 25 to 30 percent less likely to experience adverse* outcomes like heart attack, heart failure, and death. Yet, when Duke University repeated the same study in 2004 by having Christian, Muslim, Jewish, and Buddhist groups pray for 371 of 700 patients, researchers found that those who received prayers were no less likely to avoid later complications. The results of this study were similar to those of a 2001 Mayo Clinic study of 799 heart patients. Half of the patients were unknowingly assigned to a prayer group, half were not. All were evaluated after twenty-six weeks. Researchers found little difference between the two groups' rates of death, cardiac arrest,* or rehospitalization. (Sources of information: Kevin Christopher, "'No Effect' Prayer Study from Mayo Clinic Ignored by Media," *Skeptical Inquirer*, March 2002, www.findarticles.com/p/articles/mi_m2843/is_2_26/ai_83585945; "Prayer, Noetic Studies Feasible; Results Indicate Benefit to Heart Patients," www.dukemednews.org/news/article.php?id=5056.)

Paragraph Type a. just the facts

b. question and answer

c. competing points of view

d. comparison and contrast

e. results of research

---

*adverse: negative.
*cardiac arrest: the stopping of the heart.

Implied Main Idea a. Research on heart patients has confirmed that intercessory prayer improves the health of those who are prayed for.

b. Despite the claims of the faithful, intercessory prayer actually has no effect on the health of those being prayed for.

c. So far, scientific studies haven't been able to conclusively prove or disprove the effectiveness of intercessory prayer.

5. When a cute and cuddly panda cub was born at Washington, D.C.'s National Zoo in 2005, the public snapped up the 13,000 tickets offered for two-hour daily viewing sessions in just two hours. To help satisfy the public's passion for panda bears, both the National Zoo and the San Diego Zoo offer online "panda cams" that allow observation of the animals 24 hours a day. The cameras are so popular viewers are asked to limit viewing to just 15 minutes so everyone gets a chance to see the bears. Pandas also appear in the logos* of many organizations and businesses, such as the World Wildlife Fund, the Panda Express fast food chain, and Panda Energy International. The panda is likewise the national symbol of China, which is why a cartoon panda named Jing Jing is one of the mascots for the 2008 Summer Olympics in Beijing. Back in the 1960s and 1970s, the adorable bears helped China establish diplomatic relations with other nations. In 1972, for instance, President Richard Nixon returned from China with pandas Hsing-Hsing and Ling-Ling. The gift gave birth to the term "panda diplomacy." (Source of information: Kitty Bean Yancey, "Panda Fever Has Broken Out," *USA Today*, December 15, 2005, www.usatoday.com/travel/destinations/2005-12-15-pandas_x.htm.)

Paragraph Type a. just the facts

b. question and answer

c. competing points of view

d. comparison and contrast

e. results of research

Implied Main Idea a. Pandas have always been the most popular animals at America's zoos, and visitors seem to dote on the cuddly creatures.

b. China has long used its national symbol, the panda bear, for political purposes.

c. Around the world, the popular panda has long inspired feelings of affection and good will.

---

*logos: symbols representing institutions or companies, e.g., Apple Computer's apple or the Hartford Insurance Company elk.

▢ EXERCISE 6 Inferring the Implied Main Idea

DIRECTIONS Read each paragraph. Identify the type of paragraph used to imply the main idea. Then write the implied main idea in the blanks.

EXAMPLE It's distressing but true that thousands of species of cockroaches are living in all kinds of places: at busy schools, under mossy stones, in subway stations, among fallen leaves, at fancy restaurants, in stinky sewer pipes. The cockroach's flattened body makes it easy for the insect to fit into tiny cracks in walls or slip into spaces under objects. In addition, cockroaches are fast runners, with nervous systems that allow the bugs to get moving as soon as they sense danger. The cockroach's survival is also aided by the long, sensitive antennae that help the insect collect information about its surroundings. In lab experiments, cockroaches have even used those antennae to detect and avoid areas sprayed with poison. Their antennae also ensure that cockroaches can locate food and water. Eating, however, is seldom a problem. To survive, cockroaches munch on a wide variety of substances, including pet food, wallpaper glue, house insulation, and paper. If necessary, the insects can do without food and water for weeks at a time. (Adapted from Doris, *Insects*, p. 42.)

Paragraph Type __just the facts__

Implied Main Idea __Cockroaches are masters of survival.__

EXPLANATION The paragraph offers a series of specific facts about cockroaches. Every specific statement in the paragraph describes how well adapted they are. Thus, the implied main idea suggests their ability to survive under any conditions.

1. How do you fight the urge to underachieve? Start by reflecting on and evaluating messages you received from family and friends while growing up. Did family members or friends resent those who experienced career success or were wealthy? Did they tell you to let other children win at games or various contests, otherwise no one would like you? Once you get a sense of how a "fear of success" pattern might develop, think about how you might showcase your abilities. This might involve volunteering to work on a new project that will allow you to demonstrate your skills. Finally, learn how to sell yourself to people who make decisions about your earnings and your advancement. In other words, don't be afraid to toot your own

horn. (Adapted from Reece and Brandt, *Effective Human Relations in Organizations*, p. 190.)

Paragraph Type _____

Implied Main Idea _____

2. Each year during the 1900s, an average of 54 swimmers worldwide were attacked by sharks at America's beaches. During 2000, there were, on average, 80 attacks. As a result scientists are wondering why more sharks seem to be preying on humans. Commercial fishermen and their supporters argue that fishing restrictions designed to protect sharks have created a safe zone for the deadly predators in coastal waters. In 1997, for instance, the federal government outlawed all attempts at catching the great white shark. Catching of other shark species has been limited to one or two per person. Thus, sharks, particularly the dangerous kind, have been left alone to breed and multiply, causing the increase in shark attacks. However, there are those who insist that the commercial fishermen themselves are the source of the increase. According to this argument, fishermen have overfished some species of shark like the sandbar and blacktip, and this has changed the whole ecosystem by removing much of the competition for food among all shark species. Fewer sharks of one type mean more food for others, such as the deadly bull shark. As other shark species dwindle, the bull shark, which is particularly vicious when it encounters humans, is able to feed more and grow both in strength and numbers. Spokespeople for the fishing industry respond by saying that there is no reliable data to prove this theory.

Paragraph Type _____ competing points

Implied Main Idea That Sharks attacks _____

3. In 2002, Americans were worried about a sagging economy, threats of terrorism, and a pending war with Iraq. Even so, two-thirds of all American households donated an average of $2,499 apiece to charitable organizations. While corporations and foundations gave about $39 billion, individuals' contributions totaled just under $184 billion. Gifts willed by the deceased added another $18 billion; therefore, over 80 percent of all charitable donations came from individuals. All together, U.S. citizens gave about $241 billion, a record-setting amount that was 1 percent higher than the previous year's total. And Americans don't just write checks to help fund charities' work. Almost half of this country's adults—about 84 million people—serve

as volunteers to help those in need. (Sources of information: Joellen Perry, "Giving Lessons," *U.S. News & World Report,* December 8, 2003, p. 46; DMA Nonprofit Federation, "Charitable Giving Increases in 2002, 'Giving USA' Reports," June 23, 2003, www.the-dma.org/cgi/dispnewsstand?article=1267.)

Paragraph Type _____

Implied Main Idea _____

_____

4. Who was the greatest baseball player of all time? Well, that depends. If we ask sports fans, many would probably name Babe Ruth number one. Thanks to his astonishing home-run record and colorful personality, Ruth was voted baseball's Greatest Player Ever in a 1969 poll. Thirty years later *The Sporting News* still put Ruth at the top of its list of "Baseball's 100 Greatest Players." In 1999, The Associated Press named him "Athlete of the Century." However, if we look at statistical achievements, we might have to conclude that one of Ruth's teammates, Lou Gehrig, is equally deserving of the greatest player title. Although it's been seventy years since Gehrig played, many of his accomplishments—such as his twenty-three grand slams—remain at or near the top of the record books. Then again, limiting ourselves to batting averages and home runs from what were once all-white leagues would mean leaving out a man like the black player Satchel Paige. Widely believed to be the greatest pitcher in the history of the Negro League, Paige's achievements included pitching sixty-four consecutive scoreless innings. Finally making it to the Major League in 1948 as its first black pitcher, he promptly led his team to a World Series victory that same year. From Paige's perspective, though, the legendary Joe DiMaggio was "the best and fastest pitcher I've ever faced." (Sources of information: Babe Ruth Biography, www.baberuth.com/flash/about/biograph.html; Lou Gehrig, www.lougehrig.com/home.php; Satchel Paige Biography, www.satchelpaige.com/bio2.html.)

Paragraph Type Comparison & Contrast/competing points

Implied Main Idea _____

_____

5. As most parents or teachers know, boys and girls begin school with different mental and physical abilities. Boys tend to have better spatial reasoning and hand-eye coordination than girls, and they are

usually more active and energetic. Girls tend to have more advanced verbal and organization skills, and they are less impulsive. Despite their strengths, however, boys are twice as likely as girls to have problems with reading and writing. By eighth grade, boys are scoring an average of 11 points lower than girls on standardized reading tests and 21 points lower on writing tests. This gap has been blamed on everything from society's differing expectations to inappropriate teaching methods. However, recent research has revealed that the prefrontal cortex, the part of the brain responsible for organizing complex thoughts and controlling impulses, processes information differently in boys than in girls. Tests on eleven- to eighteen-year-olds show that when boys are shown pictures of fearful faces, they register activity on both sides of their prefrontal cortex. Girls, however, use only one side, just like adults. By age eighteen, of course, boys' and girls' brains are processing information with the same speed and sophistication. But brain scans have revealed that the prefrontal cortex reaches its maximum thickness in girls by age eleven. In boys, this development happens later on.

Paragraph Type _____

Implied Main Idea _____

_____

 # More on Evaluating Your Inferences

Any time you infer the main idea of a paragraph, you need to make sure your inference is logical. **Logical inferences** are firmly based on statements in the paragraph. They do not contradict or undermine what the author actually says, and they keep the reader in touch with the author's intended meaning. **Illogical inferences** are based more on the reader's personal experience or common sense than on the author's actual words. In fact, they are likely to ignore or contradict what the author actually says. Illogical inferences often divert readers from the writer's train of thought, leading them to develop a meaning the writer never intended.

To see the difference between logical and illogical inferences, read the following passage about Joan of Arc. Then look carefully at the two possible implied main ideas that follow. One is a logical inference that follows from, or is based on, the paragraph. The other is not. It reflects the reader's point of view more than the author's. Your job is to decide which is which:

Joan of Arc, the national heroine and patron saint* of France, was born in 1412 to a family of poor peasants. In 1425, at the age of thirteen, Joan claimed to hear voices that she believed belonged to the early Christian saints and martyrs.* Four years later, in 1429, those same voices told her to help the young king of France Charles VII fight the British, who were trying to take control of France in the Hundred Years War.* When the king believed her story and gave her troops to command, Joan put on a suit of armor and led her soldiers to victory. Yet when the British captured Joan in 1430 and tried her for heresy* and wearing masculine dress, Charles refused to help her, allowing her to be condemned to death. On May 30, 1431, Joan was burned at the stake, still swearing loyalty to the king of France.

Now which of the following implied main ideas effectively sums up the above paragraph?

Implied Main Idea 1 Even though Joan of Arc sacrificed her life to save his throne, the king of France failed to return her loyalty.

Implied Main Idea 2 Although she died swearing her loyalty to the king of France, Joan of Arc must have hated him for his betrayal.

Did you decide that the first implied main idea was a more logical inference than the second? If you did, you are absolutely correct. The paragraph definitely implies that Joan sacrificed everything for a king who did not return her loyalty. Because we can safely say that statement 1 sums up the message of the paragraph in the same way that a topic sentence might have, we can also say that it's the implied main idea of the paragraph.

Statement 2, in contrast, is an illogical inference. It could easily lead the reader away from the writer's real point. There is simply no evidence in the paragraph to support the notion that Joan hated the king for his betrayal. True, many people might well despise someone who betrayed their loyalty as Charles VII did Joan's. Yet a reader's inferences can't be based on what many—or even most—people might feel. Logical inferences have to be grounded primarily on the author's words. Inference 2 does not fulfill this requirement. Thus it's not the implied main idea of the paragraph.

---

*patron saint: the saint protecting or guarding a nation, a place, an activity, or a person.
*martyrs: people who choose death rather than give up their religion or cause.
*Hundred Years War (1337–1453): an episodic struggle over land that varied from times of peace to periods of intense violence.
*heresy: challenging church law.

Logical and Illogical Inferences

Logical Inferences

- follow from or are based on what's said in the paragraph.
- do not favor the reader's experience or knowledge over the author's words.
- are not contradicted by any statements appearing in the paragraph.
- do not divert the reader from the author's intended meaning.

Illogical Inferences

- give more weight to the reader's feelings than they do the author's words.
- are based on a few stray words rather than several different sentences.
- are likely to be contradicted by one or more statements appearing in the paragraph.
- are likely to lead readers far from the author's intended meaning.

▄▆ EXERCISE 7 Identifying the Implied Main Idea

DIRECTIONS Read each paragraph. Then circle the letter of the more logical implied main idea. *Note*: Make sure that the answer you choose fits the criteria for a logical inference.

EXAMPLE Increasing numbers of Americans are turning to hypnosis to stop smoking or to lose weight. Similarly, arthritis sufferers are using acupuncture, an ancient method of Chinese healing, to gain some relief from their pain. Cancer patients have also been using nontraditional medical treatments like creative visualization to fight their disease. Some cancer sufferers, for example, imagine themselves as huge and powerful sharks. They imagine their cancer cells as much smaller fish that easily fall prey to the larger and more dangerous sharks. Even some businesses are supporting nontraditional medical treatments and encouraging employees to use meditation in order to ward off migraine headaches and high blood pressure.

Implied Main Idea   a. In the United States, an ever-growing number of people are turning to nontraditional medical treatments that often do more harm than good.

(b.) In the United States, more and more people are turning to non-traditional medical treatments to deal with medical problems.

EXPLANATION Inference *b* better expresses the implied main idea because all the sentences in the paragraph introduce or explain examples of Americans who are turning to nontraditional treatments. Inference *a* is inappropriate because the author never discusses the failure or the success of those treatments.

1. During World War I, India took the side of Great Britain. After the war ended in 1918, many Indian citizens dreamed of liberation* from British rule, hoping that Britain would show its gratitude and grant India independence. Instead, the British government enacted the 1919 Government of India Act. This act specified that all matters of local and lesser importance would be controlled by the Indian government. Major policies and decisions, however, would continue to be made by the British. Following the passage of the Government of India Act, there was widespread protest throughout most of India.

Implied Main Idea a. After World War I, the British disappointed Indian hopes for independence.

b. Because of their disappointment with the Government of India Act, Indian citizens staged a series of protests that only made matters worse.

2. In the early days of making movies, Westerns were extremely popular, and stars such as Tom Mix and William S. Hart made cowboy life seem dangerous and daring. In the early films, the daily life of a cowboy consisted mainly of shootouts with stagecoach robbers and cattle rustlers. Meanwhile, in real life, most cowboys were tending sprawling cattle herds under a hot, blazing sun. They didn't use their guns much, and, when they did, it was usually to shoot a coyote or a rattlesnake.

Implied Main Idea a. Most stars in early Westerns never left the East Coast and knew little or nothing about life on the range.

b. Early Westerns did not offer audiences a realistic view of cowboy life.

---

*liberation: the state of being given freedom.

■ EXERCISE 8 Identifying the Implied Main Idea

~~DIRECTIONS~~ Read each paragraph. Then circle the letter of the implied main idea.

1. The drug called cocaine was formally identified in 1855. By the 1870s, surgeons used it as an anesthetic for minor surgery. In the 1880s, it was used to treat opium addiction and alcoholism. The drug came to the notice of the young Sigmund Freud when he read reports of how small doses could restore exhausted soldiers. Trying it out on himself, Freud was enthusiastic, calling cocaine a wonder drug and recommending it to his wife. Freud was so enthusiastic that he prescribed cocaine for a young colleague who was addicted to morphine. The drug, however, did not produce a cure. Instead, the young man began hallucinating wildly. Believing that snakes were crawling under his skin, he committed suicide, leaving Freud devastated.

Implied Main Idea a. Sigmund Freud never got over his guilt about driving a colleague to suicide.

   b. Sigmund Freud never got over the mistake he made when he prescribed cocaine for a colleague who then killed himself.

   c. Sigmund Freud was sadly mistaken in his early enthusiasm for cocaine.

2. Entrants in the Little Miss of America beauty contest—girls between the ages of three and six—are not asked to pay a fee. Their indulgent* parents, however, willingly pay hundreds of dollars just to have their children's photographs included in the pageant catalog. They also must pay for the singing and dancing lessons that will allow their child to participate in the talent section of the contest. But perhaps even more costly than the lessons are the extensive wardrobes of party dresses that the girls must have in order to participate in the contest and its related functions. Furthermore, traveling expenses for the children and the relatives who accompany them can easily run into thousands of dollars.

Implied Main Idea a. It costs a lot of money to enter the Little Miss of America beauty contest.

---
*indulgent: lenient, inclined to spoil.

b. Little girls should not be encouraged to participate in beauty pageants.

c. When parents enter their little girls into beauty pageants, they have no idea of the costs associated with being in the pageant.

3. On January 30, 1889, young Crown Prince Rudolf of Austria was found shot to death in his hunting lodge on the outskirts of Vienna. Lying next to him was the body of his lover, seventeen-year-old Baroness Maria Vetsera. She, too, had been shot. In the years since that tragic event, some have claimed that Rudolf ended his life because he was depressed over a terminal illness. According to this theory, when Maria found him, she decided to take her life. Others insist, however, that Rudolf was murdered by members of the court who feared his progressive* beliefs would become public policy when Rudolf reached the throne. According to another theory, Maria and Rudolf entered into a suicide pact when their parents forbade the couple to marry.

Implied Main Idea a. Although there are many theories about how Crown Prince Rudolf and Maria Vetsera died, the theory that they were murdered makes the most sense.

b. No one really knows for sure how Crown Prince Rudolf and Maria Vetsera died.

c. Love drove Crown Prince Rudolf of Austria to suicide.

4. Can babies remember sounds heard when they were in the womb? Anthony DeCasper and Melanie Spence (1986) asked pregnant women to read Dr. Seuss's *The Cat in the Hat* to their unborn infants twice a day for the last six weeks of their pregnancies. After birth, the researchers tested the newborns by using a nipple connected to a tape recorder. By sucking in one pattern of short and long sucks, a baby could hear a recording of the mother reading *The Cat in the Hat*. Another sucking pattern produced a recording of the mother reading a different rhyming story. The babies, some only hours old, chose *The Cat in the Hat* most often. (Rubin et al., *Psychology*, p. 222.)

Implied Main Idea a. The research of Anthony DeCasper and Melanie Spence suggests that babies do remember sounds they hear in the womb.

---

*progressive: supporting social or political change.

b. Without question, babies remember everything they experience in the womb.

c. One study proved that babies have a special fondness for the sounds of Dr. Seuss.

▪ EXERCISE 9 Drawing a Logical Inference

DIRECTIONS Read each paragraph. Then, in the blanks that follow, write the implied main idea of the paragraph.

EXAMPLE The plow was invented during the Middle Ages. Thanks to its invention, farmers could dig more deeply into the soil and do it with much greater ease. That meant they could farm more land, using less labor. Another important invention in the Middle Ages was the collar harness. The old yoke harness had worked well with oxen, but tended to choke horses. With the collar harness, farmers could exchange oxen for horses. Horses had more stamina* and worked faster than oxen. Thus farmers could work fewer hours while still covering the same amount of ground. The Middle Ages also saw the invention of the water mill. With water-powered mills, farmers could grind more corn with less effort.

Implied Main Idea _During the Middle Ages, several important inventions made farming easier and more productive._

EXPLANATION The paragraph describes three separate inventions that appeared in the Middle Ages. Each of those inventions helped farmers do more work with less effort. Because this inference is general enough to include all three inventions, it effectively sums up the implied main idea of the paragraph.

1. During World War II, women of childbearing age had, on average, 2.5 children. But the 1950s saw an increase in the fertility rate. It edged up to more than 3.3 children per woman in the first half of the decade and then peaked at 3.6 children in the decade's last half. Fifteen years later, the fertility rate had dropped to the point where the average woman had 1.7 children. This trend has reversed in the past ten years, with fertility increasing to 2.0 children per

---

*stamina: ability to stay strong over time.

woman of childbearing age in 1989. However, this apparent baby boomlet may be the result of baby-boom women having children. (Adapted from Richard J. Gelles, *Contemporary Families*. Thousand Oaks, CA: Sage Publications, 1995, p. 261.)

Implied Main Idea <u>Threw the years the amount of children has fluaten threw the years.</u>

2. Anyone who orders a milk shake in Rhode Island and expects a drink made with ice cream is in for a surprise. In Rhode Island, a "milk shake" contains no ice cream. It's made of milk and flavored syrup. That's all. If you want ice cream in your drink, you'd better call it a "cabinet." The name comes from the wooden cabinet encasing the mixer that shakes up the milk. Similarly, anyone in search of a long sandwich made with layers of meat and cheese should ask for a "sub" or a "hero" in the North. But in the South, you had better request a "poor boy," or the waiter will be confused. If you want a soda in Boston, you should probably ask for a "tonic." However, if you are in Minneapolis, you'd better ask for a "pop," or else you're likely to get a glass of flavored seltzer water.

Implied Main Idea _____

_____

3. When Annie Sullivan first arrived to teach her young pupil, Helen Keller, she found a little girl who could not see or hear or speak. Cut off from the rest of the world around her, the child behaved like a little savage, biting and kicking whenever anyone approached her. In less than a month, however, Sullivan had taught the wild little girl that things had a name and that human beings could use those names to communicate with one another. In the years that followed, with Sullivan as a teacher and friend, Helen Keller learned to read Braille* in English, Latin, Greek, French, and German. She learned to use sign language and, above all, she learned to speak.

Implied Main Idea _____

_____

4. The Beatles' song "I Am the Walrus" was inspired by Lewis Carroll's classic work of children's literature, *Alice's Adventures in Wonderland*.

_____

*Braille: a system of printing for those who are visually impaired.

The same book also gave rock group Jefferson Airplane the idea for its song "White Rabbit" and Steely Dan its idea for "The Mock Turtle's Song." Mary Shelley's great science fiction novel, *Frankenstein*, inspired songs performed by rock band Blue Oyster Cult and singer-songwriter Bob Dylan, who also got many of his ideas for lyrics from great works of literature like Samuel Taylor Coleridge's "The Rime of the Ancient Mariner," Dante's *The Inferno*, and the poetry of William Blake. Several of Led Zeppelin's songs are derived from J. R. R. Tolkien's *The Lord of the Rings*. The band Styx also performed a song based upon that same fantasy classic. Rock group Pink Floyd's entire *Animals* album was inspired by George Orwell's classic, *Animal Farm*. Homer's *The Odyssey* has influenced songs by Steely Dan, Cream, and others. (Source of information: www.artistsforliteracy.org/famous.html.)

Implied Main Idea _____

_____

Check Your Understanding
Explain the difference between logical and illogical inferences.
_____
_____
_____
_____
_____

■ **DIGGING DEEPER**

BLACK BASEBALL

LOOKING AHEAD Page 251 introduced the name of Satchel Paige, considered by many to be one of the greatest baseball players of all time. The following reading describes the Negro League, which flourished in the years before Jackie Robinson broke the color barrier in baseball. After reading the selection, decide which inference more effectively sums up the implied main idea.

1 In 1947, the general manager of the Brooklyn Dodgers, Branch Rickey, decided to integrate the major leagues by hiring Georgia-born infielder Jackie Robinson. Ignoring death threats, Robinson made his debut on April 15 at Brooklyn's Ebbets Field, and major league baseball was never the same again. The color bar separating black and white players had finally been broken, and it was down for good.

2 For decades now, Robinson's story has been told and retold—and rightly so, for it illustrates how discrimination can be eradicated when people decide it has to be. Yet, as James A. Riley, the author of *The All-Time Stars of Black Baseball*, has written, great black players in the tradition of Hank Aaron, Willie Mays, and Willie Stargell didn't just spring up out of nowhere as a result of Robinson's debut. From the beginning, Jackie Robinson was standing on the shoulders of countless black players who came before him. Unfortunately, the players' names and their struggles to make a living playing the game they loved have been largely ignored.

3 As early as the 1860s, mixed crowds were watching championship games played by all-black teams like the Uniques, the Pythians, and the Excelsiors. Yet despite the obvious skill of the players and the enthusiasm shown by fans of both races, the National Association of Base Ball Players (NABBP), organized in 1868, would not accept the all-black teams for membership. Instead the association established the first official "color line" in baseball by voting unanimously to bar "any club which may be composed of one or more colored persons."

4 Fortunately for black players, the association only had amateur status. Thus, professional players weren't bound by its rules, and black ballplayers continued to appear on integrated teams (some black teams even played in integrated leagues). The noose, however, was tightening: Black players were slowly being cut off from all integrated team play. The year 1876 saw the birth of the

National League, and it was clear from the start that the league was going to remain lily white. When talented black players like the brothers Moses and Wellday Walker, Frank Grant, and the near-legendary pitcher George Stovey began flocking to the International League's integrated teams, editorials began to appear, asking questions similar to the one posed in the magazine *Sporting Life:* "How far will this mania* for engaging colored players go?"

5   After a few more such editorials, some protests by angry fans, and several on-field confrontations, integrated teams quickly became a thing of the past. To be sure, black players could found their own teams, like the Cuban Giants, organized in 1885. They could also start their own leagues, like the Negro National League established in 1920 by Rube Foster, the father of black baseball. But black players weren't going to appear on the field with white players. Talent wasn't the issue; race was what mattered.

6   Had talent been the issue, only the most die-hard racists would have argued that black players weren't the equal of white ones. It's revealing that in the era prior to Robinson's debut, many white players publicly proclaimed their admiration for their black counterparts. When the great Pittsburgh Pirates shortstop Honus Wagner heard that black shortstop John Henry Lloyd was called "the black Wagner," he called the comparison "an honor and a privilege."

7   In fact, some white players, including the celebrated Babe Ruth, were so anxious to have black players on the field, they organized their own exhibition games. Because the teams weren't paid, blacks could participate, and Ruth, for one, could test his mettle against the likes of Josh Gibson, considered the most dangerous hitter in black baseball. Following Ruth's example, the famed pitcher Dizzy Dean organized numerous exhibition games, largely because they allowed him to compete against Satchel Paige, the black pitcher widely known as the "Mound Magician." In 1934, Dean got a taste of the magician's magic when Paige beat him 1–0 in an exhibition game that went down in sports history.

8   Ironically,* the Negro leagues, which had done so much to foster the talent of players like Paige and Gibson, became a thing of the past once Robinson broke the color barrier. The Negro National League, for example, folded just one year after Robinson ran onto Ebbets Field. Robinson had led his team to the World

---

*mania: madness.
*ironically: contrary to what one might expect, implying the opposite of what one says. If asked how your day went, you might make a face and say "Oh, just great," meaning it was a horrible day.

Series, and the once all-white leagues were now eager to sign young black players who showed signs of talent. The era of two separate baseball leagues, one black and one white, was finally over. Sadly, the end of that era had been a long time coming, much longer than many people realize.

Sharpening Your Skills

DIRECTIONS Answer the following questions by circling the letter of the correct response.

1. Based on the context, what is the meaning of *mettle* in paragraph 7?
   a. dislike and anger
   b. courage and strength
   c. past and present
   d. string of awards

2. What is the main idea of paragraph 2?
   a. Nobody before or after his time has ever been a match for the great Jackie Robinson.
   b. James A. Riley's book *The All-Time Stars of Black Baseball* has managed to preserve the true story of black baseball.
   c. Jackie Robinson was a creation of newspaper reporters who needed a good story; he was never as talented as the press claimed.
   d. Many great black ballplayers came before Jackie Robinson; they just never got a chance to show their ability.

3. What is the main idea of paragraph 6?
   a. With a few exceptions, no one ever doubted that black ballplayers could play as well as white ones.
   b. Honus Wagner was one of the few ballplayers to openly acknowledge the talent of black ballplayers.
   c. Black shortstop John Henry Lloyd was a great admirer of the Pittsburgh Pirates shortstop Honus Wagner.
   d. Honus Wagner was insulted at hearing that a black ballplayer was called "the black Wagner."

4. In paragraph 7, which sentence is the topic sentence?

a. In fact, some white players, including the celebrated Babe Ruth, were so anxious to have black players on the field, they organized their own exhibition games.

b. Because the teams weren't paid, blacks could participate, and Ruth, for one, could test his mettle against the likes of Josh Gibson, considered the most dangerous hitter in black baseball.

c. Following Ruth's example, the famed pitcher Dizzy Dean organized numerous exhibition games, largely because they allowed him to compete against Satchel Paige, the black pitcher widely known as the "Mound Magician."

d. In 1934, Dean got a taste of the magician's magic when Paige beat him 1–0 in an exhibition game that went down in sports history.

5. What's the implied main idea of the entire reading?

a. For almost a century, black ballplayers were forced to create their own baseball teams and leagues in order to play ball, even though they were clearly superior to the all-white teams.

b. We should not forget the many black baseball players who paved the way for Jackie Robinson's triumphant civil rights breakthrough in 1947.

c. In the early years of the game, baseball was open to any player who had talent.

d. Without the courage of Jackie Robinson and Branch Rickey, baseball would have remained a segregated sport for at least another decade.

INTERNET RESOURCE

For more practice with supporting details, see **college.hmco.com/ pic/flemmingRFR10e**, where you will find three levels of interactive quizzes: *Getting Down the Basics*, *Checking Your Progress*, and *Taking the Challenge*. You can find additional interactive practice with inferences at **laflemm.com**, *Reading for Results*: Online Practice for Chapter 5.

 # Test 1: Recognizing the Implied Main Idea

DIRECTIONS Read the paragraph. Then circle the letter of the implied main idea.

1. The word *natural* in advertisements clearly sells products. Juices and foods filled with "natural" goodness along with "natural" vitamins and herbs are big sellers. Consumers seem to believe that anything coming straight from nature has to be good for you. Yet if you're one of those consumers, you might want to reconsider your trust in Mother Nature. Aflatoxin, one of the most potent cancer-causing substances that exists, is a natural product of mold. Ricin, one of the deadliest poisons on earth, comes from nature's own castor beans. Take just one bite of the naturally growing mushroom *Amanita phalloides,* and you won't be around long enough to discuss its bitter aftertaste. Next time you're thinking of buying an herbal supplement because it's "natural"—and therefore has to be good for you—just remember, bee stings and poison ivy are also part of nature.

Implied Main Idea a. Synthetic products are better for you than natural ones are.

b. We shouldn't just assume that "natural" products are safe.

c. The word *natural* is a big selling point for all kinds of products.

2. After Timothy J. McVeigh was convicted of bombing a federal office building in Oklahoma City, causing the deaths of 168 people, reporters swarmed to McVeigh's hometown of Pendleton, New York.* The journalists sought comments on the verdict from McVeigh's friends, family, and acquaintances in the small town which has about five thousand residents. The reporters also wanted to ask if Pendleton people thought McVeigh deserved the death penalty. But in short order, community members slammed their doors in the journalists' faces. McVeigh's family pulled down the shades and refused to leave the house. When television crews approached Pendleton folks at a supermarket, the shoppers tried to slam their carts into expensive TV equipment. One woman grabbed a phone and started dialing local police. Other Pendleton residents just pressed their lips together and stared.

Implied Main Idea a. People in Timothy McVeigh's hometown didn't want to talk to reporters.

*The bombing took place on April 19, 1995; McVeigh was convicted in June of 1997. He was executed on June 11, 2001.

     b. People in Timothy McVeigh's hometown thought he was inno-
cent.

     c. People in Timothy McVeigh's hometown were ashamed to have
known him.

3. In 1995 gray wolves, listed as an endangered species, were reintro-
duced into Yellowstone Park, where they had once roamed freely. To
the surprise of biologists, the wolves multiplied faster than
expected, so much so that their status is now listed as "threatened"
rather than endangered. Perhaps because of the population spurt,
the wolves have begun to stray outside the park's boundaries. In a
few cases, they have ventured onto bordering ranch lands and
killed domestic livestock. The U.S. Fish and Wildlife Service
responded quickly by shooting or capturing the wolves believed to
be preying on livestock. But some ranchers have taken the law into
their own hands and shot the wolves themselves. The ranchers
want the legal right to shoot any wolf that ventures onto their property. Many are furious that the Fish and Wildlife Service insists on
fining and prosecuting any rancher caught wolf hunting.

Implied Main Idea   a. The reintroduction of gray wolves was a bad idea from the
beginning.

     b. The reintroduction of gray wolves into Yellowstone Park proves
that endangered animals can be saved by human intervention.

     c. The 1995 reintroduction of gray wolves into Yellowstone Park
has saved them from extinction; however, it has also caused
some serious problems.

4. Currently, children in the United States receive more vaccinations
than ever before. On average, they get nineteen inoculations for ten
different diseases. As a result, potential killers such as polio and
diphtheria are all but unknown in the United States. One would
think that would be cause for gratitude among parents anxious to
protect their children from illness. But some parents are not so
thrilled. Instead, they want to know more about the possible
adverse effects. One such parent is Barbara Loe Fisher, president
of the National Vaccine Information Center, who pointedly asks if
the vaccines children receive "could be doing something else which
isn't so good." Fisher charges that parents don't get enough information about the relationship between vaccines and chronic physical and mental disorders. Lisa Mayberry is another parent troubled
by the numerous vaccines given to children. She watched her child

develop autism* after he was inoculated against measles, mumps, and rubella (MMR). Although a study of 498 autistic children found no connection between the MMR shot and autism, the Centers for Disease Control is continuing to investigate. The CDC has recommended that physicians discontinue use of the oral vaccine against polio because it has been proven to induce polio in several instances. It has also called a halt to the new rotavirus vaccine designed to eliminate gastrointestinal ailments in infants. As it turns out, the vaccine causes bowel obstructions in some recipients. (Source of information: Claudia Kalb and Donna Foote, "Necessary Shots," *Newsweek*, September 13, 1999, p. 73.)

Implied Main Idea a. Although vaccinating America's children has had obvious benefits, some parents are worried about possible adverse reactions.

b. All the vaccination programs for children should come to an immediate halt.

c. Anxious about their children's health, some parents have launched a fight against vaccinations.

*autism: a disorder that makes it hard for affected children to make contact with the world around them.

 ## Test 2: Recognizing the Implied Main Idea

DIRECTIONS Read the paragraph. Then circle the letter of the implied main idea.

1. According to the rules of their order, Carmelite nuns begin their days at the crack of dawn. Rising at 5:00 AM, they sing hymns and eat breakfast. Breakfast, like the rest of their meals, is simple. The nuns are not allowed to eat meat. In addition, they have taken a vow of poverty, so rich food is out of the question. Once breakfast is over, the Carmelites spend their days doing chores or saying prayers. Conversation of any sort is forbidden, as are visitors. If the nuns speak at all to outsiders, it is through an iron grill that symbolizes their separation from the world. As one might expect, radio, television, and computers are not usually found among the Carmelites.

Implied Main Idea   a. In time, the rules of the Carmelite order are bound to become less strict.

b. Most Carmelite nuns enter the order because they have been wounded by the world.

c. The Carmelites will never change the strict rules of their order.

d. The rules of the Carmelite order ensure that the nuns lead a life of solitude and simplicity.

2. History books have long insisted that the Spanish explorer Hernando Cortés defeated the Aztec Empire after Montezuma, the empire's too trusting king, welcomed Cortés into Tenochtitlan (now Mexico City) and extended him his hospitality. Cortés returned the courtesy by throwing Montezuma into jail. Then with the help of a few hundred men and the arrival of European diseases like typhus and small-pox, he turned the Aztec Empire into a Spanish colony. That, in any case, is the conventional version of events. But now researchers at an archaeological dig about one hundred miles east of modern Mexico City have unearthed hundreds of skeletons, bones, and arti-facts* that tell another story. The remains found are from a 1520 caravan of Spanish conquistadors, their families, and servants, all of whom were on their way to Tenochtitlan, probably to help put the finishing touches on Cortés's defeat of the Aztecs. According to Enrique Martinez, director of the dig, the newfound evidence strongly suggests that the travelers were set upon and captured by

*artifacts: remnants of lost civilizations.

Aztec warriors. The captors then apparently kept their victims in cages for an extended period of time, perhaps up to six months. During that time, Aztec priests made regular selections of those who were to be used as human sacrifices in religious rituals. Close examination also suggests that the caravan's captors engaged in cannibalism, eating the bodies of those who had been sacrificed. This seems to explain why Cortés named the town where it all happened "Tecuaque," which means "where people were eaten." (Source of information: http://news.independent.co.uk/world/americas/article1221635.ece.)

Implied Main Idea a. Historians have long underestimated the courage of Montezuma's warriors.

b. Enrique Martinez has found conclusive evidence that cannibalism was part of Aztec society.

c. A new archaeological discovery disputes the notion that the Aztecs let themselves be conquered without a fight.

d. In at least one instance, Cortés's followers got exactly what they deserved for plundering the great Aztec Empire.

3. Spectacled cobras—six-foot-long brown snakes that can kill with a single bite—are everywhere in the country of Sri Lanka. It's not surprising, therefore, that thousands of people are bitten yearly. Many victims are children, and some of them die. What's surprising is that most Sri Lankans will not harm a cobra that happens to venture into a nearby woodpile or rice field. The majority of Sri Lankans are Buddhists. According to their religion, the spectacled cobra once gave shelter to Buddha by opening the hood at the back of its neck. To show that the cobra was under his protection, Buddha is said to have given the snake the spectacles-like red mark that appears on the back of its head.

Implied Main Idea a. Given the number of people who die from snake bites, the people of Sri Lanka should stop worshipping cobras.

b. The people of Sri Lanka should do something about the threat of cobra bites to their children.

c. The people of Sri Lanka do not kill cobras because they believe the snakes are under the protection of Buddha.

d. Should the number of victims suffering from cobra bites continue to rise, the people of Sri Lanka are bound to change their attitudes toward cobras.

4. Listeria is a food-borne bacterium that has been found in hot dogs; deli meats; soft cheeses; and undercooked meat, poultry, and seafood. On a yearly basis, listeria sickens about 2,500 Americans. One serious outbreak of listeria poisoning, in 1998, was traced to meat processed at a Sara Lee Corporation plant in Michigan. The company had to recall 15 million pounds of hot dogs and luncheon meats. More recently, in 2002, seven people died from eating Wampler brand turkey tainted by listeria. In the healthy, listeria is an unpleasant nuisance, causing flu-like symptoms that last several days. But if the elderly are stricken by listeria poisoning, they can die from it. If a pregnant woman ingests the bacterium, a miscarriage or a stillbirth often results, even if the mother herself experiences no symptoms. In the 1998 outbreak, at least one hundred people got sick, and fifteen of those died. (Source of information: www.cspinet.org/new/20021016/html.)

Implied Main Idea a. Processed meats have long been the source of food poisoning.

b. Given the high incidence of listeria poisoning, it is amazing that meatpacking plants are not required to test for it.

c. Outbreaks of listeria poisoning are bound to increase.

d. Depending on who is stricken, listeria poisoning can be an unpleasant nuisance or a horrible tragedy.

 **Test 3: Recognizing the Implied Main Idea**

DIRECTIONS Read the paragraph. Then circle the letter of the implied main idea.

1. Researchers at the University of Kentucky wanted to find out if public service announcements (PSAs) on television have an impact on teenagers' use of the drug marijuana. To test the effectiveness of PSAs, researchers created dramatic, attention-getting anti-drug ads targeted toward sensation-seeking teens. The assumption was that kids having this personality trait were inclined toward drug use. Then the researchers began interviewing randomly selected public school students in grades seven through ten. The goal of the interviews was to identify sensation seekers and determine the extent of their marijuana use. These interviews, which began eight months before the PSAs began airing, involved more than three thousand students. Next, researchers began broadcasting their anti-marijuana PSAs during television programs that were favorites of the high-sensation-seeking teenagers. At least 70 percent of the sensation-seeking group was exposed to a minimum of three PSAs per week. Researchers continued to interview groups of one hundred students each month during the campaign and for eight months after it ended. By the study's end, researchers found that 26.7 percent of the high-sensation-seeking teenagers who had been using marijuana had stopped using the drug. (Source of information: National Institute on Drug Abuse, "Research Shows TV PSAs Effective in Reducing Teen Marijuana Use," January 31, 2001, www.nida.nih.gov/MedAdv/01/NR1-31.html.)

Implied Main Idea a. Researchers have found that drug users tend to be sensation seekers who like dramatic TV shows.

b. Research suggests that anti-marijuana public service announcements may be effective in reducing teenagers' use of the drug.

c. Research has shown that adolescents who are sensation seekers prefer marijuana to other kinds of drugs.

d. A growing body of research shows that public service announcements can persuade people to change or eliminate bad habits.

2. A phonics-based reading program teaches children how to match up sounds with letters. Once children know the sound or sounds of the letters of the alphabet, they are encouraged to break unfamiliar words into separate sounds, blend the sounds together, and pronounce them as a means of word recognition. However, critics of

phonics argue that using this method can diminish, even destroy, children's interest in reading. Bored by sounding out words, they give up on reading. Opponents of the phonics-based approach prefer what's called the "whole-language" method. They claim that children can recognize words by using context clues. Freed from the need to sound words out, young readers can read at a faster pace and learn to enjoy the act of reading. Critics of the whole-language approach insist, however, that it leaves kids without any tools to identify words they haven't seen in print before forcing them to rely on memorization to build their reading vocabulary.

Implied Main Idea a. Phonics-based reading programs are better than whole-language reading programs.

b. Whole-language reading programs are better than phonics-based reading programs.

c. Phonics-based reading programs and whole-language reading programs both have their defenders and their critics.

d. Neither approach to reading—phonics or whole language—has been successful in teaching children to read.

3. Prisons have always had elderly inmates. However, the number of elderly inmates is rapidly increasing: From 1992 to 2002 alone, the number of convicts age fifty and older doubled to 8.6 percent of all prisoners. As inmates begin to age, they often require additional health care and more expensive medications. Many states must offer their elderly prisoners special diets and exercise programs, and some have had to create special wings or units for their older convicts. Sixteen states have even opened entire geriatric* prisons. In 2000, Texas provided around-the-clock nursing care for two hundred inmates, and in many states prisons are providing hospice care for inmates who are terminally ill. When older convicts die in prison, correctional facilities often have to conduct funeral services and provide cemetery burial plots. At many institutions, such as the Louisiana State Prison at Angola, as many as 90 percent of the inmates will die while in the custody of the state. As a result, states are paying an average of $69,000 per year to incarcerate each elderly inmate, compared to $22,000 for a younger inmate. (Source of information: Patrick McMahon, "Aging Inmates Present Prison Crisis," *USA Today*, August 10, 2003, www.usatoday.com/news/nation/2003-08-10-prison-inside-usat_x.htm.)

---

*geriatric: related to aging.

Implied Main Idea   a. We need an alternative to prison for punishing older criminals who have not committed a violent crime.

b. Elderly prisoners should be released from penal institutions.

c. Correctional institutions are expected to do too much for inmates.

d. The increase in elderly prison inmates comes with a high price tag.

4. In national surveys, more than 80 percent of all American youth admit to consuming alcohol before their twenty-first birthday, and four out of every five college students say they drink alcohol. Even worse, 40 percent of college students engage in binge drinking—the consumption of five or more alcoholic drinks in one sitting for males and four or more for females. With this many young people abusing alcohol, it should come as no surprise to anyone that every year over two million college students drive while intoxicated. Thus binge drinking leads to an annual 1,700 accidental deaths and 599,000 injuries among college students eighteen to twenty-four years old. Students themselves report that drinking increases sexual assaults and incidents of unprotected sex, along with academic and health problems. As a result, both college students and college presidents identify alcohol abuse as even more worrisome than rising tuition rates. The U.S. Surgeon General and the U.S. Department of Health and Human Services (USDHHS) are so concerned about binge drinking among college students that they have set the goal of cutting the binge drinking rate in half by 2010. (Sources of information: Steve Wieberg, "Colleges Are Reaching Their Limit on Alcohol," *USA Today*, November 16, 2005, p. 1A; National Institute on Alcohol Abuse and Alcoholism, www.collegedrinkingprevention.gov.)

Implied Main Idea   a. Drinking while driving is the leading cause of accidents among people under the age of thirty.

b. Binge drinking among college students is a dangerous and deadly trend.

c. Alcohol abuse on campus is viewed with more concern now then it was in the past.

d. The Surgeon General's office has a plan to eliminate binge drinking on campus.

 **Test 4: Recognizing the Implied Main Idea**

DIRECTIONS Read the paragraph. Then circle the letter of the implied main idea.

1. Some people claim that declawing a cat does no real harm, but for reasons of their own, they are denying the obvious. Cats remove old skin and dry hair by scratching themselves. A cat without claws can't groom itself properly. Cats also need their claws to jump. Their claws are like landing gear. They help cats maintain their balance. If deprived of claws, the animals find it hard to jump from place to place. Worst of all, if a declawed house cat escapes its home, it could quickly die of starvation. Grabbing for a mouse or bird would be an empty gesture, leaving the cat to go hungry. An even more horrible fate awaits the declawed cat who gets into a fight with another animal.

Implied Main Idea   a. It's a mistake to declaw a cat.

b. Cats need their claws for grooming.

c. Too many pet owners don't consider their animals' needs.

d. The practice of declawing cats is increasing.

2. On December 18, 1912, an amateur archaeologist named Charles Dawson and his friend Arthur Smith Woodward presented what they claimed were extraordinary findings to the Geological* Society of London. Woodward and Dawson presented the skeleton of a creature alleged to be half man and half ape. The two men claimed they had discovered what was believed to be the missing link on the evolutionary* scale. With relatively little investigation, Piltdown man—as the skeleton came to be called—was accepted as genuine. As time went by, however, doubts began to surface, and paleontologists* examined and reexamined the skeleton. In 1953, close analysis of the skeleton revealed that someone had created it by fusing together the bones of a human being and an orangutan.

Implied Main Idea   a. Dawson and Woodward were con men.

b. The Piltdown man was a fraud.

c. The Piltdown man hoax illustrates a basic truth in science: The experts are often the easiest to fool.

------

*geological: involved in the study of Earth.
*evolutionary: related to the development of human beings as they changed from apes into humans.
*paleontologists: people who study ancient life forms.

d. Dawson knew the Piltdown man was a hoax, but Woodward believed the skeleton was the real thing—the missing link.

3. In the eighteenth century, the English economist Thomas Malthus predicted that future populations would increase faster than food supplies—with disastrous results. But in the past two hundred years, technological advances* have profoundly influenced food-production methods. In industrialized* countries, the same amount of food can be produced in less time than it took half a century ago. Similarly, increased knowledge of agriculture has helped grow more food on less land. By the same token, land once considered unfit for food production has become fertile. With time, as we learn more about the ocean, we may be able to produce food not just from the land but from the sea as well.

Implied Main Idea a. Malthus's prediction may yet be proven true.

b. Technology will always outwit Mother Nature.

c. The theory that population increases faster than food supplies has not proved true for industrialized countries.

d. Malthus inaccurately predicted a problem with overpopulation.

4. Vitamin A helps with vision, bone growth, and healthy skin. A deficiency in vitamin A can produce eye diseases. Dairy products, nuts, and yellow vegetables all contain vitamin A. Vitamin C helps fight colds and is essential to healthy teeth. Oranges, lemons, tomatoes, and strawberries all contain this important vitamin. Vitamin D, the sunshine vitamin, helps keep bones and teeth strong; a lack of this vitamin can contribute to arthritis. Fish and eggs are the best sources of vitamin D. The vitamin B complex—B_1, B_2, B_6, and B_{12}—is also extremely important. It keeps the skin healthy and develops muscle tone. Vitamin B may even help reduce stress and tension. Green, leafy vegetables, milk, and grains help supply this important group of vitamins.

Implied Main Idea a. Of all the vitamins, the B complex is the most important.

b. Vitamin A is the key to good health.

c. We can get all the vitamins we need from a balanced diet; vitamin pills are unnecessary.

d. Vitamins are important for maintaining good health.

---

*technological advances: progress based on the application of science to industry.
*industrialized: relying heavily on machinery to produce goods and services.

 **Test 5: Recognizing the Implied Main Idea**

DIRECTIONS Read each paragraph. Then write the implied main idea in the blanks that follow.

1. Left on his own at a young age, the comedian Charlie Chaplin quickly learned how to survive on London's city streets. Living in part from money earned as a mime,* he also charmed friends and strangers alike into giving him food and shelter. Above all, he learned how to outwit the police, who were not fond of a young boy without a home or a job. Arriving in the United States in 1910, Chaplin quickly got work in silent films. After that, it did not take him long to develop the character that made him famous—the "Little Tramp." Dressed in shabby clothes, begging for money and food wherever he could find it, the Little Tramp spent most of his twenty-five years onscreen avoiding the police, who pursued him in one hilarious scene after another.

Implied Main Idea _____

_____

2. During the Civil War, the first war to be covered by newspaper journalists, some reporters considered it their duty to rally the troops. During the famous battle of Bull Run, for example, Edmund Clarence Stedmen of the *New York World* would wave the regiment flag whenever he thought the troops he was covering were losing their will to fight. Junius Brown from the *New York Tribune* went a step further. If he thought a rebel sniper was in the surrounding area, he would pick up a gun and start firing. Aware that Union* leader Ulysses S. Grant liked to drink, Sylvanus Cadwallader of the *Chicago Times* did his part to win the war: He locked himself and Grant in the bathroom to keep the general from hitting the bottle. Even more than his colleagues, Samuel Wilkeson of the *New York Times* participated in the war he covered. After the bloody battle of Gettysburg, Wilkeson wrote his report standing beside the grave of his oldest son.

Implied Main Idea _____

_____

---

*mime: a performer who acts out situations without speaking.
*Union: loyal to the United States government during the Civil War.

3. In the stable and moist conditions of the tropical rain forests, plants and animals are more varied and diverse than anywhere else on Earth. The variety and diversity of the rain forest makes it a treasure trove for all kinds of riches, from exotic perfumes to cures for deadly diseases. Yet every year, a rain forest region the size of Belgium is cut down to make way for agriculture. The cutting occurs despite the fact that the soil in the rain forest is not particularly suitable for either growing or grazing. The soil is sandy. Lacking nutrients from the trees, it quickly becomes too dry to be useful for farming or herding. Still, the cutting continues, although no one knows what miraculous cure for disease has been lost in the process.

Implied Main Idea _____

_____

4. Lasers, devices that produce an intense, focused beam of light, have been around since 1960, when Theodore H. Maiman put the first one together. At the time, however, no one quite knew what to do with the laser. In fact, in the sixties and early seventies, the laser was often described as a solution looking for a good problem. But nowadays, no one makes that little joke any more. Laser technology is being used with increasing frequency on people who wear glasses. Many who undergo laser surgery discover that once it is over, they can see without glasses. Lasers are also now commonly used to remove cataracts and gallstones, and heart surgeons employ them to remove blood clots from coronary arteries. In addition to medical uses, lasers are important tools of the military. They are central to all kinds of weaponry, including the so-called smart bombs. Moreover, traveling at the speed of light, lasers can burn a hole in missiles or their warheads and thereby render them ineffective. They are also a central part of military warning and detecting systems. In addition, lasers have found their place in industry. They play a key role in machine-tool operations, communication systems, tunnel construction, and welding.

Implied Main Idea _____

_____

5. The first successful blood transfusion was performed in the seventeenth century, but the practice was outlawed because of the dangers it posed to the patient. The practice was revived in the nineteenth century, but it was accompanied by terrible risks, like blood clots and kidney failure. Austrian-born Karl Landsteiner (1868–1943), however, had a theory. He argued that the blood of humans had inborn differences and similarities. The key, from Landsteiner's perspective, was to understand both the differences and the similarities. Once they were understood, Landsteiner thought the risks of blood transfusion might be eliminated. To that end, he analyzed numerous blood samples. By 1901, he had classified blood donors into three different categories called A, B, and O (AB was added in 1902). Following that discovery, the transfusion of blood became a relatively safe procedure.

Implied Main Idea _____

_____

 **Test 6: Vocabulary Review**

DIRECTIONS Here are twenty of the words introduced in Chapter 5. Use them to fill in the blanks. Words introduced in previous chapters are marked with an asterisk. *Note*: As before, the form of the word used here may differ from the form used in the chapter.

respiratory	terrain	irreparable	stamina
mania	progressive	liberate	indulgent
geriatric	artifacts	adverse	catapult
mettle	paleontologists	ironically	palpitations
logos	geological	evolutionary	industrialized

1. The Spanish Flu Pandemic of 1918–1919 killed 50 to 100 million people worldwide and was one of the worst flu outbreaks in history. Caused by two viral strains also found in poultry and pigs, the disease became deadly when it jumped to humans. Infection caused victims' lungs to fill up with fluid, producing severe ___respiratory___ problems such as pneumonia. ___Ironically___, it was the very young who, despite the advantages of youth, were vulnerable* and most likely to die from the flu. Not that ___geriatric___ members of the population were left in safety, but it was the young and healthy who were hardest hit.

2. Sneakers, first invented in 1893 for boaters, have evolved into a major fashion statement, with companies such as Nike, Adidas, and Reebok now selling athletic shoes for over $100 a pair. Of course, teenagers who buy these brands are interested more in what their ___logos___ represent than in the shoes' actual fitness for sports. A $150 pair of sneakers is more a trendy status symbol than a guarantee of better speed, balance, or the ability to ___catapult___ one's body into the air while on a basketball

court. While it is possible to understand why someone might pay a high price for hiking shoes, good on all kinds of _terrain_, it's harder to grasp why a person would spend that kind of money for sneakers. Certainly only the most _indulgent_ parent could consider that a sensible purchase.

3. In 1912, American historian Hiram Bingham found the ruins of the "Lost City of the Incas," forgotten for centuries, and rescued it from obscurity.* The city's palace and recovered _artifacts_ suggest that it was used as a country retreat for Incan royalty. Temples to Incan gods and local _geological_ features, such as a nearby mountain range shaped like a man gazing at the sky, indicated that it was also used for religious purposes. (www.mnsu .edu/emuseum/prehistory/latinamerica/south/sites/machu_ picchu.html.)

4. By unearthing fossils of ancient humans, Richard Leakey established himself in the 1970s as one of the world's foremost _paleontologists_. His discoveries—including a two million-year-old skull, the nearly complete 1.6 million-year-old skeleton of a child, and the skull of a new species called Australopithecus aethiopicus—helped scientists understand human beings' _evolutionary_ progression. (www.leakeyfoundation.org/ foundation/fl_4.jsp.)

5. Newly _industrialized_ in the early 1900s, America still didn't have any rules or laws for the workplace. This generally "lawless" situation perfectly suited newly wealthy industrialists, like John D. Rockefeller and Andrew Carnegie. Appropriately nicknamed "robber

barons," these men had a lust for money that bordered on
manic . They were determined to extract* huge profits
from their industries, even if their predatory* methods did
adverse harm to industry workers, who suffered from
chronic* breathing problems, dehydration,* skin disease, and heart
palpitations among other cardiac problems. But the
implacable* men who ruled industry with iron fists didn't reckon
with the commitment* of a group of investigative reporters and writers known as muckrakers, who had enough _stamina_
and _mettle_ to take on big business and expose the
respiratory conditions workers needed to survive in
order to scrape out a living. Muckrakers like Ida Tarbell, Lincoln
Steffens, and Upton Sinclair even went undercover to get the
information for their stories, all the while hoping they would
shock the public into protest and pave the way for
irreparable reforms that would _liberate_
working men and women from an inhumane system. And the
American public did not disappoint. When, for example, Americans read in Upton Sinclair's novel _The Jungle_ about the bent
backs, missing fingers, and scarred skin that was the norm in the
meat packing industry, there was a public outcry that only diminished when reforms were begun.

INTERNET BONUS QUESTIONS
While Upton Sinclair took on the meat packing industry, muckraker Ida Tarbell took on what famous industrialist?

_____

What incident from her childhood motivated Tarbell's crusade?

_____

_____

_____

What search terms did you use to find the answers to these two questions?

_____

CHAPTER 6

More on the Function of Supporting Details

In this chapter, you'll learn

- **more about the relationship between topic sentences and supporting details.**

- **how to distinguish between major and minor supporting details.**

- **how supporting details require reader-supplied inferences to fully communicate the author's meaning.**

- **how visual aids can function as supporting details.**

- **how concluding sentences differ from supporting details.**

Chapter 5 described the relationship between supporting details and the main ideas they imply. In this chapter, we'll look more closely at the relationship between supporting details and the topic sentences they clarify and develop. We'll also examine the way readers add supporting details to paragraphs by drawing logical inferences. And, finally, we'll look at concluding sentences, which may not directly support the main idea but can still be significant.

Supporting Details Develop Topic Sentences

Paul: I thought June's behavior at that meeting was extraordinary.

Monique: I thought the same thing. I couldn't believe how rude she was. She's too outspoken for my taste.

Paul: That's not what I meant at all. I thought she was great. When she believes in something, she's not afraid to speak her mind.

When the conversation between Paul and Monique stays on a general level, both speakers tend to agree. It's only when Monique moves to a more specific level that the speakers realize they actually disagree. This is a good example of how much good communication depends on supporting details.

As you might suspect, the kind of confusion that happens between Monique and Paul isn't restricted to conversations. It can also occur between readers and writers.

When writers communicate their ideas in paragraphs, they also run the risk of being misunderstood if they don't supply enough supporting details. **Supporting details** are specific sentences that explain or prove the topic sentence by providing reasons, examples, studies, definitions, and so on. Although supporting details can take many different forms, their function is always the same. They help clarify, prove, or suggest a topic sentence.

To see how topic sentences and supporting details work together, read the following statement:

Prolonged unemployment can create serious psychological problems that, in the long run, actually contribute to continued joblessness.

By itself, the sentence tells us that long-term unemployment can do psychological damage. But what does the author mean by the general phrase "prolonged unemployment"? Is she talking about six months or six years? Exactly what kind of psychological problems does she have in mind? After all, that general phrase covers a good deal of ground. Also, how do psychological problems contribute to continued joblessness?

On its own, the sentence raises several questions. However, when it's followed by specific supporting details, those questions are answered:

[1]Prolonged unemployment can create serious psychological problems that, in the long run, actually contribute to continued joblessness. [2]In a society that stresses the relationship between productive work and personal value, it is easy enough to equate long-term unemployment with personal worthlessness. [3]That is, in fact, precisely what many unemployed men and women begin to do. [4]Out of a job for a year or more, they begin to see themselves as worthless human beings without any value to society. [5]In what amounts to a vicious cycle, their sense of personal worthlessness further diminishes their chances of gaining employment. [6]Sometimes they stop looking for work altogether, sure in their despair that no one will hire them. [7]Or else they go on interviews, but they present themselves in such a defeated and hopeless way that the interviewer cannot help but be unimpressed and reject their application.

Do you see how the specific sentences in the paragraph help readers understand the topic sentence? Sentences 2 and 3, for example, limit the ways in which readers can interpret the phrase "serious psychological problems." Sentence 4 then defines "prolonged unemployment."

Sentence 5 explains the second half of the topic sentence by telling us how a sense of personal worthlessness can "contribute to continued joblessness." Sentences 6 and 7 provide two specific illustrations of how this happens.

The supporting details in the paragraph define key phrases like "prolonged unemployment" and "serious psychological damage." They also illustrate the author's main idea and thereby answer a question readers might raise about the topic sentence, "How does prolonged unemployment contribute to continued joblessness?"

When reading a paragraph, you should always search for the author's topic sentence. However, by itself, that topic sentence is bound to raise some questions that only the supporting details can answer.

Actually, if you don't recognize and understand the supporting details the author uses to develop the topic sentence, you haven't understood the paragraph. Imagine, for example, that you were asked this question on an exam: "Explain how prolonged unemployment can contribute to continued joblessness." Without a thorough understanding of the supporting details included in the paragraph, you wouldn't be able to answer the question.

After locating the topic sentence in a paragraph, you also need to figure out what the supporting details contribute to your understanding of that topic sentence. You can usually determine what supporting details contribute by asking two questions: (1) What type of supporting details does the author supply—examples, reasons, studies, definitions, statistics? (2) What questions about the topic sentence do the supporting details answer?

The following exercises give you practice in seeing the relationship between a topic sentence and the supporting details that explain it.

Reading Tip   Once you think you have identified the topic sentence, ask yourself which of the remaining sentences provide clarification or evidence for that sentence. If the remaining sentences don't do either, you need to re-think your choice of topic sentence.

■ EXERCISE 1   Recognizing Supporting Details

DIRECTIONS   The first sentence in each group of sentences is the topic sentence. That topic sentence is followed by five supporting details. Circle the letters of the three sentences that make the topic sentence clear and convincing.

EXAMPLE

Topic Sentence   In April 1986, a tragic accident occurred at a nuclear power plant known as Chernobyl.

Supporting Details   (a.) An explosion ripped through one of Chernobyl's four reactors and radiation entered the atmosphere.

(b.) The plant burned for two weeks because technicians were unable to plug the leak caused by the explosion.

c. America had had its own nuclear scare when a meltdown occurred at Pennsylvania's Three Mile Island.

d. Immediately following the explosion at Chernobyl, thirty-one people died; several weeks later, 135,000 people were evacuated from the area.

e. Western Europe relies on nuclear power for much of its electricity.

EXPLANATION The three supporting details that are circled tell us more about the tragic accident mentioned in the topic sentence. These are the three sentences that help make the topic sentence clear and convincing. The other two do not help explain the topic sentence.

Topic Sentence **1.** The life of the Masai, a group of people who make their home in East Africa, is tightly linked to the raising of cattle.

Supporting Details

a. The diet of the Masai consists mainly of the blood and milk of cattle.

b. Because they consider cattle sacred, the Masai do not slaughter or sell them.

c. Through a series of treaties, the British evicted the Masai from most of their homeland.

d. The Masai follow their cattle from grazing site to grazing site.

e. The Masai are known to be fierce and proud warriors.

Topic Sentence **2.** After close to forty years on NASA's* drawing boards, the Hubble space telescope went into orbit in 1990; but the telescope was plagued with problems throughout its voyage.

Supporting Details

a. Edwin Hubble, for whom the telescope was named, was the son of a Missouri lawyer.

b. The Hubble's ninety-four-inch mirror was off, and it sent blurred images back to earth.

c. By 1993, some of the telescope's navigational equipment had begun to fail.

d. The current generation of land-based telescopes can do anything the Hubble can.

e. During its early voyages in space, the Hubble telescope responded poorly to temperature change.

---

*NASA: a word formed from combining the initial letters in the words National Aeronautics and Space Administration. Another example of an acronym.

Topic Sentence **3.** During World War I, new technology made war deadlier than it had ever been before.

Supporting Details

a. During World War I, the czar of Russia took the Russians under his personal command.

b. When World War I began, the U.S. Army consisted of only 92,710 men.

c. In World War I, new technology allowed both sides to launch airplanes filled with explosives.

d. After the Germans used poison gas in 1915, France, England, and the United States also began using it.

e. New gasses were invented that could maim and kill faster than ever before.

Topic Sentence **4.** Before the introduction of a vaccine in 1954, the spread of polio terrorized the nation.

Supporting Details

a. In 1916, a polio epidemic hit New York City; twenty-seven thousand people were paralyzed and six thousand died.

b. The virus that causes polio was identified in 1908.

c. In the 1700s, physicians believed that polio was associated with the teething of infants, despite the fact that plenty of infants cut new teeth with no signs of fever or paralysis.

d. Twenty-five thousand cases of polio were reported in 1946; most of them were children who were left paralyzed.

e. Between 1952 and 1953, close to one hundred thousand people were struck down with polio.

EXERCISE 2   Identifying Irrelevant Details

DIRECTIONS Read each paragraph and write the number of the topic sentence in the first blank. Each paragraph includes a sentence that has no relationship to the topic sentence. Write the number of that sentence in the second blank.

EXAMPLE [1]Orthorexia nervosa is a new eating disorder that occurs when health-conscious individuals become obsessed with the quality of the food they eat. [2]People who suffer from this disorder base their self-esteem on their ability to maintain a diet of only healthy foods. [3]They decide, for example, that beans and rice are healthy and restrict themselves to eating only those two foods. [4]If they deviate from their restricted diet, they feel intensely guilty and depressed. [5]Bulimics overeat, and then feel guilty until they are able to purge.* [6]Victims of orthorexia nervosa don't seem to realize that excessive reliance on a few select foods can deprive their bodies of critical nutrients.

Topic Sentence <u> 1 </u>

Irrelevant Detail <u> 5 </u>

> **EXPLANATION** With the exception of sentence 5, the supporting details in the sample paragraph all describe the eating disorder orthorexia nervosa. Sentence 5, however, talks about the eating disorder bulimia and never relates it to orthorexia, making detail 5 irrelevant to the rest of the paragraph.

1. [1]In 1894, Japan waged war with China for the control of Korea; the Chinese, however, were no match for their opponents. [2]Within one year, the war was over, and the Japanese had almost completely destroyed the Chinese naval forces. [3]As a result of the war, China had to pay large sums of money to Japan and recognize the full independence of Korea; it also had to give up the resource-rich island of Taiwan. [4]Although the war was brief, it proved without a doubt that Japan was a military power to be reckoned with. [5]During World War II, Japan invaded China.

Topic Sentence <u>   </u>

Irrelevant Detail <u>   </u>

2. [1]Child abuse can take several forms. [2]Sometimes the child is injured physically and may suffer from an odd or disturbing combination of cuts, burns, bruises, or broken bones. [3]Usually the parents or guardians claim that the child "had an accident," even though no normal accident could cause such injuries. [4]Abused children have a greater chance of becoming abusive parents. [5]But child abuse may also take the form of emotional neglect; the parents will simply ignore the child and refuse to respond to bids for attention. [6]Children suffering from this kind of neglect often show symptoms of the *failure to thrive* syndrome, in which physical growth is delayed. [7]In still other cases of maltreatment, the child may be emotionally abused.

---

*purge: remove waste from the bowels or stomach, also to eliminate or get rid of.
*thrive: grow.

[8]One or both parents may ridicule or belittle the child. [9]In this case, physical problems may be absent, but the child's self-esteem will be seriously undermined.

Topic Sentence ____

Irrelevant Detail ____

3. [1]Do you need to memorize a list of items in a particular order? [2]If you do, you should take the *serial position effect* into account. [3]The serial position effect refers to the tendency of many people to make the most errors when trying to remember the middle of a list or series. [4]If, for example, you are introduced to a long line of people, you are most likely to forget the names of those in the middle of the line. [5]People who deal with the public a lot can't afford to be forgetful. [6]Anytime you need to learn a long poem or speech, be sure that you take the serial position effect into account. [7]Give the middle of the speech or poem extra attention and practice.

Topic Sentence ____

Irrelevant Detail ____

4. [1]Most people run or scream in terror when they see a snake. [2]Yet if snakes are examined without prejudice, they prove to be fascinating and relatively harmless members of the reptile family. [3]Like other reptiles, they are cold-blooded, and their temperatures change with the environment. [4]Although most people think that snakes are slimy and wet, the opposite is true. [5]Their skins are cool and dry, even pleasant to the touch. [6]The Hopi Indians perform ritual dances with live rattlesnakes in their mouths. [7]Despite their reputation, most snakes do more good than harm by helping to control the rodent population.

Topic Sentence _1-2_

Irrelevant Detail _6_

 ## Understanding the Difference Between Major and Minor Details

There are two kinds of supporting details, *major* and *minor*. To understand the difference between the two, read the following paragraph. The major supporting details appear in **boldface**, the minor in *italics*.

Psychologists have identified three basic styles of parenting. **Controlling parents think their children have few rights and many responsibilities.** *They tend to demand strict obedience to rigid standards of behavior and expect their children to obey their commands unquestioningly.* **Permissive parents, in contrast, require little responsible behavior from their children.** *Rules are not enforced, and the child usually gets his or her own way.* **Effective parents find a balance between their rights and their children's rights.** *They control their children's behavior without being harsh or rigid.*

In this paragraph, the topic sentence announces that psychologists have identified three different parenting styles. The natural response of most readers would be a question: "What are the three styles of parenting?" Notice how all the major details (printed in boldface) speak to that question.

Based on this illustration, we can say then that **major details** define key terms and clarify general words or phrases in the topic sentence. They further explain or develop those parts of the topic sentence that might otherwise confuse or even mystify the reader. To express it another way, major details answer the questions suggested by the topic sentence. They are, therefore, essential to understanding the main idea and should be included in your notes.

The Role of Minor Details

Look now at the minor details in the sample paragraph. Notice how they help flesh out, or further explain, the major details. They are, however, not essential to explaining the topic sentence. Based on the example given, we can say then that **minor details** help make major ones more specific. But they can also repeat a key point for emphasis or add a colorful fact to hold the reader's interest. What minor details don't do is directly contribute to clarifying or explaining the main idea.

Reading Tip If you eliminate a minor detail from a paragraph, the main idea expressed by the topic sentence should remain clear and convincing. If it doesn't, the detail you eliminated is probably more major than minor.

Evaluating Minor Details

Unlike major details, minor details may or may not be essential to your understanding of the paragraph. If you need a minor detail in order to fully understand a major one, then, yes, include it in your reading notes. However, if the minor detail simply repeats or slightly expands a point clearly stated in a major detail, then you can safely leave it out.

To test your ability to recognize major and minor details, read the next sample paragraph. It contains only one minor detail. When you finish the paragraph, write the number of that sentence in the blank that follows.

[1]In the last forty-odd years, Native Americans have made numerous attempts to gain more political power. [2]In late 1969, a group of Native Americans publicized their grievances by occupying Alcatraz, the abandoned prison in San Francisco Bay, for nineteen months. [3]In 1963, tribes in the Northwest waged a campaign to have their fishing rights recognized in parts of Washington. [4]These were eventually granted by the Supreme Court in 1968. [5]In 1972, a group of Native Americans marched on Washington, D.C., to dramatize what they called a "trail of broken treaties" and present the government with a series of demands. [6]In 1973, members of AIM, the American Indian Movement, took over Wounded Knee, South Dakota, for seventy-two days to protest the government's treatment of Native Americans. [7]Since the early 1980s, several tribes have filed lawsuits to win back lands taken from their ancestors. _____ (Adapted from Thio, *Sociology*, p. 255.)

In this paragraph, the topic sentence tells us that in the last few decades, Native Americans have begun to demand more political power. Sentences 2, 3, 5, 6, and 7 are all major details that answer the obvious question raised by the topic sentence: How have Native Americans gone about demanding more political power?

The exception is sentence 4. This sentence provides an interesting detail: In at least one case, Native Americans triumphed in the Supreme Court. However, if that sentence were eliminated from the paragraph, we would still be able to answer the question "How have Native Americans gone about demanding more political power?" Thus, sentence 4 is clearly a minor detail. It gives us relatively little information about the author's main idea. Instead, it adds an interesting fact to an idea already introduced in sentence 3.

Diagrammed to show the relationship between major and minor details, the above sample paragraph would look like this:

In the last few decades, some Native Americans have begun to assert their political power.

| Late 1969: publicized grievances by taking over Alcatraz | 1963: started campaign to get back fishing rights in Washington | 1972: marched on Washington, D.C., to dramatize trail of broken treaties and to outline demands | 1973: took over Wounded Knee, South Dakota, to protest government treatment | Since 1980s: have filed lawsuits to reclaim tribal lands |

Granted by Supreme Court in 1968

Major Details

- are less general than topic or introductory sentences.
- provide the examples, reasons, statistics, and studies that help make the topic sentence clear and convincing.
- answer readers' questions about the topic sentence.
- must be included in reading notes.

Minor Details

- are the most specific sentences in the paragraph.
- further explain major details.
- repeat key points and add colorful details.
- may or may not be important enough to include in reading notes.

Study Tip

When taking notes, always evaluate the minor details, deciding which ones you need to include and which ones you can leave out.

EXERCISE 3 **Diagramming Major and Minor Details**

DIRECTIONS Read each paragraph and fill in the boxes by paraphrasing and abbreviating the sentences.

EXAMPLE It seems impossible that large prehistoric creatures are alive today. Yet huge creatures from the dinosaur age may still exist beneath the sea. After all, as fossil remains show, dinosaurs had relatives who lived in the sea. They were huge and had long necks and snakelike heads. People who maintain that dinosaurs still live point to recent accounts of strange sea creatures that fit the description of ancient sea monsters. According to reports, the modern-day sea creatures also have long necks and snakelike heads.

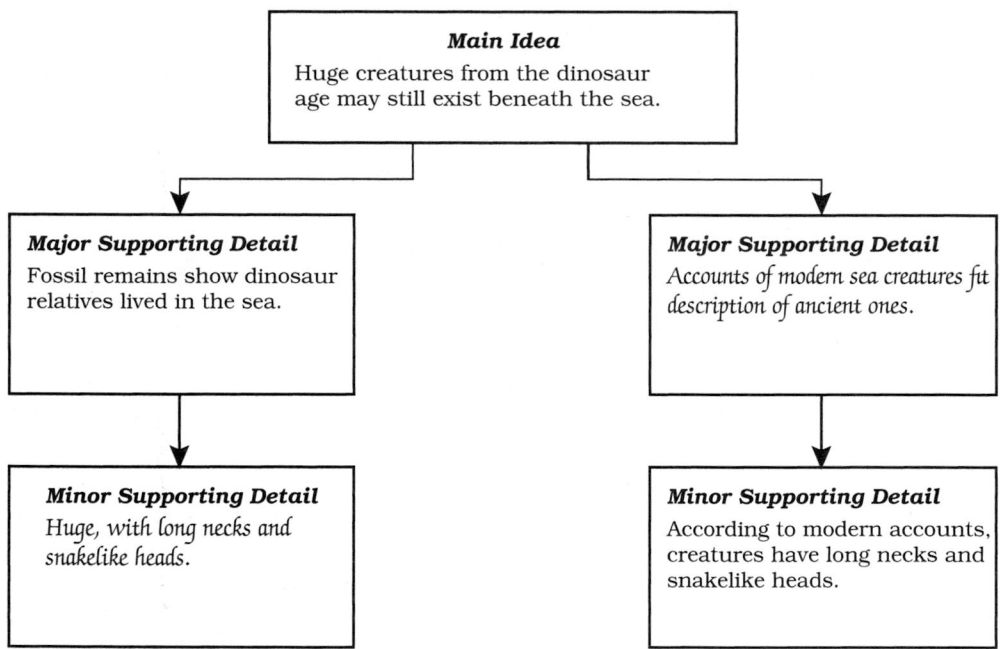

Main Idea
Huge creatures from the dinosaur age may still exist beneath the sea.

Major Supporting Detail
Fossil remains show dinosaur relatives lived in the sea.

Major Supporting Detail
Accounts of modern sea creatures fit description of ancient ones.

Minor Supporting Detail
Huge, with long necks and snakelike heads.

Minor Supporting Detail
According to modern accounts, creatures have long necks and snakelike heads.

EXPLANATION The topic sentence claims that huge creatures from the dinosaur age might still exist beneath the sea. Two major supporting details help make that statement more convincing. Each major detail is followed by a minor one that adds more information.

1. To the ordinary observer, the earth appears to be a solid mass. Scientists, however, know that the earth is composed of several distinct layers. Called the *outer crust,* the layer closest to the surface consists of lightweight rock that extends for about twenty miles beneath the earth's surface. Just underneath the crust is a second layer, about two thousand miles thick, known as the *mantle.* Portions of the mantle are extremely hot. The third layer, or the *core* of the earth, is made up of nickel and cobalt, and it too reaches extremely high temperatures. The temperatures are hot enough to melt both metals, but the sixty pounds of pressure borne by each square inch keeps them solid.

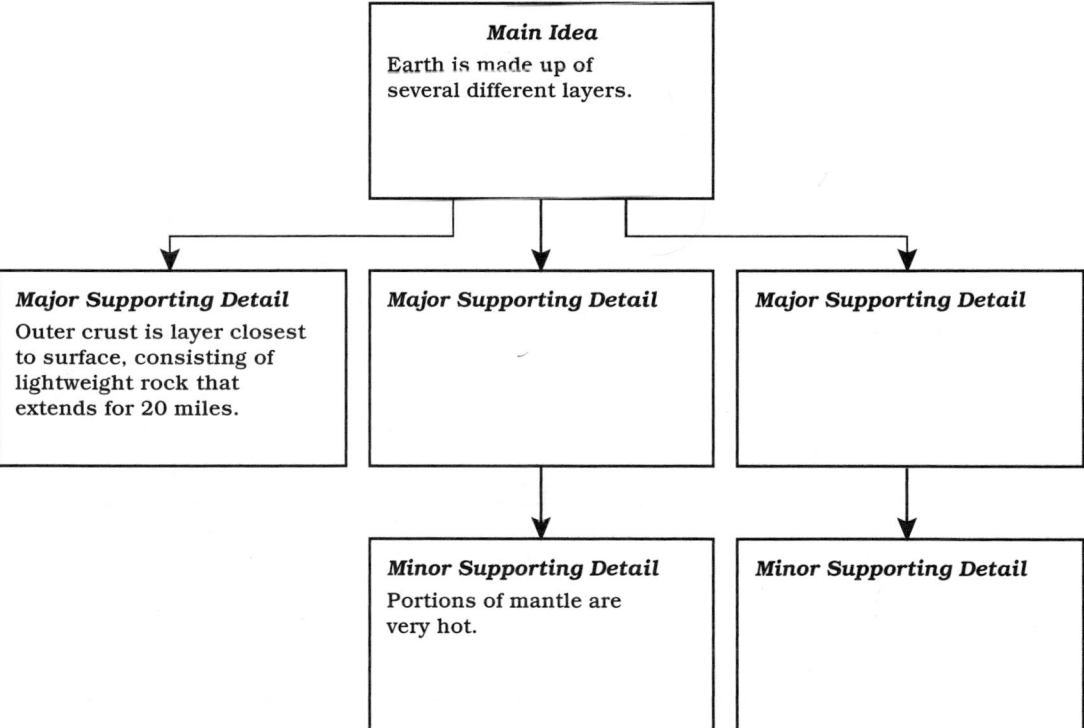

2. Latin American music has had a powerful influence on popular music around the world. Since the 1930s, for example, Latin rhythms have been popular among West, Central, and East African musicians. Latin rhythms have also turned up in some Middle Eastern countries. In fact, they have had a particularly strong impact on the music used by Middle Eastern belly dancers. American hip hop reflects significant Latin American musical influences. The use of Latin American rhythms is a big change from earlier times, when popular music relied almost exclusively on the beat of the blues.

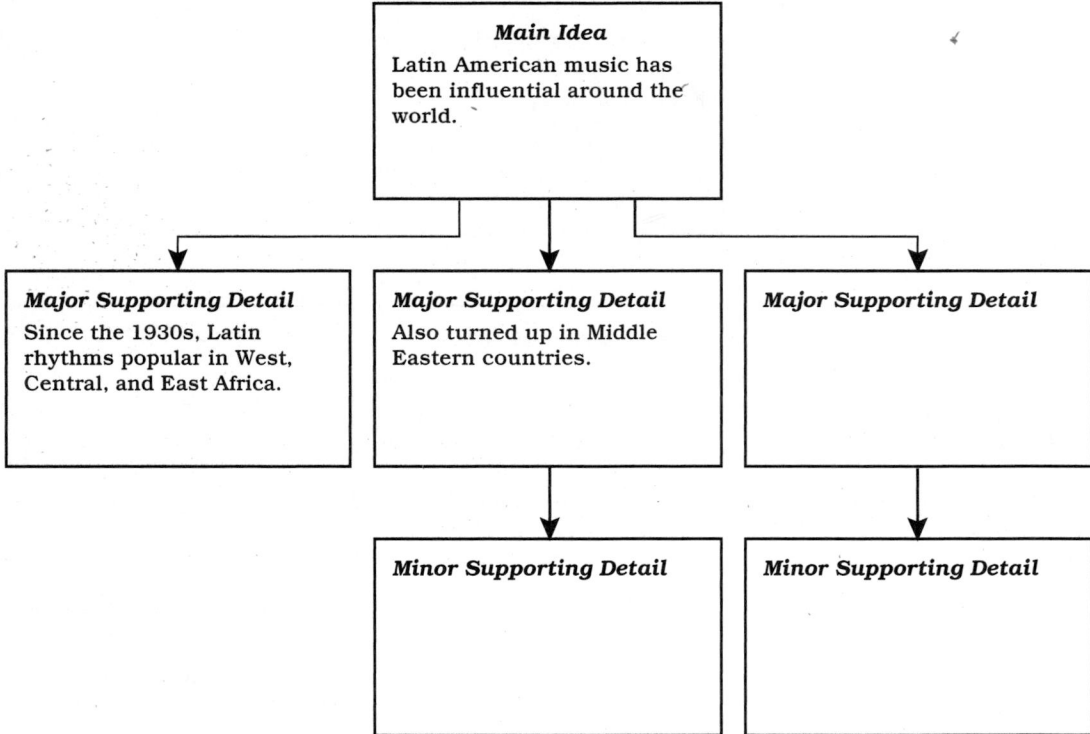

EXERCISE 4 Diagramming Major and Minor Details

DIRECTIONS Read each paragraph and fill in the boxes by paraphrasing and abbreviating the sentences.

1. Scientists who study identical twins have generally come to a similar conclusion. Even when identical twins are reared in different homes, they share many similarities. Observers are often struck by twins' identical facial expressions and personal habits. If, for example, one twin is a nail biter, the other is likely to be one too. Identical twins who have been separated are also likely to have similar IQ scores. They are even likely to share similar talents. If one excels* in art, music, dance, or drama, the other is also likely to excel in the same artistic fields.

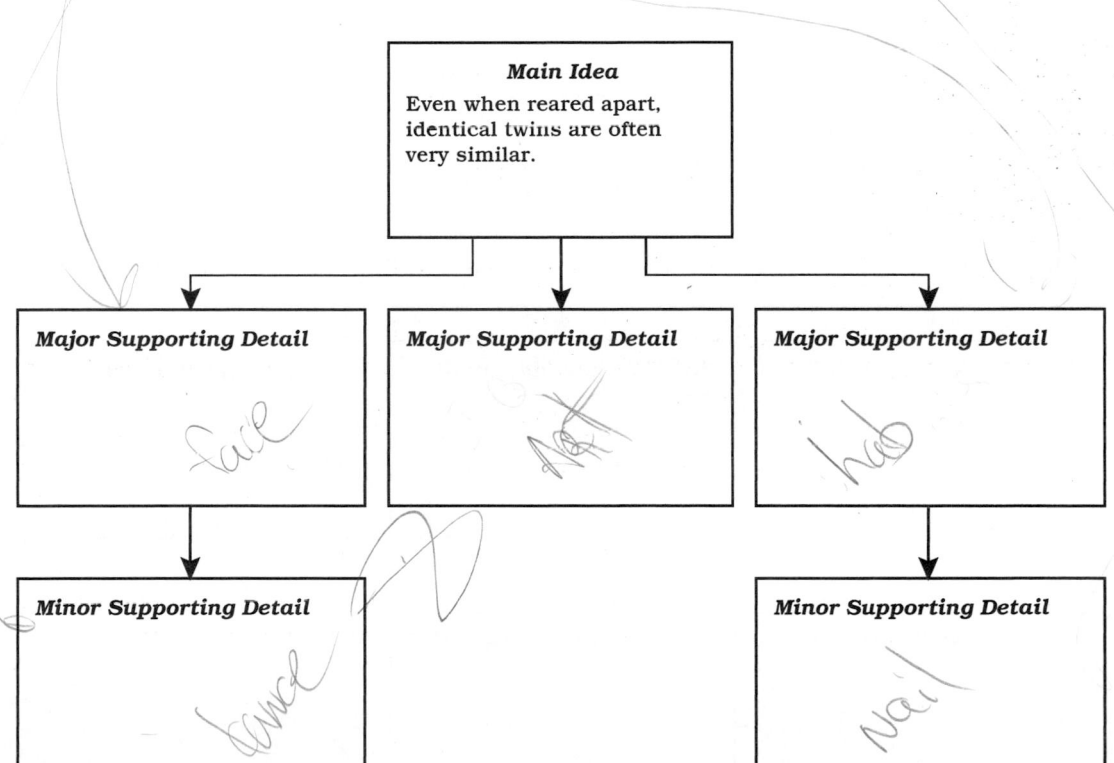

Main Idea
Even when reared apart, identical twins are often very similar.

Major Supporting Detail

Major Supporting Detail

Major Supporting Detail

Minor Supporting Detail

Minor Supporting Detail

*excels: does well.

2. A little over a decade ago, the government of India started a program designed to clean up the Ganges River. The program failed because the Indian states did not have the money to keep it afloat. However, there is new hope on the horizon: Impressed with the scavenging behavior of carnivorous turtles, Indian officials in some states are using them to clean up river waste. According to officials, the turtles happily eat both animal and human carcasses. This is significant because among some religious groups, disposing of bodies in rivers is a common practice. In addition to their willingness to consume flesh, turtles also loosen the earth along the river banks, making it easier for plants to survive at the water's edge. The plants, in turn, help fight erosion at the banks, and some plants actually contribute to the water's purification. If the turtle experiment succeeds in a few states, it will be implemented throughout India, and even the Ganges may once again flow without pollutants.

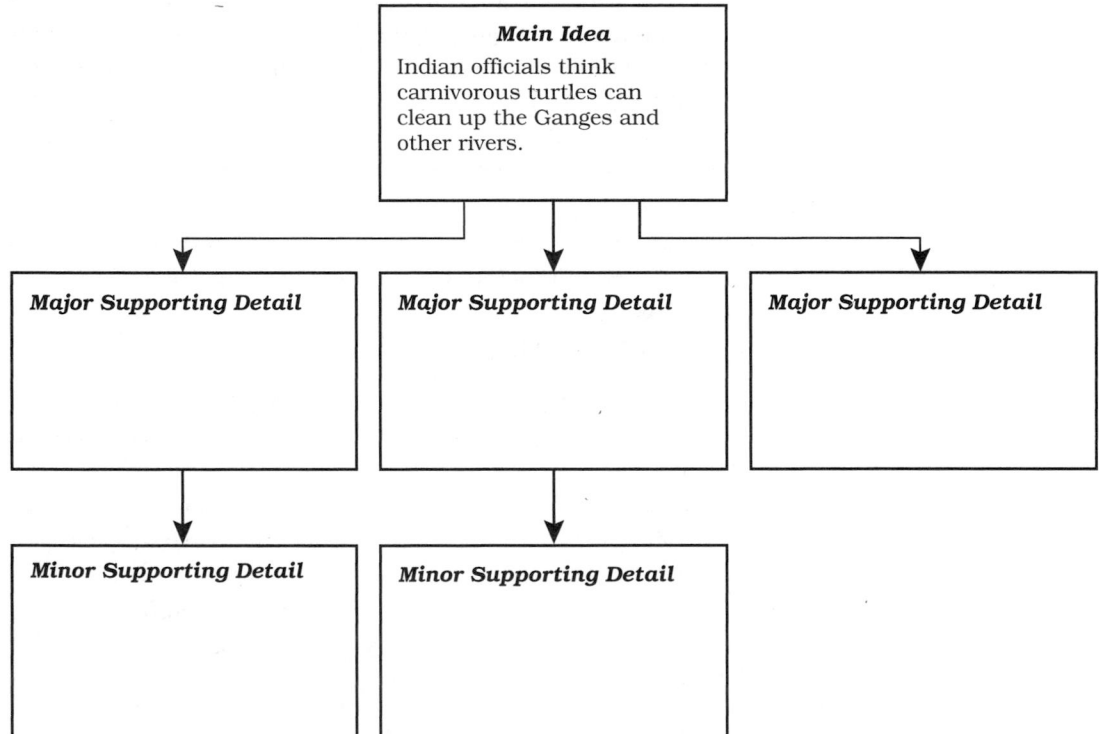

Main Idea
Indian officials think carnivorous turtles can clean up the Ganges and other rivers.

Major Supporting Detail

Major Supporting Detail

Major Supporting Detail

Minor Supporting Detail

Minor Supporting Detail

 # Topic Sentences Help Identify Major Details

One way to distinguish between major and minor details is to imagine the questions that a topic sentence is likely to raise in a reader's mind. Then look for the sentences that answer those questions. The sentences providing answers are likely to be major details.

It also pays to be alert to words and phrases in topic sentences that help readers identify major details. Note, for example, the underlined phrases in these three topic sentences:

1. Child abuse can take <u>several different forms</u>.
2. Psychologists have identified <u>three styles of parenting</u>.
3. Even when identical twins are reared in different homes, they show <u>many similarities</u>.

All of the underlined phrases—<u>several different forms</u>, <u>three styles of parenting</u>, and <u>many similarities</u>—refer to some larger group that can be broken down into smaller subgroups. Such words and phrases are important because they tell you what kind of major supporting details you need to look for. In other words, each time you locate a different *form*, another *style*, or an additional *similarity*, you have also found a major detail.

For an illustration, read the next paragraph. Circle the word or phrase in the topic sentence that tells you what type of major detail you need to locate. Then label each of the supporting details as a major (*M*) or a minor (*m*) detail.

Topic Sentence
[1]Feminists scored two impressive legal victories in the 1970s. [2]In 1974, Congress passed the Equal Credit Opportunity Act, which enabled women to get bank loans and obtain credit cards on the same terms as men. _____ [3]Many states also revised their laws on rape, prohibiting defense lawyers from trying to discredit rape victims by revealing their previous sexual experience. _____ [4]Prior to this time, a woman's sexual history could be used to challenge her accusation of rape. _____ (Adapted from Norton et al., *A People and a Nation*, p. 1045.)

If you circled the phrase "two impressive legal victories," you're right; that is the key phrase. What about the supporting sentences? Did you label sentences 2 and 3 as major details and sentence 4 as a minor one? Correct again. Sentences 2 and 3 are major details because they introduce the two legal victories referred to in the topic sentence. Sentence 4 is a minor detail because it further explains the victory described in sentence 3.

Check Your Understanding

Explain the difference between major and minor details

_____

_____

_____

Whenever you locate a topic sentence, look for words or phrases telling you that some larger group can be broken down into smaller parts. Usually, if you can identify the individual members of the larger group mentioned, you have also identified all the major details. Although there are many such words and phrases, the following chart lists some of the most common. Watch for them as you read.

Topic Sentence Words and Phrases That Are Clues to Major Details

Among the causes, results	Motives
A number of ways	Numerous cases, people,
Categories	studies
Causes	Precautions
Characteristics	Reasons
Classes	Several advantages, cases,
Components	studies, goals
Consequences	Similarities
Differences	Skills
Effects	Stages
Elements	Steps
Examples	Studics
Factors	Symptoms
Groups	Tactics
Kinds	Traits
Methods	

 # Transitions and Major Details

In addition to topic sentences that tell readers what type or kind of major detail they need to look for, there are other clues that can help you decide if a detail is major or minor. Transitions like *furthermore*, *moreover*, and *also* are the author's way of saying to readers, "Here's another major reason, illustration, advantage, or consequence to consider." Look, for example, at the following passage and pay close attention to the italicized transitions.

[1]There are a number of reasons why parents should not allow young, impressionable children to watch televised wrestling. [2]Wrestling suggests to children that physical violence causes no real harm. [3]*After all,* in a wrestling match, no one seems to get hurt because most of the wrestlers come back the following week. [4]*Furthermore,* wrestling suggests that people are valued according to the damage they can do since the superstars of wrestling are

those men and women who most effectively hurt and humiliate their opponents. [5]This is not an especially good message to be giving children. [6]*In addition*, wrestling celebrates incredibly loutish behavior. [7]Watching a wrestling match on television, viewers must find it difficult to say whose behavior is more disreputable, the wrestlers shouting at the top of their lungs that they are going to demolish their opponent, or the scantily clad women who parade around exhibiting score cards and occasionally jump in the ring to join the fray.*

In this paragraph, the author opens with a topic sentence that sends a clear message: Young, impressionable children should not be allowed to watch televised wrestling. Then the transition *after all* announces that the author is following up on that claim. However, she also wants to be sure that the remaining reasons stand out. To that end, she signals their presence with the transitional words *furthermore* in sentence 4, and *in addition* in sentence 6. They are her way of telling readers, "I'm continuing with the same train of thought. Here are additional reasons why you should share my point of view."

As you might suspect, transitions like the ones listed below don't always introduce major details. However, they introduce them often enough for you to be aware of the relationship between the two.

Transitions That Signal Addition or Continuation

After all	For one thing	Second, Third,
Also	For this reason	Fourth
And	Furthermore	Similarly
Finally	In addition	Then
First	Last	Therefore
First and foremost	Last of all	Thus
First of all	Lastly	Too
For example	Moreover	
For instance	Next	

---

*fray: battle, contest, test.

◆ EXERCISE 5 **Using Topic Sentences and Transitions to Identify Major Details**

> **DIRECTIONS** Read each paragraph. Circle any phrases in the topic sentences that offer a clue to the major details, and circle as well the transitions that signal continuation or addition. Then fill in the boxes by paraphrasing and abbreviating the sentences. *Note*: Not all topic sentences will include a phrase identifying the major details.

1. According to the sociologist Emile Durkheim, deviance (the violation of social rules) can serve a number of functions for society. First, it helps enhance conformity as a whole. Deviant behavior allows us to see the boundaries between right and wrong more clearly. Once aware of these boundaries, we are more likely to conform to standards of correct social behavior. Second, deviance strengthens solidarity among law-abiding members of society. Collective outrage against deviant behavior can unite people with different points of view. Third, deviance provides a safety valve for discontented people. Through relatively minor forms of deviance, those unhappy with society's rules can strike out at or insult the social order without doing major harm. Fourth, deviance can induce social change. As the civil rights movement has shown, people sometimes have to engage in deviant behavior in order to make society aware of its errors. (Adapted from Thio, *Society, Myths and Realities*, pp. 172–173.)

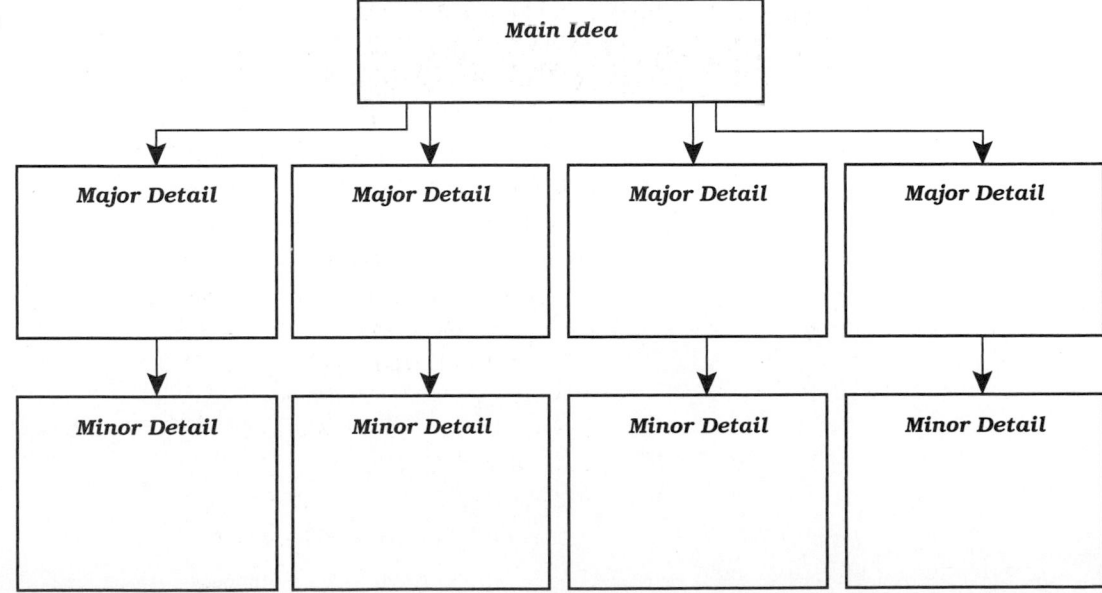

2. There are four main reasons why scientists believe that life on Mars may currently exist or may have existed in the past. For one thing, photographs taken by several probes suggest that the planet once had water. The *Viking* orbiters, the *Mars Pathfinder*, and the *Mars Global Surveyor* all sent back images of surface features—channels, canyons, and what appear to be lake shorelines—that seem to have been formed by flowing water. Second, although the planet is now cold and encased in a thin atmosphere of mostly carbon dioxide, some evidence suggests that Mars was once warmer, with a thicker atmosphere. The discovery of microbes* in extreme environments on Earth has also led scientists to conclude that life could exist in harsh conditions on other planets. In the past twenty years, scientists have found bacteria living miles beneath Earth's surface and in Arctic climates, where the organisms survive without oxygen or light. Plus, a meteorite from Mars may contain the fossilized remains of bacteria-like organisms. Although this conclusion is controversial, some scientists believe that the microscopic bacteria-like impressions in the meteorite are evidence that life existed on Mars more than 3.6 billion years ago. (Sources of information: "Mars, Water, and Life on Earth," *Riverdeep*, September 9, 2002, www.riverdeep.net/current/2002/ 09/090902_mars.jhtml.)

---

*microbes: minute forms of life such as the bacteria that cause disease.

```
                        ┌─────────────────────────────┐
                        │          Main Idea          │
                        │                             │
                        └──┬────────┬────────┬──────┬─┘
          ┌────────────────┘        ↓        ↓      └────────────┐
          ↓                         ↓        ↓                   ↓
┌──────────────────┐ ┌──────────────────┐ ┌──────────────────┐ ┌──────────────────┐
│ Major Supporting │ │ Major Supporting │ │ Major Supporting │ │ Major Supporting │
│      Detail      │ │      Detail      │ │      Detail      │ │      Detail      │
│                  │ │                  │ │                  │ │                  │
│                  │ │                  │ │                  │ │                  │
│                  │ │                  │ │                  │ │                  │
└────────┬─────────┘ └──────────────────┘ └────────┬─────────┘ └────────┬─────────┘
         ↓                                          ↓                    ↓
┌──────────────────┐                      ┌──────────────────┐ ┌──────────────────┐
│ Minor Supporting │                      │ Minor Supporting │ │ Minor Supporting │
│      Detail      │                      │      Detail      │ │      Detail      │
│                  │                      │                  │ │                  │
│                  │                      │                  │ │                  │
│                  │                      │                  │ │                  │
└──────────────────┘                      └──────────────────┘ └──────────────────┘
```

3. There are several benefits to having music education as part of the school curriculum. One benefit of musical training is that it seems to improve thinking skills. Students who have had music lessons score an average of 59 points higher on the verbal portion of the SAT and 44 points higher on the math portion than students who have not had music lessons, and studies show that youthful musicians tend to get good grades. Another important benefit of musical training is enhanced self-esteem. Researchers have also found that children who have had music education have more confidence in their own potential than do those who have not had music education and therefore are more likely to graduate from high school and less likely to use drugs. In addition music education helps children develop a host of other important skills. Learning to play an instrument requires self-discipline, concentration, and time management while learning to make music with others helps young people learn how to cooperate and, above all, how to listen.

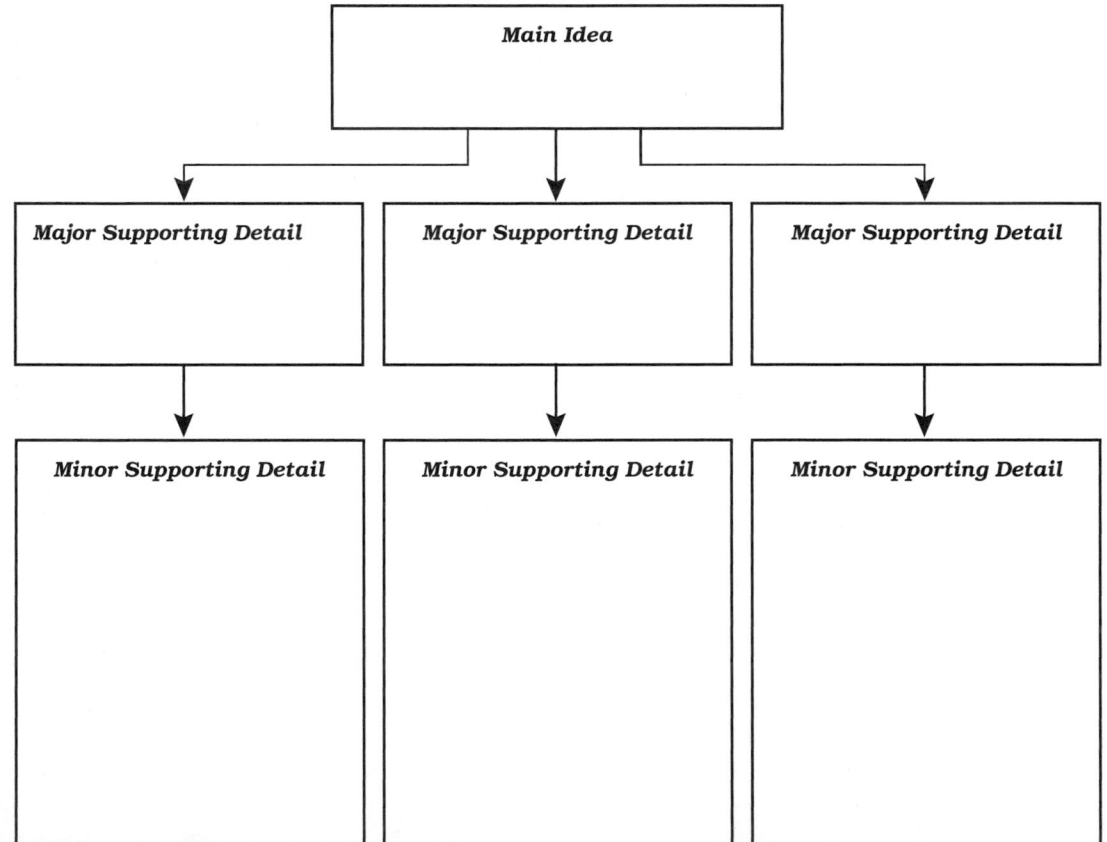

4. A 2003 poll sponsored by the American Automobile Association and other highway safety organizations has revealed that most Americans are bad drivers who don't want to get better. Most drivers do little or nothing to improve their driving knowledge or skills. As a matter of fact, because the majority of states do not require motorists to periodically refresh their skills, adult drivers have generally not taken a test on road rules, road signs, or driving skills since they first got their driver's license as teenagers. In addition, motorists in our fast-paced society, pressed for time and in a hurry, drive recklessly. The poll reveals, for example, that more than 70 percent of drivers admit to speeding, and one-third say they have run yellow or even red lights. Finally, many drivers engage in distracting behaviors while behind the wheel. Sixty percent of drivers eat while they drive, 37 percent talk on cell phones while driving, and 14 percent say they even read while driving. (Source of information: Deborah Sharp, "A Poll Highlights Road Recklessness," *USA Today*, May 27, 2003, p. 3A.)

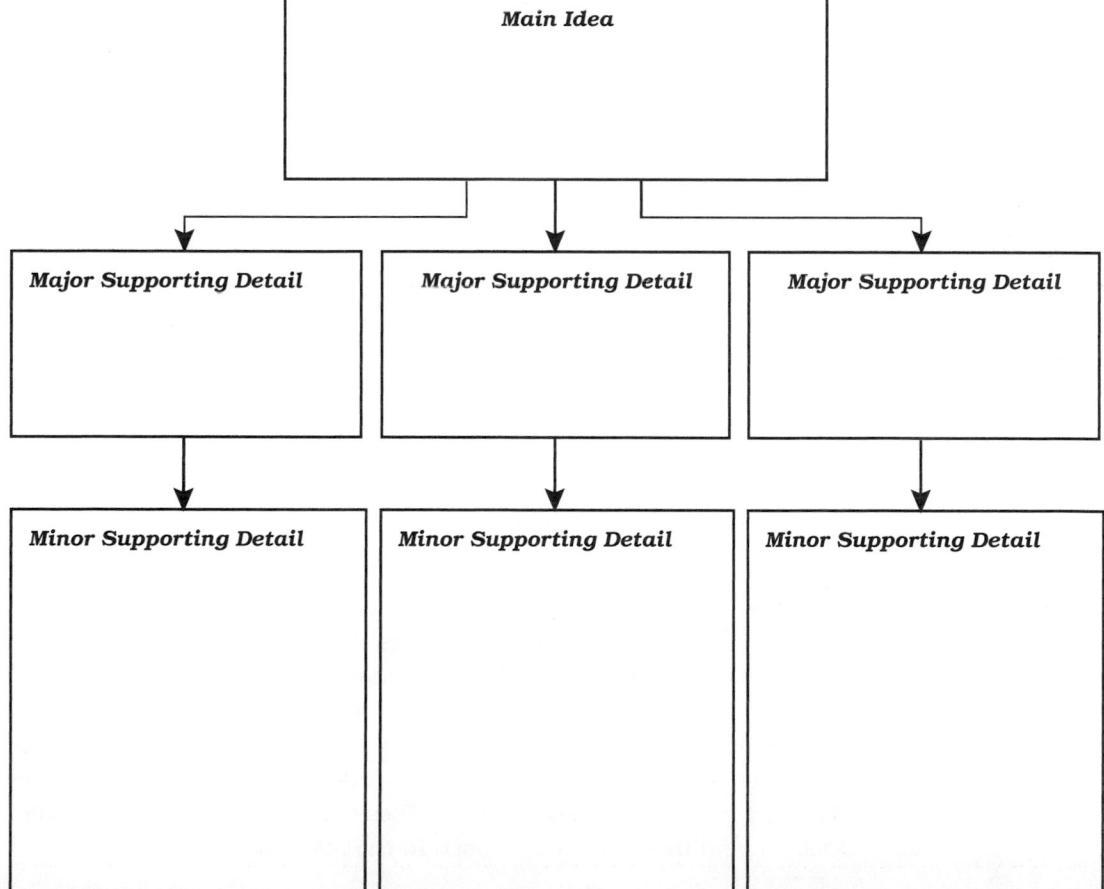

EXERCISE 6 Identifying Topic Sentences and Major Details

> **DIRECTIONS** Read each paragraph and answer the questions about the topic sentence. Then paraphrase and list all the major details. Circle any transitions that signal continuation or addition.

EXAMPLE ¹Although the famed magician Harry Houdini could have benefited from his audience's belief in the world of spirits, he tried in a number of ways to expose the fakery behind supposed supernatural happenings. ²Throughout his career, Houdini carefully investigated and proved false hundreds of claims by people who said they could communicate with the spirit world. ³(Moreover,) he kept a file of fake mediums* and he instructed that after his death, the file be made public. ⁴To ensure that his wishes were carried out, Houdini entrusted a key to the file to his friend and fellow magician Joseph Dunninger. ⁵Houdini (also) liked to dispel the "magic" behind his tricks and explain how they were performed. ⁶This was his way of proving to people that miracles could actually be faked.

a. Sentence __1__ is the topic sentence.

b. What word or phrase in the topic sentence provides a clue to the major details?

   a number of ways

c. Number and list all the major details according to the order in which they appear.

   1. *Houdini investigated and disproved hundreds of fake claims*
      about people in touch with spirits.

   2. *Houdini kept a file on people claiming to be in touch with*
      the spirits and left instructions that the file should be
      published on his death.

   3. *Houdini explained how his tricks were performed.*

> **EXPLANATION** The topic sentence is the first sentence in the paragraph. It's the only sentence general enough to sum up the rest of the paragraph. The phrase "a number of ways" is a clue to the major details. It tells you that each way, or method, of exposing trickery is a major detail. Sentences 2, 3, and 5 all describe different techniques Houdini used to uncover fakes. These three sentences are major details, and they are paraphrased in the blank lines.

---

*medium: people who claim they can communicate with the dead.

1. ¹The honeybee is a social insect that can survive only when it is part of a community. ²Within that community, all of the honeybees have a number of special functions that help ensure survival. ³The queen, for example, is the only sexually productive female; she gives birth to all of the drones, workers, and future queens. ⁴Her capacity for laying eggs is enormous, and her daily output often exceeds 1,500 eggs. ⁵Although lacking the ability to mate or reproduce, worker bees secrete wax, build the honeycomb, gather food, turn nectar into honey, guard the hive when necessary, and regulate its temperature. ⁶When, for instance, the hive becomes too hot, worker bees cool the air by fanning their wings. ⁷In contrast to the worker bees, drones have only one function—to mate with the queen. ⁸After mating, which always takes place in flight, a drone immediately dies; he has served his sole function and is no longer necessary to the community.

   a. Sentence _____ is the topic sentence.

   b. What word or phrase in the topic sentence provides a clue to the major details?

   _____

   c. Number and list all the major details according to the order in which they appear.

   _____

   _____

   _____

   _____

   _____

2. ¹The religion of the Hopi Indians includes several different ceremonies intended to influence or pay respect to nature. ²In the Bear Dance, for example, as many as two hundred masked and painted dancers represent the Kachinas, spirits associated with growing and distributing food.* ³The purpose of the Bear Dance is to ensure that spring will bring a lush harvest. ⁴The Snake Dance, which takes place every second August, is a plea for rain. ⁵During the ceremony, the dancers twine live rattlesnakes around their shoulders. ⁶Once open to visitors, the Snake Dance is now closed to all outsiders. ⁷Visitors, however, may still be present for the Corn Dance, which is supposed to encourage a rich crop.

   _____

   *The word *Kachinas* can also refer to the spirits of ancestors and the forces of nature.

a. Sentence _____ is the topic sentence.

b. What word or phrase in the topic sentence provides a clue to the major details?

_____

c. Number and list all the major details according to the order in which they appear.

_____

_____

_____

_____

_____

3. [1]To write his book *Hindsights: The Wisdom and Breakthroughs of Remarkable People,* author Gary Kawasaki interviewed thirty-two people he considered out-of-the-ordinary. [2]According to Kawasaki, the men and women he interviewed had a number of traits in common that had helped make them successful. [3]One of the most critical traits was a willingness to tolerate failure without giving up. [4]Instead of giving up, the people Kawasaki interviewed analyzed their mistakes and figured out what they had done wrong. [5]Then they tried again. [6]For them, failure did not equal defeat. Kawasaki's subjects were also willing to learn from others, and they were never too proud to ask for help or advice. [7]In addition, Kawasaki discovered that people with remarkable lives refused to call themselves victims, no matter what the circumstances. [8]From their perspective, any obstacle could be overcome.

a. Sentence _____ is the topic sentence.

b. What word or phrase in the topic sentence provides a clue to the major details?

_____

c. Number and list all the major details according to the order in which they appear.

_____

_____

_____

_____

_____

4. ¹To many people, a life sentence without parole has definite advantages over the death penalty. ²First of all, a life sentence without parole protects society without taking human life. ³Second, it eliminates lengthy court appeals of a death sentence. ⁴Finally, a life sentence without parole ensures that criminals really pay for their crimes by staying in jail. ⁵With parole allowed, a life sentence can be as short as fifteen years. ⁶However, a life sentence without parole means just that. ⁷It lasts a lifetime.

a. Sentence _____ is the topic sentence.

b. What word or phrase in the topic sentence provides a clue to the major details?

_____

c. Number and list all the major details according to the order in which they appear.

_____

_____

_____

_____

_____

EXERCISE 7 Identifying Topic Sentences and Minor Details

DIRECTIONS After reading each paragraph, identify the topic sentence by writing the correct number or numbers into the blank at the end of the paragraph. Then go back and fill in each blank within the paragraph with the letter of the appropriate minor detail.

EXAMPLE ¹The human ear is a complicated structure that can be divided into three main parts. ²The first part is the outer ear. ³It collects sound waves and directs them to the auditory canal. ⁴_c_ ⁵The middle ear contains three small bones. ⁶_a_ ⁷The middle ear is connected to the throat by a small tubelike structure known as the Eustachian tube. ⁸The inner ear contains the actual hearing apparatus, a small, shell-like organ filled with fluid and nerve endings. ⁹It is called the cochlea. ¹⁰_b_

Topic Sentence <u> 1 </u>

Minor Details   a. These are called the hammer, anvil, and stirrup.

     b. When the nerve endings receive vibrations from the fluid in the cochlea, they transmit them directly to the hearing portion of the brain.

     c. At the very end of that canal is a membrane called the eardrum, or tympanum.

> **EXPLANATION** In this case, sentence 1 is the only sentence that could effectively sum up the paragraph. Choosing the correct minor supporting detail is easy if you use the right clues. Sentence 3, for example, mentions the auditory canal. Therefore we put sentence *c*, which refers to the canal, into the first blank. Sentence 5 mentions three small bones. Therefore, the next sentence logically should be answer *a*, which identifies those bones. Sentence 9 introduces the cochlea. Therefore, answer *b*, which mentions the cochlea, is the appropriate choice to follow sentence 9 as a minor supporting detail. (Note, too, the importance of the minor details.)

1. [1]In October 1957, the Russians leaped into the space age with the launching of a satellite that became world famous as *Sputnik*. [2]Awed by this breakthrough, America intensified its efforts to improve its satellite technology. [3]Since that time, the United States has rivaled Russia by launching its own share of satellites. [4]Hundreds of American satellites have been successfully propelled into the air. [5]As our technology improves, scientists expect that many more satellites will be used. [6]_____ [7]The military, which already makes extensive use of satellites, will also continue to do so in the future. [8]_____ [9]Although they possess no satellites of their own, less industrialized countries have already laid claim to precious air space. [10]_____

Topic Sentence _____

Minor Details   a. If they gain the technology to launch satellites in the future, these countries do not want to discover that all usable orbits have been taken.

     b. Certainly the use of satellites in global communication will continue to increase.

     c. Military satellites are essential to intelligence gathering.

2. [1]The Galapagos are volcanic islands located about six hundred miles from South America's Pacific coast. [2]With their barren landscape,

the islands do not seem the ideal spot for a summer vacation. [3]Nevertheless, the Galapagos have begun to attract growing numbers of tourists, and that increase in tourism has caused a variety of problems. [4]Some tourists, planning a long stay, have brought their pets with them. [5]_____ [6]In addition, many tourists have decided that the tortoises inhabiting the island make splendid souvenirs. [7]_____ [8]Even the tourists who bring no pets and steal no tortoises have managed to injure the island's fragile environment. [9]They do not realize, for example, that killing a stray spider can actually harm the balance of nature. [10]_____

Topic Sentence _____

Minor Details a. Hundreds of tortoises have been captured and taken off the island.

b. Unfortunately, those pets have often destroyed vegetation needed to support the wildlife population.

c. Spiders are needed in great numbers to keep numerous island pests under control.

3. [1]Progeria is a genetic disorder that strikes children. [2]Victims of the disease experience rapid aging. [3]_____ [4]First mentioned at the turn of the century, progeria is extremely rare. [5]_____ [6]Usually the disease goes undetected until just past infancy, when children suddenly stop growing. [7]_____ [8]Death usually occurs in the teens, often from a disease associated with aging, such as hardening of the arteries.

Topic Sentence _____

Minor Details a. It occurs about once in eight million births.

b. Children with progeria seldom reach a weight of more than fifty pounds.

c. For every one year, their bodies age ten.

4. [1]In 1954, the Supreme Court ruled in *Brown v. Board of Education* that "separate educational facilities are inherently* unequal." [2]The Supreme Court's *Brown* decision encouraged African Americans to integrate all public facilities. [3]As a result, the civil rights movement officially began in Montgomery, Alabama, in December 1955 when Rosa Parks refused to give up her seat on a city bus to a white man. [4]_____ [5]Led by the Reverend Martin Luther King Jr., African Americans reacted to her arrest by organizing a boycott. [6]_____ [7]The

_____
*inherently: at the core, by nature.

protests continued, with civil rights workers fanning out all over the South. [8]However, the civil rights bill designed to end segregation in all public facilities remained stalled in Congress. [9]_____

Topic Sentence _____

Minor Details a. The bill finally passed in 1964.

b. Consequently, Parks was arrested and taken to jail.

c. The boycott lasted a year and ended when the federal court ruled that Alabama's bus segregation laws were unconstitutional.

5. [1]For centuries, the shroud of Turin has been an object of fascination to Christians and non-Christians alike, and so far, the many tests performed on the shroud have served only to increase its mystery. [2]A fourteen-foot piece of linen fabric, the shroud is believed to have been the cloth in which Jesus of Nazareth was wrapped after his death on the cross. [3]Normally it lies hidden behind the iron grille on a Turin altar. [4]But in 1978, an exhibition was held to celebrate the four hundredth anniversary of the shroud's discovery. [5]_____ [6]Markings on the shroud revealed the faded image of a naked man laid out for burial. [7]_____ [8]For a while, experts were puzzled when special photographs revealed bulges around the eyes. [9]_____ [10]The shroud of Turin was also exhibited in 1998, when Pope John Paul II knelt before it in silent prayer. [11]Two years later, it was on exhibit again, from August 12 to October 22, 2000.

Topic Sentence _____

Minor Details a. But that mystery was solved when someone pointed out that the Romans placed coins over the eyes of the dead.

b. Strongly built and with regular features, his face is partially covered by a beard.

c. During the anniversary celebration, scientists were allowed to examine the cloth.

 # Reader-Supplied Inferences and Supporting Details

Drawing inferences isn't limited to figuring out implied main ideas. To thoroughly understand a paragraph, good readers also draw inferences about supporting details that are implied but not explicitly stated. For an illustration, read the following paragraph. As you do, consider where you have to read between the lines to fully understand the passage.

Topic Sentence   [1]According to social exchange policy, the development and ontinuation of intimate relationships are associated with the rewards and costs involved. [2]Research has shown that dating couples who experience increases in rewards as their relationship progresses are likely to stay together. [3]In contrast, dating couples who experience fewer reward increases are less likely to stay together. [4]Rewards and costs, however, do not arise on their own and in isolation. [5]People bring to their relationships certain expectations. [6]John Thibaut and Harold Kelley coined the term "comparison level" (CL) to refer to the expected outcome in relationships. [7]A person with a high CL expects his or her relationships to be rewarding. [8]Someone with a low CL does not. [9]Even a bad relationship can look pretty good to someone who has a low CL. (Adapted from Brehm et al., *Social Psychology*, p. 208.)

In this paragraph, the main idea is spelled out in the opening topic sentence. However, for the supporting details to fully clarify the topic sentence, readers have to add to the details by supplying a number of inferences.

To connect sentences 2, 3, and 4 to the topic sentence, readers need, first of all, to infer the appropriate meaning for the words *rewards* and *costs*. Within this passage, both words need to be read as more emotional than financial, otherwise the social exchange theory doesn't make any sense when applied to intimate relationships. Note, however, that the writers do not specifically define the meanings of those two key words. They just supply the context or setting for the two words and leave it up to readers to draw the right conclusions about the appropriate meanings.

The need for reader-supplied inferences, however, does not end with these two definitions. Sentences 2 and 3 only develop the topic sentence if readers are willing to infer a cause and effect relationship whereby one event produces another. Dating couples who get an increased number of rewards stay together *because* they like the rewards. Similarly, couples who experience fewer rewards are less likely to last *because* there aren't enough rewards in the relationship. Even sentence 4, which looks so simple, requires readers to infer an additional piece of information: Rewards and costs within couple relationships do not arise on their own or in isolation *from all other influences.*

In sentence 6, to thoroughly understand the meaning of the phrase *comparison level* and how it affects relationships, you also have to infer the source of a high or low "CL." For the notion of a comparison level to make sense, the reader needs to infer that high or low expectations are based on *what people have previously experienced*. That's where the comparison comes in. In other words, if you come from a relationship with lots of rewards, you will expect them to be present in your new relationship. Similarly, if your last relationship had more costs than benefits, there is a good chance you won't have high expectations for your next one. Significant as that piece of information is to understanding the theory, it is still implied rather than stated.

Reading Tip

Never assume the writers provide you with every single word or phrase you need to create their intended meaning. Stay alert and ready for those places in the text where you have to fill in the gaps with the right inference.

EXERCISE 8 **Drawing Inferences About Supporting Details**

DIRECTIONS After reading the passage, identify the topic and underline the topic sentence. Then identify the inferences readers need to add to the supporting details.

EXAMPLE According to sociologist Robert Merton, U.S. culture <u>places too much emphasis on success as a valued goal.</u> From kindergarten to college, teachers prod students to achieve the American dream. Parents and coaches pressure Little League players not just to play well but to win. The media often glorify winning not only in sports but also in business, politics, and other arenas of life. This emphasis on success motivates hard work, thereby contributing to society's prosperity. But at the same time, people are not equally provided with the legitimate means (such as good jobs and other opportunities) for achieving success. There is, then, an inconsistency between too much emphasis on the success goal and too little emphasis on the availability of legitimate means for achieving that goal. Such inconsistency produces a strain among some people, pressuring them to achieve through what Merton calls *innovation*—using illegitimate means of achieving success, such as committing robbery to selling drugs. (Adapted from Thio, *Society, Myths, and Realities*, p. 175.)

Topic <u>Robert Merton's theory about the role of success in U.S. culture</u>

1. Which one of these inferences is the reader expected to add to the supporting details?

    a. As Merton defines it, success involves establishing personal goals and achieving them, regardless of what others are doing.

    (b.) Merton's idea of success centers on making money and earning social prestige.

    c. Merton defines success as the feeling of personal peace that comes with fulfilling a long-held, childhood dream.

2. Which one of these inferences is the reader expected to add to the supporting details?

    a. The word *innovation* means "the act of beginning or introducing something new," and this is precisely the definition Merton has in mind.

    b. Merton's use of the word *innovation* suggests that those who innovate are not willing to use new or novel means in order to achieve success.

    (c.) Merton's use of the word *innovation* suggests being forced to try socially unacceptable routes to success.

EXPLANATION The topic here is sociologist Robert Merton's theory about the role of success in American culture. Every sentence refers to this topic as the author tries to explain what Merton had in mind. The topic sentence is the first sentence because all of the sentences that follow further explain that first sentence in more specific detail. To make sense of Merton's idea, readers have to infer a specific definition for the American Dream, which is traditionally defined as "An American ideal of a happy and successful life to which all may aspire."* The traditional definition leaves open the meaning of the word "successful," but Merton expects readers to limit the meaning (as many people do) to financial success and social acclaim, making *b* the best answer for question 1. The word *innovation* usually has positive connotations, but Merton's theory gives it negative overtones, by suggesting that the U.S. emphasis on success and the simultaneous lack of means to attain it force people to go outside the law, making *c* the best answer to question 2.

1. Violence depicted in the media has been a target of attack and counterattack for decades. But the amount, intensity, and graphic nature of the violence in the media have continued to escalate.

---

*See, for instance, *The American Heritage Dictionary of the English Language.*

Testifying before a U.S. Senate subcommittee, social psychologist Leonard Eron estimated that by the end of elementary school, a typical American child would have seen 8,000 murders and more than 100,000 other acts of violence. And the numbers seem only to rise. A 2003 study by the Parents' Television Council, for example, counted 534 separate episodes of prime-time violence on the six major American networks during the first two weeks of November 2002, compared to 292 from the year before, and also found preliminary evidence suggesting that the trend toward increased violence continued in 2003.

Topic _____

1. Which one of these inferences is the reader expected to add to the supporting details?

   a. Violence is a constant presence in American society.

   b. Elementary school children must watch a lot of television.

   c. Television programmers have begun to reduce the medium's violent content due to long-standing parental pressure.

2. Which one of these inferences is the reader expected to add to the supporting details?

   a. The major networks are seriously worried about the continual criticism of television's violent content.

   b. The major networks have not been especially influenced or affected by the long-standing criticism of television's violent content.

   c. Violence on America's six major networks is no greater than it is on European networks.

2. Because many athletes enjoy supersized salaries and owners of teams are generally wealthy, fans are often far less sympathetic to sports labor disputes than they are to other labor disputes. Baseball lost a large number of fans after the 1994 strike, a fact that players and owners kept in mind as they successfully resolved differences in 2002 without disrupting any games. Ultimately, fans are likely to continue as an invisible but important influence on sports as the players and the owners negotiate collective-bargaining agreements for the future. (Pride et al., *Business,* p. 355.)

Topic _____

1. Which one of these inferences is the reader expected to add to the supporting details?

   a. Sports fans don't understand the issues involved in sports labor disputes.

   b. Sports fans support strikes in basketball but not in baseball.

   c. Sports fans don't sympathize because they think the disputes are about money that neither side deserves or needs.

2. Which one of these inferences is the reader expected to add to the supporting details?

   a. Fans will continue to influence negotiations between players and managers because both sides are worried about losing fans angered by a prolonged strike.

   b. It was pure coincidence when the 2002 baseball labor dispute did not disrupt the schedule.

   c. Baseball fans generally think both players and management have enough money, should stop complaining, and should just play ball.

3. When crime news is emphasized by news programs, it almost certainly reinforces what is a current trend toward victimization. Mass communications researchers have studied the degree to which television cultivates a particular view of crime in viewers. As a result, we know that viewers who watch a lot of television consider themselves to be likely victims of crime or wrongdoing to a greater extent than is actually probable in the real world. Viewers often live in the TV world of violent crime. This is not to say that crime is not a problem in American society, because it most certainly is. But not everyone is guaranteed victim status. Is it any wonder that so many trivial lawsuits are filed over spilled coffee or hurt feelings? How can the public place the various aspects of life in any sort of realistic context when television news, in particular, suggests that the most important news is crime-related? (Adapted from Leslie, *Mass Communication Ethics*, p. 170.)

Topic _____

1. Which one of these inferences is the reader expected to add to the supporting details?

   a. People who watch a lot of television are more likely to engage in violent crimes because they believe that everyone else is doing the same thing.

b. People who watch a lot of television cannot tell the difference between what they imagine and what they actually experience.

c. People who watch a lot of television are inclined to think that the life they see portrayed on television mirrors the real world.

2. Which one of these inferences is the reader expected to add to the supporting details?

a. The author believes that lawsuits are turning an even greater number of people into victims.

b. The author believes that people who watch a lot of television are quick to engage in lawsuits because television inclines its heavy viewers to see themselves as victims.

c. The majority of the lawsuits being filed in the United States today are trivial and not worth the court's time.

4. In his book *Mortal Lessons* (1993), surgeon Richard Selzer described his near-death experience. His electrocardiogram was flat for 4 1/2 minutes and no amount of resuscitation* had any effect. The nurse wrote the time of death on his chart. A few minutes later his body shuddered, his electrocardiogram returned, and his breathing became regular. Clearly the judgment of death had been a mistake. A flat electrocardiogram is the sign of a deep coma. Sometimes people come out of a deep coma, as Richard Selzer did; other times the coma is terminal. We are not used to thinking of death as a judgment call, but it is. *Death* used to be defined by the absence of heartbeat and respiration, and still is in most places in the world. But since the 1960s, when the development of artificial respirators made it possible to sustain vital processes artificially, this definition of death has been challenged. In technologically advanced countries, the criteria for determining death have focused instead on *brain death.* (Adapted from Seifert, *Lifespan Development*, p. 680.)

Topic _____

1. Which one of these inferences is the reader expected to add to the supporting details?

a. Richard Selzer's experience illustrates that no human being can rightfully make decisions involving the right to die; the risk of a mistake is too great.

---

*resuscitation: the act of bringing someone back to consciousness or life.

    b. Richard Selzer's experience illustrates why the pronouncement of death is a "judgment call."

    c. Richard Selzer wrote *Mortal Lessons* in order to show the world that death is nothing but a "judgment call."

2. Which one of these inferences is the reader expected to add to the supporting details?

    a. The author labels the pronouncement of death a "judgment call" because of the Richard Selzer case in which a nurse showed poor judgment and labeled Selzer dead when he was still very much alive.

    b. The author labels death a "judgment call" because it is after death that we face judgment.

    c. The author says that the pronouncement of death is a "judgment call" because the definitions of death can change as a result of geographical location and technological advances.

 **Visual Aids as Supporting Details**

Often visual aids simply reinforce what's said in the text. Look, for example, at the following paragraph and accompanying drawing.

> In the late 1960s, Professors Phillip Tichenor, George Donahue, and Clarice Olen of the University of Minnesota came upon a sobering survey finding that relates to the difference in the amount of current events information that different people learn from the media. They found that people who are information-rich to begin with will get richer faster than people who are information-poor. If the difference in the amount of knowledge between the two types of people grows wider so does the difference in financial success. (Source of information: Turow, *Media Today,* p. 150.)

Media discussion of a developing issue

Information-poor media consumer

Information-rich media consumer

START

In this case, the drawing gives you a visual image to accompany the verbal explanation: People rich in information can, in financial terms, often charge ahead of those who are less well informed. The visual image is useful on two counts: (1) If you had any trouble understanding the point of the paragraph, the drawing should eliminate any confusion and (2) looking at the drawing right after you read the text is a good way to anchor the information in your long-term memory.

However, the drawings, tables, graphs, charts, and so on, that appear in a textbook do not always repeat, in visual form, the printed material. Sometimes they add to the text and give you additional supporting details to clarify or prove the main idea of the paragraph or section. For an example, read the following paragraph. Then look at the table that accompanies it on the facing page.

> As you can see from the table, salaries vary considerably from state to state. Each school district determines what it will pay its teachers, with many states setting a minimum base salary below which the school district cannot go. Generally, the large and middle-size school districts pay better than the small ones, and urban and suburban school districts pay better than rural ones. Many school districts offer extra pay for special duties such as directing the band or coaching athletic teams. Some offer summer teaching or curriculum development jobs. Most states and school districts provide public school teachers with a number of fringe benefits, including sick leave, health and life insurance programs, and retirement benefits. When applying for a teaching position, be sure to ask about these benefits. (Ryan and Cooper, *Those Who Can, Teach*, p. 405.)

Table 1 Average and Beginning Teacher Salaries, by State and Region

State	Average Salary ($) (2001–2002)	Beginning Salary ($) (2000–2001)	State	Average Salary ($) (2001–2002)	Beginning Salary ($) (2000–2001)
New England			**Southeast**		
Connecticut	53,551	32,203	Georgia	44,073	31,314
Rhode Island	49,758*	29,265	North Carolina	41,991	29,786
Massachusetts	49,054	26,290	Virginia	41,262*	28,139
New Hampshire	38,911*	25,020	Alabama	39,268*	28,649
Vermont	39,240	26,152	South Carolina	38,943*	26,314
Maine	37,300	23,689	Florida	39,275	25,786
Mideast			Tennessee	38,554	28,074
New Jersey	51,186	30,937	Kentucky	37,847	25,027
New York	53,081	32,772	West Virginia	36,751	24,889
Pennsylvania	50,599	31,127	Louisiana	34,505*	26,124
Delaware	48,363	32,281	Arkansas	37,140*	24,469
Washington, D.C.	47,049	31,889	Mississippi	32,800*	23,292
Maryland	46,200	30,321	**Rocky Mountains**		
Great Lakes			Colorado	40,222*	26,479
Michigan	52,037*	29,401	Wyoming	37,841	24,651
Illinois	50,000	31,222	Idaho	37,482*	23,386
Ohio	44,029	24,895	Utah	37,414*	24,553
Indiana	44,195	27,311	Montana	34,379*	21,728
Wisconsin	42,232	26,232	**Far West**		
Great Plains			California	53,870*	33,121
Minnesota	43,330*	27,003	Alaska	49,418	36,293
Iowa	38,230	26,058	Oregon	46,039	27,903
Missouri	37,904	27,173	Washington	43,474	27,284
Kansas	36,673	26,010	Hawaii	42,615	29,204
Nebraska	36,236	24,353	Nevada	41,524*	29,413
North Dakota	31,709*	20,675	**U.S. Average**	44,449	28,986
South Dakota	31,295	22,457			
Southwest					
Texas	39,232	29,823			
Arizona	39,973	26,801			
New Mexico	36,440	25,999			
Oklahoma	34,744	27,016			

*estimated

Sources of figures: Average salaries from "Ranking Estimates of the States and Estimates of School Statistics 2002," Update Fall 2002 (Washington, DC: National Education Association, 2002), available at **http://www.nea.org/edstats/reupdate02.html**. Beginning salaries from F. Howard Nelson, *Survey and Analysis of Salary Trends, 1998, 2001.* Table 1-8, p. 8.

The topic sentence of the paragraph on page 322 tells you that salaries vary considerably from state to state. The supporting details in the passage then explain that large and middle-size school districts pay better than small ones while urban and suburban school districts pay better than rural ones. But if you want to understand just how much teachers' salaries can vary, *it's the table that really tells the story:* According to the table, a new teacher living in Connecticut starts out at more than $32,000 a year in contrast to a new teacher in North Dakota who starts out at a salary over one-third less than that of a Connecticut teacher. This is very specific support for the claim made in the topic sentence: Teachers' salaries vary a lot from state to state. It's the kind of specific information you would want to record to use in an answer to a test question

---

Steps in Reading a Table

1. Read the title of the table to be sure you understand what's being illustrated. If there's a caption, read that as well. Check, if you can, the source of the figures to see how up-to-date they are.

2. If the table is highly detailed, be prepared to spend a few minutes studying the columns and getting accustomed to the facts and figures presented here.

3. Compare and contrast the different columns, looking for similarities and differences.

Identify the Function of the Visual Aid

The previous sample passages (pages 321–323) and accompanying figures illustrate a key principle of reading: Visual aids appear in a text for different purposes. Sometimes the author includes a visual aid to emphasize a key point. But just as frequently, the author includes a visual aid to add information that is best displayed as a drawing, table, chart, or graph. Make sure you understand the function or purpose of every visual aid. Is it there to repeat a key point or to add new information? If its purpose is to add new information, be sure you know how that information connects to the ideas in your textbook.

Three Ways to Use Visual Aids

When you are reading, you should look at visual aids in three different ways:
1. Look them over before you read as part of your survey, asking yourself what they suggest about the chapter's contents.
2. Study them while you read to make sure you understand their relationship to the written text.
3. Review the visual aids when you are finished. For each one, ask, "What purpose did this graph, table, chart, etc., serve?" If you can answer that question, then you know you have understood the related text.

Bar Graphs

Like drawings and tables, bar graphs* like the one accompanying the passage below can help speed up comprehension.

> **Magnitude of Pay** In union negotiations, of considerable importance is the *magnitude*, or amount, of pay that employees receive as both direct and indirect compensation. The union attempts to ensure that pay is on par with that received by other employees in the same or similar industries, both locally and nationally. The union also attempts to include in the contract clauses that provide pay increases over the life of the agreement. The most common is the *cost-of-living*, which ties periodic pay increases to increases in the cost of living, as defined by various economic statistics or indicators. Of course, the magnitude of pay is also affected by the organization's ability to pay. If the firm has posted large profits recently, the union may expect large pay increases for its members. If the firm has not been profitable, the union may agree to smaller pay hikes or even to a pay freeze. (Pride et al., *Business*, p. 353.)

---

*For more on bar graphs, see pages 721–723.

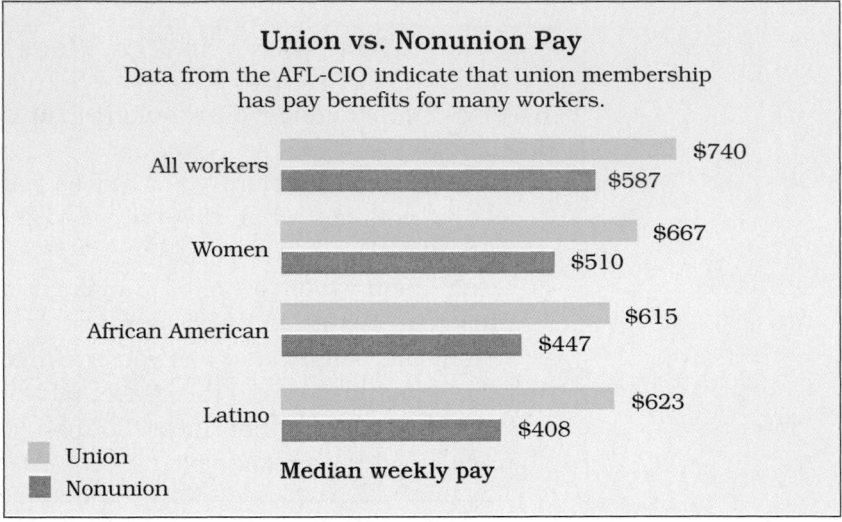

Union vs. Nonunion Pay

Data from the AFL-CIO indicate that union membership has pay benefits for many workers.

(Sources of information: Pride et al., *Business*, p. 353; www.aflcio.org/aboutunions/joinunions/whyjoin/uniondifference.)

Look where each blue bar (representing weekly pay of union workers) ends. Then note how far each blue bar extends over each gray bar (representing nonunion workers). The comparison tells you that in addition to being concerned about pay, unions have been effective in winning increases for members. This piece of information adds to the author's main idea. Still, it's contributed by the graph and its caption rather than the text.

Steps in Reading a Bar Graph

1. Read the figure title, caption, and source note. Pay close attention to any dates mentioned.
2. Identify the purpose of the graph. Is it comparing and contrasting different substances or quantities? Or is it tracing increases and decreases over time?
3. If the graph measures changes or quantities over time, determine the time span and look for the longest and shortest bars to discover the largest increases or decreases.
4. If the graph compares and contrasts different products or substances, look carefully at the horizontal axis for the names of those products or substances. Then look for the longest and shortest bars to determine the degree of difference or similarity between each substance or product.

⊣▬ EXERCISE 9 Understanding Visual Aids

DIRECTIONS Read each passage and underline the topic sentence. Then study the visual aid that accompanies the paragraph. Circle the appropriate letter to indicate what the illustration adds to your understanding of the text.

EXAMPLE <u>Though presidential popularity is an asset, its value tends inescapably to decline.</u> Between 1975 and 2004, every president except Reagan and Clinton lost popular support between his inauguration and the time that he left office, except when his reelection gave him a brief burst of renewed popularity. Ford was hurt by having pardoned Nixon for his part in Watergate; Carter was weakened by continuing inflation, staff irregularities, and the Iranian kidnapping of American hostages. George H. W. Bush was harmed by an economic recession. Remarkably, Clinton's approval rating was not greatly harmed by his affair with Monica Lewinsky and his impeachment. (Source of information: Wilson and DiIulio Jr., *American Government*, pp. 392–393.)

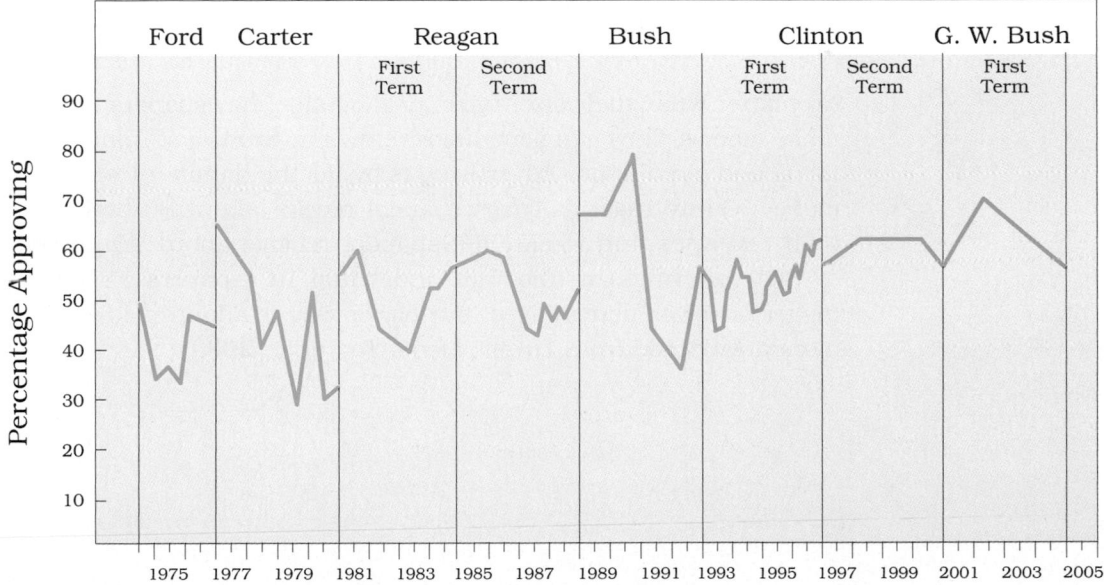

The line graph adds which piece of information to your understanding of the paragraph?

a. Bill Clinton's ratings did not experience a decline in his second term.

b. All presidents experience a decline while in office.

c. George W. Bush's public support was at its peak in 2001, after the tragedy of 9/11, and it began to decline steadily by 2002.

EXPLANATION The illustration on page 327 is actually a series of short line graphs. Each jagged line for the term (or terms) of each president has to be read from left to right. Do that, and you'll see how the graph essentially repeats what's said in the text. If you look at the year ending each president's last term in office and let your eye travel to the jagged line, you can clearly see that Ford, Carter, and George H. W. Bush all experienced a drop in popular support. But the graph tells you even a bit more. It tells you that Bill Clinton's popular support during the year of his impeachment and his affair with Monica Lewinsky was exactly the same as at the time of his inauguration. The graph also tells you something else not mentioned in the paragraph: George W. Bush's popularity peaked in 2001, the year of the terrorist attack on the United States, and then began to decline.

1. No matter what their size, topic, or language, newspapers need to make money. They can generate revenues in two ways: from advertising and circulation. Advertising is by far the dominant source of money. On average, daily newspapers receive about 80 percent of their revenues and weekly newspapers receive about 90 percent of their revenues in this way. Individual newspapers may have higher or lower percentages, but either way it adds up to a lot of money. (Adapted from Turow, *Media Today*, p. 298.)

Table 2 U.S. Daily Newspaper Advertising Revenues

Year	National Advertising ($ millions)	Local Advertising ($ millions)	Classified Advertising ($ millions)	Total Newspaper Advertising ($ millions)
1965	$ 783	$ 2,429	$ 1,214	$ 4,426
1970	$ 891	$ 3,292	$ 1,521	$ 5,704
1975	$1,109	$ 4,966	$ 2,159	$ 8,234
1980	$1,963	$ 8,609	$ 4,222	$14,794
1985	$3,352	$13,443	$ 8,375	$25,170
1986	$3,376	$14,311	$ 9,303	$26,990
1987	$3,494	$15,227	$10,691	$29,412
1988	$3,821	$15,790	$11,586	$31,197
1989	$3,948	$16,504	$11,916	$32,368
1990	$4,122	$16,652	$11,506	$30,349
1992	$3,834	$16,041	$10,764	$30,639
1993	$3,853	$16,859	$11,157	$31,869
1994	$4,149	$17,496	$12,464	$34,109
1995	$4,251	$18,099	$13,742	$36,092
1996	$4,667	$18,344	$15,065	$38,075
1997	$5,315	$19,242	$16,773	$41,330
1998	$5,721	$20,331	$17,873	$43,925
1999	$6,732	$20,907	$18,650	$46,289
2000	$7,652	$21,404	$19,608	$48,664

Sources of information: NAA, U.S. Department of Commerce.

The table adds what piece of information to your understanding of the paragraph?

a. Advertising has not always been such a major source of revenue for newspapers.
b. Local advertising has long been the largest source of advertising revenues.
c. Advertising was not always such an important source of revenue to newspapers.

2. The notion that the pursuit of self-interest can sometimes be self-destructive forms the basis of what is called a *social dilemma*. In a social dilemma, what is good for one is bad for all. If everyone makes the most self-rewarding choice, everyone suffers the greatest loss.

Social dilemmas involve very large groups—a city, a nation, the whole world. In these circumstances, the factors listed in the table below may be the most influential. (Adapted from Brehm et al., *Social Psychology*, p. 297.)

Table 3 Solving Social Dilemmas

Behavior in a social dilemma is influenced by both psychological factors and structural arrangements. The characteristics listed here contribute to the successful solution of social dilemmas.

Psychological Factors
- Individual and cultural differences
  - Having a prosocial, cooperative orientation
  - Trusting others
  - Being a member of a collectivistic culture
- Situational factors
  - Being in a good mood
  - Having had successful experience managing resources and working cooperatively
  - Seeing unselfish models
  - Having reason to expect others to cooperate
- Group dynamics
  - Acting as an individual rather than in a group
  - Being in a small group rather than in a large group
  - Sharing a social identity or overall goals

The table adds what piece of information to your understanding of the paragraph?

a. Some social dilemmas can prove dangerous to large groups, driving a wedge into the group that ultimately destroys it.

b. An egocentric attitude is at the core of a social dilemma.

c. Trusting others and being in a good mood encourage the solution of social dilemmas.

 ## Concluding Sentences and Supporting Details

At this point, you are familiar with every kind of sentence that can appear in a paragraph except for one—the concluding sentence. As the name implies, **concluding sentences** come at the very end of paragraphs containing topic sentences. Unlike the supporting sentences that precede them, concluding sentences don't directly develop the topic sentence or modify a major detail. Instead, they describe a result or make a prediction about some problem or event mentioned in the paragraph. Although not all paragraphs end with concluding sentences, a good many do. You need to recognize them when you see them because concluding sentences usually contain significant information, even if they do not directly support the main idea expressed in the topic sentence.

The following paragraph illustrates how a concluding sentence differs from a supporting detail.

> In 1692, Salem, Massachusetts, was the scene of a series of witchcraft trials. The trials began when two young girls who appeared to be suffering fits accused several men and women in the town of dealing with the devil. The girls' accusations were believed, and before the townspeople came to their senses, nineteen men and women had been hanged and hundreds of others had been cruelly tortured and imprisoned. Following the Salem experience, witchcraft trials practically disappeared from the colonies.

The topic of the paragraph is witchcraft trials in Salem; the topic sentence of the paragraph tells readers that in 1692 Salem was the scene of witchcraft trials. All the remaining sentences in the paragraph, except the last one, tell us more about the Salem trials. The last sentence tells us what happened in the colonies *after* the Salem experience. The last sentence is a good example of a concluding sentence.

If you're reading a paragraph and encounter a concluding sentence, don't assume it's unimportant because it does not directly develop the main idea. Concluding sentences can include significant information about the topic under discussion. Thus they deserve your attention. At the very least, you need to decide whether or not they are essential to your understanding of the paragraph.

The following exercise will give you practice in recognizing concluding sentences. But don't be fooled. Not all paragraphs end with concluding sentences. Many end with a major or minor supporting detail.

◄█ EXERCISE 10 Recognizing Concluding Sentences

DIRECTIONS The topic sentence in each paragraph has been underlined. After reading the paragraph, circle the letter of the answer that best describes the final sentence of the paragraph.

EXAMPLE In 1856, Henry Bessemer invented a new method for manufacturing steel, one that consisted of three basic steps. First, a blast of cold air was forced through the mass of hot melting iron. The enormous heat created then burned out the impurities in the iron and left it ready for the final step—the addition of carbon, manganese, and other substances that produced good-quality steel. The introduction of the Bessemer process revolutionized the steel industry, making steel an important commodity* for American export.

a. The last sentence in the paragraph provides a supporting detail.

(b.) The last sentence in the paragraph is a concluding sentence.

EXPLANATION   The last sentence does not further explain the topic sentence. It does not describe one of the three basic steps in the Bessemer process. That eliminates answer *a*, making answer *b* the correct choice.

1. In 1886, French chemist Louis Pasteur believed that he had found a vaccine to combat the dreaded disease called rabies. <u>Pasteur, however, was fearful of using the rabies vaccine on human beings until the decision to do so was forced upon him</u>. On July 6, 1886, a young boy named Joseph Meister was brought to Pasteur for treatment. The boy had been bitten on the arms and legs by a rabid dog. Pasteur consulted with several physicians who assured him that the boy was going to die. It was only then that Pasteur decided to use his rabies vaccine. Meister lived to become gatekeeper of the Pasteur Institute and committed suicide fifty-five years later.

a. The last sentence in the paragraph provides a supporting detail.

b. The last sentence in the paragraph is a concluding sentence.

2. <u>While human beings like to think of themselves as the only animals who possess total control over all their actions, this belief is not based on fact</u>. A strong emotion such as fear can cause reactions that are totally beyond human control. For example, it is well known that human beings often tremble when frightened. The trembling is involuntary and ceases only when danger is past. Similarly, children and adults have been known to urinate when placed in fear-producing situations.

a. The last sentence in the paragraph provides a supporting detail.

b. The last sentence in the paragraph is a concluding sentence.

---

*commodity: something that is bought or sold in the market.

3. Until the sixteenth century, people believed that the earth was the center of the universe. <u>However, in 1543, Nicolaus Copernicus, a Polish astronomer, challenged the traditional worldview</u>. In his book *Concerning the Revolutions of the Heavenly Bodies,* Copernicus insisted that the earth revolved around the sun and that the sun was the real center of the universe. He further argued that the apparent revolution of the sun around the earth was caused by the earth's daily rotation on its own axis. Although Copernicus' theory was essentially correct, it was not accepted until well into the seventeenth century.

   a. The last sentence in the paragraph provides a supporting detail.
   b. The last sentence in the paragraph is a concluding sentence.

4. Whether or not a war should have been fought can always be debated. The prowar forces can always come up with a reason why a war should be waged; the antiwar forces are perfectly able to prove the opposite. <u>However, there was one war that everybody agreed had to be fought; that was World War II</u>. In the face of Hitler's murder of millions of human beings, few people were willing to question the need to stop him. And anybody who thought he could be persuaded by peaceful means just had to look at the promises he had broken when dealing with England and Russia.

   a. The last sentence in the paragraph provides a supporting detail.
   b. The last sentence in the paragraph is a concluding sentence.

5. Because viruses are difficult to classify, several different systems have been put forward. <u>Probably the most commonly used system classifies viruses according to their host cells; according to the system, there are three groups of viruses: animal, plant, and bacterial</u>. On the whole, animal viruses are much more complex than plant viruses and have, therefore, been given distinct names like *poxvirus* and *parvovirus*. In contrast, plant viruses are named according to the host they invade, for example, the tobacco virus. Bacterial viruses, also called *bacteriophages,* or *phages*, are usually identified by a system of letters and numbers, like the T-2 bacteriophage.

   a. The last sentence in the paragraph provides a supporting detail.
   b. The last sentence in the paragraph is a concluding sentence.

■ DIGGING DEEPER

CHALLENGING THE DIGITAL DIVIDE

LOOKING AHEAD The paragraph on page 321 describes what can happen when some people are information-rich while others remain information-poor. This reading addresses a related problem, the growing divide between those who have access to a home computer and those who don't. The first paragraph expressing the main idea of the reading is missing, but you should be able to identify that paragraph based on the supporting details that follow.

1   The founder of Microsoft and possibly the world's richest man, [Bill] Gates built his empire of technology on the premise that computers would make the world a better place. Since stepping down as CEO of Microsoft, Gates and his wife, Melinda, have turned much of their attention to philanthropic endeavors. They became concerned about research that showed a major global digital divide—that people without the means to integrate computers and the Web into their lives are becoming more and more disadvantaged compared to those with access. They began donating computers to some of the world's poorest people in hopes of narrowing that gap, with the idea that being "connected" would provide the most impoverished people with the power and mobility they so desperately needed.

2   Lately, though, Bill Gates has changed his tune and begun to criticize the very ideology he used to preach. Though he continues his philanthropic work, the Gates Foundation doesn't see computers as the solution to all the world's problems. Gates has been quoted as saying that poor families trying to live on $1 a day "are not going to like, sit around and browse eBay or something. What they want is for their children to live." Now Gates's priorities are health care and distribution of vaccines, which are expected to make up two-thirds of the grants handed out by the $21 billion Gates Foundation. The integration of technology globally, he says, can be seen as a long-term goal, but in the meantime, more effort must be made to accommodate crucial basic human needs.

3   Some people in Mr. Gates's industry have commended him for his recent comments, while others claim that there's no reason to slow efforts to "wire" the whole world, because new media products are increasingly being used to satisfy even people's most fundamental needs. Can technology really improve the quality of life

everywhere? Gates thinks so, but not before more important concerns like health care and food are seriously addressed.

Adapted from Joseph Turow, Media Today. Boston:
Houghton Mifflin, 2003, pp. 152–153.

Sharpening Your Skills

DIRECTIONS Answer the following questions by circling the letters of the correct response or filling in the blanks.

1. Which of these three main ideas matches the supporting details you just finished reading?

   a. Bill Gates became a billionaire by making the world want Microsoft products, but today it's not clear that he would do the same thing all over again if he could. Gates, whose philanthropy has become legendary, is now focused less on making money and more on giving it away.

   b. Professors Phillip Tichenor, George Donahue, and Clarice Olien have argued in an influential paper, "Mass Media Flow and the Differential Growth of Knowledge," that making information widely and inexpensively available through mass media can fill in the gap between those who have information and those who don't. To the surprise of many, Bill Gates seems to agree.

   c. Even when people don't dispute the findings of research, they may dispute the effect or importance of those findings. Bill Gates's current take on the digital divide is a good example.

2. Paraphrase the definition of "digital divide" introduced in paragraph 1.

   _____

   _____

   _____

3. In your own words, explain how Bill Gates has, as the author says, "changed his tune" (paragraph 2). What did he used to say, and what is he currently claiming?

   _____

   _____

   _____

4. The word *ideology* was introduced earlier in Chapter 2. Please define the term on the lines below.

Ideology: _____

_____

5. Based on the reading, what inference or conclusion could you draw about the kind of charity the Gates husband and wife team are more likely to support?

a. a program for bringing AIDS drugs to hard-hit countries like Botswana, but at one-quarter their usual cost.

b. a program for giving every school child access to a computer during the time they are in school.

INTERNET RESOURCE

For more practice with supporting details, see **college.hmco.com/ pic/flemmingRFR10e**, where you will find three levels of interactive quizzes: *Getting Down the Basics*, *Checking Your Progress*, and *Taking the Challenge*. You can also find additional interactive practice with supporting details at **laflemm.com**, *Reading for Results*: Online Practice for Chapter 6.

 # Test 1: Recognizing Supporting Details

DIRECTIONS The first sentence in each group of sentences is the topic sentence. That topic sentence is followed by five supporting details. Circle the letters of the three sentences that help make the topic sentence clear and convincing.

Topic Sentence **1.** Over the years, salamanders—small, lizardlike creatures that walk on four legs—have been the focus of numerous legends.

Supporting Details

    a. In England, a salamander is also the name of a portable stove.

    b. The philosopher Aristotle claimed that salamanders could put out fires simply by walking through them.

    c. The word *salamander* comes from the Greek word *salamandra*.

    d. It was once believed that twining a salamander around a tree would kill the tree and poison its fruit.

    e. According to legend, four thousand soldiers died when they drank from a stream into which a salamander had fallen.

Topic Sentence **2.** The Walt Disney film *Pinocchio* is based on a novel by nineteenth-century Italian writer Carlo Collodi, but the novel was far more violent than the film.

Supporting Details

    a. In both the novel and the film, Pinocchio is transformed into a donkey.

    b. Disney's *Pinocchio* did not achieve the popularity of the fabulously successful *Snow White*.

    c. In Collodi's novel, when Pinocchio is attacked by a cat, he bites off the cat's paw.

    d. In the Italian version, Pinocchio kills a talking cricket when the insect tries to keep him from getting into trouble.

    e. In the novel, when Pinocchio falls asleep by the fire, he wakes up with his wooden feet burned off.

Topic Sentence **3.** Until a cure was discovered in the nineteenth century, scurvy, a disease caused by a lack of vitamin C, plagued sailors on long sea voyages.

Supporting Details

    a. In the late 1490s, the explorer Vasco da Gama lost more than half of his crew to scurvy.

    b. In his autobiography, *Two Years Before the Mast,* nineteenth-century writer Richard Henry Dana described the sufferings of a fellow sailor who had contracted scurvy: "His legs swelled . . . his flesh lost its elasticity . . . and his gums swelled until he could not open his mouth."

c. Scurvy no longer plagues sailors who spend long periods of time at sea.

d. During the Napoleonic wars (1803–1814), French soldiers who did not have daily doses of vitamin C suffered from scurvy, but British soldiers, who drank daily doses of lime juice, escaped the disease.

e. British sailors became so associated with the drinking of lime juice that they were nicknamed "limeys"; the name stuck with them.

Topic Sentence **4.** For centuries, dogs have held a very special place in the hearts of humans.

Supporting Details

a. In the fifteenth and sixteenth centuries, no high-born lady was complete without her lap dog, and many women took their pets to church.

b. Unlike most dogs, border collies would rather work than play.

c. The eighteenth-century poet and scholar Samuel Johnson was quick to put humans in their place, but he doted on his pet dog.

d. Even the French Emperor Napoleon (1769–1821) claimed that his beloved Josephine preferred her dog Fortuné to him.

e. Some people do not understand the bond that can develop between human beings and their pets.

 **Test 2: Distinguishing Between Major and Minor Details**

DIRECTIONS Read each paragraph and fill in the boxes with abbreviated versions of the major and minor details.

1. Parents worry about the violence in video games that require kids to shoot enemies, but research shows that these games benefit children by improving their visual attention skills. After as few as ten hours of play, kids show a 30 to 50 percent improvement in identifying objects in their peripheral vision. These games also help children develop their brains' ability to shift attention rapidly from one thing to another. And such shooting games improve players' ability to track many different items at one time. This skill, in particular, is helpful in tasks such as driving. (Source of information: Sandra Blakeslee, "Video-Game Killing Builds Visual Skills, Researchers Report," *New York Times*, May 29, 2003, p. A1, www.nytimes.com/2003/05/29/science/29VIDE. html.)

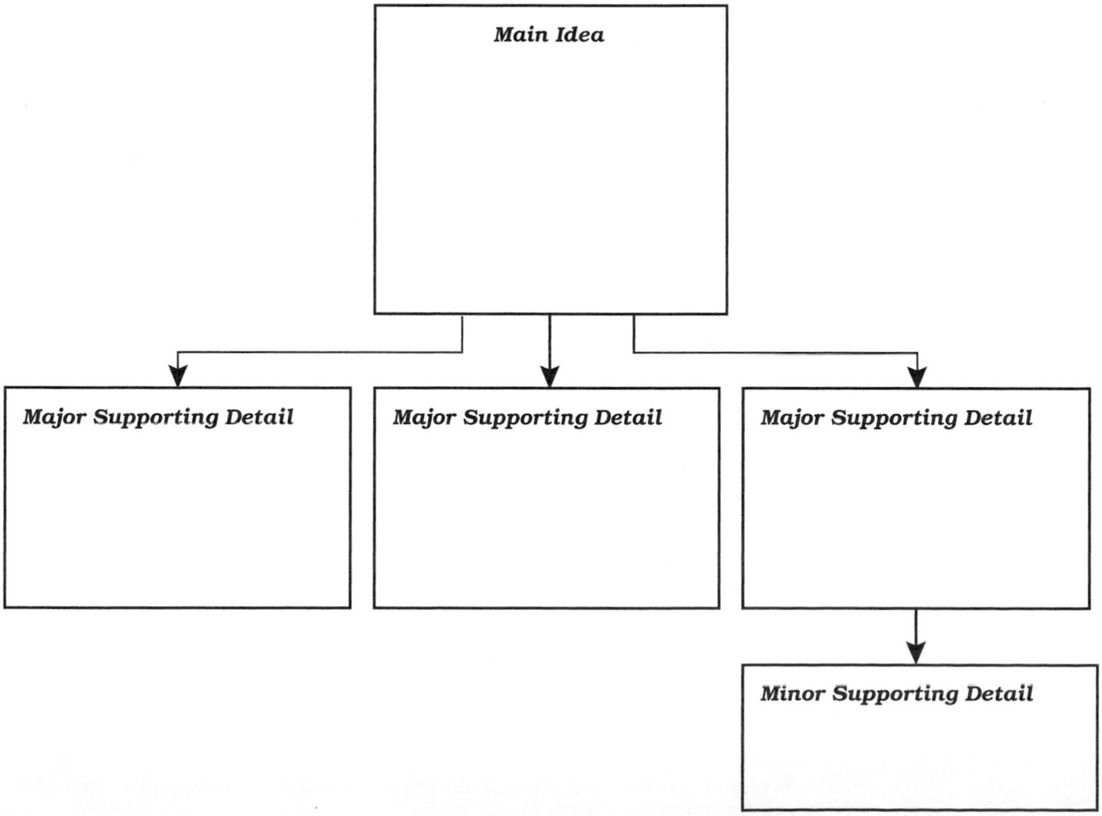

```
                    ┌─────────────────────┐
                    │     Main Idea       │
                    │                     │
                    │                     │
                    │                     │
                    │                     │
                    └─────────────────────┘
         ┌──────────────┼──────────────┐
         ▼              ▼              ▼
┌──────────────┐ ┌──────────────┐ ┌──────────────┐
│ Major        │ │ Major        │ │ Major        │
│ Supporting   │ │ Supporting   │ │ Supporting   │
│ Detail       │ │ Detail       │ │ Detail       │
│              │ │              │ │              │
└──────────────┘ └──────────────┘ └──────┬───────┘
                                         ▼
                                  ┌──────────────┐
                                  │ Minor        │
                                  │ Supporting   │
                                  │ Detail       │
                                  │              │
                                  └──────────────┘
```

2. Several dogs have actually helped determine the course of human history. In the sixteenth century, Cardinal Wolsey's greyhound Urian forced King Henry VIII to begin the English Reformation.* Wolsey had gone to Pope Clement VII to ask for an annulment of Henry's marriage, but when Urian bit the pope's foot, negotiations ended; consequently, Henry had no choice but to declare himself head of the Church of England so that he could have his divorce. Another dog may have contributed to the American Revolution and the creation of the United States. Had Scotland's Robert Bruce not been saved from death by one of his dogs, his family would not have taken over the English throne. The Stuarts' hereditary mental disorder would not have influenced the English king's treatment of the American colonies. Likewise, several other dogs saved the lives of great people who went on to influence history. A Newfoundland rescued nineteenth-century explorers Lewis and Clark from a charging buffalo, a greyhound saved Alexander the Great from a rampaging elephant, another Newfoundland dove off the deck of a boat and rescued Napoleon Bonaparte from a stormy sea, and Abraham Lincoln's mixed-breed dog alerted passersby when her eleven-year-old master fell into a dark cave. (Source of information: Larissa MacFarquhar, "Bark," *The New Yorker*, February 3, 2003, pp. 89–90.)

---

*Reformation: a sixteenth-century movement aimed at reforming practices of the Roman Catholic church.

	Main Idea	

Major Supporting Detail	*Major Supporting Detail*	*Major Supporting Detail*

Minor Supporting Detail	*Minor Supporting Detail*	*Minor Supporting Detail*

3. Biologically, chimpanzees and humans differ by little more than one percent of their DNA, which means that chimpanzees are actually more closely related to humans than they are to gorillas. The anatomy of a chimpanzee's brain and central nervous system is amazingly like that of humans. Therefore, chimpanzees can and do create and use tools, make decisions, and cooperate in groups, just like humans. Chimpanzees also demonstrate many of humans' communication skills. Not only can they learn to use languages such as American Sign Language, but they also use nonverbal behaviors such as kissing, hugging, back patting, and fist shaking in the same ways humans do. Furthermore, chimpanzees feel and express human emotions such as happiness, sorrow, fear, and despair. These animals are like us in many of their behaviors, too. For example, mother chimpanzees care for their offspring during their long childhood, and chimps also divide into groups that go to war against one another. (Source of information: "Similarities Between Chimpanzees and Human Beings," *Chimpanzee Central,* www .janegoodall.org/chimp_central/chimpanzees/similarities/.)

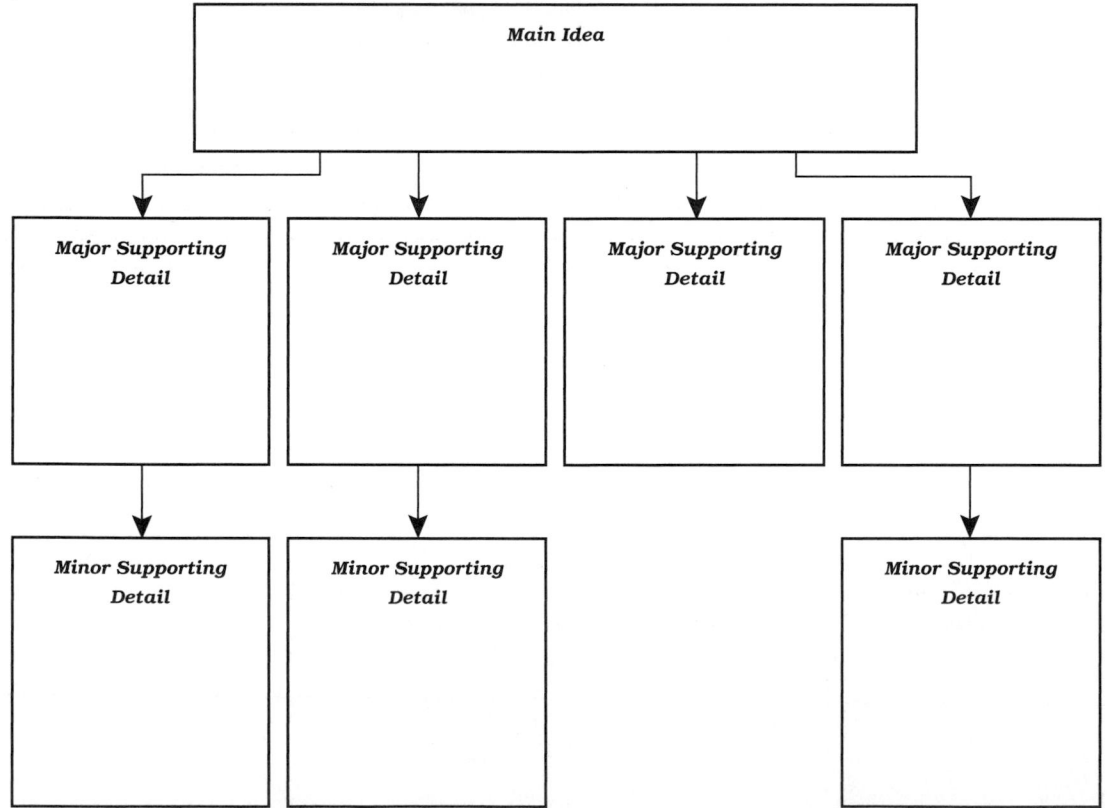

4. Four categories of monarchies still exist in the world today. The first category includes monarchies in which the king (or queen) is both head of the government and head of state, and the monarch is directly involved in ruling the country. This type of monarchy, found mostly in the Middle East, includes Jordan, Saudi Arabia, and Morocco. The second type of monarchy is one based on religious authority. In Japan, Thailand, Nepal, and Bhutan, for example, monarchs are actually above the government, and they remain remote from politics and the public while observing formal rituals of conduct. Monarchs in the third category, which includes democracies of Northern Europe and the Scandinavian states, have no political or religious role, serving instead as symbols of national unity. The Netherlands, Denmark, and Luxembourg all have this type of monarch. The fourth and final category of monarchy is the hybrid type illustrated by Britain, where the queen has some political authority, serves a religious role as head of the Anglican Church, and also functions as a symbol of her nation's identity. (Source of information: Ben Partridge, "Can Monarchy Survive in the 21st Century?" *Radio Free Europe/Radio Liberty*, www.rferl.org/nca/features/1999/02/F.RU.990222142810.html.)

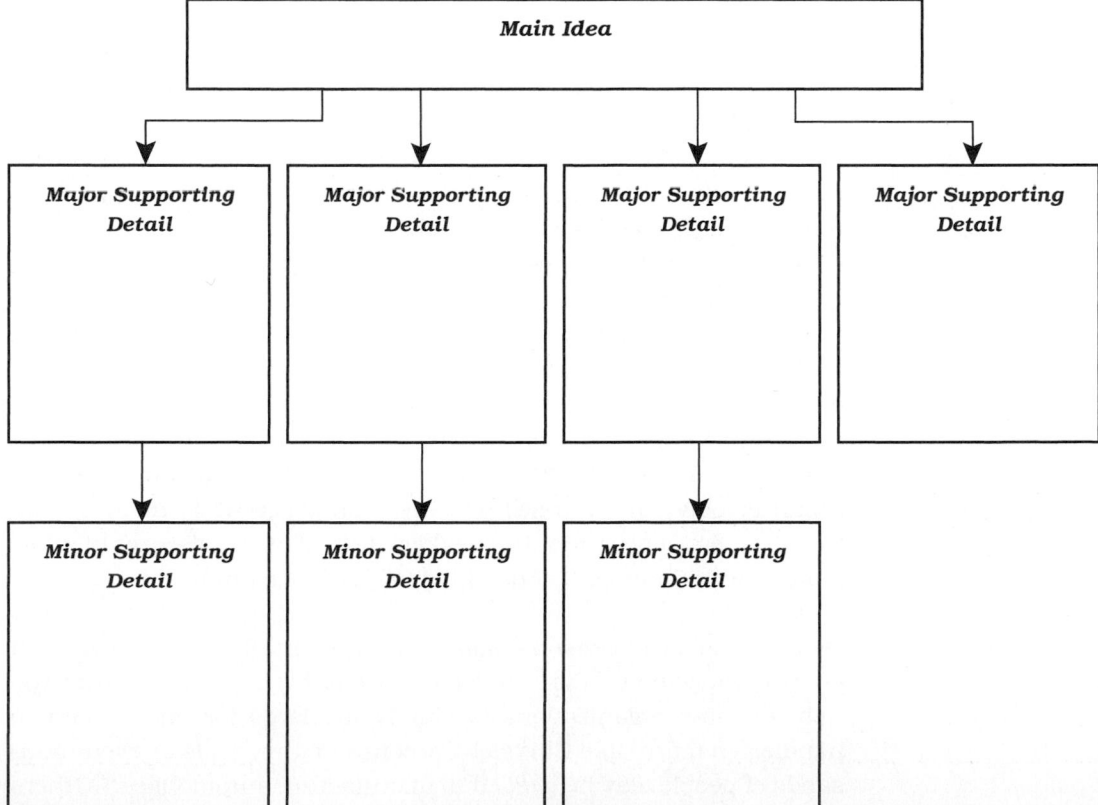

 **Test 3: Recognizing Topic Sentence Clues to Major Details**

DIRECTIONS Read each paragraph and underline the topic sentence, making sure to circle the word or phrase that provides a clue to the major supporting details.

1. [1]Many of us use recitation as a memory aid. [2]Having finished reading an essay, for instance, we mentally repeat the key points. [3]But even those of us who use recitation to remember, don't realize that there are two different kinds: active and passive. [4]When we use *active* recitation, we paraphrase the material, repeating key points in our own words. [5]When we use *passive* recitation, we simply repeat what we see before us in the text. [6]We don't even attempt to replace the author's words with our own. [7]Over the years, numerous studies have shown that active recitation, especially when combined with visualization, is a much better device for remembering than passive recitations.

2. [1]Most middle-class Americans generally maintain four principal zones of distance in their personal and professional relationships. [2]*Intimate distance* covers a space varying from direct physical contact with another person to a distance of six to eighteen inches. [3]This is the distance considered appropriate for close friends, romantic partners, and family members. [4]It's the one used for intimate situations. [5]Personal distance—eighteen inches to four feet—is the distance married couples use in public; it's also the distance used for conversation about things not considered especially private. [6]Social or business distance covers a four-to-twelve-foot zone that is used for casual social exchanges and business negotiations. [7]Eye contact is almost always maintained at this distance, since the lack of it suggests that someone's attention is wandering. [8]Public speaking distance can be a separation of only twelve feet, but usually it's not more than twenty-five. [9]The goal of public speaking distance is to put a barrier between one's self and one's audience while making sure that listeners stay within the speaker's field of vision. (Source of information: www.linus-geisler.de/dp/dpo3_distance.html.)

3. [1]For a number of reasons, some job specialization is necessary in every organization. [2]First and foremost is the simple fact that the "job" of most organizations is simply too large for one person to handle. [3]In a firm like Chrysler Corporation, hundreds or even thousands of people may be needed to manufacture automobiles. [4]Others

will be needed to sell cars, to control the firm's finances, and so on. [5]Second, when a worker has to learn only a specific, highly organized task, the individual should be able to do it very efficiently. [6]Third, the worker who is doing the same job over and over does not lose time changing from one operation to another. [7]Fourth, the more specialized the job, the easier it may be to design specialized equipment for those who do it. [8]And finally, the more specialized the job, the easier it is to train new employees when an employee quits or is absent from work. (Pride et al., *Business*, p. 689.)

4. [1]What everyday rules for behavior guide parents' efforts to socialize their children? [2]To answer that question, Heidi Gralinski and Claire Kopp (1993) observed and interviewed mothers with their children. [3]The research by Gralinski and Kopp suggests that maternal rules at least vary with the child's age. [4]They found that for fifteen-month-olds, mothers' rules and requests centered on ensuring the children's safety, respecting basic social niceties ("Don't bite; "No kicking"), and learning to accept delays. [5]As children's ages and thinking abilities increased, the numbers and kinds of prohibitions and requests expanded. [6]The focus now was on family routines, self-care, and other concerns regarding the child's independence. [7]By the time children were three, new kinds of rules emerged: "Do not scream in a restaurant, run around naked in front of company, pretend to kill your sister, hang up the phone when someone is using it, fight with children in school, play with guns or pick your nose." (Adapted from Seifert, *Lifespan Development*, p. 179.)

 ## Test 4: Recognizing Supporting Details and Concluding Sentences

DIRECTIONS Read each paragraph. The topic sentence in each paragraph is underlined. Label each of the following sentences as a major (*M*) or minor (*m*) detail. If you think the paragraph ends with a concluding sentence, write a *c* in the final blank.

1. ¹Surprising as it may seem to those of us who grew up with him, Santa Claus was not always pictured as a roly-poly figure with chubby cheeks, a big belly, and a long white beard. ²<u>The Santa Claus we know today was created in the mid-nineteenth century by the cartoonist Thomas Nast</u>. ³The European ancestor of our Santa Claus, Saint Nicholas, was always pictured as a tall, lean, and bearded bishop who bore no trace of extra fat. _____ ⁴However, during the years 1863 to 1885, Nast was commissioned by *Harper's Weekly* to do a series of Christmas drawings; during that twenty-two-year period, he created the pudgy figure so beloved by children today. _____ ⁵It was Nast who decided that Santa should wear a fur-trimmed red suit and hat. _____ ⁶Nast's cartoons also showed the world how Santa spent his entire year—making toys, checking on children's behavior, and reading their letters. _____ ⁷Ultimately, however, Nast's fame rests not on his Santa Claus drawings but on his cartoons attacking political corruption.* _____

2. ¹<u>Although we associate penguins with the Antarctic, only two of approximately twenty species live on the continent of Antarctica.</u> ²These are the two largest, the emperor and the king penguins. _____ ³Both of them stand about four feet high. _____ ⁴Most other species are found on the islands in the Antarctic region, but a few breed as far north as Australia, New Zealand, South Africa, and South America. _____

3. ¹<u>Leadership and management are in some ways similar forms of influence, but in one very crucial way they are quite different</u>. ²Managers can direct the efforts of others because of their status or power within an organization. _____ ³Simply put, employees follow the directions of a manager largely because they know that not to do so would endanger their jobs. _____ ⁴Leaders, in contrast, don't have to rely on their position or rank; often it is the power of their personality that makes them an influence to be reckoned with. _____ ⁵At the

---

*corruption: dishonesty, wrongdoing.

Marriott Corporation, for example, employees often go beyond their normal duties largely because they respect and admire Bill Marriott. _____

4. [1]The first American comic strip appeared in 1894. [2]<u>Comic books, however, arrived after the turn of the century, and it wasn't until the 1930s that comic books successfully became part of American culture</u>. [3]The first comic book, published by Dell Publishing Company, was a huge failure, but the second one, also published by Dell, succeeded. _____ [4]Called "Famous Funnies," the comic book cost ten cents, and all thirty-five thousand copies quickly sold out. _____ [5]Not surprisingly, many more comic books followed, most of them featuring cartoon characters, such as Popeye and Flash Gordon, that had originally appeared in newspapers. _____ [6]The biggest comic book breakthrough, however, came in 1938 with the introduction of a red-caped, blue-suited figure called Superman. _____ [7]Appearing in the first issue of *Action Comics,* Superman was an immediate sensation. _____ [8]Today, that first issue of *Action Comics* can fetch its owner around one hundred thousand dollars. _____

 ## Test 5: Topics, Topic Sentences, and Inferring Supporting Details

DIRECTIONS Identify the topic, underline the topic sentence, and circle the appropriate letters to identify the two inferences supplied by readers.

1. [1]More than half a century has passed since John Steinbeck wrote the novel The Grapes of Wrath. [2]In it, he depicted the sorrows and trials of the Joads, an impoverished* family of migrants*. [3]When Steinbeck wrote the book, there were no laws protecting migrant workers, and they were almost uniformly mistreated by their employers. [4]After *The Grapes of Wrath* was published and widely read, the public's outcry for change was clear and strong, and reforms were undertaken; but most of the reforms never took effect, and even today many migrant workers still live under the worst possible conditions. [5]Every year, the Department of Labor receives numerous complaints about improper recruitment procedures and failure to pay proper wages. [6]But the charges are hard to prove, and workers often give up on getting justice. [7]In addition, housing provided for migrant workers is frequently substandard. [8]Migrant workers often live in barn-like dormitories or shacks, and overcrowding is the norm. [9]Meals are equally inadequate, and poor nutrition causes widespread disease. [10]Owners of farms employing migrant workers are often absent, leaving them in the hands of crew leaders. [11]Unfortunately, crew leaders, paid according to the amount they harvest, sometimes abuse their authority.

Topic _____

Which two of these inferences is the reader expected to add to the supporting details?

a. Steinbeck's book was not emotionally powerful enough to keep the desire for reform alive.

b. Steinbeck's book was so emotionally powerful, it made the public care about the unhappy lives forced upon migrant workers.

_____

*impoverished: reduced to poverty, completely without resources.
*migrants: people who are seasonally employed and must travel from place to place to make a living.

c. After the initial outpouring of sympathy for migrant workers, public outrage died down, and those who could improve the living conditions for migrant workers no longer felt the need to make an effort.

d. Farm owners would like to maintain better conditions, but the crew leaders they hire don't share their compassion.

e. The working conditions for migrant workers have actually gotten much worse since Steinbeck's book caused such an uproar.

2. [1]Although foot binding is no longer practiced in China, the custom took a long time to disappear. [2]References to foot binding first appear in the tenth century, when palace dancing girls had their feet broken and then permanently bound in order to please their emperor. [3]Their bound feet supposedly made their dancing more graceful. [4]However, the practice began in earnest during the Ming dynasty (1368–1644). [5]At this point, all upper-class women began having their feet bound. [6]Women who wanted to marry well were expected to have bound feet, and women who wanted wealthy husbands did not quibble over the pain involved. [7]Between 1644 and 1911, foot binding spread to all social classes, and only the poorest of women were allowed to walk on unbound feet. [8]A poor family, after all, could not afford to hobble even one of its workers. [9]It wasn't until 1912 that foot binding was finally banned, but even then the practice was slow to die out.

Topic _____

Which two of these inferences is the reader expected to add to the supporting details?

a. Foot binding was also practiced by the men of ancient China.

b. The first women to practice foot binding would have done so even if it didn't please their emperor.

c. During the Ming dynasty, women had their feet bound to prove their class status to prospective husbands.

d. Poor women escaped foot binding because their labor was needed for the family to survive, and a woman with bound feet was next to useless as a worker.

3. [1]By 1939, gospel singer Marian Anderson had sung before most of Europe's royalty, but when she tried to rent Washington, D.C.'s Constitution Hall for a concert, her request was denied because of racism. [2]The building was owned by the all-white Daughters of the American Revolution (DAR), and Anderson was the descendant of

slaves. [3]Appalled by the thought of Anderson singing in their hall, the board of the DAR refused. [4]Fortunately, the DAR's refusal aroused considerable protest. [5]Eleanor Roosevelt, wife of President Franklin D. Roosevelt and a long-time champion of civil rights, promptly gave up her membership in the DAR. [6]In addition to Mrs. Roosevelt's very public protest, Interior Secretary Harold Ickes arranged an outdoor performance for Anderson on the steps of the Lincoln Memorial. [7]The concert was a smashing success, winning Anderson rave reviews. [8]In the end, it was Marian Anderson who had the last laugh.

Topic _____

Which two of these inferences is the reader expected to add to the supporting details?

a. In 1939, everyone in the DAR had the same racist attitude as the board that refused Anderson's request.

b. Marian Anderson sang on the steps of the Lincoln Memorial.

c. Eleanor Roosevelt was known to champion the cause of the underdog.

d. Interior Secretary Harold Ickes did not like what the DAR had done.

4. [1]Early on in their career, Wilbur and Orville Wright, the inventors of the airplane, weren't exactly an impressive pair. [2]Seeing them on the beach staring at birds in flight and flapping their arms in imitation, passersby made fun of the brothers. [3]As John T. Daniels, an early observer put it, "We couldn't help thinkin' they were just a pair of poor nuts." [4]But Wilbur and Orville Wright were anything but nuts— and on December 17, 1903, they proved every one of their detractors wrong. [5]On that day, their 745-pound invention, the *Flyer*, climbed ten feet into the air. [6]True, the flight came to a sudden halt when the plane nose-dived to the ground after only twelve seconds. [7]Still, the Wright brothers had proved that men could fly like those birds they had watched on the beach. [8]By 1908, the Wright brothers were ready to sign contracts to produce their flying machine with both the U.S. Army and a French industrial firm. [9]Wilbur, however, did not live long enough to really enjoy his triumph. [10]By 1912, he was dead of typhoid fever. [11]Luckier than his brother, Orville lived to continue his research; he died in 1948 at the age of seventy-seven.

Topic _____

Which two of these inferences is the reader expected to add to the supporting details?

a. Wilbur and Orville Wright were remarkably unattractive men.

b. Orville Wright survived the typhoid fever that killed his brother.

c. By 1908, people were no longer dismissing the brothers as nuts.

d. Passersby who made fun of the brothers because they thought the two looked silly flapping their arms didn't understand what the brothers were really doing.

5. [1]The Cuban hero Jose Martí devoted his life to making Cuba a free country. [2]Born in 1853, he was exiled to Spain at the age of seventeen for protesting Spanish domination of Cuba. [3]While in exile, he published a pamphlet describing the pain and humiliation of the political imprisonment he had suffered for demanding Cuban independence. [4]In 1878, Martí was allowed to return to Cuba under a general amnesty* for political prisoners. [5]But he was soon banished once again for conspiring* against the Spanish authorities. [6]After fleeing to the United States, where he stayed for a year in New York City, Martí left for Venezuela. [7]But his political work for Cuban independence made him unwelcome there, and he returned to New York City, where he lived from 1881 to 1895. [8]In 1895, he returned to Cuba to join the war for Cuban liberation and died in one of the first skirmishes.* (Source of information: www.fiu.edu./~fcf/marti.html.)

Topic _____

Which two of these inferences is the reader expected to add to the supporting details?

a. Martí was banished the second time for again conspiring to free Cuba of Spanish rule.

b. Martí was not alone in his determination to make Cuba independent of Spain.

c. While Martí lived in New York, his every move was watched by the government.

d. If he could have, Martí would have become an American citizen.

---

*amnesty: release from a crime.
*conspiring: plotting.
*skirmishes: brief battles.

 ## Test 6: Visual Aids as Supporting Details

DIRECTIONS Read the passage and study the accompanying visual aids. Write the main idea in the blank, then circle the appropriate letter to indicate what the visual aid adds to your understanding of the main idea.

1. **American Federation of Labor** In 1886, several union leaders in the Knights of Labor joined with a number of independent craft unions to form the *American Federation of Labor* (AFL). Samuel Gompers, one of the founders, became the AFL's first president. Gompers believed that the goals of the union should be those of its members rather than those of its leaders. The AFL did not seek to change the existing economic system as the Knights of Labor had. Instead, its goal was to improve union members' living standards within that system. Another major difference between the Knights of Labor and the AFL was their positions regarding strikes. The Knights did not favor the use of strikes, whereas the AFL strongly believed that striking was an effective labor weapon. (Adapted from Pride et al., *Business*, p. 340.)

Main Idea _____

_____

Protesting for better work conditions, these women picket during the 1910 Ladies Tailors strike in New York.

George Grantham Bain/© Corbis

The accompanying visual aid adds what information to readers' understanding of the main idea?

a. Women were among the most dedicated members of the AFL.

b. Women were allowed to join the AFL, and they went out on strike with the men.

c. Women made up a significant portion of the Knights of Labor, which took great pains to encourage female membership.

2. In the United States, physical appearance is a very important attribute, especially for females. The average American woman is five feet four inches tall and weighs 162 pounds, but teenage girls describe their ideal body as five feet seven inches, weighing 110 pounds, and fitting into a size five dress. Although this ideal is far from the actual statistics for body size among American women, it is consistent with the image portrayed in mass media. It is estimated that only about 5 percent of American women can achieve the size required for fashion models. Yet millions of American women suffer because they have unrealistic expectations about their bodies. (Adapted from Sue et al., *Understanding Abnormal Behavior*, p. 538.)

If the proportions of the Barbie doll were applied to the woman on the left, she would have to be a foot taller, increase her breast size by four inches, and reduce her waist by five inches.

Source: From Jill Greenburg, © The Walt Disney Company/Discover Magazine.

Main Idea _____

_____

The accompanying visual aid adds what information to readers' understanding of the main idea?

a. Barbie dolls encourage women to have unrealistic expectations about their bodies.

b. Only a small percentage of women achieve the mass media version of female proportions.

c. Teenage girls believe they can wear a much smaller size than is really possible.

Test 7: Vocabulary Review

DIRECTIONS Here are ten of the words introduced in Chapter 6. Use them to fill in the blanks. Words introduced in previous chapters are marked with an asterisk. Note: The form of the word used here may differ from the form used in the chapter.

purge   thrive
excelled   resuscitate
fray _to wear down noisy fight_   commodity
corruption   impoverished _to make poor_
mediums   migrants _to move around person_

1. Famed magician and escape artist Harry Houdini _excelled_ at exposing anyone engaged in hoodwinking the unsuspecting public. Making a commitment* to _purge_ the world of disreputable* frauds, he debunked many psychics, _mediums_, and just plain frauds who fooled even scientists and academics into believing they could read minds or _resuscitate_ the dead. As a magician, Houdini's logic was simple: It was perfectly valid* to fool the public on stage when the audience knew trickery was involved. But doing it off stage, when they didn't know, was the work of scoundrels.

2. In the mid to late 1800s, the German-born cartoonist Thomas Nast (1840–1902) waded into the political _fray_ and took aim at the _corruption_ that seemed to be blighting* the country. His graphic* illustrations of fraud and scandals helped expose despicable* politicians who were selling their influence like a _commodity_ that could be bought by the highest bidder.

3. After a series of huge dust storms in the 1930s, many Oklahoma farmers could no longer _thrive_ on the dry, barren

terrain.* ___impoverished___ and forced from homes they couldn't pay for, the ___Migrants___ fled west to California, where they were insultingly referred to as "Okies," and life become even more unbearable.   (www.livinghistoryfarm.org/farmingin the30s/water_06 .html)

INTERNET BONUS QUESTION

Thomas Nast had a huge influence on what national holiday, and he helped end the career of what famous New York politician?

_____

_____

Beyond the Paragraph: Reading Longer Selections

In this chapter, you'll learn

- **how to adapt paragraph reading to longer, multiparagraph selections.**

- **how to monitor your comprehension with informal outlines.**

- **how to take notes on longer readings.**

Chapter 7 shows you how to adapt everything you have learned about paragraphs to longer readings. The chapter also introduces two methods for note-taking so that you can make your notes fit the material. Finally, Chapter 7 introduces a crucial element of writing we have not discussed in relation to paragraphs—the writer's purpose.

 # Moving Beyond the Paragraph

Reading longer, multiparagraph selections takes more time than reading single paragraphs. However, the extra time needed should not suggest to you that reading essays, articles, or chapter sections requires a brand new set of skills totally different from the ones you use to read paragraphs. What you need to do, instead, is adapt the skills you practiced on paragraphs to make them suitable for longer, multiparagraph selections. That means you need to understand exactly how the structure and content of multiparagraph readings differ from single paragraphs, so that's where we'll start.

Titles and Headings Are Tip-offs

Single paragraphs don't usually have headings or titles. Longer readings do. Longer readings are likely to have titles, headings, even subheadings. Fortunately for readers, these titles and headings usually say a good deal about the reading's topic. For instance, if you are asked to read a chapter section titled "Brand Loyalty," you could correctly predict that the topic of the chapter section is "consumer attachment to a particular brand." Similarly, many textbooks use questions as titles, e.g., "Is Romance Essential to Marriage?" The answer to the question is almost always the main idea of the reading.

One Main Idea Controls and Unifies the Others

Like paragraphs, longer readings are unified by one general main idea. In composition classes, this main idea is often called a "thesis," and it usually appears in the first two or three paragraphs (if the reading is longer, the introduction of the main idea can also be delayed). The paragraphs that follow state or imply a new series of main ideas. However, these main ideas fulfill the function of supporting details. They clarify or prove the overall main idea. Your goal as the reader is to discover the overall or controlling main idea of the entire selection. Then you need to determine what the other paragraphs contribute to that overall point.

Topic Sentences versus "Thesis Statements"

When you read a single paragraph, you should be on the lookout for topic sentences that sum up the main idea. With longer readings, you need to do the same. However, in extended readings the main idea is not always summed up in one sentence. The longer the reading, the more likely it is that the author will need several sentences to develop the overall main idea. That's why the controlling or unifying main idea of a multiparagraph reading is called the **thesis statement**.

Double Vision Is Essential

Longer readings require you to maintain a type of double vision. On the one hand, you need to get a sense of a reading's overall or controlling main idea as quickly as possible. But you also need to determine the main ideas of each individual paragraph and figure out how these individual main ideas relate to the central thought of the entire reading.

Once you think you have a sense of the main idea that governs or controls the entire reading, keep asking yourself: "What does each remaining paragraph contribute to my understanding of the controlling main idea?" If the remaining paragraphs elaborate on or flesh out the main idea you have in mind, you know you're on the right track. If they don't, you probably have to revise your main idea, rather than struggling to make it fit.

Implied Main Ideas Are Slow to Emerge

Writers usually introduce the thesis statement at the beginning of a selection. Depending on the length of the reading, the thesis statement could be in the first paragraph or as far down as the fifth. While most writers almost never hold off the main idea until the very end of the reading, some do. So, yes, if by the third or fourth paragraph you haven't spotted a thesis statement, consider inferring a controlling main idea. Still, you can't be completely sure that the main idea is unstated until you have finished the entire reading.

Major Supporting Details Expand Their Territory

When writers have more space at their disposal, they are free to explain their ideas at greater length. Thus, you'll notice in several of the following readings that the main idea of one supporting paragraph may be developed in two paragraphs rather than one. The author might, for instance, introduce a main idea, offer an illustration or two in one paragraph, and then provide two more illustrations of the same idea in the next paragraph.

Concluding Paragraphs Fulfill More Functions

In paragraphs, concluding sentences are likely to describe the outcome of some event or problem mentioned by the author. They don't necessarily provide direct support to the main idea. In longer readings, concluding paragraphs might also describe an outcome. But they are just as likely to summarize what came before and predict what's going to appear next.

Summary   In sum, the problem of air pollution is both serious and complex; it's not going to be completely resolved any time soon. True, as we have outlined here, some improvement has already been made.
Prediction   But environmental legislation will have to be markedly tightened to improve the quality of the air we all breathe.

In textbooks, concluding paragraphs often restate the controlling idea for emphasis and then offer a preview of what's coming in the next section. In effect, they behave like transitions, signalling where the author's train of thought is going.

Summary   The preceding section briefly summarized the work of Hermann Ebbinghaus, a nineteenth-century researcher who revolutionized
Transition   the study of memory and learning. In the pages that follow, we move into the twentieth century to focus on the work of George Miller, who, like Ebbinghaus, revolutionized thinking on memory.

Reading Tip

When you spot a concluding paragraph in a chapter section, check to see if it contains a prediction, consequence, or solution you should record in your notes. If the paragraph functions as a transition, use that information to make some predictions about what the upcoming chapter section will accomplish.

The Writer's Purpose Becomes Clearer

When you are dealing with single paragraphs, it's hard to make a decision about whether the author's **primary purpose**, or main intention in writing, is *to inform* or *to persuade*. Usually, you don't have enough information to make that call. Some readings begin with a paragraph offering a description of events and suggesting a purely informative intent. However, by the time you are through reading, a paragraph can switch to a call for action and end up with persuasion being its primary purpose. With longer readings, you have a number of paragraphs on which to base your inference or conclusion about the author's overall purpose. You also have more chances to study the author's word choice and relationship to readers, two key clues to use when determining purpose. (There's more on purpose in Chapter 10.)

Reading Tip

As soon as you see a title or heading, consider what it reveals about the material. Some titles keep main ideas, along with the author's purpose, to themselves, e.g., "Shadow Juries."* Others all but announce both, e.g., "We Need to Question the Ethics of Shadow Juries."

Reading Tip

If the author maintains a formal, impersonal style and does not offer a judgment or call for change, the primary purpose is probably informative, rather than persuasive.

Diagramming Major and Minor Details

To understand how paragraphs work together to develop one main idea, read the following selection. Then study the diagram that accompanies it.

---

*Shadow juries mimic real juries as closely as possible. Lawyers assemble shadow juries to decide how jury verdicts might turn out.

Anorexia Nervosa: The Starvation Disease

Introductory
Sentences

Thesis Statement

1   When their children begin talking about dieting, most parents smile indulgently and do not worry. In figure-conscious America, it is quite natural for young people to desire a slim figure. How-ever, for some teenagers, dieting is no laughing matter. For them, dieting is not a momentary whim to be pursued and forgotten; instead, it is the symptom of a serious emotional disorder called *anorexia nervosa,* a disease that can have terrible, even fatal con-sequences.

2   The disease usually strikes adolescent and preadolescent girls who have no reason to diet. They are not overweight, nor have they been told to diet by their doctors. They are not preparing to take part in specialized sports activities requiring a slender figure. These girls stop eating because, despite all evidence to the con-trary, they believe they are fat. Determined to lose the imaginary excess poundage, they refuse to eat more than a few morsels of food. Usually, the weight loss is rapid, sometimes more than fifty pounds in a few months.

3   Some teenagers who are obsessed with the need to diet seek treatment because they or, more typically, their parents realize that the diet is leading to starvation. Others do not seek treatment but simply begin eating normally again on their own. However, because the disease comes in waves, or bouts, a few victims manage to keep it a secret and so avoid both exposure and treatment.

4   Unfortunately, members of this group are in the most serious danger. Although they may be able to keep their secret into adult-hood, the disease, if untreated, almost always goes out of control, with tragic results. In fact, some victims—like gymnast Christy Henrich and pop singer Karen Carpenter—die from the physical effects of prolonged starvation. Mortality rates are high: One in ten anorexia patients will die within ten years of the disease's onset.

5   To date, the actual cause of the starvation disease has not been determined. According to one theory, teenagers may be starving themselves in order to rebel against parental authority. Tradition-ally, the refusal to eat has been a young child's weapon against parental discipline. The parent may plead and even demand that the child eat, but by refusing, the child demonstrates his or her power over the situation. Unconsciously, teenagers who diet to the point of starvation may be attempting to teach their parents the same lesson: Control is not in the hands of the parents.

6   According to another theory, anorexia may indicate a young girl's deep-rooted fear of growing up. From this perspective, starv-ing the body can be viewed as a way of maintaining its childish

contours and rejecting adult femininity. Yet another hypothesis views the disease as a form of self-punishment. The victims may have extraordinarily high standards of perfection and punish themselves for failing to meet their goals.

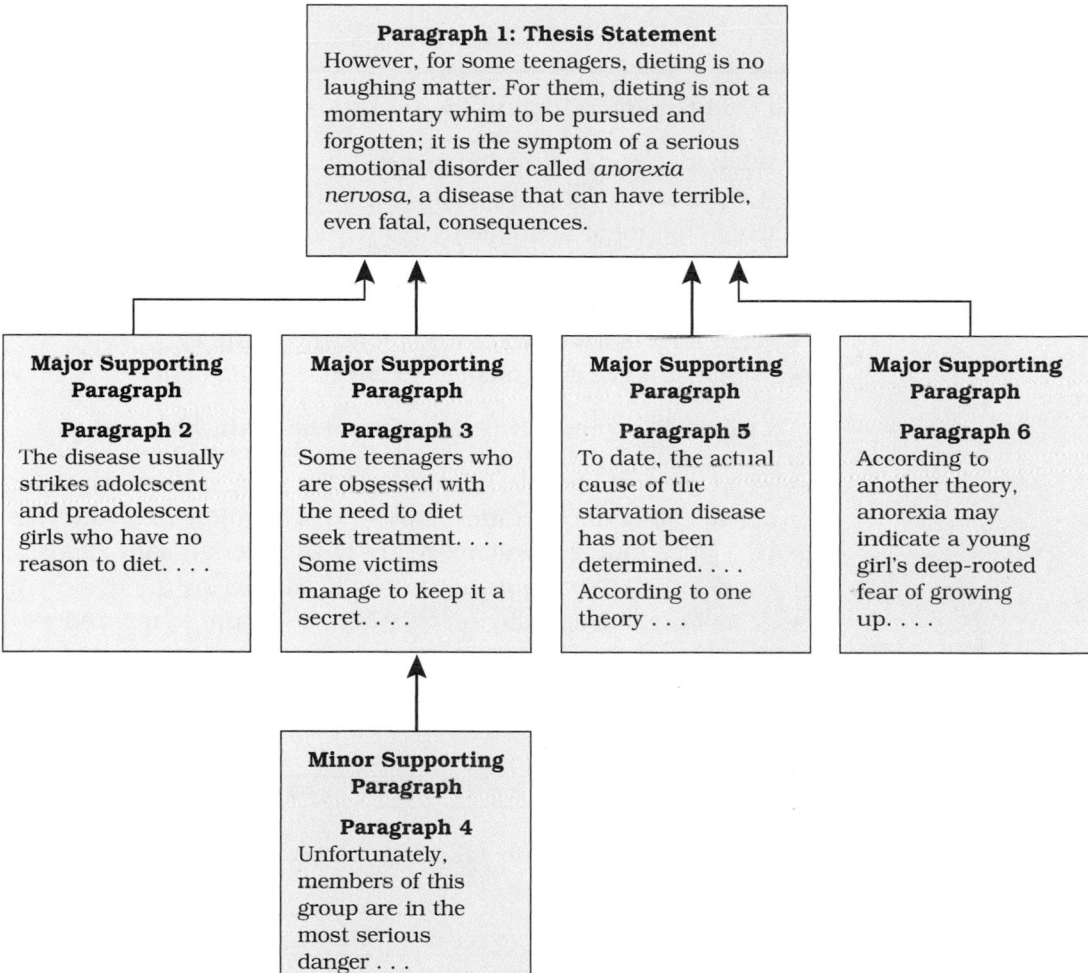

Paragraph 1: Thesis Statement
However, for some teenagers, dieting is no laughing matter. For them, dieting is not a momentary whim to be pursued and forgotten; it is the symptom of a serious emotional disorder called *anorexia nervosa,* a disease that can have terrible, even fatal, consequences.

Major Supporting Paragraph

Paragraph 2
The disease usually strikes adolescent and preadolescent girls who have no reason to diet. . . .

Major Supporting Paragraph

Paragraph 3
Some teenagers who are obsessed with the need to diet seek treatment. . . . Some victims manage to keep it a secret. . . .

Major Supporting Paragraph

Paragraph 5
To date, the actual cause of the starvation disease has not been determined. . . . According to one theory . . .

Major Supporting Paragraph

Paragraph 6
According to another theory, anorexia may indicate a young girl's deep-rooted fear of growing up. . . .

Minor Supporting Paragraph

Paragraph 4
Unfortunately, members of this group are in the most serious danger . . .

As the diagram shows, the first paragraph of this reading introduces the thesis statement. Keep in mind, however, that longer readings sometimes open with one or more introductory paragraphs that pave the way for the thesis statement.

The reading on page 362 also contains four major supporting paragraphs. They answer the questions "Which teenagers get this disease?" and "What are its symptoms and causes?" One minor supporting paragraph fleshes out, or further explains, a point made in a major supporting paragraph: Some victims keep their illness a secret, which can be deadly.

As the selection and the diagram illustrate, reading multiparagraph selections does not require a new set of reading strategies. Longer readings require you to refine the reading skills you already have.

To find the overall main idea, ask:

- What idea is developed in general and specific terms?
- If there is no general statement that sums up the reading, what statement is implied?

To find the thesis statement, ask:

- What idea is developed throughout the reading?
- What sentence or sentences express that idea?

To relate the supporting details to the main idea, ask:

- What *kind* of specific information does the author supply: examples, studies, stories, statistics, quotations, reasons?
- How does that information relate to the overall main idea of the reading? What questions does it answer for the reader?
- What does the specific information contribute to my understanding of the thesis statement or implied main idea?

Check Your Understanding

What are the two main differences between topic sentences and thesis statements?

_____

_____

_____

◾ EXERCISE 1   **Recognizing Main Ideas in Longer Readings**

DIRECTIONS Read each selection. Then circle the letter of the sentence that best expresses the main idea of the selection.

EXAMPLE

On the Trail of Typhoid Mary

1 On November 11, 1938, a woman called Mary Mallon died of a stroke. She was seventy years old at the time. During her seventy years on earth, death and disease had followed in her wake.* By the time Mary Mallon died, at least three deaths and fifty-three cases of typhoid had been attributed to her, and the press had dubbed* her "Typhoid Mary."

2 In 1906, while working as a cook for New York city banker William Henry Warren, Mallon prepared a sumptuous* dinner— cold cucumber soup, lobster, wild rice, and strawberry ice cream with peaches. Warren and his guests ate heartily. But less than ten days later, several guests ended up in the hospital. All of them were eventually diagnosed with typhoid fever.

3 Careful research and some clever detective work by Dr. George Soper, a sanitary engineer employed by the New York Department of Health, traced the disease to Mary Mallon. Unfortunately, by the time Soper had identified Mallon as the source of infection, she was gone, on to yet another job as a cook or housekeeper. Hot on Mallon's trail, Dr. Soper discovered that the woman changed jobs frequently; wherever she worked, someone developed typhoid fever.

4 When Soper finally caught up with Mallon in 1907, she was hardly apologetic. On the contrary, she chased him away with a carving knife. Mallon only submitted to testing when Soper returned with three policemen. Tests done over her objections showed Mallon carried the bacteria that caused typhoid, but for some reason she herself showed no symptoms of the disease. Told to have her gall bladder removed—the gall bladder was believed to be the site of the infection—Mallon refused and began a lengthy court battle to gain her freedom.

5 In 1910, Mary Mallon was released. However, she had to promise never to work as a cook again. She also had to report to the New York Department of Health every ninety days. But by now, the newspapers all knew who Mallon was. Hounded by reporters, Mallon disappeared again only to resurface in 1915 when an outbreak of typhoid was reported at the Sloane Hospital for Women.

---

*wake: the course or track left behind by someone or something that has passed.
*dubbed: named.
*sumptuous: delicious, rich, fancy.

6   As George Soper had suspected, Mary Mallon had been working in the hospital kitchen shortly before the outbreak. This time, when police caught up with Mallon, they arrested her. By order of the courts, she was confined to Riverside Hospital in New York, where she spent the rest of her life.

Main Idea   a. In the United States, typhoid fever was once a dangerous disease that took many lives.

b. Mary Mallon, also known as "Typhoid Mary," fought a lengthy court battle to win her freedom.

c. By the time she died, Mary Mallon had truly earned her nickname "Typhoid Mary."

EXPLANATION   Statement *c* is correct because it's the answer that best states the main idea of the selection. Statement *a* is incorrect because the selection does not discuss typhoid in general but focuses on how Mary Mallon spread the disease. Statement *b* is inappropriate because the reading has only one sentence about Mary's court battle.

1. Is Romance Essential to Marriage?

1 The majority of Americans and Europeans believe that couples should first fall in love and then get married. Yet in many other countries, including India and China, the reverse is much more common. First, an individual marries someone chosen by family members; *then* the couple find love. Anthropologists say that the arranged marriage is actually common throughout history, with even colonial Americans approaching matrimony in this way. Today, in fact, as many as 60 percent of the world's marriages are still arranged. There appear to be two main reasons why arranged marriages have never gone out of fashion.

2   First of all, in many cultures marriage is viewed as the union of two families, rather than just two people. Because marriage is a valuable tool for creating alliances that benefit both parties, the selection of a mate is considered too important to be left up to the young and inexperienced. Often with the help of professional matchmakers, parents search for someone who possesses the specific temperament, interests, and background that will suit both their child *and* their family. Unlike western relationships, which usually begin from chance encounters between two people who may or may not have much in common, the arranged marriage involves a focused search that ends by matching up two very compatible

people. Thus, children are raised with the expectation that their parents will help them find the best possible husband or wife so that the blending of the two families will be permanent.

3   The other reason why the tradition of arranged marriage remains strong is the belief that romantic love can hinder the establishment of a lasting partnership. Proponents of arranged marriage believe that in a union based on romance, serious problems can arise when the excitement of courtship begins to fade and the partners' flaws and differences become more apparent. Because arranged marriages are not based on love to begin with, they are not usually dissolved, as many western marriages are, once passion dies. Thus, while about half of romantic marriages end in divorce, only about 5 percent of arranged marriages fail.

4   Still, arranged marriages are not necessarily loveless. On the contrary, in societies that arrange marriages, couples often become loving life partners. Because the spouses were matched based on compatible characteristics, they usually possess the necessary foundation for building mutual respect, affection, and even love. In western marriages, passionate love is often damaged by the intrusion of everyday life. In arranged marriages, however, couples begin their courtship *after* the wedding as they blend gradually blossoming affection with the realities of day-to-day existence.

5   Today, more and more Americans, disillusioned with the dating scene and failed relationships, are beginning to explore some of the methods used in arranged marriages. It's no coincidence that participants of one television reality show called *Married By America* agreed to give viewers the power to decide whom they would marry, based on assessments of the contestants' compatibility. Online dating and matchmaker services, especially those that allow participants to search for someone with very specific qualities, have also grown in popularity. While most Americans are unlikely to change their belief that marriage requires love, they are less scornful of the idea that a successful, happy marriage can be arranged by family, friends, or an interested third party.

Main Idea a. Unlike Americans, people in other countries do not believe that romance is essential to marriage.

b. Americans and Europeans both believe that romantic love is essential to a good marriage.

c. Generally speaking, two essential advantages account for the longstanding popularity of arranged marriages.

2. Blind Tom: A Forgotten Prodigy*

1   Born blind and the son of slaves, Thomas Greene Wiggins (1849–1908) was unusually musical. Even as an infant, he could mimic whatever tune he heard. By the age of five, he was composing music. Surprisingly, the boy's owner, a lawyer named James Neil Bethune, fostered Wiggins's obvious talent. As might be expected, however, Bethune, an avid supporter of slavery, had a less than altruistic* motive in mind. Bethune hoped to exhibit the boy around the country as a musical oddity and earn money from the boy's special ability. As it turned out, Bethune was right about the promise of financial gain. Over the years his investment in Thomas Wiggins paid off handsomely: Bethune exploited Wiggins's natural talent for huge profits.

2   It wasn't very long before Wiggins, whose stage name was "Blind Tom," was earning Bethune around $100,000 annually, a munificent* sum for the nineteenth century. Needless to say, Wiggins never collected a penny of the money he earned. It all went directly into the pockets of Bethune and Perry Oliver, the white planter who managed Wiggins's career.

3   Although Wiggins could play serious classical music, and his early compositions show real musical merit, both owner and manager insisted on portraying him as a musical oddity. While on stage, Wiggins would sing one song while playing a different one with his right hand. With his left hand, he played still a third. He also performed classical favorites with his hands crossed, imitated famous political speakers, and did on-the-spot imitations of musical instruments, animals, or objects. Labeled by Bethune and Oliver as a freak of nature with a flair for imitation, Wiggins was actually a gifted musician, who could play serious music and needed no weird noises to please the audience.

4   He could play the music of Bach, Beethoven, and Liszt. Even the Europeans, notably critical of American artists, were enthralled by Blind Tom. Respected musicians like Charles Halle and Ignaz Moscheles glowingly praised both the African American's wit and his technique. Still, no amount of money or praise seemed capable of winning Wiggins the thing he prized most—his freedom.

5   When the end of the Civil War brought freedom within Wiggins's grasp, Bethune found a way to maintain his income at the musician's expense. He persuaded the young man's parents to sign an

---

*prodigy: a person of unusual gifts.
*altruistic: unselfish.
*munificent: generous.

agreement that bound him over to Bethune for a period of five years. The Bethune family then regularly renewed those contracts until, by 1887, Blind Tom had been in service to his former owners for thirty-eight years. He only managed to escape their clutches by retiring from the stage and refusing to perform. Although he did return to the stage occasionally to lay to rest rumors about his death or to challenge the performance of impersonators, he made almost no money from any of those infrequent appearances. Those profits went to Eliza Bethune, James's daughter-in-law. When he died in 1908 of a stroke, Thomas Greene Wiggins was still under the legal guardianship of Eliza.

6   If there is a bright side at all to Wiggins's sad story, it is this: Almost one hundred years after his death, he has finally found a champion. The acclaimed pianist John Davis has released a CD called "John Davis Plays Blind Tom." It contains fourteen pieces of Wiggins's original music, and all of them attest to his skill and originality. In addition, Mr. Davis has created a one-man show devoted to Wiggins's performing life. It is titled "Will the Real Thomas Wiggins Please Stand Up." (Source of information: Thomas L. Riis, "The Legacy of a Prodigy Lost in Mystery," *New York Times*, March 5, 2000, pp. 35–36.)

Main Idea a. The life of Thomas Greene Wiggins—also known as"Blind Tom"— is a superb illustration of how spirit can battle circumstance.

b. Unfortunately, the talents of Thomas Greene Wiggins were exploited by others for most of his life.

c. In his heart, James Bethune thought he was being generous to allow a slave to play the piano; he never realized what a terrible thing he had done to Thomas Greene Wiggins, the man who made Bethune rich.

EXERCISE 2 Recognizing Main Ideas in Longer Readings

DIRECTIONS Read each selection. Then circle the letter of the sentence that best expresses the main idea of the passage.

1. No Diet Books on the Fiji Islands

1 On the Fiji Islands of the South Pacific, diet books would never be the big sellers they are in the United States. Although Fiji Islanders have definite ideas about how a person should look, they don't much care about being overweight. On the contrary, Fijians like sturdy muscles and a generally well-fed look in both

men and women. To a large degree, the preference for plumpness among Fijians stems from their culture's emphasis on community rather than appearance.

2   Unlike Americans, who prize individualism, the Fijians care more about the good of the community than they do about themselves as individuals. For them, standing out in a crowd is never as important as showing a nurturing and caring attitude toward friends. And what is the primary vehicle for showing your friends you care for them? It's serving them food, of course. For the Fijians, offering food to friends and family is a way of showing you're concerned about their physical and emotional well-being. At dinnertime, Fijians routinely open their windows and doors so that the aroma of the meal will waft outside and attract passersby. Extra food is always prepared so that anyone attracted by the smell of dinner can stop by for a snack. It is, in fact, a social disgrace not to have enough food for drop-in guests.

3   Because of their perspective on food and its cultural significance, Fijians consider dieting socially unacceptable. Dieting prevents the person invited to dine from accepting the invitation. In addition, what dieter would willingly prepare huge, tempting meals for friends and family? Thus, parents watch their children carefully for signs that they might be losing weight. They do so not because they want their children to achieve and maintain a certain weight, but because they want to make sure their children are fully participating in the community, which is expressed by the sharing of food.

4   As a result of the Fijians' attitude toward food, children in particular are spared the painful experience so common to Americans of all ages—the failed diet. They aren't obsessed by their personal appearance and they don't constantly compare themselves to those a bit trimmer or thinner. If anything, they pity others for failing to be appropriately plump. However, the Fijian emphasis on food and the celebration of body fat does have one drawback. Children who need to limit their intake of calories for reasons of health—say, a child with diabetes—can become anxious or depressed because they are unable to fully participate in the community's common feasting. (Source of information: Seifert et al., *Lifespan Development*, pp. 264–265.)

Main Idea   a. Thanks to Fijians' attitudes toward dieting, children don't feel that their personal appearance is all that counts in life.

b. The Fijians don't care about being overweight because for them the sense of community created by the sharing of food is more important than one's personal appearance.

c. Americans are extremely individualistic; as a result, they tend to place too much emphasis on personal appearance and are overly obsessed with being thin.

d. On the whole, Fijian children are happier and more confident than American children.

2. The Ebbinghaus Experiments

1 At the end of the nineteenth century, a German psychologist named Hermann Ebbinghaus became interested in the carefully controlled laboratory experiments being used to do research in the fields of physiology* and physics. He was so impressed with the experiments' results that he decided to introduce similar methods into the study of human memory.

2 Using only himself as a subject, Ebbinghaus devoted six years of research to his experiments. In one of his experiments, he memorized lists of nonsense syllables, put them aside for specified amounts of time, and then relearned them. By comparing the time taken to learn the lists with the time taken to relearn them, Ebbinghaus was able to reach several important conclusions about the role of memory in learning. After more than a century of research, these conclusions have been repeatedly confirmed.

Rates of Forgetting

3 As a result of his research, Ebbinghaus maintained that the rate of forgetting becomes progressively slower over time. A list of nonsense syllables that he had memorized and put aside for an hour required more than half the original study time to relearn. But a list that had been put aside for nine hours was not, as one would expect, totally forgotten. The rate of forgetting had slowed down, and only two-thirds of the original study time was required to relearn the nonsense syllables.

4 Since 1885, when Ebbinghaus first published his work, investigators have studied the rate of forgetting. They have used not only nonsense syllables but also passages of prose, lists of facts, and excerpts from poetry. Like Ebbinghaus, they have discovered that the rate of forgetting slows down over time. It is rapid at first but becomes slower as the amount of time between learning and relearning increases.

---

*physiology: the study of how the body functions.

Overlearning

5 Another of Ebbinghaus's conclusions confirmed by modern research is that overlearning during the initial learning period makes relearning at a later time easier. Based on his experiments, Ebbinghaus maintained that the more repetitions involved in the original learning, the fewer repetitions needed for relearning. Later investigators have come to a similar conclusion. However, they have also concluded that each repetition will not produce an equal return in time saved during the relearning period. After a point, the repetition of material already memorized does not produce a sufficient reward.

Distributed Learning

6 Research that followed Ebbinghaus's experiments by more than half a century also confirmed his belief that learning sessions devoted to memorizing are more effective if they are distributed over time. In 1940, an American psychologist, A. P. Bumstead, decided to do a series of experiments to determine whether it was better to have several short learning sessions spaced out over a period of time or one long, unbroken learning session. Using only himself as a subject, Bumstead memorized several different poetry selections, spacing his learning sessions at intervals that varied from one hour to eight days. After finishing the experiment, Bumstead concluded that increasing the time between learning sessions actually decreased the amount of time needed to memorize the material.

Main Idea a. Thanks to Ebbinghaus, we know how to do controlled laboratory experiments that test the power of human memory.

b. More research is needed to confirm Ebbinghaus's early conclusions about the nature of memory.

c. Research has shown that Ebbinghaus's claims about learning and memory are correct.

d. Research has proven that Ebbinghaus was right when he claimed that the rate of forgetting slows down with the passage of time.

 # Implied Main Ideas in Longer Readings

In longer readings, the controlling main idea is usually expressed in a thesis statement. Much of the time, that statement appears somewhere in the first three or four paragraphs, right after the title, heading, or introduction.

However, authors do sometimes expect readers to infer the implied main idea that unifies the entire reading. Here's an example:

The Gorilla's Two Faces

1 Even die-hard wrestling fans don't remember his name anymore, but in the mid-sixties, the wrestler Gorilla Monsoon was a major star. He weighed more than four hundred pounds and fought some eight thousand bouts. When announcers said his name, their voices tended to quaver a little, for Gorilla was wrestling's first real "bad guy." He was the wrestler audiences loved to hate because he was tougher and meaner than anyone else around.

2 Wearing a body suit with one strap draped over his massive shoulder, Gorilla would enter the ring looking as if he could, in a hungry moment, chew rusty nails and easily digest them. After toying with his opponent for a while, he liked to end the bout with the wrestling hold that helped make him famous. Knocking his opponent to the floor, he would wrap the man's feet around his enormous waist. Seemingly without effort, he would then lift and twirl his opponent round and round, keeping the man just about at waist level for at least thirty seconds. To further embroider his image of pure evil, Gorilla would cackle with laughter the entire time. Staged or not, it was a terrifying display, and the audience couldn't get enough of it.

3 Out of the ring, however, Gorilla Monsoon was Robert Marella. Quiet and soft-spoken, he had a college education. Prior to becoming a wrestler, he had been a high school teacher. But the money was bad, and wrestling was more lucrative. Mr. Marella, as he liked to be called, also had a way with words. When asked why anyone would ever pay to see grown men throw one another around in a ring, he paused for a moment and then paraphrased St. Augustine:* "For those who believe in our sport, no explanation is necessary."

4 He was equally articulate when interviewed, long past his heyday, about the current state of wrestling. Asked about the new and more profitable face of wrestling, he didn't have to think twice before shrugging it off as little more than people from the pages of "comic books." From his perspective, wrestling in the old days was a more serious sport, and "people really thought I was the Devil incarnate."* (Source of information: David Hadju, "When Wrestling Was Noir," *New York Times Magazine,* January 2, 2000, p. 43.)

---

*St. Augustine (354–430): Catholic saint who, when questioned about his faith, responded, "For those who believe, no explanation is necessary."
*incarnate: in the flesh.

Generally speaking, this reading breaks into two sections. In the first section, we learn about Gorilla Monsoon's professional image as the wrestler everyone loved to hate. But in the second, a new image emerges along with Gorilla's real name, Robert Marella. Out of the ring, Marella was anything but the hulking bully he portrayed in it. Yet if we look for a thesis statement that sums up both sides of Gorilla's personality, we won't find it. Almost all the sentences in the reading are equally specific, and there is no general statement summarizing them. On the contrary, we have to infer one like the following: "Sixties wrestler Gorilla Monsoon may have looked like the Devil incarnate in the ring, but out of it, he was a thoughtful man who took his profession seriously."

Much of the time, longer, multiparagraph readings will contain a thesis statement. But just like paragraphs, they won't always. If you read an article, an essay, or a chapter section and don't find any general statements that combine and summarize the meaning of the more specific ones, you need to infer a main idea that sums up the reading.

EXERCISE 3 Recognizing Implied Main Ideas

DIRECTIONS Read each selection. Then circle the letter of the sentence that best expresses each reading's implied main idea.

EXAMPLE

Traveling the Information Highway

1 In its early stages, the Internet was wildly celebrated for its ability to enlarge our intellectual universe. Through the aid of the Net we could contact people in all parts of the world, and they, in turn, could reach us as well. There was no subject we could not explore on the Internet, and the world seemed to be opening up before us in vivid and wonderful ways. The Internet was our information superhighway, and it was going to take us anywhere and everywhere we wanted to go.

2   Flash forward now to June 23, 2003, when the Supreme Court upheld a law called the Children's Internet Protection Act requiring public libraries receiving federal funds to install antipornography filters in all computers with Internet access. Greeted with much controversy because of concerns about its effect on the right to free speech, the law had never gone into effect after it was

enacted in 2000. Presumably, now that it has, parents won't have to worry that their children, on a supposedly harmless visit to the library, are being exposed to websites which introduce kids to pornography or prejudice. Parents still need to be aware, however, that the law does not prescribe the kind of software that has to be installed, leaving libraries to make their own choices. Since some of the filters just don't do what they claim, parents can't quite relax their vigilance yet.

3   Still, you don't have to leave your home to get a sense of where the information superhighway might be taking us. How many times have you opened your e-mail only to discover ads for mega-vitamins, sexual potency drugs, or cheap tropical vacations? In other words, how many times have you downloaded what's known as spam, or junk mail? Desperate to stop the flood of daily spam, many computer owners have installed software like SpamAssassin, the purpose of which is to keep our e-mail boxes free of junk mail we didn't request and don't want to read.

4   Then, too, there are alarming statistics about the proliferation of hate-group websites that have been expressly created to encourage prejudice against anyone perceived to be different. An equal-opportunity purveyor of information, good or evil, the Internet has something for everyone, from the misogynist to the anti-Semite. When Al Gore was running for president and burbling about his invention of the Internet, these sites were definitely not the ones he wanted to take credit for.

5   In time, no doubt, software filters will probably improve to the point that we will indeed be able to block out websites that peddle hatred, violence, and filth. Certainly, spam filters are steadily improving, a sign that such software can be effective. Filters will probably never be perfect, but at some point they will be good enough to block out a large percentage of what consumers don't want to find on their computers or their children's computers. But until that day comes, we may need to curb our enthusiasm for what's becoming a pileup on the information superhighway.

Implied Main Idea (a.) Our initial optimism about the Internet as the information highway has diminished.

b. The Internet has not proven to be the information gold mine we once expected it to be.

c. Software filters are now at the stage where they can block out objectionable material.

EXPLANATION The selection opens with a description of the public's early optimism about the Internet as a source of information. Then, in paragraph 2, the author introduces the first of three criticisms about information found on the Internet. By the time readers finish the central paragraphs, they can draw only one inference: Our initial optimism about the Internet as an ideal source of information may need to be revised.

1. Is Local News Really News?

1   News is frequently defined as the telling of factual stories, meant to inform the public about significant events. Thus, when you turn on your local television newscast every evening, you probably expect to hear about recent events in your community. You might even consider yourself an informed citizen because you're in the habit of watching your local news program. However, while watching your local news, it's unlikely that you will see or hear many reports about significant events concerning politics, culture, business, and government. Instead, you're probably learning about violent crimes, major accidents, deadly disasters, and celebrity breakups.

2   In a half-hour local news broadcast, only about fifteen minutes are left once the time for commercials, weather, sports, traffic, and bantering by news anchors is subtracted. This is not much time to relate all of the news of the day. Therefore, each individual news story is necessarily quite short. In fact, studies have shown that 70 percent of all news stories are no more than a minute long. Forty-three percent are less than thirty seconds long. Only about 16 percent of stories are longer than two minutes; in the television news industry, any story more than a minute and a half long is billed as an "in-depth" report.

3   Typically, the television news anchors who introduce or read these stories are not experts in any of the fields—such as education, the environment, business, government, and health—that are covered. Most are hired not for their understanding of the news but for their ability to read a story well while conveying the specific emotion (anger, fear, sympathy, admiration, disgust, etc.) appropriate to that story. The reporters who gather the stories are not experts either. They are hired primarily for their ability to communicate well on camera, as well as for their writing skill and general common sense. Plus, reporters are under tremendous pressure to produce a story. They are usually assigned a particular story about midmorning; then they have but a few hours to gather the facts and write the story so that it can be edited with

video and ready for a 5:00 or 6:00 p.m. broadcast. As a result, reporters have little time for research, and their sources tend to be thin: only 25 percent of TV news stories have more than one source. Not surprisingly, news directors avoid assigning hundreds of important stories that would require some real research.

4   The truth is that television news broadcasts feature stories that readily lend themselves to videotape footage and pictures. This is why there's so little coverage of events that are important but difficult to illustrate, such as political speeches, school board meetings, or city council sessions. One survey revealed that only about 7 percent of news stories cover economic issues. Another study of 6,000 news stories showed that only 9 percent of them concerned poverty or welfare. Instead, TV news focuses on events that are relatively trivial but also very visual, and it tends to sensationalize those events by making them look even more dramatic than they actually were.

5   In addition to avoiding nonvisual news stories, TV newscasts seldom include negative stories about their advertisers or about police officers and firefighters. According to one survey, more than half of news directors interviewed said that they had been pressured by advertisers to either kill critical stories or promote favorable ones. The largest number of consumer complaints concern new car dealerships, but because car dealers buy a lot of commercial airtime, they are rarely subjected to a news station's scrutiny. Neither will viewers see many critical stories about grocery and clothing stores, shopping malls, banks, insurance and health care providers, soda manufacturers, or fast-food restaurants, all of which buy a significant amount of commercial airtime. Police and firefighters are also rarely cast in a negative light on local TV news stations because reporters need the cooperation of law enforcement and public safety officials to get the crime stories that are their lifeblood. That's why viewers see few, if any, stories about issues like radar traps, brutality, and/or police or firefighter mistakes. (Sources of information: Amy Mitchell, "The Big Picture," *Columbia Journalism Review*, January/February 1999, www .archives.cjr.org/year/99/1/pej/picture.asp; Greg Byron, "TV News: What Local Stations Don't Want You to Know," www.tfs.net/ ~gbyron/tvnews1.html.)

Implied Main Idea   a. For a number of reasons, local television news broadcasts don't really serve to inform the public.

b. Local television news broadcasts are sensationalized, and the information they offer is usually, if not always, inaccurate.

    c. Local television news broadcasts serve an important purpose in communities all over the country.

2. What Makes a True Believer?

1 If astrology and handwriting analysis have no scientific basis, why do they remain so popular? One explanation is the "Barnum effect"—the tendency for people to accept vague, ambiguous,* and general statements as accurate descriptions of their personalities (French, Fowler, and McCarthy, 1991). The Barnum effect is named after the famous circus owner P. T. Barnum, who declared, "There's a sucker born every minute."

2 Handwriting analysis and astrological readings often sound something like this (based on Forer, 1949):

> You have a great need for other people to like you and admire you. You have a tendency to be critical of yourself. You have a great deal of unused capacity, which you have not used to your advantage. At times, you are extroverted,* affable, and sociable. At times, you are shy, wary, and reserved. Some of your aspirations* tend to be pretty unrealistic. Security is one of your major goals in life.

3 People are often amazed by how "accurate" such reports are. As a result, they may conclude that there must be something to horoscopes or handwriting analysis (French, Fowler, and McCarthy, 1991; McKelvie, 1990). The trick is that such a general statement is likely to sound accurate to just about *anyone.* In P. T. Barnum's words, it has "a little something for everyone."

4 The Barnum effect goes hand in hand with another aspect of human reasoning that encourages illogical beliefs. We tend to give the most credence* to information that confirms our expectations and to discount information that doesn't confirm our expectations (Nisbett and Ross, 1980). So we are likely to remember the few times that our horoscope precisely matched our experience and forget the many other times it didn't. Or we focus on the two or three accurate statements in our handwriting analysis and ignore the seven or eight inaccurate ones. The mass media reinforce these biases. If an astrologer correctly predicts the date a world leader is assassinated, for example, the prediction will be picked up as "news," but the thousands of times such predictions are false do not make the headlines. (Rubin et al., *Psychology*, p. 35.)

———————
*ambiguous: having more than one meaning.
*extroverted: outgoing.
*aspirations: hopes, desires.
*credence: belief.

Implied Main Idea a. There are two different reasons why people believe in pseudo-sciences like astrology and handwriting analysis.

b. The public's belief in astrology continues to grow despite the fact that there is no scientific basis for astrological forecasts.

c. The term "Barnum effect" refers to the readiness of people to believe what they wish to believe, avoiding all evidence to the contrary.

▄▃ EXERCISE 4 **Recognizing Implied Main Ideas**

DIRECTIONS Read each selection. Then circle the letter of the sentence that best expresses the reading's implied main idea.

1. **The Future of Genetic Testing**

1 In August 2000, a test-tube baby named Adam Nash was born in Denver, Colorado. After cutting Adam's umbilical cord, doctors collected some cells from that cord. A month later, they infused those same cells into the circulatory system of Adam's six-year-old sister, Molly. The procedure was necessary to save Molly's life.

2 Afflicted with a rare bone marrow disease called Fanconi anemia, Molly's only hope was a cell transplant from a sibling. Because both parents carried the Fanconi gene, which gave them a 25 percent chance of giving birth to a child carrying the same disease as Molly, doctors needed to select an embryo not affected by the disease-carrying gene. That selection process could only be carried out in an in vitro–produced pregnancy followed by sophisticated gene testing. Doctors would test embryo cells to discover which of them did not carry the diseased gene and then impregnate the mother with only those cells that tested normal.

3 In part at least, the Nash case resembles a similar one from 1989, which involved sixteen-year-old Anissa Ayala, a young girl diagnosed with a lethal form of leukemia. In an effort to save her life, the girl's father, Abe Ayala, had his vasectomy reversed so that he and his wife, Mary, could have a third child who would be a bone marrow donor for Anissa. Although the Ayalas had a one-in-four chance of having a child with the right cells to be a donor, luck was on their side. Genetic testing showed that Anissa's newborn sister, Marissa, had inherited all the right genes, and she did, in fact, prove to be an ideal donor. Thanks to Marissa, Anissa got a new lease on life.

4 In situations like these, genetic testing does indeed seem a god-send. Certainly, this perspective is promoted by Charles Strom,

director of the Illinois Masonic Medical Center, which was heavily involved in both cases. Thanks to genetic testing, lives can be saved and tragedy avoided. As long as the children born to be donors are loved, says Strom, that's all that matters; and in both cases, the children born to save their siblings are very much cherished.

5   Yet both cases raise a serious question: Are the increasing sophistication and use of genetic testing always a cause for celebration? If you ask Jeffrey Kahn, director of the University of Minnesota's Center for Bioethics,* the answer is no. Mr. Kahn takes issue not with the subject of children who come into the world to be donors but with the use of genetic testing to search out or avoid specific traits. He fears a future in which reproductive technology allows some parents—primarily those who can afford it—to choose their children's physical and mental makeup. Kahn, who is as pessimistic as Strom is optimistic, claims that having a child "is quickly becoming like buying a car." Parents can choose the options they do or do not want. He believes that as genetic tests become more available to the public, there will be more and more parents asking for "embryos without a predisposition* to homosexuality or for kids who will grow to more than six feet tall."

6   Although Kahn's argument smacks of slippery slope* logic, it does seem plausible that some parents, intent on shaping their children's future, would insist on genetic testing in order to select or reject certain traits. The question is, Will those researchers and doctors currently involved in creating even more sophisticated forms of genetic testing allow parents easy access to the tests, or will they restrict access to cases of dire emergency? Since there's no guarantee that genetic tests won't become available for a price, it's hard not to share Kahn's concerns that the tests will be used not solely to save lives, but also to create "designer babies" tailored to suit their parents' specifications.* (Sources of information: Rick Weiss, "Test-tube Baby Born to Save Ill Sister," *Washington Post*, October 3, 2000; Abigail Trafford, "Miracle Babies Draw Us into an Ethical Swamp," *Washington Post*, November 14, 2000, p. 28.)

---

*bioethics: the study of moral and ethical implications caused by new scientific discoveries.
*predisposition: leaning.
*slippery slope: an error in logic in which it's assumed that one event will lead to similar, and even more serious, events no matter what the context.
*specifications: requirements, desires.
Note: As of 2006, Adam and Molly were both doing well.

Implied Main Idea   a. The negative consequences of genetic testing far outweigh its positive uses.

        b. Genetic testing can be positive or negative, depending on the uses to which it's put.

        c. Thanks to genetic testing, children like Molly Nash now have a chance to lead a normal life.

        d. Genetic testing has rightly become the center of a serious ethical controversy.

2. Side Effects of Using Physical Punishment on Children

1 Concerned about how to safely and effectively discipline their children, most parents, even the highly authoritarian* ones, want to know if there is a drawback to using a physical punishment like spanking. The answer to that question is not simple. Certainly, one problem with physical punishment has to do with the pain and discomfort it causes. As a result, both the parents who punish and the situation that brings punishment about become associated with fear, resentment, and dislike, sometimes all three. This negative response to physical punishment makes it especially ineffective to use when toilet training children or teaching them table manners.

2 **Learning Avoidance Techniques** A second problem is that aversive stimuli* encourage escape or avoidance learning. With *escape learning,* the child responds to the threat of punishment by misbehaving and then disappearing. With *avoidance learning,* the child finds a way to postpone or prevent the pain of punishment. Children who run away from punishing parents (escape learning) may start to lie about their behavior or spend long stretches away from home (avoidance learning).

3 **Encouraging Aggression** A third problem with physical punishment is that it often increases *aggression* in the same way that animals react to pain by attacking whomever or whatever else is around (Azrin et al., 1965). Likewise, humans who are in pain have a tendency to lash out at others.

4 We also know that aggression is one of the most common responses to frustration. Generally speaking, punishment is painful, frustrating, or both. Punishment, therefore, sets up a powerful environment for learning aggression. Children who are spanked often feel angry, frustrated, and hostile. Then they engage in aggressive acts like slapping other children in order to

---

*authoritarian: demanding strict obedience.
*aversive stimuli: things that provoke avoidance or escape behavior.

release feelings of anger and frustration. In this vicious cycle, aggression gets rewarded and will tend to occur again in similar situations.

5   One study found that children who are physically punished are more likely to engage in aggressive, impulsive, antisocial behavior (Straus & Mouradian, 1998). Another study of overtly angry adolescent boys found that the boys had been severely punished at home. The harsh physical discipline suppressed their misbehavior when at home, but it made them more aggressive elsewhere while the parents were often shocked to learn that their "good boys" were in trouble for fighting at school (Bandura & Walters, 1959). Yet another study of classroom discipline problems found that physical punishment, like yelling and humiliation, are generally ineffective. Positive reinforcement, in the form of praise, approval, and reward, is much more likely to quell classroom disruptions (Tulley & Chiu, 1995). (Source of information: Dennis Coon, *Essentials of Psychology*. Belmont, CA: Wadsworth/Thompson Learning 2003, pp. 258–259.)

Implied Main Idea a. The problem with physical punishment is that it greatly increases aggressive behavior in children.

b. Punishment, particularly physical punishment, encourages children to lie.

c. Parents who physically punish their children are likely to become objects of fear.

d. Using physical punishment to control behavior has several major drawbacks.

3. The Presidency of John F. Kennedy

1   President John F. Kennedy was, as novelist Norman Mailer wrote, "our leading man." Young and handsome, the new chief executive was the first president born in the twentieth century. Considered an intellectual by the public, he had a genuinely inquiring mind, and, as a patron of the arts, he brought wit and sophistication to the White House.

2   In contrast to the Eisenhower administration, the new president surrounded himself with young men who had fresh ideas for invigorating* the nation. (Kennedy appointed only one woman to a significant position.) Secretary of Defense Robert McNamara, age forty-four, had been an assistant professor at Harvard at twenty-four and later the whiz-kid president of the Ford Motor Company. Kennedy's special assistant for national security affairs, McGeorge

---

*invigorating: energizing.

Bundy, age forty-one, had become a Harvard dean at thirty-four with a bachelor's degree. Kennedy was only forty-three, and his brother Robert, the attorney general, was thirty-five.

3   Still, Kennedy's ambitious program, known as the "New Frontier," promised more than the president could deliver: an end to racial discrimination, federal aid to education, medical care for the elderly, and government action to halt the economic decline the country was suffering. Only eight months into his first year, it was evident that Kennedy lacked the ability to move Congress, which was dominated by a conservative group of Republicans and southern Democrats. In that year, Kennedy saw the defeat of bills providing for federal aid to education and a boost in the minimum wage.

4   Struggling to please conservative members of Congress, the new president did not pursue civil rights with vigor. Kennedy did establish the President's Committee on Equal Employment Opportunity to eliminate racial discrimination in government hiring. But he waited until late 1962 before honoring a 1960 campaign pledge to issue an executive order* forbidding segregation in federally funded housing. The struggle for racial equality was the most important social issue of the time, and Kennedy's performance disappointed civil rights supporters. (Adapted from Norton et al., *A People and a Nation*, p. 620.)

Implied Main Idea   a. During his short term as president, John F. Kennedy introduced far-reaching social legislation that still affects our lives today.

b. There has never been another president as handsome and cultured as John F. Kennedy.

c. Despite his glamorous image and brilliant administration, John F. Kennedy never fulfilled his plans for the New Frontier.

d. Over time, John F. Kennedy's image has been tarnished.

4. The Pros and Cons of Tort Reform

1 In Houston, a woman who scalded herself with hot coffee sued McDonald's and won $2.9 million (later reduced to a "mere" $480,000). In Maine, a woman golfer hit a shot that bounced off an obstacle and struck her in the face. She sued the country club and won $40,000. In Connecticut, a twelve-year-old Little League baseball player uncorked a wild throw that conked a woman in the stands. The woman promptly sued the player and the local

*executive order: an order issued by the president and having the force of law.

government. In New York City, several prison inmates somehow shot themselves in the feet and then sued the city for negligence.

2   Such stories seem to be increasingly common, as 800,000 lawyers in the United States seek to justify their existence and citizens look for an easy dollar instead of for a sense of personal responsibility. The results are a reduction in the gross national product of an estimated $2.5 million per attorney, personal and corporate financial tragedies, and local governments that must hike taxes to cover legal fees and liability settlements.

3   The biggest problem is that of *torts,* damage suits over product liability, personal injury, medical malpractice, and related claims. Throughout the twentieth century, state courts gradually eliminated restrictions on tort liability and substituted legal doctrines favoring plaintiffs* over defendants. For example, nearly all states have a strict liability rule for product safety. This means that manufacturers of defective products (or even very hot coffee) may be held fully liable for damages caused by their product, whether or not the manufacturer was negligent.

4   Today, state legislatures are actively engaged in tort reform that shifts the advantage more toward defendants. Punitive damage awards have been capped in Alabama, New Jersey, Illinois, Texas, and other states. Laws protecting local governments and their employees from exorbitant* liability awards have been adopted in several states. There has been a surge of business interest in judicial* elections in California and other states, as judges known for generous tort decisions have come under electoral* attack and, in some cases, gone down to defeat.

5   Aligned against tort reform are powerful trial lawyers; litigation,* product liability, and personal injury suits are their bread and butter. Also against tort reform are certain consumer groups, who see unlimited tort liability as a fundamental right for injured citizens and a means to hold individuals and firms accountable for shoddy and dangerous practices and merchandise. These opponents of tort reform are fighting against insurance companies, manufacturers, and others in courtrooms and in state capitols. Recently, the supreme courts of several states (e.g., Indiana, Ohio, Oregon) have overturned tort reforms. (Adapted from Bowman and Kearney, *State and Local Government,* p. 268.)

---

*plaintiffs: people who bring the suit to court wanting damages.
*exorbitant: excessive.
*judicial: related to the courts and judges.
*electoral: related to voting.
*litigation: lawsuits.

Implied Main Idea   a. Tort reform has been a long time coming, but the public, fed up with lawsuits, has decided to take the plunge and reduce the rewards of litigation.

b. While many states are actively engaged in tort reform, both lawyers and consumers fear that the reforms will go too far.

c. Lawsuits over product liability are a menace to the economy and to citizens' sense of personal liability; they are fueled more by the lure of easy money than by any real harm done by a product.

d. While state legislators are working hard to protect companies from lawsuits over product liability, consumers are worried that injured citizens will lose their right to sue those who caused the damages.

Reading Tip   Look at the beginning of paragraphs for the answer to two questions that should *always* be on a reader's mind: Why does this paragraph follow the previous one? What connects them to one another?

EXERCISE 5   Inferring the Main Idea

DIRECTIONS   Read each selection. Then infer the implied main idea and write it in the blank lines that follow.

EXAMPLE

Are You Sure You Want to Be a Leader?

1 The word *leader* has positive connotations for most people. Thus, most of us, if asked whether we would like to be in a position of leadership, will say yes. To be sure, being a leader has its satisfactions. Leadership brings with it power and prestige. Often it brings status, respect, and opportunities for professional advancement and financial gain. Yet those of us intent on pursuing leadership roles in our professional lives don't always take into account the fact that leaders are usually expected to work longer hours than other employees are. Actually, people in organizational leadership positions typically spend about fifty-five hours per week working. During periods of peak demand, this figure can rise to eighty hours per week.

2   Being a leader is also a good way to discover the validity of Murphy's law: "If anything can go wrong, it will." A leader is

constantly required to solve numerous problems involving both people and things. Because of those problems and the difficulties attendant on solving them, many people find leadership positions enormously stressful. As a result, many managers experience burnout and abandon their positions.

3   In addition, people in managerial positions complain repeatedly that they are held responsible for things over which they have little control. As a leader, for example, you might be expected to work with an ill-performing team member, yet you might not have the power to fire him or her. You might also be called on to produce a high-quality service or product but not be given the staff or the funds to get the job done effectively.

4   In a sense, the higher you rise as a leader, the more lonely you are likely to be. After all, leadership limits the number of people in whom you can confide. It is awkward, not to mention unprofessional, to complain about one of your employees to another employee. Then, too, you need to be wary about voicing complaints against your superiors to the people who work for you. Such complaints are bad for morale. Even worse, they can threaten your job security. Not surprisingly, people in leadership positions complain that they miss being "one of the gang."

5   People at all levels of an organization, from the office assistant to the chairperson of the board, must be aware of political factors. Yet you can avoid politics more easily as an individual contributor than you can as a leader. As a leader you have to engage in political byplay from three directions: below, sideways, and upward. Political tactics such as forming alliances and coalitions are a necessary part of a leader's role. (Adapted from Dubrin, *Leadership*, pp. 16–17.)

Implied Main Idea Although being a leader has some very positive consequences, it also has some negative ones that need to be carefully considered.

EXPLANATION Although the first paragraph opens by describing the positive consequences of being a leader, most of the paragraphs describe the negative effects of assuming a leadership role. But if you look for a general statement that sums up both the positive and the negative consequences of leadership, you won't find it. What this means is that the reader has to draw an inference like the one shown above.

1. The Reality of Prison Life

1 Many Americans firmly believe that prison inmates spend their days lifting weights, watching television, or playing basketball while hard-working taxpayers pay for prisoners' food, clothing, shelter, education, and health care. However, in a minimum-security prison, the day typically begins with a wake-up call at 6:00 a.m. Prisoners then head for the community bathrooms. Because hundreds of men often share a bathroom, they usually wait in line to use the facilities. Inmates are also expected to make their beds and clean their cells.

2 Prisons are noisy. Arguments, fistfights, and robberies among convicts are common. Many prisons, even those in sweltering southern states, are not air-conditioned. In spite of regular cleaning, they often smell of urine and body odor because fresh air cannot enter the sealed buildings.

3 At many institutions, prisoners might attend psychological counseling or educational programs for part of the day. But everyone who is able usually works between four and eight hours daily. At some of this country's penal institutions, inmates labor in prison factories where they are paid somewhere between $0.25 and $1.35 per hour. Others are assigned to food service, laundry, maintenance, or janitorial service. A typical workday lasts from 7:30 a.m. to 3:30 p.m., with a break for lunch. Yet the majority of prisoners earn less than $25 a month, out of which they must buy their snacks, sodas, aspirins, and toiletries.

4 At 4:00 p.m. every day, prisoners must be in their cells and on their feet while guards count heads and make sure everyone is present. From 4:30 p.m. until the evening meal and then again until about 9:30 p.m., prisoners read mail, watch one of three available television channels, exercise, play cards and board games, or receive visitors. After these visits, prisoners are strip-searched before going back to their cell blocks, where they can watch television, wait in long lines to use the telephone, or visit with other inmates until lights out at 11:30.

Implied Main Idea _____

_____

2. Tyrannosaurus Rex

1 The *Tyrannosaurus rex* has always had a reputation for being one of the fiercest predators to ever walk the earth. Every school child

learns how this vicious, six-ton killing machine once ruled the dinosaur world. Typically, in many museums, reconstructed *T. rex* skeletons reveal huge mouths filled with rows of teeth that seem perfect for ripping the flesh from prey.

2   But some paleontologists now believe that those huge teeth were actually designed to crush bone and tough cartilage rather than slice meat. The *T. rex*'s teeth were cylinder shaped and not as sharp or jagged as those of other known predators, such as the velociraptor, a six- to ten-foot dinosaur that hunted in packs. The current thinking is that after dinosaurs like the velociraptors had their fill, the *T. rex* may have moved in to scavenge what was left of the carcass. Further evidence for this new scenario is the fact that scientists have never found any bones that have been scratched or otherwise damaged by a *T. rex*'s teeth.

3   Many of the *T. rex*'s other body parts, too, were inadequate for predatory behaviors but perfect for scavenging. Two-legged predators usually have short thighs and long shins, a combination that allows them to run fast, so they can catch fleeing prey. But *T. rex*'s huge legs had longer thigh bones than shin bones, which means that it could have walked long distances in search of food but could not have outrun most other dinosaurs. Plus, *T. rex*'s arms were tiny and weak, so it would not have been able to grab and hold prey. In addition its eyes were too small for it to see prey at any great distance.

4   Yet the *T. rex* did have an excellent sense of smell. Paleontologists have studied *T. rex* skulls and determined that the creature had a huge olfactory lobe, the part of the brain used for smell. Although it couldn't see well, it could pick up a scent—such as that coming from a dead animal—at long distances. As a matter of fact, *T. rex*'s olfactory lobe is very similar to that of the greatest scavenger of them all—the vulture, which can smell decaying flesh twenty-five miles away. (Sources of information: Robert Locke, "T. rex May Have Been a Scavenger, Not a Predator," *USA Today*, September 2, 2001, www.usatoday.com/news/science/dinos/ 2001-09-02-trex.htm; Ben Waggoner, "Tyrannosaurus Rex!" www.ucmp.berkeley.edu/trex/specialtrex2.html.)

Implied Main Idea _____

_____

Monitoring Comprehension with Informal Outlines

If you are reading a single paragraph, it takes very little time to monitor your comprehension by checking the relationship between the supporting details and the topic sentence or implied main idea you think unifies the passage. But try doing that with longer readings, and you are likely to give up. It takes too much time to check every sentence in every paragraph. Fortunately, there is a better way to make sure that you and the author are following the same line of thought. If you complete a chapter section and want to check your comprehension, try making a quick informal outline. Then test the overall main idea against the supporting main ideas in the remaining paragraphs. Attempting to match up the main idea to the supporting details will tell you if you are in tune with the author or not.

Making a Sentence Outline

Start your outline by writing the main idea of the reading at the very top of a loose-leaf notebook page. Then, indented beneath the main idea, jot down the main ideas of at least three supporting paragraphs. Here to illustrate is a sentence outline for the reading about Fijians on pages 369–370.

Main Idea of the Entire Reading	Fijians don't diet because the sharing of food is too important to their culture.
Supporting Paragraph Main Idea 1	Serving good food is an essential way of showing people you care for them.
Supporting Paragraph Main Idea 2	Dieting is socially unacceptable because it prevents people from accepting invitations to eat with friends.
Supporting Paragraph Main Idea 3	Because of Fijians' cultural attitude, everyone in general, and children in particular, is spared the misery of failing on a diet.

If you check the main idea of the entire reading against the main ideas of the supporting paragraphs, you don't have to struggle to see the connections. Supporting detail 1 makes more specific the last half of the overall main idea: "food is too important to their culture." Supporting detail 2 explains the first part of the overall main idea by describing exactly *why* Fijians "don't diet." Supporting detail 3, in turn, describes a positive effect of the Fijians' refusal to diet.

An informal sentence outline like the one on page 389, where it's easy to understand what the supporting details add to the main idea of the reading, shows that the reader is staying in touch with the author rather than going off in the wrong direction. But look what happens when a reader has a completely different main idea, such as the one that opens the sentence outline below.

Main Idea of the Entire Reading	Unlike Americans, Fijians don't believe diet books help people lose weight.
Supporting Paragraph Main Idea 1	Serving good food is an essential way of showing people you care for them.
Supporting Paragraph Main Idea 2	Dieting is socially unacceptable because it prevents people from accepting invitations to eat with friends.
Supporting Paragraph Main Idea 3	Because of Fijians' cultural attitude, everyone in general, and children in particular, is spared the misery of failing on a diet.

Try to match the supporting main ideas to the overall main idea of the selection, and they just don't connect. That's because in this sample, the reader's overall main idea is not in tune with the main idea intended by the author.

Now, you might be saying to yourself, "Well, couldn't the supporting main ideas be wrong?" The answer is yes, they could be. But it would be rare for the reader to get all of the supporting main ideas wrong. If you monitor your reading with a sentence outline and most of the main ideas in the supporting paragraphs don't seem to fit the overall main idea of the reading, it's probably the overall, or controlling, main idea that needs revision.

 # Taking Notes with Informal Outlines

Even when you don't create a skeletal outline to test your comprehension, think about using informal outlining for note-taking. Informal outlines are an excellent device for readings with lots of details that are more abstract* than concrete.*

Making an Informal Outline

As you know from Chapter 1, informal outlines have no fixed format. You can mix phrases with sentences and leave an *a* without a *b*. The only test of an informal outline is how well it works for you. If your outline (1) records the main idea of the entire reading, (2) identifies the details essential to understanding that idea, and (3) shows the relationship between them, it's perfect.

Here's an informal outline based on the reading on pages 382–383 about John F. Kennedy's New Frontier.

Main Idea   Kennedy's New Frontier made promises it couldn't keep.

Supporting Details

1. <u>Failed Promises</u>: ① end to racial discrimination, ② more federal aid to education, ③ medical care for elderly, ④ government intervention in economy

   a. lacked ability to move Congress

   b. 1961: defeat of federal aid to education and increase in minimum wage

2. K. didn't pursue civil rights agenda.

   a. waited until '62 before issuing an executive order stopping segregation in federally funded housing

   b. did establish Commission on Equal Employment Opportunity

To a large degree, how you organize an informal outline is up to you. Still, there are some definite guidelines to follow if you want to take notes that are brief, complete, and well organized.

---

*abstract: describes ideas that cannot be understood or felt by the physical senses, e.g., justice, honesty.
*concrete: describes ideas that can be comprehended by one or more physical senses.

Guidelines for Informal Outlining

1. **Indent to show relationships.** Even with a quick glance, your outline should clearly identify the main idea of the entire reading. Always start off by writing the main idea close to the left-hand margin. Underneath and indented, list the supporting details used to explain it.

2. **Condense and abbreviate.** Whenever you can, use phrases instead of sentences. If possible, make up your own shorthand for common words and use it consistently. If a name appears several times, spell it out once, then use initials. For example, in the sample notes on page 391, Kennedy becomes K.

3. **Paraphrase the author's words.** If you just copy the author's words into your outline, you can't be sure you've understood them. An outline of ideas you haven't completely grasped is not going to do you much good when finals roll around.

4. **Leave plenty of space.** Think of your outline as a work in progress. As you gather additional information from lectures or outside reading, you may want to add to it, so leave plenty of space in your initial outline in the margins and between sentences.

5. **Reorder the material if it helps you remember it.** There's no law saying you have to re-create the author's original pattern of presentation. If you think combining facts or ideas that actually appear in separate paragraphs will help you remember them more easily, then, by all means, do it.

EXERCISE 6   **Note-Taking with Informal Outlines**

DIRECTIONS Read and outline each selection.

EXAMPLE

Harriet Tubman and the Underground Railroad*

1   Even though the famed abolitionist* Harriet Tubman (1820?–1913) gave several interviews about her early life, the facts are hard to verify.* There are, for example, no exact records of her birth,

---

*Underground Railroad: an underground organization that helped slaves escape to freedom.
*abolitionist: a person who wanted to end slavery.
*verify: prove true.

although most history books cite 1820 as the year she was born. However, one item in Harriet Tubman's biography needs no verification: Because of her efforts, hundreds of slaves found their way to freedom.

2   According to Tubman's own account, she decided on her life's work when she was only thirteen years old. Badly beaten and wounded in the head by her owner, she prayed that guilt would make him repent and see the light. But when he came to visit her, intent only on seeing if she was well enough to sell, the girl realized that prayers were not enough. From that moment on, she knew that she had no choice but to escape to the North and wage a battle against slavery.

3   Although Tubman married in 1844, she did not forget her vow to fight. Quiet as she seemed to those around her, she was only biding her time until she could escape with her two brothers, and, in 1849, the three set out together. Although her brothers eventually gave up, Tubman did not. Hunger and exhaustion could not deter her. From her point of view, death was a better alternative than slavery. Spending long nights alone in the woods, Tubman traveled hundreds of miles until she arrived in Philadelphia, a free woman. The year was 1850, and Tubman was just thirty years old.

4   Before long, Tubman made contact with members of the Underground Railroad, learning the names of people and places that could guarantee safety for fleeing slaves. With her knowledge of the underground network, Tubman returned to the South for her sister and her sister's children. One year later, in 1851, she returned again for her brothers. That same year, she returned for her husband, only to find that he had a new family and was content to stay where he was.

5   During the next ten years, Tubman traveled back and forth between the free and slave states, making about twenty secret journeys in all. Ultimately, she was personally responsible for the escape of more than three hundred men, women, and children.

6   Because some of the escapes were extraordinary and because she was subject to strange seizures, some people thought Harriet Tubman had magical powers. But those who traveled with her knew otherwise. To them, Tubman's success was not mysterious. It was the result of brains, daring, and ingenuity. Magic had nothing to do with it.

7   Tubman planned her rescues with enormous attention to detail and flatly refused to take any chances that might endanger her charges. If, for example, wanted notices were posted describing the number and appearance of her group, she would change the group's makeup. If the description said one man and two women,

she would dress one of the women in men's clothes to outwit her pursuers. If any member of her party aroused her suspicions, she would refuse to take that person. It was this attention to minute detail that made her rescue attempts so successful and earned her the nickname "Moses."

8   Yet another black American to escape slavery and become an influential abolitionist was Frederick Douglass, whose contributions are outlined in the section that follows.

Main Idea Harriet Tubman enabled hundreds of slaves to gain freedom.

Supporting Details

1. After being badly beaten, she decided to escape slavery and take action against it.

2. 1844; got married but did not forget her vow to fight.

   a.   1849, escaped.

   b.   1850; arrived in Philadelphia a free woman at the age of thirty.

3. Made contact with the Underground Railroad to learn who could guarantee safety.

   a.   Made twenty secret journeys.

   b.   She was so successful, people thought she had magical powers.

4. Planned her rescues with great attention to detail.

   a.   If wanted notices described her party, she would change the group's appearance.

   b.   If she had doubts about a person, she wouldn't take that person.

   c.   Earned the nickname "Moses."

EXPLANATION Because most of the reading deals with Tubman's efforts to free other enslaved people, the last sentence in paragraph 1 is the thesis statement. It effectively sums up the reading. Although there are eight paragraphs, only four of them contain major details that are essential to explaining the main idea. Note, too, the transitional sentence that ends the reading. This kind of transition could help you focus your reading of the next section, but it need not appear in your notes.

1. **Journalist and Activist: Ida B. Wells**

1 Ida B. Wells is not as well known as early black civil rights advocates Frederick Douglass,* W. E. B. Du Bois, or Booker T. Washington.* However, she is gaining recognition today for being a trailblazing black female, noteworthy for her accomplishments as a journalist but above all for her passionate commitment to civil rights.

2 Born a slave during the Civil War, Wells grew up in an era when few women pursued careers outside of the home. However, she discovered a love of journalism while working as a schoolteacher and launched her writing career with a series of articles about an 1883 experience in which she refused—seventy-two years before Rosa Parks's civil disobedience aboard a Montgomery, Alabama, bus—to sit in a train car designated for black passengers. When the conductor insisted that she move to the other car, she bit him. It took three men to forcibly remove her from the train as white onlookers applauded. The next year, she sued the railroad and won, although her victory was later overturned. Her articles about the case led Wells to begin writing a column for African-American newspapers, and she eventually bought part-ownership in the *Free Speech*, a black Memphis newspaper, becoming its coeditor. When she was thirty-two years old, she bought a Chicago newspaper called *The Conservator.*

3 In addition to her work in journalism, Wells was also a tireless social activist. She established the Negro Fellowship League, which assisted southern blacks who moved to Chicago. In 1909, she became one of the founders of the National Association for the Advancement of Colored People (NAACP). In 1913, Wells organized what was probably the first black female suffrage group in America, inspiring black women all over the country to organize and form the National Association of Colored Women. In 1930, at age sixty-seven, she became the first black woman to run for public office in the United States when she tried but failed to win a seat · in the Illinois state senate.

4 However, Wells is also remembered today for risking her own life in a crusade to end the practice of lynching by vigilante mobs. Between 1830 and 1930, about 3,220 black Americans were murdered in this way. One of the victims, grocery-store owner Thomas Moss, was a close friend of Wells. When Moss was lynched in 1892, an angry and grief-stricken Wells launched a campaign to eliminate this atrocity. She plunged into a wide-ranging investigation of lynching practices, interviewing witnesses and researching

---

*Frederick Douglass (1817–1895): Douglass escaped slavery and went on to become a famous writer and abolitionist.
*Booker T. Washington (1856–1915): Washington was a former slave who went on to become a famous educator.

newspaper accounts. She published the results of her study in a pamphlet titled *Lynching in All Its Phases* that she later expanded into a book. Wells even toured Great Britain in 1893 and 1894, delivering lectures that caused British citizens to threaten a boycott of U.S. goods if lynching did not end.

5   Wells's militant tactics were effective, and lynching did decline as the result of her campaign. However, she often outraged her fellow Americans with her frank and forceful response to the injustices suffered by her race. She was both black and female, so she was expected to be silent. Instead, Wells wrote candidly about the horrors of lynching. Her scathing editorials were met with hatred and death threats. Yet decades before the Civil Rights movement of the 1950s and 1960s gathered momentum and produced lasting change, Wells was a powerful leader in the fight for equality, compassion, and justice. (Source of information: Clarissa Myrick-Harris, "Against All Odds," *Smithsonian*, July 2002, pp. 70–78.)

Main Idea _____

_____

Supporting _____
Details

_____

_____

_____

_____

_____

_____

_____

_____

_____

_____

_____

_____

_____

_____

_____

_____

2. Visual Displays

1   *Visual displays* are diagrams that represent information in a manner that helps readers (1) see changes over time, (2) make comparisons, and (3) understand the parts of a larger whole. The type of visual display used for a report, book, or project depends on the information being interpreted.

2   *Line graphs* show how something changes by plotting values to scale along vertical and horizontal axes (see pages 716–720). They are most effective for presenting information about one or more variables* that change with time (such as variations in sales figures for a business over a five- or ten-year period). Line graphs are good at illustrating trends or changes that have deep lows and extreme highs, like the sale of luxury cars.

3   In a *bar chart*, each variable is represented as a vertical or horizontal bar (see pages 720–724). The longer the bar, the greater the value and vice versa. This type of display is useful for presenting things that are to be compared, such as the salaries of male and female college administrators. The eye can quickly pick out the longest and shortest bars and even those that seem to be of average size. Bar charts make it easy to see the similarity or difference between the things being compared.

4   A *pie chart* is a circle ("pie") divided into "slices," each of which represents some part of a larger whole. The circle represents the whole—for example, Texas Democrats. The size of each slice shows the contribution of each part to the whole; for instance, Texas Democrats divided according to income. By their nature, pie charts are most effective in displaying what each part contributes to a larger whole. For example, if the total federal budget is the pie, military spending would be one slice. (See pages 713–716.)

_____

*variables: things subject to change, having no fixed or permanent value.

5   A *table* presents verbal or numerical information in columns and rows (see page 470). It is most useful in presenting information about two or more related variables. A table, for example, can be used to illustrate the number of vetoes used by all the U.S. presidents. Information that can be manipulated, or altered—for example, the terms of a loan—is also usually displayed in tabular form. Information displayed in tables could often be presented in other ways, as pie charts for instance, but alternatives would take up too much space. For example, displaying the information that could be contained in a three-column table would require several bar or pie charts. (Adapted from Pride et al., *Business*, pp. 513–514.)

Main Idea _____

_____

Supporting _____
Details

_____

_____

_____

_____

_____

_____

_____

_____

_____

_____

_____

 # Introducing Graphic Organizers

Not everyone learns in the same way. Some people prefer learning from lectures because they remember what they hear better than what they read. Others are convinced they can't learn or remember anything unless they write it down. How one absorbs new information, in other words, is often a matter of personal style. The same principle applies to note-taking. For some people, outlines are the favored method of recording information. Others rarely use outlines, preferring instead to rely on graphic organizers. **Graphic organizers**, also called concept or mind maps, are the reader's picture of the writer's words.

Graphic organizers are valuable because they force you to look closely at the text in order to figure out what visual form would best match the material. With a graphic organizer, it's all but impossible to fall into the bad habit of mindlessly listing details as if they were all equally important.

Here's an example of a reading that describes the information processing model of memory. Read the selection. Then study the graphic organizer that follows.

Information-Processing Model of Memory

1   Historically, the most influential and comprehensive theories about memory have been based on a general **information-processing model** (Roediger, 1990). The information-processing model originally suggested that in order for information to become firmly embedded in memory, it must pass through three stages of mental processing: sensory memory, short-term memory, and long-term memory (Atkinson & Shiffrin, 1968).

2   Information from the senses—sights or sounds, for example—is held in *sensory memory* for a very brief period of time, often for less than a second. To be remembered, information in the sensory memory must be attended to, analyzed, and encoded as a meaningful pattern. This is the process of *perception*. If the information in sensory memory is consciously perceived, it enters short-term memory. If new information is not made the focus of attention, it will disappear in less than twenty seconds. If information in short-term memory is then processed further, it enters long-term memory, where it may remain indefinitely.

3 The act of reading illustrates all three stages of memory processing. As you read any sentence in this book, light energy reflected from the page reaches your eyes, where it is converted to neural* activity and registered in sensory memory. If you pay attention to these visual stimuli, your perception of the patterns of light can be held in short-term memory. This stage of memory holds the early parts of the sentence so that they can be integrated* and understood as you read the rest of the sentence. As you read, you are constantly recognizing words by matching your perceptions of them with the patterns and meanings you have stored in long-term memory. In short, all three stages of memory are necessary for you to understand a sentence.

4 Today's versions of the information-processing model emphasize these constant interactions among sensory, short-term, and long-term memory (Massaro & Cowan, 1993; Wagner, 1999). For example, sensory memory can be thought of as that part of your knowledge base (or long-term memory) that is momentarily activated by information sent to the brain via the sensory nerves. And short-term memory can be thought of as that part of your knowledge base that is the focus of attention at any given moment. Like perception, memory is an active process, and what is already in long-term memory influences how new information is encoded (Cowan, 1988). (Bernstein et al., *Psychology*, pp. 241–242.)

Graphic Organizer

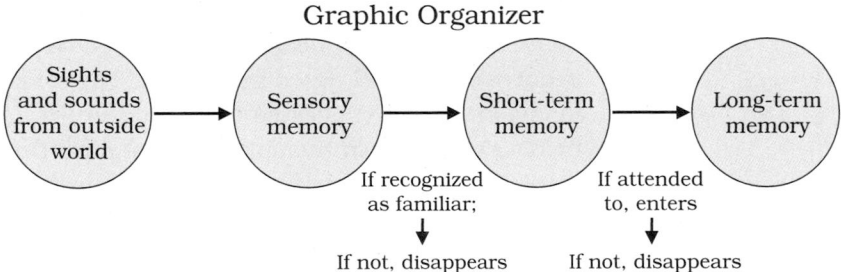

This graphic organizer is similar to a **flow chart**, the visual aid often found in textbooks that describes how things function. Flow charts represent the steps or stages in a process by showing each one a circle or a box. The circles or boxes are accompanied by arrows indicating what happens when.

---

*neural: related to the nerves.
*integrated: connected to or made part of something else.

Whenever you use boxes or symbols to represent the steps in a process, the symbols should be arranged in a way that highlights the order in which each stage occurs. This graphic organizer does just that, which is what makes it an effective learning tool. You can look at it and easily identify each individual stage information goes through as it makes its way into long-term memory.

Here's another example of a reading followed by a graphic organizer. Note how the form of the graphic organizer changes to match the change in content and organization.

Three Classes of Mammals

1 There are three major groups of mammals: the monotremes, the marsupials, and the eutherians. **Monotremes** are egg-laying mammals (most mammals are born rather than hatched) and the duck billed platypus is one of the three existing species. The platypus lives along rivers in eastern Australia and on the nearby island of Tasmania. It eats mainly small shrimp and aquatic insects. The female usually lays two eggs and incubates them in a leaf nest. After hatching, the young nurse by licking up milk secreted onto the mother's fur.

2 **Marsupials** are the so-called "pouched" mammals, which include kangaroos and koalas. These mammals have a brief gestation* and give birth to tiny embryonic offspring that complete their development while attached to the mother's nipples. The nursing young are usually housed in an external pouch called the marsupium on the mother's abdomen. Nearly all marsupials live in Australia, New Zealand, and Central and South America. Australia has been a marsupial sanctuary for much of the past 60 million years.

3 **Eutherians** make up almost 95 percent of the 4,500 species of living mammals. Dogs, cats, cows, rodents, bats, and whales are all examples of eutherian mammals. One of the eutherian groups is the order Primates, which includes monkeys, apes, and humans. (Adapted from Neil A. Campbell and Jane B. Reece, *Biology.* San Francisco: Benjamin Cummings, 2001, pp. 378–379.)

---

*gestation: period of pregnancy.

Sample Graphic Organizer

There are 3 major groups
of mammals.

Monotremes

Egg-laying mammals

Platypus, one of 3 species

Female lays 2 eggs

Marsupials

Pouched animals like kangaroos

Nursing young live in an
external pouch called a marsupium

Eutherians

95% of living mammals

humans, monkeys,
apes, dogs, cats

Now the graphic organizer you might make from this reading could very well look quite different. That doesn't matter. What does matter is how you answer these questions: Does my graphic organizer include the essential information? And, are the relationships between ideas clear? If you can answer yes to both questions then your graphic organizer is perfect for you.

Chances are that with a detailed reading making a graphic organizer will be time-consuming, particularly in the beginning. That's not a bad thing. The more time you spend thinking about how to best display the content of the reading, the better chance you have of understanding and remembering what you have read.

Reading Tip

✔

Any time you read descriptions of physical characteristics or chains of events, try to visualize the characteristics and/or events while you read.

INTERNET RESOURCE

You can find some great ideas for graphic organizers at **www .writedesignonline.com/organizers**. This site specializes in matching the organizers to the material.

EXERCISE 7 Using a Graphic Organizer

DIRECTIONS Read the selection and answer the questions. Then take notes using a graphic organizer.

EXAMPLE

Why Join a Union?

1 A *labor union* is an organization of workers who act together to negotiate their wages and working conditions with employers. Some workers, especially those with dull or repetitive jobs, decide to start or join a union because they feel they are merely parts of a machine. Therefore, they band together with others to avoid losing their sense of identity as individuals while they are on the job. Another reason for joining a union is to increase job security. Unions cannot completely guarantee their members' jobs, but they can enforce rules that protect workers from being fired for no good reason. Finally, workers start or join unions to improve unsatisfactory aspects of their jobs. For example, they may believe that a union will get them better pay, benefits, or working conditions.

2 The first step in forming a union is to conduct an organizing campaign. The goal of this campaign is to stimulate employee interest in having a union. The campaign may begin when a national union sends organizers to a particular firm to talk to employees. Or, the employees of a firm might contact a national union to get help with organizing. During the organizing campaign, the organizers ask employees to sign authorization cards. These cards indicate, in writing, the employees' support for the union.

3 If at least 30 percent of eligible employees sign authorization cards, the National Labor Relations Board (NLRB) holds an election. The NLRB distributes secret ballots to the employees at the workplace during normal working hours and then counts the votes. The vote of the majority determines the outcome of the election.

4 If the majority of eligible employees vote *against* having a union, a year must pass before another election can occur. If the majority of employees vote *for* having a union, the union becomes the official bargaining agent for its new members. In the final step of the process, the NLRB certifies the results of the election. Then, the union begins the process of negotiating a labor contract with the employer. (Source of information: Pride et al., *Business*, pp. 335–337.)

1. What's the main idea of the reading?

There are a number of reasons why people form a union.

2. Take notes using a graphic organizer.

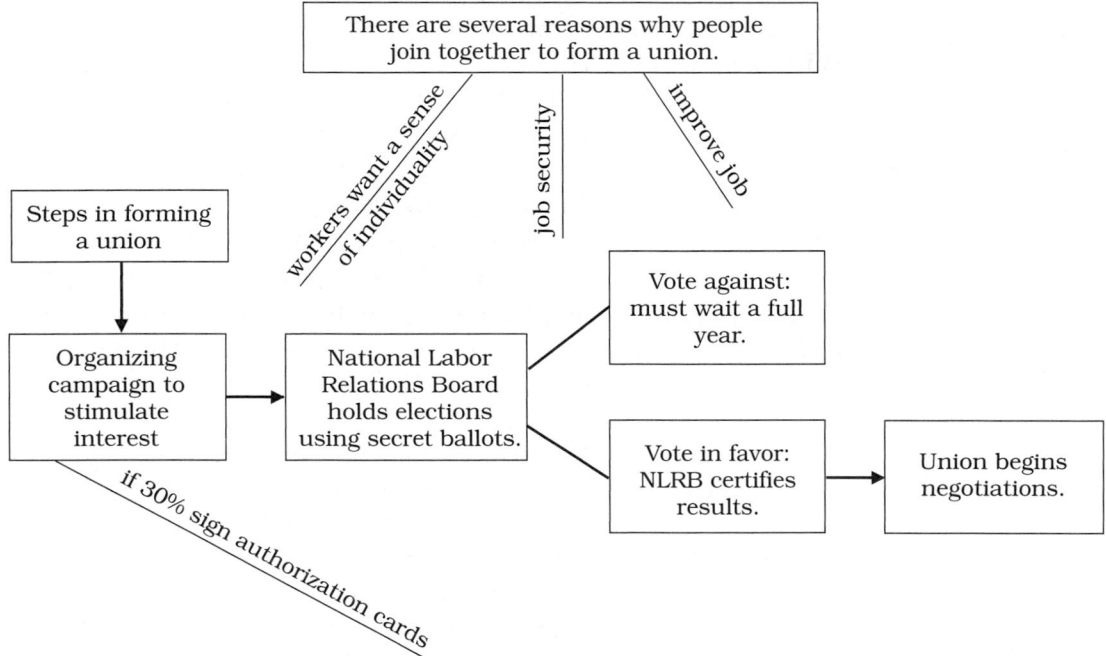

EXPLANATION Your graphic organizer for this reading might not look exactly like the one shown here. But if it identifies the reasons why people form a union along with the steps involved in creating one, it effectively fulfills its function. Exactly how you "picture" the material and its underlying organization is up to you.

1. The Jury Deliberation Process

1 During a courtroom trial, the jury listens as both the defense and the prosecution present their witnesses and their evidence. Both sides finish presenting their cases by making closing arguments to the jury. Then, the judge sends the jury to the jury room to decide on a verdict of "guilty" or "not guilty." To reach this verdict, the jurors must deliberate, discussing the information presented

in the courtroom. Their decision-making process usually goes through three stages.

2   The first stage is a relaxed period of *orientation*. The jury begins its deliberation process by selecting a group leader (the foreperson), setting an agenda, and discussing the judge's instructions. Next, jurors begin to explore what they heard in the courtroom. They talk about the facts and the evidence the lawyers presented. They raise questions. This initial discussion ends with a vote, and each jury member reveals his or her opinion about the verdict.

3   If the necessary consensus, or agreement, is not reached, the jury shifts into a period of *open conflict*. During this phase, the discussion becomes more argumentative. The two opposing groups go over the evidence and try to construct stories to explain it. The majority group tries to convince the members who disagree to change their minds by presenting information to support its argument. The majority group may also try to pressure the minority group to conform to the majority's opinion.

4   When a consensus* is finally reached, the group enters a *reconciliation* phase. During this period, group members smooth over the conflicts between them. They express their satisfaction with their decision. On some juries, however, the majority is not able to persuade the holdouts to change their minds. In that case, the jury is "hung." A hung jury causes a mistrial, and the case must be retried with a new jury. (Source of information: Brehm et al., *Social Psychology*, p. 460.)

1. What's the main idea of the reading?

_____

2. Take notes using a graphic organizer.

_____
*consensus: form of group agreement.

Reading Tip   Even if you don't use diagrams for taking notes, use them to process information while you read. Drawing diagrams in the margins is an excellent way to clarify difficult concepts.

■ DIGGING DEEPER

LEGAL RIGHTS FOR ANIMALS

LOOKING AHEAD The reading on pages 383–384 suggested that there might be too many lawyers at work in the U.S. This reading suggests that their number might well increase due to an increase in lawsuits.

1 A little more than two decades ago, something called "animal law" started gaining public notice. There were several pet custody and wrongful death cases mentioned in the press that immediately became fodder* for late-night comedians. Except for those involved, almost everyone seemed to think that talking about the legal rights of animals was a huge joke. In addition to the comic monologues, there were numerous cartoons showing a dog or cat sitting in the witness chair of a courtroom with paw raised in preparation for taking an oath. These were often accompanied by editorials with titles like "It Really Is a Kangaroo Court."*

No Joke Anymore

2 But make no mistake; these days, no one is laughing. Animal law, once unheard of both in and out of law school, is now being taught at more than a dozen law schools. Among them are some of the most prestigious: Georgetown, Harvard, and the University of California at Los Angeles. According to Stephen Wise, a Boston lawyer who teaches animal law at Harvard, the number of animal law classes is "sky-rocketing," and the first animal law casebook* is now in publication. Wise himself, the former president of the Animal Legal Defense Fund, has also written a book on animal law. It's called *Rattling the Cage: Toward Legal Rights for Animals.* The New York City Bar Association has even scheduled a conference on the legal rights of animals, and additional conferences are expected around the country.

3 In August 1999, for the first time ever, an appellate* court in New York awarded custody of Lovey, a ten-year-old cat, on the basis of the cat's "best interests." This is in direct contrast to what used to be the basis for awarding pet ownership: the animal would go to whoever came up with the bill of sale or certificate of adoption. In other words, the animal was a piece of property. The

---

*fodder: feed.
*kangaroo court: a court that's dishonest or illegal.
*casebook: a collection of source materials, often used in teaching or research.
*appellate: having the power to hear appeals and review decisions.

New York decision, however, challenges the long-held assumption that, like jewelry or furniture, animals are property, devoid of interests or rights. As Jeffrey Dallied, the New York City lawyer who won the case, pointed out, "It's huge. This is the first time an appellate court has accepted the idea that you can't treat a pet as a piece of property."

4   Tennessee became the first state in the nation to approve emotional-distress damages for a pet's loss. But rest assured, other states are sure to follow, especially since attorneys specializing in animal law are intent on making the legal system recognize and respond to the human suffering caused by the loss of a beloved pet.

5   The noticeable toughening of anticruelty laws is further evidence that animal law is no longer a laughing matter. In 1994, all but six states considered cruelty to animals a misdemeanor* and punished it with small fines or short jail sentences. At the present time, "aggravated cruelty" to animals has been elevated from a misdemeanor to a felony* in twenty-seven states. In other words, if someone intentionally kills or causes serious physical injury to a pet or other animal, that person can end up paying a large fine and spending time in prison. Such tough sentencing is a far cry from the days when hurting or killing an animal was punished with a fifty-dollar fine. It is also a further indication of the justice system's changing attitude toward animals.

6   If the toughening stance vis-à-vis* animal cruelty wasn't evidence enough, there is also this simple statistic: The number of lawyers registered with the Animal Legal Defense Fund is currently around seven hundred, and no one thinks that number has anywhere to go but up. Significant, too, is the first-ever publication of an animal-law textbook. (Sources of information: David Abel, "Lawyers Seek Legal Protection for All?" *Minneapolis Star Tribune,* February 8, 2000, p. 4E; Daphne Eviatar, "Animal Rights: Law and Natural Order," *Newsday,* December 9, 1999, p. A69; Richard Marosi, "More Pet Owners Going to Court," *Dallas Morning News,* June 6, 2000, p. 12A.)

---

*misdemeanor: a misdeed, an offense less serious than a felony.
*felony: major crime.
*vis-à-vis: in the face of or in view of.

Sharpening Your Skills

DIRECTIONS Answer the following questions by circling the letters of the correct response.

1. Which statement best expresses the main idea of the entire reading?

   a. Animal law is not yet taken seriously by legal scholars.

   b. Pets are the main obstacle in resolving a divorce amicably.

   c. If animal law gains full legal recognition, all experimentation with animals is likely to be abandoned.

   d. Animal law is now being taken seriously by many members of the legal profession.

2. Which sentence best sums up the main idea of paragraph 3?

   a. The 1999 appellate court decision awarded Lovey to the person who had the cat's best interests at heart.

   b. The 1999 appellate court decision undermines the notion that pets are property.

   c. There was a time when pets involved in divorce cases were treated as just another piece of property.

   d. Thanks to the 1999 appellate court decision involving Lovey the cat, attorney Jeffrey Dallied has become a leading figure in the struggle to revise the legal system's view of animals.

3. Which statement best paraphrases the topic sentence of paragraph 5?

   a. While a few states have made cruelty to animals a felony, the majority have not followed suit.

   b. Anyone who purposely injures an animal deserves to serve time in prison.

   c. The growing tendency to make animal cruelty a serious crime is another indication that animals are winning legal rights.

   d. There was a time when people who purposely injured animals would be punished with a small fine and nothing more.

4. To make sense out of paragraph 5, readers have to add what inference?

   a. No one laughs at anticruelty laws these days.

   b. Harsh punishment for a crime indicates that society takes the crime seriously.

   c. Many people still think animal cruelty is a joke, despite fines and jail sentences.

5. The author's primary purpose is

   a. to inform readers about the laws that pertain, or relate, to animals.

   b. to persuade readers that animal law is becoming an established branch of the law.

INTERNET RESOURCE

For more practice with supporting details, see **college.hmco.com/ pic/flemmingRFR10e**, where you will find three levels of interactive quizzes: *Getting Down the Basics*, *Checking Your Progress*, and *Taking the Challenge*. You can find additional interactive practice with extended readings at **laflemm.com**, *Reading for Results*: Online Practice for Chapter 7.

Test 1: Recognizing Controlling Main Ideas and Supporting Details

DIRECTIONS After reading each selection, answer the questions by circling the appropriate letter.

1. Henry Ford's Model T

1   Long before he invented the car known as the Model T, Henry Ford made the American public a promise: "I will build a car for the great multitude." Ford kept his promise. Using an assembly-line method of production, which he refined for maximum efficiency, Henry Ford produced a car that ordinary working people could afford. The first Model T appeared in 1908. By the following year, close to ten thousand Model Ts were putt-putting their way across America's frequently bumpy roadways. Unlike in earlier years, the drivers were no longer wealthy tycoons* but farmers and factory workers.

2   Light in weight, the Model T was still strong enough to be driven on rough country roads that had never known pavement. At a price of less than $900, even farmers could afford to save up and buy one. And buy them they did, using their cars for everything from carting eggs to making Sunday calls. As one farmer's wife delightedly wrote to Ford, "Your car has lifted us out of the mud."

3   To be sure, the Model T was not restricted to rural areas. As cities continued to spring up across the nation, more and more people began using cars to drive to and from work. When the weekend rolled around, what could be cheaper than piling the family into the Model T for an excursion? By the time production stopped in 1927, more than 15 million Model Ts had been sold, and the price had been reduced, making the cars even more affordable for the masses of people who wanted to buy them.

4   What made the Model T so cheap to produce for a mass audience—and ultimately such a gold mine—was the interchangeability of its parts. Every Model T was like the previous one. That meant the Model T could be mass produced on assembly lines, whereas other cars had to be put together one by one. But Ford didn't stop there. Always looking to cut production costs, he introduced the *moving* assembly line, making it easier and quicker for factories to turn out Model Ts, again at a cheaper price.

---

*tycoons: wealthy businessmen.

5   An astute businessman, Ford was also willing to pass on his savings to consumers because he knew full well that lowering the price of the Model T would increase its sales, which is exactly what happened. The decrease in price boosted sales and broadened the spectrum of ordinary working people who could afford to buy a car. By 1923, the price of a Model T, which had started out selling for $850, was at an all-time low of $290, a price not beyond the range of average working people. Thus, between 1908 and 1927, Ford sold a whopping 15.8 million Model Ts. He also established a production record that was not shattered until the arrival of the Volkswagen Beetle during World War II.

1. Which sentence best expresses the main idea of the entire reading?
   a. Henry Ford was an excellent businessman who knew the value of a good public relations campaign.
   b. Henry Ford did what he set out to do: He built a car that ordinary working people could afford.
   c. Henry Ford refused to build automobiles for the rich; instead he built cars that working people could afford to drive.
   d. Henry Ford was a superb businessman, but he was also a racist and a crackpot.

2. Which of the following statements accurately describes the quote from the farmer's wife in paragraph 2?
   a. The quotation is a major detail in both the paragraph and in the reading as a whole.
   b. The quotation is a major detail in the paragraph but a minor detail in the reading as a whole.
   c. The quotation is a minor detail in both the paragraph and in the reading as a whole.

3. Which sentence best expresses the main idea of paragraph 4?
   a. Henry Ford invented the assembly line.
   b. Henry Ford may have developed ways to cheapen the price of the Model T, but he also turned factory life into a worker's nightmare.
   c. The Model T's ability to be mass produced on an assembly line made the car both cheap and profitable.
   d. Henry Ford revolutionized factory production in America.

4. Which sentence best expresses the main idea of paragraph 5?

a. Ford was smart enough to boost sales by passing his savings on to consumers.

b. When it came to passing on his savings to consumers, Ford was an exception to the general rule of millionaire businessmen who never cut prices no matter how cheap the labor costs.

c. Ford's production record was not challenged until the arrival of the Volkswagen Beetle.

d. Like Ford's Model T, the Volkswagen Beetle was very much a "people's car."

5. Which of these inferences does the reader need to add to paragraph 4?

a. Producing Models Ts on an assembly line meant the cars all looked exactly alike.

b. Producing Model Ts on an assembly line meant more cars could be produced in less time, thereby earning Ford more profit.

c. Model Ts not produced by an assembly line cost more, but they were better cars.

2. Dating Online

1 If you're interested in meeting a person to date or even marry, how would you go about finding that special someone? In the past, you could go to a club and hope to run into someone interesting. Or, you could ask your friends to fix you up with a blind date. You could also take out a personal ad in a newspaper or pay a matchmaking service to find someone suitable.

2 These days, however, you can also sit down in front of your computer and log on to one of a growing number of online dating services. In 2003, more than 45 million Americans visited at least one Internet matchmaking website, such as Match.com, Kiss.com, or Date.com. These sites are steadily increasing in popularity as single people discover the advantages of finding potential mates in cyberspace.

3 One benefit of online dating sites is the huge number of people to choose from. Match.com, the largest of these sites, offers 8 million profiles of individuals who are all looking for love. Yahoo! Personals is the second largest, with 2.9 million subscribers. It would take months or years to meet 100 people you find interesting, but on the Internet, you can view 100 profiles in an hour. Then you

can decide which ones you want to correspond with and you have many more chances of meeting an individual who is right for you.

4   Online dating sites also allow you to search for people with very specific qualities, interests, or backgrounds and screen out those who don't have what you're looking for. Many sites allow you to search for people with specific income levels, religious beliefs, or hobbies. By reading what other subscribers write about themselves, you can learn right away whether their interests and goals are similar to your own. Therefore, Internet dating services provide a more efficient way to assess potential compatibility.

5   What's more, a number of "niche" online dating sites are catering to even more specific tastes. If you want to meet people who have earned a minimum of a master's degree, you can go to Advanceddegreessingles.com. Largeandlovely.com is for overweight singles, Blacksingles.com is for African Americans, and Sassyseniors.com is for older people. There's even Doggiedating.com, a site where single pet lovers might meet a kindred soul. Jdate.com, a meeting place for Jewish singles established in 1997, already has 350,000 members. Psychologists say that such niche sites are particularly practical because they increase the odds of finding the perfect match.

6   Once you locate individuals who might be compatible with you, corresponding with them via the Internet is an efficient and effective way to get acquainted. By exchanging photos, messages, and even videos through e-mail, chat rooms, and personal websites, you can get a thorough understanding of potential partners' personalities and preferences. It's true that cyberdating will not allow for an assessment of personal chemistry between two people; however, if they are encouraged by the information they gain during their correspondence with each other, two individuals can always arrange to meet in person to see if there's a spark. Cyberdating gives two people plenty of opportunities to get to know each other intellectually before entering into a relationship.

7   Yet another advantage of online dating services is the reduction of the costs involved in exploring possible new relationships. Some of these costs, of course, are financial. In traditional dating, a couple spends a lot of time and money on food and entertainment. But online dating provides people with a setting in which they can converse and become better acquainted without having to spend any money. Cyberdating also reduces the emotional and mental costs of getting to know others face-to-face. Meeting someone through the Internet significantly reduces the awkwardness that often comes with meeting an individual in person. Later, if one

partner decides to end a relationship that existed only online, the break is often easier on both parties because they don't have as much invested as they might have in a traditional dating situation.

8   The best reason, though, to try online dating services is probably the undeniable success found by many other cyberdaters. Word is spreading that participation in these sites does indeed lead to new romance. For a growing number of Americans, cyberdating is also resulting in marriage. And as more and more people prove that online dating services are not just for losers, the embarrassment of advertising for a partner online is rapidly fading.

9   There are about 85 million single people in the United States alone. Many of them are becoming disillusioned with traditional methods of finding a soul mate. Others—such as busy professionals, single parents, and physically disabled people—just need better ways to connect with others. It appears that the Internet will be able to fulfill some of their needs. (Sources of information: Amy Harmon, "Online Dating Dumps Its Losers.com Image," *International Herald Tribune,* July 1, 2003; Helena Oliviero, "More Singles Looking to Click Online," *The Atlanta Journal and Constitution,* July 15, 2002, p. E1; Jim Krane, "The New Courtship: Targeted Romance Via Internet," *AP Worldstream,* July 21, 2002.)

1. Which sentence best expresses the main idea of the entire reading?

   a. The online dating service is the most profitable type of Internet business.

   b. Online dating services offer many advantages to people who are looking for romance.

   c. Online dating services allow singles to search for romantic partners with certain characteristics.

   d. Compared to traditional dating, cyberdating results in more successful relationships.

2. Which sentence best expresses the main idea of paragraph 6?

   a. Cyberdating has some drawbacks.

   b. Cyberdating is more effective than traditional dating.

   c. Two people should get to know each other intellectually before beginning a physical relationship.

   d. Cyberdating is a convenient way for like-minded people to get to know one another.

3. Which sentence best expresses the main idea of paragraph 7?

   a. Online dating services don't cost anything.

   b. Most people cyberdate for financial reasons.

   c. Online dating services decrease the financial, emotional, and mental costs of beginning and ending relationships.

   d. Ending an online relationship is easier than ending a traditional relationship, and that's one of the main reasons online dating is becoming so popular.

4. Which of the following statements accurately describes this sentence from paragraph 3: "It would take months or years to meet 100 people you find interesting, but on the Internet you can view 100 profiles an hour"?

   a. The sentence is a major detail in both the paragraph and the reading as a whole.

   b. The sentence is a major detail in the paragraph but a minor detail in the reading as a whole.

   c. The sentence is a minor detail in both the paragraph and the reading as a whole.

5. Which of these inferences does the reader need to add to paragraph 4?

   a. Most people looking for someone to date want someone completely opposite from themselves.

   b. Whether it's for a date or a mate, most people are looking for someone with similar interests and plans.

   c. When people describe themselves for an online dating site, they always tell the truth.

 ## Test 2: Recognizing Controlling Main Ideas and Supporting Details

DIRECTIONS After reading each selection, answer the questions by circling the appropriate letter.

1. Tips on Time Management

1   Ron has known for months that his research paper is due on Monday, but he didn't start working on it until the Friday before. Sherrie never begins to study for even major exams until the night before the test. Michael has a great idea for a novel, but he always has a reason for not sitting down to write it. Juanita never finishes her tax return until minutes before the midnight deadline on April 15. Tyrone checks his e-mail frequently but rarely replies to his friends' messages.

2   These people are among the one in five individuals who are chronic procrastinators. They habitually postpone doing something until it's difficult or impossible to get it done; meanwhile, they are overwhelmed with guilt and they worry about the consequences of putting off important tasks. The problem is especially widespread among college students; about 70 percent have admitted to submitting papers late or having to cram for an exam. As a result, students tend to smoke and drink more, and they suffer from more insomnia, stomach problems, colds, and flu. Why do so many people make life harder for themselves by putting things off? Psychologists say that a problem with procrastination arises from an individual's anxieties and misconceptions about productivity.

3   According to procrastination expert Neil Fiore, Ph.D., fear of failure is the main reason why people postpone the inevitable. Thus, procrastinators delay because of their anxiety about not having the required talent, skills, or knowledge to complete the task at hand. They would rather not try at all than be exposed as incapable of completing a task well. When they flunk tests, procrastinators can blame their failure on inadequate study time rather than on lack of intellect. When they force themselves to write entire research papers in one weekend, they can attribute their papers' low grades to time pressures rather than lack of ability.

4   Another type of anxiety that causes procrastination is perfectionism. If perfectionists can't do something flawlessly, they don't want to do it at all. They put off a task because they feel anxious about producing anything less than perfect. It is for this reason

that many people keep postponing work on projects—from novels to quilts to home renovations—that they'd like to finish.

5   It is also quite common to put off those tasks that cause anxiety because they are unpleasant or painful. Even people who don't usually procrastinate will delay dental appointments and physical exams simply because of the discomfort involved.

6   In addition to one or more of these anxieties, false beliefs about productivity could be at the root of a procrastination problem. Many procrastinators are convinced that the pressure of an impending deadline causes them to work faster and better. This idea, however, is a myth because work quality usually suffers if a task is completed at the last minute. Papers are more poorly written, and tax returns are often filled with errors if done in a hurry while trying to beat a deadline. Nor does the adrenaline rush that results from being forced to finish a last-minute task improve one's performance. Again, the finished product usually suffers. People who enjoy feeling this rush are often thrill seekers who are not doing themselves any favors by putting things off. (Source of information: Maia Szalavitz, "Stand and Deliver," *Psychology Today*, July/August 2003, pp. 50–54.)

1. Which sentence best expresses the main idea of the entire reading?

   a. Procrastination is responsible for a lot of the stress Americans suffer.

   b. Fear of failure causes procrastination.

   c. A number of different anxieties are at the root of procrastination.

   d. Procrastination can be caused by anxieties or by false ideas about the right conditions for being productive.

2. Which sentence best expresses the main idea of paragraph 3?

   a. Neil Fiore, Ph.D., is an expert on procrastination.

   b. Most people procrastinate because they are afraid of failing.

   c. Students' number one anxiety is looking foolish in front of their peers.

   d. Procrastination is the main cause of poor test performance.

3. Which sentence best expresses the main idea of paragraph 6?

   a. Anxieties are the cause of procrastination.

   b. Misconceptions about productivity can result in a tendency to procrastinate.

    c. The quality of procrastinators' work is usually poor.

    d. Procrastinators tend to be thrill seekers.

4. Which of the following statements accurately describes this sentence from paragraph 6: "Papers are more poorly written, and tax returns are often filled with errors if done in a hurry while trying to beat a deadline"?

    a. The sentence is a major detail in both the paragraph and the reading as a whole.

    b. The sentence is a major detail in the paragraph but a minor detail in the reading as a whole.

    c. This sentence is a minor detail in both the paragraph and the reading as a whole.

5. Which of these inferences does the reader need to add to paragraph 2?

    a. Student procrastinators feel guilty about submitting papers late and cramming for exams.

    b. Student procrastinators cram for exams because they drink too much.

    c. There is a link between an addiction to cigarettes and procrastination.

2. Medical Remedies: Leeches, Maggots, and Dirt

1 If a patient became ill with a fever in the eighteenth century, a surgeon might prescribe leeches. Several of these glossy black worms would be placed on the patient's body, where they would puncture the skin and draw small amounts of blood. If the doctor thought that the patient should be drained of more blood than leeches could drink, he would next turn to bloodletting, which involved cutting a vein and allowing ounces or even whole pints of blood to flow from the body, often until the patient fainted.

2   During the Civil War, physicians sometimes treated a soldier's open wound by putting maggots, the wormlike larvae of flies, directly onto the patient's damaged flesh. If a patient complained of intestinal problems, the physician might order him to eat dirt.

3   Do you shudder when you think of such revolting remedies? Are you relieved that advances in medical knowledge have put a stop to these kinds of barbaric* treatments? You may be surprised to know that scientists have discovered that many of these old

*barbaric: primitive.

cures actually work; in some cases, they are actually more effective than other, more modern techniques. As a result, a number of disgusting medical remedies are making a comeback in today's hospitals.

4   Because leeches offer so many benefits, doctors are again beginning to use them for bloodletting. Leeches are proving to be particularly useful after surgeries involving the reattachment of severed body parts. When areas swell with congested blood, leeches are applied to relieve the pressure by sucking up the blood. Leech saliva contains a natural anesthetic, so the bite is pain free. The saliva also contains substances that prevent bacteria from infecting the wound area and cause blood vessels to open wider. Therefore, the worms promote the circulation of blood necessary for healing. Leech saliva also contains a chemical that keeps blood from clotting. Thus the creatures also have been used to unclog blood vessels during heart surgery.

5   Another creepy-crawly making a comeback in doctors' offices is the maggot. In the nineteenth and early twentieth centuries, battlefield physicians noticed that maggot-infested wounds healed better than those injuries that were bug free. It turns out that maggots eat dead flesh and kill harmful bacteria that cause infection. Today's laboratories grow the larvae and put them into special bandages that keep the creatures in a wound. Then they ship the bug-filled bandages to the more than 200 hospitals in the United States and Europe that have prescribed maggots for patients with bedsores, leg ulcers, stab wounds, or any other injury that won't heal. The practice is even referred to now as *biosurgery.*

6   One more disgusting treatment that actually works is *geophagy,* or dirt eating. For thousands of years, people suffering from intestinal disorders have eaten a little soil to settle their stomachs. As a matter of fact, geophagy has always been relatively common in central Africa and in the southern United States. Scientific research has confirmed that some forms of clay and earth neutralize acid, which is why the antidiarrhea product Kaopectate contains a white clay called kaolin, and the laxative-antacid milk of magnesia contains a little of the soil found around Magnesia in Greece. Dirt also contains phosphorus, potassium, copper, zinc, manganese, and iron—minerals that are essential to the body's functions—so doctors may even prescribe geophagy for patients suffering from deficiencies of these nutrients.

7   They may not have known *why* these therapies worked, but doctors of days gone by knew their remedies were effective. Today, of course, modern scientific research has revealed the reasons for these treatments' success. The next time you're in one of our

modern, sterile hospitals, don't be surprised if you see a few bugs and a little dirt. (Sources of information: Maia Weinstock and Mark Bregman, "Gross Medicine," *Science World*, October 19, 1998, http://teacher.scholastic.com/researchtools/articlearchives/humanbody/grossmedicine.htm; Robert Root-Bernstein and Michele Root-Bernstein, "Honey, Mud, Maggots and Other Medical Marvels," www.msu.edu/unit/msuaa/magazine/s98/honey.htm.)

1. Which sentence best expresses the main idea of the entire reading?

    a. Geophagy is making a comeback because it helps people with stomach disorders or mineral deficiencies.

    b. Sick people will sometimes try just about anything to be cured of their illness, and that includes submitting to some really disgusting treatments.

    c. Research has shown that some old remedies like bloodletting and eating dirt are actually much more beneficial than more modern remedies like milk of magnesia and penicillin.

    d. Research has shown that some old remedies, including leeches, maggots, and dirt, are actually effective, so modern doctors are prescribing them again.

2. Which sentence best expresses the main idea of paragraph 4?

    a. Leeches are particularly helpful to people undergoing surgery for the reattachment of body parts.

    b. Leeches may one day make surgery unnecessary.

    c. The saliva of leeches is beneficial to humans.

    d. Leeches are now a required element of all microsurgeries.

3. Which sentence best expresses the main idea of paragraph 6?

    a. Over-the-counter remedies like Kaopectate are actually not very safe.

    b. Geophagy is an age-old treatment for stomach problems.

    c. Geophagy can help patients suffering from intestinal disorders or mineral deficiencies.

    d. Dirt eating is common the world over.

4. Which statement accurately describes this sentence from paragraph 5? "It turns out that maggots eat dead flesh and kill harmful bacteria that cause infection."

    a. The sentence is a major detail in both the paragraph and the reading as a whole.

    b. The sentence is a major detail in the paragraph but a minor detail in the reading as a whole.

    c. The sentence is a minor detail in both the paragraph and the reading as a whole.

5. Which of these inferences does the reader need to add to paragraph 5?

    a. Biosurgery is more popular in Europe than in the United States.

    b. Maggots cannot be used with all kinds of wounds.

    c. The maggots will escape the bandages and eat away any bacteria in the wounds.

Test 3: Recognizing the Main Idea, Supporting Details, and Author's Purpose

DIRECTIONS After reading each selection, answer the questions by circling the appropriate letter.

1. Driving While Old

1 In July 2003, eighty-six-year-old George Weller drove his car through a busy farmer's market in Santa Monica, California. Confusing the gas pedal with the brake, Weller sped for three blocks through the market's crowds. By the time he finally stopped his vehicle, dozens of people had been hurt, eight died at the scene, and two more died later at the hospital. The incident immediately sparked debate about whether drivers as old as Weller should still be behind the wheel.

2 About 10 percent, or 19.1 million, of America's drivers are seventy or older. As the population continues to age, that number is expected to reach 30.7 million by the year 2020. In 2002, this age group was responsible for 8.1 percent of all accidents with fatalities. Even though teenage drivers still cause more fatal crashes, the number of wrecks involving drivers seventy and older increased 20 percent in the 1990s alone, indicating that as the elderly population continues to grow, more accidents may occur as well.

3 State officials have been reluctant to discriminate against senior citizens by removing the driver's licenses of motorists who reach a certain age. Understandably, older Americans do not want to give up their freedom and independence by surrendering their licenses voluntarily. Perhaps the best solution is to follow the lead of those states that are adding provisions to the licenses of older drivers.

4 Some old drivers suffer age-related ailments that can make driving more dangerous. To address the problem of visual deterioration, a few states require older motorists to have more frequent eye tests. Maine and Utah, for example, instituted mandatory vision screenings for drivers over sixty-two or sixty-five who want to renew their licenses. To ensure that aging drivers still possess the necessary mental competence for operating a vehicle, many states require older motorists either to renew their licenses more frequently or to renew them in person rather than by mail, as younger drivers can. These additional requirements effectively help states identify drivers who should no longer operate a vehicle.

5   To address the problem of slower reflexes that often come with age, a few states are adding road tests as a condition for older drivers' license renewals. Both Illinois and New Hampshire, for example, require a road test of every driver over seventy-five. These tests help examiners recognize older drivers whose decreased reaction time might make them a hazard.

6   But even the handful of states that already have additional licensing requirements for older citizens may need to further strengthen their laws. As America's streets and highways become more and more crowded, it would be wise to do whatever is necessary to make sure that unfit drivers of any age are off the roads. (Sources of information: Janet Kornblum, "Age Catches Up with Drivers," *USA Today,* July 22, 2003, p. 8D; Scott Bowles, "More Older Drivers in Accidents," *USA Today,* July 17, 2003, www.usatoday.com/news/nation/2003-07-17-older-drivers-usat_x.htm.)

1. Which sentence best expresses the main idea of the entire reading?

a. Older drivers are to blame for causing the most serious accidents on America's highways today.

b. More states should add stricter requirements for elderly Americans who want to renew their driver's licenses.

c. A driver's license is much too easy to obtain, so tests for licensing should be made a lot more rigorous.

d. Older drivers have no business behind the wheel of a vehicle.

2. The main idea of the reading is

a. stated.

b. implied.

3. Which sentence best expresses the main idea of paragraph 5?

a. Some states are trying to identify those drivers whose reflexes have slowed.

b. Road tests for drivers are not rigorous enough.

c. Illinois and New Hampshire have the strictest driver's license requirements.

d. Older drivers should have to pass road tests in order to renew their licenses.

4. Which of the following statements accurately describes this sentence from paragraph 4: "To address the problem of visual deterioration, a few states require older motorists to have more frequent eye tests"?

a. The sentence is a major detail in both the paragraph and the reading as a whole.

b. The sentence is a major detail in the paragraph but a minor detail in the reading as a whole.

c. The sentence is a minor detail in both the paragraph and the reading as a whole.

5. The primary purpose of this reading is to

a. describe new laws for aging drivers.

b. persuade readers that new laws for aging drivers are necessary.

2. America Cools Off

1 In 1902, mechanical engineer Willis Carrier needed to solve a problem for one of his employer's clients, a printing company that was having trouble with its paper, which expanded and contracted in the heat and humidity. As Carrier pondered the problem, he figured out the relationship between temperature, humidity, and dewpoint. Then he invented the air conditioner, which cooled the printing plant for the first time on July 17, 1902, solving the paper problem. Carrier's system was the first one that chilled, cleaned, and dried the air, resulting in an indoor climate that could remain a comfortable 72 degrees even on the hottest of summer days.

2 But the printing industry was not the only one that benefited from the invention of air conditioning. This new control over interior climates resulted in increased efficiency and productivity for a variety of industries, including textiles, cigars, chocolate, pasta, and celluloid film, among many others. As a result, air conditioning was in common use in commercial buildings by the 1940s. The technology also had a significant economic impact on the retail and entertainment industries. Department stores, movie theaters, sports arenas, and shopping malls have grown and prospered thanks in part to their ability to entice customers into their comfortably cool buildings. Air conditioning allowed businesses—such as movie theaters—that were once forced to close during the sweltering summer months to stay open year-round. And air conditioning itself has grown to a huge $32-billion-a-year industry.

3   The technological impact of air conditioning, too, has been profound. It not only opened up many new areas of medical and scientific research, but it made space travel possible as well. Without air conditioning, astronauts could never have explored the moon.

4   Air conditioning affected where Americans lived, opening up the steamy South and the desert Southwest for settlement. As a result, migration from southern states reversed in the 1960s, and cities such as Phoenix, Houston, Las Vegas, and Miami grew in size. Without air conditioning, these booming cities would probably still be small towns.

5   All over the country, air conditioning caused significant changes in architecture. Thanks to climate control, skyscraper windows could be sealed, allowing buildings to rise higher and higher. Residential architecture was transformed, too. Windows that were once placed in order to provide cross-ventilation were rearranged and reduced in size, the overhanging eaves and large porches that once helped cool a house were eliminated, and two-story Victorian homes with high ceilings were replaced by suburban, single-story ranch homes.

6   These architectural changes went on to produce profound social changes. People who once sought relief from the heat out on their front porches, where neighbors could interact regularly with one another, began staying inside their cooler, air-conditioned houses. As the streets emptied, social interaction outside the home diminished. America became a much more private society. (Source of information: Gene Collier, "Air Conditioning Changed Society with Chilling Effects," *Post-Gazette* (Pittsburgh), July 17, 2002, www.post-gazette.com/columnists/2002717gene4.asp.)

1. Which sentence best expresses the main idea of the entire reading?

    a. The invention of air conditioning caused a number of dramatic changes in the way Americans lived and worked.

    b. Willis Carrier was a technological genius, who single-handedly figured out how to protect paper from the effects of heat and humidity, thereby saving the printing industry from bankruptcy.

    c. Thanks to Willis Carrier, the printing industry was saved from complete financial ruin.

    d. The invention of air conditioning gave birth to the great American symbol—the skyscraper.

2. The main idea of the reading is

    a. stated.

    b. implied.

3. Which sentence best expresses the main idea of paragraph 2?

    a. The invention of the air conditioner had a profound effect on the tobacco industry.

    b. The printing industry doubled its profits thanks to the invention of air conditioning.

    c. A variety of industries benefited from the invention of air conditioning.

    d. The food industry reaped huge profits from the invention of air conditioning.

4. Which sentence best expresses the main idea of paragraph 6?

    a. Air conditioning had a dramatic effect on architecture.

    b. Air conditioning changed American architecture, and those architectural changes produced social ones.

    c. Porches became a thing of the past once families could buy air conditioners.

5. The primary purpose of this reading is

    a. to describe the effect of air conditioning's arrival on industry and society.

    b. to persuade readers that the invention of air conditioning was the most important invention of the twentieth century.

Test 4: Vocabulary Review

DIRECTIONS Here are twenty words introduced in Chapter 7. Use them to fill in the blanks. Words introduced in previous chapters are marked with an asterisk. Note: The form of the word used here may differ from the form used in the chapter.

wake	plaintiffs	munificent	extroverted
dubbed	exorbitant	barbaric	incarnate
prodigy	sumptuous	aspirations	authoritarian
litigation	unambiguous	predisposition	consensus
credence	abolitionists	invigorating	fodder

1. When the *Titanic* first set sail on April 10, 1912, promptly at noon, most of the passengers were jubilant.* They envisioned their voyage as one long delight, filled with _munificent_ dinners, _invigorating_ sea air, and the pleasure of being among the first to travel on a ship already famous for its innovative* design and sleek beauty. But as everyone knows, those expectations were cruelly dashed when the *Titanic* hit an iceberg on April 14 and sank into the icy waters of the North Atlantic, killing 1,517 people. The only good to come out of the disaster was that in its _wake_, new regulations required ships to carry enough lifeboats for all passengers.

2. President Abraham Lincoln agreed with _abolitionists_ who argued that slavery in the United States was evil _incarnate_. Lincoln gave no _credence_ to the slaveholders' claim that slavery was a form of protection for those unable to care for themselves. Because of his _aspirations_ position on the slavery question, Lincoln was _dubbed_ the Great Emancipator, but there certainly was no

_____ concerning his character and reputation. He was wildly admired by those who shared his hatred of the despicable* institution and utterly detested by those who considered it a necessary fact of life.

3. Thanks in part to his ___extroverted___ father Leopold, the composer Wolfgang Amadeus Mozart (1756–1791) was a child ___prodigy___, who displayed his ___aspirations___ for musical composition at the ripe old age of five. _____ except when he was composing and needed quiet, Mozart was already performing throughout Europe at the age of six. Despite the fact that his audience was made up of royalty, Mozart's career as an entertainer was never particularly lucrative. While his patrons might be kings and queens, they were not inclined to be ___Sumptuous___ when giving to others, and Mozart was in need of money until the day he died.

4. Although high school science teacher and football coach John T. Scopes ended up being charged with a less than _____ one hundred dollar fine, he still may be one of the most famous ___litigations___ in legal history. The _____ involving Scopes began when he allegedly made references to the theory of evolution while teaching his high school general science class. Unfortunately for Scopes, Tennessee had recently created a law called the Butler Act (1925), which forbade the teaching of Darwin's theory. Scopes, who was hardly a radical,* seems to have done little more than make some casual references to human beings as *animals* or *mammals*. But that was _____ enough for the foes of Darwinism, who

decided that the state needed to take punitive* action. Scopes was

hauled into court for allegedly claiming that human beings could

have _____ apes as their ancestors. His lawyer, how-

ever, was Clarence Darrow, the sharpest legal mind in the country,

and Darrow made legal mincemeat of the opposing attorney,

William Jennings Bryan, whose presidential _____

were destroyed by his pitiful performance in court.

BONUS QUESTION

In passage 4, the author says that Darrow "made legal mincemeat"
of the opposing attorney, William Jennings Bryan. Explain the
expression "to make mincemeat" out of a person, an idea, or an
argument.

_____

_____

_____

 C H A P T E R   8

Recognizing Patterns of Organization in Paragraphs

 **In this chapter, you'll learn**

- **how to identify five patterns commonly used to organize paragraphs: definition, time order, comparison and contrast, cause and effect, and classification.**

- **how to recognize topic sentences and transitions that signal these patterns.**

- **how to make your notes match the patterns.**

- **how to determine the *primary* pattern of organization.**

Chapter 8 introduces five patterns of organization that authors commonly use to explain ideas. Recognizing these organizational patterns will serve you by helping you (1) make predictions to guide your reading, (2) identify key points, (3) decide how best to take notes, and (4) give you a framework for remembering details.

 # Pattern 1: Definition

As you already know from Chapter 1, the **definition pattern** includes a key term—usually highlighted in boldface, color type, or italics—followed by a detailed definition that can consist of several sentences. It also frequently includes examples or illustrations to make the meaning clearer.

Because textbook authors need to identify the specialized vocabulary of their subject, paragraphs like the following appear in almost every college textbook:

> **Epithelial tissue**, or *epithelium* (ep-ih-THE-le-um), forms a protective covering for the body and all the organs. It is the main tissue of the outer layer of the skin. Epithelial tissue forms the lining of the intestinal tract, as well as that of the respiratory and urinary passages. It also lines the blood vessels, the uterus, and other body cavities. (Adapted from Ruth Memmler et al., *The Human Body in Health and Disease*. Philadelphia: Lippincott-Raven Publishers, 1994, p. 40.)

Typically for the definition pattern, the authors have highlighted the term they are defining, **epithelial tissue**. Then that highlighted term is followed by a definition. The authors also provide examples of where the tissue can be found in the body.

Typical Topic Sentences

Sentences like the ones that follow are a strong indication that the definition pattern plays an important role in the paragraph.

> **1.** Nineteenth-century America was guided by the concept of **Manifest Destiny**, the belief that the United States was on a mission from God to occupy North America from coast to coast.

2. The *greenhouse effect* is the name for what happens when excessive carbon dioxide and other gases build up in Earth's atmosphere.

3. Ozone is the name for a specific form of oxygen containing three atoms instead of the two found in regular oxygen.

4. A "browser" is software that allows you to travel on the Internet and find out what is available.

Taking Notes on Definition Paragraphs

Notes on the definition pattern should include three or four elements:

1. the term being defined
2. a complete definition
3. at least one example
4. any other details that might help clarify the definition

To illustrate, here are notes on the definition paragraph on page 432:

Main Idea *Epithelial tissue* is the main tissue covering the skin and organs; it protects the body and its organs.

Supporting Details
1. Lines the intestinal tract along with respiratory and urinary passages.
2. Lines the blood vessels, uterus, and other body cavities.

Sometimes authors include background material about how a word came into being, or they define a key term by telling you what it is *not*. This information is not always essential, so look at it carefully and decide if it needs to be included in your notes.

Note-Taking Tip

When taking notes in your textbook, it's a good idea to make the word or words being defined stand out by circling, boxing, or underlining them. This way, during review, you'll be sure to study important key terms.

If you are a fan of graphic organizers, you'll be happy to learn that definition passages readily lend themselves to that format, for instance:

lines respiratory
and urinary passages

Epithelial tissue:
main tissue covering the
body, form of protection

lines intestines

lines blood vessels,
uterus, and body cavities

EXERCISE 1 Understanding Definition Patterns

DIRECTIONS Read and take notes on each paragraph, making sure to paraphrase and abbreviate in your notes.

EXAMPLE The psychiatric term **psychodrama** refers to a particular kind of group therapy created and developed by therapist Jacob Moreno in the early 1950s. In a psychodrama, individuals act out disturbing incidents from their lives, often playing multiple roles. The purpose of a psychodrama is to help patients better understand the troubling situations that may have contributed to their psychological problems. Moreno believed that the insights gained during a psychodrama could then be transferred to real life. For example, a teenager jealous of and in conflict with a twin might better understand both his own feelings and the feelings of his brother by acting out one of their quarrels.

Main Idea In the 1950s, Jacob Moreno developed a special kind of group

therapy called psychodrama.

Supporting 1. During psychodrama, individuals act out disturbing real-life
Details
situations.

2. Objective is to better understand situations that may contribute

to psychological disturbance.

3. Moreno thought insights gained during a psychodrama could

be applied to real life.

a. A teenager in conflict with his twin might gain understand-

ing by acting out a typical quarrel.

EXPLANATION Here, the key term is *psychodrama* and our notes clearly define it. They also include some essential background about the word—the name of Jacob Moreno and the approximate time when the term came into being. Note, too, that an example clarifying the key term has also been included.

1. A **self-concept** is a person's perception, or view, of his or her personality and character traits. It consists of all your ideas and feelings about how you define yourself. To discover your self-concept, you might ask yourself, "What kind of person am I? Am I compassionate?* Selfish? Stubborn?" Self-concepts are built out of daily experiences and our reactions to those experiences. For example, let's say that as a child you consistently do well in sports but find it hard to be part of a team. You might then begin to describe your self-concept in the following terms: "I'm a good athlete, but I'm not much of a team player." Self-concepts, however, can—and sometimes should—be revised, particularly if they are overly negative.

Main Idea _____

_____

Supporting _____
Details
_____

_____

_____

_____

_____

_____

_____

2. During the nineteenth century, the absence of effective government in many of the newly settled parts of the West created a vacuum that was often filled by **vigilante groups**—private citizens taking the law into their own hands at almost any provocation.* Vigilante groups, which typically consisted of a few hundred people led by the town elite, would track down criminals or people creating disorder in the

_____

*compassionate: caring of others.
*provocation: stimulus to anger or punishment.

settlement and administer "justice" to them. At some "trials" the captured outlaws were given a chance to present a defense. Determination of guilt most often resulted in the execution of the "defendant," usually by hanging. Vigilante groups were generally well organized along military lines and had written manifestos or constitutions to which the members would subscribe. (Adapted from Adler et al., *Criminal Justice*, p. 136.)

Main Idea _____

_____

Supporting Details _____

_____

_____

_____

_____

_____

3. By definition, **blood pressure** is the force exerted against the walls of the arteries as the heart contracts and relaxes. The force is measured in millimeters of mercury (mm Hg), and a "typical" blood pressure is 120/80 (read 120 over 80). The "120" refers to the force exerted by the blood just as the heart contracts and is called the **systolic** pressure. The "80" refers to the force exerted when the heart muscle is relaxed and is called the **diastolic** pressure. (Kathleen D. Mullen et al., *Connections for Health*. New York: McGraw-Hill, 1996, p. 349.)

Main Idea _____

_____

Supporting Details _____

_____

_____

_____

_____

_____

4. The word *Spanglish* is said to be the creation of the Puerto Rican linguist Salvador Tió. Tió coined the word to describe the mix of English and Spanish spoken by Spanish-speaking people who live among or have heavy contact with native English-speakers. Spanglish is common along the U.S.-Mexico border and in places with large bilingual communities like Texas and Florida. Spanglish is also spoken in Panama, where America's control of the Panama Canal brought Panamanians into close contact with English. Spanglish can also be found wherever American or British movies and music have become popular. Although the characteristics of Spanglish can vary according to where it is spoken and who is describing it, the main feature is the combining of English and Spanish grammar and vocabulary in the same sentence or conversation. For instance, a speaker of Spanglish might say "Ya me voy a get up" instead of "Ya me voy a levanter" ("I'm just getting up"). (Source of information: wikipedia.org/wiki/Spanglish.)

Main Idea _____

_____

Supporting _____
Details
_____

_____

_____

_____

_____

_____

_____

Pattern 2: Time Order

Two different types of paragraphs rely heavily on the **time-order pattern**. The first paragraph type lists a sequence of dates and events according to when they happen (or happened) in real time.

The other type explains a process, telling readers how something works or develops.

Sequence of Dates and Events

Textbook authors in all fields frequently use a **sequence of dates and events** to (1) describe how a smaller series of events led up to a larger and more major event; (2) chart the career of an important figure; or (3) explain how some theory, invention, or activity came to be part of culture or history. Here, for example, is a time-order paragraph that traces a sequence of dates and events according to the order in which they occurred.

> What we now call the Internet began in 1969 when the U.S. Defense Department linked up computers at four universities to create ARPANET (Advanced Research Projects Agency Network). By 1972, thirty-seven universities were connected over ARPANET. In 1983, ARPANET interlinked with other computer networks to create the Internet. Between 1983 and 1990, the Internet was used mainly to transmit messages known as electronic mail, or *e-mail*, among researchers. In 1991, a group of European physicists devised a system for transmitting a wide range of materials, including graphics* and photographs, over the Internet. By 1994, households all over the United States were "surfing the net." (Adapted from Janda et al., *The Challenge of Democracy*, p. 181.)

The topic of this paragraph is the growth of the Internet. The implied main idea suggests that the Internet as we know it did not happen overnight. Rather, it took more than twenty years to develop. Notice how the dates and events in the paragraph all contribute to this implied main idea.

Transitions

Many of the sentences in the previous paragraph open with transitions that help readers follow the order of events. Phrases like "by 1972," "in 1983," and "between 1983 and 1990" tell readers to pay attention because the next significant event is coming up. They are the author's way of saying, "I've finished describing the previous event and I'm ready to tell you about the one that followed it." Since they usually introduce major details, time-order transitions are worthy of your attention. Here's a list of transitions likely to appear in a paragraph tracing a sequence of dates and events.

---

*graphics: visual images.

Transitions Commonly Used to Organize Dates and Events

After that

At that time, point

Before

Between _____ and _____

By the end of the year

By the year _____*

During _____

During that time, period

Finally

From _____ to _____

In January (etc.) _____

In the days, weeks, months, years, century following

In the spring, summer, fall, winter of

In the following year

In the next year

In the years since

In the year _____

On the day, afternoon, evening of _____

Until

When

While

_____ years later

---

*In the context of a text, blanks would include dates or numbers.

Typical Topic Sentences

Transitions like those shown above are clues to the time-order pattern. So, too, are the topic sentences like the following. Note how they all identify a particular period of time.

1. The life of painter Frida Kahlo is a lesson in how art can be an antidote to pain.
2. The years leading up to the Great Depression were filled with a sense of both optimism and progress.
3. Between 1939 and 1944, most of Europe descended into a nightmare world of terror, violence, and death.
4. In their youth, the inventors of the airplane, Wilbur and Orville Wright, seemed destined for failure.

Any time a topic sentence mentions a specific period of time or evaluates a life or career, there's a good chance the organization is a sequence of dates and events.

Telltale Visual Aids

Timelines like the one shown below indicate that the sequence of dates will likely play a heavy role in the material you are reading.

Chronology of Events	
1860	Lincoln elected president
	Secession begins
1861	Fort Sumter attacked
	Lincoln institutes martial law in the border states
	First Battle of Bull Run
	Trent Affair
1862	Peninsular campaign
	Battle of Shiloh
	Union navy seizes Memphis and New Orleans
	Battle of Antietam
	Battle of Fredericksburg
	Confederate Conscription Act
	Homestead Act
	Morrill Land Grant Act
1863	Emancipation Proclamation
	Union army enrolls black enlistees
	Federal Conscription Act
	New York City draft riot
	Battle of Chancellorsville
	Battle of Gettysburg
	Vicksburg falls
1864	Grant made commander of all Union forces
	Grant's wilderness campaign
	Lincoln reelected president
	Grant lays siege to Petersburg
	Sherman takes Atlanta, begins his march to the sea
1865	Confederacy enlists black troops
	Petersburg and Richmond fall
	Lee and Johnston surrender

(Adapted from Steven M. Gillon and Cathy D. Matson, *The American Experiment.* Boston: Houghton Mifflin, 2006, p. 571.)

Taking Notes on Dates and Events Patterns

When you take notes on paragraphs devoted to dates and events, include the following information:

> **1.** the main idea
> **2.** the dates and events used to develop the main idea
> **3.** any other supporting details that lack dates but still seem essential to developing the main idea

Here, to illustrate, are notes on the paragraph about the Internet.

Main Idea The Internet was developed over an extended period of time.

Supporting Details

1. 1969: The first step toward developing the Internet came when the Defense Department linked computers at four universities to form ARPANET (Advanced Research Projects Agency Network).

2. 1972: Thirty-seven universities were connected over ARPANET.

3. 1983–1990: ARPANET interlinks with other computers to create Internet, used primarily for e-mail among researchers.

4. 1991: A group of European physicists created a standardized system for encoding and transmitting graphics.

5. By 1994: Families all over the U.S. were exploring the Net.

Note-Taking Tips

1. The supporting details in the sample notes above all start off with the dates mentioned in the paragraph. This is a good format to use when taking notes on paragraphs devoted to dates and events. It will help you keep the sequence of dates and events clear in your mind.

2. When you take notes, consider making a timeline like the one on page 440.

▬ EXERCISE 2 Understanding Dates and Events Patterns

> **DIRECTIONS** Read and take notes on each paragraph. Circle the time-order transitions.

EXAMPLE The son of a Spanish immigrant, Cuban leader Fidel Castro quickly rose to power. Castro was educated at a Roman Catholic school in Santiago, and from 1945 to 1950 he attended the University of Havana. In 1947, he participated in an unofficial raid on the Dominican Republic, and in July 1953 he organized an attack on the army barracks in Santiago. The attack was unsuccessful, and Castro was sentenced to fifteen years in prison. In 1955, Castro was released from prison, and the following year he went to Mexico to build a Cuban revolutionary movement. In December 1959, he returned to Cuba, and in January 1960 he led a successful attempt to overthrow dictator Fulgencio Batista. Since that time, Castro has ruled Cuba with an iron hand although in 2006, he was rumored to be close to death.

Main Idea   It did not take many years for Fidel Castro to rise to power in

Cuba.

Supporting Details

1. 1945–1950: Attended University of Havana

2. 1947: Took part in unofficial raid on Dominican Republic

3. July 1953: Organized attack on army barracks in Santiago

4. 1955: Released from prison

5. 1956: Went to Mexico to organize Cuban revolution

6. December 1959: Returned to Cuba

7. January 1960: Overthrew Batista

8. Since 1960: Rules with iron hand, although rumors of death

   began in 2006

EXPLANATION To prove the claim made in the topic sentence—that Castro's rise to power was rapid—the paragraph provides a sequence of dates and events. Using the "date-first" format, the sample notes briefly record all the significant events in Castro's rise to power. *Note:* The year 1956 is not mentioned in the paragraph, but you can figure out when Castro went to Mexico because of the phrase "the following year." Sometimes, authors don't include specific dates but instead expect you to figure them out.

1. It took some time before American colonists learned how to grow their own tea. The first tea shrub was planted in the early nineteenth

century, sometime between 1810 and 1820. In 1848, more extensive* experiments with tea production were carried out; ten years later, plans were made to distribute tea seed throughout the South. These experiments, however, were cut short by the Civil War (1861–1865), and it was not until 1880 that the United States Department of Agriculture resumed tea production. In 1890, Charles U. Shepard of Summerville, South Carolina, devoted his private fortune to growing tea. By 1900, he had planted sixty acres and harvested five thousand pounds of tea. However, despite the efforts of Shepard and others who came after him, tea has never successfully competed with coffee as America's favorite drink.

Main Idea _____

_____

Supporting _____
Details
_____

_____

_____

_____

_____

_____

_____

2. Born in 1912, future German rocket scientist Wernher von Braun demonstrated his interests early on. As a boy, he tried to make his wagon fly by attaching rockets to its sides. By 1932, von Braun— a fresh-faced youth of twenty—had earned an engineering degree and was heading a newly created rocket program in Kummersdorf, Germany. By 1934, von Braun had received a doctorate in physics and was being funded by the new German leader, Adolf Hitler, who was enthusiastic about the potential of rocket science. It was only four years later that von Braun's team had developed the deadly V-2 missile, which could carry explosives almost two

_____
*extensive: large, wide ranging.

hundred miles. The V-2, in fact, was instrumental in Germany's deadly bombing raids on London. However, by 1945, the Nazi regime was collapsing. Von Braun, who was always careful to advance his own interests, decided to get on the winning side and surrendered to American troops. At first skeptical of von Braun, who had helped Hitler wage his bloody and horrific war, the Americans quickly realized how valuable he was to their own rocket program and decided to overlook his dubious past. After all, the Cold War was heating up, and von Braun was a gold mine of information. By 1960, von Braun was the head of NASA's George C. Marshall Flight Center. Von Braun was jubilant when his agency landed a man on the moon in 1969, and the country celebrated with him. In 1975, he was awarded the National Medal of Science. Wernher von Braun's story is worth remembering the next time anyone tells you with great certainty that "what goes around, comes around."

Main Idea _____

_____

Supporting _____
Details
_____

_____

_____

_____

_____

_____

3. Although the idea of constructing a canal across Panama dates back to the sixteenth century, the canal did not become a reality until the twentieth century. As early as 1534, Holy Roman Emperor Charles V suggested that building a waterway across the narrowest part of Central America would allow ships to travel more easily to Peru and Ecuador. His idea was revived now and then as the years went by, but construction was not actually attempted until 1880, when the French broke ground on January 1. Thirteen years later,

in 1893, they abandoned the project as too difficult. In 1903, the United States, under President Theodore Roosevelt, gained control of the unfinished Panama Canal, and in 1904 construction resumed. Over the next ten years, workers built the canal's foundation and system of locks. On August 15, 1914, the canal formally opened when the cargo ship *Ancon* became the first to use it. After World War II, controversy swirled around the canal over who the rightful owners were, the Americans or the Panamanians. In 1977, U.S. President Jimmy Carter signed a treaty returning control of the canal zone to Panama. (Source of information: "A History of the Panama Canal," Panama Canal Authority, 2001, www.pancanal.com/eng/history/history.)

Main Idea _____

_____

Supporting _____
Details
_____

_____

_____

_____

_____

_____

_____

_____

4. The civil rights, student, and antiwar movements of the 1950s and 1960s produced large numbers of young women activists.* Like the women in the earlier abolitionist movement, these activists called attention to their own inequality in America. Thus, the 1960s saw significant advances in the rights of women. Responding to increased lobbying by women, President John F. Kennedy, in 1961, created a Commission on the Status of Women. The commission's report openly criticized the fact that women continued to be second-class citizens in America, and it led to the establishment of similar

_____

*activists: people devoted to fighting for a cause.

state commissions. In 1966, Betty Friedan, author of the best-seller *The Feminine Mystique,* led a movement to form the first important national feminist organization in America since Susan B. Anthony's* National Women's Suffrage* Association. The new organization was called the National Organization for Women (NOW). Even today, it continues to be a vocal and visible force in America on such issues as equal employment opportunity for women. In 1967, pressured by NOW, Lyndon Johnson formally prohibited sex discrimination in federal employment. Although the decades that followed the sixties have seen progress in women's rights, none quite equals the sixties. (Adapted from Harris, *American Democracy,* pp. 170–171.)

Main Idea _____

_____

Supporting Details _____

_____

_____

_____

_____

_____

_____

_____

_____

_____

Process

Writers use the **process pattern** of development to tell their readers how something works, happens, or develops. Thus the process pattern is particularly common in science and business textbooks.

---

*Susan B. Anthony (1820–1906): a nineteenth-century leader in women's fight for the right to vote.
*suffrage: legal right to vote.

For an illustration of the process pattern, see the following paragraph, where the author describes the three stages of growth in identical twins.

> There are three basic stages involved in the development of identical twins. Their growth begins when the father's sperm pierces the egg of the mother. The fertilized egg then splits and divides into equal halves, each half receiving exactly the same number of chromosomes* and genes.* The halves of the egg then develop into two babies who are of the same sex and who are identical in all hereditary traits, such as hair and eye color.

The topic of this paragraph is "the development of identical twins." The topic sentence tells us there are three specific stages. The supporting details then describe each of the three stages.

Transitions

Whenever an author explains how something develops over time, look for transitions that help readers keep track of the individual steps or stages. The transitions listed below are some of the most common.

Transitions That Describe a Process		
After	In	Once
At the onset	In the beginning	Over time
At this point	In the early stages	Right after
Before	In the end	Shortly after
By	Last	Soon
During	Later	Then
Eventually	Meanwhile	Today
Finally	Next	When
First, second, third	Now	Within hours
Following	On	(or days)

Typical Topic Sentences

In addition to the transitions listed above, topic sentences like the following also suggest the process pattern.

---

*chromosomes: bodies within a cell that consist of hundreds of clear, jellylike particles strung together like beads. They carry the genes.
*genes: the elements responsible for hereditary characteristics, such as hair and eye color.

> 1. Children go through several different stages before arriving at a sense of gender.
> 2. The process of photosynthesis is essential to plant life.
> 3. Storing information in long-term memory involves several distinct steps.
> 4. The red-headed owl follows an intricate courting ritual.

Any time a topic sentence uses words and phrases like *process* or *sequence of steps* or *series of stages,* you are probably dealing with a paragraph that employs the time-order pattern.

Telltale Visual Aids

Flow charts like the ones described in Chapter 7 are a dead giveaway to the process pattern. If you see a paragraph or chapter section accompanied by a flow chart, it's more than likely that the process pattern organizes the selection.

Taking Notes on Process Patterns

Notes on paragraphs describing a process should include the following:

> 1. the main idea
> 2. the specific steps in the process
> 3. the order in which they are presented
> 4. any specialized vocabulary used to describe the steps or stages

As you can see, the following sample notes identify all four essential elements of this pattern. The sample notes also indicate that each stage is a major detail.

Main Idea There are three stages in the development of identical twins.

Supporting Details
1. Father's sperm pierces mother's egg.
2. Fertilized egg splits and divides into equal halves; each half receives same number of chromosomes and genes.
3. Halves of egg develop into two babies of same sex, identical in all hereditary traits, such as hair and eye color.

<table>
<tr>
<td>Note-Taking Tip
</td>
<td>You might also try using a flow chart to take notes on a process. Just make sure to include arrows and brief but complete explanations of each step with one box or circle per step.</td>
</tr>
</table>

EXERCISE 3 Understanding Process Patterns

DIRECTIONS Read and take notes on each paragraph. Circle the time-order transitions.

EXAMPLE (In spring,) the stickleback, a small fish found in both fresh and salt water, goes through a strange courtship ritual. (With the coming of) the spring months, the male stickleback begins to look for a place where he can build his nest. (Once he has found it,) he grows aggressive and fights off all invaders. (After) finishing the nest, he searches for a female. (When he finds one,) he leads her to the nest, and she enters it. The male (then) hits the tail of the female, forcing her to deposit her eggs. (Once) she lays the eggs, the female swims off, and the male enters the nest.

Main Idea *In spring, the stickleback goes through an odd courtship ritual.*

Supporting Details
1. *Male stickleback looks for place to build nest.*
2. *Finding one, he grows aggressive.*
3. *After finishing nest, he looks for female.*
4. *Leads her to nest, which she enters.*
5. *Male hits female's tail, forcing her to deposit eggs.*
6. *Once eggs are laid, she swims off and male enters nest.*

EXPLANATION Because the notes contain the main idea and all the steps described in the paragraph, we have everything of importance.

1. The first act of a newly hatched queen bee is to seek a mate. Three to five days after hatching, she attempts her first flight, flying far from the hive to avoid inbreeding.* When she is far enough, the

*inbreeding: reproducing by mating with a closely related individual.

queen produces a scent that attracts drones from distant hives. Once a drone arrives, mating takes place at an altitude of about fifty feet. Following the mating, the queen flies home to lay her eggs. A queen who does not mate by the time she is two weeks old will never mate and will remain barren.

Main Idea _____

_____

Supporting _____
Details

_____

_____

_____

_____

_____

_____

2. The psychological disorder known as paranoia develops in four basic stages. At the illness's onset, victims begin to distrust the motives of others. The paranoid are constantly alert for ulterior, or secret, motives in the actions of others. If suspicion marks the first stage, self-protection is central to the second. At this point, any personal failure is seen as the fault of others, and victims no longer take responsibility for their actions. In the third stage, paranoia sufferers become hostile; they are openly angry at their supposed ill treatment at the hands of others. This period of anger usually leads to a moment of paranoid illumination.* In this final stage, everything falls into place, and the truly paranoid wholeheartedly believe that a plot or conspiracy is being directed against them. Seeing enemies everywhere, they are now convinced that someone, often a whole group, is trying to do them bodily harm and perhaps even kill them.

Main Idea _____

_____

_____

*illumination: understanding.

Supporting
Details

_____

_____

_____

_____

_____

_____

_____

_____

3. A volcanic eruption begins when lava, or liquified rock, in a volcano becomes charged with steam and gas. The lava then shoots upward and falls back to earth in fragments of stone. In the next stage, the lava in the volcano's center builds up and flows over the rim. At this point, the volcano's eruption is at its crisis, or critical, point. After a final massive explosion of lava, the volcano begins to cool. During the cooling stage, the volcano emits gases and vapors. This phase is often followed by the appearance of hot springs or geysers, like the ones that can be seen in Yellowstone National Park. Eventually the last traces of volcanic heat disappear, and cold springs may appear around the volcano.

Main Idea

_____

_____

Supporting
Details

_____

_____

_____

_____

_____

_____

_____

_____

_____

_____

4. The eggs of the king salmon hatch in freshwater streams; within a year after hatching, however, the young salmon head out to sea. During their journey, many are killed by bears, ducks, raccoons, and industrial waste. Only a small portion of the salmon actually reaches the sea. Those that do, stay anywhere from four to six years. Then they begin their journey back to the river in which they hatched. When they reach that river, they lay thousands of eggs that will hatch and go through the exact same life cycle. Once the adult king salmon have laid their eggs, life is over for them. They change color and turn slimy. Slowly, they float downstream with their tails forward. Within days, they are dead.

Main Idea _____

_____

Supporting _____
Details

_____

_____

_____

_____

_____

_____

_____

 # Pattern 3: Comparison and Contrast

Paragraphs based on comparison and contrast mention the similarities and/or differences between two people, events, animals, or objects. Take, for example, the following paragraph:

> Much attention, perhaps too much, has been paid to the differences between Japanese and American workers. *But* perhaps we should examine more carefully the differences between Japanese and American management at the highest levels of decision making. In Japan, the heads of companies are discouraged from earning more than fourteen times the salary of their highest-paid workers. In America, *in contrast*, the company's chief officer can be expected to earn as much as fifty times more than the highest-salaried worker. In Japan, if someone in top management makes a serious blunder, he is in public disgrace. If the same thing happens, *however*, in America, the company may suffer bankruptcy, but no one would expect the person who erred to publicly take responsibility.

While the introductory sentence suggests a paragraph that will focus on the differences between Japanese and American workers, the transition *but* reverses the opening train of thought and paves the way for the topic sentence—"But perhaps we should examine more carefully the differences between Japanese and American management at the highest levels of decision making." That topic sentence makes it clear that the paragraph will concentrate on differences between Japanese and American management. The major supporting details then cite specific differences.

In some cases, paragraphs do both: They compare *and* contrast two topics. Here's an example:

> The African or so-called killer bees have entered the United States, and their arrival has, for good reason, aroused intense fear. *Although* in some ways the African bees are similar to harmless honeybees, they are different in a significant and dangerous way. *In terms of similarities,* the African bee's venom is no more poisonous than the honeybee's, and individually the African bee is not much more aggressive than the honeybee. What distinguishes the African bee from the American honeybee is its determined defense of territory. If African bees are disturbed in their nest, they mount a furious attack and pursue intruders for miles, *whereas* honeybees quickly give up the chase.

In this paragraph, the topic sentence tells readers to expect a discussion of both similarities and differences: "Although in some ways the African bees are similar to harmless honeybees, they are different in a significant and dangerous way." The supporting details fulfill the promise of that sentence, specifically identifying two similarities and one dangerous difference.

Transitions

Notice, too, the italicized transitions that signal both comparison and contrast. Such transitions are useful clues to the comparison and contrast pattern. They can also help you distinguish between major and minor supporting details. Transitions signaling comparison or contrast almost always introduce major rather than minor details.

Transitions That Signal Similarity

Along the same lines	In like fashion, manner	Just as
Also	In much the same	Like, just
By the same token	way, manner	like
Comparatively	In terms of similarities	Likewise
In comparison	In the same vein	Similarly

Transitions That Signal Difference

Actually	In reality	Opposing
Although	Instead	that position
And yet	Ironically	Rather
But	Just the opposite	Still
Conversely	Nevertheless	Though
Despite that fact	Nonetheless	Unfortunately
Even though	On the contrary	Unlike
However	On the one hand	Whereas
In contrast	On the other	While
In opposition	hand	Yet

Typical Topic Sentences

Transitions like those listed above are good clues to the comparison and contrast pattern. So, too, are topic sentences like the following.

1. Scientists Enrico Fermi and Robert J. Oppenheimer had very different feelings about the success of the Manhattan Project.*
2. Unlike African Americans, Mexican Americans were not forced into segregated military units during World War II.
3. France and Germany were both against the 2003 war with Iraq, but they showed their disagreement in very different ways.
4. Roy Cohn and Joseph McCarthy showed the same approach to the truth: If it stood in their way, they just ignored it.

Topic sentences that identify two topics and mention either similarities and/or differences are a dead giveaway to the comparison and contrast pattern.

Taking Notes on Comparison and Contrast Patterns

Notes on a paragraph using a comparison and contrast pattern should clearly identify three essential elements:

1. the two topics being compared and/or contrasted
2. the similarities and/or differences between the two
3. the main idea they explain or support

Here, to illustrate, are notes on the paragraph on page 453.

Main Idea Although there are some similarities between American honeybees and African bees, there is an important and dangerous difference.

Supporting Details
1. African bees' venom no more poisonous than honeybees'.
2. The two bees just about equally aggressive.
3. What makes African bees different and dangerous is determined defense of territory.
   a. Attack in a group and pursue for miles.
   b. Honeybees quickly give up the chase.

*Manhattan Project: the name given to the research group that focused on building the atom bomb.

When taking notes on the comparison and contrast pattern, consider as well a graphic organizer that looks something like this:

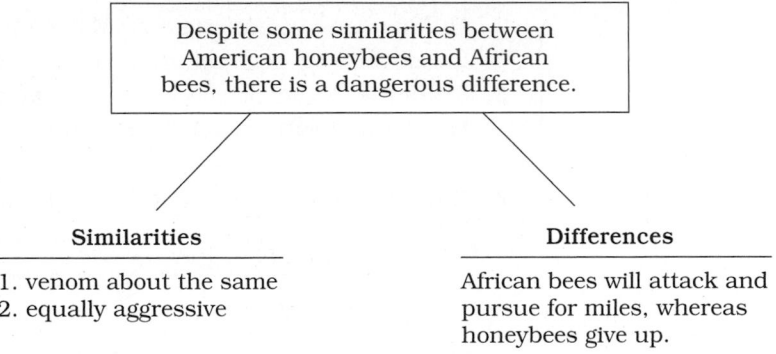

| Despite some similarities between American honeybees and African bees, there is a dangerous difference. |

Similarities

1. venom about the same
2. equally aggressive

Differences

African bees will attack and pursue for miles, whereas honeybees give up.

Reading Tip

Make sure you know what main idea is developed by the description of differences and similarities.

EXERCISE 4 Understanding Comparison and Contrast Patterns

DIRECTIONS When you finish reading each paragraph, circle the appropriate letter to indicate whether the author has (1) compared two topics, (2) contrasted two topics, or (3) compared *and* contrasted two topics. Circle all comparison and contrast transitions, and use the blank lines to take notes on the paragraph.

EXAMPLE Between 1890 and 1900, millions of people from southern and eastern Europe left their homes in search of the American dream. The new immigrants hoped to find a comfortable place where they could settle and live out their lives. (But) the cities to which they came were not prepared for the new arrivals, and many immigrant families ended up in ugly apartments that were poorly supplied with light, heat, and water. The new arrivals had dreamed of finding work that could make them independent, even rich. (Instead,) they found that jobs were scarce. Immigrants often had to take jobs for which they were unsuited, and the work left them exhausted and depressed. (Moreover,) many found that they were treated as outsiders, and their accents were subject to insults or ridicule.

In this paragraph, the author

a. compares two topics.

(b.) contrasts two topics.

c. compares and contrasts two topics.

Main Idea Immigrants who came in search of the American dream between 1890 and 1900 were terribly disappointed.

Supporting Details 1. Instead of comfortable place to live, had to settle for ugly apartments with little light, heat, or water.

2. Instead of suitable jobs, found unemployment or exhausting, depressing work.

3. Instead of warm welcome, treated as outsiders with odd customs and odd way of speaking.

EXPLANATION The paragraph contrasts what immigrants hoped to find in their new country with what they actually found. Each difference reinforces the implied main idea: "Immigrants who came in search of the American dream, between 1890 and 1900, were terribly disappointed."

1. The ancient Greek philosophers Plato and Aristotle differed widely in their worldviews. Plato, the mystic, was a believer in intuition rather than reason. For him, nature was only a dark reflection of a higher, more spiritual world revealed in occasional flashes of insight. Aristotle, on the other hand, was a firm believer in logic and hard evidence. Unlike Plato, he believed that truth could be found through the observation of nature. Yet despite their basic differences, the two had a similarly negative effect on scientific progress during the Middle Ages and early Renaissance. Thanks to their teaching, the scientific understanding of astronomy and physics slowed to a standstill. Insisting that all motion was in perfect circles completed at a uniform speed, both Plato and Aristotle delayed the recognition of what the astronomer Johannes Kepler proved in the seventeenth century: Kepler demonstrated that the planets moved in oval rather than circular orbits. Kepler's discoveries laid the groundwork for the laws of motion later discovered by Isaac Newton. Yet both Kepler's description of the planets and Newton's laws of motion might have come a good deal sooner had the ideas of Plato and Aristotle not been influential for so many centuries.

In this paragraph, the author

a. compares two topics.

b. contrasts two topics

c. compares and contrasts two topics.

Main Idea _____

_____

Supporting _____
Details
_____

_____

_____

_____

_____

_____

_____

_____

2. Gerald Ford, the thirty-eighth president of the United States, was fond of alluding* to one of his predecessors, Harry S. Truman. Ford used the allusions to emphasize what he believed were similarities between himself and Truman. A less than charismatic president, Ford seemed to think that likening himself to Truman would increase his hold on the public's imagination. Like Ford, Truman had been a vice president who became president only by chance. Truman took over when Franklin Roosevelt died in office, a circumstance that resembled Ford's own ascent* to the presidency when Richard Nixon resigned from office. Neither Truman nor Ford was an intellectual, and both men tended to exaggerate their lack of learning, insisting that they were just simple men with simple tastes. Ford also liked to emphasize that both he and Truman came

_____
*alluding: referring, mentioning.
*ascent: climb.

to office at a difficult time. Truman led the nation during the final months of World War II, and Ford entered office in the wake of the Watergate scandal that destroyed Nixon's career.

In this paragraph, the author

a. compares two topics.

b. contrasts two topics.

c. compares and contrasts two topics.

Main Idea _____

_____

Supporting _____
Details
_____

_____

_____

_____

_____

_____

3. Laws and ethics are not quite the same. In general, laws are society's attempt to formalize—reduce to written rules—the general public's ideas about what is considered right and wrong conduct in various spheres of life. However, it is rarely possible for written laws to capture all of the subtle shadings that people include in the codes of ethics they use to govern their lives. Ethical concepts, or moral principles—like the people who believe in them—are more complex than written rules of law. Ethical concepts are ideas about right or moral conduct, and they cannot always be expressed in the formal language of law or in rules. (Adapted from William C. Frederick et al., *Business and Society.* New York: McGraw-Hill, 1992, p. 68.)

In this paragraph, the author

a. compares two topics.

b. contrasts two topics.

c. compares and contrasts two topics.

Main Idea _____

_____

Supporting _____
Details
_____

_____

_____

_____

_____

4. To some degree, all societies are altered by time. But for Nigerian society, the changes between life in early-nineteenth-century Nigeria and now are especially striking. Most notable is the shift in economic and political power, which was originally in the hands of local leaders who governed Nigeria's twenty-three individual states. Currently, power is concentrated in the hands of a small group of business and military leaders. While local leaders in the early nineteenth century often waged war in pursuit of expanding their territory or province,* modern tribal leaders exert influence through behind-the-scenes political wheeling and dealing rather than military conquest. Although the power and influence of local leaders has been dramatically curtailed by the arrival of democratic traditions, one thing has not altered. Community leaders are still regarded as the custodians of past tradition and are seen as the final word on questions about what it means to be a Nigerian in moral or ethical terms. Another area where dramatic change has occurred is in the conduct of courtship. In the past, there was no such thing as dating. If a couple was seen together in public, they were expected to marry. City couples, at least, are now free to date without expectations of marriage. In the countryside, however, courtship rules are somewhat stricter, and dating as we know it is not encouraged.

_____

*province: area governed as a unit of a country or an empire; area of knowledge or interest.

In this paragraph, the author

a. compares two topics.

b. contrasts two topics.

c. compares and contrasts two topics.

Main Idea _____

_____

Supporting _____
Details
_____

_____

_____

_____

_____

_____

_____

Pattern 4: Cause and Effect

Whatever type of reading you do, you are bound to run across passages that explain how one event—the **cause**—leads to or produces another event—the **effect**. Look, for example, at the following paragraph:

> Fear has a profound effect on the human body. When you become frightened, you breathe more deeply, thereby sending your muscles more oxygen and energy. *Consequently*, your heart beats faster, making your blood circulate more quickly and thereby rushing oxygen to all parts of your body. *In response* to fear, your stomach and intestines stop contracting and all digestive activity ceases. Your saliva also stops flowing, causing your mouth to become dry. Fear also causes the body's blood vessels to shrink, making your face lose its natural color.

In this paragraph, the topic sentence identifies the cause and effect relationship under discussion: Fear has a profound effect on the human body. The supporting details then describe those effects more specifically. Note, too, that some details also describe *cycles of causes and effects* in which one effect turns into the cause of another. Fear, for example, causes your blood vessels to shrink, which, in turn, produces another effect—your face loses color. If diagrammed, the relationships among these statements would look like this:

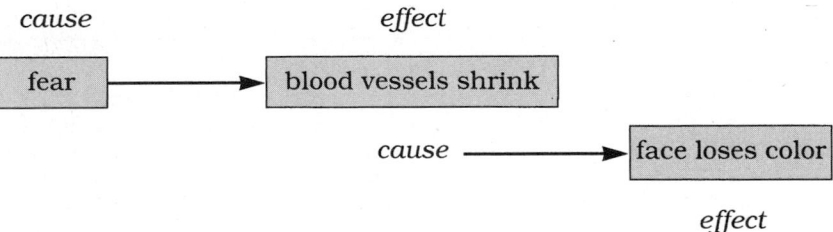

Transitions

As the italicized transitions in the paragraph on page 461 suggest, transitions are often clues to the cause and effect pattern. Should you see any of the following in a paragraph, there's a good chance that the cause and effect pattern is at work.

Cause and Effect Transitions		
As a result	For this reason	In response to
As a side effect	Hence	Thanks to
Consequently	In the aftermath of	Therefore
Due to	In consequence	Thus

Cause and Effect Verbs

In addition to the above transitions, watch for the following verbs. They, too, are clues to the cause and effect pattern. Like the transitions, they can also help you sort out the individual causes and effects mentioned in a paragraph.

Verbs Frequently Used to Link Cause and Effect		
Affect	End	Result
Begin	Foster	Revolutionize
Bring about	Generate	Set in motion
Cause	Halt	Set off
Change	Increase	Spur
Contribute	Induce	Start
Create	Introduce	Stimulate
Decrease	Lead to	Stop
Encourage	Produce	Trigger

Typical Topic Sentences

Topic sentences like those listed below all suggest a cause and effect pattern.

1. General Alfredo Stroessner took control of Paraguay in 1954 and turned the country into a haven for international outlaws.
2. Artist Andy Warhol's paintings of ordinary objects like the Campbell's soup can revolutionized modern art.
3. In the eighties and nineties, rock star Madonna profoundly affected the image of women in pop music.
4. File sharing among music fans poses a major threat to the recording industry.
5. At least three factors have contributed to the decline in union membership.

If you encounter a topic sentence that says one event led to or caused another, you are undoubtedly dealing with a cause and effect pattern.

Taking Notes on Cause and Effect Patterns

As you might expect, cycles of causes and effects such as the one illustrated on page 461 should be included in your notes along with the following:

> **1.** The general cause and effect relationship described by the topic sentence.
> **2.** The specific causes and/or effects mentioned in the paragraph.

For an illustration, look at the following sample notes:

Main Idea Fear has a powerful effect on the human body.

Supporting **1.** Breathe more deeply, sending muscles more oxygen and energy.
Details **2.** Heart beats faster, making blood circulate more rapidly.

  a. Blood rushes oxygen to all parts of body.

3. Stomach and intestines stop contractions so that all digestion ceases.

4. Saliva stops flowing and mouth gets dry.

5. Blood vessels shrink.

  a. Causes face to lose color.

Note-Taking Tip

When taking notes on a cause and effect passage, consider using a graphic organizer like the diagram shown on page 462.

EXERCISE 5   Understanding Cause and Effect Patterns

DIRECTIONS Read each paragraph. Circle the cause and effect transitions. Then take notes on each pattern.

EXAMPLE No one would deny that several events led to America's Revolutionary War. But one of the most important was the introduction of the Coercive* or Intolerable Acts. The Coercive Acts, which were designed to punish Americans for the Boston Tea Party,* treated Bostonians with great severity. The Port of Boston was closed until the tea that had been destroyed was paid for. In addition, any English officials accused of committing murder in the course of suppressing a riot or enforcing the law could no longer be tried in the colony where

---

*coercive: forcing someone to do something against his or her will.
*Boston Tea Party: In 1773, Bostonians angry over British taxes on tea hurled 342 chests of English tea into the ocean.

the incident had taken place. Moreover, Massachusetts officials would no longer be locally elected; instead, they had to be appointed by the king. Perhaps most offensive to the Americans was the new Quartering Act. It specified that British troops could be housed in all inns or homes even without the owners' permission. As a result of the Coercive Acts, many Americans who had been undecided about rebellion became committed to the idea of throwing off British rule.

Main Idea   *The Coercive Acts played a key role in America's decision to rebel against the British.*

Supporting Details   *1. Port of Boston closed until tea was paid for.*

2. English officials who committed murder while putting down a riot or enforcing the law tried outside of the colony where murder had occurred.

3. Massachusetts officials had to be appointed by king rather than locally elected.

4. Most offensive was the Quartering Act, which said that British troops could be housed in inns and homes without owners' permission.

EXPLANATION This paragraph tells readers that Americans fought the Revolutionary War, in part at least, because of the hated Coercive Acts. The major details describe the acts so that readers understand the source of the hatred.

1. In his book *The Bounty of the Sea*, Jacques Cousteau, the underwater explorer, writer, and filmmaker, painted a terrifying portrait of what will happen if, in his words, we let the ocean "sicken and die" from pollution. From Cousteau's point of view, the death of the ocean, or extinction of sea life, will have terrifying consequences for all of humanity. Without sea life, the ocean would become a rotting grave. Billions of decaying bodies would create a stench* that would make its way into coastal regions. Consequently, people would have

---

*stench: smell, stink.

to abandon their homes to escape the smell. In addition, the death-filled seas would no longer be able to maintain a balance between the gases that make life possible. The carbon dioxide in the atmosphere would increase, trapping the heat that normally radiates outward from Earth into space. As a result, temperatures at sea level would dramatically increase. Yet another consequence would be visible on the ocean's surface. It would be covered with a thick film of decayed matter. Thus, the ocean would no longer give water to the skies through evaporation. Rain would be a rarity. Drought would range* over the land, and multitudes would starve.

Main Idea _____

_____

Supporting _____
Details
_____

_____

_____

_____

_____

_____

_____

2. There are at least two different, though occasionally overlapping, reasons why people decide to join groups. In some cases, the group's activities offer a chance to fulfill civic* or religious obligations we consider valuable. Thus, a person concerned about the plight of the homeless might decide to become part of a community soup kitchen to fulfill her sense of social responsibility. Then, too, we frequently join groups because we care more about the group's members than we do about the group's goals. For example, a person might decide to join a bowling group even if he's not all that fond of bowling. The appeal here is a chance to get together with friends—not the dream of winning a bowling tournament.

_____

*range: move about, travel.
*civic: relating to the city or citizenship.

Main Idea _____

_____

Supporting _____
Details

_____

_____

_____

_____

_____

_____

3. By the 1830s and 1840s, the growth of cities and the increase in literacy* had dramatically changed the face of American newspapers. Initially, newspapers had been written primarily for the well-to-do who wanted news about the arts, social events, and commerce.* But thanks to the growing urban landscape and the increase in the reading public, papers like the New York *Sun* started a trend toward cheap, mass-produced newspapers. The new "penny press," as it was called, broadened the range of topics covered in newspapers, telling of everyday events, sensational crimes, gossip, sports, and human-interest stories. By the 1890s, some penny papers had more than a million readers.

Main Idea _____

_____

Supporting _____
Details

_____

_____

_____

_____

_____

*literacy: ability to read and write.
*commerce: trade.

_____

_____

_____

4. The causes for the dinosaurs' extinction remain one of science's great mysteries. Although there are several theories as to why the dinosaurs disappeared, only one seems truly sound. According to this theory, dinosaurs became extinct because a comet or an asteroid crashed into Earth, producing huge quantities of dust. As a result, clouds of dust blocked out sunlight for many months, and plants dependent on photosynthesis* for survival died out. Thus, the dinosaurs, who lived mainly on vegetation, were left without much food. The absence of sunlight would have also caused temperatures to drop sharply, subjecting the dinosaur to twin forces of destruction—freezing and starvation.

Main Idea _____

_____

Supporting _____
Details
_____

_____

_____

_____

_____

Pattern 5: Classification

When authors use the **classification** pattern, they begin by explaining how some larger group can be broken down or divided into smaller subgroups or categories. Then they describe each category

_____

*photosynthesis: process conducted by plants during which they utilize the sun's energy to convert carbon dioxide and water into food.

in specific detail. For example, in the following paragraph, the authors classify voting methods in the House of Representatives.

> Members of the House of Representatives may vote in four different ways. The most common method is the *voice vote*. Members in favor of a bill say "yea," while those opposed say "nay." The Speaker of the House then judges which side has the most voice votes and announces the result. If any member feels that the Speaker is mistaken, the Speaker can be forced to call for a *standing vote* in which the members stand to be counted for or against. A third method is the *teller vote*. If one-fifth of the members present demand, all the members of the House pass between "tellers" and are counted as they do so, first those in favor and then those opposed. The *roll call* is the procedure used for important measures. The Clerk of the House calls the roll, and each of the members responds by answering "yea" or "nay." Roll-call voting takes about forty-five minutes. (Adapted from Shick and Pfister, *American Government: Continuity and Change*, p. 29.)

As is typical of the classification pattern, the authors open by telling their readers two things: (1) the larger group to be subdivided and (2) the number of categories produced by classification. They then proceed to describe each category in more specific detail.

Typical Topic Sentences

Topic sentences like those listed here practically guarantee that the classification pattern organizes the paragraph.

---

1. Scientific experiments fall into four different categories.
2. Bestsellers can be divided into three types.
3. Researchers in interpersonal communication have come up with four kinds of conversations.
4. The Indian caste system once assigned human beings to four different groups, with Brahmans at the top of the heap and the untouchables at the bottom.

If a topic sentence announces that some larger group can be divided into separate categories or groups, you should prepare to take notes on the classification pattern.

Frequently Used Words in Classification Topic Sentences			
Categories	Groups	Elements	Types
Components	Parts	Features	Kinds
Fields	Factors	Problems	Classes
Ranks			

Telltale Visual Aids

Tables like the one below frequently signal the presence of the classification pattern. Keep in mind, though, that you can also use them to review (just cover the right-hand side and see what you can remember about each classification category) or as a model for note-taking.

Table: The Four Basic Components of a Strategy

Scope	• Identifies the markets or industries in which firm will compete
Resource Deployment	• Indicates how company will allocate or use resources
Competitive Advantage	• Specifies what advantages a firm has relative to competitors
Synergy	• Reflects extent to which businesses inside the firm can draw upon one another

(Source of Information: VanFleet and Peterson, *Contemporary Management*, pp. 73–74.)

Taking Notes on the Classification Pattern

To be complete, notes on the classification pattern require the following information:

1. The name of the larger group being broken down into subgroups
2. The names of the categories if they are supplied
3. A brief description of each category

Here to illustrate are notes on the paragraph on page 469:

Main Idea Members of the House have four different ways to vote.

Supporting Details

1. "Voice vote." Members voting in favor say "yea," those opposed say "nay," and the Speaker judges who has the stronger voice.

2. "Standing vote." If someone thinks the Speaker is mistaken, then members must stand to be counted.

3. "Teller vote." If 1/5 of all present members demand, members must be counted as they walk between tellers.

4. "Roll call." Used for really important measures; the House clerk calls the roll and each member responds "yea" or "nay."

Note-Taking Tip

✔

If names of categories do appear in the classification paragraph, put those names first in your notes. This note-taking format nicely highlights the individual categories. However, you should also be aware that the subgroups in this pattern are not always named.

 EXERCISE 6 **Understanding Classification Patterns**

DIRECTIONS Read and take notes on each paragraph.

EXAMPLE Psychological problems are generally classified into two categories: externalizing disorders and internalizing disorders. The **externalizing disorders** are characterized by aggression diverted outward, such as striking out at other people or the environment. People suffering from these kinds of disorders exhibit behaviors such as lying, stealing, disobedience, and delinquency. Other common symptoms of externalizing disorders include fighting, cruelty to animals, property destruction, temper tantrums, hostility toward authority figures, and violating the rights of others. The **internalizing disorders** are directed inward. These affect the individual rather than other people or the environment. These disorders include anxiety, depression, worrying, withdrawal, phobias, and panic attacks. (Source of information: Kaplan, *Adolescence*, pp. 463–464.)

Main Idea Psychological problems are generally divided into two groups:

externalizing disorders and internalizing disorders.

Supporting Details

1. Externalizing disorders are directed toward others or the

environment.

a. Include lying, stealing, disobedience, and delinquency.

b. Also include violence, fighting, animal cruelty, property damage, temper tantrums, hostility, and violation of others' rights.

2. Internalizing disorders are directed inward, toward self.

a. Include anxiety, depression, worrying, withdrawal, phobias, and panic attacks.

EXPLANATION As you can see, the notes contain the essential elements of the classification pattern. The larger group is divided into two smaller categories, and the names and characteristics of each group are listed.

1. In the human body, blood circulates through elastic, tubelike canals called *blood vessels.* Consisting of three different types, blood vessels are well adapted to their functions. The vessels called *arteries* carry blood away from the heart to all parts of the body. The largest artery in the human body is the *aorta.* Arterial blood appears bright red because it is filled with oxygen. In contrast, blood in the *veins,* another type of blood vessel, appears purplish because it is no longer carrying a supply of oxygen. Veins, which carry blood back to the heart, contain small valves that prevent the blood from flowing backward. This is important in the lower parts of the body where the blood has to move against the pull of gravity. The third type of blood vessel is the *capillary.* Capillaries are tiny vessels connecting arteries and veins. Capillary walls are extremely thin. They have to be thin so that digested food can pass through them to the cells of the body.

Main Idea _____

_____

Supporting _____
Details
_____

_____

_____

_____

_____

_____

_____

_____

_____

2. Studies indicate that learning can be divided into two categories: incidental learning and intentional learning. *Incidental learning* takes place by chance; there is no clearly defined intention to learn. For example, a student wanting to check if he knows the first sixteen presidents of the United States may ask a friend to listen while they are named. During the recitation, the friend may, by chance, also learn the names of the first sixteen presidents. *Intentional learning* occurs when a clearly defined purpose exists from the very beginning. For example, a student may sit down with a list of the fifty states and their capitals because she needs to learn them for a test. Current research suggests that intentional learning is more effective because it stays with us over time.

Main Idea _____

_____

Supporting _____
Details

_____

_____

_____

_____

_____

3. In management, the phrase "downward communication" refers to messages from superiors to subordinates. According to D. Katz and R. Kahn, authors of the text *The Social Psychology of Organizations*, there are five different types of downward communication in organizations. (1) **Job instructions** are messages that specify how tasks should be conducted: "Always submit budget requests two months in advance." (2) **Job rationale** messages explain why tasks must be performed and how they relate to other activities of the organization: "We require advance notice so that we can plan ahead." (3) **Procedures and practices** messages inform members about organizational responsibilities, obligations, and privileges: "According to the procedures manual, we follow affirmative action* guidelines to the letter." (4) **Feedback** messages inform employees of their performance in the organization: "I am happy to note that your last project was a real success." (5) **Instruction about goals** messages teach employees the mission, goals, and objectives of the organization: "As you can see from our shared-values list, we feel that customer service is our number-one job." Downward communication may seem simple and clear-cut on the surface, but it is a complicated process that doesn't always go smoothly. (Adapted from O'Hair, Friedrich, and Shaver, *Strategic Communication*, p. 58.)

Main Idea _____

_____

Supporting _____
Details

_____

_____

_____

_____

_____

_____

_____

4. The sociologist Max Weber (1864–1920) classified authority into three major types. **Traditional authority** is authority based on custom and accepted practice. In England, for example, the authority to be the head of government is traditionally a birthright. The person who becomes the king or queen does so because a parent or

_____

*affirmative action: term for a variety of efforts to ensure employment opportunities for women and minorities.

some other ancestor reigned before. **Charismatic authority** stems from the personality or personal appeal of the individual. Salvador Allende,* Martin Luther King Jr., and Princess Diana are examples of people whose power stemmed partly or wholly from their *charisma.* **Legal-rational authority** comes from rules or laws created to make institutions function effectively. Elected government officials hold this type of authority. Neatly divided as Weber's categories are, however, it should be pointed out here that all three types of authority are present in most societies, and they do occasionally overlap. (Adapted from Poponoe, *Sociology,* pp. 436–437.)

Main Idea _____

_____

Supporting _____
Details
_____

_____

_____

_____

_____

_____

_____

_____

_____

_____

 ## Identifying the "Primary" Pattern

Until now, you've been working with one organizational pattern at a time. But from now on you'll be asked to select one particular pattern among several possibilities. You need to be aware that, at this

_____

*Salvador Allende (1908–1973): The first democratically elected Marxist head of government, he ruled Chile between 1970 and 1973.

point, you are being asked to identify the *primary* pattern. The primary pattern organizes all or *most* of the details. If, for instance, a paragraph describes a cause and effect relationship for six of seven sentences and sentence seven makes a comparison, the primary pattern—and the correct answer—is cause and effect, not comparison and contrast.

◄■ EXERCISE 7 Recognizing Primary Patterns of Organization

DIRECTIONS Identify the primary organizational pattern for each paragraph by circling the appropriate letter.

EXAMPLE With the arrival of twentieth-century technology, medical professionals were able to think seriously about creating artificial replacements for damaged human hearts that no longer functioned effectively. In 1957, Dr. Willem Kolff created the first artificial heart and implanted it in a dog, who promptly died from the experiment. Still, animal research continued, and, in 1969, Dr. Denton Cooley implanted the first artificial heart into the body of a human. The device, made largely of plastic, only had to function for a brief period of time, while the patient awaited a transplanted human heart. In 1979, Dr. Robert Jarvik patented the first artificial heart. Three years later, the Jarvik heart, as it came to be called, was implanted in the body of Barney Clark, a retired dentist dying of heart disease. Clark lived for 112 days after the surgery, and his survival raised hopes for the future success of artificial hearts. But, by 1985, it was clear that artificial-heart patients were prone to fatal strokes and infections. Still, to this day, researchers—among them Robert Jarvik—are convinced that artificial heart transplants will one day be successful.

a. definition
b. time order: dates and events
c. time order: process
d. comparison and contrast
e. cause and effect
f. classification

EXPLANATION Because the paragraph is heavily laced with dates marking major events, time order: dates and events is the primary pattern.

1. A **generic product** (sometimes called a **generic brand**) is a product with no brand name at all. Its plain package carries only the name of the product—applesauce, peanut butter, potato chips, or whatever—in black type. Generic products, available in supermarkets since 1977, usually are made by the major producers that manufacture name brands. They appeal mainly to consumers who are willing to sacrifice consistency in size or quality for a lower price. However, generic products are not necessarily lower in quality. Even though generic brands may have accounted for as much as 10 percent of all grocery sales several years ago, they currently represent less than 1 percent. (Pride et al., *Business*, p. 403.)

   a. definition

   b. time order: dates and events

   c. time order: process

   d. comparison and contrast

   e. cause and effect

   f. classification

2. The painting known as the *Mona Lisa* has fascinated art lovers for centuries. But it wasn't until the twentieth century that one man fell so in love with the *Mona Lisa* that he decided to steal her from the Louvre.* In 1909, Italian-born Vincenzo Peruggia was employed by the Louvre to do some painting; it was at this point that Peruggia first got a look at the masterpiece that was to get him into so much trouble. On August 21, 1911, Peruggia returned to the Louvre as a visitor and headed straight for the *Mona Lisa*. Twenty minutes later, he left the museum with the painting tucked inside his jacket. For more than two years, investigators hunted unsuccessfully for the painting. Then, on November 29, 1913, a wealthy Italian art dealer received a letter saying the *Mona Lisa* would be returned for a price. On December 10, 1913, the art dealer arranged to meet with the painting's new owner. After Peruggia produced the painting, police took him into custody. At his trial in 1914, Peruggia explained that he had stolen the *Mona Lisa* because he couldn't forget her smile.

---

*Louvre: a famous museum in Paris.

The unsympathetic judge sentenced the would-be art collector to three years in jail.

a. definition

b. time order: dates and events

c. time order: process

d. comparison and contrast

e. cause and effect

f. classification

3. Child psychologists are inclined to divide aggressive behavior into two kinds, *overt* and *relational* aggression. Overt aggression harms others through actual physical damage or the threat of physical harm. Children who engage in overt aggression are likely to push, hit, or kick a peer. At the very least, those who are overtly aggressive will make explicit threats to do some kind of physical harm in the future. Relational aggression is more psychological than physical and it revolves around threats to or criticism of peer relations. Children who use relational aggression, for example, may taunt a peer by saying that he or she is unlikable and has no friends. At one time, parents and educators focused on strategies to avoid overt aggression among children, because this kind of aggression seemed the more harmful of the two. But research has shown that children also suffer from being the target of relational aggression.

a. definition

b. time order: dates and events

c. time order: process

d. comparison and contrast

e. cause and effect

f. classification

4. The term **alluvial deposits** refers to layers of broken rocky matter formed from material that has been carried by the waves of a river or stream and dropped when the current's speed lessened. River plains and deltas consist of alluvial deposits. The elements that make up alluvial deposits can range widely in size, from chunks of boulders, to small pebbles, to grains of sand. A large portion of the world's richest farmland is located on top of alluvial deposits, which can also be the source of minerals such as gold or tin. These mineral deposits are called "placer deposits." (Source of information: *Scientific American Desk Reference*, 1999, p. 289.)

a. definition

b. time order: dates and events

c. time order: process

d. comparison and contrast

e. cause and effect

f. classification

5. When Elvis Presley, the acknowledged king of rock-and-roll, died, he was horribly overweight, addicted to countless drugs, and subject to fits of uncontrollable rage. Exactly what caused Elvis to degenerate so terribly is still unknown; in fact, there seems to have been a complicated variety of causes. Throughout his career, Presley longed to be considered a serious actor, but all his movies were critical disasters. Films such as *Blue Hawaii* earned money yet never earned the critics' praise. Devoted to his mother, who protected him throughout his childhood and youth, he was grief stricken over her death in 1958 and never quite recovered from her loss. Oddly enough, although he never complained, Elvis's spirit seems to have been broken by his highly publicized stint* in the army. On his return to civilian life, his music seemed to have lost its original spark. Yet, despite the failure of Elvis's later years, many of his fans have remained faithful. Even today, they flock to Graceland, the mansion in which he lived and died.

a. definition

b. time order: dates and events

c. time order: process

d. comparison and contrast

e. cause and effect

f. classification

6. The human brain has two hemispheres—the right and the left. Although the hemispheres cooperate for many functions, research suggests that they control highly different activities. Thanks to the left side of our brain, we are able to master and manipulate language, using it to communicate our thoughts. The left side of our brain helps us make sense by giving order and logic to our utterances.* The right hemisphere is less crucial to language production and appears to be more concerned with the

---

*stint: period of time.
*utterances: verbal statements.

creation of images. Research suggests that the right brain dominates during infancy. Babies make sense of the world by visualizing, rather than naming, and visualization is controlled by the right side of the brain.

a. definition

b. time order: dates and events

c. time order: process

d. comparison and contrast

e. cause and effect

f. classification

7. Adolescent rape victims seem to have more subsequent behavior problems than do other victims. This is probably because the adolescent experiences the attack at the time when she is trying to develop a sense of self. Immediate reactions to rape can include loss of self-trust, turning away from friends, retreating to the protection of the family, and avoiding social activities. Long-term reactions include anxiety, sleep disturbances, and abnormal fears. (Adapted from Greenberg et al., *Sexuality*, p. 513.)

a. definition

b. time order: dates and events

c. time order: process

d. comparison and contrast

e. cause and effect

f. classification

8. An attacker has put you in a wristlock to force you to submit. He has grabbed your wrist, pressing hard on the bones and nerves to cause you pain. If you try to pull away, you cause yourself more pain, and you could actually break your own wrist in an attempt to escape. However, if you remember a simple self-defense technique, you can free yourself. First, fight your instinct to tighten the muscles in your hands and arms. Doing so will actually cause you more pain because the tension will exert more pressure. If you are in pain, you cannot strike out to free yourself from your opponent. Second, let your hand and wrist relax and go limp. This will lessen the pain you're experiencing long enough for you to punch, kick, or bite your attacker to force him to let you go. Relaxing your hand may also surprise him, causing him to loosen his grip for a

moment. Third, the thumb is the weakest link in a person's grip, so rotate your arm and pull your hand toward your attacker's thumb for the best chance of breaking free.

a. definition

b. time order: dates and events

c. time order: process

d. comparison and contrast

e. cause and effect

f. classification

9. The death of a spouse is bound to be a painful emotional experience for the surviving mate, but it appears that men have a harder time adjusting to widowhood than women do. True, both sexes suffer a profound sense of shock, and both must survive long periods of loneliness and painful adjustment. But men seem to have a harder time handling household chores like laundry, shopping, and food preparation. They also have more difficulty maintaining the circle of friends that was once part of their married life. Often, it was the wife who kept up the couple's social network. With her death, the husband must learn a whole new set of social skills.

a. definition

b. time order: dates and events

c. time order: process

d. comparison and contrast

e. cause and effect

f. classification

10. Samuel Gompers was born in London in 1850. After only four years of elementary school, he was apprenticed to a cigar maker and learned the trade that he followed for more than a quarter of a century. But it was as a labor leader rather than a cigar maker that Samuel Gompers made his mark on history. Gompers moved to America with his family in 1863. The next year, he became a member of the Cigar Makers' International Union. Young as he was, he took an immediate interest in the union's progress and began speaking at local meetings. The hard times of the 1870s only strengthened Gompers' belief in the importance of unions, and he became even more active. Elected president of the local union in

1874, he was ousted* from that position by the socialist* opposition in 1880. But this defeat left him free to take a prominent role in founding the Federation of Organized Trades and Labor Unions, established in 1881 to influence legislation on behalf of labor. When the American Federation of Labor (AFL) was created in 1886, Gompers was elected president. Until his death in 1924, Gompers was repeatedly reelected as president of the AFL.

a. definition

b. time order: dates and events

c. time order: process

d. comparison and contrast

e. cause and effect

f. classification

---

*ousted: removed.
*socialist: a person who believes that the means of production in a society should be owned by a large group rather than an individual.

■ DIGGING DEEPER

TYPES OF LOVE

LOOKING AHEAD You probably know that the way a person loves a dog or cat is quite different from the way he or she loves a parent or spouse. But did it ever occur to you that there might actually be six different kinds of love?

1. Although there are many theories about love, one in particular has captured the attention of researchers in interpersonal communication. According to this theory, there are actually six different kinds of love.

Eros: Beauty and Sexuality

2. Like Narcissus, who fell in love with the beauty of his own image, the erotic lover focuses on beauty and physical attractiveness, sometimes to the exclusion of qualities you might consider more important and more lasting. Also like Narcissus, the erotic lover has an idealized image of beauty that is unattainable in reality. Consequently, the erotic lover often feels unfulfilled. Not surprisingly, erotic lovers are particularly sensitive to physical imperfections in the ones they love.

Ludus: Entertainment and Excitement

3. Ludus love is experienced as a game, as fun. The better he or she can play the game, the greater the enjoyment. Love is not to be taken too seriously; emotions are to be held in check lest they get out of hand and make trouble; passions never rise to the point where they get out of control. A ludic lover is self-controlled, always aware of the need to manage love rather than allow it to be in control. Perhaps because of this need to control love, some researchers have proposed that ludic love tendencies may reveal tendencies to sexual aggression (Sarwer, Kalichman, Johnson, Early, et al. 1993). Not surprisingly, the ludic lover retains a partner only as long as the partner is interesting and amusing. When interest fades, it's time to change partners. Perhaps because love is a game, sexual fidelity is of little importance. In fact, recent research shows that people who score high on ludic love are more likely to engage in "extradyadic" dating and sex than those who score lower (Wiederman and Hurd 1999).

Storge: Peaceful and Slow

4 Storge love lacks passion and intensity. Storgic lovers don't set out to find lovers but to establish a companionable relationship with someone they know and with whom they can share interests and activities. Storgic love is a gradual process of unfolding thoughts and feelings; the changes seem to come so slowly and so gradually that it's often difficult to define exactly where the relationship is at any point in time. Sex in storgic relationships comes late, and when it comes, it assumes no great importance.

Pragma: Practical and Traditional

5 The pragma lover is practical and seeks a relationship that will work. Pragma lovers want compatibility and a relationship in which their important needs and desires will be satisfied. They're concerned with the social qualifications of a potential mate even more than with personal qualities; family and background are extremely important to the pragma lover, who relies not so much on feelings as on logic. The pragma lover views love as a useful relationship, one that makes the rest of life easier. So the pragma lover asks such questions of a potential mate as "Will this person earn a good living?" "Can this person cook?" "Will this person help me advance in my career?" Pragma lovers' relationships rarely deteriorate. This is partly because pragma lovers choose their mates carefully and emphasize similarities. Another reason is that they have realistic romantic expectations.

Mania: Elation and Depression

6 Mania is characterized by extreme highs and extreme lows. The manic lover loves intensely and at the same time intensely worries about the loss of the love. This fear often prevents the manic lover from deriving as much pleasure as possible from the relationship. With little provocation, the manic lover may experience extreme jealousy. Manic love is obsessive; the manic lover has to possess the beloved completely. In return, the manic lover wishes to be possessed, to be loved intensely. The manic lover's poor self-image seems capable of being improved only by love; self-worth comes from being loved rather than from any sense of inner satisfaction. Because love is so important, danger signs in a relationship are often ignored; the manic lover believes that if there is love, then nothing else matters.

Agape: Compassionate and Selfless

7 Agape is a compassionate, egoless, self-giving love. The agapic lover loves even people with whom he or she has no close ties. This lover

loves the stranger on the road even though they will probably never meet again. Agape is a spiritual love, offered without concern for personal reward or gain. This lover loves without expecting that the love will be reciprocated. Jesus, Buddha, and Gandhi practiced and preached this unqualified love, agape (Lee 1976). In one sense, agape is more a philosophical kind of love than most people have the strength to achieve. (Joseph A. DeVito, *The Interpersonal Communication Book.* New York: Addison Wesley Longman, 2001, pp. 343–345.)

Sharpening Your Skills

DIRECTIONS Answer the following questions by circling the letter of the correct response or filling in the blanks.

1. Which statement best expresses the main idea of the entire reading?
   a. Unlike erotic love, storge love is gradual and not particularly intense.
   b. Most people do not realize that there are six different kinds of love.
   c. Experts in interpersonal communication generally embrace the notion that there are six different kinds of love.
   d. Although there are six different kinds of love, only erotic love gets much attention from researchers involved in interpersonal communication.

2. What's the primary pattern of this reading?

   _____

3. What's the main idea of paragraph 4?
   a. Storge love is based on companionship.
   b. Storge love does not involve sex.
   c. Storge love is not as lasting as erotic love.
   d. Storge lovers are usually middle aged.

4. What's the main idea of paragraph 6?
   a. The manic lover is never happy even when loved in return.
   b. Manic lovers make the lives of those they love utterly miserable.
   c. Manic lovers are psychologically unbalanced.
   d. Manic lovers love with great passion and are always anxious about losing those they love.

5. In the last sentence of paragraph 5, the author says, "Another reason is that they have realistic romantic expectations." To make sense of that statement, readers need to infer that *they* refers to

_____ and the expectations are about

_____.

INTERNET RESOURCE

For more practice with organizational patterns, see **college.hmco.com/pic/flemmingRFR10e**, where you will find three levels of interactive quizzes: *Getting Down the Basics, Checking Your Progress,* and *Taking the Challenge.* You can also find additional interactive practice with organizational patterns at **laflemm.com**, *Reading for Results*: Online Practice for Chapter 8.

Test 1: Predicting Patterns

DIRECTIONS Read each topic sentence. Then circle the letter of the most likely pattern of organization.

1. Writers Norman Mailer and James Baldwin both knew success early in their careers; however, Baldwin chose to break new literary ground in his later work, whereas Mailer returned to his original themes again and again.

   a. definition

   b. time order: dates and events

   c. time order: process

   d. comparison and contrast

   e. cause and effect

   f. classification

2. Now that telephone companies are offering high-speed Internet access, the increase in services may be one reason why consumer complaints about telephone companies are also increasing.

   a. definition

   b. time order: dates and events

   c. time order: process

   d. comparison and contrast

   e. cause and effect

   f. classification

3. **Ethics**, one of the five classical fields of philosophical inquiry, refers to the study of moral principles and behavior.

   a. definition

   b. time order: dates and events

   c. time order: process

   d. comparison and contrast

   e. cause and effect

   f. classification

4. In his famous book *Childhood and Society,* Erik Erikson outlined eight stages of psychological and social development.

   a. definition

   b. time order: dates and events

   c. time order: process

   d. comparison and contrast

   e. cause and effect

   f. classification

5. For Sigmund Freud, the mind consisted of three parts: the id, the ego, and the superego.

   a. definition

   b. time order: dates and events

   c. time order: process

   d. comparison and contrast

   e. cause and effect

   f. classification

6. Unlike his well-born predecessor, George Herbert Walker Bush, Bill Clinton came from a working-class family.

   a. definition

   b. time order: dates and events

   c. time order: process

   d. comparison and contrast

   e. cause and effect

   f. classification

7. The first step in the process of perception is a simple awareness of the outside world.

   a. definition

   b. time order: dates and events

   c. time order: process

   d. comparison and contrast

   e. cause and effect

   f. classification

8. Gas prices have increased and, as a result, many consumers have simply stopped buying premium gas, even when automakers have recommended its use.

a. definition

b. time order: dates and events

c. time order: process

d. comparison and contrast

e. cause and effect

f. classification

9. Writer Rushworth Kidder divides dilemmas into four different kinds.

a. definition

b. time order: dates and events

c. time order: process

d. comparison and contrast

e. cause and effect

f. classification

10. Like the music industry, the film industry may find itself financially hammered by online piracy.

a. definition

b. time order: datcs and events

c. time order: process

d. comparison and contrast

e. cause and effect

f. classification

 **Test 2: Patterns and Transitions**

DIRECTIONS For each pair of sentences, fill in the blank with the appropriate transition. Then identify the pattern suggested by both the transition and the sentences.

1. In Eastern religions such as Buddhism and Hinduism, enlightenment is the quest for spiritual knowledge or understanding.

   _____, in European and American history, the word *Enlightenment* refers to a period of time when there was great confidence in the power of reason to solve social problems.

   a. Thus

   b. However

   c. In the first place

   Pattern a. time order

   b. comparison and contrast

   c. cause and effect

2. The Austrian psychoanalyst Sigmund Freud demanded strict obedience from his followers. _____, he promptly broke with Carl Jung, whom he had once treated as a son, after Jung began questioning Freud's theory of the unconscious.

   a. In the beginning

   b. In contrast

   c. Consequently

   Pattern a. time order

   b. comparison and contrast

   c. cause and effect

3. In 1962, the Soviets had two one-man capsules orbiting the earth.

   _____, they sent the first woman into space.

   a. A year later

   b. Consequently

   c. In contrast

Pattern a. time order

  b. comparison and contrast

  c. cause and effect

4. An exhibition of ancient Middle Eastern artifacts at New York's Metropolitan Museum of Art has caused a heated controversy. The origin of some of the objects is unknown. _____, some critics insist that the exhibit could encourage the theft of national treasures.

  a. Nevertheless

  b. Therefore

  c. In the beginning

Pattern a. time order

  b. comparison and contrast

  c. cause and effect

5. The Beatles' first single, "Love Me Do," was released in September 1962 and got to number seventeen on the pop charts. Their second, "Please Please Me," reached number two; and their third, "From Me to You," hit number one. _____, the Beatles were the most popular musicians in British history.

  a. However

  b. First

  c. By 1963

Pattern a. time order

  b. comparison and contrast

  c. cause and effect

 **Test 3: Recognizing Primary Patterns**

DIRECTIONS Identify the primary pattern of organization by circling the appropriate letter.

1. The meaning of silence can vary with one's culture. Americans, for example, often view silence as negative. At business meetings, participants frequently force themselves to speak; they fear that being silent will make it appear as if they had nothing to say. On a personal level, silence is often interpreted as a sign that things are not going well. In a group, for example, members frequently mistrust the person who remains silent. It's assumed that he or she is bored or disinterested in the group's activities. In Japan, however, silence is viewed in an altogether different light. Silence, in a personal or a professional context, is often interpreted as positive. People who are silent at meetings are thought to reflect more deeply on the issues under discussion. During personal conversations, remaining silent so that the other person has a chance to speak is considered the height of politeness and courtesy. The Japanese, in general, prefer silence to speech.

   a. definition

   b. time order: dates and events

   c. time order: process

   d. comparison and contrast

   e. cause and effect

   f. classification

2. New York City's size and layout changed greatly between 1728 and 1890. A flourishing center of trade, New York grew in the early and mid-1700s without a definite plan. Farmers sold land for buildings plot by plot, as need demanded, and this stop-and-start development is reflected in lower Manhattan's irregular streets. After the Revolutionary War, the 1782 Act of Confiscation took land away from anyone who had sided with the British, leaving many areas of New York available for organization and urban planning. A commission was set up in 1807 to create a street layout that would keep New York orderly, no matter how much trade or industry boomed. In 1811, the commission revealed its plan: a simple pattern of horizontal and vertical lines that didn't follow the natural landscape. A piece of wasteland purchased in 1853 was eventually turned into the 843-acre Central Park.

Otherwise, little open land remained for games or sports. By 1890, the island of Manhattan had grown into a thriving checkerboard of streets and buildings.

a. definition

b. time order: dates and events

c. time order: process

d. comparison and contrast

e. cause and effect

f. classification

3. During the Middle Ages (600–1500) in Europe, most ordinary people could not read. They had to rely on village gossip and on tales relayed by bands of storytellers. During this period, four main types of storytellers developed, each specializing in particular themes and characters. In northern Europe, *bards* recited poems about heavenly gods and earthly heroes. The poem *Beowulf,* for example, was probably first recited by an English bard. In France and Spain, *minstrels* related the great deeds performed by King Charlemagne's knights in stories like the *Song of Roland.* In France and Italy, *troubadours* spun tales of courtly romance that placed women on a pedestal and men at their command. In Germany, *minnesingers* told stories of passion and romance.

a. definition

b. time order: dates and events

c. time order: process

d. comparison and contrast

e. cause and effect

f. classification

4. In Northern India, a wasp known as *Rogas indiscretus* kills the gypsy moths that harm trees in the foothills of the Himalayas.* Scientists say the wasp's methods are simple yet quite efficient. The female wasp stings a gypsy moth caterpillar and deposits an egg inside it. After hatching, the wormlike baby wasp eats the moth's insides. The infant wasp then spins a cocoon inside the moth's dead body; the cocoon is protected by the mummified husk. A few weeks later, the infant wasp grows into an adult—which, if female, is ready

*Himalayas: mountains in south central Asia.

to lay at least two hundred eggs in other gypsy moth caterpillars. (Adapted from *U.S. News & World Report*, April 7, 1997, pp. 70–71.)

a. definition

b. time order: dates and events

c. time order: process

d. comparison and contrast

e. cause and effect

f. classification

5. Jon Krakauer's best-selling book *Into the Wild* tells the story of Chris McCandless, an idealistic young man who traveled to a remote region in Alaska to live off the land. McCandless cut himself off from the world and vowed to make his way with no money or map. In August 1992, four months after he walked into the Alaskan wilderness, McCandless's body was discovered by hunters who were hiking by an abandoned bus. At the time, no one knew how or why McCandless had died until Krakauer, investigating McCandless's case for a national magazine, uncovered the cause: poisoning from the seed pods of wild potato plants. As was his habit, McCandless had used a field guide to identify edible plants, and the book said nothing about any ill effects from eating potato seeds. But, as Krakauer found after taking some seeds for laboratory tests, the seeds contain a poisonous substance that causes weakness, depression, muscle fatigue, and nervousness. The poison also makes it hard to eat and drink and prevents the body from turning food into usable energy. McCandless was already very thin because his wilderness diet consisted of berries he had gathered, and the potato-seed poison hit him hard. Unable to leave his remote campground or call for help, he slowly starved to death.

a. definition

b. time order: dates and events

c. time order: process

d. comparison and contrast

e. cause and effect

f. classification

 ## Test 4: Recognizing Primary Patterns

DIRECTIONS Identify the primary pattern of organization by circling the appropriate letter.

1. Industrial psychologists who have studied work teams have come up with five different categories. First, *production teams* consist of the employees who actually produce a product or service. These are the employees who make the ball bearings, computer chips, or automobile parts. Second, *management teams* coordinate workers who report to them while the product is being made, developed, or refined. Unlike members of the production team, the members of the management team are not on the front line. Instead, they are responsible for the planning, staffing, budgeting, and logistics* of work projects. *Service teams* consist of employees who work together to serve the needs of customers. An example of a service team is the technical support group that addresses a software problem customers call or e-mail about. Fourth, *project teams* carry out specific projects and are dissolved upon project completion. For example, book publishers might assign the publication of a book to a specific team that no longer exists once the book is in stores. Finally, there are *advisory teams*. These teams offer advice about a specific problem, e.g., the presence of low morale in the workplace. (Adapted from Levy, *Industrial/Organizational Psychology*, pp. 368–369.)

   a. definition

   b. time order: dates and events

   c. time order: process

   d. comparison and contrast

   e. cause and effect

   f. classification

2. The body's response to flesh wounds is remarkably quick and efficient. The first stage in the body's response occurs when the blood begins to clot. Next, tiny bodies in the bloodstream called **platelets** rush to the wound site and disintegrate.* Fibrous proteins begin to form, and the blood that has already escaped hardens into a scab. Once the bleeding stops, the body releases chemicals called **pyrogens**. These chemicals cause the area surrounding the wound to grow warm. In turn, blood vessels grow wider, allowing nutrients,

---

*logistics: plan of action or organization.
*disintegrate: dissolve.

oxygen, and white blood cells to flood the wounded area and start the formation of new tissue.

a. definition

b. time order: dates and events

c. time order: process

d. comparison and contrast

e. cause and effect

f. classification

3. Few events are more bizarre or unbelievable than sudden death said to be caused by "voodoo" or "magic." Nevertheless, death caused by voodoo does, indeed, seem to occur. Here is one account of what happened in a tribe when a man discovered that he had been cursed. "His body begins to tremble and the muscles twitch involuntarily. He sways backwards and falls to the ground. . . . From this time onwards he sickens and frets, refusing to eat and keeping aloof from the daily affairs of the tribe. Unless help is forthcoming in the shape of a countercharm, death is only a matter of a comparatively short time (Basedow, 1925; cited in Cannon, 1942)."* It has been argued that voodoo deaths seem to require belief in the power of magic. But all they really require is belief in the power of emotion. Walter Cannon, a well-known medical researcher, studied many voodoo deaths and concluded that they are explained by the bodily changes that accompany strong emotion. More specifically, Cannon argued that intense fear and its effects on the body are what causes someone to die from a curse.

a. definition

b. time order: dates and events

c. time order: process

d. comparison and contrast

e. cause and effect

f. classification

4. **Syndicates** provide important materials for newspapers. A syndicate is a company that sells editorial matter that is not hard news to newspapers. Hundreds of syndicates supply a variety of content

---

*Dennis Coon, *Introduction to Psychology* (St. Paul: West Publishing, 1989), p. 308.

for different departments and different audiences. The Washington Post Writers Group, the syndication arm of the *Washington Post,* circulates the work of columnists such as Ellen Goodman, George Will, and David Broder. Copley News Services sells editorial cartoons. Universal Press Syndicate offers a wide range of choices from "Dear Abby" and Jeane Dixon's "Your Horoscope" to Marshall Loeb's "Your Money" column to the "Doonesbury" strip. As you might imagine, syndicates supply some of the most popular parts of a paper. (Adapted from Turow, *Media Today,* pp. 132–133.)

a. definition

b. time order: dates and events

c. time order: process

d. comparison and contrast

e. causc and effect

f. classification

5. First ladies Eleanor Roosevelt and Hillary Rodham Clinton shared many similarities. While their husbands served as U.S. presidents, both women actively assisted and advised their spouses. Mrs. Roosevelt frequently made fact-finding trips to gather information for her husband, and Mrs. Clinton helped her husband by advising him during his political campaigns. She also assisted him in his efforts to establish affordable health care for all Americans. Both women engaged in humanitarian work. Mrs. Roosevclt advocated equal rights for minority groups and worked with children and the poor. Mrs. Clinton served as national chairperson for the Children's Defense Fund, an organization dedicated to helping neglected children. Finally, both first ladies became role models for women in politics and public affairs by pursuing distinguished careers of their own. After her husband's presidential term ended, Mrs. Roosevelt went on to serve as a delegate to the United Nations General Assembly, where she chaired the Human Rights Commission. Mrs. Clinton was elected a U.S. senator for New York State.

a. definition

b time order: dates and events

c. time order: process

d. comparison and contrast

e. cause and effect

f. classification

 **Test 5: Recognizing Primary Patterns**

DIRECTIONS Identify the primary pattern of organization by circling the appropriate letter.

1. Several characteristics distinguish African elephants from Asian elephants. African elephants, the largest land mammals on Earth, may stand thirteen feet tall and weigh up to seven tons. Asian elephants never get quite so big or so heavy. African elephants have large, rounded ears that billow from their heads like sails. In contrast, the ears of Asian elephants are smaller, with square edges that don't jut out quite so far. African elephants also have much flatter foreheads than their bumpy Asian cousins. Near their mouths, African elephants boast long, sharp tusks. When Asian elephants do have tusks, they are much less developed than those of African elephants. The trunks of African elephants split into two fingerlike projections at the end, but Asian elephants have trunks with only one such feeler. African elephants usually have three nails on each back foot, whereas Asian elephants have four nails in the same spot.

   a. definition

   b. time order: dates and events

   c. time order: process

   d. comparison and contrast

   e. cause and effect

   f. classification

2. No one really knows for sure when table tennis, more commonly known as *Ping-Pong,* actually came into being. But some authorities on the game believe that it originated in 1890, when British Army officers began playing it in India. By 1900, table tennis was popular throughout the world. Although table tennis was called a variety of names, among them *Whiff Whaff* and *Gossimar,* by 1902 most amateur players referred to it as Ping-Pong (the name was taken from the patented trademark of a company that produced table tennis equipment). By 1910, table tennis—under any name—had become a popular pastime. In fact, in the United States, it was practically a craze.* But like so many fads, its popularity quickly faded. In 1921, however, a movement started in several parts of the

---

*craze: a short-lived popular fashion.

world, the goal of which was to make table tennis a serious sport. In 1926, seven nations came together in Berlin, Germany, for a meeting that resulted in the formation of a group called the International Table Tennis Federation. By 1933, the U.S. had its own governing group called the U.S. Table Tennis Association. To this day, the group governs all tournament competition in the United States.

a. definition

b. time order: dates and events

c. time order: process

d. comparison and contrast

e. cause and effect

f. classification

3. Traditionally, musical instruments are grouped into five categories, based on the way sound is produced. When the sound results from the vibration of air through a tube or mouthpiece, the instrument is known as an *aerophone.* Clarinets, flutes, and trumpets belong to this musical family. A second type, *idiophones,* make sound when they are stamped, shaken, scraped, or rubbed. Members of this group include rattles and washboards. A third classification, *membranophones,* produce sound through the movement of a stretched membrane, or skin. All drums are membranophones. Another category is the *chordophones.* These instruments create sound through the movement of strings. Harps, violins, and cellos are good examples of chordophones. *Electrical instruments* comprise the fifth group, which includes electric organs and guitars, keyboards, and chimes.

a. definition

b. time order: dates and events

c. time order: process

c. comparison and contrast

e. cause and effect

f. classification

4. In June 1955, *The $64,000 Question* made its debut broadcast on CBS. By July, it was the top-rated show on American TV, attracting a weekly audience in excess of forty-seven million viewers. Revlon, the show's sponsor, enjoyed an enormous surge in sales and profits. Largely as a result of its hit show, Revlon seized a huge lead in the battle for sales among cosmetics makers. Given its success, what sort of magic did *The $64,000 Question* possess? What caused so many Americans to turn on a quiz show each and every week? One answer is that Lou Cowan, the independent television packager who came up with the idea for the show, knew the power of the get-rich-quick daydream. But Cowan also believed that Americans would be drawn to the spectacle of ordinary people like themselves displaying extraordinary knowledge in a particular field. It was no accident, therefore, that among the show's early winners were a New York City policeman (Shakespeare), a grandmother (the Bible), a shoe repairman (opera), and a Marine captain (cooking). The show also made a winner of Lou Cowan: He became the president of CBS. (Adapted from David Wallechinsky, *The Twentieth Century.* Boston: Little, Brown, 1995, p. 440.)

a. definition

b. time order: dates and events

c. time order: process

d. comparison and contrast

e. cause and effect

f. classification

5. Edgar Schein's model for looking at organizational change and growth is evolutionary in nature; that is, it describes distinct stages of change. Schein created a model that identified three separate stages. In the first stage, the organization's founders are the source of inspiration. Their ideas guide the organization and hold it together. The second stage is often defined by an identity crisis. At this point, members sometimes doubt their commitment to the group, and the organization's goals frequently come under fire. In stage two, the organization needs to redefine its underlying rules and objectives; otherwise, it may simply disappear. Organizations that survive stage two and enter stage three often disavow some of the early ideas that motivated or guided the group's behavior. New rules and goals that reflect a changing world take the place of the old.

a. definition

b. time order: dates and events

c. time order: process

d. comparison and contrast

e. cause and effect

f. classification

 **Test 6: Recognizing Primary Patterns**

DIRECTIONS Identify the primary pattern of organization by circling the appropriate letter.

1. If you're talking about e-mail, a *flame* is a message that makes an unfair attack or criticism on a person or a person's ideas. Unfortunately, messages not meant to be flames are sometimes taken as flames. At other times, people go out of their way to "flame" or insult someone. Flames can range from mildly rude to hateful and mean. For example, "Don't you know you're not wanted, fool" is the kind of flame you might get if you wander into a chat room to which you haven't been invited. The best thing to do if you think you've been flamed is to ignore it for a day and then respond, but without flaming back. Instead, use patience and wit. If flames recur, simply ignore them. (Adapted from Crump and Carbone, *English OnLine*, p. 10.)

   a. definition

   b. time order: dates and events

   c. time order: process

   d. comparison and contrast

   e. cause and effect

   f. classification

2. It is easy enough to confuse cheetahs with leopards. Even in Africa, where people are used to seeing these animals, they are often called by the same Swahili name, *ngari*. The confusion is understandable. On a superficial level, the two have much in common. Both have light tan fur and dark spots. Both have about the same body weight, approximately 110 to 130 pounds. However, on closer inspection, there are clearly more differences than similarities between the two. The cheetah has longer legs and a much smaller head. An agile climber, the leopard climbs trees to hunt monkeys; the cheetah, one of the fastest animals on Earth, takes its prey on the ground, running it down at full speed. The leopard consumes a varied diet. Even when game is scarce, it can subsist on mice and fruits. The cheetah, by contrast, relies primarily on antelope for food.

   a. definition

   b. time order: dates and events

   c. time order: process

   d. comparison and contrast

    e. cause and effect

    f. classification

3. The process of human digestion begins at the very moment that food enters our mouth. At this point, both teeth and saliva begin preparing the food for safe entry into the intestine. Once the chewed and liquefied food is swallowed, it moves downward through the esophagus by means of muscle contractions. When it reaches the stomach, the food is mixed with enzymes and acid that ready the partially digested food for entry into the small intestine. There, more enzymes will be added, and digestion will essentially be completed. After all the food nutrients have been absorbed by the body, the indigestible parts will move on to the large intestine in preparation for being excreted from the body.

    a. definition

    b. time order: dates and events

    c. time order: process

    d. comparison and contrast

    e. cause and effect

    f. classification

4. In the next decade, hundreds of thousands of convicted felons who were locked up as a result of tough anticrime policies in the 1980s and 1990s will be released from America's prisons. Their release in such large numbers is bound to challenge government and community reentry programs created to help former inmates adjust to life outside of prison. Most of these programs are already underfunded and understaffed. As a result, it will be hard to arrange adequate social services for all those who need them. Yet if former inmates do not receive psychological counseling, job training, and some help finding employment, they are bound to drain community welfare programs and food banks. Ex-prisoners left to sink or swim on their own will probably see no alternative except returning to the criminal behavior that got them into trouble in the first place. Although some increased funding for reentry programs is already in the works at both the state and federal level, much more is desperately needed.

    a. definition

    b. time order: dates and events

    c. time order: process

    d. comparison and contrast

    e. cause and effect

    f. classification

5. The nineteenth-century composer Johannes Brahms started out in the poorest of circumstances, but by the end of his life, his music had brought him success and fame. Born in Hamburg, Germany, in 1833, Brahms was the son of a poorly paid musician who played for the city's theater. In 1840, at the age of seven, Brahms began playing the piano; he gave his first concert in 1843. Forced to make his own way as a teenager, Brahms played in a succession of cheap bars to earn money. But in 1853, he toured with the Hungarian violinist Eduard Remenyi and was discovered by the German composer Robert Schumann, who gave Brahms a wildly enthusiastic review that helped make the young composer's reputation. In 1859, Brahms performed his Piano Concerto* no. 1 in D Minor, but it was not well received. It wasn't until 1868, when his *German Requiem** was performed that Brahms gained the European critics' respectful attention. He further cemented his reputation with a series of magnificent symphonies* composed between 1873 and 1885. Brahms died in 1897, at the age of sixty-four, but his method of composition remained somewhat mysterious even after his death. A fiercely private man, Brahms had burned many of his personal papers.

    a. definition

    b. time order: dates and events

    c. time order: process

    d. comparison and contrast

    e. cause and effect

    f. classification

---

*concerto: a piece of music composed for an orchestra and one or more solo instruments.
*requiem: music composed to honor the dead.
*symphonies: long or extended pieces of music usually consisting of three or more individual movements, or parts.

 **Test 7: Vocabulary Review**

DIRECTIONS Here are fifteen of the words introduced in Chapter 8. Use them to fill in the blanks. Words introduced in previous chapters are marked with an asterisk. *Note*: The form of the word used here may differ from the form used in the chapter.

stench	province	provocation	oust
suffrage	range	utterance	civic
commerce	compassionate	stint	logistics
extensive	coercive	activists	

1. In pursuit of women's _Suffrage_, nineteenth-century feminists in both Britain and America showed both mettle* and stamina.* The threat of public ridicule and the possibility of social stigma* failed to discourage them from their efforts to win the vote for women. In an attempt to end what they saw as obvious discrimination* against their gender, the British _province_ were especially militant and carefully planned their _coercive_ of rebellion. They would, for instance, chain themselves to public buildings and wait for government officials to walk by so that the outraged men would be forced to hear the women's complaints about their plight* as poor, voteless creatures, the helpless, put-upon subordinates* of men.

When the occasion called for it, women would even lie down in the streets in order to stop all _commerce_ for an _extensive_ period of time. The goal of such aggressive measures was to force an often uninterested public into paying attention. It was also a message that the women were serious about their cause. To be sure, they weren't intimidated by the _activists_ measures employed by those who found their demands repellent.* If the women were hauled off for a _____ Stint _____ in jail, they would respond by staging a hunger strike. Force-fed, they would plead for forgiveness, promise to mend their ways, and head for home, only to be back again the subsequent* week with some new _Utterance_.

2. If American women were less aggressive in their demands for women's rights, they were no less determined to extend their _____ logistics _____ beyond the home. While they were willing to accept the role of _____ Compassionate _____ helpmate created to orbit* around men, they argued as well that their supposedly natural warmth and kindness could perform a _____ civic _____ duty outside the home. Modest and well-spoken, American feminists like Elizabeth Cady Stanton and Lucretia Mott had been thoroughly socialized* to behave like "ladies." But despite their ladylike appearance, they were rebels through and through who didn't care all that much about the opinions of polite society.

Although they never said they wanted to _____ oust _____ men from their positions of power, they both wanted a society that allowed women a wider _____ range _____ for their interests and abilities. Stanton and Mott wanted to live among men who didn't treat every _provocation_ from a woman as superfluous chatter.

For those of us living in the twenty-first century, the aspirations* of the early feminists may seem almost timid. After all, most women were not openly demanding equality with men—no matter what they might have thought in private. Yet to many in the nineteenth-century world, feminism had about it the _____ Stench _____ of socialism,* that radical* theory of equality that at mid-century had left the Europeans shaking in their boots.* Viewed from that perspective, feminist thinking was dangerous, and feminists had to be subdued.* And for a time they were. Women did not get the vote until 1918, seventy years after the early feminists made their wishes known at the first ever American convention for women's rights.

INTERNET BONUS QUESTION

The author refers to the first convention for women held seventy years before women got the vote. Create a search term that helps you answer these two questions: Where was the convention held, and what was it called?

_____

_____

_____

---

*In the mid-nineteenth century, Europe had witnessed socialist-inspired uprisings.

Combining Patterns in Paragraphs and Longer Readings

In this chapter, you'll learn

- how to recognize two or more patterns in a paragraph.

- how to take notes on paragraphs that combine patterns.

- how to recognize patterns in longer readings.

- how to take notes on readings that combine two, three, or even four patterns.

Until now, you've worked with paragraphs based primarily on one organizational pattern. But if their ideas require it, writers often use more than one pattern.

507

Particularly in longer readings, authors frequently combine two, three, or even four patterns, instead of relying solely on one. Thus, it's important for you to learn how to (1) identify the different patterns used in a reading; (2) figure out which pattern or patterns are primary, or central, to developing the main idea; and (3) record in your notes the essential elements of the most important patterns.

 ## Combining Patterns in Paragraphs

The following paragraph combines two different patterns. Read it through. Then, on the blank line below it, identify the two patterns you think are at work in the paragraph.

[1]Increased spells of warm weather and decreased use of a pesticide called Mirex have resulted in a plague of what laypeople call fire ants. [2]Indeed, pleasant weather and an absence of pesticides have encouraged whole armies of ants to make their homes in farmers' fields, where they can leisurely munch on potato and okra crops. [3]Should a tractor overturn one of their nests, the furious ants swarm over the machine and attack the driver. [4]Using their jaws to hold the victim's skin, they thrust their stingers into the flesh, holding the same position for up to twenty-five seconds. [5]The sting produces a sharp burning sensation and frequently produces painful infections that can last weeks and even months. [6]Some victims who were especially allergic to the ants' poison have not survived a fire ant attack.

_____

The first clue to a pattern in the paragraph is the verb *resulted* in the first sentence. That verb suggests a cause and effect pattern. And, in fact, that is exactly the pattern that first appears in the paragraph. In the opening sentence, the author explains how two causes—more warm weather and decreased pesticide use—have produced an effect—a plague of fire ants.

But look what happens in sentence 3. At this point, the author starts to describe a process—an attack by angry fire ants. Step by step in the remaining sentences, the paragraph outlines what happens when fire ants attack. Thus, we can rightly say that the paragraph is organized according to two different patterns, cause and effect *and* time order (process).

Because the paragraph describes a cause and effect relationship and outlines the steps in a process, you need to first identify the key elements in each pattern. Then you need to decide if all of those elements are essential to the main idea.

Because cause and effect is central to the main idea—more warm weather and decreased use of the pesticide Mirex have made fire ants a serious threat—we definitely need to identify and link both cause and effect in our notes. However, to further illustrate the threat posed by the ants, we also need to include the steps in their attack. Complete notes would look something like this:

Main Idea More warm weather and decreased use of the pesticide Mirex have produced a plague of fire ants.

Supporting Details
1. Whole armies of ants have moved into farmers' fields and are eating potatoes and okra.
2. If tractor overturns nest, ants swarm over machine and attack driver.
3. They thrust stingers into flesh, holding the same position for up to 25 seconds.
4. Sting produces painful burning sensations and can cause infections.
5. Some especially allergic victims have died following fire ant attacks.

Not All Patterns Are Equal

When taking notes on a paragraph with two or more organizational patterns, don't assume all patterns are equal. Instead decide which pattern or patterns are most important based on two questions: (1) which pattern is most central to explaining the main idea? and (2) which one organizes the most sentences? The answers to those two questions will tell you which patterns are essential to explaining the main idea. The key elements of those patterns should appear in your notes.

INTERNET BONUS QUESTION

Which site would be a better choice when it comes to getting information about how to eliminate fire ants?

a. <u>Texas Imported **Fire Ant** Research and Management Project</u>

> The Texas Imported **Fire Ant** Research and Management Plan is a state-funded program developed to find effective methods to eliminate the red imported **fire**...
> <u>fireant.tamu.edu/</u>

b. <u>Imported **Fire Ant**-FAQ</u>

> Frequently asked questions about **Fire Ants** from University of Texas.
> <u>uts.cc.utexas.edu/~gilbert/research/fireants/faq.html</u>

Please explain.

_____

_____

EXERCISE 1 Recognizing Combined Patterns

DIRECTIONS Read and take notes on each paragraph. Circle the letters of the patterns used in each paragraph.

EXAMPLE By 1913, tennis had become a popular American sport, but only one year later, it was to undergo a profound change. In the early part of the twentieth century, tennis had been considered a delightful, if slightly too strenuous, pastime, a game to be played by the wealthy in their leisure moments. However, 1914 saw the entrance of young players like Maurice E. McLoughlin, a tennis champion whose competitive and aggressive playing style helped change the game's very nature. In contrast to players of an earlier era, those who followed in McLoughlin's footsteps played to win. In 1915, the national tennis championship was transferred from the privileged environment of Newport, Rhode Island, to the far less sophisticated West Side Tennis Club at Forest Hills, New York. This move signaled that tennis was ready to break free of its earlier role as an upper-class diversion.*

a. The paragraph defines a key term or terms.

(b.) Time order: The paragraph outlines a sequence of dates and events.

c. Time order: The paragraph describes a process.

---

*diversion: pastime; a pleasant activity.

(d.) The paragraph compares and/or contrasts two topics.

(e.) The paragraph explains a cause and effect relationship.

f. The paragraph explains a system of classification.

Main Idea By 1913, tennis had become popular in America, but it was about to change dramatically.

Supporting Details

1. 1914: Players like Maurice McLoughlin entered the game.

    a. These players were aggressive and competitive.

    b. Before McLoughlin, tennis was a relaxing diversion.

    c. After McLoughlin, players wanted to win.

2. In 1915, national tennis championship moved from Newport, Rhode Island, to Forest Hills, New York.

    a. Move signaled that tennis was no longer a pastime for the wealthy.

EXPLANATION This paragraph describes a cause and effect relationship. It explains how players such as Maurice McLoughlin helped change the face of tennis. Because that cause and effect relationship is central to explaining the main idea expressed in sentence 1, it is included in our notes. But the paragraph also contrasts tennis before and after players like Maurice McLoughlin entered the game. Because the difference in style is central to explaining the main idea, it also appears in our notes. So, too, do the dates and events that help explain how tennis changed over time.

1. Anyone who has ever cheered on his or her favorite athlete knows that yelling can produce hoarseness. When a person yells or screams, the vocal cords—two thick, muscular strings—close tightly and create a tremendous amount of air pressure. As they open to let out a sound, the sudden release of air causes the cords to slam together. When the cords hit each other, especially over a long period of time, they can bruise and swell. If this happens, they will not fit together properly. Air then leaks between the cords, and the voice sounds hoarse. Hoarseness is a sign that the vocal cords need rest. Trying to talk as a way of getting rid of the hoarseness only makes matters worse, for the cords may begin bleeding. Many vocalists, especially rock singers who shout a lot, suffer from bleeding and irritated cords.

   a. The paragraph defines a key term or terms.

   b. Time order: The paragraph outlines a sequence of dates and events.

   c. Time order: The paragraph describes a process.

   d. The paragraph compares and/or contrasts two topics.

   e. The paragraph explains a cause and effect relationship.

   f. The paragraph explains a system of classification.

Main Idea _____

_____

Supporting Details _____

_____

_____

_____

_____

_____

_____

2. Hurricanes and tornadoes both pack a wallop. But of the two, tornadoes have become the more deadly. On average, tornadoes kill at least 100 people a year. In the worst tornado on record, the Tri-State tornado of 1925, a mile-wide killer tornado hurtled through Missouri, Illinois, and Indiana, destroying over 15,000 homes, killing 695 people, and injuring 2,207. Like tornadoes, hurricanes can sweep through several states, but today's improved weather tracking systems have made it easier to prepare for and avoid death and destruction from hurricanes, usually by evacuating those in danger. In 1928, however, such tracking systems did not exist. When a hurricane struck Lake Okeechobee in Florida, it killed 1,836 people. Still even with modern tracking systems, 1999's Hurricane Floyd caused 56 deaths. And those locations lacking sophisticated weather monitoring systems are still in serious danger when a hurricane hits. In 1991, a typhoon (as hurricanes are called in the western Pacific and Indian oceans) tore through Bangladesh and left in its wake 140,000 deaths.

a. The paragraph defines a key term or terms.

b. Time order: The paragraph outlines a sequence of dates and events.

c. Time order: The paragraph describes a process.

d. The paragraph compares and/or contrasts two topics.

e. The paragraph explains a cause and effect relationship.

f. The paragraph explains a system of classification.

Main Idea _____

_____

Supporting _____
Details
_____

_____

_____

_____

_____

_____

_____

_____

_____

_____

3. The venom of a bee resembles the venom of a snake, and the sting of a bee can, in some instances, prove dangerous. Yet while most people react quickly to a snake bite, they tend to ignore a bee sting. That failure to act, however, can be a mistake. Bee stings can actually have deadly consequences if a person is allergic to bee venom. Thus it is better not to take any chances with bee stings. Anyone who gets stung by a bee should react quickly, just as he or she would in reaction to a snake bite. First, remove the stinger by brushing it away; don't try to pull it out. Then apply one of the several professional bee-sting remedies to the whitish swelling that appears almost immediately following the sting. If the swelling

continues throughout the day or if it becomes difficult to breathe, call a doctor.

a. The paragraph defines a key term or terms.

b. Time order: The paragraph outlines a sequence of dates and events.

c. Time order: The paragraph describes a process.

d. The paragraph compares and/or contrasts two topics.

e. The paragraph explains a cause and effect relationship.

f. The paragraph explains a system of classification.

Main Idea _____

_____

Supporting _____
Details
_____

_____

_____

_____

4. The Hollywood propaganda* films created during World War II fall into three general categories: (1) films that praise American traditions, (2) films that introduce World War II allies, and (3) films that criticize the enemy. Around 1938, Hollywood began producing a series of biographical* films that glorified the American democratic tradition. John Ford's *Young Mr. Lincoln* (1939) and John Cromwell's *Abe Lincoln in Illinois* (1940) were Hollywood tributes to an America that gave everyone an equal chance at success. In the early forties, Hollywood began to introduce America's British allies. Films such as *Mrs. Miniver* (1942) and *Journey for Margaret* (1942) presented a sympathetic picture of the British people. During the mid-forties, Hollywood concentrated on introducing American audiences to the enemy, and movies like *Hitler's Children* (1943) and *Behind the Rising Sun* (1943) portrayed German and Japanese brutality. Many of these later films have since been criticized because of their distorted and simplistic themes that presented the German

_____

*propaganda: a method of persuasion that relies on emotional appeal and discourages logical thinking.
*biographical: related to a person's life.

and Japanese people as half-mad beasts. It has been argued that vicious stereotypes are not appropriate, even during wartime when propaganda supposedly serves a useful, if not a positive, function.

a. The paragraph defines a key term or terms.

b. Time order: The paragraph outlines a sequence of dates and events.

c. Time order: The paragraph describes a process.

d. The paragraph compares and/or contrasts two topics.

e. The paragraph explains a cause and effect relationship.

f. The paragraph explains a system of classification.

Main Idea _____

_____

Supporting _____
Details
_____

_____

_____

_____

_____

_____

_____

_____

 ## Seeing Patterns in Longer Readings

Longer, multiparagraph readings do occasionally rely on a single pattern of organization. Look, for example, at the following selection, which relies almost exclusively on the cause and effect pattern of development. As you read, note the italicized transitions that are clues to the cause and effect pattern.

Hunger and the Ik

1 The Ik are a small tribe located in East Africa. Formerly a society of hunters, the Ik were forced to become farmers when their government confiscated most of their land for a national park. Deprived of their right to hunt and unable to support themselves through farming, the Ik have learned to live with constant hunger and the threat of starvation. As the anthropologist Colin Turnbull has shown in his book *The Mountain People,* starvation brought profound changes to Ik society.

2 Painfully aware of every extra mouth to feed, the Ik do not regard children as a blessing. They know that children expect to be fed, and that is exactly what Ik parents cannot do. *Therefore,* children are forced from home around the age of three. Left to fend for themselves, the children run in packs, constantly searching for food. They fight among one another, squabbling over scraps.

3 Understandably, children treated in this fashion harbor no great love for their parents or grandparents. *Thus* Turnbull's book contains numerous examples of starving parents being turned away when they sought their grown-up children's help. From the children's point of view, they have enough trouble feeding themselves and cannot possibly feed their aging parents. The parents, apparently remembering their own attitude toward their children, do not consider such behavior unusual. They simply accept it and go away.

4 *Another consequence of starvation* is that married love seems to have disappeared from Ik lives. Men care little or nothing for their wives, valuing the women only if they are able to provide food. The women share this practical attitude. They will quickly abandon a husband who does not provide food or money and will search for a mate who can. To the Ik, the idea of caring for an aging or ailing spouse is ridiculous. Unable to take care of themselves, they find it hard to care for others.

5 *Like love,* sex doesn't interest the Ik. Sex is viewed primarily as a way of getting food or gifts from neighboring tribesmen who are better off than the Ik. It's important only when it puts food on the table. Otherwise, sex requires far too much energy, energy that could be better spent in search of something to eat.

In this reading, the thesis statement tells us that the Ik, at least according to Colin Turnbull, have been profoundly affected by the starvation that haunts their society. Each major supporting paragraph then describes a different tragic effect. Basically, the whole reading follows a cause and effect pattern of development.

Now, what about the following reading? Would you say that it, too, relies on only one pattern?

Ancient Beliefs About Mental Illness

1   Some half a million years ago, ancient societies apparently did not recognize any difference between mental and physical disorders. Abnormal behaviors, from simple headaches to convulsions,* were believed to be caused by evil spirits that lived in the victim's body. According to this system of belief—called *demonology*—those suffering from disease were considered responsible for their misfortune.

2   For this reason, some Stone Age cave dwellers appear to have treated behavior disorders by a surgical method called *trephining*. During this procedure, part of the skull was chipped away to make an opening. Once the skull was opened, the evil spirits could escape. It was believed that when the evil spirit left, the person would return to his or her normal state. Surprisingly, several trephined skulls that healed over have been found. This indicates that some patients survived what had to be an extremely crude operation. (Adapted from Sue et al., *Understanding Abnormal Behavior*, p. 16.)

In this example, the authors' thesis statement identifies a cause and effect relationship: In early societies, illness was considered to be a result of demonic possession. The second paragraph then defines and describes a primitive surgical procedure—*trephining*— that our ancestors may have used to free the body from evil spirits. All together, the authors use three different organizational patterns: (1) cause and effect, (2) definition, and (3) process.

Generally, most of the longer readings you encounter in textbooks, magazines, and newspapers are going to resemble the second sample selection rather than the first. They will rely, that is, on two, three, and, occasionally, even four patterns of organization. True, one pattern may be primary, or be more important, than the rest. But that doesn't mean you should ignore the others. Instead, search out and evaluate the elements of each pattern.

Taking Notes on Mixed Patterns

To take complete notes on a reading that combines two or more patterns, you need to (1) identify the essential elements of each pattern,

---

*convulsions: uncontrolled fits in which the muscles contract wildly.

(2) select the elements that are essential to explaining the overall main idea, and (3) record those elements in your notes.

To illustrate, here are some sample notes on the above reading.

Main Idea According to prehistoric beliefs, disease was a result of possession by demons, and the victims were responsible for their illness.

Supporting **1.** Because they believed demons caused illness, Stone Age cave
Details dwellers treated illness with a procedure called "trephining."

2. Part of the skull was chipped away to make an opening for evil spirits to escape.

a. Surprisingly, some patients appear to have survived.

As you can see, complete notes on the reading clearly describe the cause and effect relationship central to the reading. They also define and describe the process of trephining.

EXERCISE 2 Identifying Patterns in Longer Readings

DIRECTIONS Read the following selections. Circle the letter of the pattern or patterns you see at work in the readings.

EXAMPLE

Scott Joplin: The King of Ragtime

1   Born in 1868 in Texarkana on the Texas-Arkansas border, musician and composer Scott Joplin began his career playing piano in the saloons of St. Louis, Missouri, at the age of seventeen. During the next ten years, he perfected the style of jazz that came to be known as ragtime. Then, from 1896 to 1900, Joplin studied at George R. Smith College in Sedalia, Missouri, so that he could write down the music he played so naturally.

2   In 1899, Joplin published his first piece of music, "Maple Leaf Rag." Less than a year later, ragtime—a unique American blend of African and European musical forms—took the country by storm. Suddenly, everyone wanted to hear "Maple Leaf Rag," and Scott Joplin became the first composer in the world to sell more than one million copies of a single tune.

3   But the King of Ragtime didn't want to devote his life to writing popular music. A serious artist, he was hurt by white Americans' tendency to dismiss his music because it had black origins. To prove the value and beauty of ragtime, Joplin decided to compose

an opera. By doing so, he was demanding direct comparison with the greatest European composers.

4 Joplin's opera, *Treemonisha,* is the story of a black orphan girl educated by whites. The opera combines elements of ragtime with black work songs and rousing gospel music. When Joplin published it at his own expense in 1911, it was called "an entirely new form of operatic art."

5 But the timing was wrong. Joplin had invested his hopes in a work based solely on black music just as ragtime was declining in popularity. The one disastrous performance in New York City in 1915 humiliated him, and two years later he was dead.

6 Had he lived to see it, Joplin would have been overjoyed to read the review of *Treemonisha* that appeared in 1972 in the *New York Times.* According to the reviewer, "the audience went out of its mind," applauding what Joplin believed was his greatest failure.

a. definition

(b.) time order: dates and events

c. time order: process

d. comparison and contrast

(e.) cause and effect

f. classification

EXPLANATION In this reading the author has two goals: (1) to trace Scott Joplin's career and (2) to explain why writing a successful opera was so important to him. To fulfill those goals, she employs two patterns: a time-order pattern to trace the composer's career, and a cause and effect pattern to explain why *Treemonisha* meant so much to him.

1. The Chernobyl Catastrophe

1 In April 1986, technicians at a Swedish nuclear power plant were puzzled by the abnormally high levels of radiation in the air. They were even more puzzled when an inspection turned up no evidence of a leak. Then reports began to come in from Denmark, Finland, and Norway that they too were experiencing unusually high levels of radiation. Horrified, the technicians now realized that somewhere—they had no idea where—a full-scale nuclear meltdown was taking place. Then, on the night of April 16, the Russian government announced that an accident

had taken place at Chernobyl, a nuclear power plant in Ukraine.

2   Actually the disaster had started days earlier when an explosion ripped through one of Chernobyl's four reactors* and sent 100 million curies* of radiation into the air. For some reason, once the explosion occurred, the plant's cooling system did not work well enough to put out the resulting fire, and the plant had been burning for two weeks. According to the government, thirty-one people died during that period from radiation sickness, but the figure may well have been a good deal higher. As a result of the explosion, 135,000 people were evacuated from a three-hundred-square-mile area. In addition, the land and water within twenty miles of the reactor were now contaminated.

3   Later investigations of the disaster revealed that plant managers had been lax* about safety controls and that human error, along with poor design, had played a key role in the explosion. Consequently, officials in charge of the plant were put on trial in 1987, and several of those responsible were sentenced to long prison terms. But the real result of Chernobyl was the lurking fear that it could happen again someplace else, with even more horrifying consequences.

a. definition

b. time order: dates and events

c. time order: process

d. comparison and contrast

e. cause and effect

f. classification

2. The Donner Party

1   In 1846, two brothers named George and Jacob Donner, along with a prosperous businessman named James Reed, organized a party to travel to California. They, like many others of the time, hoped to buy land and make a better life for themselves. Their group grew to include a number of families and individuals, reaching a total of eighty-seven people, thirty-nine of them children, all of whom set out from Illinois in May of the same year.

---

*reactors: devices using heat to generate power.
*curies: units of radioactivity.
*lax: careless.

However, the Donner Party, as the group came to be known, would meet with disaster and become infamous in American history.

2   During the first leg of their journey, the group experienced the expected hardships that accompanied wagon-train travel. It was difficult to transport all of their belongings, which included furniture, clothing, food, and cattle. River and creek crossings were especially hazardous. Wagons often became stuck and had to be pulled free of obstacles like mud and rocks. Yet despite these complications, the Donner Party was still on schedule when it reached Wyoming in June.

3   Unfortunately, however, the party's leaders then made an ill-fated decision. They decided to take a little-used shortcut to save time. Ignoring an experienced wilderness explorer named James Clyman, who advised James Reed not to travel the shortcut, the Donner Party decided to try the more direct route. In August, the pioneers faced their first serious obstacle, eighty miles of desert near the Great Salt Lake. Although they were able to successfully cross the barren land, they suffered terribly, enduring sweltering daytime heat and freezing nighttime cold. In addition, many of the livestock suffocated during sandstorms.

4   By October, the group had managed to reach the Sierra Nevada outside California. Tensions, however, were running high. After killing another man in a fight, James Reed had been banished. Exhausted, frustrated by the many delays they had encountered, and increasingly concerned about the approaching winter, the travelers pressed on into the mountains. Although the food supply was getting low, members of the group assured the rest of the party that the route through the Sierras would be passable for another month. The travelers decided to rest their livestock for a few days before continuing. It was their second bad decision.

5   They were just below the summit of the Sierra Nevadas and only 150 miles from Fort Sutter in California when a blizzard struck on October 31. By the next day, the party could not locate the road under several feet of snow, let alone move the wagons. The group quickly erected makeshift cabins and shacks, and butchered the few remaining cattle for food. But the weather continued to worsen, and the situation quickly grew desperate. The first death from starvation occurred on December 15.

6   Seventeen of the group's members decided to make one last-ditch effort to walk the trail to California. But they got lost in heavy snow, and after three of the men died of starvation in one

night, the desperate survivors resorted to cannibalism to stay alive. When their grisly provisions ran out, the starving band turned on their Native-American guides, killed them, and ate them, too.

7   Meanwhile, back at the Sierra Nevada camp, twelve people had starved to death by February, and others had gone mad from hunger. When rescuers finally reached the camp on February 19, they found a ragged group of emaciated survivors who had also been desperate enough to resort to cannibalism.

8   Four different relief parties journeyed to the Donner camp over the next several weeks. The first two rescue groups were each able to take only about twenty survivors with them due to limited supplies. The second group was beset by another blizzard, which killed four more people, and that group, too, was forced to cannibalize the dead before the third relief party arrived. By the time the third group of rescuers arrived at the camp, fewer than ten people were still alive. A few refused to leave those who were sick or were too ill themselves to travel, so they stayed behind. By the time a fourth rescue team arrived, after a month's delay, only one survivor remained.

9   Following their ordeal, the survivors told their stories to the newspapers, horrifying the entire nation and even briefly putting a stop to westward migration. Those who lived through the experience disagreed about who was to blame for their disastrous trip. However, it seems clear that this group of Midwestern flat-landers seriously underestimated the dangers of mountain travel. They probably also underestimated the lengths they would go to in order to stay alive. (Source of information: Sara Ann McGill, "Donner Party," *American History & Politics, 1850–1914*, pp. 5–8.)

    a. definition

    b. time order: dates and events

    c. time order: process

    d. comparison and contrast

    e. cause and effect

    f. classification

3. Key Management Skills

1 The skills that typify effective managers tend to fall into five general categories: technical, conceptual, interpersonal, diagnostic, and analytic.

Technical Skills

2 A technical skill is a specific skill needed to accomplish a specialized activity. For example, the skills that engineers, lawyers, and machinists need to do their jobs are technical skills. Lower-level managers (and, to a lesser extent, middle managers) need the technical skills that are relevant to the activities they manage. Although these managers may not have to perform the technical tasks themselves, they must be able to train subordinates, answer questions, and otherwise provide guidance and direction.

Conceptual Skills

3 Conceptual skill is the ability to think in abstract terms. Conceptual skill allows the manager to see the "big picture" and to understand how the various parts of an organization or an idea can fit together. In 1951, a man named Charles Wilson decided to take his family on a cross-country vacation. All along the way, the family was forced to put up with high-priced but shabby hotel accommodations. Wilson reasoned that most travelers would welcome a chain of moderately priced, good-quality roadside hotels. You are no doubt familiar with what he conceived: Holiday Inns.

Interpersonal Skills

4 An interpersonal skill is the ability to deal effectively with other people, both inside and outside the organization. Examples of interpersonal skills are the ability to relate to people, understand their needs and motives, and show genuine compassion. When all other things are equal, the manager who is able to exhibit these skills will be more successful than the manager who is arrogant and brash and who doesn't care about others.

Diagnostic Skills

5 Diagnostic skill is the ability to assess a particular problem and identify its causes. The diagnostic skills of the successful manager are like those of the physician, who assesses the patient's symptoms to pinpoint the underlying medical problem. We can take this comparison one step further, too. In management as in medicine, correct diagnosis is often critical in determining the appropriate action to take. All managers need to use diagnostic skills, but top managers probably use them most.

Analytic Skills

6 Analytic skills are used to identify the relevant issues in a situation to determine how they are related, and to assess their relative importance. All managers, regardless of level or area, need

analytic skills. Analytic skills often come into play along with diagnostic skills. For example, a manager assigned to a new position may be confronted with a wide variety of problems that all need attention.

7   Although effective managers tend to have all five skills described in this reading, they don't have them all in equal measure. A good manager, for example, can have strong interpersonal skills but weak diagnostic ones. In effective managers, however, the stronger and weaker skills balance one another. (Adapted from Pride et al., *Business*, pp. 143–144.)

a. definition

b. time order: dates and events

c. time order: process

d. comparison and contrast

e. cause and effect

f. classification

4. Personality and Body Type

1   In the 1940s, some researchers tried to revive a much-debated theory of human behavior called *constitutional typology*. According to this theory, body type determines personality. Although the theory has been severely criticized over the years, it still has numerous supporters who believe that human beings fall into three basic categories of physique, or body type, with each one producing a particular set of character traits.

2   According to constitutional typologists, *endomorphs* tend to be round and soft, with protruding abdomens. They love gracious living and good food. They have gentle, relaxed temperaments and prefer to keep life uncomplicated. Said to embody the cliché about fat people being friendly, endomorphs like to be surrounded by their friends and are not comfortable being alone for any length of time.

3   The exact opposite of the endomorph, the *ectomorph* is described as all skin and bones, with a flat belly and long legs. Much less gregarious than the fun-loving endomorph, the ectomorph prefers intellectual pursuits, especially if they can be carried on in relative isolation from people. Less good natured than the endomorph, ectomorphs are nervous and high strung. Given to quick reactions and high-intensity relationships, they suffer from the aftermath of tension and have difficulty relaxing and falling asleep.

4   The *mesomorph* is neither fat nor thin, but broad and muscular, with a strong, rugged physique. People in this category are said to love physical activity—the more daring and fast paced, the better. They also enjoy games of risk or chance. Domineering by nature, mesomorphs like to be around people but prefer to be in situations they can control.

a. definition

b. time order: dates and events

c. time order: process

d. comparison and contrast

e. cause and effect

f. classification

Reading Tip   In a reading that combines several patterns, one pattern might well dominate, or be primary, but you still need to find and evaluate the key elements in the less important patterns. Then you can decide which of those elements should appear in your notes.

EXERCISE 3   Identifying the Primary Patterns

DIRECTIONS Identify the main idea of each reading along with the patterns used to develop it. Then decide which patterns are primary.

EXAMPLE

The Dual Nature of Curare

1 *Curare* is a blackish, powderlike substance made from the roots and bark of a woody vine that grows in South America. Although many people know that curare is a deadly poison, they do not know that it can save life as well as take it. Once known only as the "flying death," curare has become one of medicine's most trusted weapons in the fight against disease.

2   Rumors of curare's deadly powers began to circulate as early as the sixteenth century, when explorers came back from journeys to the Amazon. Upon their return, they described Indian hunters who could bring down prey with a single blow from a dart gun. According to eyewitness accounts, hunters boiled the roots and bark of a woody vine into a heavy syrup. Then they dipped darts

into the thick liquid. Expert hunters, capable of finding a target more than a hundred yards away, would blow the darts through hollow reeds, killing their prey almost instantly. Birds died in less than five seconds, and human beings in less than five minutes.

3   Because the jungles were all but unreachable to everyone but the Indians, no one really understood how curare worked until the mid-nineteenth century, when experimenters began to uncover its secrets. It was found that curare, if swallowed, is fairly harmless. But if it penetrates the skin, curare is lethal. Because it relaxes all the muscles in the body—including those that control breathing—the victim quickly suffocates and dies.

4   Once researchers knew how curare worked, they were in a better position to figure out how it might be used to more beneficial ends. However, researchers were reluctant to experiment with curare imported from South America. Its strength varied, and one could never be sure how strong a dosage to use.

5   During World War II, Daniel Bovet, an Italian pharmacologist, developed the first synthetic* form of curare, and the stage was set to discover if curare could prove beneficial to humans. In 1942, Dr. Harold Griffith successfully used it as an anesthetic during surgery. From that time on, a synthetic and diluted* form of curare was used in many operations because its ability to relax the patient's muscles made the surgeon's work easier. Eventually, it was also used to treat rabies and tetanus, diseases that produce severe muscle cramps.

1. What is the overall main idea of the reading?

    a. Curare is an incredibly dangerous poison that can kill in seconds.

    (b.) A deadly poison, curare can also save lives.

    c. Curare has a long and ancient history.

    d. The jungle kept curare a secret for centuries.

2. Which four patterns does the author use to develop the main idea?

    (a.) definition

    (b.) time order: dates and event

    (c.) time order: process

    d. comparison and contrast

    (e.) cause and effect

    f. classification

---

*synthetic: artificial, man-made.
*diluted: weakened.

3. Of those four, which pattern or patterns are the most important?

Cause and effect; definition; sequence of dates and events

Please explain.

Without definition and the cause and effect pattern, the writer couldn't explain how curare kills and cures. Without the sequence of dates and events, the writer couldn't explain how scientists unraveled the poison's secrets with the passage of time.

EXPLANATION Everything in the reading, including the title, points to answer *b* as the overall main idea: Curare has a double nature: It can kill *and* it can heal. To explain that main idea, the author needs the definition pattern to tell readers what curare is. The cause and effect organizational pattern is central to explaining curare's dual nature as killer and healer. The sequence of dates and events pattern plays a key role in organizing the description of how curare's other, more beneficial, uses came to light. Process, probably the least important pattern, helps explain how hunters turned curare into a poison so that they could dip their arrows into it.

1. Schizophrenia, the Mind in Two

1 The term *schizophrenia* was coined in 1911 by the Swiss psychiatrist Eugene Bleuler. Literally, the word means "split mind." Bleuler thought the term effectively expressed one of the disease's central symptoms—a split between the patient's internal world and the external world of social reality.

2 Since Bleuler's time, researchers still have not figured out what causes this mysterious and devastating disease. However, they have been able to identify and name three distinct types.

3 *Disorganized schizophrenia* expresses itself through bizarre and childlike behavior. Victims pay little attention to personal grooming. Sometimes they remain unwashed for days. Behaving like children, they are prone to making faces and given to bouts of giddiness.*

4 Those suffering from a second form of the disease, called *catatonic schizophrenia,* can remain immobile for hours. Mentally withdrawing from their environment, patients adopt rigid postures and fall silent for days, even months. Sometimes, without reason, sufferers will suddenly grow violent and attack anyone who comes near.

---

*giddiness: silliness.

5   In *paranoid schizophrenia*, the most marked symptom is the presence of delusions or fantasies that bear no relation to reality. Patients suffering from this form fear that a person or group is trying to harm them. They often think they are surrounded by enemies and may, in response, become violent.

6   As research continues, it's becoming more and more likely that schizophrenia is not a single disease but a family of diseases that may arise from a variety of causes. By learning more about each type of schizophrenia, researchers hope to find more effective treatments.

1. What is the overall main idea of the reading?

   a. The term *schizophrenia* means "split mind," and was coined by Eugene Bleuler.

   b. Schizophrenia may well be a family of diseases.

   c. Although no one knows the cause of schizophrenia, researchers have identified three distinct types.

   d. Paranoid schizophrenia is perhaps the worst and most debilitating form of the disease.

2. Which three patterns does the author use to develop that main idea?

   a. definition

   b. time order: dates and events

   c. time order: process

   d. comparison and contrast

   e. cause and effect

   f. classification

3. Of those three patterns, which pattern or patterns are the most important?

_____

Please explain.

_____

_____

_____

2. The Johari Window

1 The Johari Window, named after its inventors, Joseph Luft and Harry Ingham, is a useful model for describing the complex process of human interaction. The window, or box, is divided into four panes, or areas, with each area labeled to indicate the kind of information that can be revealed or concealed when we communicate or interact with others: (1) open, (2) blind, (3) hidden, and (4) unknown. Because each person's window reflects his or her psychological makeup, the size of each pane varies with the individual.

2 The **open area** of the Johari Window represents your "public" or "awareness" area. This section symbolizes the information about yourself that both you and others recognize. It includes the information that you are willing to admit or make public. For example, you and everyone you know may be aware that you are a competitive person who doesn't like losing an argument or that your temper is easy to trigger.

3 The **blind area** in the Johari Window represents the information about yourself that others may know, or think they know, but that you are not aware of. For instance, you may think that you have a tendency to be shy and a bit withdrawn, whereas others may see you as open, relaxed, and friendly. Over time, information in the blind area can shift to the open area if other people are willing to mention their view of your behavior.

4 The **hidden area** in the Johari Window shows information that you know but that others do not. This area reflects the private thoughts and feelings you prefer to keep to yourself. For example, you may not want people to know that you are terrified of public speaking despite the fact that you do it frequently. Unlike the open and blind areas, the hidden area may not change over time. In other words, you may always choose to keep certain things about your life a secret.

5 The **unknown area** of the Johari Window is made up of things unknown both to you and to others. This area is reserved for those feelings, talents, and motives that are below the surface of awareness and have never been acknowledged or displayed. For example, you may have a talent for verbal expression, but if you are shy and avoid speaking a lot, you may never know that you have the ability. To offer another example, you may know that you grow angry when conversing with authority figures but have no idea that your anger stems from an unhappy relationship with your older brother. Obviously, if you don't recognize the cause and effect relationship between your childhood and your adult behavior, no one else is likely to either.

1. What is the overall main idea of the reading?

   a. The Johari Window is the creation of Joseph Luft.

   b. The Johari Window consists of four separate panes, or sections.

   c. The Johari Window offers an effective way to describe the human psyche.

   d. The size of the panes in the Johari Window varies with the individual.

2. Which four patterns does the author use to develop that main idea?

   a. definition

   b. time order: dates and events

   c. time order: process

   d. comparison and contrast

   e. cause and effect

   f. classification

3. Of those four, which pattern or patterns are the most important?

   _____

   Please explain.

   _____

   _____

   _____

   _____

■□ **EXERCISE 4   Using Organizational Patterns to Take Notes**

> **DIRECTIONS** Read each selection and identify the pattern or patterns used. Then take complete notes, using the blanks provided.

> **EXAMPLE**

What's in a Name?

1 Over the past three hundred years, from the time they first arrived in America as slaves, African Americans have referred to themselves in a variety of ways (Ghee, 1990). In the seventeenth and eighteenth centuries, the accepted term was "African." Later, "colored" and "Negro" came into common usage.

2   In the mid-1960s, the Black Power movement initiated a nationwide shift from "Negro" to "black." This change was part of a consciousness-raising movement that gave many black people a new sense of pride. "Say it loud—I'm black and I'm proud!" was its rallying cry (see Cross, 1979).

3   Today, in contrast, many African Americans believe that the term "black" has outlived its usefulness and have urged adoption of "African American." Psychologist Kenneth L. Ghee (1990) is an African American who advocates this change for several reasons.

4   In many languages, the term "black" is associated with dirt, wickedness (a "black soul"), and darkness. From Ghee's point of view, thirty years of political change cannot undo three thousand years of negative thinking associated with the concept of blackness.

5   In addition, the colors black and white are total opposites. Ghee believes that constant emphasis on the "oppositeness" of races cannot help race relations.

6   And, finally, most racial and ethnic groups in America label themselves in ways that acknowledge their origins—Mexican Americans, Japanese Americans, Italian Americans, and so on. Only blacks describe themselves without reference to their geographical and cultural origins. Ghee believes that the label "black" conveys an unfortunate message: "Forget your ancestry, remember your skin color. Forget you are African; remember you are black."

7   Not all black Americans agree with Ghee's call for a new label. Many believe that the term "black" remains a powerful way to encourage self-pride and positive self-definition, especially among black children. (Adapted from Rubin et al., *Psychology*, p. 404.)

a. definition
b. time order: dates and events
c. time order: process
d. comparison and contrast
e. cause and effect
f. classification

Main Idea Like many African Americans, psychologist Kenneth L. Ghee prefers the label "African American" instead of "black." Dr. Ghee has several reasons for his belief.

Supporting
Details

1. In many languages, the word "black" is associated with evil and darkness, and it's hard to ignore those associations.

2. The terms "black" and "white" are total opposites and could interfere with improved race relations.

3. The label "black" conveys the message "It's not your origin; it's your skin color that counts."

4. Many black Americans still believe that using the word "black" helps encourage a sense of pride.

EXPLANATION Overall, the reading relies on three different patterns of organization. The sequence of dates and events pattern leads up to the thesis statement. To develop that statement, the authors rely heavily on the cause and effect pattern. But they also occasionally mention points of contrast between Dr. Ghee's position and that of other African Americans. Because the dates and events serve primarily as an introduction, complete notes on this reading need not include any dates and events. However, they should indicate all the reasons offered for rejecting the label "black." They should also identify any significant points of contrast between Dr. Ghee's position and that of other African Americans.

1. The Industrial Revolution in America

1 A young British mechanic named Samuel Slater helped jumpstart the Industrial Revolution in America. In 1790, Slater decided to sail to America. To protect the English textile industry, British law forbade the export of machinery, technology, and skilled workers. To get around that law, Slater memorized the plans for the water-powered spinning machine that had revolutionized the British textile industry. Then he left England disguised as a farmer. A year later, he set up a textile factory in Pawtucket, Rhode Island, to spin raw cotton into thread. Slater's ingenuity resulted in America's first use of the **factory system** of manufacturing, in which all the materials, machinery, and workers required to manufacture a product are assembled in one place. Thanks to Samuel Slater, America's Industrial Revolution was born.

2 By 1814, Francis Cabot Lowell had established a factory in Waltham, Massachusetts, to spin, weave, and bleach cotton all under one roof. He organized the various manufacturing steps

into one uninterrupted sequence, hired professional managers, and was able to produce thirty miles of cloth each day! Lowell's success was a result of the manufacturing technique called specialization. **Specialization** is the separation of a manufacturing process into distinct tasks and the assignment of different tasks to different individuals. The purpose of specialization is to increase the efficiency of industrial workers.

3   The three decades from 1820 to 1850 were the golden age* of invention and innovation in machinery. The widespread use of the cotton gin, invented by Eli Whitney, greatly increased the supply of cotton for the textile industry. Elias Howe's sewing machine, invented in 1846, became available to make material into clothing. The agricultural machinery of John Deere and Cyrus McCormick revolutionized farm production.

4   At the same time, new means of transportation greatly expanded the domestic* markets for American products. The Erie Canal was opened in the 1820s. Soon afterward, thanks to Robert Fulton's invention of the steam engine, steamboats could move upstream against the current and use the rivers as highways for hauling bulk goods. During the 1830s and 1840s, the railroads began to extend the existing transportation system to the west, carrying goods and people much farther than was possible by waterways alone. Between 1860 and 1880, the number of miles of railroad track tripled; by 1900, it had doubled again. (Adapted from Pride et al., *Business,* p. 23.)

a. definition

b. time order: dates and events

c. time order: process

d. comparison and contrast

e. cause and effect

f. classification

Main Idea _____

_____

Supporting _____
Details
_____

_____

*golden age: period of peace, happiness, and wealth; originally used in Greek mythology.
*domestic: related to the home or to a country's internal affairs.

_____

_____

_____

_____

_____

_____

_____

_____

_____

_____

_____

_____

_____

_____

_____

_____

_____

_____

2. Farming the Earth's Jungles

1 Not too many years ago, it was thought that food shortages could readily be solved by cultivating* the world's jungles. Because the lush region of the Amazon Basin of Brazil seemed the perfect site,

_____

*cultivating: in this context, improving and preparing land for planting; also encouraging or promoting.

an agricultural colony was formed and farming was begun. To the surprise of many, the project failed—and failed badly. Yet, in retrospect, several major causes of that failure can be readily identified.

2   The first and most fundamental problem is the tropical soil. Although rain forests are lush and rich in foliage, the soil itself is poor. When foliage falls to the ground, very little is absorbed by the soil because of heavy rains. When the rains come—and they come often—most of the decaying foliage is washed away before it can enrich the earth. As a result, the soil in the tropical jungles never has enough time to absorb nutrients from fallen leaves, making it less appropriate for cultivation than one might assume.

3   Then, too, there is the problem of how quickly the jungle grows. Workers on the project would spend a day clearing a space for planting, only to return a day or two later and find it partially overgrown. The jungle is simply too powerful for humans' puny efforts to make any lasting imprint. One can fly over the area for hours and see no sign of human settlement.

4   Finally, there is the effect of sunlight on jungle soil. In many areas, when the soil is exposed to sunlight, it first hardens, then it turns into *laterite*, a red, rocklike substance containing high concentrations of aluminum and iron. While laterite is so beautiful it has been used to build temples in places such as Cambodia and Vietnam, it is all but impossible to till.*

a. definition

b. time order: dates and events

c. time order: process

d. comparison and contrast

e. cause and effect

f. classification

Main Idea _____

_____

Supporting _____
Details
_____

_____

_____

_____

*till: to prepare for crop raising.

———————————————————————————

———————————————————————————

———————————————————————————

———————————————————————————

———————————————————————————

■ **DIGGING DEEPER**

THE DEVELOPMENT OF SELF IN CHILDHOOD

LOOKING AHEAD Ever say "I'm not myself today" or "I know myself; I don't do well in high-stress situations"? Most of us talk about our "self" without ever really asking the question that underlies this reading, "How do we become who we are?"

1 How do we acquire a sense of identity, or self? Well, it doesn't happen overnight. In Europe and the United States, at least, identity formation is a process that involves several different steps, each occurring at a different age. By the second year of life, for example, most children can correctly label their gender, a key component in identity formation. Around two, children start to make statements like "I am a boy" or "I am a girl." Labels like these then pave the way for a later, more complete and more sophisticated sense of identity.

2   Initially, however, such labels lack permanence. Between the ages of two and three, a boy may claim he can become a girl under certain circumstances—"when I grow up" or "if I grow my hair long." Similarly, a girl might imagine she can change her gender by changing her name—"I'm going to call myself Bob and become a boy." At this early stage in identity formation, children are also prone to thinking they can throw off human identity and become an animal: "Bow-wow, I'm a dog."

3   After the age of five or six, however, children begin to develop a sense of **self-constancy** (the belief that identity remains permanently fixed). At this point, children start to believe that they will stay the same person indefinitely on into the future. They now believe that they will remain human forever and maintain the same gender under all circumstances. Permanent beliefs like these are the most basic and earliest core of a personal identity.

4   Around the age of eight, children begin to include psychological characteristics in their description of self. They say, for example, "I am brave" or "I am happy." What's missing from this early description of self is any sense of context. The child does not realize that he or she is brave in certain situations and fearful in others. Nor does the child recognize that he or she can be brave and fearful at the same time. Rather, the tendency is to focus on one particular feeling or trait and disregard all others. At this point, ambiguous, or conflicting, feelings seem too

threatening to be expressed or even acknowledged, perhaps because the child's internal sense of identity still feels weak and fragile.

5   By the end of middle childhood, both boys and girls are clearly able to think of themselves in more complicated ways. They can, for example, describe themselves as relaxed and skillful when in the classroom but ill-at-ease or uncomfortable in social settings. They are now much less likely to define themselves in simplistic terms, i.e., "I am always angry." Instead, they are more likely to describe themselves in relation to particular situations: "I get angry when I think people are not listening to what I have to say." But generally speaking, it isn't until adulthood that children develop a more flexible sense of self and are able to integrate, or combine, conflicting traits: "I am a friendly person and like to be around people, but I also need some time alone on a regular basis."

6   It's worth pointing out, however, that the process of creating and maintaining a sense of identity does not appear to be the same in all cultures. In Asian countries like India, Japan, and Nepal, for example, three distinct senses of self appear to develop in childhood and persist on into adulthood—the familial, the spiritual, and the individual. The familial self relates only to how one appears or behaves within the context of the family: "I am very obedient to my parents' wishes." In contrast, the spiritual self is defined and organized strictly in terms of religious beliefs: "My relationship to my god is central to my life." As one might expect, the individual self is closest to the European sense of identity described in the preceding paragraphs: "I am a generally happy person." (Source of information: Seifert et al., *Lifespan Development*, pp. 301–302.)

Sharpening Your Skills

DIRECTIONS Answer the following questions by circling the letter of the correct response or filling in the blanks.

1. How would you paraphrase the main idea of the entire reading?

_____

_____

2. Overall, what is the primary pattern in this reading?

    a. definition

    b. time order: dates and events

    c. time order: process

    d. comparison and contrast

    e. cause and effect

    f. classification

3. In order to connect paragraph 5 to paragraph 4, readers have to draw what inference?

    a. By the end of middle childhood, children are better able to express their feelings.

    b. By the end of middle childhood, children's intelligence has increased.

    c. By the end of middle childhood, children have a sense of context when describing themselves.

4. What two patterns of organization do you see at work in the last paragraph?

    a. definition

    b. time order: dates and events

    c. time order: process

    d. comparison and contrast

    e. cause and effect

    f. classification

5. Which statement better describes the purpose of this reading?

    a. The author wants to describe the stages we go through to develop a sense of personal identity.

    b. The author wants to persuade readers that our society over-emphasizes the sense of personal individuality.

INTERNET RESOURCE

For more practice with mixed patterns, see **college.hmco.com/ pic/flemmingRFR10e**, where you will find three levels of interactive quizzes: *Getting Down the Basics*, *Checking Your Progress*, and *Taking the Challenge*.

 ## Test 1: Identifying Main Ideas and Patterns of Organization

DIRECTIONS Read each selection. Then circle the appropriate letter to identify the main idea along with the patterns used to organize the reading.

1. Rattlesnakes

1 The rattlesnake's tail is ringed with several rattles that make a whirring sound when the snake is disturbed and about to attack. Each time the snake molts and loses its skin, a new ring is added to the rattle. However, after several years, the end rattle becomes worn and falls off. Therefore, it is a myth that the age of the snake can be determined by the number of its rattles.

2 What's not a myth, however, is that rattlesnakes can be dangerous. In general they prefer to hide from humans, but they will attack if threatened, and their venom can be deadly.

3 The venom of the rattler contains two different poisons. One stops the action of both heart and lungs. The other destroys tissue. The rattler's venom is contained in two glands, one in each cheek. Long ducts connect the glands to two hollow fangs in the upper jaw. The fangs protrude, or stick out, if the rattler is ready to strike, but they fold back into the mouth when the snake is at rest.

4 Unlike other poisonous snakes—copperheads, water moccasins, and coral snakes—rattlers have never been known to attack human beings without reason. They will attack only if they are disturbed by some sudden intrusion. They also always warn in advance that they are about to strike. Although a rattler's venom is indeed deadly, no one need die of a rattlesnake bite if medical attention is available. There are several antidotes for the snake's poison, all of which render it harmless. The main thing is for the victim to receive the antidote as soon as possible.

1. What is the main idea of the entire reading?
   a. It's not true that the age of a rattler can be determined by counting the number of rings.
   b. Rattler attacks are dangerous and can be deadly.
   c. There are many myths surrounding rattlesnakes.
   d. Rattlers are famous for attacking without reason.

2. Which patterns does the author use to develop that main idea?

   a. definition

   b. time order: dates and events

   c. time order: process

   d. comparison and contrast

   e. cause and effect

   f. classification

2. Open Versus Closed Questions

1 The questions we ask can be open or closed (Goodman and Esterly, 1988). *Closed questions* are ones that people can answer with a "yes" or a "no" or some other equally short answer. If we meet other people for the first time and ask them, "How long have you lived here?" we are asking a closed question. *Open questions,* in contrast, are designed to obtain more information than closed questions. Open questions are asked in such a way so that people cannot give a one-word answer. Asking someone "What kinds of experiences have you had since you moved here?" is an open question that would produce more information than a closed question such as "Do you like your new school?"

2   If we really want a direct answer, we should ask a closed question. To illustrate, if we want to know if our spouse or partner wants to go to a movie tonight, we shouldn't ask, "When's the last time we went to the movies?" The answer to this question may or may not lead the other person to suggest that we go to the movies. But if we really want to go to the movies that night, a closed question such as "Would you like to go to a movie tonight?" would prove more effective.

3   Keep in mind, too, that asking several closed questions instead of one good open question can make a small problem seem like a big one (Goodman and Esterly, 1988). To illustrate, suppose you are in conflict with your roommate, and you have just explained your position. Now you want to know how your roommate feels about what you have just said. Unfortunately, if you ask a number of closed questions, your roommate is likely to feel like she or he is being interrogated.* To get more information, you could ask an open question such as "How do you feel about what I just said?" (Gudykunst et al., *Building Bridges*, p. 281.)

---

*interrogated: required to answer questions as if in a police station.

1. What is the main idea of the entire reading?

  a. There are two types of questions: open and closed.

  b. Closed questions are always better than open ones.

  c. Open questions almost never produce the necessary information.

  d. To get honest answers, we need to ask closed questions.

2. Which patterns does the author use to develop that main idea?

  a. definition

  b. time order: dates and events

  c. time order: process

  d. comparison and contrast

  e. cause and effect

  f. classification

3. Radio Rescues

1 The invention of radio had a profound effect on the safety of ships at sea. When ships got into trouble, it became possible to summon aid by radio. One of the first such cases occurred in 1898, when radio signals were used to help a sinking vessel.

2 A truly dramatic rescue at sea took place in 1909. When the SS *Republic* began to sink off New York, the wireless* operator immediately sent out a distress signal. Other ships detected it and came to the position indicated. Luckily, all the passengers were rescued. The rescue made newspaper headlines, and the public was thrilled.

3 Unfortunately, a historic rescue effort in 1912 was less successful. When the "unsinkable" *Titanic* struck an iceberg in the North Atlantic, the wireless operator tried to alert nearby ships. Unfortunately, their radio crews had gone to bed for the night. However, he was able to make contact with a station on shore (in Wanamaker's department store in New York City), whose stronger signal could reach more distant points. The young operator, David Sarnoff, stayed at his post for many hours, making contact with other vessels. Unfortunately, by the time the ships he had contacted arrived the next morning, the great passenger liner had sunk to the bottom of the ocean. Some 1,500 people drowned, including the *Titanic*'s heroic wireless operator, who tried all night to summon aid until he went down with the ship. (Adapted from DeFleur and Dennis, *Understanding Mass Communication*, pp. 190–191.)

_____

*wireless: a radio telegraph.

1. What is the main idea of the entire reading?

    a. When the *Titanic* sank, the wireless operator went down with the ship.

    b. The dramatic rescue of the *SS Republic* dramatically illustrated the effect of radio on ship safety.

    c. Even radio communication could not help the *Titanic.*

    d. Although the invention of radio profoundly improved ship safety, even radio communication could not help the *Titanic.*

2. What patterns does the author use to develop that main idea?

    a. definition

    b. time order: dates and events

    c. timc order: process

    d. comparison and contrast

    e. cause and effect

    f. classification

4. Creativity: Not Just for the Few

1 **Creativity** is thinking in ways that lead to original, practical, and meaningful solutions to problems or that generate new ideas or forms of artistic expression. The creation of a new product, for example, may solve a problem in a novel and useful way. Creativity is not limited to a few creative geniuses. Psychologists recognize that virtually all of us have the ability to be creative in our daily lives (Simonton, 2000; Ward, Smith, & Vaid, 1997). For example, a parent who invents a new activity for a four-year-old, a chef who combines ingredients in innovative ways, a worker who improves on a production method—all demonstrate creativity.

2 Though most of us have the potential to be creative, some people are clearly more creative than others (Gelade, 1995). More creative people typically have at least an average to high-average IQ. However, there doesn't seem to be any relationship between creativity and IQs in the high range (above 120) (Csikszentmihalyi, 1996). As psychologist Robert Sternberg (2001) notes, products developed by highly intelligent people may be of high quality, but they are not necessarily novel. Creativity goes beyond general intelligence.

3 Creativity is measured in different ways but most commonly through tests that tap *divergent thinking.* **Divergent thinking** is the wellspring of invention; it is the ability to conceive of new ways of viewing situations and new uses for familiar objects

(Guilford, 1977; Runco, 1991). By contrast, **convergent thinking** is the attempt to find the one correct answer to a problem. . . .

4   Creativity typically springs from the expansion or modification of familiar categories or concepts. Even creative geniuses incorporate existing knowledge in producing something fresh and original. Would Monet* have experimented with splashes of color to create impressions of water lilies if he had lived several hundred years earlier in a time of more representational* art? Would Mozart have composed his masterpieces if he hadn't had the opportunity of hearing Haydn's music? The ability to take what is given in our knowledge structures and modify and expand on it is one of the basic processes of creative thinking.

5   Do you have a creative personality? Psychologist Mihaly Csikszentmihalyi (1996) studied creative individuals in the arts, science, politics, and business. He looked for similarities among them and found one word that best captured their personalities: *complexity. Complexity* refers to "contradictory extremes" within the personality. In Csikszentmihalyi's view, creative people are able to move between extremes of aggressiveness or competitiveness on the one hand and nurturance or cooperativeness on the other, between intelligence and naivety, between convergent and divergent modes of thinking, between playfulness and discipline, and between having a hard-nosed view of reality and a sense of innocence or wonder. Csikszentmihalyi believes extreme sides are present in each of our personalities but that we tend to let one side wither because others perceive it as "bad" and the other extreme as "good." In his view, creative people can tap both dimensions of their personality at the same time or at different times, depending on the situation. (Adapted from Nevid, *Psychology: Concepts and Applications*, pp. 270–271.)

1. What is the main idea of the entire reading?

   a. Ironically, being in familiar surroundings is likely to bring out originality and creativity.

   b. People with high IQs are likely to be more creative than most.

   c. Creativity is not limited to one specific group of people; to one degree or another, many people have the ability to be creative.

   d. Because they have a gift for divergent thinking, geniuses show the kind of creativity most of us cannot even recognize, let alone exhibit.

---

*Claude Monet (1840–1926): French Impressionist painter famous for paintings of water lilies.
*representational art: art meant to reflect or represent the real world.

2. Which patterns does the author use to develop the main idea?

    a. definition

    b. time order: dates and events

    c. time order: process

    d. comparison and contrast

    e. cause and effect

    f. classification

5. Is It Wise to "Treat" Shortness?

1 It's hard to be a short person in America. We live in a country where kids seem to grow just a little taller every year, and our society idealizes the tall. To make things even worse, short people are often subjected to ridicule and discrimination. Studies have even shown that short people are generally viewed as less competent than the tall. However, shortness may soon be a thing of the past. Growth-hormone treatments are making it possible for shorter-than-average children to grow more than they would have without treatment. Not everyone agrees, though, about whether the advantages of this treatment outweigh the disadvantages.

2 The drug that has sparked the debate about the wisdom of manipulating children's height is called Humatrope. Used since the 1980s to treat children with growth-stunting diseases, it was approved by the Food and Drug Administration in 2003 for use with boys who are predicted to grow no more than 5 feet 3 inches and with girls who are predicted to grow no taller than 4 feet 11 inches. For these children, Humatrope can add anywhere from one to three inches in height.

3 Proponents of Humatrope say that giving shorter-than-average kids the opportunity to grow a few extra inches will have positive benefits. For one thing, adding height allows children to escape the stigma that comes with being short. Thus, kids avoid not only their peers' teasing but also the discrimination that short people frequently encounter as adults.

4 As a result, growth-hormone treatments can prevent the psychological damage that often results from being unusually short. Many kids who have taken Humatrope report that their additional height halted the taunts of other children and ended their status as social outcasts. Growing taller also improved their self image and increased their confidence. Humatrope patients also report an improvement in their overall quality of life. As they grow taller, their struggles to reach out-of-reach objects like water fountains

and gas pedals diminish, allowing them to function more easily in the everyday world.

5   Critics of growth-hormone treatments, however, argue that the positive effects of Humatrope do not outweigh the drug's drawbacks. They point out that Humatrope has both known and unknown side effects. A few patients have developed chronic headaches, arthritis, and even diabetes while undergoing treatment. And although the drug has been in use for more than fifteen years and appears to be safe, its long-term side effects are still not known.

6   Humatrope's high price is another disadvantage. The drug costs $10,000 to $25,000 per year, and a child must take the drug for several years. Because insurance companies will not pay for cosmetic uses of growth-hormone therapy, the expense may prove to be too great for many families with smaller children.

7   The frequency of injections and the overall length of treatment, too, may not justify the potential gain of a few more inches. Children must endure as many as six shots a week for four or more years. Critics argue that the effort required to keep up with this treatment schedule, along with the pain and suffering involved with getting so many shots, is not worth the end result.

8   Humatrope's opponents also criticize the drug for helping perpetuate the idea that shortness is an abnormality or a disease in need of a cure. They claim that the use of growth-hormone treatments may ultimately reinforce the stigma attached to being short and encourage people to pass negative judgment on those who do not take advantage of the remedy. Some medical professionals worry that the ability to "heal" short people will lead to increased pressure to change other characteristics—such as large feet or the shape of one's head—which are simply human traits, not illnesses. (Sources of information: Lauren Neergaard, "FDA Approves Hormone Shot for Short Kids," *Salon*, July 25, 2003, www.salon.com/mwt/wire/2003/07/25/hormone/print.html; "Growth Hormones for Kids?" *CBSNews.com*, June 12, 2003, www.cbsnews.com/stories/2003/06/11/earlyshow/health/printable558240.shtml.)

1. What is the main idea of the entire reading?

   a. Advocates of Humatrope insist that escaping the consequences of being short makes the benefits worth the risk of side effects.

   b. Growth hormone treatments will make being short a thing of the past.

    c. Humatrope, the drug that may well do away with being under average height, has strong supporters and equally strong critics.

    d. Patients who take Humatrope say that their quality of life has improved.

2. Which patterns does the author use to develop that main idea?

    a. definition

    b. time order: dates and events

    c. time order: process

    d. comparison and contrast

    e. cause and effect

    f. classification

 **Test 2: Identifying Main Ideas and Patterns of Organization**

DIRECTIONS Read each selection. Then circle the appropriate letters to identify the main idea along with the patterns used to organize the reading.

1. The Origin of Ice Cream

1 References to ice cream already appear in the time of Alexander the Great (356–323 BC), yet no one really knows who invented the frozen dessert. The earliest written records suggest that ice cream evolved gradually, in response to the human desire for foods both cool and sweet.

2 Biblical allusions to ice cream show that King Solomon was a lover of cool, sweet drinks. Historians also note that Roman emperor Nero Claudius Caesar (AD 37–68) would frequently send teams of runners into the mountains for freshly fallen snow. When they returned, palace cooks would flavor the snow with honey, fruits, and juices. The result was something like our modern-day snow cone.

3 More than a thousand years later, the Italian explorer Marco Polo returned from the Far East with a recipe for a dessert very like our modern sherbet. By the sixteenth century, the Italians had tinkered* with the original recipe and had become devoted lovers of ice cream. In 1553, when the Italian Catherine de Medici married Henry II of France, she brought the Italian recipe for ice cream with her to her adopted country. As a result, French royalty also began eating ice cream. By 1670, the general public could purchase dishes of ice cream in local cafes.

4 In the eighteenth century, ice cream became increasingly popular throughout Europe. By 1768, a number of recipes had been collected and made into a popular book titled *The Art of Making Frozen Desserts.*

5 Always eager to mimic the British, Americans also began eating ice cream in the early eighteenth century. By the middle of the nineteenth century, the treat was so popular that Americans were manufacturing it in bulk. The first ice cream cone, however, did not appear until 1903, when an Italian ice cream salesman named Italo Marioni patented the mold for the cone.

---

*tinkered: experimented or played with.

1. What is the main idea of the entire reading?

    a. Human beings, like chimpanzees, love all things cool and sweet.

    b. The explorer Marco Polo introduced ice cream to Europe after he returned from the Far East.

    c. Ice cream has been around for centuries.

    d. The first reference to ice cream appears in an account of Alexander the Great's reign.

2. Which patterns does the author use to develop that main idea?

    a. definition

    b. time order: dates and events

    c. time order: process

    d. comparison and contrast

    e. cause and effect

    f. classification

2. Communication Between the Sexes

1 According to Deborah Tannen, the best-selling author of *You Just Don't Understand*, men and women engage in different types of talk. In Tannen's terms, women engage in more *rapport* talk*, while men engage in *report talk*. Men feel comfortable doing "public speaking," whereas women are more at ease with "private speaking."

2 From Tannen's perspective, men view talk as a way of asserting one's independence; report talk is their way of exhibiting knowledge and skill, thereby gaining power in social situations. Tannen maintains that even as little boys, men use talk to get and keep attention in a group. Quite naturally, then, men grow up feeling more comfortable speaking in public. Consequently, they are likely to use their public-speaking techniques in private situations, even if those techniques are inappropriate to the context.

3 In contrast, Tannen believes that women use language primarily to establish and maintain relationships. Women see talk as a way of moving closer to others; a conversation's content is less important than the feeling communicated by the words. Here again, Tannen maintains that the different uses of language are already apparent in childhood. Girls tend to be critical of peers who assert themselves by speaking out. Perhaps as a result, girls

---

*rapport: agreement or harmony.

often grow up feeling uncomfortable when called on to do public speaking.

4   If Tannen is correct, then the prescription for a better future is simple. Men and women need to understand and learn the other's language. Whereas women have to grow more adept at report talk and more comfortable speaking in public, men have to learn the art of rapport talk and use it to connect with others. When each sex can speak the other's language, then perhaps men and women can truly communicate with one another.

1. What is the main idea of the entire reading?

    a. According to Deborah Tannen, men and women need to spend more time learning the other's language.

    b. According to Deborah Tannen, men use language to prove their authority; women use language to show support.

    c. According to Deborah Tannen, men and women will probably always talk at cross purposes.

    d. According to Deborah Tannen, men and women use language in different ways.

2. Which patterns does the author use to develop that main idea?

    a. definition

    b. time order: dates and events

    c. time order: process

    d. comparison and contrast

    e. cause and effect

    f. classification

3. American Lifestyles

1 Paul Ray, vice president of the firm American Lives Inc., spent a decade studying the values and lifestyles of modern Americans. In the process, Ray identified three distinct groups that play major roles in today's society.

2   Most traditional are the *heartlanders,* who represent a sizable portion of the population—nearly fifty-six million people. Heartlanders are conservative and slow to accept change. They cling to the idea that America's small-town past represents all that is good and desirable. Accordingly, heartlanders value antique furniture and old-fashioned clothes more than the latest technology or newest fashion.

3   *Modernists* are the direct opposite of heartlanders. As their name suggests, modernists focus on what's happening now instead of looking fondly to the past. Their political views are liberal. Concerned for the welfare of others less fortunate, they also enjoy spending money. Modernists believe that living in a big city gives them status, as does buying new gadgets and luxury items. Ray estimates that about eighty-eight million people are modernists.

4   *Cultural creatives* make up a third, highly independent group. Politically, they lean neither to the right nor to the left. Unlike the heartlanders, they do not revere* the past. In contrast to the modernists, cultural creatives don't celebrate the trendy. Instead, they try to lead a life they consider natural and genuine. For example, cultural creatives like houses that fit the natural landscape and scorn both antiques and high-tech gadgetry. Cultural creatives prefer handmade objects to mechanically perfect ones, rejecting anything plastic, imitation, or throwaway. Ray calculates that about forty-four million Americans fit the profile of cultural creatives.

1. What is the main idea of the entire reading?

    a. For more than a decade, Paul Ray studied the lifestyles of today's Americans.

    b. Heartlanders represent the largest percentage of the population.

    c. In his study of American lifestyles, Paul Ray came up with three different groups.

    d. Cultural creatives lead the most independent, free-wheeling kind of life.

2. Which patterns does the author use to develop that main idea?

    a. definition

    b. time order: dates and events

    c. time order: process

    d. comparison and contrast

    e. cause and effect

    f. classification

---

*revere: hold sacred.

4. America's Bumpy Economic Ride

1 The Roaring Twenties ended with the sudden crash of the stock market in 1929 and the near collapse of the economy. The Great Depression that resulted in the 1930s was a time of misery and human suffering. The unemployment rate varied between 16 and 25 percent in the years between 1931 and 1939. The value of goods and services produced in America fell by almost half. People lost their faith in business and its ability to satisfy the needs of society without government interference.

2 After the election of President Franklin D. Roosevelt, the federal government developed a number of programs to get the economy moving again. By creating these programs, the government got deeply involved in business for the first time. Many business people opposed this intervention, but they reluctantly accepted new government regulations.

3 In 1939, World War II broke out in Europe and helped America recover from the Depression. The need for vast quantities of war materials—first for our allies and then for the American military as well—spurred industrial expansion. This rapid economic pace continued after the war, and the 1950s and 1960s witnessed both increasing production and a rising standard of living. **Standard of living** is a measure of how well off an individual or a society is, mainly in terms of satisfaction through goods and services.

4 In the mid-1970s, however, a shortage of crude oil led to a new set of problems for business. Petroleum products supply most of the energy required to produce goods and services and to transport goods around the world. As the cost of petroleum increased, so did the cost of energy and the cost of goods and services. The result was **inflation**—a general rise in the level of prices—at a rate well over 10 percent per year during the early 1980s. (Pride et al., *Business*, p. 24.)

1. What is the main idea of the entire reading?

    a. Between 1931 and 1939, America went into a deep economic slump.

    b. The U.S. economy has known many ups and downs.

    c. After the highs of the Roaring Twenties came the Great Depression.

    d. Despite economic lows, the U.S. economy always comes back strong.

2. Which patterns does the author use to develop that main idea?

a. definition

b. time order: dates and events

c. time order: process

d. comparison and contrast

e. cause and effect

f. classification

5. Power and Relational Styles

1 The different balances of power in relationships create three potential styles: complementary, symmetrical, and parallel.

2 The **complementary style** represents an imbalance in power such that one person is dominant and the other is submissive. This might sound like a terrible arrangement, but such relationships are satisfactory if both parties are agreeable to the arrangement. Your relationship with your instructors is probably complementary. The instructor gives you assignments and exams and you comply. Think about your personal relationships. Some of them are probably complementary in that either you or your friend is always the one who initiates interactions, calls the other, and decides when to go out together and what to do.

3 A **symmetrical style** is a relational style in which both parties have fairly equal power. If you and your friend are both active in initiating interactions and deciding when to go out and what to do, that is a symmetrical style. You may be inclined to think that symmetrical relationships are inherently better than complementary relationships. However, imagine what happens in a marriage if both parties want to be responsible for deciding how to spend their money. Reaching a decision about what to buy and how much to spend would sometimes produce conflict and a need for negotiation. Having two individuals with equal power can produce problems when they have different goals.

4 In a **parallel style** relationship, one partner sometimes has more power or less power than the other, and sometimes both partners are equal. The style varies according to the situation and the needs and skills of each person. Working out who has power in a given situation is one of the relational dynamics that couples must negotiate as they develop a more intimate relationship. Parallel styles are continually developing as couples encounter new situations and decide whether to approach them in a complementary or symmetrical manner.

5   Each of the styles related to power is reflected in interpersonal communication. In a complementary relationship, we would likely hear one partner giving commands or directions and the other asking questions of clarification; communication would almost seem unbalanced. Symmetrical relationships and parallel relationships would incorporate a fair amount of disagreement and conflict as the partners tried to work out decisions. Well-developed parallel relationships would eventually resolve many issues, and the amount of conflict could be expected to subside. (Redmond, *Communication: Theories and Applications,* pp. 147–148.)

1. What is the main idea of the entire reading?
   a. Relationships all have their own unique style.
   b. Relationships balance power in three different ways.
   c. The complementary balance of power is the one all couples should strive for.
   d. Relationships usually balance power in different ways, depending on the time and situation.

2. Which patterns does the author use to develop that main idea?
   a. definition
   b. time order: dates and events
   c. time order: process
   d. comparison and contrast
   e. cause and effect
   f. classification

Test 3: Identifying Main Ideas and Patterns of Organization

DIRECTIONS Read each selection. Then circle the appropriate letters to identify the main idea along with the patterns used to organize the reading.

1. Styles of Leadership

1 For many years, leadership was viewed as a combination of personality traits, such as self-confidence, intelligence, and dependability. A consensus on which traits were most important was difficult to achieve, however, and attention turned to styles of leadership behavior. In the last few decades, three styles of leadership have been identified: authoritarian, laissez-faire, and democratic.

2 The **authoritarian leader** holds all authority and responsibility, with communication usually moving from top to bottom. This leader assigns workers to specific tasks and expects orderly, precise results.

3 At the other extreme is the **laissez-faire leader**, who waives responsibility and allows subordinates to work as they choose with a minimum of interference. Communication flows equally among group members. The **democratic leader** holds final responsibility but also delegates authority to others, who participate in determining work assignments. In this leadership style, communication is active both upward and downward.

4 Each of these styles has its advantages and disadvantages. For example, democratic leadership can motivate employees to work effectively because it is *their* decisions that they are implementing.* However, the decision-making process takes time that subordinates could otherwise be devoting to their tasks. (Pride et al., *Business*, pp. 186–187.)

1. What is the main idea of the entire reading?

    a. It's been difficult to identify the kind of personality that makes for a better leader.

    b. No leadership style is completely effective on its own; it has to be combined with other qualities.

    c. Over the last decades, three leadership styles have been defined by researchers.

    d. Most people think that the ability to lead requires a certain kind of personality.

---

*implementing: putting into practice.

2. Which patterns does the author use to develop that main idea?

   a. definition

   b. time order: dates and events

   c. time order: process

   d. comparison and contrast

   e. cause and effect

   f. classification

2. How a Lake Becomes Land

1 As soon as a lake is created, natural forces begin to fill it in. Although the process can take from a few years to several centuries, over time every lake is bound to become dry land.

2   A lake is born when water fills a depression in the land. The first creatures to enter a newly born lake are usually tiny drifting water plants and animals called *plankton.* In time, the plankton increase their numbers and begin to support larger colonies of animals such as mussels, insects, fish, and birds.

3   As generations of animals succeed one another, some plant and animal remains are recycled by scavengers, but inevitably some of the remains fall to the lake floor. Thus, the bottom is built up, perhaps a foot or two a century. Gradually, the lake becomes shallower.

4   Once the lake becomes shallow, submerged water plants begin to take root in those parts of the lake where the bottom has built up the most. They slow the currents, speeding up the accumulation of debris* on the bottom. At the same time, plants such as cattails, bulrushes, and burr reeds begin to sprout at the water's edge. Over time, the rising debris and the shoreline plants meet. Eventually, they combine forces and transform the lake into marshy land.

1. What is the main idea of the entire reading?

   a. Every lake is in the process of becoming dry land.

   b. A lake is born when the earth sinks and the water builds up in the resulting hollow.

   c. Lakes build up from the bottom thanks to the work of scavengers.

   d. Plankton is the key element that changes a lake back into land.

---

*debris: the scattered remains of broken or destroyed objects.

2. Which patterns does the author use to develop that main idea?

   a. definition

   b. time order: dates and events

   c. time order: process

   d. comparison and contrast

   e. cause and effect

   f. classification

3. The Absence of Sunlight

1 Because they do so many things that seem to prepare them for the approach of winter, plants and animals seem to know that winter's coming, but of course neither knows about the future the way humans do. So what causes these behavioral changes? According to biologists, both animals and plants are profoundly affected by the decrease in the amount of sunlight they receive in autumn.

2 Among animals, the change in the day's length and the resulting decrease in sunlight are both registered* in the *hypothalamus*, the "master control" gland of the brain. In response, the hypothalamus secretes hormones that trigger chemical reactions throughout the animal's body. Among deer, for example, autumn brings on mating urges. Thus, fall is the season when bucks lock antlers and compete for females.

3 Another instinctive animal response to messages from the hypothalamus is the urge to eat more. During the autumn months, birds and squirrels increase their food-gathering activities. By eating more, they build up additional layers of fat, which will nourish the animals during the winter.

4 Plants also respond to the decrease in sunlight; however, they do it without the help of a master control gland. The leaves of deciduous* trees respond to the lack of light by changing color, drying out, and falling to the ground. The fallen leaves then protect and nourish the tree's roots.

1. What is the main idea of the entire reading?

   a. Amazingly, animals and plants know when winter is on the way.

   b. Biologists believe that plants and animals are affected by the amount of sunlight they receive and this causes them to prepare for winter.

---

*registered: recognized.
*deciduous: falling off or shedding at a particular season.

    c. Plants and animals respond to sunlight because they both have a control gland called the hypothalamus.

    d. Biologists don't understand how it is that plants and animals know when winter is on the way.

2. Which patterns does the author use to develop that main idea?

    a. definition

    b. time order: dates and events

    c. time order: process

    d. comparison and contrast

    e. cause and effect

    f. classification

4. Staying Healthy in the Nineteenth Century

1 Prior to 1860, no one in the United States really understood how deadly communicable diseases like cholera and yellow fever were transmitted. At a loss for an explanation, doctors offered up different theories about contagious diseases—that they were transmitted by touch or poisonous gases given off by dead animals and rotting vegetation. Unfortunately, those same theories were quickly disproved by practical experience. Quarantines did nothing to prevent either cholera or yellow fever, which strongly suggested that touch was not the source of contagion.* In addition, many of the country's poorest residents, who often lived in the most abject* conditions, were not stricken during epidemics. This simple fact all but eliminated the poisonous gases theory of disease.

2   Physicians' inability to come up with convincing explanations for contagious diseases caused the general public to be highly cynical of medical expertise. As a result, in the first half of the nineteenth century, many Americans turned to more unorthodox* therapies that promised good health and a long life. Two of the most popular therapies of the time were hydropathy and the Graham diet.

3   Practitioners of *hydropathy,* or the water cure, claimed to improve their patients' health by making them drink five to ten glasses of water while being immersed in hot or cold baths. The

---

*contagion: disease transmission.
*abject: miserable, wretched, poorest.
*unorthodox: unusual, untraditional.

reasoning behind this so-called cure was that water absorbed in heavy doses could flush out any poisons in the system. Whether or not the cure had any scientific basis, it was highly popular in the mid 1850s, when there were twenty-seven hydropathic sanatoriums* in the United States. These sanatoriums were particularly popular with wealthy women. They seemed to like the idea of escaping their responsibilities at home and whiling away a few hours in the bathtub.

4   Unlike the water cure, which required money and time, the *Graham diet*, created by temperance* advocate Sylvester Graham,* was popular with rich and poor alike. Alarmed by the cholera epidemic of 1832, Graham decided that Americans could protect themselves from disease by adopting a new diet. Insisting that his countrymen ate too much red meat, he urged his followers to eat more vegetables and fruit. He also urged them to consume several daily servings of a coarse, whole-grain bread he called "Graham bread." It was the bread, primarily, that would flush out the digestive system, thereby removing any bodily poisons that might cause disease.

5   Some of Graham's most enthusiastic followers were members of reform movements.* Like Graham, many nineteenth-century reformers were convinced that society's evils could be traced to dietary habits. Some abolitionists, for example, argued that red meat encouraged lust and violence in white men and thereby contributed to the brutality of slavery. Yet Graham's followers were not limited to social reformers. On the contrary, his books sold well throughout the United States, and all classes of people attended his lectures. There were even boarding houses that claimed to set "a Graham table."

6   On the whole, the Graham diet was a good deal more popular than hydropathy. It also had more staying power, remaining fashionable until the early twentieth century. Still, what made both therapies especially desirable to the American public was their absence of medical approval. In the mid-nineteenth century, many of the treatments advocated by doctors were thought to do more harm than good, and a lack of medical acceptance was considered a virtue rather than a failing.

---

*sanatoriums: institutions for treatment of disease.
*temperance: in this context it means restraint in the use of alcohol, moderation.
*Sylvester Graham: yes, this is the origin of the Graham cracker.
*reform movements: groups devoted to social change.

1. What is the main idea of the entire reading?

   a. Before 1860, the causes of deadly communicable diseases were unknown and the death rate soared, but doctors could do nothing to cure their patients.

   b. Nineteenth-century America did not hold doctors in great respect.

   c. The public's general mistrust of doctors led many nineteenth-century Americans to try highly unorthodox medical treatments like the Graham diet and hydropathy.

   d. Quarantines did nothing to protect nineteenth-century Americans from disease; as a result, many men and women tried alternative methods.

2. Which patterns does the author use to develop that main idea?

   a. definition

   b. time order: dates and events

   c. time order: process

   d. comparison and contrast

   e. cause and effect

   f. classification

Test 4: Identifying Main Ideas and Primary Patterns

DIRECTIONS After reading each selection, identify the main idea and the patterns used to explain it. Then decide which of those patterns are most essential.

1. Laura Bassi's Breakthrough

1   In the eighteenth century, the field of science was virtually* closed to women. In France, the Marquise du Chatelet might write a highly regarded book about Newtonian physics,* but its very excellence spoke against her. The manuscript was so good it was widely assumed that it had been written by the countess's tutor rather than by the countess herself. Sadly enough, the tutor, Samuel König, did nothing to discourage the rumors about the book's authorship. Instead, he took full credit for the marquise's efforts. In England, the leading nation in science, the situation was worse. Women were strictly prohibited from admission to scientific societies. Indeed the English denied women access to all forms of scientific inquiry.*

2   Italy, however, was something of an exception to the general European rule, and a number of provincial* scientific societies did admit women. It's perhaps not surprising, then, that the one woman who crashed the barriers erected against her gender was an Italian, Laura Bassi (1711–1778). Bassi actually became a respected scientific figure at a time when women were generally thought to be too intellectually limited for the rigors* of scientific study. By all accounts, she thoroughly disproved the sexist notion that women and the sciences were opposed to one another.

3   Bassi was one of the lucky women of her era. Her father was an enlightened* lawyer in Bologna, Italy, who believed that women should be educated. Thus, young Laura was schooled by the family physician, Gaetano Tacconi. By the age of twenty she was familiar with the scientific concepts of the times, particularly Newtonian physics. Because her father encouraged her to display her erudition* at social gatherings, Bassi's reputation as a learned

---

*virtually: practically, for all purposes.
*Newtonian physics: Isaac Newton's (1642–1727) explanation of universal gravitation and the laws of motion.
*inquiry: study, exploration.
*provincial: situated away from the capital.
*rigors: difficulties.
*enlightened: educated, open to change.
*erudition: knowledge.

woman grew. Tested by a group of professors and scholars anxious to prove that a woman could not possibly be so clever, Bassi astonished the disbelievers with her intelligence, learning, and eloquence.* Local scholars were so impressed that in 1731 they invited her to join the Bologna Institute of Sciences and to study for a degree at the University of Bologna. On May 12, 1732, Bassi became only the second woman ever to gain an academic degree. A few months later, she became the world's first female professor.

4   But despite her breakthrough, those in charge of the University of Bologna had very rigid ideas about what Bassi could or could not do as a professor. For example, she had no say over her schedule. For the university's leaders, she was an intriguing oddity. They might trot her out for display to curious visiting scholars, but they would not let her lecture on a regular basis. Nor, for that matter, could she pursue her own studies or research. Still, Bassi was not an easy woman to control, and to a degree, she managed to go her own way.

5   In 1749, to escape university restrictions, Bassi began offering private lessons in experimental physics. She also began championing Newtonian physics at a time when it was relatively unknown in Italy, and she promoted Newton's findings about gravity even in the face of widespread intellectual resistance. In addition, Bassi corresponded with the leading physicists of the day—men like Roger Boscovitch, who founded the idea of a universal force of nature, and Alessandro Volta, who pioneered electrical research. Thus, she was crucial to keeping her country abreast of new scientific theories.

6   In 1776, when Bassi was sixty-five, the university acknowledged her contributions to scientific thought by bestowing upon her an unheard of honor for a woman: She was appointed to a chair in experimental physics, and her husband, Giovanni Veratti, father of her eight children, was appointed as her assistant.

7   Although it would be nice to learn that Bassi's achievements paved the way for other women, they did not. On the contrary, many of Bassi's male colleagues had been disturbed by her extraordinary progress and were reluctant to let any other female follow in her footsteps. After Bassi's death in 1778, it took more than a century, and the arrival of Marie Curie,* for another woman to find herself at home in the male-dominated world of

---

*eloquence: gifted way of speaking.
*Marie Curie (1867–1934): Polish-born French chemist, who, with her husband, Pierre, and another researcher, won the 1903 Nobel Prize for research on radioactivity. In 1911, she also became the first person to win a second Nobel, this time for chemistry.

physics. (Source of information: Margaret Wertheim, *Pythagoras' Trousers*. New York: W. W. Norton, 1995, pp. 135–137.)

1. What is the main idea of the entire reading?

a. In the eighteenth century, science was closed to women.

b. In the eighteenth century, Laura Bassi defied the stereotypes to become a respected scientist.

c. In the eighteenth century, if a woman did good work in science, it was assumed a brother or father had done it for her.

d. Thanks to her father, Laura Bassi became a respected scientist.

2. Which patterns are used to develop that main idea?

a. definition

b. time order: dates and events

c. time order: process

d. comparison and contrast

e. cause and effect

f. classification

3. Which pattern or patterns are the most essential to developing the main idea of the entire reading?

_____

Please explain.

_____

_____

_____

2. **Motivation and Morale**

1 A **motive** is something that causes a person to act. A successful athlete, for example, is said to be "highly motivated." A student who avoids doing homework is said to be "unmotivated." Generally, **motivation** is defined as the internal process that energizes, directs, and sustains behavior. It is the personal "force" that causes you or me to act in a particular way. Thus, job rotation may increase your enthusiasm for your work so that you devote more energy to it. Job rotation, however, might not have the same effect on me.

2   **Morale** is sometimes confused with motivation, but it is different. Morale refers to an employee's attitude or feelings about the job, his or her superiors, and the firm itself. High morale results mainly from the satisfaction of needs met by the job or its rewards. One need that might be satisfied, for instance, is the desire to be recognized for a job well done. Another need that can be satisfied by work is the longing for financial security. Whereas high morale can fuel motivation, low morale can do the opposite. It can lead to shoddy work, absenteeism, and high turnover rates as employees leave to seek more satisfying jobs with other firms.

3   Beginning in the late nineteenth century, both motivation and morale became the subjects of research as employers sought to increase productivity. Probably the most famous studies of motivation and morale were performed by Frederick Taylor, considered the father of scientific management. After studying worker behavior at two different steel companies, Taylor claimed that most people work only to earn money. He therefore reasoned that pay should be tied directly to output. Taylor's theory made an impression on employers and gave rise to the **piece-rate system**, under which employees were paid a certain amount for each unit produced. Today, however, Taylor's theory is considered overly simplistic. It is generally acknowledged that people work for a variety of reasons other than pay.

1. What is the main idea of the entire reading?

    a. When it comes to worker productivity, morale is more important than motivation.

    b. The most famous studies of motivation and morale were conducted by Frederick Taylor.

    c. Motivation and morale may differ in meaning, but both are important to job satisfaction.

    d. The piece-rate system was based on an inaccurate notion of what motivates people to work.

2. Which patterns are used to develop that main idea?

    a. definition

    b. time order: dates and events

    c. time order: process

    d. comparison and contrast

    e. cause and effect

    f. classification

3. Which pattern or patterns are the most essential to developing the main idea of the entire reading?

_____

Please explain.

_____

_____

_____

3. Ordering Needs

1 Both biological and psychological needs play important roles in human motivation. But how do these needs relate to each other? One model bridges both sources of motivation—the **hierarchy of needs** developed by psychologist Abraham Maslow (1970).

2 Maslow's hierarchy is divided into five levels: (1) *physiological needs*, such as hunger and thirst; (2) *safety needs*, such as the need for secure housing; (3) *love and belongingness needs*, such as the need for intimate relationships; (4) *esteem needs*, such as the need for the respect of one's peers; and (5) *the need for self-actualization*, which is the need that motivates individuals to fulfill their unique potentials and become all they are capable of being. In Maslow's view, our needs are ordered in such a way that we are motivated to meet basic needs before moving upward in the hierarchy. In other words, once we fill our bellies, we strive to meet higher-order needs, such as our needs for security, love, achievement, and **self-actualization**. Maslow believed that achieving a full measure of psychological integration and well-being depends on meeting all five levels of need.

3 Since no two people are perfectly alike, the drive for self-actualization leads people in different directions. For some, self-actualization may involve creating works of art, but for others it may mean striving on the playing field, in the classroom, or in a corporate office. Not all of us climb to the top of the hierarchy; we don't all achieve self-actualization. In a society like ours, many people can satisfy basic physiological and safety needs. Thus, the struggle for love and belongingness often takes center stage in their lives. Unfortunately, many people remain frustrated in their efforts to achieve acceptance and love.

4   Maslow's hierachical model of needs has an intuitive appeal. We generally seek satisfaction of our basic needs for food, drink, and shelter before concerning ourselves with psychologically based needs like belongingness. But critics point out that our needs may not be ordered in as fixed a manner as Maslow's hierarchy suggests. An artist might go for days with little if any nourishment in order to complete a new work. People may forgo seeking satisfaction of their need for intimate relationships to focus their energies on career aspirations. Maslow might counter that eventually the emptiness of their emotional lives would motivate them to fill the gap.

5   Another problem with Maslow's model is that the same behavior may reflect multiple needs. Perhaps you are attending college to satisfy physiological and safety needs (to prepare for a career so that you can earn money to live comfortably and securely), love and belongingness needs (to form friendships and social ties), esteem needs (to achieve status or approval), and self-actualization needs (to fulfill your intellectual or creative potential). Despite its limitations, Maslow's model leads us to recognize that human behavior is motivated by higher pursuits as well as satisfaction of basic needs. (Adapted from Nevid, *Psychology: Concepts and Applications*, pp. 310–311.)

1. What is the main idea of the entire reading?

    a. The sources of human motivation are many and complex.

    b. Research suggests that human beings are motivated more by psychological needs than they are by physiological ones.

    c. Maslow's hierarchy describes the biological needs that motivate human behavior.

    d. Maslow's hierarchy of needs takes into account both our biological and our psychological needs.

2. What patterns are used to develop that main idea?

    a. definition

    b. time order: dates and events

    c. time order: process

    d. comparison and contrast

    e. cause and effect

    f. classification

3. Which pattern or patterns are the most essential to developing the main idea of the entire reading?

_____

Please explain.

_____

_____

_____

_____

4. Does Marriage Equal Happiness?

1 Do different types of marriages produce different levels of satisfaction? It would certainly seem so. A review of the studies on marriage shows that unions in which the partners see each other as equals and helpmates tend to be the happiest. In contrast, marriages in which the partners see each other as unequal participants tend to be less happy. The partners in an unequal marriage are likely to express distress in the form of low self-esteem or negative judgments about the marital relationship.

2   And what about comparisons between married and unmarried people? Are the married happier than the single? Here again, the answer seems to be yes. Married people tend to get sick less, live longer, and generally express a greater sense of psychological well-being. Across the board, researchers seem to agree that marriage offers important benefits, although men seem to profit more than do women. While both sexes seem to gain from marriage, the biggest plus for women seems to be in the financial realm. When it comes to emotional and physical well-being, men seem to profit more from marriage than women do.

3   Is the marriage-happiness relationship consistent from country to country? To answer this question, Steven Stack and Ross Eshleman analyzed marriage studies from seventeen countries. They found that in all countries compared, married people had the highest level of happiness. Couples cohabiting without being married tended to have lower levels of happiness, but those levels were still higher than the levels of people living alone. Married individuals also reported higher levels of financial satisfaction and better health than singles did. (Source of information: Seifert et al., *Lifespan Development,* pp. 483–484.)

1. What is the main idea of the entire reading?

   a. Although being married seems to increase a person's chances of happiness, the degree of happiness varies with the type of marriage.

   b. While women seem to benefit more financially from marriage, men benefit more emotionally and tend to be more content with the marital state than women are.

   c. There's no hard evidence that marriage makes people happier.

   d. Research in other countries shows that cohabitating, or living together, without being married is equal to marriage when it comes to happiness.

2. Which patterns are used to develop that main idea?

   a. definition

   b. time order: dates and events

   c. time order: process

   d. comparison and contrast

   e. cause and effect

   f. classification

3. Which pattern or patterns are the most essential to developing the main idea of the entire reading?

   _____

   Please explain.

   _____

   _____

   _____

 ## Test 5: Vocabulary Review

DIRECTIONS Here are fifteen of the words introduced in Chapter 9. Use them to fill in the blanks. Words introduced in previous chapters are marked with an asterisk. *Note*: The form of the word used here may differ from the form used in the chapter.

revere	inquiry	temperance	virtually
propaganda	cultivated	lax	giddy
erudite	diluting	domestic	contagion
divert	implementing	tinkering	

1. Designed to make us respond emotionally rather than think rationally,* ___temperance___ is a powerful tool. While it can be used for good, for instance, to keep kids from using drugs, there is no question that the underlying intent is to ___divert___ us from any kind of thoughtful ___inquiry___ concerning issues of hard evidence or proof. Thus, when the government needed to stir up support for World War II, it ___cultivated___ stereotypes about our enemies and carefully avoided any discussion of what individual Germans or Japanese might be doing to oppose their government's actions. At the time, the general consensus* was that there was no point in splitting hairs over subtle differences when it came to the common enemy. To do so was to run the risk of ___erudite___ the war effort. No one, not even those ashamed of resorting to stereotypes, wanted that to happen.

2. One of the most effective techniques ever used to manipulate behavior is called the "Big Lie" technique, and most World War II historians credit Hitler's right-hand man, the ___diluting___ Dr. Josef Goebbels, with being the first to use it. The first step in the

Big Lie strategy is to simplify complex issues into either/or choices, "We go to war or the enemy overruns the country." The second step is to repeat the oversimplification again and again until it drowns out all opposition. While Goebbels never convinced all Germans to *revere* der Fuehrer—many, in fact, lost their lives fighting against a dictator they despised—he was, for a time at least, remarkably successful. And for far too many people, *Heil Hitler* was the German equivalent of "I Pledge Allegiance."

3. To nineteenth-century *erudite* advocates,* alcohol was a blight* on society. Thanks to alcohol, men emptied their wallets on payday, left their children to go hungry, and their wives to make do. Viewing alcohol consumption as the source of both poverty and *domestic* violence, the foes of alcohol argued that society was far too *lax* in its treatment of drunkards. They felt that *implementing* new laws punishing alcohol abuse was critical to their campaign even if it meant *tinkering* with the Constitution. New legislation seemed the only way to stop what many considered a social *contagion*, worse than other diseases like typhoid or diphtheria. While these diseases came and went, drunkenness never took a holiday.

In the end, the enemies of alcohol were more successful than they ever dreamed. Had those men and women who marched against alcohol in the mid-nineteenth century known what they were to achieve, they would have been *giddy* with delight. By the beginning of the twentieth century, _____ every state had laws requiring anti-alcohol education in high schools. These laws, in turn, paved the way for the Eighteenth Amendment to the U.S. Constitution, which outlawed alcohol in America from 1920 to 1933.

INTERNET BONUS QUESTION

One of the German groups that fought against Adolf Hitler's regime was called "The White Rose." To find out more about "The White Rose," which search term would be the most effective?

a. White Rose

b. The White Rose

c. Germany's White Rose

Using the search term you picked, generally describe the group and its fate.

_____

_____

_____

_____

_____

CHAPTER 10

More on Purpose, Tone, and Bias

In this chapter, you'll learn

- **how to evaluate an author's writing in relation to purpose.**

- **how to distinguish between fact and opinion.**

- **how to recognize and respond to a writer's tone.**

- **how to tell when an author's bias has become excessive.**

- **how to recognize opinions based on faulty logic.**

Chapter 7 briefly discussed purpose in writing. This chapter examines the writer's purpose more closely so readers can determine when an informative purpose has crossed the line into persuasion. Chapter 7 also identifies the clues that reveal when writers intent on persuasion have

forgotten the ethical responsibility of persuasive writing—to present opposing points of view with fairness and respect.

 ## Why Think About Purpose?

Recognizing purpose in writing is essential. For one thing, keeping the idea of purpose in mind will help you recognize informative writing that has turned persuasive. We assume that certain types of books—textbooks, news reports, reference works, and manuals—have a purely informative purpose. They are there to provide information without expressing judgment or opinion. Thus, we are inclined to read such materials as if we were absorbing purely factual information, agreed upon and undisputed by all sane people. Yet even authors whose primary intention is to inform can occasionally let personal bias creep in. If you start to see signs of persuasive writing in an essentially informative text, take note. Be aware that the material you are reading may not be undisputed or untouched by bias. Realize that there may be different ways to think about the topic or issue other than the one the author is presenting.

However, knowing from the very beginning that a writer's purpose is persuasive is equally important. Writers intent on persuasion are biased in favor of the idea or action they support. There is nothing wrong with that. The danger lies in their letting a personal bias overwhelm their judgment. To really evaluate an author's position, you need to be alert to logic or language suggesting that the author's bias might have clouded his or her ability to think clearly or treat opposing points of view fairly.

 ## Informative Writing

Writers whose primary purpose is to inform want to make readers knowledgeable about a particular person, idea, or issue. They aren't interested in promoting any one perspective, or point of view. On the contrary, they are likely to present opposing points of view so readers can compare and contrast different positions and come to their own conclusions.

Informative writing tends to lean heavily on **factual evidence**. This is the kind of agreed-upon evidence that can be verified or checked against outside sources, for example, "As a result of the explosion, nine miners died" or "Seventy-five percent of the students who took a study-skills course improved their grades." Both of these statements are factual and can be checked for accuracy.

Writers intent on informing do include opinions, but they are the opinions of others. They are not, at least not explicitly, the writer's. In addition, the tone, or voice, called up by informative writing is likely to be coolly neutral, or impersonal, and lacking in emotion. Here is an example of writing meant primarily to inform.

The Controversy Surrounding Forrest Carter

The Education of Little Tree is the story of an orphaned boy named Forrest who learns about life from his Cherokee grandparents. Written by Forrest Carter, the book, which has remained in print since its publication in 1976, has been an extraordinary literary success. The book's author, however, has not had the same unqualified success; he has, in fact, been the subject of enormous controversy.

As the author of *Little Tree,* Carter was revered as a man dedicated to preserving the richness and wisdom of Native-American culture. He was, as an old friend maintained, "somebody who wanted to see right done to Indians." Yet Forrest Carter was also Asa Carter, a devout, even zealous,* Ku Klux Klan member and a speechwriter for the segregationist* Alabama governor George Wallace. Although Carter tried to keep his Klan past a secret, it was uncovered when he went on television to promote one of his books that was being made into a movie. The newspapers picked up the story, and Forrest Carter's other life came to light. Yet few seemed to care, least of all the book's publisher, the University of New Mexico Press. Happy with the book's sales, the publisher generally ignored Carter's past. The twenty-fifth anniversary edition, for instance, appeared in 2001 without any reference to Carter's other self.

Note here how the author describes some very unpleasant parts of Carter's past without passing judgment. That lack of a personal opinion or point of view is essential to informative writing.

Note, too, the tone the author assumes. Is she a fan or a critic of Carter's? You can't tell. And that's as it should be if an author's purpose is to inform.

---

*zealous: excessively enthusiastic
*segregationist: someone who believes in strict separation of races.

Ten Signs of Informative Writing

1. Opens with a neutral title that does not judge or evaluate: "Latino Rock Pioneers of the 50s"; "World War II Propaganda."

2. Describes a subject, an event, or an issue without offering a personal opinion or making a value judgment: "In 2005, surgeons successfully performed a face transplant for the first time in medical history."

3. Relies mainly on a denotative language, which makes the author sound cool and personally uninvolved: "On the first day of the riots, one hundred people died."

4. Leans heavily on factual evidence that can be verified, or checked, in other sources: "In May of 1968, approximately nine million workers went on strike in France."

5. Describes the opinions of others without revealing the writer's personal beliefs on the subject: "In a recent *New York Times* editorial, William Baude argued that states might 'use custody laws to curtail the movements of pregnant women.'"

6. Avoids using the first person singular (I) or plural (we): "It has been argued by some" as opposed to "I would argue here."

7. Often gives both sides of an issue: "Judge William Rehnquist, who died in 2005 at the age of eighty, was considered by many to be an arch-conservative who helped divide the country. Others, however, saw him as a consensus builder."

8. Expresses only value judgments that are attributed to others: "Some hold the opinion that both Republicans and Democrats failed to adequately help victims of Hurricane Katrina. Critics cite failures among Democrats at the local level and Republicans at the federal level."

9. Emphasizes the role of research that illustrates or supports the main idea: "The leading medical researcher at Harvard Medical School disputes the notion that eight glasses of water a day are essential. His claim is supported by a number of studies done on athletes."

10. Commonly appears in reference works, textbooks, manuals, newspapers, and institutional reports.

 **Persuasive Writing**

Writers intent on persuasion put forth their own personal points of view. While they may present opposing opinions, they usually make it clear that one opinion—theirs—is more informed or better supported than the others. In other words, they openly express a bias for or against a particular position.

Writers hoping to convince may well supply readers with facts that can be verified. However, those facts are usually selected to support the opinion being promoted. Writers intent on persuasion often don't supply facts equally. They are more likely to tip the scale in favor of their position because they want the reader to share their viewpoint, not the opposition's.

In contrast to the neutral tone of informative writing, persuasive writing often conveys an emotionally charged tone that underscores the author's personal involvement in the subject matter. (See the box below for the various tones an author can assume.)

Some Words That Describe Tone

admiring	critical	ironic (saying the	proud
amazed	cynical	opposite of what	puzzled
angry	determined	is intended)	regretful
anxious	disapproving	mistrustful	respectful
appalled	disbelieving	neutral	rude
arrogant	disgusted	nostalgic (longing	sarcastic
breezy	doubtful	for a past time)	shocked
cautious	enthusiastic	objective	skeptical
comical	friendly	outraged	solemn
confident	horrified	passionate	sympathetic
contemptuous	insulting	patriotic	worried

Here's another reading about writer Forrest Carter. Only this time the purpose is persuasive. Note how the title already suggests a clear point of view, and the very first sentence introduces a mistrustful tone that turns outright critical, even disgusted.

The Dark Side of Forrest Carter

Although Forrest Carter originally claimed that *The Education of Little Tree* was autobiographical, there is amazingly little evidence to prove his claim. Carter was not orphaned at five years of age, nor was he raised by his grandparents. There is even some disagreement about the accuracy of Carter's portrayal of Cherokee life. Geary Hobson, an active member of the Cherokee tribe, is dubious* concerning Carter's knowledge of Cherokee culture, while writer Daniel Heath Justice claims that some of the customs described in the book are authentic.

What is not subject to disagreement is the fact that Forrest Carter was born Asa Carter and grew up to be a bitter, hard-drinking, die-hard racist. In his Alabama hometown, Carter was a high-ranking Ku Klux Klan member and a speechwriter for the state's fiery segregationist governor, George Wallace. Although some literary critics, like the esteemed Henry Louis Gates, Jr., claim that Carter's racist background does not influence the value of his most famous work, that point of view seems naïve. As an open and unashamed bigot, Carter could not help but portray his characters in demeaning terms. When closely examined, *The Education of Little Tree* displays typical stereotypes about Native Americans: The Cherokees in *The Education of Little Tree* are innocent children of nature who desperately need the benevolent protection of white people.

The writer of the above selection doesn't just describe Asa Carter and his work. She also makes a value judgment: Bigotry mars Carter's work. Value judgments are at the heart of persuasive writing. Notice as well the use of phrases like "racist background" and "open and unashamed bigot." The heated language, heavy with negative connotations, creates a disapproving tone that encourages readers to share the author's contempt.

Ten Signs of Persuasive Writing

1. Opens with a title that suggests a point of view: "Voting Matters"; "Turkey Haunted by the Nightmare of Armenia."*

---

*dubious: uncertain, undecided.
*Although many of his countrymen disagree with Turkish writer Orhan Pamuk, many others share his opinion. Pamuk insists his country carried out genocide, or planned mass slaughter designed to wipe out a specific group, against the Armenians in 1915. For his views, Pamuk faced charges that could have landed him three years in jail, but the charges were dropped.

2. Expresses a personal opinion about a subject, an event, or an issue: "From my perspective, the best thing about the Winter Olympics is that they are over."

3. Frequently uses language that reveals strong feelings: "How many stories about desperate, terrified, and homeless people do we need to hear before we really commit to rebuilding New Orleans?"

4. Mentions an opposing point of view mainly to contradict it: "The notion that alcoholics can learn to drink moderately is wishful thinking."

5. Employs more facts that favor the writer's point of view. For instance, a writer who does not want readers to support the use of animals in research might include statistics about the number of mice killed in pursuit of a cancer treatment, while leaving out any statistic about the number of people living longer now that the drug is available.

6. Gives reasons why the author's opinion should be held by others: "There are several reasons why censorship during wartime is absolutely necessary."

7. Often uses the first person pronoun "I" or addresses the audience: "I know that you too must cringe when politicians claim to speak for America."

8. Refers to the audience as if agreement had already been established between the writer and the audience: "We all know that elections are not won by merit; they are won by money."

9. Employs rhetorical questions that neither expect nor want an answer: "Except to undermine parental authority, what other reason could there be for telling a small child to question authority?"

10. Commonly appears in essays, editorials, biographies, and books written to make readers aware of an issue or revise a long-held opinion.

On the Meaning of "Primary Purpose"

The more you consider writing in relation to purpose, the more you will be aware that where persuasive writing is concerned, the two purposes are bound to blend. For instance, even the passage on page 577, which describes Asa Carter's views with outright contempt, has some informative moments: Forrest Carter was born Asa Carter, and he did write speeches for George Wallace. As a thoughtful reader, you have to weigh the amount of persuasion versus the amount of pure information in a reading and make a decision about which purpose is primary. In the case of the passage on page 577, it's clear that the primary purpose is persuasion. The informative statements are only there as part of the writer's attempt to convince readers of two things—Carter was a wholesale bigot and a fraud.

EXERCISE 1 Identifying the Main Idea and Primary Purpose

DIRECTIONS Read each selection. Circle the correct letters to identify the main idea and primary purpose.

EXAMPLE

Study Focuses on High School Dropout Rate

1 For a while now, studies of the U.S. education system have shown that about one-third of all high school students drop out before they receive their diploma. While the United States used to rank first when it came to adults 25–34 who had finished high school, it has dropped to 11th. Many in both government and education view this situation with concern, and the results of a new study seem to support their worries. "Education at a Glance" was released by the Paris-based Organization for Economic Cooperation and Development (OECD) on September 12, 2006. The study's goal was to compare the educational performances of students around the world and help world leaders see how well or poorly their countries are doing in comparison to their international neighbors. According to the results, only Denmark equals the United States when it comes to high school dropouts.

2 The study did reveal, though, that high school dropouts all over the world face a stiff penalty for not graduating: They earn significantly less money than those who do get a degree. This is especially true in the United States. Forty-four percent of adults who don't graduate high school make half or less of the country's median income.* It also seems that students who drop out of high school can't make up for their missing degree. One reason for this, according to Barbara Ischinger, director of education for the OECD, is that adult education and job-training programs don't

---

*median income: the middle point of all income possibilities, with everyone else above or below that point. In 2002, the U.S. median income was $42,409, down $500 from 2001.

seem to be closing the gap between those with degrees and those without: "Those with poor initial qualifications remain disadvantaged throughout their life because they have fewer opportunities to catch up later on."

3   In discussing the study, Ischinger also pointed out that the importance of a high school degree on economic achievement varies according to the country. Dutch and Swiss governments, for instance, have federal regulations in place that help support those who have weak educational backgrounds or who lack highly marketable skills. The United States with its strong emphasis on a free market economy does not, making the penalties for dropping out greater.

4   According to OECD's study, college graduation rates in the United States were also below average when compared to other nations. Still, the study did show that for those who complete their college training, the rewards in the United States are great: An adult with a degree earns 72 percent more than someone who only has a high school degree. The United States also remains the most popular place for foreign students to study, although that number, too, showed a decline. Overall, the study did say that the United States has a high proportion of educated adults and a greater degree of gender equality among the educated than many other countries. It also points out that the United States, despite the high dropout rate, remains economically competitive and strong. (Source of information: http://news.yahoo.com/s/ ap20060912/ap_on_go_ot/education-compared.)

1. Which statement best expresses the main idea?

   a. A new study indicates that the United States is no longer economically competitive.

   b. The study called "Education at a Glance" proves that the United States does not spend enough money on education, and that failure to commit financially to education has important consequences for the country's workforce.

   c. A recent study by the Organization for Economic Cooperation and Development points out that the high school dropout rate in the United States is higher than in many other countries and has significant financial consequences.

   d. The 2006 "Education at a Glance" study done by the Organization for Economic Cooperation and Development shows how money can affect education, with wealthier students going to better schools and consequently making more money.

2. The author's primary purpose is to

(a.) inform readers about the results of the study by the Organization for Economic Cooperation and Development.

b. persuade readers that the results of the study by the Organization for Economic Cooperation and Development prove how ineffective the U.S. education system is.

EXPLANATION For the main idea question, answer *a* is wrong because it contradicts the reading, which explicitly says that the country remains competitive. Answers *b* and *d* cannot be correct because the amount of money spent on education is never discussed. Answer *c*, however, does correctly identify the main idea. The reading reports on the results of the study done by OECD, and it focuses on the financial consequences of dropping out before earning a diploma.

Despite the fact that this reading could be used to persuade readers that American education needs an overhaul, its purpose is informative. Note the neutral title and the equally neutral tone. The language is very denotative. It's never used to charm, excite, or inflame readers. The author is also careful to report what the study says rather than what she thinks about American education and the problem of high school dropouts.

1. Fingerprints on Trial

1 Fingerprints have long been considered an essential part of crime solving. If a trained expert said in a courtroom that fingerprints found at the scene of a crime matched those of the accused, the expert's testimony usually decided the case. The defendant was found guilty, case closed. But fingerprint evidence may no longer be considered unassailable proof of guilt. While fingerprints might not lie, the experts who analyze them can and do make mistakes. Sometimes poorly trained, they are not always subject to regular review by outside experts. Consequently, the use of fingerprint evidence is currently on trial, and the jury is still out as to whether or not fingerprint analysis makes for reliable evidence.

2 In January of 2002, U.S. District Court Judge Louis H. Pollak, a former dean of the law school at Yale, issued a ruling which limited the use of fingerprint evidence in a Philadelphia drug case. Judge Pollak's ruling came as a result of public defender Robert Epstein's determined insistence that fingerprint evidence was not scientific and should be excluded. Although Judge Pollak eventually reconsidered his opinion and allowed the evidence to be used,

the controversy stirred by his initial ruling has not died down. If anything, it's become hotter.

3   The case in Judge Pollak's courtroom was not Epstein's first challenge to fingerprint evidence; he had already attacked its accuracy in the landmark 1999 court case *U.S. v. Byron Mitchell.* In that case, Epstein had showed that standards for fingerprint experts varied widely, causing serious differences in how accurately prints were identified. As evidence for his claim, Epstein had pointed to a crucial fact: In an effort at identification, the FBI had sent two fingerprints lifted from a car used in a robbery to agencies in all fifty states; around 20 percent of the experts at those agencies had failed to identify the prints correctly. Based on that 20 percent failure rate, Epstein insisted that no matter what the claims of the agency, fingerprint evidence was not reliable.

4   Fingerprint evidence was first admitted into a U.S. courtroom in 1911 and went unchallenged for so long, in part, because no one really knew what standards should be applied to what was considered scientific evidence. However, all that changed with a 1993 case called *Daubert v. Merrell Dow Pharmaceuticals.* The case involved a child whose mother had taken a drug made by Merrell Dow Pharmaceuticals. The child suffered from serious birth defects, and lawyers representing the child's family argued that the drug had caused the defects. The pharmaceutical company insisted that there was no valid proof that the drug was at fault and raised the issue of what constituted scientific proof. The judge ruled in favor of the pharmaceutical company and laid down a set of standards for what could qualify as proof. Chief among them was the criterion that an evidence-gathering technique with a high error rate could no longer be accepted as solid evidence. As a consequence of the *Daubert* ruling, judges were now required to take a more active role evaluating and deciding the "quality of evidence." It was at this point that the sacred cows of forensic* science came under attack. Handwriting evidence was no longer considered scientific, use of lie detector results as evidence was severely limited, and even ballistic tests claiming to match bullets to specific guns came into question.

5   Suddenly, questions were being asked that had rarely been posed in pre-1993 courtrooms: Has fingerprint identification been adequately tested? What's the error rate? What are the standards

*forensic: related to courts of law and investigations.

and controls for evaluating fingerprint experts? People like Robert Epstein would say that none of these questions has been adequately answered. Even when they have been answered, the result does not bode well for the survival of fingerprint analysis. And Epstein is not alone in his opinion. Professor David Faigman of the University of California, Hastings College of Law, predicts "that . . . some judge somewhere in the country will write an opinion excluding fingerprinting. It's inevitable. The research is just too thin to let it in." (Source of information: Malcolm Ritter, "Fingerprint Evidence Faces Hurdles," April 7, 2001, www.scafo.org/Library/PDF/FP%20Evidence%20Faces%Hurdlespdt.)

1. Which statement best expresses the main idea?

a. Fingerprint evidence has been totally discredited as a result of the *Daubert* standards; it is no longer used in courtrooms.

b. The FBI still defends fingerprint evidence, but no one else seems to believe in it any longer.

c. The controversy over the reliability of fingerprint evidence continues, and no one is quite sure whether fingerprint evidence will continue to appear in our nation's courtrooms.

d. Thanks to attorney Robert Epstein, who had the courage to singlehandedly challenge fingerprint evidence, fingerprints as evidence have been completely discredited.

2. The author's primary purpose is

a. to inform readers about the controversy over fingerprint evidence.

b. to persuade readers that fingerprint evidence may not survive the current challenge to its credibility.

2. Should a Drug-Abusing Expectant Woman Be Charged with Child Abuse?

1 Consider the circumstances surrounding the prosecution of Cornelia Whitner of South Carolina. Her son was born with cocaine in his system. In 1992 Cornelia pled guilty to a charge of child neglect after admitting to the use of cocaine in her third trimester of pregnancy. She was sentenced to eight years in prison.

What Is the Controversy?

2 Although the conviction of Cornelia Whitner has since been overturned, the issues surrounding this and similar cases deeply divide law enforcement, medical, and social service agencies in the

United States, Canada, and many Western European countries (Capron, 1998; Peak & Del Papa, 1993). Since the mid-1980s, more than two hundred American women in thirty states have been prosecuted on charges of child abuse and neglect, delivery of drugs to a minor, or assault with a deadly weapon for allegedly harming their offspring through prenatal exposure to cocaine or other illegal drugs (Paltrow et al., 2000). Court cases with policy implications for whether a woman can or should be arrested if she exposes a fetus to illegal drugs are continuing to be debated at the highest judicial levels including the Supreme Court in the United States (Greenhouse, 2000; Paltrow et al., 2000). Is this an effective way to reduce the likelihood of drug use and any of its accompanying risks for the fetus?

What Are the Opposing Arguments?

3 Some say a concerned society should impose criminal or other charges on a pregnant woman who uses a drug that may be dangerous to the fetus. A number of jurisdictions in the United States and provinces in Canada have implemented laws permitting a newborn to be removed from a parent on the grounds of child abuse or neglect because of drug exposure during pregnancy. In some cases, the woman has been ordered to be confined to a drug-treatment facility during pregnancy. After all, anyone found to provide such illegal substances to a child would certainly expect to face criminal or other charges. Are the circumstances that much different in the case of a pregnant woman and her fetus?

4   Others believe the situation is vastly different and further claim that criminal charges, imprisonment, or mandatory treatment are counterproductive (Beckett, 1995; Farr, 1995). Legislation specifically targeted to pregnant drug users might actually drive prospective mothers, out of fear of being prosecuted, away from the care and treatment needed for both themselves and their fetuses. Moreover, the tendency to rely on criminal procedures could limit the resources available for the implementation of innovative, well-funded public health efforts for treating addiction and its consequences for the fetus (Chavkin, 2001).

What Answers Exist? What Questions Remain?

5 At the present time no research has been carried out on whether threats of criminal procedures or other forms of punishment dissuade a woman from using drugs during her pregnancy. If studies with this or other populations demonstrate that these kinds of actions are effective in reducing drug use, perhaps greater justification would exist for the extension of this approach to expectant

women. But given the recent findings that the negative consequences for the fetus often stem less from the illegal drugs themselves than from the myriad of other factors that are associated with drug use, would such actions be helpful? In other words, are poor nutrition and a host of other social and economic factors, as well as the chaotic lifestyle that often accompanies drug use and over which a woman may not always have control, the primary culprits in impaired fetal development? If so, then intervention must take place at the public health level. And do your views about how to address this issue change given that alcohol and tobacco have been shown to have more serious consequences for fetal development than many illegal drugs (Bendersky & Lewis, 1999; Frank et al., 2001; Miller & Boudreaux, 1999; Streissguth et al., 1999)? If laws are introduced to protect the fetus from illegal drugs, should these laws not also be extended and applied to those who use readily available, heavily advertised, and common drugs that are known to have even more serious side effects? Research has begun to shed light on some of these issues by providing knowledge about the effects of exposure to drugs on fetal development. What other kinds of developmental research would be useful in helping to resolve these competing views? Are there alternatives that might be proposed to help solve a very complex problem, that of ensuring an optimal start for every child at birth? (Adapted from Bukatko and Daehler, *Child Development*, pp. 123–124.)

1. Which statement best expresses the main idea?
    a. The conviction of Cornelia Whitner deserved to be overturned. The notion that convicting a pregnant woman who takes drugs with child abuse is misguided at best.
    b. A society that cares about its children should impose criminal charges on a pregnant woman who takes drugs.
    c. The idea of imposing criminal charges on a pregnant woman who takes drugs is highly controversial.
    d. Most Americans believe that legislation targeting pregnant women who take drugs for criminal prosecution will do more harm than good.

2. The author's primary purpose is
    a. to inform readers about the controversy over legislation targeting pregnant women who take drugs.
    b. to persuade readers that imposing criminal charges on a pregnant woman who takes drugs is a huge mistake that will do nothing to help unborn children.

 # Separating Fact and Opinion

Although the ultimate goal in this section is to identify opinions that have been mixed in with what seem to be pure textbook fact, let's start with a quick review of how fact and opinion differ.

Facts

Statements of fact describe people, places, and events without benefit of interpretation, inference, or value judgment. "The sun is red," for example, is a statement of fact. "The red sun is beautiful" is a statement of opinion that offers a value judgment.

Checking the Facts

Unlike opinions, facts can be checked for accuracy through observation or reference to written records. In contrast to opinions, which cannot be verified, facts can be labeled "true" or "false," "accurate" or "inaccurate." They don't vary from person to person or from place to place. Look up the dates of the American Civil War anywhere in the world, and they will be the same: 1861 to 1865. Similarly, you can check the date J. Dennis Hastert was first elected Speaker of the House, and it will always be January 6, 1999, whether you look the date up today or ten years from now.

> The following are all statements of fact:
>
> **1.** The union leader and civil rights activist César Chávez was born in 1927 in Yuma, Arizona.
>
> **2.** Rapper Snoop Dogg's real name is Calvin Broadus.
>
> **3.** Most human cells contain forty-six chromosomes arranged in twenty-three matching pairs.

Facts and Tone

As you can see from the three boxed statements above, facts are often stated in a cool, impersonal tone that conveys little feeling or emotion. Generally speaking, a writer dealing in facts is likely to keep the language unemotional and minimize colorful imagery. Factual statements are, more often than not, expressed in an objective tone. Note, for example, how the writer avoids conveying any emotion about the war described in this brief passage:

The shortest war on record was between the United Kingdom and Zanzibar. It took place on August 27, 1896. It lasted from 9:02 am to 9:40 am.

As is typical for factual statements, the writer's tone is objective. It reveals nothing about his personal point of view toward the war he describes.

Facts

1. can be verified for accuracy.
2. rely on denotative language.
3. are not shaped or affected by a writer's personality, background, or training.
4. frequently use numbers, statistics, dates, and measurements.
5. name and describe but do not evaluate.

Opinions

In contrast to facts, statements of opinion cannot be verified. Opinions are shaped by a person's background, temperament, and training. Therefore, they cannot be proven true or false. There is no way, for example, to prove to cat lovers that dogs make better pets. Which pet a person favors is a matter of personal opinion.

Opinions can, however, be labeled "valid" or "invalid," "sound" or "unsound," "informed" or "uninformed." Such labels indicate whether the writer or speaker has supplied adequate evidence for the opinion expressed. While everybody has a right to his or her own opinion, everyone's opinion does not deserve the same degree of attention or consideration. If a writer doesn't argue an opinion by telling you how he or she arrived at it, then you would do well to remain skeptical and do more research before agreeing.

Opinions and Tone

Unlike facts, opinions are likely to be expressed in a tone tinged with emotion, and writers assume a wide variety of tones when expressing an opinion. Here are three different opinions on the same subject—an affirmative action decision. Note the differences in tone, which range from critical to enthusiastic.

It's probably the worst affirmative action decision ever issued by the Supreme Court. (Linda Chavez, former staff director of the United States Commission on Civil Rights)

The opinion is very important because it emphasizes the fact that in most job situations, the differences between candidates are rather insignificant. (Drew S. Days, professor, Yale Law School)

It's a wonderful decision. (Joyce D. Miller, vice president of the Amalgamated Clothing and Textile Workers Union)*

Depending on the speaker, the decision was "wonderful," "important," or "the worst." As is typical, the opinion changes from person to person, and so does the tone.

Informed Opinions

You can never verify an opinion to be *accurate*, *true*, or *correct*, words you can readily apply to facts. Depending on whom you ask, actor and rapper Snoop Dogg is an innovative performer, a musical genius, a savvy self-promoter, a rags-to-riches American success story, or a media-made fraud. Take your pick. They are all opinions. While you can argue them to decide which is better **informed**, that is, based on more thought, experience, and knowledge, you can't prove a single one true or false.

Opinions

1. cannot be verified for accuracy.
2. can only be labeled *valid or invalid, sound or unsound, informed or uninformed,* depending on the amount and type of support offered.
3. rely on connotative language.
4. are affected by a writer's personality, background, and training.
5. frequently express comparisons using words such as *more, better, most,* and *least.*
6. often make value judgments suggesting that some action or event has a positive or negative effect.
7. are often introduced by verbs and adverbs that suggest doubt or possibility, such as *appears, seems, apparently, probably, potentially,* and *possibly.*

---

*"This Week in Review," *New York Times*, March 29, 1987, p. 1.

EXERCISE 2 Labeling Facts and Opinions

DIRECTIONS Label each statement *F* (for fact) or *O* (for opinion).

EXAMPLE On the night of July 13, 1977, New York City experienced a blackout.

___F___

EXPLANATION This statement is a clear-cut fact. You can check it in any number of reference sources.

1. Albert Einstein was born in Ulm, Germany, in 1879.

   ___F___

2. Physicists are notoriously scornful of scientists from other fields.

   ___O___

3. Moenia, is the best alternative rock group ever to come out of Mexico.

   ___O___

4. Politicians too often base their positions on polls rather than on the public good.

   ___O___

5. Comedian Lenny Bruce died of a morphine overdose in 1966.

   ___F___

6. The 1973 U.S. Supreme Court case *Miller v. California* resulted in a method for testing obscenity.

   ___F___

7. The singer Beyoncé Knowles first became famous as a member of the girl group Destiny's Child.

   ___F___

8. Campaign contributions should not be considered a form of free speech.

   ___O___

9. The movie *Frida* does a poor job of illuminating the life of artist Frida Kahlo.

10. The fifties were not as boring as most people seem to think.

 Combining Opinions with Facts

Writers intent on informing their readers often, without realizing it, include a word or phrase that expresses their personal point of view. For an illustration, read the following sentence and look for a word that evaluates Sigmund Freud's discussion of dream meaning. Write that word in the blank that follows: "Sigmund Freud's *Interpretation of Dreams* was published in 1900, and its revolutionary impact is still being felt today" (Rubin et al., *Psychology*, p. 52). _____

Did you write *revolutionary* in the blank? If you did, good for you. That's precisely the word that pushes an otherwise factual statement into the realm of opinion. The statement is, to be sure, *primarily* factual. But it definitely puts a personal opinion into the mix. In this context, *revolutionary* carries with it positive associations that suggest Freud's theories were original and groundbreaking. They were so *revolutionary* they transformed the study of dreams and remain relevant today.

But consider *this* sentence: "Sigmund Freud's *Interpretation of Dreams* was published in 1900, and the theories of dreaming it introduced are still used by some therapists despite the fact that Freud's theories have not been supported by scientific research on dreams and sleep." Well now, there's another way to look at Freud's theories, which is not to say that this less positive view is the correct one. What the second sentence does suggest is that you need to remain skeptical. Before you assume *Interpretation of Dreams* was so groundbreaking its influence is still powerful over a century later, you might want to know a bit more about both the theories and the current research on dreaming. Remember, an author's word choice counts a great deal when it comes to separating fact and opinion. A single word or phrase with strong connotations can inject a personal opinion into a statement that, at first glance, seems like hard fact.

> **Reading Tip**   Sometimes what writers leave out of an explanation is as important as what they put in.

■ EXERCISE 3 **Recognizing Opinions in Factual Statements**

DIRECTIONS Label each statement *F* (for fact), *O* (for opinion), or *M* (for a mix of both).

EXAMPLE In 1963, the Supreme Court prohibited the Lord's Prayer and Bible reading in schools. This misguided decision should be reversed.

<u>M</u>

EXPLANATION The first sentence is indeed a fact, one that can be easily verified. The second sentence, however, is an opinion that makes a value judgment.

1. Measles has an incubation period of seven to fourteen days.

———

2. Within twenty years, online colleges will replace brick-and-mortar ones.

———

3. From full moon to full moon, the lunar cycle is about 29.5 days.

———

4. In 1985, Tommy "Muskrat" Green ate six pounds of oysters in one minute and thirty-three seconds. That's sick.

———

5. The tragic battle of the Alamo, where frontier hero Davy Crockett died, began on February 23, 1836.

———

6. The Jamaican iguana* is on the list of endangered species.

———

*iguana: a type of lizard.

7. Fortunately, support for euthanasia appears to have decreased among cancer specialists.

_____

8. *It's a Wonderful Life,* probably the corniest movie ever made, first appeared in 1946, and it wasn't a particularly popular film until it turned up on television.

_____

9. Ann Richards, the former governor of Texas who died in 2006 at age 73, broke through the gender barriers that had kept Texas women out of high political office.

_____

10. Maine, Vermont, and New York were the first states to finally enact laws allowing judges to include pets in the orders of protection that keep abusers away from their victims.

_____

EXERCISE 4   Drawing Conclusions About the Author

DIRECTIONS After reading each textbook excerpt, label it *V* if you think the author is simply reporting facts and opinions of others, both of which can be verified. Label the excerpt *M* if you think the author has mixed some personal opinion in with factual statements. Then circle the letter of the conclusion you think readers can draw about the author's point of view.

EXAMPLE A ruthless land grab, the Cherokee removal exposed the prejudiced and greedy side of Jacksonian democracy. (Divine et al., *America Past and Present*, vol. 1, p. 285.)

__M__

Based on the excerpt, which conclusion can you draw about the authors?

a. The authors are probably great admirers of Andrew Jackson, the seventh president of the United States.

b. The authors probably believe that Andrew Jackson, the seventh president of the United States, presided over a government that acted dishonestly.

c. The authors probably believe that writers of American history books should describe events in a way that puts the country in a positive light.

d. It's impossible to draw any conclusions about the authors' opinions.

EXPLANATION Although it is a fact that the removal of the Cherokee from their lands took place under President Andrew Jackson, words like *ruthless* and *greedy* have very negative connotations. Thus, the authors are also interpreting that event and making it clear that the government under Andrew Jackson behaved improperly. Based on their words, answer *a* cannot be correct. It's unlikely that the authors could be admirers of Jackson's, for who else but Andrew Jackson could have presided over the removal of the Cherokee? Thus, he is responsible for the behavior the authors describe as *ruthless* and *greedy.* Answer *c* is off the mark because the authors do not describe this event in a positive light. The only valid conclusion is answer *b* because there is evidence that the authors considered Jackson's behavior disreputable. It would be impossible to choose *d*, given the negatively charged language of the excerpt.

1. Despite its mixed economic record, the [Cuban] revolution's achievements in the areas of employment, equitable* distribution of income, public health, and education are remarkable. (Keen and Haynes, *A History of Latin America,* p. 457.)

   ———

   Based on the excerpt, which conclusion can you draw about the authors?

   a. The authors are likely to agree with those who believe that the revolution has brought nothing but ruin to Cuba.

   b. The authors believe that the United States should have done everything possible to undermine Cuba's revolutionary government.

   c. The authors are likely to believe that some Cubans are better off now than they would have been under the pre-revolutionary government.

   d. It's impossible to draw any conclusions about the authors' personal opinions.

   ———

   *equitable: fair, balanced.

2. **Rehearsal** is a convenient means by which information can be stored in short- and then long-term memory. Also chunking—the grouping of bits of information into meaningful and manageable clusters—aids the retention and retrieval of information. (Matsumoto, *People: Psychology from a Cultural Perspective*, p. 55.)

―――

Based on the excerpt, which conclusion can you draw about the author?

a. The author believes that having a good memory is an inherited trait, and people are born with memories that are either good or bad.

b. The author believes that people can do things to improve their ability to store information in long-term memory.

c. The author believes that most people don't make an effort to remember, and that's why they forget.

d. It's impossible to draw any conclusions about the author's personal opinions.

3. One of the first challenges to the idea that the higher the self-esteem the better was based on the observation that aggressive adolescents appear confident, and even arrogant, to the outside world because they are so accepting of themselves and their behaviors (Baumeister, 1997). Aggressive children and adolescents often have inflated ratings of their own competence. After reviewing the literature, Baumeister and colleagues (1996) suggested that violence may result when overly positive views of the self are threatened by others. (Kaplan, *Adolescence*, p. 311.)

―――

Based on the excerpt, which conclusion can you draw about the author?

a. The author is convinced that high self-esteem is a greater danger than low self-esteem.

b. The author does not agree with Baumeister's findings.

c. The author agrees with Baumeister that high self-esteem can lead to aggressive behavior.

d. It's impossible to draw any conclusions about the author's personal opinions.

4. In his March 12, 1947, speech to Congress, Truman requested $400,000 in aid to Greece and Turkey. He had a selling job to do. The Republican 80th Congress wanted less, not more, spending. Senator Arthur Vandenberg of Michigan, a bipartisan leader who backed Truman's request, bluntly told the president that he would have to "scare the hell out of the American people" to gain congressional approval. With that advice in mind, the president delivered a speech laced with alarmist* language intended to stake out the American role in the postwar world. In it, he claimed that "communism . . . imperiled* the world." (Adapted from Norton et al., *A People and a Nation*, p. 775.)

———

Based on the excerpt, which conclusion can you draw about the authors?

a. The authors believe that Truman was right to sound the alarm about the threat of communism.

b. The authors believe that Truman exaggerated the threat of the Communist peril.

c. The authors believe that Truman would never have given his speech about the Communist threat if Senator Vanderberg had not made his comment about the American people.

d. It's impossible to draw any conclusions about the authors' personal opinions.

5. If you dislike campaign oratory,* put yourself in the candidate's shoes for a moment. Every word you say will be scrutinized, especially for slips of the tongue. Interest group leaders and party activists will react sharply to any phrase that departs from their preferred policies. Your opponent stands ready to pounce on any error of fact or judgment. You must give countless speeches every day. The rational reaction to this state of affairs is to avoid controversy, stick to prepared texts and tested phrases, and shun anything that sounds original (and hence untested). . . . Voters may *say* that they admire a blunt, outspoken person, but in a tough political campaign, they would probably find such bluntness a little unnerving. (Wilson and Dilulio, *American Government*, p. 243.)

———

*alarmist: given to exaggerating real or potential danger.
*imperiled: endangered.
*oratory: speech making.

Based on the excerpt, which conclusion can you draw about the authors?

a. The authors probably believed that 2004 presidential candidate Howard Dean, the governor from Vermont who was outspoken about his opposition to the Iraq war, was very likely to sweep the primaries and win the Democratic nomination.

b. The authors probably didn't believe that Howard Dean was likely to sweep the primaries and win the Democratic nomination.

c. The authors believe that many Americans are waiting for a presidential candidate who is willing to speak his or her mind, but the candidates are too worried about polls to recognize what the public wants.

d. It's impossible to draw any conclusions about the authors' personal opinions.

 # Evaluating Bias in Persuasive Writing

By definition, persuasive writing has a bias, and no one expects otherwise. Bias only becomes a drawback of persuasive writing when (1) the reader is oblivious, or unaware, of it; (2) the author's belief in a particular point of view has turned him or her into a verbal bully, someone who won't let readers even consider an opposing point of view; or (3) the author consciously misrepresents opposing opinions.

When Bias Goes Overboard

In the following reading the author has a stake in the long-running controversy over who actually got to the North Pole first, Robert E. Peary or Frederick A. Cook. The author's on Peary's side, and he's not about to let his readers so much as wonder if there might be another way of looking at things.

Who Got There First Is Not in Question

1 On September 6, 1909, Robert E. Peary announced to the world that he had just returned from the Arctic, where he had been the first person to reach the North Pole. He claimed that he had arrived at the Pole on April 6, 1909, and had then spent the next five months traveling back to civilization. To his

astonishment, however, Peary learned that just five days before, Frederick A. Cook had made the exact same announcement, claiming that he had been the first human being to discover the North Pole. Cook insisted that he had reached the Pole on April 21, 1908, a full year before Robert Peary did. According to Cook, he had been unable to communicate the news for more than a year because he had been lost in the Arctic wilderness, where he had spent the winter in a cave.

2   Which man was telling the truth? That question has generated controversy to this day. Yet the controversy is somewhat inexplicable, given that Peary was backed by the scientific community and Cook was not. Even the rather staid National Geographic Society deemed Peary more believable than Cook. And while it's true that Cook's description of the Pole's geography and physical conditions was accurate, his rather shady past doesn't exactly lend him credibility. The man was, after all, imprisoned for mail fraud.

3   Ask some current scholars what they think of the controversy, and they might argue that both Cook and Peary were lying. That's certainly the point of Robert Bryce's book *Cook and Peary: The Polar Controversy.* But Bryce, who is even-handed when it comes to Cook, seems to have an ax to grind when he discusses Peary's achievements. He fails to take into account evidence that supports Peary's claim, evidence that is overwhelming to all but the most biased fan of that milkman-turned-doctor, Frederick Cook.

In this reading, the author does not initially acknowledge that he is taking sides. Particularly in the first paragraph, he appears to be intent on telling readers something about the controversy surrounding the claims of both Peary and Cook. But as the reading develops, it's clear that he is excessively biased in favor of Peary. More to the point, the author's bias has made him an unreliable source of information because he doesn't adequately address opposing points of view.

After mentioning that Cook did in fact give accurate descriptions of the North Pole, the author insists that this is not meaningful proof because Cook had been imprisoned for mail fraud. This response is an example of faulty logic in which the author substitutes a **personal attack** for evidence. Writers sometimes launch an attack on a person's character or beliefs when they have no convincing reasons or evidence to prove their point or challenge an opposing position. Some writers even stoop to insults in place of solid reasons or hard evidence for their claims. However, if they were able to supply those, they wouldn't need to engage in personal attacks.

Note, too, how the author concludes by telling readers that only biased Cook fans could ignore the "overwhelming" proof that Peary made it to the Pole first. If the evidence were so overwhelming, we should have seen a lot more of it in this reading.

An Example of Acceptable Bias

In the reading that follows, the writer has a definite bias. But this time the bias isn't excessive. The author doesn't use a personal attack to undercut the opposition. Instead, the author uses evidence to convince readers that Peary was telling the truth.

Charisma or Not, Peary's the One

1   On September 6, 1909, Robert E. Peary jubilantly announced to the world that he had done what no man before had accomplished. He had reached the North Pole. According to Peary's account, he had reached the North Pole on April 6 and had spent the next five months making his way back to civilization. To his annoyance and astonishment, however, Peary learned that, just five days earlier, Frederick A. Cook had made the same claim. Cook insisted that he had reached the Pole on April 21, 1908, a full year before Peary. According to Cook, he had been unable to communicate the great news because he had been lost in the cold Arctic wilderness and had survived by taking shelter in a cave.

2   The question these competing claims raised was obvious: Who was telling the truth? Established experts like the National Geographic Society took Peary's part, insisting that his photographs and journals proved his claim. *The New York Times* put Peary on the front page while the various naturalist societies of the day pinned medals on him.

3   Yet somehow, the general public wouldn't, or couldn't, give up its faith in Cook. Even the *New York Herald* took his side. In part at least, Cook had his champions because no one liked Peary very much. Selfish, vain, and greedy for glory, Peary was too desperate to be famous and too unwilling to give any credit to others. From his very first expedition, he had been accompanied by an African American named Matthew Henson. A skilled dog and sled handler, Henson was also fluent in the Inuit* language, which Peary hadn't bothered to learn. Henson's help, in other words, was invaluable, particularly after Peary had lost most of his toes to frostbite. But

---

*The people living in the Arctic regions prefer *Inuit* to *Eskimo*.

Peary was forever trying to pretend that Henson played a completely subordinate role in the quest to reach the Pole. In Peary's accounts, he was more servant than fellow-explorer.*

4   Despite his stint in jail, Cook by many accounts was charming, courageous, and charismatic. So much so that Robert M. Bryce, the author of *Cook & Peary: The Polar Controversy Solved,* started writing the story of both Cook and Peary in order to prove that Cook had been the first one at the Pole. Yet whatever his aspirations, Bryce ended up believing that neither man told the truth. According to Bryce, Peary couldn't have made it in the time he claimed—thirty-seven days—because later explorers with better equipment and technology hadn't been able to match or beat that record. Unfortunately, when Bryce got a look at a heretofore undiscovered diary written by Cook, along with some of Cook's private papers, he was forced to admit that his hero occasionally doctored the evidence to prove his claims.

5   Critically heralded and widely read, Bryce's book seemed to have resolved the controversy over who got to the North Pole first. The key word here, though, is *seemed* because, like it or not, the vain, overbearing, glory-hound Peary apparently was the one who made it to the Pole first. Conclusive proof for that claim came from a team of five explorers who arrived at the North Pole in April of 2005, using the same equipment Peary had used, huskies and wooden sleds. The four men and one woman arrived there in a little under the thirty-seven days Peary had claimed for his journey. They made the trip because they were long-time Peary fans, who wanted to give their man his due. As leader Tom Avery expressed it, "We hope we have restored Peary's name to its rightful place and put the controversy to rest once and for all." While diehard Cook fans may not like the idea, it was indeed Robert E. Peary who made it to the North Pole ahead of everyone else. (Sources of information: members.tripod.com/PolarFlight/ controversy1.htm; http://news.bbc.co.uk/1/hi/england/ southern_counties/4505333.stm.)

In this reading, readers can infer from the title that the author is going to take Peary's side. But taking sides in persuasive writing is expected. The question is how strong is the writer's bias? Is it so strong that this author, like the previous one, can't be considered a reliable source of information?

---

*According to Robert M. Bryce, in one of history's typical ironies Henson's account of the journey is much read. Peary's isn't.

The answer is no. Look at the way the reading challenges the opposing position of Robert Bryce. Instead of ridiculing Bryce's opinion, the writer contradicts it with factual evidence. Writing before the 2005 expedition, Bryce argued that Peary wasn't telling the truth because no one had matched his record in getting to the Pole. In response to Bryce, the author points to an expedition that disproves his argument. In April of 2005, five people, traveling exactly like Peary did, made it to the North Pole in almost the same time the earlier explorer had claimed it took him.

That's not to say that Cook's supporters won't still claim that Cook should also be believed. But that's not the issue here. The point is that this reading reveals a bias but doesn't go overboard defending it. The author refuses to insult the opposition or launch personal attacks. Instead, she treats the opposing point of view with respect and counters it by giving readers a solid, factually based reason for thinking Peary should be believed. That's what a persuasive piece of writing should do. It shouldn't browbeat the reader or disparage the opposition. Instead, it should offer readers the kind of logic and evidence that rightfully sways opinions.

Reading Tip

Any time a writer decides to do your thinking for you by saying that a particular point of view is "undeniable" or evidence is "overwhelming," it probably means that he or she hasn't really built a convincing case.

Check Your Understanding

Explain the difference between acceptable and excessive bias.

_____

_____

_____

_____

━◼ EXERCISE 5 Recognizing Excessive Bias

DIRECTIONS All of these excerpts have a persuasive purpose. Your job is to identify (1) what opinion the author wants readers to share, (2) the tone used to sway readers in the author's direction, and (3) the degree of bias.

EXAMPLE Americans seem always to have lusted for rags-to-riches heroes. Failing to find them, we are too often inclined to invent them. This certainly seems to be the case when it comes to the man born Joel Hagglund and christened Joe Hill. A poet and songwriter, Hill first came to public attention when he wrote a series of songs that were adopted by the early American labor movement. His name, however, did not become notorious until he was arrested for armed robbery and murder. According to the legend, Hill never committed the murder; he was executed in an attempt to destroy the labor movement. Although it is true that Hill was tried and convicted on circumstantial evidence, it is equally true that his story contained numerous distortions and loopholes. At his best, he was a man unfairly tried and convicted; at his worst, he was a criminal who boldly proclaimed himself innocent. But in neither case was he a legendary hero, and the ridiculous tendency to call him heroic is a misguided attempt to create a hero where none existed.

The author wants to persuade readers that

a. Joe Hill was really guilty of the murder for which he was executed.

(b.) Joe Hill should never have been given heroic status.

c. Joe Hill was a liar, and that alone should eliminate him from the category of American hero.

The tone is

a. ironic.

b. mystified.

(c.) disgusted.

For a persuasive piece of writing, the author's bias is

a. acceptable.

(b.) excessive.

EXPLANATION The author opens by saying that Americans are too ready to find a hero where none exists. Joe Hill is an illustration of that point, making *b* the correct answer. Answer *a* is not correct because the author admits Hill might not have been guilty. Answer *c* is also incorrect because lying is not the sole reason the author won't grant Hill heroic status. The author says exactly what he means, so an ironic tone cannot be correct. He is so confident of what he believes that answer *b* has to be wrong. Answer *c* is correct because the author's language drips with contempt for Hill and the people who admire him. It's the contempt and the last line of the passage that make the bias excessive. The author never explains why some people admire Hill; he simply dismisses them and their "ridiculous tendency" to call Hill heroic. This is another form of attacking your opposition by insulting them. Name-calling and insults should never persuade readers of anything—except that the writer hasn't got the evidence to prove his or her point.

1. Several high-profile celebrities, such as television weatherman Al Roker and singer Carnie Wilson, have undergone weight-loss surgery and lost hundreds of pounds in very short amounts of time. Such success stories are inspiring more and more obese Americans to consider going under the knife to have their stomach size reduced in what's known as a gastric bypass operation. They're convinced that going to this extreme is the only way for them to shed their excess fat.

   However, the media's profiles of stars' amazing transformations don't always mention the drawbacks of weight-loss surgery, and this is a detail that should not be ignored. The reports fail to point out, for example, that the operation can be quite dangerous. Many physicians refuse to perform operations on significantly obese people because of the risks involved, and one or two patients out of every two hundred actually die as the result of gastric bypass surgery. Those patients who survive their operation can face serious side effects; about 7 percent of gastric bypass patients suffer from problems such as infections, blood clots, respiratory failures, and hernias. Many require second or even third operations to correct the subsequent complications. Thirty percent of patients suffer from nutritional deficiencies such as anemia because their bodies don't absorb enough vitamins and minerals any more. Plus, the long-term effects of the surgery are not yet known. The media has also failed to report that about 10 to 15 percent of patients undergo all of this suffering for nothing: either they don't lose much weight, or they end up gaining back most or all of the pounds they initially shed. (Source of information: Julia Sommerfeld, "Weight-Loss Surgery Means Weighing Risks," *Seattle Times*, June 5, 2003, http://seattletimes.nwsource.com/html/localnews/134644627_obeserisks03m0.html.)

The author wants to persuade readers that

a. Americans' obsession with losing weight has led many people to undergo a dangerous form of surgery, which may not even be successful.

b. celebrities who want to undergo bypass surgery should do so if they wish, but they should not encourage others to follow suit.

c. in leaving out the drawbacks of bypass surgery, the media has been irresponsible.

The tone is

a. accusing.

b. friendly but firm.

c. puzzled.

For a persuasive piece of writing, the author's bias is

a. acceptable.

b. excessive.

2. When architectural student Maya Lin won the contest to design the Vietnam Veterans Memorial in 1981, many people—especially veterans—were shocked and angry. Her design, a long black wall inscribed with the names of those who died, was described as a "black gash of shame," and the resulting opposition and controversy came close to preventing Lin's design from ever being built. However, when people now visit Lin's completed monument, they see a black granite wall that, although it makes no political statement about the war, cuts into the earth like the shiny scar of a deep wound. The wall lists the names of all of the men and women who lost their lives in the conflict. It is long and low, and every name is within reach. In its effect, the memorial invites the living to reach out and touch the names of the dead. When visitors look at the wall, its polished mirrored surface reflects the ghosts of their own faces behind the names of fallen friends and loved ones. As a result, many visitors openly grieve, demonstrating the monument's ability to evoke powerful emotional responses that can help assuage grief. Even the memorial's opponents have changed their initial opinion about the monument's design. They now agree that the wall is a

moving tribute that encourages visitors to reflect on the price of war while still honoring those who served. The pity is that it took so long for Lin's critics to recognize her achievement.

The author wants to persuade readers that

a. Maya Lin produced exactly the right design for the Vietnam Veterans Memorial, and the recognition of her accomplishment took much too long.

b. Maya Lin's design for the Vietnam Veterans Memorial was meant to elicit powerful emotions.

c. if Maya Lin had not been a woman, people would have recognized her accomplishment sooner.

The tone is

a. impressed.

b. ironic.

c. disbelieving.

For a persuasive piece of writing, the author's bias is

a. acceptable.

b. excessive.

3. Since 1971, Columbus Day has been a federal holiday celebrating the achievement of Christopher Columbus, the first European explorer to land in the New World. But how can we American citizens, in good conscience, continue to honor a man whose greed and brutality were legendary among the people he conquered?

When Columbus set sail in 1492, King Ferdinand and Queen Isabella of Spain wanted him to spread Christianity while fulfilling his promise of finding a route to Asia. Columbus, as it turned out, did neither. When Columbus first made land, he thought he was somewhere in the East Indies, but he was actually stepping on shore of what is now Barbados. Claiming everything in sight as the property of Spain, Columbus demanded that the indigenous* population pay tribute, preferably in gold. If they refused outright or seemed to be making insufficient efforts to pay, their hands were to be chopped off per order of the admiral—Christopher Columbus.

In 1493, as the governor of Hispaniola, now Haiti, Columbus gifted the New World population with imported European diseases, malnutrition, overwork, and harsh punishments. Eventually, Columbus's

*indigenous: native to the region.

rule and its aftermath took a terrible toll, reducing the population to 22,000 people.

With time even the Spanish missionaries, sent to help Columbus spread God's word, were alarmed by his behavior. One missionary reported that Columbus was guilty of "robbing and destroying the land." Columbus apparently thought nothing of cutting down a whole forest in order to have enough wood for building and heat. By 1500, even his Spanish sponsors knew their man to be a failure. The missionaries had written Ferdinand and Isabella, saying that peace would never be possible as long as Columbus remained in power. Stripped of his authority, Columbus was returned to Spain in chains at the command of the new governor.

In light of these facts, we have to wonder about those people who claim that Columbus's voyage began a new era of exploration and that his great achievement is worthy of a federal holiday. Who will they honor next, the serial killer Charles Manson? (Sources of information: The Library of Congress, "Columbus Day," http://memory.loc.gov/ammem/today/oct12.html; Felipe Fernandez-Armesto, "Columbus—Hero or Villain?" *History Today*, May 1992, pp. 4+.)

The author wants to persuade readers that

a. Columbus was a terrible leader.

b. Columbus was generally incompetent.

c. Columbus is not deserving of a federal holiday.

The tone is

a. outraged.

b. discontented.

c. soothing.

For a persuasive piece of writing, the author's bias is

a. acceptable.

b. excessive.

4. When former President Jimmy Carter lost his bid for a second term in 1980, he left behind a host of serious economic, political, and international problems for his successor to clean up. Had he gone the way of most ex-presidents, who usually spend their time playing golf or earning cash for speaking engagements, he might have been best remembered for his ineffectual administration. But Carter obviously decided not to rest until he had qualified for sainthood. Thus, he has been working relentlessly to salvage his place

in history. Although his own administration was characterized by questionable foreign policy decisions, he has insisted on peddling his so-called "expertise" to nations for which he negotiates treaties and monitors democratic elections. Carter has used his star status as a platform from which he has criticized other presidents' policies and undermined our leaders with his unsolicited and inappropriate proposals. For example, he is the only current or former president to unofficially visit Communist Cuban dictator Fidel Castro, an avowed enemy of democracy. Carter also directly contradicted U.S. policy by noisily advocating an end to America's trade embargo of Cuba. Perhaps Carter's time would be better spent hammering nails for the Habitat for Humanity organization he supports instead of traipsing around the globe and giving advice he hasn't been asked for.

The author wants to persuade readers that

a. former President Jimmy Carter has done a great deal of good since leaving office.

b. former President Jimmy Carter may well go down in history as a man of achievement despite his failures while in office.

c. Jimmy Carter was an incompetent president and is an annoying nuisance as an ex-president.

The tone is

a. contemptuous.

b. curious.

c. ironic.

For a persuasive piece of writing, the author's bias is

a. acceptable.

b. excessive.

 # Backing Opinions with Arguments

Despite the old saying "Everyone has the right to an opinion," all opinions aren't equally worthy of your respect. If someone can't argue an opinion with convincing reasons or evidence, then you should think twice before letting yourself be persuaded.

Imagine, for example, that a friend saw you taking an aspirin for a headache and told you that chewing a garlic clove was a far better remedy. When you asked why, he shrugged his shoulders and said: "I don't know. I heard it someplace." Given your friend's inability to argue his position with reasons or evidence, you probably wouldn't be too quick to chew garlic in order to relieve your discomfort.

Opinions and Sound Arguments

To be persuasive, writers need to put forth a sound argument. They need to clearly identify the opinion they would like you to share or consider and provide reasons and evidence for their position. Look, for example, at the following passage:

> For decades, we Americans have shunned the $2 bill and the $1 coin. Although both are still legal tender, they are rarely used. Most of us prefer to throw them in our drawers at home rather than spend them. There are, however, some very good reasons to start using these two forms of currency more. The best reason is that both the $2 bill and the $1 coin save taxpayer dollars. Because the government can print half the number of $2 bills than $1 bills to put the same amount of money in circulation, production costs are lower. The same is true of the $1 coin. Although it costs three times as much as a paper dollar to make, it lasts twenty times as long. In the long run, then, fewer new coins must be produced, and the government again saves money. Another reason to spend our $2 bills and $1 coins is their lack of value as collectors' items. Apparently, many of us assume that because these forms of currency are unusual, they must be keepsakes that could one day be worth more than their face value. This idea causes many people to hoard them for the future. However, expert collectors like the editor of *Money Talks* say that this belief is a mistake. Thus, saving $2 bills and $1 coins makes no sense. (Sources of information: "Money for Sale," editorial, *USA Today*, June 13, 2003, 15A, www.usatoday.com/usaonline/20030613/5240970s/html; Associated Press, "Government May Revive $2 Bill," *The Atlanta Journal-Constitution*, May 12, 2003, www.ajc.com/news/content/news/0603/12twodollar.html.)

The author of the above paragraph believes that people should stop hoarding the $2 bill and the $1 coin. But notice that she doesn't just state her opinion and expect you to accept it without reasons or evidence. Respecting her readers' right to an argument—instead of an unsupported assertion, or claim—she carefully supplies reasons for her belief.

Shaky Arguments

Now that you've seen an example of a solidly argued opinion, you'll probably be less impressed by the shaky, or poorly supported, arguments that follow.

Hasty Generalizations

Convinced that they are correct in their opinions, writers intent on persuasion sometimes forget to convince their readers. They forget, that one example or, for that matter, a few instances are never enough to prove a broad generalization about huge numbers of people. In other words, writers who want to persuade can sometimes be guilty of offering readers a hasty generalization. Here's an example:

Generalization <u>Without a doubt, the 1.5 to 2 million American children who are being home-schooled are learning more and learning it faster than children who are attending public or private schools</u>. According to a study conducted in 2004 by the Home School Advocates organization, which examined the progress of 102 home-schooled children in 50 families, students who are taught at home by their parents consistently score in the 80th percentile or above on standardized achievement tests. This same study also revealed that 75 percent of these 102 home-schooled children are enrolled in one or more grades higher than their public- and private-school counterparts of the same age. Clearly, a home-school education is far superior to that of an education in any institutional setting.

Now don't be fooled by the presence of a study supporting the idea that children who are home-schooled do better than children who are not. To begin with, one small study seldom proves anything. And in this case, readers are being asked to accept a generalization about more than a million children based on a single study of 102 kids. Where broad generalizations are concerned, writers need to give readers lots of examples. *The broader the generalization the more examples required.* Look, for instance, at the following paragraph to see an illustration of a generalization that is not hasty.

Generalization

What has come to be known as the Forer effect may well explain why people, despite all evidence showing that astrologers don't know anymore than the rest of us, continue to read the astrology columns of their local newspapers: <u>They do so because they, like most people, are ready to believe any statement that is positive and vague enough to apply to just about anyone.</u> In 1948, psychology instructor Bertram R. Forer gave his students a personality test, ignored their answers, and gave them all the same evaluation. The evaluation read as follows:* "You have a need for other people to like and admire you, and yet you tend to be critical of yourself. While you have some personality weaknesses you are generally able to compensate for them. You have considerable unused capacity that you have not turned to your advantage. Disciplined and self-controlled on the outside, you tend to be worrisome and insecure on the inside. . . ." Almost everyone in the class agreed with their "personality assessment," despite the fact that everyone received the same one. The first such experiment was done in 1948 but has been repeated hundreds of times since. On every occasion at least 80 percent of the people tested have rated the descriptions of themselves as accurate. (Source of information: http://skepdic.com/forer.html)

The generalization in this paragraph is based on numerous studies conducted over a long period of time. It is well supported rather than hasty.

Irrelevant Evidence

When you analyze a piece of persuasive writing, always be on the lookout for irrelevant, or unrelated, evidence. Authors in the grip of excessive bias will sometimes supply you with a fact or reason that fills up space but has no particular bearing on the subject at hand. Look, for example, at the following paragraph, where the writer argues that John F. Kennedy does not deserve his high ranking on surveys of best presidents. Can you find a piece of irrelevant evidence?

When surveyed for its opinion about America's best presidents, the public consistently and mistakenly ranks John F. Kennedy either first or second. In reality, Kennedy was not a particularly effective president. No doubt, much of his appeal rests upon his image. He was seen as a dynamic leader reigning over a new

---

*The evaluation is too long to quote in its entirety here.

"Camelot."* Kennedy's quick wit, excellent speaking skills, and good looks helped make him the media's darling, and his charm and charisma played well on television. Yet while the press portrayed him as a devoted family man, Kennedy actually was a womanizer who had a number of extramarital affairs, including one with a nineteen-year-old White House intern. He suffered from chronic health problems and took many drugs, including painkillers, to relieve colitis, back pain, and Addison's disease. His precarious physical state made him ill-suited to the nation's highest office, yet he irresponsibly duped the American people into believing that he was capable and fit. In truth, Kennedy was living on borrowed time; had he lived to be reelected to a second term, his failings eventually would have been exposed, and his house of cards would have come tumbling down.

The author of this passage argues that John F. Kennedy was, in fact, not a particularly good president. To support that opinion, she offers two reasons: Kennedy was a womanizer, and he had serious health problems that he kept hidden.

John F. Kennedy may well have been a womanizer, but unless the author can explain to you how it interfered with Kennedy's performance of his duties, the author has not supplied you with evidence relevant to her claim. To make Kennedy's immoral behavior matter, the author would have to describe how Kennedy's affairs with women kept him from the business of the presidency. Since she doesn't do that, this particular piece of evidence is not related to the opinion she puts forth.

More relevant to the author's point are Kennedy's hidden health problems and the medications he was forced to take. Painkillers are notorious for clouding a person's ability to think clearly, so they may well have interfered with Kennedy's performance. But even this piece of supporting evidence needs to be fleshed out in order to be truly convincing. The author needs to cite some instance in which President Kennedy seemed to have been affected by the drugs he took. By failing to do so, she simply assumes that you will infer Kennedy was not up to the job because of his health. The author, however, offers no evidence that this was the case. John F. Kennedy may not have been an effective president, as the author claims. Still before making that opinion your own, you need a better argument, one with more relevant reasons.

---

*Camelot: According to legend, King Arthur's royal court.

Circular Reasoning

The author of the following passage is convinced that the government should regulate nightshift work hours. The question is, How does he try to convince his readers to share that point of view?

> The government of the United States should regulate the number of hours a worker can put in on a nightshift. It is a disgrace that this has not been done already. The United States is one of only six industrialized countries that do not regulate nightshift hours. This lack of regulation is a dangerous and costly oversight that will one day prove disastrous.

It's easy to determine the opinion expressed in this paragraph: The U.S. government should regulate nightshift hours. What's not so clear is why the author takes this position. Much of the paragraph simply repeats the opening opinion. That's why the reasoning is circular. The opinion and the reason for holding it are one and the same.

But imagine now that the author had recognized his failure to provide an argument and revised the above paragraph to make it more persuasive.

> The government of the United States should regulate the number of hours a worker can put in on a nightshift.* According to studies completed by the National Commission on Sleep Disorders, the loss of sleep, whether voluntary or involuntary, is a dangerous and deadly threat. The commission concluded that literally millions of accidents are caused every year by drivers and workers trying to function normally on too little sleep. Yet another study by the Congressional Office of Technology pointed to the importance that changes in the sleep cycle play in human errors within the workplace. Additional studies suggest that people are more likely to make errors of all kinds if they have not slept seven to eight hours within the last twenty-four hours. These studies strongly suggest that limits be placed on disturbances in the human sleep cycle. Although the government cannot determine how many hours employees sleep, it can and should place limits on the number of hours they spend on nightshifts.

In this paragraph, the author now anticipates and answers the question he rightly assumes his readers might pose: "Why should I accept this opinion?" To argue his claim and make it persuasive, he tells his readers about some studies that helped him to form his

---

*Statistics and studies drawn from Merrill M. Miller, "Punch the Clock, Hit the Hay," *New York Times*, January 11, 1992, p.19.

opinion. Although critical readers might not immediately embrace the author's opinion as their own, they would certainly give it serious consideration.

Offering False Alternatives

Authors determined to persuade may insist that there are only two possible alternatives or answers to a problem or question when, in fact, there are several. Here's an example:

> Moviemakers intent on creating a realistic atmosphere are forced to engage in *product placement*—the use of brand names in exchange for a fee. Were an actor in a scene to open a can simply labeled tuna, the audience's attention would be distracted by the label, and the effect of the scene would be destroyed. People are used to seeing brand names such as Chicken of the Sea and Bumble Bee. Filmmakers who want realism in their films aren't doing anything wrong when they engage in product placement.

According to this author's reasoning, there are only two alternatives: moviemakers must accept fees for using brand names, or they will be forced to use general names that distract the audience. Left out of this reading are two other alternatives: (1) arrange the scene so that audiences don't see labels, or (2) invent brand names and labels that resemble the real ones. Faced with the above either-or thinking, critical readers would start looking for other alternatives.

Making Careless Comparisons

Comparisons used to illustrate a point are a useful tool for writers. Look how Gail Sheehy uses a comparison between humans and lobsters in order to illustrate the stages we go through in life.

> We are not unlike a particularly hardy crustacean.* The lobster grows by developing and shedding a series of hard, protective shells. Each time it expands from within, the confining shell must be sloughed off. It is left exposed and vulnerable until, in time, a new covering grows to replace the old shell.
>
> With each passage from one stage of human growth to the next, we, too, must shed a protective structure. We are left exposed and vulnerable. (Sheehy, *Passages*, p. 24.)

Be wary, however, of authors who use comparisons not to illustrate a point but to prove it. Often the differences between the two things

---

*crustacean: shellfish.

compared are more crucial than the similarities. Here, for example, the author compares producers who get paid for product placement with athletes who get paid to wear their sponsor's clothing:

> Filmmakers who accept fees for using brand names in their films are just like athletes who are paid to wear name brands in public.

Although that reasoning might sound convincing at first, the differences between the two practices may, in fact, be more important than the similarities. Certainly that is what the writer of the following passage believes:

> Product placement and celebrity endorsements are not the same at all. Highly publicized celebrity contracts have made the public fully aware that athletes are paid large sums of money to sport a sponsor's clothing or footwear. In contrast, the average moviegoer is not so knowledgeable about the fees paid to filmmakers using brand names. Thus, the effects of product placement in films work on a far more subconscious level. Audience members have no idea they are seeing paid advertising.

As the author of this passage points out, there are some crucial differences between athletes who wear name-brand clothing and filmmakers who use brand names in their movies. Those differences considerably weaken the first author's argument for product placement.

◄■ EXERCISE 6 Recognizing Faulty Logic

DIRECTIONS The following passages all present you with arguments. But each one reveals flawed logic. Circle the appropriate letter to identify the author's error in logic.

EXAMPLE In far too many American cities, homelessness has become a major problem. In some cities, whole families live on the street. In a country this rich, homelessness is a national disgrace. In response to this social problem, Americans must dig more deeply into their pockets to support the work of local charities, or the number of homeless people will continue to grow.

a. irrelevant evidence
b. false alternatives
c. careless comparison
d. hasty generalization
e. personal attack

EXPLANATION The author insists that we have only two choices about how to treat the homeless: give to local charities or allow the problem to increase. It doesn't take a sociologist to realize that there are other alternatives, as well.

1. Stephen King is an underrated artist who is every bit as gifted as Shakespeare. Evidence of King's greatness can be found by examining the similarities in the work of both authors. Shakespeare often wrote about love and relationships. An excellent example of this is his play *Romeo and Juliet.* Stephen King also writes about relationships. *The Stand* and *It* both focus on the importance of love and the power of friendship. Both authors examine issues of morality and are interested in the power of evil. If Shakespeare were alive today, I think he and Stephen King might even work on writing a book or screenplay together. That's just how talented Stephen King is.

   a. irrelevant evidence
   b. false alternatives
   c. careless comparison
   d. hasty generalization
   e. personal attack

2. As a writer, Ernest Hemingway is overrated. His novels and short stories are of little general interest. He wrote about experiences that appeal only to a certain kind of man: the hypermasculine male who loves hunting, fishing, and safaris. Hemingway's range as a writer was very narrow. But that should come as no surprise to people familiar with Hemingway's personal life. Hemingway was a womanizer and a heavy drinker. He was the worst kind of "man's man." It's no wonder that his writing is limited and shallow: Hemingway was a limited and shallow man.

   a. irrelevant evidence
   b. false alternatives
   c. careless comparison
   d. circular reasoning
   e. personal attack

3. On July 13, 1977, the lights went out in New York City and almost as soon as it happened, the fighting and looting began. But the city would never have been the scene of such confusion had the police

done their job. It was the police's incompetence that caused the epidemic of theft, violence, and arson. Had the police been more in control, few would have dared saw off padlocks and storm into stores to steal everything that wasn't nailed down.

a. irrelevant evidence

b. false alternatives

c. careless comparison

d. circular reasoning

e. personal attack

4. Sociologists have long claimed that a lack of daily or weekly contact with a noncustodial parent has few negative effects on the children of divorce; however, new research shows that a lack of regular contact with one of the parents is actually destructive. In one study, fifty college freshmen with divorced parents completed a questionnaire about their experiences and feelings. A number of the students who were geographically separated from one of their parents following the divorce admitted to having a more difficult time adjusting. In comparison to those whose parents continued to live near each other after divorcing, they also claimed to feel more hostility. (Source of information: Mackenzie Carpenter, "Experts Disagree on Best Interests of Children of Divorce," *Pittsburgh Post-Gazette,* http://singleparents.about.com/cs/divorce/a/childofdiv81503.htm.)

a. irrelevant evidence

b. false alternatives

c. hasty generalization

d. careless comparison

e. circular reasoning

5. Currently, many health maintenance organizations (HMOs) in the United States do not adequately meet the medical needs of their participants. Part of the problem stems from the amount of money HMOs are forced to spend not on medical care but on the bureaucratic apparatus they need to function. HMOs rely heavily on disease management and review boards that advise insurers about which treatments and drugs should be allowed. The boards cost money, not just to pay the salaries of board members but also to finance the paperwork they generate. In addition to the management

and review boards, HMOs require legal services to defend against the possibilities of lawsuits that might be filed when specific treatments are disallowed. In addition to their billing agencies, HMOs rely heavily on marketing consultants to help them attract business. All of these services require substantial amounts of cash, and even in the most efficient HMOs, overhead consumes 14 percent of insurance premiums compared to only 3 percent in Canada, where there is a national health insurance and 97 percent of the premium payment goes to doctors, hospitals, and clinics.* No wonder states like Illinois are demanding the right to fill their prescriptions in Canada.

a. irrelevant evidence

b. false alternatives

c. careless comparison

d. circular reasoning

e. hasty generalization

EXERCISE 7 Recognizing Faulty Logic

DIRECTIONS Read each passage. Identify the error in reasoning by circling the appropriate letter. *Note*: Read the passages slowly. You may even need to read them twice.

EXAMPLE The media often call attention to teachers' poor working conditions and low pay. However, the teaching profession has improved in many ways during the last forty years. For one thing, today's teachers are responsible for fewer students. A National Education Association survey of the 2000–2001 school year revealed that elementary school teachers have about 21 students per class. In contrast, teachers in 1961 had an average of 29 students. Teachers in secondary schools have seen a slight increase—from 27 to 28 students in a class—since 1961; however, they teach fewer students overall. High school teachers in 1966 taught 132 students a day; by 2001, that total was down to 89. In addition, the NEA survey showed that today's teachers have more preparation time than their 1960s counterparts had. Teachers now hold more advanced degrees, too. Fifty percent of today's teachers have earned a master's degree; this percentage has more than doubled since 1961. What's more, a teacher's average salary has steadily increased

---

*James Weinstein, *The Long Detour* (Boulder, Colo.: Westview Press, 2003), pp. 240–241.

since the 1960s, when teachers made the equivalent of $32,598 in today's dollars. In 2001, the average teacher's salary was $43,262. Plus, some researchers say that when salaries are computed on an hourly basis, teachers usually earn an hourly wage exceeding that of registered nurses, accountants, engineers, and other middle-class professions. (Sources of information: Fredreka Schouten, "Public School Teachers' Hourly Pay Tops Many Professions, Study Finds," *USA Today*, June 3, 2003, p. 9D; Greg Toppo, "Teachers Have Smaller Classes But Spend More Time There," *USA Today*, August 28, 2003, p. 9D.)

(a.) irrelevant evidence

b. circular reasoning

c. false alternatives

d. careless comparison

e. hasty generalization

EXPLANATION The passage generally does a good job supporting the notion that the teaching profession has improved. However, letter *a* should be circled because the sentences about the number of teachers holding advanced degrees is irrelevant. This information would be more appropriate in a passage claiming that teachers are now more qualified than ever before.

1. Elementary school teachers often keep classroom pets such as gerbils, hamsters, guinea pigs, and reptiles. The teachers claim that these animals help young children learn about both responsibility and biology. However, animals in the classroom should be outlawed for ethical and health reasons. According to People for the Ethical Treatment of Animals and the American Society for the Prevention of Cruelty to Animals, keeping animals in cages for education or enjoyment teaches youngsters that cruelty to animals is acceptable. Therefore, either we put a stop to keeping animals in the classroom, or we destroy young people's compassion for the other creatures of our world. In addition, classroom pets pose health risks. Both the American Lung Association and the U.S. Environmental Protection Agency caution against keeping animals in schools because feathers and pet dander can trigger asthma attacks and allergic reactions in sensitive children. In addition, the animals can also transmit harmful bacteria to the kids who handle them. (Source of information: Dorren Klausnitzer, "Teachers' Pets Face Expulsion,"

USA Today, October 3, 2003, p. 20A, www.usatoday.com/usaonline/
20031003/5358619.htm.)

a. irrelevant evidence

b. circular reasoning

c. false alternatives

d. careless comparison

e. hasty generalization

2. The federal government is overstepping its bounds with the aggressive "Click It or Ticket" program that requires all motorists to wear their seatbelts or pay hefty fines. Whether or not you wear your seatbelt is not the business of the government. The choice to wear a seatbelt is an individual one, and every American should be able to decide not to wear a seatbelt if he or she so desires. Seatbelt use is really every citizen's personal decision, and the government should not make that decision for us, as though we were children incapable of making the right choices for ourselves. We must put a stop to the random searches at checkpoints because buckling up is our choice and no one else's.

a. irrelevant evidence

b. circular reasoning

c. false alternatives

d. careless comparison

e. personal attack

3. A growing number of educational programs now target very young preschool children. Sylvan Learning Centers, for example, offers reading programs for four-year-olds, and Kaplan Inc. has an early learning program for pre-K children. The Kumon Learning Centers claim to be able to teach toddlers as young as two years old fundamental reading and math skills that help their academic progress when they get to kindergarten and elementary school. Many educators argue that there is no evidence that this kind of early tutoring offers children any long-term benefits. Others warn that pressuring children to learn academic skills at such a young age can backfire, turning children against school and learning. Despite these fears, however, early tutoring is clearly working. One four-year-old enrolled at age two at the Kumon Center in Naples, Florida, could read by age three. Some of the other three-year-olds in the program are able to complete second grade math problems. These

children, says Mena Grimes, the center's director, are well above their peers by the time they get to school. (Sources of information: Melissa Keeney, "Parents Starting Early, Tutoring Toddlers at Age 2," WINK TV, December 3, 2004, www.winktv.com/x12725.xml; www .susanohanian.org/atrocity.fetch.php?id-4019.)

a. irrelevant evidence

b. circular reasoning

c. false alternatives

d. careless comparison

e. hasty generalization

4. The next time you're shopping for a car, will you pay several hundred dollars extra to get one with optional side airbags? According to the Toyota and Ford Motor companies, only about one-fifth of their customers purchase these additional airbags; however, they're definitely worth the money. Side airbags significantly increase one's chance of surviving side-impact vehicle collisions, which kill 9,000 people every year. A study of these types of accident deaths, conducted by the Insurance Institute for Highway Safety, found that for every 100,000 passenger cars involved in side collisions, 248 people died in the vehicles with no side airbags. In comparison, there were 74 percent fewer fatalities in cars with torso and head side airbags when those cars were hit by either another car or a minivan. In crashes involving a pickup truck or a sport utility vehicle, the presence of side airbags led to a 53 percent drop in the number of fatalities. Trucks and SUVs are a serious danger to other motorists, for in crashes involving a car and a truck or an SUV, the occupants of the car are twenty times more likely to be killed than are the occupants of the truck or SUV. (Sources of information: Danny Hakim, "Study Touts Side Air Bags," *New York Times*, August 26, 2003, www.nytimes.com/2003/08/26/business/26AUTO.html; Buckle Up America, July 25, 2003, www.buckleupamerica.org.)

a. irrelevant evidence

b. circular reasoning

c. false alternatives

d. careless comparison

e. personal attack

5. In an attempt to make their children good students, many parents use rewards and punishments. "Get an 'A' in history and you can take the car to school," they tell their kids. "Do your homework every night and at the end of the month, we'll pay your cell phone bill." Yet, as writer and teacher Alfie Kohn pointed out in his book *Punished by Rewards,* the system of rewarding kids for doing well in school and punishing them for not doesn't work very well. Kohn's book synthesizes years of research on the subject and repeatedly comes up with the same result—as an educational tool, rewards and punishments are a failure. Psychologist Edward Deci makes the same point in his book *Why We Do What We Do.* Deci describes a study in which he asked two groups of college students to solve a series of puzzles. One group was paid a dollar for each puzzle. The other group wasn't paid at all. The group that received payment stopped as soon as money changed hands. The other group members, in contrast, continued to tinker with the puzzles even after the experiment ended; they did it because they were intrinsically rather than extrinsically motivated. The more we make students rely on rewards for what they do, the less personal motivation they will have. They become dependent on rewards for achievement. But think about it: did we really need research to tell us that? Don't we have enough examples in the animal kingdom to make that point? Hold a biscuit over a dog's head and it will eagerly stand on its hind legs to get the treat. Take away the biscuit and the dog stays on all fours. No treat, no trick. Parents who think they are doing a good thing by rewarding their kids for achievement are really just letting their kids go to the dogs. (Source of information: www.shearonforschools.com/gold_star_junkies.htm.)

a. irrelevant evidence

b. circular reasoning

c. false alternatives

d. careless comparison

e. personal attack

■ DIGGING DEEPER

CRITICAL THINKING AND PSEUDO-PSYCHOLOGIES— PALMS, PLANETS, AND PERSONALITY

LOOKING AHEAD Psychologist and professor Dennis Coon believes that most people are not skeptical enough about what he calls pseudo-psychologies. To discover what they are and find out why many of us are all too ready to believe in them, read the selection drawn from Professor Coon's textbook *Essentials of Psychology.*

1 Most of us would be skeptical when buying a used car. But all too often, we may be tempted to "buy" outrageous claims about topics such as "channeling," dowsing,* the occult, the Bermuda Triangle, hypnosis, numerology, and so forth. Likewise, most of us easily accept our ignorance of sub-atomic physics. But because we all deal with human behavior every day, we tend to think that we already know what is true and what is false in psychology.

2 For these, and many more reasons, learning to think critically is one of the lasting benefits of a college education. **Critical thinking** refers to an ability to evaluate, compare, analyze, critique, and synthesize information. Critical thinkers are willing to ask the hard questions, including those that challenge conventional wisdom.

Pseudo-psychologies

3 A **pseudo-psychology** (SUE-doe-psychology) is any dubious and unfounded system that resembles psychology. Many pseudo-psychologies offer elaborate systems that give the appearance of science but are actually false. (*Pseudo* means "false.") Like most pseudo-sciences, pseudo-psychologies change little over time because their followers do not actively seek new data. In fact, they often go to great lengths to avoid evidence that contradicts their beliefs. Scientists, in contrast, actively look for contradictions as a way to advance knowledge.

4 Unlike the real thing, pseudo-psychologies are not based on empirical* observation or scientific testing. **Palmistry**, for instance, claims that lines in the hand reveal personality and predict a person's future. Despite the overwhelming evidence against this, palmists can still be found separating the gullible from their money in many cities. A similar false system is **phrenology**, popularized in the nineteenth century by Franz Gall, a German anatomy teacher.

---

*dowsing: the use of a divining rod to search for underground water or minerals.
*empirical: based on observation or experiment; verifiable by such means.

Gall believed that personality is revealed by the shape of the skull. However, modern research has shown that bumps on the head have nothing to do with talents or abilities. In fact, the area of the brain that controls hearing was listed on phrenology charts as the center for "combativeness" and "destructiveness"!

5   At first glance, a pseudo-psychology called **graphology** may seem more reasonable. Graphologists believe that they can identify personality traits and predict job performance from handwriting. Graphology is moderately popular in the United States, where at least 3,000 companies use handwriting analysis to evaluate job applicants. This is troubling to psychologists because studies show that graphologists score close to zero in tests of accuracy in rating personality (Ben-Shakhar et al., 1986). In fact, studies show that graphologists do no better than untrained college students in rating personality and job performance (Neter & BenShakhar, 1989; Rafaeli & Klimoski, 1983). (By the way, graphology's failure at revealing personality should be separated from its proven value for detecting forgeries.)

6   At this point, you may be asking a good question: If the pseudo-psychologies have no scientific basis, how do they survive and why are they popular? There are several reasons, all of which can be demonstrated by a critique* of astrology.

7   **Problems in the Stars**   Astrology is probably the most popular pseudo-psychology. Astrologers assume that the position of the stars and planets at the time of a person's birth determines personality traits and affects behavior. Like other pseudo-psychologies, astrology has repeatedly been shown to have no scientific validity (Crowe, 1990). The objections to astrology are numerous and devastating, as shown by the following:

8   **1.** The zodiac has shifted by one full constellation since astrology was first set up. However, most astrologers simply ignore this shift. (In other words, if astrology calls you a Scorpio you are really a Libra, and so forth.)

2. There is no connection between the "compatibility" of the astrological signs of couples and their marriage and divorce rates.

3. Studies have found no connection between astrological signs and leadership, physical characteristics, career choice, or personality traits.

4. The force of gravity exerted by the physician's body at the moment of birth is greater than that exerted by the stars. Also, astrologers have failed to explain why the moment of birth should be more important than the moment of conception.

*critique: analysis and evaluation.

5. A study of over 3,000 predictions by famous astrologers found that only a small percentage were fulfilled. These "successful" predictions tended to be vague ("There will be a tragedy somewhere in the eastern United States in the spring") or easily guessed from current events. (Sources: "Astrology and Astronomy," 1983; Culver & Ianna, 1979; Pasachoff, 1981; Randi, 1980.)

9   In short, astrology doesn't work.

10   **Uncritical Acceptance**   If you have ever had your astrological chart done, you may have been impressed with its seeming accuracy. Careful reading shows many such charts to be made up of mostly flattering traits. Naturally, when your personality is described in *desirable* terms, it is hard to deny that the description has the "ring of truth." How much acceptance would astrology receive if the characteristics of a birth sign read like this.

> Virgo: You are the logical type and hate disorder. Your nitpicking is unbearable to your friends. You are cold, unemotional, and usually fall asleep while making love. Virgos make good doorstops.

11   **Positive Instances**   Even when an astrological description of personality contains a mixture of good and bad traits it may seem accurate. To find out why, read the following personality description.

Your Personality Profile

You have a strong need for other people to like you and for them to admire you. You have a tendency to be critical of yourself. You have a great deal of unused energy which you have not turned to your advantage. While you have some personality weaknesses, you are generally able to compensate for them. Your sexual adjustment has presented some problems for you. Disciplined and controlled on the outside, you tend to be worrisome and insecure inside. At times you have serious doubts as to whether you have made the right decision or done the right thing. You prefer a certain amount of change and variety and become dissatisfied when hemmed in by restrictions and limitations. You pride yourself on being an independent thinker and do not accept other opinions without satisfactory proof. You have found it unwise to be too frank in revealing yourself to others. At times you are extroverted, affable, and sociable, while at other times you are introverted, wary, and reserved. Some of your aspirations tend to be pretty unrealistic.*

---

*Adapted and reproduced with permission of authors and publisher from Ulrich, R. E., Stachnik, T. J., & Stainton, N. R. "Student acceptance of generalized personality interpretations." *Psychological Reports,* 1963, 13, 831–834. © Southern Universities Press 1963.

12   Does this describe your personality? A psychologist read this summary individually to college students who had taken a personality test. Only five students out of seventy-nine felt that the description failed to adequately capture their personalities. Another study found that people rated this "personality profile" as more accurate than their actual horoscopes (French et al., 1991).

13   Reread the description and you will see that it contains both sides of several personality dimensions ("At times you are extroverted . . . while at other times you are introverted . . ."). Its apparent accuracy is an illusion based on the **fallacy* of positive instances,** in which a person remembers or notices things that confirm his or her expectations and forgets the rest. The pseudo-psychologies thrive on this effect. For example, you can always find "Leo characteristics" in a Leo. If you looked, however, you could also find "Gemini characteristics," "Scorpio characteristics," or whatever.

14   **The Barnum Effect**   P. T. Barnum, the famed circus showman, had a formula for success: "Always have a little something for everybody." Like the all-purpose personality description, palm readings, fortunes, horoscopes, and other products of pseudo-psychology are stated in such *general* terms that they can hardly miss. There is always "a little something for everybody." If you doubt this, read *all* twelve of the daily horoscopes found in newspapers for several days. You will find that predictions for other signs fit events as well as those for your own sign do.

15   Astrology's popularity shows the difficulty many people have separating valid psychology from systems that seem valid but are not. The goal of this discussion, then, has been to make you a more critical observer of human behavior and to clarify what is, and what is not, psychology. In the meantime, here is what the "stars" say about your future:

> Emphasis now on education and personal improvement. A learning experience of lasting value awaits you. Take care of scholastic responsibilities before engaging in recreation. The word *psychology* figures prominently in your future.

(Dennis Coon, from *Essentials of Psychology: Exploration and Application,* 6th ed. © 1994. Reprinted with permission of Wadsworth, an imprint of the Wadsworth Group, a division of Thomson Learning. Fax 800-730-2215.)

———————
*fallacy: error.

Sharpening Your Skills

DIRECTIONS Answer the following questions by circling the letters of the correct response or filling in the blanks.

1. What's the main idea of the entire reading?

   _____

   _____

2. What word part gives away the meaning of the word *pseudo-psychology*? _____

3. In your own words, paraphrase the definition for the fallacy of positive instances.

   _____

   _____

4. What inference does the author expect readers to add to the opening paragraph?

   a. We think we know a lot about psychology because we deal with human behavior all the time, but we don't know as much as we think we do.

   b. We don't mind being ignorant about physics because, for some reason, ignorance of science is accepted in our culture.

   c. Our everyday dealings with other human beings do, in fact, teach us everything we need to know about psychology.

   d. Being knowledgeable about physics is more important than being knowledgeable about psychology.

5. Based on what the author says, readers could logically draw which conclusion, or inference?

   a. The author is likely to agree that Americans are too obsessed by logic and analysis and need to rely more on pure instinct and emotion.

   b. The author may criticize astrology, but he probably reads the astrology section of the newspaper daily.

c. The author would probably agree that critical thinking should be part of every high school and college curriculum.

d. The author would probably agree that pseudo-sciences could qualify as science if they were the subject of more study and experiment.

INTERNET RESOURCE

For more practice with purpose, tone, and bias, see **college .hmco.com/pic/flemmingRFR10e**, where you will find three levels of interactive quizzes: *Getting Down the Basics*, *Checking Your Progress*, and *Taking the Challenge.*

Test 1: Fact or Opinion

DIRECTIONS Label each sentence *F* for fact or *O* for opinion.

1. Thomas Jefferson appointed James Madison to be secretary of state in 1801.

   _____

2. Adopted children should be allowed to know who their birth parents were.

   _____

3. Today's parents don't spend enough time with their children.

   _____

4. By September of 2006, Apple's sales of iTunes songs had hit 50 million with 2.5 million songs downloaded each week.

   _____

5. Russell Simmons and partner Rick Rubin founded the record label Def Jam Recordings in 1985.

   _____

6. The Food and Drug Administration should more carefully control the way drug makers advertise their products.

   _____

7. Mexican leader Benito Juárez is a heroic figure in Mexican history.

   _____

8. After the spectacular flop of her film *Swept Away*, Madonna should give up on acting and stick to singing.

   _____

9. Honolulu is the capital of Hawaii.

   _____

10. Today there are 3.3 workers supporting every Social Security recipient.

    _____

 **Test 2: Fact, Opinion, or Both**

DIRECTIONS Label each sentence *F* for fact, *O* for opinion, or *M* for a mix of both.

1. Alan Mathison Turing (1912–1954) was an English mathematician whose brilliant career was senselessly destroyed when it was discovered that he was a homosexual.

———

2. A carcinogen is any agent that increases the chances of a cell's becoming cancerous.

———

3. During World War I, Chile remained neutral.

———

4. Home shopping networks encourage viewers to engage in mindless consumerism.

———

5. Although most people don't realize it, eyewitnesses to crimes are extremely unreliable.

———

6. Reality television shows appeal to people who have no lives of their own.

———

7. A new species of land mammal has been discovered in the forests of Vietnam.

———

8. The son of an African-drummer father and a gourmet-chef mother, the talented rapper Lupe Fiasco was born Wasalu Muhammad Jaco.

———

9. The 2006 album "We Shall Overcome" is Bruce Springsteen's tribute to the legendary folk singer Pete Seeger.

   ____

10. The Japanese mushrooms called *maitake* sometimes grow as big as footballs.

    ____

 **Test 3: Identifying Tone**

> **DIRECTIONS** Identify the tone used in each passage by circling the appropriate letter.

1. In August 2006, the *New York Times* published an article titled "Tale of the Tapeworm (Squeamish Readers Stop Here)." Readers who didn't take the warning seriously made a huge mistake. What the article reported on was the story of a woman who had, in the course of making gefilte fish, ingested a tapeworm, and here's where the squeamish should have stopped reading. When the tapeworm was purged from the woman's body, it turned out to be three feet long. The source of numerous and vague symptoms like fatigue and indigestion, the worm had been happily living in the woman's stomach for who knows how long. Disgusting as the idea may be, tapeworms can, in fact, do just that: take up residence in your body without your knowing it. Unless the body gets irritated by its guest and produces some symptoms, the tapeworm can make use of it for as long as twenty years. As if that thought weren't gross enough, tapeworms can, if undetected, grow as long as thirty feet. Consider that the next time you think about eating sushi.

The tone is

a. humorous.

b. horrified.

c. neutral.

d. lighthearted.

2. For years, critics have argued about the ancient Greek play *Oedipus Rex*. Some have claimed that Oedipus knows nothing of his guilt until the end of the play, when it is revealed that he murdered his own father. Others have insisted that Oedipus is aware all along of his guilt. According to this point of view, Oedipus, the brilliant solver of riddles, could not possibly have ignored the mounting evidence that he was the king's murderer. Just how or why this debate has raged for so many years remains a mystery. The correct interpretation is so obvious. Oedipus knows from the beginning that he is guilty. He just pretends to be ignorant of the truth. For example, when a servant tells the story of the king's murder, he uses the word *bandits*. But when Oedipus repeats this story, he uses the singular form *bandit*. Sophocles provides clues like this throughout the play. Thus, it's hard to understand why anyone would think that Oedipus does not know the truth about his crime.

The tone is

a. lighthearted.

b. extremely confident.

c. neutral.

(d.) outraged.

3. Chimpanzees, who share nearly 99 percent of our DNA, are almost human, but you would never know it from the way we treat them. As photographer Michael Nichols has shown in his disturbing book *Brutal Kinship,* we use and abuse them at will for medical research, for entertainment, or simply out of personal greed. Resolutely* blind to their suffering, we refuse to grasp how like us they are. Chimpanzees nurture their young and mourn their dead. They have distinct personalities and can express a variety of emotions, from love to rage. Yet for all their similarities, we appear to think little of their pain and suffering if our interests are served. Leafing through the pages of Nichols's book, which is filled with images of chimps in cages or lying vacant-eyed with tubes dangling from their arms, it's practically impossible to understand how we can torture and maim creatures who look and behave so much like ourselves.

The tone is

a. disgusted.

b. confident.

c. ironic.

d. neutral.

4. I'm on the couch because the dog on the blanket gets worried at night. During the day she sleeps the catnappy sleep of the elderly, but when it gets dark her eyes open and she is agitated.* I'm next to her. We are in this together, the dying game, and I read for hours in the evening with one foot on her back, getting up only to open a new can of beer or take blankets to the basement. At some point I stretch out on the vinyl couch and close my eyes, one hand hanging

---

*resolutely: determinedly.
*agitated: nervous.

down, touching her side. By morning the dog arm has become a nerveless club that doesn't come around until noon. My friends think I am nuts. (Jo Ann Beard, "The Fourth State of Matter." *The Best American Essays 1997*, ed. Ian Frazier and Robert Atwan. Boston: Houghton Mifflin, 1997, p. 12.)

The tone is

a. angry.

b. sad.

c. irritated.

d. neutral.

5. Many people live in such a horror of failure that they can never embark on any great enterprise. And this inability to get going in the first place is the worst kind of failure because there is truly no way out. You can cover up. You can hide behind a mask of exquisite sensibility. You can congratulate yourself on the fact that your standards are so high that no human effort could possibly match up to them. You can make yourself unpleasant to your contemporaries by becoming expert on their shortcomings. In the end, nothing is achieved by this timidity. (James Fenton, "A Lesson from Michelangelo." *The Best American Essays 1996*, ed. Geoffrey C. Ward and Robert Atwan. Boston: Houghton Mifflin, 1996, p. 155.)

The tone is

a. disapproving.

b. questioning and unsure.

c. neutral.

d. puzzled.

6. In June 2000, the Supreme Court upheld the Boy Scouts' right to exclude gay troop leaders. After the Court's decision, several corporations, companies, and organizations that had once sponsored Scout activities stopped all funding to the organization. Furthermore, several school districts around the nation refused to sponsor any Boy Scout meetings or activities. To make sure the Boy Scouts got the message, one school board member spelled out the board's implicit message: Despite the Supreme Court's approval, the Scouts' policy was discriminatory and therefore would not be tolerated. There was no comment from the Boy Scout leadership. More important,

the Boy Scouts have shown no sign of rethinking their decision to ban the presence of gays in the Scouts.

The tone is

a. ironic.

b. disgusted.

c. neutral.

d. casual.

7. On September 26, 2000, the Motion Picture Association of America pledged not to use children under the age of seventeen in test screenings of movie violence. Jack Valenti, the association's chairman, said that a report by the Federal Trade Commission had prompted studios to look more closely at their marketing methods. What Mr. Valenti chose not to mention was that up to that point, the studios had been using children as young as nine to test kids' reactions to films that included scenes of brutality and violence. In other words, if a film sequence featuring someone being murdered with an ice pick won the approval of a group of ten-year-olds, then that sequence would be heavily publicized during the film's marketing. More than likely, it would become a selling point and be featured in ads for the film. In light of what the studios were actually doing, Mr. Valenti's comment that they had "perhaps . . . stepped over the line" was an extraordinary piece of understatement. These people were using impressionable children to evaluate and rate movie violence. And what was the purpose of the children's ratings? The purpose was to encourage other equally impressionable kids to attend movies that would bring them face to face with murder and mayhem.* We must also ask about the parents of the children evaluating the violence in R-rated movies. Didn't these parents care that their kids were being used as guinea pigs for a marketing scheme designed to find just the right degree of violence to attract hordes of youthful moviegoers? Yes, indeed, the studios did step over the line; there is no "perhaps" about it.

The tone is

a. ironic.

b. outraged.

c. neutral.

d. lighthearted.

---

*mayhem: violence, disorder.

8. In the night, when the owl is less than exquisitely swift and perfect, the scream of the rabbit is terrible. But the scream of the owl, which is not of pain and hopelessness, and the fear of being plucked out of the world, but of the sheer rollicking* glory of the death-bringer, is more terrible still. When I hear it resounding through the woods, and then the five black pellets of its song dropping like stones into the air, I know I am standing at the end of the mystery, in which terror is naturally part of life, part of even the most becalmed, intelligent, sunny life—as, for example, my own. The world where the owl is endlessly hungry and endlessly on the hunt is the world in which I live too. There is only one world. (Mary Oliver, "Owls," *Best American Essays 1996*, p. 281.)

   The tone is

   a. solemn and awed.

   b. lighthearted and comic.

   c. neutral.

   d. cool and confident.

9. I'm afraid I have noticed an alarming development at our house. The dog is trying to talk. He is not at all interested in remaining The Creature in the Household Who Barks, which, I have explained to him again and again, is the only role for which he is suited. Oh, I've done all the right things to raise his self-esteem about this: I've assured him that forever and ever he will be the only one in the house who is permitted to bark, and that, in fact, is why we hired him as the family dog in the first place, so he would bark and maybe protect us. I even told him that we *respect* him for his bark. You know what he says to this? "*Oowwww. . . .*" (Sandi Kahn Shelton, *You Might as Well Laugh*, p. 74.)

   The tone is

   a. surprised.

   b. neutral.

   c. amused.

   d. angry.

10. For cockroaches, the byword has been: Keep it simple. Consequently today, as always, they can live almost anywhere and eat almost anything. Unlike most insects, they have mouthparts that

---

*rollicking: carefree and high-spirited.

enable them to take hard food, soft foods, and liquids. They will feed on virtually any organic substance. One study, written a century ago, and still considered authoritative, lists their food preferences as "Bark, leaves, the pith of living cycads [fern palms], paper, woolen clothes, sugar, cheese, bread, blacking, oil, lemons, ink, flesh, fish, leather, the dead bodies of other cockroaches, their own cast skins and empty egg-capsules," adding that "Cucumber, too, they will eat, though it disagrees with them horribly." So much for cucumber. (Quammen, *Natural Acts*, p. 55.)

The tone is

a. horrified and disgusted.

b. neutral.

c. angry and outraged.

d. casual and comical.

 ## Test 4: Recognizing Tone and Purpose

DIRECTIONS Identify the author's tone and purpose in each passage by circling the appropriate letter.

1. **Say *No* to Fat in the Schools**

Almost one-third of America's kids are overweight, and that number is probably increasing. But experts now say that schools could play a big part in the solution to this problem.

Kids spend most of their waking hours at school, consuming 25 to 33 percent of their daily calories and getting about 20 to 30 percent of their daily physical activity there. Thus many health care experts argue that school is the logical place to begin encouraging kids to maintain healthier weight levels. The nutritionists are urging school officials to replace their cafeterias' pizza, corndogs, and French fries with more nutritious foods like fruit, salads, and sandwiches.

Health experts, like Dr. Antonia Demas of the Food Studies Institute in Trumansburg, New York, advocate ridding schools of vending machines filled with sodas, chips, cookies, and other unhealthy snacks. As Demas puts it, "Food in school frequently . . . mimics the foods in the fast food culture"—an unhealthy mistake given the link between obesity and a fast food diet. The solution, she says, is to make "food literally part of the school curriculum." In addition, groups like "Kids Health" also recommend that kids spend more time in physical education programs. For example, P.E. teachers could modify games for smaller groups of students so that each student is physically active for longer periods of time. Fitness activities could also be disguised as fun to encourage kids to work up a sweat while playing. (Source of information: Nanci Hellmich, "Name of This Game Is Healthier Kids," *USA Today*, May 20, 2003, p. 7D; www.education-world.com.)

The tone of this passage is

a. critical.

b. neutral.

c. alarmed.

d. amused.

The primary purpose is to

a. inform.

b. persuade.

2. **Canned Laughter Has a Long History**

The practice of prompting audiences to react to performances in certain ways has a long history. In ancient Rome, Emperor Nero assured that he would receive a favorable reception for his theatrical performances by establishing a school of applause, where he trained 5,000 of his soldiers to clap. In ancient Greece, contestants in comedy competitions would pay supporters to infiltrate the audience and encourage others' laughter with their own. Sixteenth-century poet/playwright Jean Daurat would give away tickets to his plays in exchange for a promise of applause. In nineteenth-century Paris, theaters hired *claques*, groups of people whose job was to applaud, laugh, or cry as appropriate to make the production seem successful to audience members.

During the 1940s, some radio shows included the sounds of both live and recorded audience laughter. In the early days of television, large red APPLAUSE signs would flash during programs like *The Johnny Carson Show* to prompt live studio audiences' laughter. Beginning in 1950, sound engineer Charles Douglass' invention of the Laff Box, recordings of giggles, chuckles, and other responses, began substituting for a live audience reaction on prerecorded TV shows like *I Love Lucy* and cartoons like *The Flintstones*.

The 1960s and 1970s saw the development and perfection of the *laugh machine*, a device that allowed engineers to select characteristics such as age, sex, laughter type, and duration to create distinct laughter sounds for different shows. Today, some sitcoms—such as *Scrubs* and *The Simpsons*—have begun to leave out the laugh track, but many other shows still use it to tell viewers when something is supposed to be funny. (Source of information: "Claque," Wikipedia, http://en.wikipedia.org/wiki/Claque; Adam Bernstein, "Charles Douglass, 93, Gave TV Its Laugh Track," *Washington Post*, April 24, 2003, p. B06.)

The tone of this passage is

a. neutral.

b. critical.

c. furious.

d. cautious.

The primary purpose is to

a. inform.

b. persuade.

3. Paul Gauguin Will Always Be a Modern Master

Paul Gauguin has always been credited with enormous artistic influence. Without a doubt, he is one of the trio of nineteenth-century painters, along with Vincent Van Gogh and Paul Cézanne, most responsible for shaping the direction of modern art. The innovative colors and forms in his paintings led directly to the development of major movements such as Impressionism and influenced such great artists as Henri Matisse and Pablo Picasso. And Gauguin's personal life, particularly his decision to leave Europe in 1891 and spend his remaining days living and painting in exotic Tahiti, contributed to the development of the romantic ideal of the artist as a heroic rebel and inspired several novels and films.

But these are not the only reasons that Gauguin should continue to interest us. A century after his death, the artist's paintings are still as popular and relevant as ever, and Gauguin's creations are prized by the museums fortunate enough to house them. Gauguin's gorgeous colors, distorted figures, and dreamlike scenes of an unspoiled, primitive paradise are still capable of inspiring not only an emotional reaction but also philosophical reflection. Uninterested in telling stories or providing answers, Gauguin used his work to ask the profound moral and intellectual questions that preoccupied him. For example, the French title of his greatest masterpiece, a huge, twelve-foot-long painting depicting a brightly colored scene of seminaked Polynesian women, is translated "Where are we from? What are we? Where are we going?" Because we twenty-first-century humans continue to struggle with these very same questions, Gauguin's work still speaks to us. (Source of information: John Whitely, "Magpie Mystic of the South Pacific," *Telegraph*, www.arts.telegraph.co.uk/arts/main.jhtml?xml=/arts/2003/05/03/bagaugm. xml&sSheet=/arts/2003/05/10/ixartarchtop.html.)

The tone of this passage is

a. nonchalant.

b. admiring.

c. objective.

d. critical.

The primary purpose is to

a. inform.

b. persuade.

4. **Francis Bellamy Pledges Allegiance**

In 1892, Baptist minister and Christian socialist Francis Bellamy (1855–1931) wrote the Pledge of Allegiance as a patriotic oath. His original wording was "I pledge allegiance to my Flag and to the Republic for which it stands, one nation, indivisible, with liberty and justice for all." Then in 1923 and 1924, the National Flag Conference changed "my Flag" to "the Flag of the United States of America." Bellamy disliked the change because he preferred the word *Republic*, but his protests were ignored.

But it wasn't until 1954 that the U.S. Congress, fearing the spread of communism, added the words "under God" after the phrase "one nation." Signing the bill that authorized this change, President Dwight Eisenhower said, "From this day forward, the millions of our schoolchildren will daily proclaim . . . the dedication of our nation and our people to the Almighty." For the five decades since then, Americans have recited this revised version of the Pledge. However, near the end of the twentieth century, the U.S. Supreme Court began to prohibit prayers in public schools and at sporting events because such prayers violated the separation of church and state, as well as the First Amendment to the Constitution. Now the Supreme Court is faced with deciding whether the words "under God" should be deleted altogether from the Pledge of Allegiance.

Opponents of editing the Pledge insist that this oath is not really a prayer and that all references to God do not constitute a government-sponsored religious exercise. However, supporters of removing the phrase "under God" argue that the Pledge amounts to professing loyalty to a set of values that includes Christianity, so it's unfair to citizens of other faiths. (Sources of information: Tony Mauro, " 'Under God' Doesn't Belong in Pledge," *USA Today*, May 5, 2003, p. 15A; John W. Baer, "The Pledge of Allegiance: A Short History," 1992, http://history.vineyard.net/pledge.htm.)

The tone of the passage is

a. neutral.

b. breezy.

c. irate.

d. alarmed.

The primary purpose is to

a. inform.

b. persuade.

5. **Laws Can Be Wrong**

Although the state of Oregon may have passed a law allowing the terminally ill to choose physician-assisted suicide, giving doctors permission to help their patients kill themselves is wrong and should not be legal. Some doctors claim that allowing patients to choose physician-assisted suicide grants dying people the power to make one final decision before their inevitable deaths. However, many of these patients are suffering from depression, a mental state that causes people to give up on life prematurely. When their depression subsides, they tend to feel very differently and often change their minds. And even when patients are not depressed, their wish to die is still a transitory* one. In Oregon, 35 percent of those who receive a prescription for a lethal drug dose don't ever use it, proving that more than a third of patients do not really want to hasten their own deaths. If patients are allowed to choose assisted suicide, then doctors could potentially rob these people of the additional days, weeks, or months of life that they would have chosen had they been given the opportunity to reconsider their decisions. (Sources of information: Andis Robeznieks, "Assisted-Suicide Numbers Continue to Rise in Oregon," *American Medical News*, March 24/31, 2003, www.ama-assn.org/amednews/2003/03/24/prs0324.htm; American Medical Association, "Physician-assisted Suicide," www.ama-assn.org/ama/pub/category/8459.html.)

The tone of the passage is

a. neutral.

b. alarmed.

c. friendly

d. puzzled

The primary purpose is to

a. inform.

b. persuade.

---

*transitory: short-lived.

Test 5: Recognizing Tone and Excessive Bias

DIRECTIONS Read each persuasive passage. Then circle the appropriate letter to identify the author's tone and degree of bias.

1. According to a report of the National Campaign to Prevent Teen Pregnancy, 20 percent of adolescents have had sex before their fifteenth birthday. The report also revealed that only a third of these adolescents' parents know that their children are sexually active. Such alarming statistics should cause us to wonder why parents aren't communicating more with their children. Communication between parents and children is important, and far too many parents seem to be falling down on the job. How can two-thirds of them not know what their own children are doing? And why aren't they talking to their kids and making them understand the risks of becoming sexually active? Are these parents that oblivious to the temptations bombarding modern young people? Or are the parents simply too lazy or self-absorbed to concern themselves with how their own kids are spending their free time? Whatever the reason for parents' apathy and ignorance, it's the kids who will ultimately pay the price. One in seven sexually active fourteen-year-old girls gets pregnant. And sexually experienced adolescents are far more likely than virgins to smoke, drink alcohol, and use drugs. Thanks to parents who won't get their heads out of the sand and watch their own kids, America's young people are growing up much too fast. (Source of information: Tamar Lewin, "One in Five Teenagers Has Sex Before Fifteen, Study Finds," *New York Times*, May 20, 2003, p. 18A, www.nytimes.com.)

The tone of the passage is

a. irate.

b. solemn.

c. ironic.

d. cautious.

For a persuasive reading, the author's bias is

a. acceptable

b. excessive.

2. Camille Claudel (1864–1943) was an extraordinary talented French sculptor who worked as an apprentice to artist Auguste Rodin, creator of the famous sculpture *The Kiss*. She also served as Rodin's

model, assistant, and mistress. Camille Claudel, however, was also a gifted sculptor in her own right, creating powerful marble and bronze sculptures such as "The Waltz," "The Wave," and "The Age of Maturity." These masterpieces have won Claudel posthumous* critical acclaim from many of today's art critics and historians. Yet, sadly, few of her own contemporaries appreciated Claudel's work. Some art historians argue that Claudel's talent was eclipsed by that of her teacher and lover. The respected and popular Rodin occupied a prominent place in French culture, and even though Claudel struggled to establish her own reputation, she never managed to emerge from his shadow. Few in the art world took her seriously, and she was openly dismissed as deranged for claiming Rodin had stolen some of her ideas.

Other historians and critics claim that Claudel's lack of success can be attributed not to Rodin but to the general problem of nineteenth-century sexism. Few female artists of that era were taken seriously. Nor were they given equal opportunities. Like Rodin, Claudel had a deep admiration for the human form, and both artists created sculptures that reflected this admiration. Claudel's *The Age of Maturity*, for instance, portrays a nude woman on her knees pleading with a departing man. While Rodin was praised for his subject matter, Claudel's sculptures were labeled inappropriately lewd* and unsuitable for display. Claudel, in the later years of her life, grew increasingly paranoid and unable to function. She spent the last thirty years of her life in an asylum for the mentally ill. (Source of information: "Camille Claudel," National Museum of Women in the Arts, www.nmwa.org/collection/profile .asp?LinkID=147.)

The tone of this passage is

a. critical.

b. cool.

c. sarcastic

d. admiring.

For a persuasive passage, the author's bias is

a. acceptable.

b. excessive.

---

*posthumous: after death.
*lewd: crudely sexual.

3. There is little doubt that urban sprawl is a health hazard. Researchers at the University of Maryland looked at some key health characteristics of more than 200,000 Americans living in major metropolitan* areas. The study showed that people living in sprawling urban areas, where they cannot walk to shops and stores, weigh an average of six pounds more than people who live in smaller, less suburban neighborhoods. People walk less when their homes are far away from stores and high-speed roads are the only link between residential and commercial areas. Less walking frequently makes suburbanites less fit. They usually drive to every destination and are more prone to obesity, high blood pressure, and other diseases. But even those suburban dwellers brave enough to walk or ride a bicycle face a significant health risk: Going on foot or on bikes in suburbia puts people in danger of being hit by cars. Cars are, in fact, the third major problem associated with urban sprawl, and it's no surprise that crowded suburbs are plagued by traffic jams that increase both air pollution and the length of drivers' commutes to work. Long commutes, in turn, produce more stress and the ailments likely to accompany high stress levels. (Source of information: Kathleen Fackelmann, "Studies Tie Urban Sprawl to Health Risks, Road Danger," *USA Today,* August 29, 2003, p. 3A.)

The tone of this passage is

a. neutral.

b. furious.

c. confident.

d. annoyed.

For a persuasive passage, the author's bias is

a. acceptable.

b. excessive.

4. In 1993, about 7 percent of America's high schools had eliminated ranking their students by grade point average (GPA); thus, the schools also did away with honoring a valedictorian—the individual with the highest GPA—at graduation. Since then, scrapping the valedictorian tradition has become a disturbing national trend. Those misinformed educational liberals who support the elimination of class rankings and valedictorians claim that ranking students

---

*metropolitan: constituting a large city or an urbanized area, including nearby suburbs and towns.

makes the lower-performing students feel inadequate. These critics just refuse to face the fact that competition is part of American society. It's the desire to be the best that makes achievement a reality. Maintaining the valedictorian tradition spurs student achievement; without it, our students have no incentive to excel. Why should they if they are not publicly rewarded for their efforts? (Sources of information: Jeremy Redmon, "Valedictorian Tradition Scrapped at High Schools," *The Washington Times*, May 7, 1999, p. A1; Jay Mathews, "A Farewell to Traditional Valedictorians," *Washington Post*, June 26, 1997, p. J01, www.washingtonpost.com/wp-srv/local/longterm/library/valedict/novdict.htm.)

The tone of this passage is

a. neutral.

b. friendly.

c. angry.

d. puzzled.

For a persuasive reading, the author's bias is

a. acceptable.

b. excessive.

 # Test 6: Locating Errors in Logic

DIRECTIONS Identify the author's error in logic by circling the appropriate letter.

1. Fast-food restaurants such as McDonald's, Burger King, and Taco Bell should be required to display warning notices about the fat content of the foods they sell. Animal studies have suggested that eating fatty foods seems to provoke addictive behavior. For example, rats fed a diet high in sugar exhibit signs of anxiety when the sugar is removed. Other research suggests that high-fat foods may stimulate the brain's pleasure centers, producing an effect similar to that of drugs such as nicotine and heroin. As a result, consumers have the right to be informed that eating fast food is just like getting hooked on drugs. The government requires cigarette manufacturers to print warning labels on every pack to inform consumers that smoking is an addictive habit that causes cancer and death. It stands to reason, then, that every fast-food wrapper and carton should be similarly labeled to make it clear that their addictive contents will lead to obesity and death. (Sources of information: Bruce Horovitz, "Fast-Food Restaurants Told to Warn of Addiction," *USA Today,* June 17, 2003, www.usatoday.com/money/industries/ food/2003-06-17warning_x.htm; "Fast Food 'as Addictive as Heroin,'" *BBC News*, January 30, 2003, http://news.bbc.co.uk/2/hi/health/ 2707143.stm.)

   a. irrelevant evidence

   b. careless comparison

   c. false alternatives

   d. personal attack

   e. hasty generalization

   f. circular reasoning

2. Kids today are being assigned far too much homework, so schools should require teachers to limit their after-school assignments to a maximum of one hour's worth of work. For one thing, when children are forced to spend school nights doing hours and hours of homework, they quickly form a dislike of both school and learning. Kids burn out quickly if their free time is filled up with assignments and projects. Children need their evenings free to play and to relax. Plus, now more than ever, children should be spending quality time with their families in the evenings. If kids are always doing homework

instead of bonding with their loved ones, how can they possibly grow up with any sense of family values? Either we limit homework now, or kids will grow up believing that academic achievement is more important than cultivating family relationships.

a. irrelevant evidence

b. careless comparison

c. false alternatives

d. personal attack

e. hasty generalization

f. circular reasoning

3. George Balanchine, the Russian-born choreographer and dance teacher, founded the School of American Ballet in 1934. Best known as the prime mover at the New York City Ballet from 1948 to 1983, Balanchine has been called one of the finest creators of ballets the world has ever known. But if we examine his career without the blinders of hero worship, it's obvious that Balanchine possessed neither enormous talent nor great artistic vision. Without a doubt, Balanchine was a cruel tyrant who worked his dancers to exhaustion and gave them little praise. His criticism during rehearsals was often so sharp it reduced young dancers to tears. Out of the studio, Balanchine ignored dancers he had trained for years, pretending not to recognize members of his troupe when he bumped into them in restaurants or stores. Even Balanchine's fellow choreographers had to endure rude treatment: He was so self-centered he could scarcely remember their names. All in all, George Balanchine was not a very nice person.

a. irrelevant evidence

b. careless comparison

c. false alternatives

d. personal attack

e. hasty generalization

f. circular reasoning

4. According to a 2001 American Management Association report, 78 percent of U.S. firms monitor their employees' communications in some way, and 47 percent read their workers' e-mail messages. Why are we Americans not more alarmed by these blatant invasions of our privacy? Companies may argue that they monitor their workers only

to guard company secrets or to protect themselves from potential lawsuits over harassment and other violations. But the fact remains that employers are spying on Americans whose privacy is protected by the U.S. Constitution, and workers are giving up their rights if they allow employers to read employees' messages, record their telephone conversations, and videotape them with surveillance cameras. Employees cannot just give up the fight and submit to this kind of snooping. They should be outraged by their employers' attempts to monitor their every move and should speak out against attempts to infringe upon their privacy. What's more, companies themselves should realize that stooping to snoop on their workers communicates a lack of trust that ultimately translates into low employee morale, diminished motivation, and reduced productivity. Given how many firms keep their employees under surveillance, it's no wonder that four out of five workers surveyed by the Johnson Foundation report dissatisfaction with their chances for professional advancement.

a. irrelevant evidence

b. careless comparison

c. false alternatives

d. personal attack

e. hasty generalization

f. circular reasoning

5. Today's zookeepers claim to have learned the lessons of the past and are creating habitats for animals that take into account the animals' needs. Unfortunately, though, no matter how many plants, trees, rocks, and waterfalls are added to create more naturalistic settings, the creatures confined in zoo exhibits are still suffering from mistreatment. They may not be cruelly locked up in cramped cages as in the past, but they are still neglected and even beaten. When an elephant handler at the Oregon Zoo inflicted 176 gashes and cuts upon one of the beasts in his care, the truth became clear. The pretty, naturalistic settings of modern zoos do nothing more than camouflage the animal abuse occurring there.

a. irrelevant evidence

b. careless comparison

c. false alternatives

d. personal attack

e. hasty generalization

f. circular reasoning

 ## Test 7: Vocabulary Review

DIRECTIONS Here are ten of the words introduced in Chapter 10. Use them to fill in the blanks. Words introduced in previous chapters are marked with an asterisk. *Note*: You will have to use one of the words three times (although you will only get credit for the first use of it). The form of the word used here may differ from the form used in the chapter.

alarmist	segregation
dubious	agitated
equitable	oratory
mayhem	posthumous
resolute	zealous

From Racism to Repentance

Although George C. Wallace, the four-time governor of Alabama (1962, 1970, 1974, and 1982), made his name as a

_____ racist, neither his career nor his views were

quite so simple. If anything, Wallace was less a racist than an

opportunist, a man who read the _____ temper of

his time and place and used it to his own advantage. Wallace

didn't start his career as a _____ racist, but he

learned a hard lesson from watching the fall from power of his

friend and teacher Governor James E. "Big Jim" Folsom. Folsom,

a real progressive* and a devout believer in the Bill of Rights,

despised racist ideology,* and he never bothered to subdue his

contempt for the minds who embraced it.

But in the end, the Alabamans who feared civil rights were

more vocal* and more volatile* than those who accepted it as the

wave of the future. Big Jim was ousted* from office. Yet Wallace,

who seemed to have considered Folsom to be something of a

father figure, wasn't about to let anything so ___zealous___

as loyalty interfere with his pursuit of power. Rather than con-

tinue Folsom's dedication to an _____ society for

all, Wallace veered in the opposite direction, basing his

_____ on the work of speechwriter Asa Carter,

whose own racist beliefs were more deeply ingrained than Wal-

lace's. It was Carter who gave Wallace the infamous inaugural line

that was to haunt the governor later in life, when he came to

regret the hatred and _____ he had brought to the

state he loved.

But in 1963, newly elected to the office his once beloved "Big

Jim" had held, Wallace was stiff and formal in the opening min-

utes of his inaugural speech. Still, it didn't take long before he

was full throttle into the _____ appeals that were

Carter's and ultimately Wallace's stock-in-trade: "In the name

of the greatest people that have ever trod this earth, I draw the

line in the dust and . . . I say _____ now . . .

_____ tomorrow . . . and _____

forever." Twenty-three years later, when George Wallace left office,

he was deaf, paralyzed from the waist down from an assassination

attempt, and in constant pain from injuries and arthritis. Above

all, he was repentant and undoubtedly worried about his

_____ reputation as a committed racist. Wallace

spent the little time he had left asking forgiveness from people like

the black politician John Cashin, who had openly acknowledged

his contempt for Wallace the man and his politics. Cashin

accepted Wallace's apology and voiced what many in his position now felt about their long-time enemy: "How can you hate a man who's been brought so low?" (Source of information: Dan T. Carter, *The Politics of Rage.* New York: Simon & Schuster, 1995.)

BONUS QUESTION

Use context to define the idiom "stock-in-trade," which appears in this reading.

_____

If you needed to look this idiom up on the Internet, which search term would get you the information faster, "stock-in-trade" or "idioms stock-in-trade"? Please explain.

_____

_____

Putting It All Together

The following readings give you a chance to practice everything you have learned about comprehension and critical reading. They will also introduce you to people and ideas that have aroused both discussion and controversy. As you read, think about where you stand on the various events and actions described. Ultimately reading is not just about understanding and remembering what other people say about the world. It's also about discovering your own point of view.

■ READING 1

THE ALTRUISTIC PERSONALITY
Sharon S. Brehm, Saul M. Kassin, and Steven Fein

LOOKING AHEAD What qualities make an individual more likely to help others? In this selection from a social psychology textbook, the authors explore the characteristics of people who are there when we need them.

WORD WATCH Some of the more difficult words in the reading are defined below. The number in parentheses indicates the paragraph in which the word appears. An asterisk marks its first appearance in the reading. Preview the definitions before you begin reading, and watch for the words while you read.

---

altruistic (2): exhibiting unselfish concern for the welfare of others

genetically (2): related to biological inheritance

longitudinal (4): long-term

empathy (5): understanding of another person's situation or feelings

fraternal twins (5): developed from two separate eggs (identical twins develop from one egg)

heritable (5): capable of being passed by birth from one generation to the next

variables (8): things that can change

conglomerate (9): a collection of different things

dispositional (9): related to mood or temperament

prosocial (9): beneficial to society

collectivist (10): valuing the group's well being over all else

individualist (10): valuing the individual person's well being over all else

extroversion (10): interest in other people, interest in the world outside one's own mind

---

FLEXIBLE READING TIP Note that the headings in this reading are questions. After reading each section, see if you can answer the question posed in the heading. If you can't, mark that section for re-reading.

Personal Influences: Who Is Likely to Help?

1 Research addressing the question "When do people help?" has been quite productive. But what about the question "Who is likely to help?" When we think about extreme acts of helping, or of failing to help, or when we think about long-term, well-planned acts of helping such as volunteering at a clinic or shelter or serving as a Big Brother or Big Sister, we tend to wonder not about the situational influences but about the nature of the people involved. Here we consider some of the individual differences between people that address the question "Who is likely to help?"

2 Researchers have tried to identify an *altruistic* personality* that distinguishes people who help from those who don't. Some of their research has focused on whether certain people tend to be more helpful across situations than others. Researchers have also asked whether and to what extent these differences might be genetically* based. Other research has sought to identify what general personality characteristics and traits comprise the altruistic personality.

"The purpose of human life is to serve and to show compassion and the will to help others."

—**Albert Schweitzer**

3 *Are Some People More Helpful Than Others?* When Daniel Santos's friends and co-workers learned of his heroics in jumping 150 feet off the Tappan Zee Bridge to save a stranger, they were not surprised. "That's just how he is," said a fellow volunteer firefighter. "If he sees something, he's going to go and try to help out that person." A receptionist at the company where he worked as a mechanic added, "He will help anyone at any place and any time." His sister noted that he leaped into the water even though he's not a strong swimmer. "He has a good heart," she said (Fitz-Gibbon & Siemaszko, 1996, p. 7).

4 Are there many people who are generally helpful across all situations? Are there others who are generally unhelpful? Although situational factors clearly can overwhelm individual differences in influencing helping behaviors (Latané & Darley, 1970), researchers have demonstrated some evidence of individual differences in helping tendencies. These tendencies seem to endure in a variety of settings. People who are more helpful than others in one situation are likely to be more helpful in other situations as well (Hampson, 1984; Rushton, 1981b). In addition, a longitudinal* study by Nancy Eisenberg and others (1999) suggests that this individual difference may be relatively stable over time. Specifically, they found that the degree to which preschool children exhibited spontaneous helping behavior predicted how helpful they would be in later childhood and early adulthood.

5   According to J. Philippe Rushton and his colleagues (1984), this individual difference in helpfulness is, in part, genetically based. Studies of twins offer some support for Rushton's argument. Genetically identical twins are more similar to each other in their helpful behavioral tendencies and their helping-related emotions and reactions, such as empathy,* than are fraternal twins* who share only a portion of their genetic make-up (Davis et al., 1994; Rushton et al., 1986; Zahn-Wexler et al., 1992). These findings suggest that there may be a heritable* component to helpfulness.

6   *What Is the Altruistic Personality?* Even if we identify some people who help others a lot and other people who don't, we have not addressed the question of what distinguishes people who help from those who don't—other than their helpfulness, of course. What are the various components of the altruistic personality? Can we predict who is likely to be altruistic by looking at people's overall personalities?

7   Consider some examples of people who have acted very altruistically. Do they seem to have very similar personality traits and characteristics? Think, for example, about Oskar Schindler[†] and how he cheated in business and in his marriage. Could anyone have predicted his altruistic actions from his overall personality? It is doubtful. What about more contemporary models of altruism? In 1997, Ted Turner, founder of numerous cable stations and owner of professional sports teams, pledged a personal donation of one billion dollars to the United Nations. Not to be outdone, by July 2000 Microsoft Chairman Bill Gates had pledged 22 billion dollars to charity. Actor Paul Newman has donated all of the millions of dollars in profits that have been generated by his brands of salad dressing, spaghetti sauce, popcorn, and the like to charities, such as his camp for children who are living with a fatal disease. And until her death in 1997, Mother Teresa devoted her life to the poor in India. These four well-known figures seem quite different from each other in overall personality—except for their concern with helping others.

8   The quest to discover the altruistic personality has not been an easy one. Much of the research conducted over the years has failed to find consistent, reliable personality characteristics that predict helping behavior across situations. Situational variables* have predicted people's helping behaviors much better than personality variables (Latané & Darley, 1970; Piliavin et al., 1981).

9   Some researchers have changed the nature of the quest, however, focusing on personality variables that predict helping in

---

[†]German businessman famous for helping Jews to escape from Nazi Germany.

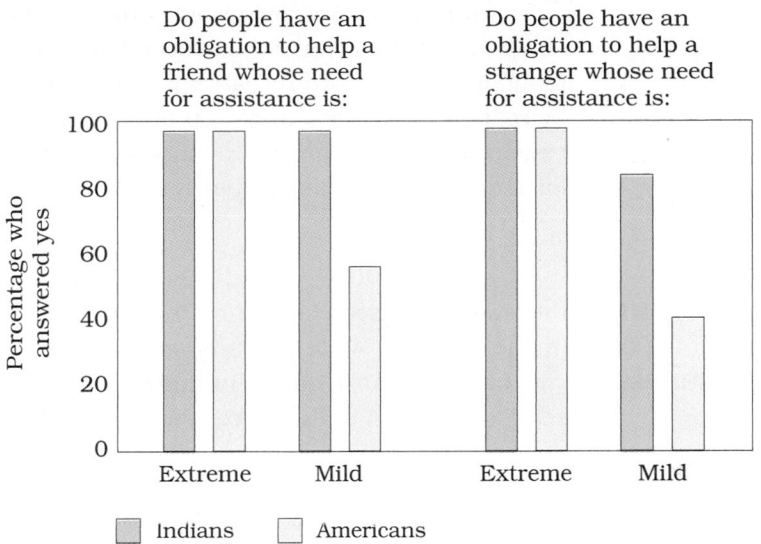

Figure 1 The Norm of Social Responsibility in India and the U.S.

These results compare the proportion of children and adults in India with the proportion of children and adults in the United States who said that people have an obligation to help others.

Source of data: J. G. Miller et al., 1990.

some specific situations rather than across all situations; and their studies have been more successful in identifying traits that predict such behavior (Carlo et al., 1991; Penner et al., 1995). George Knight and his colleagues (1994) have suggested that an interacting "conglomerate"* of numerous dispositional* traits influences prosocial* behavior and that the traits differ depending on the situation. For example, in dangerous emergencies, people who are high in self-confidence and independence are more likely to help than other people, but they are no more likely to help in response to a request to donate money to a charity (Wilson, 1976).

10   Personality variables that have been associated with greater helpfulness in some contexts include the following: empathy toward others; a tendency to attribute the causes of events to individual control rather than external circumstances; a collectivist* rather than an individualist* orientation; and extroversion,* openness to experience, and agreeableness (Bierhoff et al., 1991; Kosek, 1995; Moorman & Blakely, 1995). And whether or not people have the traits associated with prosocial behavior, if they can be convinced or motivated to believe that they are altruistic, their behavior may follow. For example, labeling someone as a helpful person increases that individual's helpful behavior (Kraut, 1973; Strenta & DeJong, 1981).

11   In sum, research provides some insight into the traits and characteristics that may be associated with helpful behavioral tendencies, but more research is needed before a conclusion can be reached about the make-up of the altruistic personality. The research thus far does point to two qualities that seem essential for such a personality: empathy and advanced moral reasoning.

Adapted from Brehm, Kassin, and Fein, *Social Psychology*, pp. 372–374.

MONITORING YOUR COMPREHENSION   Review the entire selection by making a list of the questions posed in the reading. Write out answers to each question. The question you have the most difficulty answering will identify the section or sections in need of future review.

COMPREHENSION AND CRITICAL READING QUESTIONS   Answer the following questions by filling in the blanks or circling the letter of the correct response.

Overall Main Idea   **1.** Which statement best expresses the main idea of the entire reading?

a. Research has shown that helping behavior definitely has a genetic basis.

b. Research on the elements of the altruistic personality is still going on, but evidence suggests that certain factors do seem to predispose an individual to helping others.

c. So far, researchers have been unable to construct any reliable studies for identifying the characteristics that make up an altruistic personality.

d. People who readily help others all have very similar personalities: They are affectionate by nature and like to be helpful.

Supporting Details   **2.** Why do the authors mention Oskar Schindler, Ted Turner, Bill Gates, Paul Newman, and Mother Teresa?

a. They illustrate the idea that donating large sums of money is a common behavior of people with altruistic personalities.

b. They are all examples of people who were altruistic from childhood on.

c. They illustrate the idea that people who behave in altruistic ways can have very different personalities.

d. They support the authors' point that extremely altruistic people always become quite famous.

Topic
Sentence

3. In paragraph 4, which sentence is the topic sentence?

    a. sentence 1

    b. sentence 2

    c. sentence 3

    d. sentence 6

Inferences
and
Conclusions

4. What do the authors imply with the description of Daniel Santos in paragraph 3?

    a. People with altruistic personalities do not care about risking their own lives or the lives of others.

    b. Altruistic people have certain personality traits in common.

    c. People who have altruistic personalities are liked and admired by others.

    d. People with altruistic personalities are just naturally willing to help others even in dangerous situations.

5. The authors open the reading with the question, "Who is likely to help?" What is their implied answer?

Patterns of
Organization

6. The heading "What Is the Altruistic Personality?" suggests which pattern of organization?

    a. definition

    b. cause and effect

    c. classification

    d. comparison and contrast

Paraphrasing

7. How would you paraphrase this statement from paragraph 8? "Situational variables have predicted people's helping behaviors much better than personality variables."

Understanding
Visual Aids

8. Based on the bar graph on page 655, what is the difference between Indians and Americans when it comes to helping others?

Purpose 9. What do you think is the authors' primary purpose?

     a. The authors want to describe current research suggesting that altruism may be inborn.

     b. The authors want to encourage their readers to be more altruistic.

Tone 10. How would you describe the authors' tone?

     a. confident

     b. casual

     c. skeptical

     d. neutral

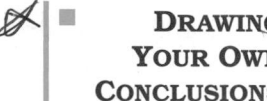

■ **DRAWING YOUR OWN CONCLUSIONS** Based on the information in this reading, what do you think the authors would say about some preschools' attempts to encourage altruism in young children? Would they say that these efforts are useful or that they might not be effective? What statements in the reading led you to your conclusion?

_____

_____

_____

■ **MAKING IT PERSONAL** On a scale of 1–10—10 being the highest degree of altruism—how would you rate yourself and why would you give yourself that rating?

■ **WRITING SUGGESTION** Write a paper in which you define and illustrate the altruistic personality. Think of people you know who might illustrate your definition. What personality traits do they have in common?

INTERNET BONUS QUESTION

Why do the authors include a quotation from Albert Schweitzer? What did he do, and why would the authors consider him an appropriate allusion?

<u>Using the quote was to show</u>

<u>that Albert Schweitzer was a Altruistic</u>

<u>person. He was born into a Alsation</u>

<u>family that was devoted to religion, music</u>

+ education. He became a minister and wrote

a book called The Quest of the Historical Jesus, He was not well known for his theology. Later on in life he donated the funds and his royalties to expand the hospital that he founded

A HERO SCORNED ■ 659

■ **READING 2**

A HERO SCORNED
USA Today Editorial

LOOKING AHEAD A *whistle-blower* is an employee or a member of an organization who reports the misconduct of his or her peers or superiors to the authorities. Some view whistle-blowers as brave, selfless souls who act according to their moral principles, regardless of the consequences. Others see them as disloyal tattletales. The writer of this editorial explains what happened after one whistle-blower stopped his fellow soldiers from killing civilians during the Vietnam War.

WORD WATCH Some of the more difficult words in the reading are defined below. The number in parentheses indicates the paragraph in which the word appears. An asterisk marks its first appearance in the reading. Preview the definitions before you begin reading, and watch for the words while you read.

---

massacre (1): the killing of a large number of people

infamous (2): having a bad reputation

pariah (2): outcast

court-martialed (3): tried for an offense in a military court of law

pardoned (3): released from punishment

icons (5): symbols

manifestation (5): display or demonstration

rationalizing (5): making excuses for

FLEXIBLE READING TIP This reading is an editorial from a newspaper. Editorials are, by definition, written to persuade. As you read, ask yourself what the writer wants you to believe as a result of reading the editorial.

1 IN 1968, HELICOPTER PILOT HUGH THOMPSON FLEW INTO THE thick of what he thought was a fierce battle in South Vietnam and discovered, instead, that a massacre* was going on—of women, children and elderly men at the hands of U.S. soldiers. Horrified, he landed his helicopter between the soldiers and the civilians, ordered his crew to fire on any American who continued shooting, called

for back-up and rescued victims, digging through corpses to scoop up one child.

2   An instant hero? It would be nice to think so. A year later, the public found out about the killings—infamous* as the My Lai massacre, exposed by journalist Seymour Hersh. But Thompson, who died of cancer in 2006 at age sixty-two, received no honors then. He was made a pariah.*

3   For years, when he walked into officers' clubs, they emptied out. He got threatening phone messages. Dead animals were left on his porch. When he was called to give closed congressional testimony, a senior lawmaker said that if anyone deserved to be court-martialed,* it was him. As it was, only one officer, Army Lt. William Calley, was convicted, spending just three years under house arrest before President Nixon pardoned* him.

4   In 1998, after a book and CBS's *60 Minutes* told of Thompson's courage, the Pentagon was shamed into giving him and his crew the Soldier's Medal, the highest award for bravery not involving conflict with an enemy. He was invited to lecture on military ethics at the U.S. Military Academy at West Point.

5   What Thompson really deserved, and never got, is the hero's recognition afforded other national icons* of moral courage, such as Rosa Parks.† Not so much for his benefit as for the nation's. The mob mentality that took over at My Lai was an extreme manifestation* of a common human instinct. It's just easier to go along with the crowd, rationalizing* corrupt behavior, than it is to face the danger of stopping it. That was true at Iraq's Abu Ghraib prison† and at corrupt Enron.†

6   Nobody likes a snitch. But when courageous people instinctively supply the moral compass missing higher up in their command—as Thompson did at My Lai, as a young soldier did at Abu Ghraib, and as whistle-blower Sherron Watkins did at Enron—they deserve recognition.

7   When Hollywood takes up that kind of plot, in movies such as *The Insider*,† it's easy to cheer. Too bad it's so different in real life.

"A Hero Scorned," Editorial, *USA Today*, January 12, 2006, www.usatoday.com/news/opinion/editorials/2006-01-12-thompson-edit_x.htm.

---

†Rosa Parks: African-American civil rights activist who became famous in 1955 for her refusal to give up her seat on a public bus to a white passenger.
†Abu Ghraib prison: the site of a 2004 scandal in which members of the U.S. military abused Iraqi prisoners.
†Enron: a large energy company that collapsed in 2001 after its fraud and corruption were revealed.
†*The Insider:* a film about Dr. Jeffrey Wigand, a tobacco company employee who exposed his company's practice of boosting the effect of nicotine in cigarettes.

MONITORING YOUR COMPREHENSION The title is "A Hero Scorned." If you can explain what the hero of the title did and why he was scorned, you've thoroughly understood the reading.

COMPREHENSION AND CRITICAL READING QUESTIONS Answer the following questions by filling in the blanks or circling the letter of the correct response.

Overall Main Idea

1. Which statement best expresses the main idea of the entire reading?

   a. American soldiers often commit immoral and disreputable acts during wartime.

   b. A hero is a person who puts himself or herself at risk to save the lives of others.

   c. Hugh Thompson displayed praiseworthy moral courage and heroism when he intervened in the My Lai massacre.

   d. Before it was cut short by cancer, Hugh Thompson's life was a hard and difficult one.

2. In this reading, the overall main idea is

   a. stated.

   b. implied.

Supporting Details

3. Why does the author mention Abu Ghraib prison and Enron in paragraphs 5 and 6?

   a. The Abu Ghraib and Enron scandals illustrate how war brings out the worst in people, making them capable of things impossible to even imagine during peacetime.

   b. The Abu Ghraib and Enron scandals prove that the public does not like whistle-blowers.

   c. The Abu Ghraib and Enron scandals show that whistle-blowers often end up being treated like outcasts.

   d. The Abu Ghraib and Enron scandals are both evidence of the terrible things people can do because they are afraid to break away from the pack.

Inferences and Conclusions

4. What is the implied main idea of paragraph 3?

   _____

5. At the end of the reading, the author says, "When Hollywood takes up that kind of plot, in movies such as *The Insider*, it's easy to

cheer. Too bad it's so different in real life." In the final sentence of the reading, the author relies on readers to infer the meaning of "it." What is the referent for that pronoun?

_____

6. The author expects readers to infer the reason for the senior law-maker's outburst referred to in paragraph 3. What inference does the author expect readers to draw?

_____

Patterns of
Organization

7. What pattern organizes paragraph 1?

   a. process

   b. comparison and contrast

   c. classification

   d. definition

Transitions

8. In paragraph 2, there are two transitions. They signal

   a. time order and comparison.

   b. addition and time order.

   c. time order and reversal.

Purpose

9. How would you describe the author's purpose?

   a. The author wants to describe Thompson's actions while he was a soldier during the Vietnam War.

   b. The author wants to persuade readers that Thompson should have been admired for his courage, not treated with contempt.

Tone

10. How would you describe the author's tone?

_____

_____

■ **DRAWING**
YOUR OWN
CONCLUSIONS

Based on what the author says, what are two reasons he might have had for telling Thompson's story so long after it happened?

I belive the author waited because Thompson was shunned enough by military people on civilans. He was also Sick and probley did not want to put him throug any more grief. Thompson was a brave man for *doing what he did but he was also probley tired of being put down for so many years.*

■ **MAKING IT PERSONAL** If you saw some of your friends or coworkers engaging in an illegal act, do you think you would confront them, attempt to stop them, or report them to authorities? Do you think you would pay a price for standing by your moral convictions? Please explain.

■ **WRITING SUGGESTION** The author writes, "It's just easier to go along with the crowd, rationalizing corrupt behavior, than it is to face the danger of stopping it" (paragraph 5). Narrate an incident from your own life to illustrate how people are inclined to go along with things they know are wrong. Or else challenge the statement by describing some person (or group) who refused to conform to immoral or unethical behavior.

INTERNET BONUS QUESTIONS

In 2002, *Time* magazine honored as its "Persons of the Year" three people who "by risking everything to blow the whistle . . . , reminded us what American courage and American values are all about." Who were these three people, and what problems did they expose?

Titled "The Whistleblowers"
Cynthia Cooper Worldcom - Coleen Rowley. FBI - Sherron Watkins Enron

What search term did you use to locate this information?

Time mag 2002 cover person of the year

Co-conspirator was a man who must be investigated when she informed the cooper exploed the bubble that worldcom had covered up 3.8 billion in losses and that the comp. had covered up 3.8 billion in losses

01

Watkis wrote a letter to Chairman Kenneth Lay in summer warning him that the Company's methods of accounting were improper Rowley sent memo to FBI Director Robert Muller about how the bureau brushed off pleas from her Minneapolis Minn. field office that Zacarias Moussaoui who is now indicted as a Sept

■ READING 3

DOES AMERICA NEED A THIRD PARTY?
Ann O'M. Bowman and Richard C. Kearney

LOOKING AHEAD According to the reading, Americans are increasingly interested in third-party candidates. The authors claim that three third-party candidates have made, in their words, a "credible" showing. As you read, consider how you would answer the question posed in the title.

WORD WATCH Some of the more difficult words in the reading are defined below. The number in parentheses indicates the paragraph in which the word appears. An asterisk marks its first appearance in the reading. Preview the definitions before you begin reading, and watch for the words while you read.

---

incumbent (1): person already in office

ideological (1): related to ideas of how people and the world function or are organized

gamut (1): range

proportional representation (2): legislative representation according to the size of all parties' popular vote

orientation (3): leaning, tendency

FLEXIBLE READING TIP The authors describe three third parties that have made a credible showing in elections. As you read, box or circle each of the three party names. Jot the characteristics of each one in the margins.

1 IN THE WEST VIRGINIA GOVERNOR'S RACE IN 2000, A CANDIDATE of the Mountain party won slightly over 2 percent of the vote. In Vermont, the incumbent* Democratic governor faced not only a Republican challenger but also a nominee of the Progressive party. Candidates of third parties are making more credible bids for public office throughout the country. Third parties run the ideological* gamut;* and they are enjoying increased electoral success.

2 Consider three third parties—the Green party, the Libertarian party, and the New party. Each has a formal platform, is recognized nationally, and has state chapters that are boasting much

success. The Green party, which grew out of the environmental movement, emphasizes citizen involvement. Citizen involvement, according to the Green platform, should be encouraged through proportional representation* and grassroots organizations.

3   The grassroots Greens call for the decentralization of government and the expansion of the power of local boards. Given this orientation* it is not surprising that the Green party has had most of its success on the local level. By 2000, seventy-nine Greens held local offices in twenty-one states, including city council positions in cities such as Santa Monica, California; Chapel Hill, North Carolina; and Madison, Wisconsin. In the coastal town of Arcata, California, Greens actually held a majority of seats on the city council, leading some to dub the town "Ecotopia."

4   While the Green party would restructure government, the Libertarian party seeks to reduce the government's size. Another difference between the two parties is the Libertarian emphasis on the freedom of the individual rather than the importance of community. Further, the message of the Libertarian platform is that our current government is hopelessly defective and needs a major overhaul. For example, Libertarians advocate abolishing the income tax and, with it, most federal programs, including Social Security. They believe that schools should be left to parental choice, reasoning that lower taxes will allow them to afford to send their children to private or home schools. Libertarians have been elected to 166 local offices in thirty-seven states, with their impact greatest in California, New Hampshire, and Pennsylvania.

5   The New party is more radical than the other two, calling for revolution to transfer power to the American people. Advocating equality, freedom, and prosperity, the New party stresses the importance of the community in achieving its goals. A unique component of the party's platform is the call for a guaranteed minimum income, or "social wage," and a shorter workweek in order to reach full employment. Women and people of color figure prominently in the New party. Like the Green and Libertarian parties, the New party's success is primarily local, in states such as Arkansas, Wisconsin, and Maryland.

6   Third parties offer alternatives, and a growing number of Americans like what they have to offer. What do you think: Should the two major parties be looking over their shoulders? Should states make it easier for third parties to get on the ballot?

Adapted from Bowman and Kearney, *State and Local Government*, p. 118.

MONITORING YOUR COMPREHENSION When you finish reading, look at each party name and see if you can remember the defining characteristics.

COMPREHENSION AND CRITICAL READING QUESTIONS Answer the following questions by filling in the blanks or circling the letter of the correct response.

Overall Main Idea

1. Which statement best expresses the main idea of the entire reading?

   a. The Green party seems to be the most credible third-party alternative.

   b. The idea of a third-party candidate seems to be growing more popular with American voters.

   c. Third-party candidates might do well in state elections, but none of them will ever enter the White House.

   d. America needs a third party because neither Republicans nor Democrats are in touch with American citizens.

Paraphrasing

2. Restate the following sentence in your own words: "Third parties run the ideological gamut; and they are enjoying increased electoral success."

   _____

Paraphrasing and Supporting Details

3. Name and describe in your own words the three parties identified in the reading.

   _____

   _____

   _____

   _____

   _____

   _____

Main Idea

4. What is the main idea of paragraph 3?

   a. The Green party focuses mainly on environmental issues and tries to enlist the aid of local governments in an effort to protect the country's natural resources.

b. The Green party has designs on the White House, but for now it is concentrating on local elections.

c. The Green party has gained national recognition because of its association with consumer activist Ralph Nader.

d. The Green party believes that local governments should have more political power and the federal government should have less.

Inferences and Supporting Details

5. In paragraph 5, the authors mention the "social wage" in order to illustrate what?

_____

Patterns of Organization

6. Which two patterns organize paragraph 4?

a. definition; comparison and contrast

b. cause and effect; classification

c. process; definition

d. comparison and contrast; classification

7. Overall, which two patterns organize the entire reading?

_____

Fact or Opinion?

8. The authors say that "candidates of third parties are making more credible bids for public office throughout the country." That statement is

a. a fact.

b. an opinion.

c. a mixture of both.

Purpose

9. What do you think is the authors' primary purpose?

a. The authors want to describe third-party candidates and point out similarities and differences.

b. The authors want to convince readers that third-party candidates will continue to play a role in elections.

Bias

10. Which statement do you think is accurate?

a. The authors are biased in favor of third-party candidates.

b. The authors are biased against third-party candidates.

c. The authors are careful not to reveal their personal feelings.

■ **DRAWING YOUR OWN CONCLUSIONS** How would you answer the authors' concluding question? Do you think Americans are moving toward a time when there are no political parties? Why or why not?

_____

_____

_____

■ **MAKING IT PERSONAL** Of the three parties described in this reading, which one would you be most likely to support and why?

■ **WRITING SUGGESTION** Write a paper in which you explain why having a third party would or would not help solve a major problem in this country: A huge number of people do not turn out to vote in the presidential elections.

INTERNET BONUS QUESTIONS

Who is the two-time third-party candidate for president who said, "If you see a snake, just kill it; don't appoint a committee on snakes."

Ross Perot

What was the point of his comment on snakes?

_____

What search term did you use to get the information?

If you see a snake just kill it

■ READING 4

THE STEREOTYPE TRAP
Sharon Begley

LOOKING AHEAD We all know by now that stereotyping people is a mistake. When we stereotype, we ignore both individual differences and the complexity of human behavior. It's only in the last decade, though, that researchers have begun to look at stereotypes from the opposite direction and focused on the targets of stereotyping. What that research suggests is that stereotypes are enormously powerful—and as you might expect, their power is not especially benevolent.

WORD WATCH Some of the more difficult words in the reading are defined below. The number in parentheses indicates the paragraph in which the word appears. An asterisk marks its first appearance in the reading. Preview the definitions before you begin reading, and watch for the words while you read.

---

ninnies (3): fools

pedophiles (3): child molesters

seminal (4): influential in an original way

subliminal (6): subconscious

pernicious (9): bad, destructive

FLEXIBLE READING TIP To answer the question "What is the stereotype trap?" this reading describes five different research studies. As you read, underline the sentences that report on the studies' conclusions.

1 THE STUDENTS HAD NO IDEA OF THE REAL PURPOSE OF THE study they had volunteered for—it is, after all, standard operating procedure in psychology to keep subjects in the dark on that little point. (If volunteers know they're being studied for, say, whether they will help a blind child cross a busy street, it tends to skew their behavior.) So when 40 black and 40 white Princeton undergraduates volunteered to play mini-golf, the psychologists dissembled a bit. This is a test of "natural ability," Jeff Stone and his colleagues informed some of the kids. This is a test of "the ability to think strategically," they told others. Then the students—non-golfers

all—played the course, one at a time. Among those told the test measured natural ability, black students scored, on average, more than four strokes better than whites. In the group told the test gauged strategic savvy, the white kids scored four strokes better, the researchers reported last year. "When people are reminded of a negative stereotype about themselves— 'white men can't jump' or 'black men can't think'—it can adversely affect performance," says Stone, now at the University of Arizona.

2   Another group of students, 46 Asian-American female undergrads at Harvard, thought they were taking a tough, 12-question math test. Before one group attacked the advanced algebra, they answered written questions emphasizing ethnicity ("How many generations of your family have lived in America?"). Another group's questionnaire subtly reminded them of their gender ("Do you live on a co-ed or single-sex dorm floor?"). Women who took the math test after being reminded of their Asian heritage—and thus, it seems, the stereotype that Asians excel at math—scored highest, getting 54 percent right. The women whose questionnaire implicitly reminded them of the stereotype that, for girls, "math is hard," as Barbie infamously said, scored lowest, answering 43 percent correctly.

3   The power of stereotypes, scientists had long figured, lay in their ability to change the behavior of the person holding the stereotype. If you think women are ninnies* ruled by hormonal swings, you don't name them CEO; if you think gays are pedophiles,* you don't tap them to lead your Boy Scout troop. But five years ago Stanford University psychologist Claude Steele showed something else: it is the targets of a stereotype whose behavior is most powerfully affected by it. A stereotype that pervades the culture the way "ditzy blondes" and "forgetful seniors" do makes people painfully aware of how society views them—so painfully aware, in fact, that knowledge of the stereotype can affect how well they do on intellectual and other tasks. Now, with half a decade of additional research under their belts, psychologists are discovering the power of stereotypes not only over blacks, but over women, members of ethnic minorities, and the elderly, too. . . .

4   In their seminal* 1995 study, Steele and Joshua Aronson, now at New York University, focused on how the threat posed by stereotypes affects African Americans. They reasoned that whenever black students take on an intellectual task, like an SAT, they face the prospect of confirming widely held suspicions about their brainpower. This threat, the psychologists suspected, might interfere with performance. To test this hunch, Steele and Aronson

gave 44 Stanford undergrads questions from the verbal part of the tough Graduate Record Exam. One group was asked, right before the test, to indicate their year in school, age, major, and other information. The other group answered all that, as well as one final question: what is your race? The results were sobering. "Just listing their race undermined the black students' performance," says Steele, making them score significantly worse than blacks who did not note their race, and significantly worse than all whites. But the performance of black Stanfordites who were not explicitly reminded of their race equaled that of whites, found the scientists.

5   You do not even have to believe a negative stereotype to be hurt by it, psychologists find. As long as you care about the ability you're being tested on, such as golfing or math, and are familiar with the stereotype ("girls can't do higher math"), it can sink you. What seems to happen is that as soon as you reach a tough par 3 or a difficult trig problem, the possibility of confirming, and being personally reduced to, a painful stereotype causes enough distress to impair performance. "If you are a white male and you find yourself having difficulty, you may begin to worry about failing the test," says psychologist Paul Davies of Stanford in an upcoming paper. But "if you are a black male . . . you begin to worry . . . about failing your race by confirming a negative stereotype." It's a sort of "Oh God, they really are right about people like me" reaction.

6   You don't outgrow it either. Becca Levy of Yale showed over-60 volunteers subliminal* messages (through words flashed quickly on a monitor) and then tested them on memory. Seniors who saw words like "Alzheimer's," "senile," and "old" always scored worse than seniors who saw words like "wise" and "sage." . . . Does it matter? In a follow-up, Levy used the same subliminal priming. But this time she asked the volunteers whether they would accept life-prolonging medical intervention. Those seniors primed with positive stereotypes usually said yes; those reminded of senility and frailty said no. "What's so frightening," says Levy, "is that the stereotype, at least in the short run, overwhelms long-held beliefs."

7   Stereotypes seem to most affect the best and the brightest. Only if you're black and care about academics, or female and care about math, will you also care if society thinks you're bad at those things. A girl whose sense of self-worth is tied up in her poetry, for instance, is less likely to freeze up when her facility with calculus is belittled. To test the effect of the "bimbo" stereotype, scientists at the University of Waterloo in Ontario showed men and women undergrads TV commercials with and without

gender stereotypes. (In one, a student says her primary goal in college is to meet "cute guys.") Then the students, who all said they were good at math and that it mattered to them, took a standardized test. Women who saw the commercials with female stereotypes not only did worse on the math problems than did women who saw gender-neutral commercials, but also did worse than men: they actively avoided math problems in favor of verbal ones.

8   Women who saw stereotyped ads expressed less interest in math-based careers like financial analysis and physics afterward, and more interest in math-free fields like writing. "Exposure to stereotypic commercials persuades women to withdraw" from fields like math and science where they are the targets of stereotypes, Davies says. Of course, if the stereotype is positive, it can induce you to persist in something you're supposed to be good at even if you're not. Steele admits sheepishly that he keeps playing sports (even though he's no Tiger Woods) because, as a black man, he's told by society that he's a natural.

9   Can the pernicious* effects of stereotypes be vanquished? If no one reminds you of a negative stereotype, your performance doesn't suffer. It can actually improve if instead you think of a positive stereotype—Steele recommends bellowing something like "You are Stanford students!" but clearly that has limited applicability. Deception helps, too: if women are told that a difficult math test reveals no gender differences . . . they perform as well as men. Otherwise, women score much lower. While such manipulations may weaken the brutal power of stereotypes, at the end of the day they remain manipulations. But until stereotypes fade away, that may be the best we can hope for.

Adapted from Sharon Begley,
"The Stereotype Trap," *Newsweek*,
November 6, 2000, pp. 66–68.

MONITORING YOUR COMPREHENSION   If you can explain what a "stereotype trap" is and provide a few examples, pat yourself on the back for your excellent comprehension.

COMPREHENSION AND CRITICAL READING QUESTIONS   Answer the following questions by filling in the blanks or circling the letter of the correct response.

Overall Main Idea   **1.** Which statement best sums up the main idea of the entire reading?

a. Stereotypes encourage the kind of bigotry and prejudice that can undermine a democratic society.

b. Research on stereotyping suggests that those inclined to think in stereotypes are more inclined to be rigid and simplistic in their thinking.

c. Those who are subjected to stereotyping are often influenced by the stereotypes applied to them.

d. High achievers are not affected by stereotypes; they know how silly such simplistic descriptions are.

Supporting Details

2. Explain why the study introduced in paragraph 2 is central to developing the main idea.

_____

_____

3. In paragraph 4, what was it that profoundly affected student performance, and why does that piece of information help illustrate the main idea of the reading?

_____

_____

_____

_____

4. What is the main idea of paragraph 3?

_____

_____

Inferences and Conclusions

5. What is the implied main idea of paragraph 4?

_____

_____

6. What can you infer about Stanford University based on Claude Steele's comment (in paragraph 9) that "You are Stanford students!" should be yelled before students take a test?

_____

_____

Patterns of
Organization

7. Overall, the reading relies on which pattern of organization?

a. comparison and contrast

b. process

c. classification

d. cause and effect

Purpose

8. What do you think is the author's primary purpose?

a. The author wants to report how stereotyping affects its victims.

b. The author wants to persuade readers not to think in stereotypes.

Tone

9. How would you describe the author's tone?

a. neutral

b. outraged

c. casual

d. disgusted

specially

Bias

10. Which statement do you think is accurate?

a. The writer is biased in favor of the researchers cited in the reading.

b. The writer is biased against the researchers cited in the reading.

c. It's impossible to determine the writer's personal bias.

DRAWING YOUR OWN CONCLUSIONS Based on the research cited in the reading, do you think freshmen girls trying out for a basketball team would perform better or worse if the tryouts took place right after the girls watched a short film about the making of the *Sports Illustrated* swimsuit edition? What led you to your conclusion?

I believe that it would have an adverse affect on the women. Women are looked at as sex objects in most cases. Showing the women this would show them how men look at other

MAKING IT PERSONAL Have you ever found yourself giving in to stereotyping, either about yourself or about other people? If so, what did you do in response? In general, what do you think people should do if they find themselves stereotyping others?

women and make them feel less attractive. At the same time it would also cause them to be less confident during the try outs. I believe this to be true

WRITING SUGGESTION Write a paragraph explaining how television programming contributes to or discourages stereotypes. Please give specific examples of programming that illustrates your point.

INTERNET BONUS QUESTIONS

What famous First Lady said, "No one can make you feel inferior without your consent."

Eleanor Roosevelt Statment was about Success and knowing how to deal with Criticism

What search term did you use to answer the question?

When did the first lady

Because of the Stereotype research that was done on good and bad stereotypes,

Stereotype

■ READING 5

WHERE DOES FREE SPEECH END?
Ann Marie Radaskiewicz and Laraine Flemming

LOOKING AHEAD Should there ever be limitations upon citizens' right to express themselves freely? In the following reading, the authors explore the case of David Irving, who was sentenced to prison for denying that the Holocaust ever happened.

WORD WATCH Some of the more difficult words in the reading are defined below. The number in parentheses indicates the paragraph in which the word appears. An asterisk marks its first appearance in the reading. Preview the definitions before you begin reading, and watch for the words while you read.

---

unicorns (1): mythical creatures pictured as horses with a single horn growing from their head

leprechauns (1): elves in Irish folklore

appalled (2): alarmed; horrified

railed against (2): criticized or condemned

affront (2): attack

crackpot (2): foolish

odious (2): awful; disgusting

refute (3): prove false

fascism (4): dictatorship form of government, powered by force

dictum (4): saying

fabricated (5): made up

FLEXIBLE READING TIP As you come to each argument for or against David Irving's jail sentence, underline it and write pro or con in the margins.

1   IN FEBRUARY 2006, AN AUSTRIAN COURT SENTENCED BRITISH historian David Irving to three years in prison. His crime? In the past, he has said that scholars writing about the Holocaust—Nazi Germany's systematic execution of six million European Jews—might as well be novelists writing about unicorns* and leprechauns.* Horrified by these views, government officials in Austria, Germany, Canada, Australia, New Zealand, and South Africa informed Irving that he was no longer welcome in their

countries. Austria went so far as to issue a warrant for his arrest in 1989 after he denied the Holocaust's existence in two of his speeches. When Irving boldly defied banishment and visited Austria in 2005, he was promptly arrested for violating a law that explicitly prohibits Holocaust denial. His subsequent conviction and imprisonment sparked strong controversy.

2   Appalled* and outraged, civil rights advocates railed against* this affront* to Irving's freedom of speech. Protecting the right to freedom of expression, they argued, demands that all citizens be allowed to speak their mind, without exception. Even misguided opinions, crackpot* ideas, and outright lies should be allowed expression, for censorship in any form must not be tolerated. Either we believe in free speech or we don't was their argument. In short, they felt Mr. Irving had a right to his opinions, no matter how wrongheaded or odious* they might be.

3   Other critics of Austria's action objected to Irving's sentence on the grounds that suppressing an idea doesn't refute* it. Locking people up for disagreeing with historical fact, they said, does nothing to get at the truth. Falsehoods and uninformed opinions need to be publicly debated and destroyed by counterarguments based on solid evidence and logical reasoning. Dangerous, hate-filled theories and thoughts need to be treated like cockroaches: They should be forced out of hiding and exposed to the light of reason, which, the supporters of free speech argue, will destroy them.

4   Those in favor of Irving's jail term took a different position. They were less concerned about free speech and more concerned about a return of fascism.* From their standpoint, the original purpose of Austria's law against denying the Holocaust had to be taken into account. The law had been formulated because the Austrians took seriously the old dictum* that those who fail to remember history are condemned to repeat it. Many feared that speech or writing that diminished the horror of the Holocaust could also drive it from public memory and pave the way for a renewal of a society rife with prejudice and hatred, in other words, a world much like Austria just prior to World War II. Considered from this perspective, Irving's persistent denial of the Holocaust minimized the tragedy that had taken place and opened the doors to its happening again. Irving's words were, then, a real and present danger to a society striving to make up for its dark past. He had to be punished for giving them voice.

5   Throughout the debate over Irving's sentence, both sides did find one piece of common ground. Each side considered Irving a disturbed individual, who had managed to deny all factual

evidence proving the Holocaust's existence in favor of his own fabricated* version of history. What neither could agree upon was how to handle Irving's insistence on speaking his mind.

MONITORING YOUR COMPREHENSION If you can summarize the arguments for and against David Irving's imprisonment for denying the Holocaust, you have successfully understood this reading.

COMPREHENSION AND CRITICAL READING QUESTIONS Answer the following questions by filling in the blanks or circling the letter of the correct response.

Overall Main Idea **1.** Which statement best expresses the main idea of the entire reading?

    a. David Irving committed no crime and should not have been punished.

    b. The Austrian court of law that convicted David Irving was justified because Holocaust deniers increase the chances that genocide can happen again in other parts of the world.

    c. Some people opposed Holocaust denier David Irving's punishment, whereas others thought it was necessary.

    d. In all the controversy over David Irving's jail sentence, no one ever mentioned a key fact. Irving was delusional.

Supporting Details and Paraphrasing **2.** According to the authors, why do countries like Austria prohibit Holocaust denial?

_____

_____

3. Paraphrase the viewpoints of those who oppose David Irving's jail sentence.

_____

_____

4. Paraphrase the viewpoint of those who supported Irving's sentence.

_____

_____

Inferences and Conclusions **5.** What inference do readers need to draw to complete the meaning of the last two sentences in paragraph 1?

_____

6. In saying that scholars writing about the Holocaust might as well be novelists writing about unicorns and leprechauns, Irving was trying to make what point?

_____

Purpose **7.** The title suggests that the reading is primarily

    a. persuasive.

    b. informative.

Fact and Opinion **8.** Which of the following best describes this sentence? "Appalled and outraged, civil rights advocates railed against this affront to Irving's freedom of speech."

    a. This is a statement of fact.

    b. This is an opinion.

    c. The statement mixes opinion with fact.

Tone **9.** How would you describe the authors' tone?

    a. angry

    b. neutral

    c. ironic

    d. anxious

Bias **10.** Which statement describes the authors' position on David Irving's views?

    a. The authors reveal a bias in favor of David Irving's viewpoint.

    b. The authors reveal a bias against David Irving's viewpoint.

    c. The authors are neutral or impartial on the subject of David Irving's viewpoint.

■ **DRAWING YOUR OWN CONCLUSIONS** In 1949, Supreme Court Justice Robert Jackson wrote a dissenting opinion in a case involving free speech. The case involved a man named Terminiello, who had given a hate-filled speech and been found guilty of disturbing the peace. Terminiello appealed, however, and the Supreme Court overturned his conviction invoking the right to freedom of speech. Jackson did not agree with the Court's decision and wrote: "There is a danger that, if the Court does not temper its doctrinaire* logic with a little practical wisdom, it will convert the constitutional Bill of Rights into a suicide pact." What did Jackson mean by calling the Bill of Rights, with its guarantee of personal freedoms, a suicide pact if it was interpreted *without* practical wisdom? Whom do you think he might have agreed with in the Irving case, and why?

_____

_____

_____

MAKING IT PERSONAL In your opinion, should David Irving have been convicted and imprisoned? Why or why not?

WRITING SUGGESTION Write a paper explaining your position on free speech. Should all kinds of speech be acceptable or should there be some limits on freedom of speech?

INTERNET BONUS QUESTIONS

What notable philosopher and Harvard University professor coined the phrase, "Those who cannot remember the past are condemned to repeat it"?

George Santayana (1863-1952)

or

What famous French philosopher is credited with saying, "I disapprove of what you say, but I will defend to the death your right to say it"?

_____

What search term did you use to answer either question?

_____

---

*doctrinaire: rigid, unbending.

■ READING 6

MEMORY, PERCEPTION, AND EYEWITNESS TESTIMONY

Douglas A. Bernstein, Louis A. Penner, Alison Clarke-Stewart, and Edward J. Roy

LOOKING AHEAD The U.S. justice system depends heavily on eyewitnesses who testify during trials. In many cases, defendants are convicted based on what those witnesses say they saw. However, in this selection from a psychology textbook, the authors point out the dangers of relying on the testimony of eyewitnesses.

WORD WATCH Some of the more difficult words in the reading are defined below. The number in parentheses indicates the paragraph in which the word appears. An asterisk marks its first appearance in the reading. Preview the definitions before you begin reading, and watch for the words while you read.

constructive (1): related to assembling or combining parts

DNA evidence (1): proof based on the body's DNA molecules, which are like a blueprint for everything in an individual's body. This means that, except in the case of identical twins, DNA evidence is unique to the person from which it was derived.

perceive (2): recognize, absorb into consciousness

stimulus (2): something that causes a response

assumption (3): belief or conviction considered to be a given

prosecution (4): related to the lawyers who make a case against a defendant during legal proceedings

inherent (6): inborn, naturally a part of

amplified (6): made more powerful

miscarriages (7): failures

arrays (7): arrangements

FLEXIBLE READING TIP In this selection, the authors are inclined to follow general statements with specific examples. Try paraphrasing the general statements in the margins. Then use arrows to point out the examples. To take your understanding a step deeper, write your own examples in the margins across from the authors' examples.

1 THERE ARE FEW SITUATIONS IN WHICH ACCURATE RETRIEVAL of memories is more important—and constructive* memory is more dangerous—than when an eyewitness testifies in court about a crime. Eyewitnesses provide the most compelling evidence in many trials, but they can sometimes be mistaken (Loftus & Ketcham 1991; Wells, Olson, & Charman, 2002). In 1984, for example, a North Carolina college student, Jennifer Thompson, confidently identified Ronald Cotton as the man who had raped her at knifepoint. Mainly on the basis of Thompson's testimony, Cotton was convicted of rape and sentenced to life in prison. After eleven years behind bars, DNA evidence* revealed that he was innocent (and it identified another man as the rapist). The eyewitness-victim's certainty had convinced a jury, but her memory had been faulty (O'Neill, 2000). Let's consider the accuracy of eyewitness memory and how it can be distorted.

2 Like the rest of us, eyewitnesses can remember only what they perceive,* and they can perceive only what they attend to (Backman & Nilsson, 1991). Perception is influenced by a combination of the stimulus* features we find "out there" in the world and what we already know, expect, or want.

3 Witnesses are asked to report exactly what they saw or heard; but no matter how hard they try to be accurate, there are limits to how faithful their reports can be (Kassin, Rigby, & Castillo, 1991). For one thing, during the time that information is encoded and stored in long-term memory, certain details can be lost (Fahsing, Ask, & Granhag, 2004). Further, the appearance of new information, including information contained in questions posed by police or lawyers, can alter a witness's memory (Belli & Loftus, 1996). In one study, when witnesses were asked, "How fast were the cars going when they *smashed into* each other?" they were likely to recall a higher speed than when they were asked, "How fast were the cars going when they *hit* each other?" (Loftus & Palmer, 1974; see Figure 7.1). There is also evidence that an object mentioned during questioning about an incident is often mistakenly remembered as having been there during the incident (Dodson & Reisberg, 1991). So if a lawyer says that a screwdriver was lying on the ground (when it was not), witnesses often recall with great certainty having seen it (Ryan & Geiselman, 1991). This

Question	Verb	Estimated mph
About how fast were the cars going when they _____ each other?	smashed into	40.8
	hit	34.0
	contacted	30.8

Original information | **External information** | **The "memory"**

About how fast were the cars going when they SMASHED INTO each other?

Figure 7.1 The Impact of Questioning on Eyewitness Memory

After seeing a filmed traffic accident, people were asked. "About how fast were the cars going when they (smashed into, hit, or contacted) each other?" As shown here, the witnesses' responses were influenced by the verb used in the question; "smashed" was associated with the highest average speed estimates. A week later, people who heard the "smashed" question remembered the accident as being more violent than did people in the other two groups (Loftus & Palmer, 1974).

misinformation effect can occur in several ways (Loftus & Hoffman, 1989). In some cases, hearing new information can make it harder to retrieve the original memory (Tversky & Tuchin, 1989). In others, the new information may be integrated into the old memory, making it impossible to distinguish the new information from what was originally seen (Loftus, 1992). In still others, an eyewitness report might be influenced by the person's assumption* that if a lawyer or police officer says an object was there or that something happened, it must be true.

4   A jury's belief in a witness's testimony often depends as much (or even more) on *how* the witness presents evidence as on the content or relevance of that evidence (Leippe, Manion, & Romanczyk, 1992). Many jurors are impressed, for example, by witnesses who give lots of details about what they saw or heard. Extremely detailed testimony from prosecution* witnesses is especially likely to lead to guilty verdicts, even when the details reported are irrelevant (Bell & Loftus, 1989). When a witness gives highly detailed testimony, such as the exact time of the crime or the color of the criminal's shoes, jurors apparently assume that

the witness paid especially close attention or has a particularly accurate memory. At first glance, these assumptions seem reasonable. However, the ability to divide attention is limited. As a result, witnesses might be able to focus attention on the crime and the criminal, or on the surrounding details, but probably not on both—particularly if they were emotionally aroused and the crime happened quickly. So witnesses who accurately remember unimportant details of a crime scene may not accurately recall more important ones, such as the criminal's facial features (Backman & Nilsson, 1991).

5   Juries also tend to believe witnesses who are confident (Leippe, Manion, & Romanczyk, 1992). Unfortunately, witnesses' confidence in their testimony often exceeds its accuracy (Shaw, 1996). Repeated exposure to misinformation and the repeated recall of misinformation can increase a witness's confidence in testimony, whether or not it is accurate (Lamb, 1998; Mitchell & Zaragoza, 1996; Roediger, Jacoby, & McDermott, 1996). In other words, as in the Jennifer Thompson case, even witnesses who are confident about their testimony are not always correct.

6   The weaknesses inherent* in eyewitness memory can be amplified* by the use of police lineups and certain other criminal identification procedures (Wells & Olson, 2003). In one study, for example, participants watched a videotaped crime and then tried to identify the criminal from a set of photographs (Wells & Bradfield, 1999). None of the photos showed the person who had committed the crime, but some participants nevertheless identified one of them as the criminal they saw on tape. When these mistaken participants were led to believe that they had correctly identified the criminal, they became even more confident in the accuracy of their false identification (Semmler, Brewer, & Wells, 2004; Wells, Olson, & Charman, 2003). These incorrect, but confident, witnesses became more likely than other participants to claim that it had been easy for them to identify the criminal from the photos because they had had a good view of him and had paid careful attention to him.

7   Since 1973, at least 115 people, including Ronald Cotton, have been released from U.S. prisons in twenty-five states after DNA tests or other evidence revealed that they had been falsely convicted—mostly on the basis of faulty eyewitness testimony (Death Penalty Information Center, 2004; Scheck, Neufeld, & Dwyer, 2000; Wells, Malpass, et al., 2000). DNA evidence freed Charles Fain, who had been convicted of murder and spent almost eighteen years on death row in Idaho (Bonner, 2001). Maryland officials

approved $900,000 in compensation for Bernard Webster, who served 20 years in prison for rape before DNA revealed that he was innocent (Associated Press, 2003). Frank Lee Smith, too, would have been set free after the sole eyewitness at his murder trial retracted her testimony, but he had already died of cancer while awaiting execution in a Florida prison. Research on memory and perception helps explain how these miscarriages* of justice can occur, and it is also guiding efforts to prevent such errors in the future. The U.S. Department of Justice has acknowledged the potential for errors in eyewitness evidence, as well as the dangers of asking witnesses to identify suspects from lineups and photo arrays.* The result is *Eyewitness Evidence: A Guide for Law Enforcement* (U.S. Department of Justice, 1999), the first-ever guide for police and prosecutors who work with eyewitnesses. The guide warns these officials that asking leading questions about what witnesses saw can distort their memories. It also suggests that witnesses should examine photos of possible suspects one at a time and points out that false identifications are less likely if witnesses viewing suspects in a lineup are told that the real criminal might not be included (Wells & Olson, 2003; Wells, Malpass, et al., 2000).

Bernstein et al., *Psychology*, pp. 256–258.

MONITORING YOUR COMPREHENSION Look at the diagram accompanying the reading. What does it illustrate, and how does it contribute to the authors' point? If you can answer those two questions, you've understood the gist of the reading.

COMPREHENSION AND CRITICAL READING QUESTIONS Answer the following questions by filling in the blanks or circling the letter of the correct response.

Overall Main Idea 1. Which statement best expresses the main idea of the entire reading?

   a. The wording of questions can distort the memories of crime victims and eyewitnesses.

   b. Because eyewitnesses can and do make mistakes, innocent people have been wrongly convicted of crimes.

   c. People's memories are, in general, not very reliable, but eyewitnesses are particularly inclined to distort reality.

   d. Many innocent people have been convicted of crimes they did not commit; fortunately, DNA evidence has been used to exonerate them and set them free.

Main Idea **2.** What is the main idea of paragraph 6?

    a. People's memories aren't always very reliable.

    b. Having crime victims look at photographs is an ineffective criminal identification technique.

    c. Procedures that police use to help victims or eyewitnesses identify criminals can encourage distorted memories of events.

    d. So many studies have revealed the flaws of both eyewitness memory and the criminal justice system that we need to consider the legality of the death penalty.

Supporting **3.** Why do the authors mention victim Jennifer Thompson and/or
Details accused rapist Ronald Cotton three times throughout the reading?

    a. They illustrate the authors' point that the wording of questions often distorts eyewitnesses' memories.

    b. Their example supports the idea that, in spite of its flaws, eyewitness testimony is usually accurate.

    c. They illustrate the idea that bystander-eyewitnesses tend to recall details more accurately than victim-eyewitnesses do.

    d. Their stories support the idea that an individual can be falsely convicted on the basis of eyewitness testimony.

4. Which statement best describes paragraphs 4 and 5?

    a. Paragraphs 4 and 5 introduce two different major details that support the overall main idea of the reading.

    b. Paragraph 4 introduces a major detail further explained by paragraph 5.

    c. Paragraphs 4 and 5 both further explain the main idea of paragraph 3.

Inferences **5.** What inference do readers need to supply in order to understand
and the following supporting detail from paragraph 3? "In one study,
Supporting when witnesses were asked, 'How fast were the cars going when
Details they *smashed into* each other?' they were likely to recall a higher speed than when they were asked, 'How fast were the cars going when they *hit* each other?'"

    a. They recalled a higher speed because they were being questioned.

    b. The change in verbs from *smashed* to *hit* affected what witnesses remembered.

    c. Being asked a question by an authority figure affected the witnesses' memory of what happened.

Inferences and Conclusions **6.** The authors use the phrase "constructive memory" in the opening sentence of the reading. That phrase is meant to imply what about how we remember?

    a. Human memory functions like a camera. The brain takes "snapshots" of the past and stores them away.

    b. Human memory is a process that pieces together or combines fragments of experience and stores away a version of what happened in the past.

    c. Human memory is a completely unreliable witness to events, subject to forgetting and distortion, it's a wonder that people can ever agree on anything.

Understanding Visual Aids **7.** The accompanying visual aid

    a. adds new information to the reading.

    b. further emphasizes an idea mentioned in the reading.

Purpose **8.** What do you think is the authors' primary purpose?

    a. The authors want to identify the various ways eyewitness testimony can be inaccurate.

    b. The authors want to persuade readers that eyewitness testimony cannot be completely trusted.

Tone **9.** The authors' tone is _____.

Bias **10.** Which of the following sentences reveals the authors' personal point of view?

    a. "Witnesses are asked to report exactly what they saw or heard; but no matter how hard they try to be accurate, there are limits to how faithful their reports can be." (paragraph 3)

    b. "Extremely detailed testimony from prosecution witnesses is especially likely to lead to guilty verdicts, even when the details reported are irrelevant." (paragraph 4)

    c. "Since 1973, at least 115 people, including Ronald Cotton, have been released from U.S. prisons in twenty-five states after DNA tests or other evidence revealed that they had been falsely convicted—mostly on the basis of faulty eyewitness testimony." (paragraph 7)

■ **DRAWING YOUR OWN CONCLUSIONS** Based on what the authors say in the reading, do you think they are or are not likely to support the death penalty? Please explain.

_____

_____

_____

_____

■ **MAKING IT PERSONAL** You are a juror in a murder trial. The prosecutor's case is weak. The only compelling evidence comes from an eyewitness account. When you enter the jury room, you realize that all the jurors are leaning toward conviction. What will you do, agree to convict or discuss the problem of eyewitness testimony with other jury members? Please explain your reasoning.

■ **WRITING SUGGESTION** Write two or three paragraphs summarizing why eyewitness testimony can be so inaccurate.

INTERNET BONUS QUESTION
The name Elizabeth Loftus turns up frequently in this reading. What does Loftus do, and why would the authors of the reading be inclined to cite her work?

_____

_____

_____

■ **READING 7**

KOHLBERG'S SIX STAGES OF MORAL JUDGMENT
Kelvin L. Seifert, Robert J. Hoffnung, and Michele Hoffnung

LOOKING AHEAD The following textbook selection explains how our sense of right and wrong develops as we move from being children to adults. As you read, consider how your own morality has evolved over time. Did you do anything as a child or an adolescent that you would now describe as morally wrong?

WORD WATCH Some of the more difficult words in the reading are defined below. The number in parentheses indicates the paragraph in which the word appears. An asterisk marks its first appearance in the reading. Preview the definitions before you begin reading, and watch for the words while you read.

> **hypothetical (1):** still in theory, not yet proven
>
> **dilemmas (1):** problems or difficult choices where each solution has a drawback
>
> **egocentric (2):** self-centered
>
> **concrete (2):** related to actual, specific things or events
>
> **conventions (2):** customs; established ways of doing things
>
> **modified (2):** changed
>
> **abstract (4):** in the realm of ideas
>
> **tyranny (4):** absolute power or authority
>
> **opportunistic (4):** taking advantage of a situation for personal benefit

FLEXIBLE READING TIP As you read, try to link each of Kohlberg's stages to a concrete example of ethical behavior, for example, children on a playground playing together without fighting because the teacher is watching. Jot your examples in the margins next to the stages they illustrate.

1 LAWRENCE KOHLBERG (1927–1987), A LONG-TIME STUDENT OF moral development, proposed six stages of moral judgment that develop slowly, well into middle adulthood (Schrader, 1990). The

stages were derived from interviews in which children and adults of various ages responded individually to hypothetical* stories that contained moral dilemmas.* The original interviewees were all males, but in later studies Kohlberg and his associates extended the research to include females.

2   The table below summarizes the six proposed stages. The stages form a progression in two ways. First, earlier stages represent more egocentric* thinking than later stages do. Second, earlier stages by their nature require more specific or concrete* thinking than later stages do. For instance, in stage 1, a child makes no distinction between what he believes is right and what the world tells him is right; he simply accepts the perspectives of the authorities as his own. By stage 4, when the child is an adolescent, he realizes that individuals vary in their points of view, but he still takes for granted the existing overall conventions* of society as a whole. He cannot yet imagine a society in which those conventions might be purposely modified,* for example, by passing laws or agreeing on new rules. Only by stages 5 and 6 can he do so fully.

Table 7.1: Kohlberg's Six Stages of Moral Judgment

Stage	Explanation
Level 1: Avoid punishments and gain rewards.	
Stage 1: Emphasis is placed on obeying authority and avoiding penalties for disobedience.	Good is following externally imposed rules to gain rewards and avoid punishment.
Stage 2: Value is placed on market exchange that benefits the individual personally along with person or group who gives or receives favors in the exchange.	Good is whatever is agreeable to the individual and to anyone who gives or receives favors; no long-term loyalty.
Level 2: Play by society's rules.	
Stage 3: Focus is on opinion of peers.	Good is whatever brings approval from friends or other peers.
Stage 4: Focus is on conforming to social system.	Good is whatever conforms to existing laws, customs, and authorities.
Level 3: Develop own moral principles.	
Stage 5: Emphasis is on balancing individual rights with the existing social contract.	Good is whatever conforms to existing procedures for settling disagreements in society without sacrificing an individual's rights.
Stage 6: Ethics are self-chosen and based on what are believed to be universal principles.	Good is whatever is consistent with personal, general moral principles.

Sources of information: www.vtaide.com/blessing/kohlberg.htm and Seifert et al., *Lifespan Development*, p. 369.

3   In the school years, children most commonly show ethical reasoning that reflects stage 2. However, some may begin showing stage 3 or 4 reasoning toward the end of high school (Colby & Kohlberg, 1987). For the majority of youth and many adults, stage 3 and stage 4 characterize their most advanced moral thinking. In stage 3, a person's chief concern is with the opinions of her peers: an action is morally right if her immediate circle of friends says it is right. Often this way of thinking leads to helpful actions, such as taking turns and sharing possessions. But often it does not, such as when a group of friends decide to let the air out of the tires of someone's car.

4   In stage 4 of moral development, there is a shift from concern with peers to concern with the opinions of community or society in the abstract.* Now something is right if the institutions approve. This broader source of moral judgment spares older children in stage 4 from the occasional tyranny* of friends' opinions. They will no longer steal hubcaps just because their friends urge them to do so. This change makes teenagers less opportunistic* than children are, less inclined to judge based on immediate rewards or punishments they experience personally. Instead they evaluate actions on the basis of principles of some sort. For the time being, the principles are rather conventional; they are borrowed either from ideas expressed by immediate peers and relatives or from socially accepted rules and principles, whatever they may be. If friends agree that premarital sex is permissible, many teenagers are likely to adopt this idea as their own, at least as a general principle. But if friends or family believe premarital sex is morally wrong, teenagers may adopt this alternative belief as a principle. (Note, however, that whether a teenager actually acts according to these principles is another matter. Moral action does not always follow from moral belief.)

postconventional moral judgment in Kohlberg's theory, an orientation to moral justice that develops beyond conventional rules and beliefs.

5   A few young adults develop **postconventional moral judgment**, meaning that for the first time ethical reasoning goes beyond the judgments society conventionally makes about right and wrong. Adolescents' growing ability to use abstract formal thought stimulates this development, though it does not guarantee it. Unlike schoolchildren, they can evaluate ethical ideas that *might* be right or wrong given certain circumstances that can only be imagined.

Issues in the Development of Moral Beliefs About Justice

6   Studies indicate that Kohlberg's six stages of moral judgment have held up well when tested on a wide variety of children, adolescents, and adults. The stages of moral thinking shown in Table 7.1 do seem to describe how moral judgment develops, at

least when individuals focus on hypothetical dilemmas posed in stories. When presented with stories about risky but fictional sexual behaviors, adolescents of both sexes evaluated the actions of the stories' characters in line with Kohlberg's stages (Jadack et al., 1995).

7   Even so, Kohlberg's theory of moral judgment leaves a number of important questions unanswered. One is whether the theory really recognizes the impact of prior knowledge on beliefs; another is whether the theory distinguishes clearly enough between conventions and morality. One especially important question has to do with gender differences: does Kohlberg's theory really describe the moral development of girls as well as that of boys?

Adapted from Seifert et al.,
Lifespan Development, pp. 359–362.

MONITORING YOUR COMPREHENSION   If you can mentally list and briefly describe the six stages, your comprehension is excellent. It's also very good if you can only remember three or four. The point is you know about the six stages and have an idea of what they are.

COMPREHENSION AND CRITICAL READING QUESTIONS   Answer the following questions by circling the letter of the correct response.

Overall Main Idea   **1.** Which statement best expresses the main idea of the entire reading?

a. To understand how moral judgment develops, Lawrence Kohlberg interviewed many adults and children and presented them with moral dilemmas.

b. According to Lawrence Kohlberg, most adults never progress beyond the stage in which their sense of right and wrong is based upon society's laws, rules, and customs.

c. Although Kohlberg's theory about six stages of moral development leave some questions unanswered, it seems to provide a fairly accurate explanation of how moral reasoning develops over time.

d. Lawrence Kohlberg's theory of moral development is inadequate for a number of reasons.

Main Ideas   **2.** Which statement best expresses the main idea of paragraph 4?

a. Adolescents governed by stage 4 are ruled by the opinions of their peers.

    b. Adolescents in the stage 4 level of moral development are inclined to steal and be promiscuous if that is what their peer group dictates.

    c. Kohlberg's theory of moral development encourages teenagers to think they are a law unto themselves.

    d. By the stage 4 level of moral development, adolescents begin to take the larger community and society into account.

Supporting Details and Inferences

3. To fully understand paragraphs 2–5, readers need to draw which inference?

    a. Kohlberg's theory presumes that everyone's moral development is exactly the same.

    b. Kohlberg's theory describes moral development in general terms and does not account for every individual.

    c. Kohlberg's theory was never designed to describe the moral development of females.

Inferences and Conclusions

4. It's often been claimed that children are more moral than adults because they are more innocent. Based on the reading, which statement do you consider accurate?

    a. Lawrence Kohlberg would have agreed that children by nature are more moral than adults.

    b. Lawrence Kohlberg would not have agreed that children are by nature more moral than adults.

    c. It's impossible to tell if Kohlberg would have agreed or not.

Patterns of Organization

5. What patterns organize paragraphs 2 and 3?

    a. classification; process

    b. process; cause and effect

    c. comparison and contrast; cause and effect

    d. definition; comparison and contrast

Transitions

6. Which transition in paragraph 4 signals reversal?

    a. in stage 4

    b. now

    c. instead

    d. for the time being

Under-standing Visual Aids

7. Which statement accurately describes the table on page 690?

    a. The table repeats information already in the reading.

    b. The table adds to the information in the reading.

Facts and Opinions

8. How would you describe the following statement: "Studies indicate that Kohlberg's six stages of moral judgment have held up well when tested on a wide variety of children, adolescents and adults" (paragraph 6)?

    a. The statement is a fact.

    b. The statement is an opinion.

    c. The statement is a mix of fact and opinion.

Purpose

9. What do you think is the authors' primary purpose?

    a. The authors want to describe Kohlberg's theory about how moral judgment develops in humans.

    b. The authors want to persuade readers that Kohlberg has accurately explained the development of moral judgment in humans.

Bias

10. Which of the following statements accurately describes the reading?

    a. The authors strongly agree with Kohlberg's view of moral development.

    b. The authors have a favorable view of Kohlberg's theory, but they are not convinced he is correct on all points.

    c. It's impossible to determine the authors' feelings.

DRAWING YOUR OWN CONCLUSIONS Based on the reading, how do you think Kohlberg would have answered this question: "Dr. Kohlberg, what role does God's rule play in your theory?"

_____

_____

_____

MAKING IT PERSONAL At what stage of moral reasoning do you think you are in right now? Explain your answer.

WRITING SUGGESTION Write a paper explaining what kind of ethical reasoning makes for a life well-lived. Do you think following society's rules for right and wrong is the key to a good life? Or, do you think people do better if they are willing to follow their own moral principles even if they conflict with society's?

INTERNET BONUS QUESTION

In 1970, Lawrence Kohlberg had a female research assistant who thought his theories did not well suit the lives of women. She went on to research the subject and eventually wrote a very influential book.

Her name was _Carol Gilligan_, and the book was _In a Different Voice: (1982)_

Psychological Theory and Women's Development

■ READING 8

MARLA RUZICKA: AN ACTIVIST ANGEL
Ann Marie Radaskiewicz

LOOKING AHEAD Would you risk your life to correct some injustice? Throughout history, many brave people have persisted in trying to right a wrong even when doing so was extremely dangerous. Many of these heroes have lost their lives as they attempted to make the world a better place. Marla Ruzicka was one of them.

WORD WATCH Some of the more difficult words in the reading are defined below. The number in parentheses indicates the paragraph in which the word appears. An asterisk marks its first appearance in the reading. Preview the definitions before you begin reading, and watch for the words while you read.

---

humanitarians (1): people who care about the welfare of other people

activist (1): person who works to change something

undeterred (2): not stopped

routed (3): defeated; drove from power

fundamentalist (3): adhering rigidly to basic religious principles

lobbied (4): tried to influence or persuade

compensation (5): payment for damage or injury

jittery (6): nervous

quantify (6): determine an amount

noncombatant (6): related to civilians during wartime

casualties (6): injuries and deaths

detonated (8): caused to explode

FLEXIBLE READING TIPS

1. The title suggests that the author considers Marla's life angelic or saintly. As you read, keep asking yourself what in the reading justifies that title. Every time you see a sentence that makes the title more meaningful and lends support to the idea that Marla's actions were above those of ordinary humans, mark that sentence with a star or an exclamation point.

2. The reading includes a number of dates. Pay particular attention to the event or events those dates identify.

1 SOME HUMANITARIANS* CRUSADE TO CHANGE LAWS OR RAISE money for charities. Others leave comfort and security behind, go to people in need, roll up their sleeves, and pitch in, often endangering their lives in the process. American activist* Marla Ruzicka did both. Before her life exploded in a car bomb, this passionate and courageous woman did whatever was necessary to help innocent civilian victims of the wars in Afghanistan and Iraq.

2 Early in life, at an age when her peers cared for little more than fashion and football games, Marla dedicated herself to saving the world. "Since the adults won't talk," she proclaimed, "the youth will lead the way." Fiercely anti-war at only fifteen, she led a protest against the first Gulf War that got her suspended from high school. Undeterred* by such punishments, Ruzicka took her protests to a wider stage. In high school, and later while enrolled in Long Island University's Friends World Program, she traveled to tense places like Cuba, Palestine, Guatemala, South Africa, and Israel.

3 Upon graduating from college in 1999, she took a job at Global Exchange, a human rights organization. With no intention of sitting behind a desk and playing it safe, she flew to the war zone in Afghanistan in 2001, just after the U.S. military routed* the Taliban, the fundamentalist* Islamic government. As stray bombs demolished buildings and sometimes whole neighborhoods, Marla went door to door and into hospitals, collecting first-person accounts of citizens who had been killed, injured, abused, or left homeless as a result. It was a heart-wrenching job, but Marla was determined to do it.

4 In early 2002, armed with thousands of stories of shattered lives, twenty-five-year-old Marla arrived in Washington, D.C. Smiling and talking to anyone who would listen, she insisted that the U.S. government had a responsibility to the innocent people injured by its weapons, especially the children. She lobbied* lawmakers relentlessly for financial aid to rebuild Afghan homes, schools, and businesses. In the end, her one-woman crusade for compassion and fairness achieved what had never before been done: the U.S. Congress agreed to pay $2.5 million to Afghan victims. Despite this amazing victory, Marla wasn't finished. Creating the Campaign for Innocent Victims in Conflict (CIVIC) soon after American forces invaded Iraq in 2003, she began raising millions of dollars in private donations for civilians in both Afghanistan and Iraq.

5 Not content to simply collect money for aid, Marla continued to return to the world's worst danger zones. From 2003 to 2005, she traveled repeatedly to Afghanistan and Iraq. Clad in the traditional

black robe of Iraqi women to better blend in, she helped locate dead and injured citizens, documented their suffering, and worked to obtain compensation* for them and their families. She kept in touch with the people she assisted, updating them when she received new information. Through her casework, she personally verified about 2,000 casualties.

6   Because of her efforts, Marla made it much harder for the U.S. military and the American public to ignore the human costs of war. Exposing the war's "collateral damage" through her large network of journalist friends, Marla told the stories of American rocket attacks that had mistakenly blown up cars or homes containing entire families, of children whose arms and legs had been ripped off in mine explosions, of nonthreatening civilians accidentally shot by jittery* soldiers. She wanted them all to be counted. As she wrote in an essay for Human Rights Watch, "A number is important not only to quantify* the cost of the war, but to me each number is also a story of someone whose hopes, dreams, and potential will never be realized, and who left behind a family." Believing that the United States should be accountable for these losses, she wanted the government to do what *she* was doing. It should take responsibility for errors, heal wounds already inflicted, and do more to prevent them from happening in the future. Marla dreamed, for example, of creating a government office responsible for maintaining records of noncombatant* casualties.*

7   Her work became increasingly dangerous. Iraqi terrorists were kidnapping and beheading Americans and other foreign citizens, and it was a rare day that did not feature at least one deadly bomb explosion. Nevertheless, Marla refused to abandon her mission. According to her closest friends, her activism was not only her calling and her obsession but also a form of self-therapy. Often battling anxiety and depression, Marla threw herself into her work, hoping to save herself by saving others.

8   But in the end, she couldn't save herself. Marla was in Iraq in April 2005 when an Iraqi suicide bomber detonated* his explosives beside her car, taking her life. She was just twenty-eight years old. All over the world reports of her death overflowed with praise for her courage, energy, persistence, and her ferocious desire to help the suffering. She was hailed as a "humanitarian angel," "a mix of Mother Teresa and Buffy the Vampire Slayer," and "the best of America."

Sources of information: Ellen Knickmeyer, "Victims' Champion Is Killed in Iraq," *The Washington Post*, April 18, 2005, p. A13; Glen Kessler, "U.S. Activist Mends Lives Torn by War," *The Washington Post*, August 23, 2004.

MONITORING YOUR COMPREHENSION In the opening paragraph, the author explains two ways that humanitarians choose to help others. If you can explain how Marla's actions illustrated both of these two methods, your comprehension was excellent.

COMPREHENSION AND CRITICAL READING QUESTIONS Answer the following questions by filling in the blanks or circling the letter of the correct response.

Overall Main Idea
1. Which statement best expresses the main idea of the entire reading?

    a. The U.S. government does not do enough to help the innocent victims of war.

    b. Marla Ruzicka sacrificed her life to help innocent victims of war.

    c. Marla Ruzicka's fundraising was her most important contribution to Afghan and Iraqi victims of war.

    d. In human terms, the war in Iraq was much more costly than the war in Afghanistan.

Context
2. Based on the context, *collateral damage* in paragraph 6 means

    a. the use of military might against civilians.

    b. the damage to buildings done by bombs.

    c. unintentional injury or damage occurring as a result of a military operation.

Main Ideas
3. Which statement best expresses the main idea of paragraph 3?

    a. Marla left behind the comfort and security of her life in America to do a very difficult job in a war zone.

    b. The war in Afghanistan took a terrible toll on innocent civilians.

    c. Global Exchange is one of the best human rights organizations in existence today.

    d. Marla went door to door to determine the number of civilian war victims.

4. What is the implied main idea of paragraph 4?

    a. Marla had a talent for persuading politicians to do the right thing.

    b. An activist can raise more money through private donations than by lobbying elected officials.

    c. Marla's CIVIC organization was amazingly successful.

d. To help the victims of war, Marla raised money from public and private sources.

Supporting Details **5.** In paragraph 2, why does the author mention Marla's protests and travels?

a. They illustrate the idea that she became an activist at a young age.

b. They show that she was fiercely opposed to war.

c. They illustrate her thirst for adventure.

d. They provide examples of her talent for persuading politicians to change their minds.

Inferences and Conclusions **6.** What inference must the readers draw to completely understand the following sentence from paragraph 2? "Fiercely anti-war at only fifteen, she led a protest against the first Gulf War that got her suspended from high school."

a. School officials did not approve of student protests.

b. The protest Marla led became destructive.

c. Anti-war sentiment in Marla's home town was not strong.

7. The author expects readers to infer the reason for civilians being shot by "jittery" soldiers in paragraph 6. What inference does the author expect readers to draw?

_____

_____

Patterns of Organization **8.** What two patterns organize the entire reading?

a. dates and events; comparison and contrast

b. definition; cause and effect

c. dates and events; cause and effect

d. cause and effect; comparison and contrast

Purpose **9.** What do you think is the author's primary purpose?

a. The author wants to inform readers about the events that led up to Marla Ruzicka's death.

b. The author wants to persuade readers that Marla Ruzicka was a very special and very heroic young woman.

Tone **10.** The author's tone is _____.

■ **DRAWING YOUR OWN CONCLUSIONS** Where would you place Maria Ruzicka on Kohlberg's scale of moral development? Please explain.

_____

_____

_____

■ **MAKING IT PERSONAL** Can you imagine yourself doing what Maria Ruzicka did? Why or why not?

■ **WRITING SUGGESTION** Write a paper in which you explain why you admire or disapprove of Marla Ruzicka's actions.

INTERNET BONUS QUESTION

What was the name of the American anthropologist who said, "Never doubt that a small group of thoughtful, committed citizens can change the world; indeed, it's the only thing that ever has"?

Margaret Mead

Wanted Housing Work group Supervisors

■ READING 9

THE WOLF CHILDREN
David Wallechinsky

LOOKING AHEAD The following reading tells the story of Kamala and Amala, two little girls who were discovered living in the den of a wolf and were then adopted by a human family.

WORD WATCH Some of the more difficult words in the reading are defined below. The number in parentheses indicates the paragraph in which the word appears. An asterisk marks its first appearance in the reading. Preview the definitions before you begin reading, and watch for the words while you read.

> **exorcise (1):** drive out
>
> **makeshift (2):** temporary, hurriedly put together
>
> **loincloths (4):** pieces of fabric that are wound around the hips
>
> **animated (4):** lively, excited
>
> **dysentery (5):** an intestinal illness
>
> **distraught (5):** miserable and upset
>
> **enhance (8):** improve
>
> **autistic (8):** mentally unable to make contact with reality
>
> **critique (8):** critical interpretation or opinion

FLEXIBLE READING TIP This reading focuses on attempts made to civilize two little girls supposedly raised by wolves. Summarize each civilizing attempt and the girls' response in the margins.

1 "TWO CHILDREN LIVE IN A WOLF'S LAIR—BISHOP'S AMAZING story—Girl who barked—Ate with mouth in dish!" So ran the front-page story in the *Westminster Gazette,* a London newspaper, on October 22, 1926—but was it a hoax? It began in India in October 1920 with the Reverend J. A. L. Singh, a missionary who ran the Orphanage of Midnapore, sixty-five miles west of Calcutta. He often combed the jungle for natives to capture and convert, and on one of these outings, he heard of the *manush-bagha* (man-beasts)—ghosts who haunted the jungle near the Santal village of Godamuri. Terrified natives asked Singh to exorcise* the demons.

2 What he found, he wrote in his diary, was "a white-ant mound as high as a two-story building," inhabited by a wolf family. While

watching them leave through holes at the base of the mound, Singh and his party saw the "ghosts"—two pale creatures running on all fours behind the animals. Some days later, on October 17, Singh's men returned, killed the mother wolf with bows and arrows, and dug out the mound. Inside were two wild children curled up with the wolf cubs, baring their teeth and resisting capture. With makeshift* nets, Singh separated them; he carried them to the orphanage in bamboo cages.

3 The girls, who were not sisters, were estimated to be three years old and five or six years old. Had the children been abandoned by their parents, or had they been stolen by the she-wolf for food, and then raised instead with her cubs? Had she nursed them? Since the girls were not sisters, the wolf had evidently repeated the experiment.

4 Singh and his wife named the girls Kamala and Amala. Attempts were immediately begun to civilize them: They were made to wear loincloths,* which they tried to tear off. They growled, bared their teeth, and would eat only with the orphanage dogs, who accepted them as their own. They refused all vegetable food, and ate only milk, raw meat, mice, and cockroaches that they caught, or dirt and pebbles. Singh built them a cage, in which they huddled during the day, avoiding the light. They became animated* only at night, pacing and howling continuously. They showed liveliness only when they were taken outside, when eating raw meat, or after dark. Slowly and steadily, Mrs. Singh made efforts to "humanize" them, but the results were minimal.

5 Almost a year after their capture, both girls fell ill with dysentery* and worms. Kamala recovered. But after two weeks Amala died. Singh said that two tears fell from Kamala's eyes, and she was severely withdrawn and distraught* for weeks after the death.

6 Kamala slowly recovered, and in the next eight years she responded bit by bit to Mrs. Singh's attention. She learned to stand on her knees, and then to walk upright, to drink from a glass, to speak about thirty words, and even to run simple errands. For all this, her closest relationships were with the orphanage animals, especially a hyena cub, which Reverend Singh had brought for her to play with.

7 The Singhs fed Kamala a mixed diet, with very little raw meat, and this may have severely weakened her health. In the last two years of her life, she was increasingly sick. Because of her ill health, Reverend Singh declined an offer to display her on tour in America. On November 13, 1929, she died at the age of fourteen or fifteen.

8 Despite decades of controversy and academic argument, it appears that Singh's diary account of Kamala and Amala's stay in

the orphanage was not a hoax. However, what remains a mystery is how he found them. More than fifty years later, author Charles Maclean tracked down a witness, Lasa Marandi, who confirmed that Singh was present when the children were removed from the ant hill. However, Singh himself often told reporters and others that Santal tribesmen had found the children and taken them to him. Singh may have made up this version to keep from his mission superiors the fact that he was out hunting and raiding villages for converts, or he may have made up the first version to enhance* his role in the discovery. It is this uncertainty that led critics to claim that Kamala and Amala had not been raised by a wolf mother, but that they were autistic* children whom villagers were trying to get rid of. There is, however, no evidence to support this critique* and the wolf girls of Midnapore remain the best-recorded case of children who were raised by animals.

David Wallechinsky, *The Twentieth Century*. New York: Little, Brown, 1995, pp. 296–297.

MONITORING YOUR COMPREHENSION Can you briefly summarize this story and then explain why some people have doubts that Kamala and Amala were actually raised by wolves? If so, your comprehension was perfect.

COMPREHENSION AND CRITICAL READING QUESTIONS Answer the following questions by filling in the blanks or circling the letter of the correct response.

Overall Main Idea **1.** Which statement best sums up the main idea of the entire reading?

a. Stories about the wolf children discovered in India in 1920 have not been verified and they could be a hoax.

b. Attempts to civilize the two "wolf children," Kamala and Amala, were a terrible mistake.

c. Attempts to civilize the two little girls known as the "wolf children" were not very successful.

d. Stories about children raised by animals seem to be part of every culture.

Supporting Details **2.** Who discovered the girls?

_____

3. How did the girls react to their discovery by humans?

_____

Inferences and Conclusions

4. What is the main idea of paragraph 6?

   a. Kamala began to behave more like a human, but she still identified with animals.

   b. Kamala responded to Mrs. Singh and tried to please her.

   c. Kamala resented being separated from her animal friends.

   d. Kamala was the more headstrong of the two girls.

5. What can you infer from Kamala's reaction to Amala's death?

   _____

6. According to the author, the girls were lively only when they were taken outside, eating raw meat, or going out after dark. What can you infer from this description?

   _____

   _____

Transitions

7. What two time-order transitions appear in paragraph 5?

   _____

Patterns of Organization

8. Which pattern helps organize this reading?

   a. definition

   b. time order

   c. classification

Purpose

9. What do you think was the author's primary purpose?

   a. The author wanted to inform readers about attempts to civilize two little girls believed to have been raised by wolves.

   b. The author wants to persuade readers that it was a mistake to try to civilize the two girls.

Bias

10. Which statement describes the author's position?

   a. The author believes the story of the two little girls raised by wolves is a hoax.

   b. The author believes that someone had to civilize the two little girls.

   c. The author remains neutral and does not reveal his personal feelings.

■   **DRAWING**   If a journalist asked the Reverend J. A. L. Singh whether or not he
    YOUR OWN   had done the right thing by taking the girls out of the den, how
    CONCLUSIONS   might Rev. Singh respond? What led you to your conclusion?

_____

_____

_____

■   **MAKING IT**   What do you think about the attempts made to civilize the two little
    PERSONAL   girls? Were the rescuers right or wrong to act as they did?

■   **WRITING**   Write a paper explaining why the girls should or should not have
    SUGGESTION   been removed from the wolf 's den.

INTERNET BONUS QUESTIONS
The most well-known case of a child growing up in the wild is

Victor Aveyron

How old was the child when he was found? *1799*

11   in Aveyron France

What search term did you use?

Most famous feral child

■ READING 10

NUCLEAR POWER AND WASTE DISPOSAL
James T. Shipman, Jerry D. Wilson, and Aaron W. Todd

LOOKING AHEAD Nuclear power plants are being built around the globe despite protests from those who consider them a threat to public safety. In the following excerpt from a physical science textbook, the authors look at both the advantages and disadvantages of this energy source.

WORD WATCH Some of the more difficult words in the reading are defined below. The number in parentheses indicates the paragraph in which the word appears. An asterisk marks its first appearance in the reading. Preview the definitions before you begin reading, and watch for the words while you read.

---

fission (2): related to the process of splitting atoms into parts to release energy

fusion (2): related to the process of combining atoms to release energy

emit (3): give or send out

turbines (4): machines that turn to generate power

theoretically (4): supposedly

entail (5): involve

cosmic (5): related to the universe beyond Earth

spent (7): used up; consumed

viable (8): capable of success or effectiveness

geologically (8): related to Earth

amended (8): changed

preliminary (8): beginning; introductory

feasibility (8): usefulness; effectiveness

repository (10): storage place

debris (10): waste

tainted (10): contaminated; spoiled

sludge (10): semisolid, mud-like material

FLEXIBLE READING TIP This reading is probably the most difficult one of the group. Read it slowly, marking difficult passages for a second reading if necessary. As you read, take marginal notes on the pros and cons of nuclear power.

1   IN THE UNITED STATES, ABOUT 23 PERCENT OF THE NATION'S electricity is generated by nuclear power. No new nuclear power plants have been built since 1978, but during the past few years, improved efficiency at the present 103 nuclear plants (at 65 locations in 31 states) has resulted in increased electrical output equivalent to what would have been obtained by building an additional 22 reactors.

2   Consequently, the 2001 energy crisis in California has caused serious consideration to giving nuclear power an increased role in the United States. In making reasoned judgments about nuclear power, we must consider the benefits and drawbacks of fission* and fusion* power.

3   Nuclear power does not produce the same problems caused by other power sources. Unlike coal, oil, and natural gas, nuclear power doesn't emit* carbon dioxide and other greenhouse gases that can cause global warming. Neither does it produce the sulfur oxides and nitrogen oxides that cause acid rain. Nor does it require drilling in environmentally sensitive areas.

4   However, nuclear power has its drawbacks, and radiation exposure from nuclear plants has long been a concern. In recent years, though, the safety of nuclear reactors has increased to the point where the risks associated with them are exceedingly small. A new reactor design called a *pebble-bed modular reactor* is supposed to be cheaper to build and safer to operate than the present light-water fission reactors. In the pebble-bed design, the core consists of radioactive pebbles of $^{238}UO_2$ surrounded by shells of silicon carbide and carbon. The pebbles heat helium (rather than water), which turns turbines* to generate electricity. A pebble-bed, helium-cooled test reactor is being built in South Africa. Theoretically,* this reactor will never need to be shut down for refueling and is practically meltdown-proof.

5   The vast majority of the average U.S. citizen's radiation exposure actually comes from *natural* sources (see Figure 1). Sources of natural radiation include cosmic rays from outer space, so frequent flying in jetliners and living in high-altitude cities such as Denver, Colorado, entail* more exposure to this part of the background radiation. Cosmic* rays also form radionuclides such as carbon-14 and potassium-40. Carbon and potassium are essential elements in living organisms, so these radionuclides become a part of all living organisms and thus another source of natural background radiation.

6   Other sources of natural background radiation include radionuclides in the rocks and minerals in our environment. One of the decay products of ^{238}U is radon gas. Radon gas and its

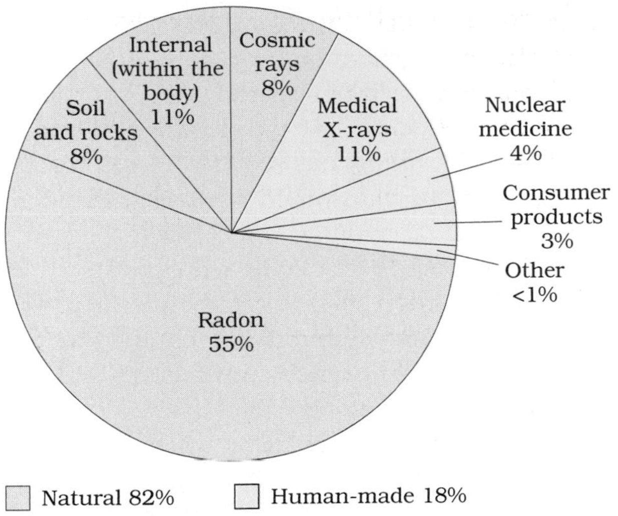

Figure 1 Sources of Exposure to Radiation
On average, each person in the U. S. receives a yearly radiation exposure of
0.2 rem, of which 82% is from the natural sources shown in the chart. The
other 18% is from human-made sources. (Source of data: Ebbing, D. D. Darrell
and R. A. D. Wentworth, *Introductory Chemistry*, 2nd ed. Copyright © 1998 by
Houghton Mifflin Company.)

radioactive daughters can be breathed into the lungs, where additional decays emit radiation. About 10,000 of the 130,000 annual
lung cancer deaths in the United States are thought to be caused
by indoor radon pollution.

7   Currently, only about 18 percent of radiation exposure comes from
human-made sources. To prevent that figure from increasing, we will
have to find effective ways to deal with nuclear power's one major
drawback. The true Achilles' heel of nuclear power is the highly toxic
radioactive waste produced by power plants. The waste must be
stored where it will be isolated from living creatures for tens of thousands of years. The waste consists of spent* fuel rods, internal
machinery from reactor cores, and the waste products of processing
nuclear fuels. For example, over 15,000 tons of spent nuclear fuel is
presently in temporary storage at plants in the United States.

8   It seems that the only viable* solution to nuclear waste disposal
is to bury it deep underground in geologically* stable formations
that can keep it isolated from the atmosphere and groundwater. In
1987, Congress amended* the Nuclear Waste Policy Act and made
Yucca Mountain in Nevada the primary potential site. Yucca
Mountain is about 90 miles southeast of Las Vegas, and preliminary* work at the mountain is testing its feasibility* as a permanent
disposal site. A thousand feet below the mountain's peak, a tunnel-
ing machine has bored a shaft into the mountain's center, and

perhaps by 2010 the site will begin to receive the nation's high-level radioactive waste.

9   As might be expected, most citizens of Nevada oppose having nuclear waste buried in their state. (It is the NIMBY argument: "not in my back yard!") Congress has the power to override any state's disapproval, but Congress may take years to make a final decision. Even if such a disposal site is approved, care must be taken to transport the waste to the site from locations across the country.

10   A repository* for relatively *low-level* radioactive waste from the defense industry (not the nuclear power industry) is located in the New Mexico desert. This Waste Isolation Pilot Plant was opened in 1999 to store radioactive debris* such as plutonium-tainted* clothing, tools, and sludge.* The low-level waste is now entombed 2,000 feet below ground, in a hollowed-out salt formation.

11   We are sure to hear about these controversial issues for many years to come. Let's hope that decisions about nuclear power will be made by knowledgeable government officials.

Adapted from Shipman et al., *An Introduction to Physical Science*, pp. 252–253.

MONITORING YOUR COMPREHENSION Can you explain the major benefits and drawbacks of nuclear power? If so, your comprehension was excellent.

COMPREHENSION AND CRITICAL READING QUESTIONS Answer the following questions by filling in the blanks or circling the letter of the correct response.

Overall Main Idea   **1.** Which statement best expresses the main idea of the entire reading?

a. The drawbacks of nuclear power outweigh its benefits.

b. Nuclear power has both benefits and drawbacks.

c. Despite its drawbacks, nuclear power is the best of all of the energy sources.

d. Each source of energy has its advantages and disadvantages.

Main Ideas   **2.** Which statement best expresses the main idea of paragraph 5?

a. Radiation exposure is a serious problem in the United States.

b. Cosmic rays are the most dangerous form of natural radiation.

c. People who fly often and people who live at high altitudes are exposed to more radiation than others are.

d. Natural sources are responsible for most of humans' radiation exposure.

Topic Sentence 3. Which sentence is the topic sentence of paragraph 4?

    a. sentence 1

    b. sentence 2

    c. sentence 3

    d. sentence 5

Supporting Details 4. Why do the authors mention the new pebble-bed modular reactor (paragraph 4)?

    a. It's an example of the increasing safety of nuclear power.

    b. It illustrates the idea that nuclear power does not contribute to pollution.

    c. It supports the idea that radioactive nuclear waste must be carefully stored.

    d. It illustrates the increased efficiency of nuclear power plants.

Patterns of Organization 5. What pattern organizes paragraph 6?

    a. dates and events

    b. comparison and contrast

    c. cause and effect

    d. classification

Transitions 6. What time order transition appears in paragraph 8?

    _____

Inferences and Conclusions 7. What do the authors expect the reader to infer about why Nevada citizens don't want nuclear waste buried in their state (paragraph 9)?

    _____

Purpose 8. What do you think is the authors' primary purpose?

    a. The authors' primary purpose is to inform readers about the advantages and drawbacks of nuclear power.

    b. The authors' primary purpose is to persuade readers that nuclear power's advantages outweigh its major disadvantage—radioactive waste.

Tone 9. How would you describe the authors' tone? _____

*Under-
standing
Visual Aids*

10. According to the pie chart,* what source is responsible for the most human-made radiation exposure?

a. radon

b. medical X-rays

c. internal (within the body)

d. nuclear medicine

■ **DRAWING YOUR OWN CONCLUSIONS** Writing about a recent Vermont vote that defeated a proposal to shut down a nuclear power plant, Marty Jezer wrote: "Ten–twenty years ago, Vermont Yankee [the nuclear power plant] would have defended nuclear power as safe, cheap, and efficient. But no one believes that anymore. . . . Their message was directed at people concerned about jobs." How do you think the authors of this reading would respond to Jezer's statement? (Source of information: www .commondreams.org/views02/0308_09.htm.)

■ **MAKING IT PERSONAL** Would you support the construction of a nuclear power plant near your home? Why or why not?

■ **WRITING SUGGESTION** Write a paper to argue for or against building additional nuclear power plants in the United States.

INTERNET BONUS QUESTION
The reading you just finished said that "highly toxic radioactive waste" was the "true Achilles' heel of nuclear power." Use the Web (or a reference book on words) to find the origin of the phrase "Achilles' heel" when it is used as an idiom rather than as a reference to the human foot. Then explain why the authors call "radioactive waste" the Achilles' heel of nuclear power.

_____

_____

_____

_____

_____

_____

*If you need any help reading a pie chart, look at pages 713–715.

 A P P E N D I X

Reading Pie Charts and Graphs

Throughout *Reading for Results* there are tips for reading visual aids. However, if you think you need more instruction, here are some additional explanations and exercises.

 ## Understanding Pie Charts

Pie charts are circles divided into slices. Each piece, or slice, of the pie represents a percentage of the larger whole. Those percentages are usually printed on or close to the individual shares of the pie. Generally, pie charts are used to show the importance or size of various groups or items within some larger whole.

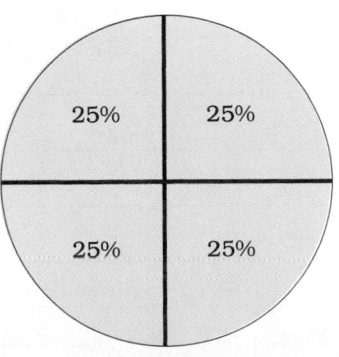

The Shares

Because we are all familiar with what it means to cut a pie into pieces, pie charts are easy to read. In fact, the process of reading a pie chart can be summed up in a few simple steps.

Steps in Reading a Pie Chart

1. Read the title, then look for the source of the chart's figures. If there is a caption, read it carefully. Pay close attention to any dates so that you know if the figures shown are recent enough to be useful.
2. Note the number of slices or pieces in the pie or pies. Look closely at how each piece is labeled or identified.
3. If there is a key indicating what each slice represents, make sure you understand it.
4. Identify the shares or percentage represented by each piece. Decide who or what accounts for the largest or smallest percentage. See if any of the percentages or shares are equal.
5. If the author provides two charts, make sure you know what each one represents. Pay attention to similarities or differences between the two.

To get a clear idea of how the steps apply, look now at Figure A.1. The title tells you that the pie charts display changes in sleep

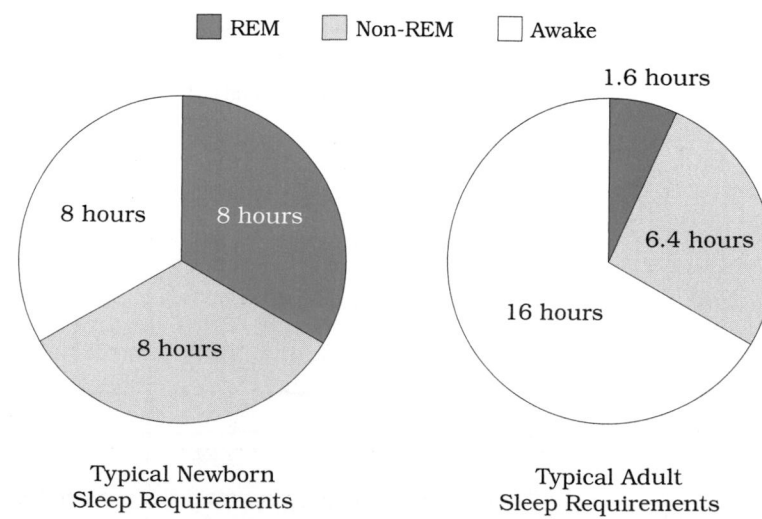

Figure A.1 Developmental Changes in Sleep Requirements

Source of data: Seifert et al., *Lifespan Development*, p. 113.

requirements. The presence of two charts along with their titles tells you the authors are making a comparison between newborn and adult sleep requirements.

On page 714, the slices in the pie charts are labeled not in percentages but in number of hours. There is also a color key telling you how to recognize the different kinds of sleep indicated on the chart: Blue represents REM sleep, gray identifies non-REM sleep, and white indicates the number of hours spent awake.

According to the pie chart for newborns, then, how many hours of REM (an active period of sleep, named for the rapid eye movements that usually accompany it) do infants usually get? To find the answer, look for the blue slice on the pie chart devoted to newborns. It tells you that the answer is eight hours. Now look at the pie chart devoted to adults and figure out how many hours of REM sleep they usually get. Quite a difference, isn't there? Adults get only about 1.6 hours.

While all of the information in the pie charts could be written out in words, it's more readily accessible to readers in the form of a pie chart. Making information easy for readers to grasp is one of the main reasons writers employ visual aids.

EXERCISE 1 Understanding Pie Charts

DIRECTIONS The pie chart in Figure A.2 on page 716 shows the types of households shared by married couples in America in 2002. Use the information in that chart to answer the following questions.

1. According to the pie chart, what portion of married-couple households in the United States were dual-income with no children in 2002?

   _____

2. What two types of households were of equal proportion?

   _____

3. Which group was larger, dual-income households with children or traditional households?

   _____

4. Which group was larger, dual-income households with children or dual-income households without children?

   _____

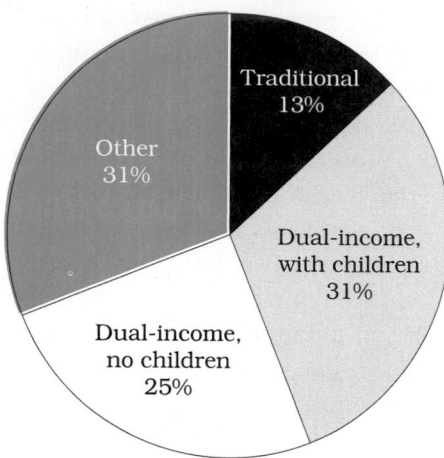

Figure A.2 Types of U.S. Married-Couple Households, 2002

Note: Traditional households include married-couple households with children where only the husband is in the labor force. Source of information: AmeriStat, analysis of data from the 2002 Current Population Survey (March Supplement).

Understanding Line Graphs

Unlike pie charts, which show parts of a larger whole, line graphs help readers visualize change over time. To understand a line graph, begin with the title. The title tells you what is being measured or tracked over time. For example, the title of Figure A.3 tells us that

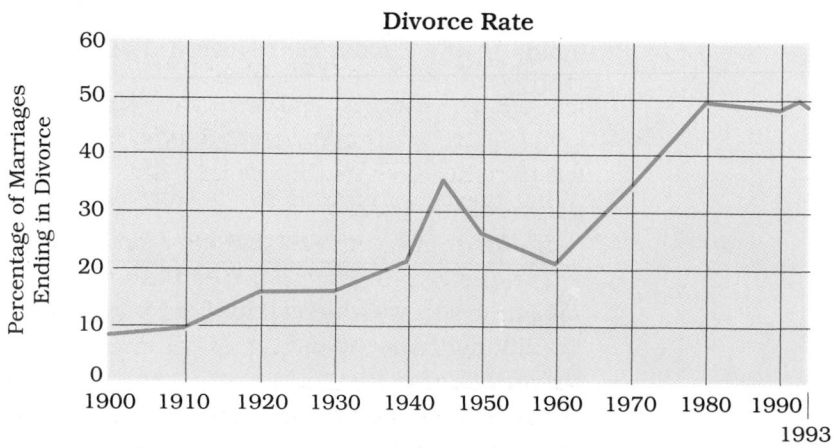

Figure A.3 Percentage of U.S. Marriages Ending in Divorce, 1900–1993

Source of data: Seifert et al., *Lifespan Development*, p. 310.

Vertical Axis

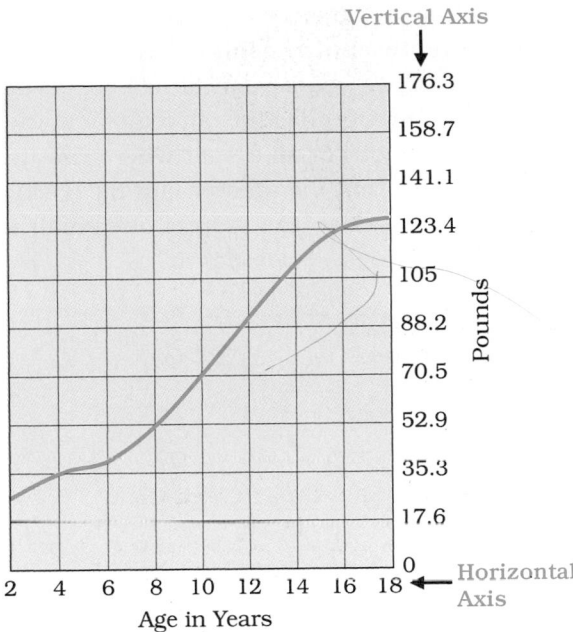

Figure A.4 Weight Increases in Girls Between Two and Eighteen Years

Source of data: Seifert and Hoffnung, *Childhood and Adolescent Development*, p. 273.

the graph will indicate the percentage of marriages ending in divorce between the years 1900 and 1993.

Look now at the graph in Figure A.4 above. Then read just the title that follows the figure-number. What can you expect to learn from reading this graph?

The title tells us that the graph will help readers "see" how the average girl's weight increases between the ages of two and eighteen. Notice how the **horizontal axis**, or the straight line going from left to right, gives us the age in years, with each block representing a span of two years.

In Figure A.4, the **vertical axis**, or the straight line from bottom to top, measures pounds rather than years, with each block representing a little over seventeen and a half pounds.

Look again at Figure A.4. What does it tell us about the average weight increase for girls between the ages of two and eighteen? For example, how much does a girl typically weigh at age four? To find the answer, look first at the number 4 on the horizontal axis. Then let your eyes travel upward until you find where the curved black line—which represents the average girl's weight increase—intersects, or crosses, with the straight line representing age four. From that point, look straight across the graph to your right and find what that point represents in pounds. The answer is 35.3 pounds.

How about two years later, at age six? What would the average girl weigh then? Because the curved black line representing weight increase does not fall on a spot where the horizontal and vertical lines meet, locating the answer is a bit tricky. But you can figure it out by paying close attention to one small section of the graph:

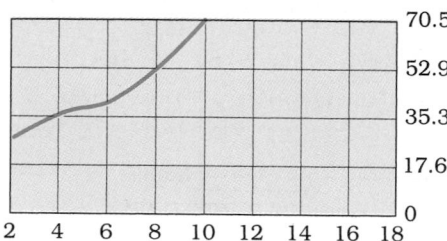

Now find age six on the horizontal axis, and let your eyes travel upward to the curved black line. Looking across to the vertical axis, representing pounds, you'll notice that the curved black line is about one-fifth of the way between two points—one representing 35.3 pounds, the other representing 52.9 pounds. Because each box represents just over 17.5 pounds, you can estimate the average girl's weight at age six by adding one-fifth of 17.5 to 35.3 pounds (35.3 + 3.5 = 38.8 pounds). From reading the graph, then, we can say that 38.8 pounds is the average girl's weight at age six.

To test your understanding of how to read a line graph, look again at Figure A.4 and determine what an average girl would weigh at age eighteen. Did you arrive at the answer 126.9 pounds? If you did, you're right on the mark. All you had to do was add 3.5 pounds to the number 123.4.

Steps in Reading a Line Graph

1. Read the title and look for the source of the graph's figures, paying close attention to dates.
2. Look at the horizontal axis to determine what kind of time intervals are measured on the graph.
3. Look at the vertical axis to discover what is measured there.
4. With your finger or a pencil, trace the curved or jagged line that connects each point on the graph. This line will tell you how the quantity measured in the vertical line has changed (or has not changed) over time.

EXERCISE 2 **Understanding Line Graphs**

DIRECTIONS The line graph in Figure A.5, on page 720 traces the American birthrate during most of the twentieth century. Read the graph and then answer the questions by circling the letter of the correct response.

1. What time period does the graph cover?

   a. 1930–2000

   b. 1965–2000

   c. 1930–1960

2. In 1965, the birthrate was approximately

   a. 125 births per 1,000 women.

   b. 105 births per 1,000 women.

   c. 95 births per 1,000 women.

3. In what decade was the birthrate the highest?

   a. 1940s

   b. 1950s

   c. 1960s

4. In what two years was the birthrate the lowest?

   a. 1935 and 1937

   b. 1945 and 1968

   c. 1975 and 1985

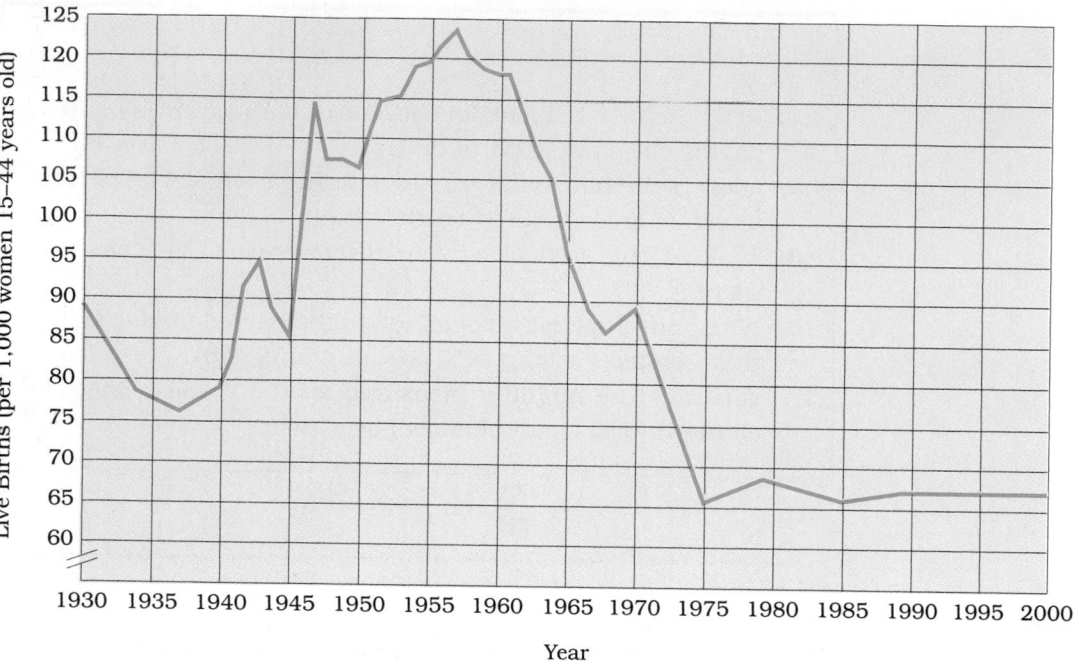

Figure A.5 Birthrate, 1930–2000

Between 1946 and 1957, rebounding from the low birthrate of the depression, families chose to have more children. This increase is often called the "baby boom." Since around 1960, the birthrate has slowed, and since the mid-1970s, it has remained fairly constant.

Source of data: Berkin, *Making America*, p. 846.

 # Understanding Bar Graphs

Bar graphs come in handy when writers want their readers to compare and contrast a number of different increases or decreases in events, populations, or transactions. Like line graphs, bar graphs are also used to trace increases or decreases over a period of time. Bar graphs, however, are more likely to be used than line graphs when many large increases or decreases need to be shown.

To understand a bar graph, you first need to determine the purpose of the graph. Does it help readers compare and contrast amounts or quantities of different products, substances, or events? Or is it designed to help readers trace increases or decreases over

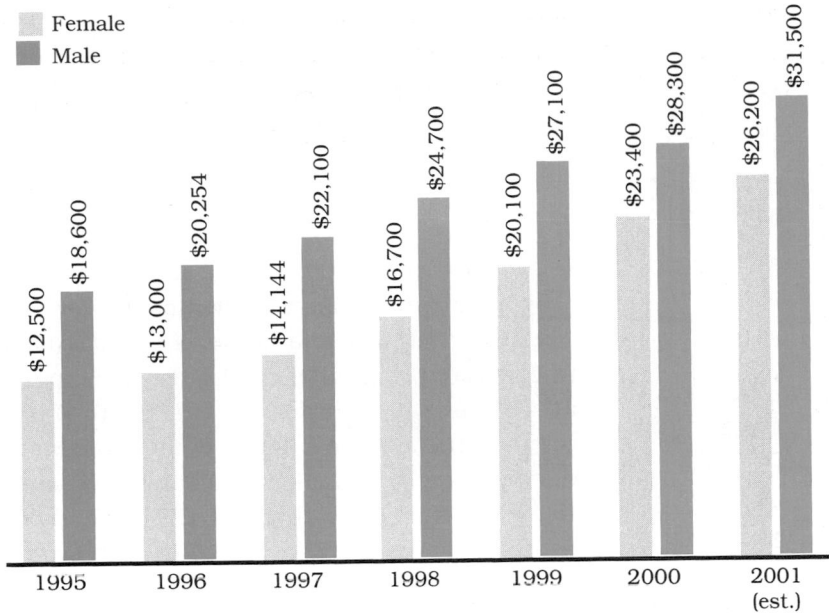

Figure A.6   Average Salaries for Males and Females, 1995–2001

Source of data: Pride et al., *Business,* p. 483.

a period of time? What, for example, is the purpose of the bar graph in Figure A.6?

The years printed along the horizontal axis tell us that the bar graph is meant to help readers track increases or decreases over time. The presence of two differently colored bars for each year says that a second purpose of the graph is to make readers aware of the differences or similarities between two groups, in this case males and females. Based on the graph, then, we should be able to tell if women, on the average, make more money than men, less money than men, or earn just about the same amount.

Even a quick glance at the graph tells us that between the years 1995 and 2001, women have lagged behind men when it comes to salaries. That's easy enough to see because the higher the bar the greater the amount or increase identified. By the same token, the shorter the bar, the smaller the increase or amount it represents. For every year identified on the graph, the bars representing male salaries are longer. It's clear, therefore, that the average salaries for men exceeded the average salaries for women.

Now here are two other questions that will test your understanding of bar graphs. Between 1995 and 2001, did the average salary for women generally increase or decrease? What about the average salary for men, did it increase or decrease? Since the bars steadily get longer for each group, the answer in both cases is the salary increased.

Rearranging the Bars

In bar graphs, the bars don't always appear in a row. Sometimes they are arranged like a ladder, as in Figure A.7.

Bars arranged like a ladder are particularly helpful if you need to compare two groups during the same period. For example, look at Figure A.7 in order to answer this question: Has the gap between the average salaries of men and women begun to increase or decrease? If you look at the bars representing each group during the years from 1995 through 1998, you can see immediately that

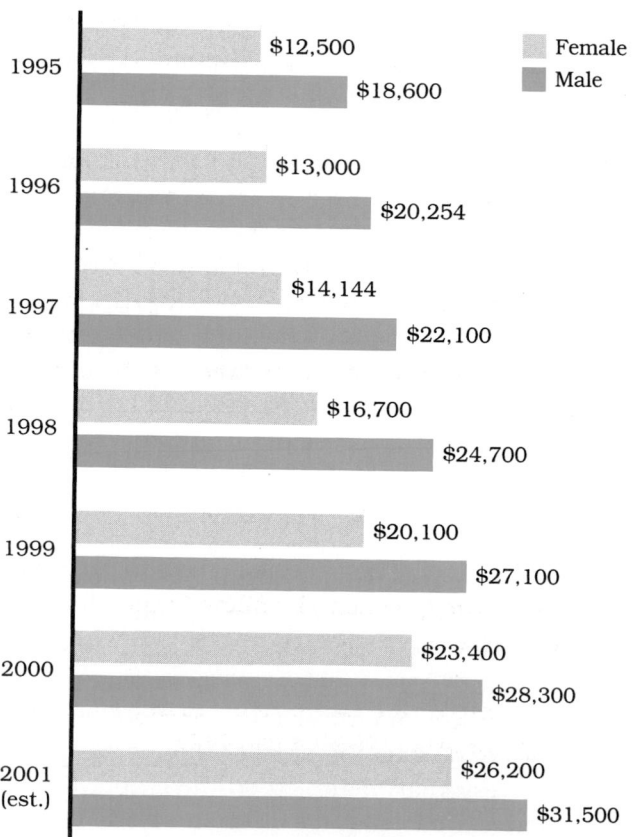

Figure A.7   Average Salaries for Males and Females, 1995–2001

Source of data: Pride et al., *Business*, p. 483.

the bars representing men's salaries are considerably longer than the bars representing women's salaries. The salary figures at the end of each bar tell you that men were sometimes making as much as $8,000 more than women from 1995 through 1998.

However, the graph also highlights that women began to catch up starting in 1999. You can see that immediately because the difference in the length of the bars obviously diminishes for that year. The point is that just a glance at the bar graph answers the question about salaries posed above. The gap between women's wages and men's wages is indeed beginning to close.

Steps in Reading a Bar Graph

1. Read the figure title, caption, and source note. Pay close attention to any dates mentioned.
2. Identify the purpose of the graph. Is it identifying large increases or decreases or comparing and contrasting different populations, events, or transactions? Or is it tracing increases and decreases over time?
3. If the graph measures changes or quantities over time, determine the time span and look for the longest and shortest bars to discover the largest increases or decreases.
4. If the graph compares and contrasts different products or substances, look carefully at the horizontal axis for the names of those products or substances. Then look for the longest and shortest bars to determine the degree of difference or similarity between each substance or product.

EXERCISE 3 Understanding Bar Graphs

DIRECTIONS Read the bar graph in Figure A.8 on page 724. Then answer the questions by filling in the blanks or circling the letter of the correct response.

1. According to the bar chart, which size car consistently outsold all others between 1983 and 1999?

   _____

2. Based on the bar graph, did the sale of luxury cars increase or decrease between 1983 and 1999?

   _____

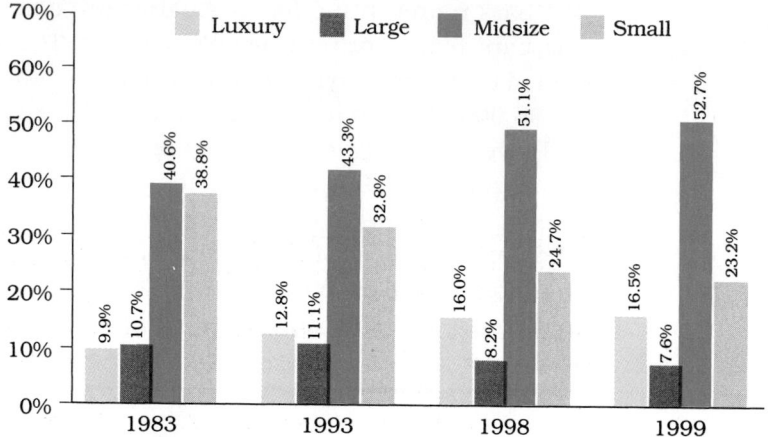

Figure A.8 U.S. Car Sales by Vehicle Size

Source of data: *World Almanac*, 2001, p. 227.

 # ACKNOWLEDGMENTS

Lorraine Ali: "Not Ignorant, Not Helpless" by Lorraine Ali from *Newsweek,* December 12, 2005, p. 33. Copyright © 2005 Newsweek, Inc. All rights reserved. Reprinted by permission.

Sharon Begley: "The Stereotype Trap" by Sharon Begley from *Newsweek,* November 6, 2000, p. 66. Copyright © 2000 Newsweek, Inc. All rights reserved. Reprinted by permission.

Roy Berko, Andrew Wolvin, and Darlyn Wolvin: From *Communicating* by Berko et al., p. 179. Reprinted by permission of Houghton Mifflin Company.

Douglas A. Bernstein, Louis A. Penner, Alison Clarke-Stewart, and Edward J. Roy: From *Psychology* by Douglas A. Bernstein et al., pp. 170, 241–242, 291–292, 299. Reprinted by permission of Houghton Mifflin Company.

Ann O'M. Bowman and Richard Kearney: From *State and Local Government, 5/e* by Bowman and Kearney, pp. 51, 260, 268. Copyright © 2002. Reprinted by permission of Houghton Mifflin Company.

Paul Boyer: From *Enduring Vision, 5/e* by Paul Boyer. Copyright © 2004. Reprinted by permission of Houghton Mifflin Company.

Sharon Brehm, Saul Kassin, and Steven Fein: From *Social Psychology, 5/e* by S. Brehm et al., pp. 248, 297, 308, 372–374, 536. Copyright © 2002. Reprinted by permission of Houghton Mifflin Company.

Danuta Bukatko and Marvin Daehler: From *Child Development* by Bukatko and Daehler, pp. 183, 505. Copyright © 2001. Reprinted by permission of Houghton Mifflin Company.

Dennis Coon: From *Essentials of Psychology* (Paperbound Edition with InfoTrac) 9/e, by Coon, pp. 258–259. Copyright © 2003. Reprinted with permission of Wadsworth, a division of Thomson Learning: www.thomsonrights.com. Fax 800 730–2215. From *Essentials of Psychology: Exploration and Application* 6/e by Coon, pp. xxxi–xxxii. Copyright ©1994. Reprinted with permission of Wadsworth, a division of Thomson Learning: www.thomsonrights.com. Fax 800 730–2215.

Joseph DeVito: From Joseph A. De Vito, *The Interpersonal Communication Book, 9/e.* Published by Allyn and Bacon, Boston, MA. Copyright © 2001 by Pearson Education. Reprinted by permission of the publisher.

Google: Reprinted by permission of Google Inc.

Alonzo L. Hamby: From AmericanPresident.org, Alonzo L. Hamby, consulting editor. Copyright 2003. The Rector and Visitors of the University of Virginia. Used by permission.

Jeffrey S. Nevid: From *Psychology: Concepts and Applications* by Jeffrey S. Nevid, pp. 10–11, 270–271. Copyright © 2003. Reprinted by permission of Houghton Mifflin Company.

Susanne Osborn and Michel T. Motley: From *Improving Communication* by Osborn and Motley, pp. 73–74. Copyright © 1999. Reprinted by permission of Houghton Mifflin Company.

William Pride, Robert J. Hughes, and Jack R. Kapoor: From *Business, 6/e* by Pride, Hughes and Kapoor, pp. 57, 317, 319. Copyright © 2005. Reprinted by permission of Houghton Mifflin Company

Frank Schmalleger: From *Criminal Justice Today: Introductory Text for the 21st Century, 6/e,* © 2001. Adapted by permission of Pearson Education, Inc., Upper Saddle River, NJ.

Kelvin L. Seifert, Robert J. Hoffnung, and Michelle Hoffnung: From *Lifespan Development,2/e.* Copyright © 2000. Reprinted by permission of Houghton Mifflin Company.

James T. Shipman, Jerry D. Wilson, and Aaron W. Todd: From *An Introduction to Physical Science, 10/e.* Copyright © . Reprinted by permission of Houghton Mifflin Company.

Joseph Turow: From *Media Today* by Joseph Turow, pp. 152–153. Copyright © 2003. Reprinted by permission of Houghton Mifflin Company.

USA Today: "A Hero Scorned" from *USA Today,* January 13, 2006, p. 10A. Reprinted with permission.

David Wallechinsky: "The Wolf Children" from *The Twentieth Century* by David Wallechinsky, pp. 296–297. Boston, MA: Little, Brown, 1985. Reprinted by permission of Ed Victor Ltd.

Thomas Whissen: Excerpt from *A Way with Words* by Thomas Whissen, pp. 54–57, 62. New York: Oxford University Press, 1982. Reprinted by permission of the author.

INDEX

addition, transitions indicating, 302
Additional Readings
  "Altruistic Personality, The,"
      652–56
  "Does America Need a Third
      Party?" 664–65
  "Hero Scorned, A," 659–61
  "Kohlberg's Six Stages of Moral
      Judgment," 689–92
  "Marla Ruzicka: An Activist
      Angel," 696–98
  "Memory, Perception, and
      Eyewitness Testimony,"
      681–85
  "Nuclear Power and Waste
      Disposal," 707–10
  "Stereotype Trap, The," 669–72
  "Where Does Free Speech End?"
      676–78
  "Wolf Children, The," 702–4
alternatives, false, 612
"Altruistic Personality, The," 652–56
annotating. *See* marginal notes
answers
  as implied main idea, 240
  writing out for *SQ3R*, 15
approximate definitions, 57
arguments
  careless comparisons, 612–13
  circular reasoning, 611–12
  false alternatives, 612
  hasty generalizations, 608–9
  irrelevant evidence, 609–10
  sound, 607–8
arguments for opinions, 607–8

background knowledge
  importance of, in reading, 21
  reading research on, 21
  search engines for, 22
  using web for, 21–23
  World Wide Web and, 21–22
bar graphs, 325–26, 720–23
bias
  acceptable, 598–600
  defined, 27

evaluating, 596–600
  unacceptable, 596–98
"Black Baseball," 261–63
boldface terms
  for specialized vocabulary, 59
  surveying of, 3
bonus questions, introducing, 33

careless comparisons, 612–13
cause and effect patterns, 461–64
  defined, 461
  note-taking for, 463–64
  topic sentences for, 463
  transitions for, 462
  verbs signaling, 462–63
  See also organizational patterns
"Challenging the Digital Divide,"
      334–35
chapter headings. *See* headings
Chapter Readings
  "Black Baseball," 261–63
  "Challenging the Digital Divide,"
      334–35
  "Critical Thinking and Pseudo-
      Psychologies—Palms,
      Planets, and Personality,"
      621–24
  "Development of Self in
      Childhood, The," 537–38
  "Going Global," 124–25
  "Jury Dodgers Beware!" 194–95
  "Legal Rights for Animals," 407–8
  "Types of Love," 483–85
  "Words Are Like Bullets," 80
circular reasoning, 611
classification
  defined, 468–69
  taking notes on, 470–71
  topic sentences for, 469
  visual aids in, 470
  See also organizational patterns
combined patterns
  defined, 508–9
  identifying primary pattern in,
      509
  taking notes on, 517–18

comparison and contrast
defined, 242
graphic organizer for, 456
implied main idea and, 242
note-taking for, 455–56
organizational patterns,
453–56
topic sentences for, 454–55
transitions indicating, 454
See also organizational patterns
competing viewpoints and
inferences, 241–42
comprehension
monitoring, 389–90
paraphrasing for, 177–78
reciting to check, 15
writing out answers to check, 15
concluding paragraphs, 360
concluding sentences, 330–33
connotations
context and, 77
denotations and, 76
in persuasive writing, 577
of words, 76–7
context
impact on connotation, 77
word meanings and, 67
context clues
combining with word
analysis, 71
contrast, 58
defined, 57
example, 57
general knowledge, 60
restatement, 58–59
contrast clues, 58
critical reading
acceptable bias and, 598–600
backing opinions with
arguments, 606–8
blending fact and opinion in,
586–88, 590
informative writing, 573–75
persuasive writing, 576–79
primary purpose in, 578–79
shaky arguments and, 597,
608–13
tone and, 574, 576–577
unacceptable bias and,
596–97
"Critical Thinking and Pseudo-
Psychologies—Palms,
Planets, and Personality,"
621–24

dashes, for restatement clues, 59
definition patterns
defined, 432
graphic organizer for, 433–34
note-taking for, 433–34
for specialized vocabulary,
59–60
topic sentences for, 432–33
definitions
approximate, 57
checking glossaries for, 75
dictionary, 56
highlighting devices for, 59–60
paragraphs devoted to, 432–34
See also word meanings
denotation
context and, 77–78
defined, 77
details. *See* supporting details
"Development of Self in Childhood,
The," 537–38
"Does America Need a Third
Party?" 664–65

evidence
irrelevant, 609–10
in persuasive writing, 575
See also arguments for opinions
example clues, 57–58

facts, 586
blending with opinions,
590–91
checking of, 586
defined, 586–87
implying main idea, 239
in informative writing, 573–74
vs. opinions, 587
tone and, 586–87
false alternatives, 612
faulty logic. *See* shaky arguments
flow charts
defined, 400
for note-taking, 400–401
process patterns and, 448
Funk, Wilfred, 56

generalize, 110
general knowledge clues, 60
general sentences
defined, 98
in first position, 118
in last position, 119–20
specific sentences and, 103–4

general words
    in context, 99
    defined, 98
    specific words and, 98
glossaries, 75
"Going Global," 124–25
graphic organizers, 399–401
    examples of, 400, 402, 404
    flow charts and, 400–401
graphs
    bar, how to read, 325–26,
        721–23
    line, how to read, 716–19

headings
    in longer readings, 358
    major and minor, 8
    surveying, 3
    turning into questions, 8
"Hero Scorned, A," 659–61
highlighting devices
    for marking text, 10–11
    for specialized vocabulary, 74–75
horizontal axis, 8, 716

illogical inferences, 252–54
implied main ideas
    clues to, 227
    in longer readings, 372–74
    in paragraphs, 226–28
    See also inferences
infer, 57
inferences
    in cartoons, 220–21
    common patterns in paragraphs,
        238–43
    defined, 220
    evaluating, 252–54
    in everyday life, 219
    likely paragraphs for, 238–43
    logical and illogical, 252–54
    in longer readings, 372–74
    of main ideas in paragraphs,
        226–28
    pronouns and, 222
    questions for evaluating, 235
    in quips and quotes, 221
    for supporting details, 314–16
    for topic sentences, 223
    of word meanings, 57
informal outlines
    defined, 19
    for monitoring comprehension,
        389–90

for note-taking, 391–92
    for reviews, 19–20
informative writing
    defined, 573
    factual evidence and, 573
    ten signs of, 575
    tone and, 574
introductory sentences
    contrasted to topic
        sentences, 153
    defined, 153
    examples, 153–54
irrelevant evidence, 609–10

"Jury Dodgers Beware," 194–95

key terms
    definition patterns for, 74–75
    recognizing, 59–60
    See also specialized vocabulary
"Kohlberg's Six Stages of Moral
    Judgment," 689–92

"Legal Rights for Animals," 407–8
line graphs, 8
    how to read, 9
logical inferences, 252–54
    defined, 228
    evaluating, 252–54
logic, errors in. See arguments
longer readings
    compared to paragraphs, 358–60
    concluding paragraphs in, 360
    example and diagram of, 362–63
    implied main idea in, 359, 372–74
    main ideas in, 358–59
    major supporting details in, 360
    organizational patterns in, 515–17
    supporting details in, 360
    taking notes on, 391–92,
        399–402, 517–18
    thesis statements in, 359
    titles and headings in, 358

main ideas
    defined, 119, 149
    implied in longer readings,
        372–74
    inferring in paragraphs, 219,
        221–23, 226–28
    in longer readings, 358
    methods for implying, 238–43
    in paragraphs, 149–51
    questions for, 364

main ideas (*continued*)
  topics and, 149–51
  topic sentences and, 151–52
  See also thesis statements; topic
    sentences
major details
  defined, 291
  diagrammed, 293, 361–63
  identified by topic sentences,
    299–300
  in longer readings, 360
  and minor details, 361–64
  relating to main idea, 364
  supporting topic sentences,
    284–86
  transitions indicating, 302
  See also supporting details
marginal notes, 5, 10
"Marla Ruzicka: An Activist Angel,"
  696–98
meaning. *See* word meanings
"Memory, Perception, and Eyewitness Testimony," 681–85
minor details
  defined, 297
  evaluating, 292–93
  vs. major details, 290–93
  See also supporting details
monitoring comprehension
  defined, 9
  techniques for, 15, 389–90

note-taking
  for cause and effect, 463–64
  for classification, 470–71
  for combined patterns, 517–18
  for comparison and contrast,
    455–56
  for definition patterns, 433–34
  informal outlines for, 391–92
  kinds of, 10
  pointers on, 10
  for process patterns, 448–49
  for sequence of dates and events,
    441
  symbols used for, 11
  underlining, 12–13
  writing out answers, 15
"Nuclear Power and Waste
  Disposal," 707–10

opinions, 587
  backing with arguments, 607–8
  combining with facts, 590

characteristics of, 588
  defined, 587–88
  vs. facts, 586–88
  informed, 588
  in persuasive writing, 576
  tone and, 587–88
  See also arguments
organizational patterns, 431–32
  cause and effect, 461–64
  classification, 468–71
  combining in paragraphs, 508–9
  comparison and contrast, 453–56
  definition, 432–34
  in longer readings, 515–17
  questions for recognizing
    primary, 509
  process, 446–49
  sequence of dates and events,
    438–41
  time order, 437–49
  See also specific patterns
outlines
  guidelines for, 392
  for note-taking, 391–92
  in review process, 19–20

paragraph patterns. *See* organizational patterns
paragraphs
  combining patterns in, 508–9
  concluding, 360
  concluding sentences in, 330–33
  implying main ideas, 238–43
  inferring main idea of, 226–28
  introductions in, 153–56
  longer readings and, 358–60
  main idea in, 149–51
  major and minor details in,
    290–92
  organizational patterns (*see*
    organizational patterns)
  reversal transitions in, 153–56
  supporting details in, 283–86
  topic sentences in, 151–53,
    161–63
  topics in, 139–40
paraphrasing
  accurate and inaccurate, 178–79
  agents and actions in, 181
  cardinal rule of, 179
  defined, 178
  examples of, 179
  flexibility in, 180
  pitfalls of, 180

for reading vs. writing, 181–82
topic sentences, 177–79
two-step method for, 180–82
parentheses, for restatement clues, 59
patterns of organization. *See* organizational patterns
personal attack, 597
persuasive writing
  arguments and evidence in, 607–8
  bias in, 576
  careless comparisons in, 612–13
  circular reasoning in, 611–12
  defined, 576
  evaluating bias in, 596–600
  excessive bias in, 596–98
  false alternatives in, 612
  hasty generalizations in, 608–9
  irrelevant evidence in, 609–10
  ten signs of, 577–78
  tone in, 576–77
pie charts, 713–15
point of view
  in informative writing, 575
  in persuasive writing, 576–77
prefixes, 68–69
preview. *See* surveying
process patterns
  defined, 446
  note-taking for, 448
  transitions in, 447
  visual aids in, 448
  topic sentences for, 448
purpose
  defined, 361
  identifying primary, 361, 578–79
  informative, 573–75
  persuasive, 576–78
  why think about, 573

questions
  checking comprehension with, 9
  for guiding reading, 7, 9, 111
  from headings, 8
  inferences and, 240
  opening paragraphs, 161
  for surveying, 4–5
  turning headings into, 7–8
  using visual aids for, 8–9

reader's response, 110–11
reading
  to answer questions, 7–9
  benefits of writing while, 12

highlighting symbols for, 11
marginal notes and, 10
marking pages and, 10–11
questions and, 7–8
rates, 13–14
in *SQR3*, 9–10
See also critical reading; longer readings; paragraphs; textbooks
reading rates
  flexibility of, 13
  four kinds of, 14
  purposes for, 14
reasoning, circular, 611–12. *See also* shaky arguments
reciting
  in *SQR3*, 15
  for testing understanding, 15
  writing out answers, alternative for, 15
restatement clues, 58–60
  in textbooks, 59–60
reversal, transitions signaling, 58, 153–54
reviewing
  informal outlines for, 19–20
  methods of, 17
  in *SQR3*, 16–20
  visual aids in, 17
Robinson, Francis, 1
roots, of words, 69

schema, 21
search engines, 22–23
  indexes and directories, 23
  search terms, 24
sentences
  concluding, 330–31
  connecting general and specific, 118–19
  general *vs.* specific, 103–4
  introductory, 153–54
  levels of specificity in, 106–7
  topic, 151
  transitional, 156
  See also topic sentences
sequence of dates and events patterns. *See also* time-order patterns
  defined, 438
  note-taking for, 441
  topic sentences typical of, 439–40
  transitions indicating, 438–39
  visual aids in, 440

shaky arguments, 608
    careless comparisons, 612–13
    circular reasoning, 611–12
    false alternatives, 612
    hasty generalizations, 608
    irrelevant evidence, 609
similarity, transitions indicating,
        454
skimming, 4
specialized vocabulary
    defined, 59
    glossaries for, 75
    methods of introducing, 59–60
    paragraphs that define, 74–75
    pointers on recognizing, 74
    recognizing in textbooks, 74–75
specific sentences
    defined, 103
    general sentences and, 103–4
    levels of, 106–7
    as supporting details, 284–86
SQR3 (survey, question, read,
        recite, review), 1–2
    flexibility of, 2
    questions used in, 5, 7, 8
    reading in, 9–14
    reciting, 15
    reviewing, 16–20
    surveying steps in, 2–3
    visual aids in, 8
    World Wide Web and, 21–31
"Stereotype Trap, The," 669–72
suffixes, 69
summaries
    concluding paragraph as, 360
    surveying, 2–5
supporting details
    clues to, 301
    compared to concluding
        sentences, 330–31
    defined, 284
    for developing topic sentences,
        284–85
    evaluating minor, 292–93
    inferences as, 314–16
    in longer readings, 360
    major and minor, 290–91
    topic sentences identifying,
        299–300
    transitions, 301–302
    visual aids as, 321–26
surveying
    defined, 2
    focus questions for, 7–8

seven steps in, 3
ten questions for, 5
three goals of, 4
visual aids in, 8
symbols, for marking text, 11
synonyms, 58–59

tables
    steps in reading, 324
test preparation, informal outlines
        for, 19–20
textbooks
    glossaries in, 75
    reading systems for (see SQR3)
    specialized vocabulary in, 59–60,
        74–75
thesis statements
    defined, 359
    locations, 359
    supporting details and, 358
    vs. topic sentences, 359
    See also main ideas
time-order patterns
    note-taking for, 441, 448
    process, 446
    sequence of dates and
        events, 438
    topic sentences for, 439, 448
    transitions for, 439, 447
    two types of, 437
    visual aids in, 440, 448
titles
    in longer readings, 358
    turning into questions, 3
tone
    facts and, 586–87
    of informative writing, 574
    opinions and, 587–88
    in persuasive writing, 576–77
    words describing, 576
topic
    characteristics, 140
    defined, 139
    identification in paragraphs,
        139–40
    in longer readings, 358
    main idea and, 149–51
    questions, 140
topic sentences
    for cause and effect, 463
    characteristics of, 152
    for classification, 468–71
    for comparison and contrast,
        453–56